RELIGIONS OF THE WORLD

A Latter-day Saint View

RELIGIONS OF THE WORLD

A Latter-day Saint View

REVISED AND ENLARGED

Spencer J. Palmer
Roger R. Keller
Dong Sull Choi
James A. Toronto

Brigham Young University
Provo, Utah
– 1997 –

Drawing of Christ (p. 186) based on Warner Sallman's painting. Used by permission.

Portrait of Joseph Smith (p. 256) based on Ted Gorka's rendering. Used by permission.

Brigham Young University, Provo, Utah 84602.
©1997 by Spencer J. Palmer. All rights reserved.
Printed in the United States of America.

Library of Congress Cataloging-in-Publication Data

Religions of the world : a Latter-Day Saint view / Spencer J. Palmer . . . [et al.].
    — 2nd general ed., rev. and enlarged.
        p. cm.
    Rev. ed. of: Religions of the world / Spencer J. Palmer and Roger R. Keller.
    Includes bibliographical references and index.
    ISBN 0-8425-2350-2
    1. Christianity and other religions.   2. Church of Jesus Christ of
Latter-Day Saints—Relations.   3. Mormon Church—Relations.
I. Palmer, Spencer J.   II. Palmer, Spencer J.   Religions of the world.
BR127.R444   1997
261.2—dc21   97-33721
                                                      CIP

Distributed by Print Services, Brigham Young University, Provo, Utah 84602.

Contents

Foreword ix

Prefaces xi

Chronology xv

PART ONE: FOUNDATIONS 1

  1   Foundations 3

PART TWO: SOUTH ASIAN RELIGIONS 15

  2   Hinduism 17

  3   Jainism 35

  4   Buddhism 49

  5   Sikhism 73

PART THREE: EAST ASIAN RELIGIONS 85

  6   Taoism 87

  7   Confucianism 99

  8   Shinto 111

GALLERY OF PHOTOGRAPHS 123

PART FOUR: SOUTHWEST ASIAN RELIGIONS 145

  9   Zoroastrianism 147

  10 Judaism 163

  11 Christianity 187

  12 Islam 213

PART FIVE: REFLECTIONS 243

  13 Religious Similarities 245

  14 Restoration Fulness 257

Bibliography 277

Index 283

Foreword

RELIGION books take up a good share of most bookstores. And books on the world's religions, the occult, New Age thinking, spirituality, and worship invite readers to join the quest for release, redemption, renewal, relief, or random access to some higher spiritual plain. So why should a quartet of Latter-day Saint scholars of world religions attempt to displace other religion books with their version of the subject? Are not the dozens of world religions texts and the infinite number of books on specific religions (or sects, or denominations, or groups within them, or meditative practices, or methods for forecasting one's future, or whatever) enough to handle the job? No; there is room for at least one more book on the subject.

The Latter-day Saint audience has grown large—with almost five million adherents in the United States and more outside—and that audience deserves a world religions text that places Latter-day Saint beliefs within the broader context of the world's important faiths. Or, better said, a book is needed that places the beliefs of the major world religions within the context of Latter-day Saint belief. This is such a book. In this new edition of *Religions of the World: A Latter-day Saint View,* the authors have not only skillfully addressed the basic doctrines of eleven major religious traditions of the world, but they have also gone to considerable effort to help Latter-day Saint readers understand the similarities and differences among the religions and between their faith and the others.

Although the label "new edition" sometimes evokes suspicion that only a few words have been changed in order to bring higher sales, this edition boasts several totally new chapters as well as major revisions to much of the text. This edition is more gender-conscious than before; of special note are new sections on the place of women in each of the religions. Revised and expanded "Latter-day Saint

Reflections" sections at the end of most chapters will bring deeper interpretive insight to the Latter-day Saint reader. And a new introductory section to the book helps students establish solid ballast when embarking on this study. A final section helps explain reasons for similarities among religions and reviews basic Latter-day Saint beliefs in comparative relief with the major world faiths.

Latter-day Saints are occasionally accused of being narrow-minded or unwilling to consider the beliefs of others. Such accusations may be true of Latter-day Saints who do not understand their own religion, but those who know the position of the church regarding the faith and beliefs of other people willingly allow them to "worship how, where, or what they may" (Article of Faith 11). Religions may be broadly placed in three categories: exclusivist, inclusivist, and pluralist. *Exclusivists* hold that their religion is the only truth and that no other ideas are needed to answer the questions of human existence. *Pluralists,* on the other extreme, claim that no religion has claim to the truth and that all religions are true, just as all cultures are acceptable—a relative position. *Inclusivists* take the middle ground, the position asserting that one religion is correct and true but that other religions do have genuine value. This is the position of the Latter-day Saints. This book is an excellent effort to clarify the inclusivist position.

Since the days of the prophet Joseph Smith, the Church has consistently held to its position that the world is filled with truth, although there is also clearly much that is not true. The responsibility of the Latter-day Saint student is to "receive truth, let it come from whence it may."[1] Further, the prophet Joseph taught: "We don't ask any people to throw away any good they have got; we only ask them to come and get more."[2] In a press conference held in Seoul, Korea, in May 1996, President Gordon B. Hinckley echoed these sentiments: "Let me say first that we respect all other churches. We do not stand out in opposition to other churches. We respect all men for all the good that they do and we say to those of all churches, we honor the good that you do and we invite you to come and see what further good we can do for you."[3] This wise and thoughtful position permeates this book.

Religions are windows that allow outsiders to see into what is most meaningful in other peoples' lives. *Religions of the World: A Latter-day Saint View* provides a clear view into these most meaningful and sensitive things.

R. LANIER BRITSCH

Notes

1. Joseph Fielding Smith, comp., *Teachings of the Prophet Joseph Smith* (Salt Lake City: Deseret Book, 1979), 313.

2. Ibid., 275.

3. Sheri L. Dew, *Go Forward with Faith: The Biography of Gordon B. Hinckley* (Salt Lake City: Deseret Book, 1996), 590.

Preface to the Current Edition

THIS revised and enlarged edition of *Religions of the World: A Latter-day Saint View* is a fulfillment of the labors, insights, and specializations of four Brigham Young University religious education faculty members over a period of years. The original version of this book was published as a preliminary edition in 1986 under the authorship of Spencer J. Palmer for use exclusively in classes at Brigham Young University. A revised edition, the first to be distributed generally, was in preparation in 1988 when Dr. Palmer was unexpectedly called to serve as president of the Seoul Korea Latter-day Saint temple. Roger R. Keller, a colleague at BYU, was invited at that time to complete the manuscript for publication and to serve as coauthor. This new edition, formally known as the second, incorporates the work of two additional authors: Dong Sull Choi, a specialist in east Asian religion, and James A. Toronto, an expert in Middle Eastern religion.

We, the authors, are deeply grateful to those who have encouraged us in the production of this book: Robert Millet, dean of Religious Education at BYU; Donald Cannon of the Religious Studies Center; Richard Cowan, former chairman of the Department of Church History and Doctrine; Larry Dahl, former associate dean of Religious Education; and Robert J. Matthews, who was dean of Religious Education when the first edition was published. We are also grateful to our colleague and friend Lanier Britsch for preparing the foreword.

No one has done more in the preparation of the manuscript for publication, nor with more skillful attention, than Howard Christy, Elizabeth Watkins, Jennifer Harrison, and Sara Lush of Brigham Young University Scholarly Publications, and the authors are deeply grateful to them. We also appreciate the labors of McRay Magleby, formerly of Brigham Young University Publications and Graphics, who designed the cover; and Bruce Patrick, presently of Publications and Graphics, and Jonathan Saltzman, who designed the interior and set the type. The sketches of the religious founders at the outset of the chapters were drawn by Jennette Purcell.

Finally, we especially express our heartfelt and lasting appreciation to our wives, Shirley Palmer, Flo Beth Keller, Kyung Choi, and Diane Toronto. Their patience, support, and understanding through the years have helped to make this book in its present form a reality.

SPENCER J. PALMER
ROGER R. KELLER
DONG SULL CHOI
JAMES A. TORONTO

Preface to the Original Edition

(CONDENSED)

LEAVING home in search of the sacred is a persistent theme in human history. Religious traditions are marked by pilgrims seeking truth, meaning, and holy places.

Latter-day Saints know that Abraham left the land of Ur with his family and household on a sacred journey to establish a new religious nation in Canaan (Gen. 12; Abr. 2). They also know that the Book of Mormon is a record of pilgrimage, describing the travels and trials of at least three groups of people (Jaredites, Mulekites, and the descendants of Lehi) who, impelled by a sacred mission, left their homes in the Old World and traversed wilderness and ocean to find a "land of promise, which was choice above all other lands" (Ether 2:7).

The epic biblical story of the struggles of Moses and the children of Israel in quest of the promised land has its analogue in the trek of the Latter-day Saint pioneers, whose arduous journey west was motivated by vibrant convictions that God would help them find their rightful place. They discovered and established Zion in the valleys of western America. They built temples to the Lord, designated as their most sacred places.

Latter-day Saints still aspire to visit the Holy Land to relive and reverence the experiences of the Old Testament prophets or of Jesus and those who associated with him. But Latter-day Saints also identify with other religious traditions beyond the Judeo-Christian tradition which summon the faithful to visit sacred places in search of truth, meaning, and personal development.

Latter-day Saints remember and celebrate the expeditions of the pioneers each July 24 with parades and pageants and sermons. They also take pilgrimages to sacred spots in America identified with the foundations of their church in this land. More than a hundred thousand pilgrims gather at the Hill Cumorah pageant held each year in New York state.

Many others attend a similar pageant at the Manti temple in Utah to listen, learn, and be inspired. Other sites of pilgrimage include Independence and surrounding areas in Missouri; Nauvoo, Illinois; Salt Lake City, Utah; and temples and temple sites worldwide. This eager quest to come in touch with the workings of the Lord in Palestine and in America is filled with benefits and blessings.

Thus, Latter-day Saints know what it is to take a pilgrimage. They have shown a capacity to reach out into the unknown. But now, in the pages of this book, we invite a new generation of Saints to venture to new places in search of religious meaning. We invite you to join us in a quest for understanding of the eleven major religions of the world: Hinduism, Buddhism, Jainism, Sikhism, Taoism, Confucianism, Shinto, Zoroastrianism, Judaism, Christianity, and Islam. This involves becoming acquainted with people beyond Europe and America.

The intent of this study of the religions of the world is to sharpen understanding of ideas, places, scriptures, doctrines, customs, practices, and thought previously little known. Although this text is an introductory survey of the world's great religions intended primarily for use by students at the university level, it is also a comparative study of these religions from the perspective of the Latter-day Saints. This poses special problems. Comparative work is inherently very difficult, since it requires equal sophistication in both sides of the comparison. Some might feel that it is impossible for a committed Latter-day Saint to be appreciative and careful in dealing with other people's beliefs. But we assume otherwise.

In making comparisons, there is always the nagging temptation to contrast the best within one's own faith with the worst or weakest within the religions of others. Invidious comparisons, drawn simply to shore up one's own religious commitments at the expense of distorting other people's belief, may be superficially satisfying in the short run, but in time they will do more damage than good. It is also easy to overreact to the immense variety of religions on earth and to try to resolve the diversity either by refusing to accept anything in others' religions or by ignoring or grossly minimizing the differences. We have striven to be above such indiscretions.

This book posits the view that the identification of both common and divergent ground through appreciative study of other religions and honest comparison of them with The Church of Jesus Christ of Latter-day Saints is of great importance and value. The interpretations and judgments in these pages are those of the authors. We do not claim that these interpretations or evaluations are the position of anyone else, and we jointly accept full responsibility for the entire contents.

Finally, this book is offered with profound admiration and respect for all God's children here on this earth. We wish no offense to anyone. If the reader, whether a Latter-day Saint or one of the faithful of any of the great religions studied or mentioned herein, would take offense or feel that any fact or interpretation in this volume is in error, we want to be so informed.

SPENCER J. PALMER
ROGER R. KELLER

A Chronology of Momentous Religious Events

Dates*	Events**
B.C.E.***	
ca. 1750	Abraham journeyed to Canaan
ca. 1500	Indo-Aryans entered India
ca. 1250	JUDAISM, **Moses,** and the *Pentateuch (Torah)*
ca. 1000	ZOROASTRIANISM, **Zarathustra,** and the *Avesta*
ca. 850–400	Period of the Hebrew prophets
ca. 800–300	Period of the Hindu sages
ca. 604–500	TAOISM, **Lao Tzu** (604–?), and the *Tao Te Ching*
	JAINISM, **Vardhamana Mahavira** (599–527), and the *Angas*
	BUDDHISM, **Siddhartha Gautama** (563–483), and the *Tripitaka*
	CONFUCIANISM, **Confucius** (551–479), and the *Chinese canon*
587–586	Jews exiled to Babylon
538	Cyrus permitted Jews to return to Jerusalem
ca. 246	King Asoka spread Buddhism

Dates*	Events**
C.E.***	
ca. 0–30	CHRISTIANITY, **Jesus Christ,** and the *New Testament*
ca. 45–65	Apostle Paul spread Christianity
ca. 90	Jewish canon, the *Old Testament,* fixed
ca. 100	Buddhism spread into China
ca. 382	*New Testament* canon fixed
ca. 500	Jewish *Talmud* completed
ca. 610	ISLAM, **Muhammad** (570–632), and the *Qur'an*
ca. 625	Buddhism spread into Tibet
ca. 651	First compilation of *Qur'an*
ca. 747	Tantric Buddhism reached Tibet
1054	Christianity split into Eastern Orthodox and Roman Catholic churches
ca. 1500	SIKHISM, **Guru Nanak** (1469–1539), and beginning of the *Adi Granth*
1517	**Martin Luther** (1483–1546) and the beginnings of Protestantism
1611	King James version of the *Bible* published
1830	MORMONISM, **Joseph Smith** (1805–1844), and the *Book of Mormon, Doctrine and Covenants,* and *Pearl of Great Price*

*Many dates are approximate.

RELIGIOUS MOVEMENT, **Religious Leader, *Scripture*

***B.C.E. ("before common era") and C.E. ("common era") have been used in compliance with the standard terminology of the literature and discourse of comparative world religions.

Part One
Foundations

It seems appropriate that a book by four Latter-day Saint scholars about the religions of other peoples should begin with an explanation of foundational principles. The foreword and prefaces have discussed in a general way the premises on which we as authors have based our study; in this introductory chapter, more groundwork is laid. It is assumed that Latter-day Saint students, to whom this chapter is primarily directed, come to this investigation with a certain degree of doctrinal uniformity, as well as certain preconceptions about God, the world, and human beings. Non–Latter-day Saint readers may be interested in learning, through this chapter, what specific Latter-day Saint doctrines support this investigation of other faiths, which preconceptions have been considered valid points of departure, and which have been discarded. We hope that, with a firm theoretical foundation established, the investigation of the world's religions which follows can be honest, informative, and enjoyable.

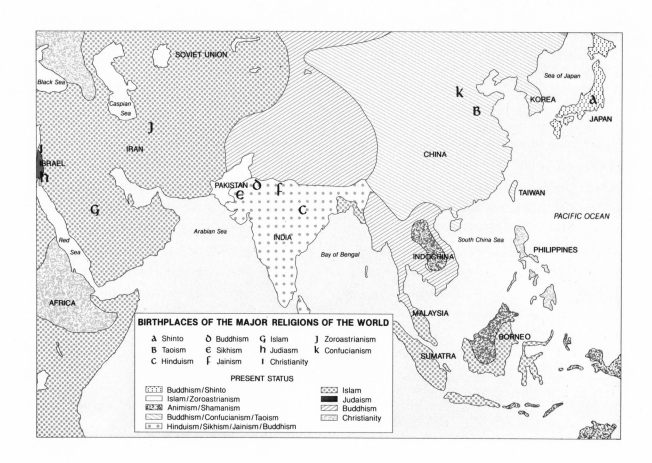

BIRTHPLACES OF THE MAJOR RELIGIONS OF THE WORLD

a Shinto   ∂ Buddhism   G Islam   J Zoroastrianism
B Taoism   ∈ Sikhism   h Judiasm   k Confucianism
C Hinduism   f Jainism   l Christianity

PRESENT STATUS

Buddhism/Shinto   Islam
Islam/Zoroastrianism   Judaism
Animism/Shamanism   Buddhism
Buddhism/Confucianism/Taoism   Christianity
Hinduism/Sikhism/Jainism/Buddhism

Foundations

Spencer J. Palmer

S INCE the earliest days of their beginnings, Latter-day Saints have been
aware of the obligation they bear to live
in the world among those of every faith
and culture, treating all with respect, understanding,
and love. In Doctrine and Covenants 88:79–80, the
instruction is given that Latter-day Saints are to
become knowledgeable

[o]f things both in heaven and in the earth, and under the
earth; things which have been, things which are, things
which must shortly come to pass; things which are at
home, things which are abroad; the wars and perplexities
of the nations, and the judgments which are on the land;
and a knowledge also of countries and of kingdoms—
That ye may be prepared in all things. . . .

In other words, Latter-day Saints are to become
actively aware of the affairs of their brethren and sisters throughout the world so as to better understand
their concerns, motivations, hardships, strengths,
weaknesses, and desires. And as we embark upon
such study in this text, it is important first that we
examine ourselves to see that we are prepared—
both academically and spiritually—to receive the
greatest possible degree of understanding and to discern truth in all its various forms and contexts.

TAKING A POSITIVE APPROACH

As we reach out to the peoples and religions of
the world, we must make a decision as to what our
approach will be. There are two ways open to us. In
following the first, or negative, way, we can take the
position of the Pharisee in the parable of Jesus and
thank God that we are "not as other men are" (Luke
18:11). We can exercise stern judgment and do all
within our power to look for ways to diminish
them. We can express intolerance and disgust by
comparing the best within our faith to the worst

within theirs. Consistent with a tendency in human
relations, we can regard that which is outside ourselves with suspicion and distrust. Because we have
the many special privileges of the fulness of the
gospel, it could sometimes seem "right" for us to
identify with forces of intolerance and bigotry.

Those who are determined to denounce blasphemy, sacrilege, and evil in others, while at the
same time claiming an exclusive corner on spirituality and truth among themselves, somehow find
it easy to justify such behavior. We need not go
back to the pride and prejudice of the ancient
Israelites to make the point. Intolerance and violence
in the name of God is widely evident in today's
world: Jews against Arabs, Arabs against Jews; Sikhs
and Hindus against each other in the Punjab;
Catholics and Protestants contending with each
other in Ireland; Muslims, Jews, and Christians
in confrontation in the Middle East; Tamils and
Buddhists against each other in Sri Lanka; the Aryan
Nation and the Ku Klux Klan against people not
like themselves.

In his efforts to bridge the gap between Latter-
day Saints and Protestant Christians living alongside
each other in the western United States, Roger
Keller has emphasized that "peacemaking is Christ's
call to all persons in all walks of life" and that "the
animosities that have existed over the past 150 years
between Christians of the '[mainstream] denominations' and Christians of the [Latter-day Saint] tradition are both inexcusable and unnecessary," but such
intramural Christian recrimination is sometimes
difficult to resolve.[1] At local levels, some Latter-day
Saints and members of some Protestant denominations have repeatedly responded with prejudice
based on ignorance and misunderstanding. Latter-
day Saints have frequently suffered abuse and excessive criticism at the hands of Protestant ministers,
some of whose misinformation on Latter-day Saint

theology has gone so far as to suggest that Latter-day Saints are not really Christians at all. Similarly, Latter-day Saints have often failed to extend the full hand of fellowship, love, and respect to neighbors who are not of their faith. The key to the solution on both sides is a positive approach, based on reliable information obtained through study, appreciation, and loving personal associations.

President Spencer W. Kimball has warned the Latter-day Saint faithful that the negative approach toward people of other faiths always bears a flavor of intolerance and that it is unacceptable for members to harbor feelings of racial, cultural, or religious superiority in the guise of religious zeal. "What a monster is prejudice!" he said. "It means prejudging. How many of us are guilty of it? Often we think ourselves free of its destructive force, but we need only to test ourselves. Our expressions, our voice tones, our movements, our thoughts betray us."[2] Intolerance is not only evil, as President Kimball pointed out, but it is unnecessary. The people of God need not defend themselves by attacking and belittling other people's faiths. "Intolerance is a sure sign of weakness," Richard P. Lindsay observes. "Only the confident can afford to be calm and kindly; only the fearful must defame and exclude."[3] With the negative approach, the focus is always upon suspicion because of differences—both imaginary and real—and not upon shared values.

In this book we have taken a positive approach. This means that we have attempted to present an appreciative study of each religion at its best. Although the criticism of a religion by its nonmember observers is understood and has been kept in mind, by and large we have striven to let the religion speak for itself in the spirit of the eleventh article of faith as expressed by Joseph Smith: "We claim the privilege of worshiping Almighty God according to the dictates of our own conscience, and allow all men the same privilege, let them worship how, where, or what they may." Further, we have sought to follow the Golden Rule set forth by Jesus: "Therefore all things whatsoever ye would that men should do to you, do ye even so to them" (Matt. 7:12).

In 1948, while church president George Albert Smith was visiting Los Angeles, unflattering accusations against him and the Latter-day Saints by some of his relatives in the Reorganized Church of Jesus Christ of Latter Day Saints, headquartered in

Independence, Missouri, were printed on the front page of the *Los Angeles Examiner*. When President Smith visited the church mission home on Hobart Street in Los Angeles, representatives of the press were waiting for him, expecting an angry—and newsworthy—retort. But when the reporters asked the president for his response to the criticisms, he replied: "My policy has always been one of friendship. The Latter-day Saints have had enemies enough. I respond with feelings of love and respect to my friends who have been critical of me and my religion. They are my brothers and sisters, and I can harbor no feelings of ill will against them."[4] In other words, for faithful Latter-day Saints there is no room for pettiness and prejudice against others on the basis of religious beliefs. The prophet Joseph Smith insisted: "A man filled with the love of God, is not content with blessing his family alone, but ranges through the whole world, anxious to bless the whole human race."[5]

In working to establish brotherhood and in savoring truth wherever it is found, Latter-day Saints are expected to interface positively with people of other religions. The authors of this book believe that President Gordon B. Hinckley's approach should be emulated by students, teachers, and all other members of the church in every country:

We want to be good neighbors; we want to be good friends. We feel we can differ theologically with people without being disagreeable in any sense. We hope they feel the same way toward us. We have many friends and many associations with people who are not of our faith, with whom we deal constantly, and we have a wonderful relationship. It disturbs me when I hear about any antagonisms. . . . I don't think they are necessary. I hope that we can overcome them. . . .

Be friendly. Be understanding. Be tolerant. Be considerate. Be respectful of the opinions and feelings of other people. Recognize their virtues; don't look for their faults. Look for their strengths and their virtues, and you will find strength and virtues that will be helpful in your own life.[6]

It is so easy and thoughtless to give offense to others on the basis of their religious beliefs and practices. As Gerald E. Jones has said, Latter-day Saints "owe respect to all churches and organizations that lead men to act more righteously than they otherwise might, even if they don't hold the keys of salvation and even if there is much error in their teachings." He suggests six useful guidelines in considering the beliefs of other peoples:

1. "We can treat things that are sacred to them with respect." This includes the rosaries and crucifixes of the Roman Catholics, the yarmulkas and phylacteries of the Orthodox Jews, the mosques of the Muslims, the icons of the Greek Orthodox, the fire temples of the Parsis, the shrines of Confucius, and the temples and images of the Hindus and Buddhists.

2. "So far as it does not offend our own religious understanding, we can observe the customs of other people when we are their guests." Among other things, this means that when we enter sacred premises of other faiths we should take off our hats, or our shoes, if that is the common practice.

3. "We must never ridicule another person's manner of worship." Our own practices and ceremonies might also seem peculiar to others.

4. "We can avoid arguing and quarreling over religious ideas." People rarely change their minds in the midst of a heated argument.

5. "We can be kind to representatives of other religions." A Jehovah's Witness proselytizing at our door or a Salvation Army representative soliciting donations on a street corner at Christmas time should meet with the same kind of respect and courtesy we hope Latter-day Saint missionaries will receive when they meet others.

6. "We [will be] judged according to how well we love our neighbor. . . . In the Savior's parable, it was not the priest or the Levite who was a true neighbor to the wounded Jew—it was the Samaritan, a member of a much-despised sect."[7]

As we approach our study of the religions of the world, we must go forward with positive, loving feelings. Contemplate these words of the prophet Joseph Smith:

We ought always to be aware of those prejudices which sometimes so strangely present themselves, and are so congenial to human nature, against our friends, neighbors, and brethren of the world, who choose to differ from us in opinion and in matters of faith. Our religion is between us and our God. Their religion is between them and their God.

There is a love from God that should be exercised toward those of our faith, who walk uprightly, which is peculiar to itself, but it is without prejudice; it also gives scope to the mind, which enables us to conduct ourselves with greater liberality towards all that are not of our faith, than what they exercise towards one another. These principles approximate nearer to the mind of God, because it is like God, or Godlike.[8]

How Can We Best Know Them?

One difficulty in discussing world religions is in knowing what to discuss. What is the most effective way to study religion? How best can we know the religions of the world as they are? To what can we compare the diversity among the world's living religions? Wayne Ham's metaphors provide provocative possibilities: Are they a forest of trees? Islands in the sea? A symphony orchestra? Different dialects of the same language? A string of beads? Spokes of a great wheel? Persons working on different jigsaw puzzles? Persons working on the same jigsaw puzzle?[9]

Clearly, the religious picture is complex. There seems to be no single way to examine fully and understand accurately the religions of the world. There is no simple formula for knowing which are "good" and which are "bad," or which are neither of these. As already mentioned, value judgments are often counterproductive. But at least Latter-day Saints can prayerfully study them and, by applying guidelines in the scriptures and in the teachings of the living prophets, identify ways in which they resemble each other, or ways in which they clearly disagree. This provides a very helpful frame of reference for deeper insights and understanding and for improved communication between members of The Church of Jesus Christ of Latter-day Saints and other religious groups.

In attempting to approach the religious systems of the world most effectively, it may be useful to consider them within categories and types. Paul Hutchinson makes the point that humankind's religions have taken an infinite variety of forms. They include temples and other places of worship; "rituals through which [people have] sought protection or blessing [which] run the gamut from the horrible to the sublime"; holy men, including prophets, gurus, shamans, and priests; symbols; organizations and institutions; sacred books of scriptures; sacred shrines; private and liturgical prayers and meditation; public services; a variety of doctrines, philosophies, and thoughts; and "the names of [so many] gods and goddesses [that they] will never be completely catalogued."[10]

Many have approached the religions of the world one at a time, assuming that there is *one* Hinduism, *one* Buddhism, *one* Judaism, *one* Islam, *one* Taoism, or *one* Christianity. Each is a separate tree in the forest. The conventional approach is to assume that they are so distinct from one another that each can almost be defined in terms of its size and geographical location. In fact, as Hutchinson inquires, if one speaks of "Buddhism," the question is *which* Buddhism—Theravada, Mahayana, or the Lamaism of Tibet? If one refers to "Islam," is the Sunni or the Shi'ite version of the faith meant? By "Judaism" should one assume the strictly traditional faith of Orthodox Jews, the middle-of-the-road teachings of Conservative rabbis, or the liberal, modernized beliefs of Reformed congregations? When reference is made to Chinese "Taoism," is it to the mystical thought of the Tao Te Ching or the bevy of religious nostrums and elixirs which are used by those in search of physical immortality? What is really meant when one says "Hinduism"—the transcendent mysticism of the holy men, the profound ideas of the Hindu philosophers, or the animism practiced by India's common villagers? And in the case of Christianity, how can anyone speak as though the Roman Catholic and Eastern Orthodox churches, the dozens of Protestant churches, and the hundreds of Christian splinter groups are all the same thing?[11] The answer to all these questions is obvious. There is a plethora of religions and an excess of confusion regarding them. Still, it is possible to propose some useful categories.

Traditional or New

It can be argued that there are only two styles of religion in the world: conventional religions and the novel, popular faiths.

The first category Robert Ellwood calls "The Temple." It fits the paradigm of Solomon's temple in Jerusalem: stable and fixed, with people dwelling together in happy harmony. This is mainstream religion—normative, large, and established. It is the great mosques of the Muslim world, the Altar of Heaven of the old Chinese emperors in Beijing, the Grand Shrine of Ise in Japan, and the Christian cathedrals in Europe and America. In the United States it is the Catholics, Episcopalians, Methodists, Baptists, Muslims, and Jews. The religions of the temple are historic, traditional, respectable, stable, large, and of significant institutional influence in society, politics, and economic affairs.

Then Ellwood identifies the metaphor of "The Marketplace," of the exotic and lively folk religions. Whereas the temple religions are traditional and of

long standing, the religions of the marketplace are still emerging. Here the groups are small, often short-lived, centered around a charismatic leader, basically concerned with mystical personal experience, and holding beliefs very different from those of the larger community outside. The alternative altars of unconventional spirituality in the world derive much from folk elements of animism and shamanism and from individualized spiritual experiences that characterize beliefs and practices unconcerned with science and technology. The merchants of the marketplace have shrines on the walls of their shops, or they deal in talismans, omens, geomancy, sorcery, healing, exorcism, trances, and ritual walks. The focus is like that of the unpredictable shaman of old who reveals and promotes the unseen powers and who provides the techniques by which believers may gain intense spiritual experience.[12] For the most part, this book will explore the "temple" religions, with only brief glimpses of the religions of the "marketplace."

Sacred Text or Popular Practice

There is often an enormous gap between the thought of the official religious scriptures and the popular beliefs and traditions of people at large. There is a difference between philosophical ideas and the unorganized customs and superstitions of popular religion. There is a disparity between priests, monks, scholars, and theologians on the one hand, and diviners, shamans, and uninformed and uneducated believers on the other. The disparity is found in the difference between those few who can read, interpret, and explain the truth—the principles and ideas of the faith laid out in holy writ—and those who sometimes see a nebulous and unpredictable world wherein spirits, demons, ghosts, leprechauns, taboos, magic, and spells abound. Thus, religious reality in the world can be divided between an overlay of theology and a substratum of popular experience. In the final analysis, folk religion underlies all the formalities of the great religions of the world. Once again, however, this book will focus first on the "formal and the proper" before turning to the popular manifestations within the religions.

Eastern or Western

The view that the religions of the world are either "Eastern" or "Western" is the interesting suggestion of Swiss psychologist Carl G. Jung, amplified by Arnold Toynbee and others. It is the familiar claim that there is a division between the self-denying faiths and the life-affirming faiths. This is to say, one is asked to contrast the underlying beliefs of followers of the Eastern faiths, who hold that "man's salvation rests in his escape from the torments of life," with the beliefs of those of Western faiths, who hold that "man finds in this life a field for spiritual attainment and preparation for life in the hereafter."[13]

This also echoes the famous refrain attributed to Rudyard Kipling, "East is East, and West is West, and ne'er the twain shall meet." Thus we are told that followers of Eastern (Asian) faiths dwell on introverted, self-negating experience and are satisfied with a relaxed existence and a resignation to what is. On the other hand, Western religions are extroverted and self-affirming. They motivate people to change their world through aggressiveness and determination. Eastern religion is prone to focus on nature; Western religion is prone to focus on people and their confrontation with nature.

This view of differences between the Eastern and Western mind has been expressed in broad brush strokes by Hari Dam, a citizen of India studying at the University of Minnesota, in an article written to American friends and published in the school newspaper:

You live in time; we live in space. You're always on the move; we're always at rest.

You're aggressive; we're passive. You like to act; we like to contemplate.

We always hark back to the past; you always look forward to the future. We pine for the lost paradise; you wait for the millennium.

We accept the world as it is; you try to change it according to your blueprint. We live in peace with Nature; you try to impose your will on her.

Religion is our first love; we revel in metaphysics. Science is your passion; you delight in physics.

You believe in freedom of speech; you strive for articulation. We believe in freedom of silence; we lapse into meditation.

You first love, then you marry. We first marry, then we love. Your marriage is the happy end of a romance; our marriage is the beginning of a love affair. Your marriage is a contract; our marriage is an indissoluble bond.

Your love is vocal; our love is mute. You delight in showing it to others; we try hard to conceal it from the world.

Self-assertiveness is the key of your success; self-abnegation is the secret of our survival.

You're urged every day to want more and more; we're taught from the cradle to want less and less. *Joie de vivre* is your ideal; conquest of desires is our goal.

We glorify austerity and renunciation; you emphasize gracious living and enjoyment. Poverty to you is a sign of degradation; it is to us a badge of spiritual elevation.

In the sunset years of life, you retire to enjoy the fruits of your labor; we renounce the world and prepare ourselves for the hereafter.[14]

Generalizations such as these must be considered with caution; the exceptions are almost as numerous as the examples used to support the hypothesis. However, when judiciously applied they do say much to us.

SOUTHWEST ASIA, INDIA, OR CHINA

In today's religious world, E. L. Allen has argued that the most fundamental difference in outlook is between the monotheistic faiths of southwest Asia (Judaism, Christianity, Zoroastrianism, and Islam) and the religions of India (Hinduism, Jainism, and Buddhism). It is a clash between *theism*—that is, a belief in one God who is personal, worthy of adoration, and separate from the world but continuously active in it—and *monism*—a belief that god, mind, and matter are not different. Jews, Christians, Zoroastrians, and Muslims hold that God is the creator and lord of the universe. To them the world is a real, tangible place with an identifiable beginning and an expected historical end. They believe that the God they worship is not "out there somewhere," but one who actually involves himself in history through such historical events as Israel's Exodus from Egypt, Christ's crucifixion on the cross under Pontius Pilate's direction, and Muhammad's night flight (Hijra) from Mecca to Yathrib (Medina).

On the other hand, the religions of Hinduism, Jainism, and Buddhism hold that humanity's goal is some form of unity with an impersonal divine principle. For them the world is not concrete but illusory, and thus it has no identifiable beginning or end. Time is merely an unending succession of cycles known as kalpa. Life is viewed through philosophical and metaphysical spectacles, not through historical ones. Consequently, the view of humanity becomes a metapsychological one, a view that transcends categories and merges with the ultimately inexplicable universe.[15]

A third dimension of religious expression, which is different from either theism or monism but has greatly influenced Asians and the world—despite its paucity of interest in God, eschatology, and afterlife—has originated in China. It is Confucianism, a religious philosophy that has powerfully impressed Chinese, Koreans, Japanese, and adjacent peoples for many centuries. Confucius was not a theologian, a prophet, or a god. He did not speak of the divine, but was person-centered in his concerns. He was devoted to the moral refinement of people in society as a key to universal harmony and peace. His philosophy of life and his doctrines of filial piety, benevolence, loyalty, virtue, and ritual have contributed greatly to civilization and stability in the world.

Thus, the religious traditions of the world may be viewed in a variety of ways; no one way is adequate in itself. Each method has insights to offer. Each approach is useful; but to examine such diverse religions adequately, one should integrate the above methods, thereby deriving the broadest possible understanding. And, of course, one must study the separate religions themselves with respect and appreciation, which is the aim of the following chapters.

WHY SHOULD LATTER-DAY SAINTS STUDY THE RELIGIONS OF THE WORLD?

Latter-day revelation has made it clear that the Lord was and is not pleased with the state of world religiosity (JS–H 1:19; D&C 1:15–16). Since the deaths of the apostles shortly after the time of Christ, all religious experience had fallen away from the truth; and if the essential truths and ordinances were to be available to humanity, a restoration had to occur. This Restoration began in 1820—and the rest of the story is well known. Given this obvious condition, why, then, should Latter-day Saints study the religions of the world? There are good arguments *against* such a study. Should we not spend more time studying our own faith? Do not the restored gospel and the Restoration scriptures require a lifetime of study? If faith in a false god produces false results, why learn about false gods? If faiths other than that of the Latter-day Saints are not founded by God, why should we have anything to do with them? If not all wrong, are they not at least irrelevant? They will not bring exaltation in the celestial kingdom, so of what value are they? We are sent forth to teach, not to be taught by others (D&C 43:15). The study

of "outside" religions, particularly the false philosophies of the non-Christian faiths, can be confusing and might possibly weaken our testimonies of the gospel of Jesus Christ.

And yet, although some of the opinions stated above contain elements of truth, there are a number of compelling reasons why Latter-day Saints *should* study the religions of humankind. Let us consider these.

The World: A Close Neighborhood

A few decades ago the terms Buddhist, Hindu, mosque, Sikh, pagoda, and synagogue were unfamiliar labels filled with mystery. Today, however, the world is a close neighborhood. Few societies or religions are any longer distant or foreign. The study of the religions of the world is no longer a matter of reading about exotic lands to which only the most intrepid travelers have voyaged. Almost any faith from anywhere is a presence in our lives—and an immediate option. Even a youngster in a Latter-day Saint home is not surprised when he sees on his television screen a bearded Sikh in a turban; a dancing devotee of the Hare Krishna movement; a Hassidic Jew with dangling curls and a curious black hat at the Western Wall in Jerusalem; the Roman Catholic pope reciting mass before throngs at Saint Peter's Square or kissing the ground in Africa or the United States; or a congregation of Japanese seated in the lotus posture, chanting in unison before a Buddhist or Shinto shrine. These are all familiar scenes in today's world.

Wherever Latter-day Saints live on earth, we are in close proximity to believers and proponents of all major religions. They have an impact, either directly or indirectly, upon our own religious thoughts, emotions, morals, and spirituality. The incredible speed of travel and the new media of instantaneous communication are commonplace. They draw people of the earth into an intimacy and interaction unique in history. No one is any longer totally isolated or confined to a single geographical location or cultural tradition. We unavoidably interface with people everywhere. For The Church of Jesus Christ of Latter-day Saints and its people to remain strong and stable, members must seek understanding of our next-door neighbors in New York, Seoul, Cairo, Rome, Guatemala City, Katmandu, and all the other villages and cities of the earth. It is foolishly unrealistic to ignore this reality or to think otherwise.

We live in a golden age for the study of the many human ways of faith. In the past, when knowledge of almost all religions but one's own was for the most part limited to books, it was inevitable that the encounter was chiefly on the level of ideas. For most, comparative religion was comparative doctrine, or at best comparative philosophy. We were content to say, "The Buddhists believe this," or "The Hindus believe that," as we sought to understand the Buddhists or the Hindus. What little we knew about worship services, styles of family or social life, or the attitudes of those who believed this or that was relegated to the realm of "quaint customs" of the sort described in travel magazines. Rarely was there any attempt to connect intellectual belief with concrete practice to gain a full picture of the religions as a unified human experience. It was always easy to fall back into a stereotyped pattern, to be flippant or glib, as though "all Buddhists" and "all Hindus" were equally well informed and equally pious in the beliefs and practices ascribed to them. Personal experience today brings Buddhists of Thailand, Cambodia, and Vietnam or Hare Krishnas and gurus of India into our schools, neighborhoods, and homes on an almost ordinary basis. Latter-day Saints throughout the world now personally associate with Chinese, Japanese, and Koreans of Confucian, Taoist, Shinto, shamanistic, and Buddhist backgrounds, often without being aware of these backgrounds. Since we see only what we are prepared to see in life, we are often not able to recognize or respect others' religious values and beliefs. What is said here about the religions of eastern and southeastern Asia can also be said about devout Christians, Muslims, Sikhs, and Parsis of southern or southwestern Asia whom we now see and hear in movies, on television, and on radio in increasingly personal ways.

Missionary Work

Latter-day Saints have been commanded through divine revelation to teach the gospel of Jesus Christ to all human beings on earth. The Lord has enjoined us to engage in missionary work in every nation, and with every kindred, tongue, and people (see D&C 42:58). Representatives of the church are going forth with conviction and force to the farthest reaches of the earth because of a commitment to share the message of redeeming love with any who are willing to receive it.

We are seeking to instill Christian faith among people who live in a diversity of nations, languages, races, and cultures heretofore beyond our historical experience. As a church founded and nurtured in the United States, with an early concentration on missionary work among Americans, Europeans, and the peoples of Polynesia, it is understandable that traditional Latter-day Saints have been slow in developing a personal appreciation of the non-Christian world or establishing any fixed ideas about the relation between the gospel and the religions of the Eastern world. Our literature heretofore has been almost entirely confined to an explanation of our religion within the context of European and American history. The writings of our gospel scholars have dealt with Catholic and Protestant backgrounds—or with the classical cultures of ancient Greece, Egypt, or Rome—and the European apostasies and reforms that preceded Joseph Smith. It has been a partial and fragmentary view, not a universal perspective. We have looked at the history of religion and of The Church of Jesus Christ of Latter-day Saints from the vantage point of a Western background. Many people—not only outside the church, but even many within it—have looked upon the Lord's dealings with man only within the limited framework of American history.

Eastern peoples were targeted in divine revelations from an early date, but knowledge born of a global view of the gospel has developed among the membership at large only gradually since the internationally conscious presidencies of David O. McKay and Spencer W. Kimball.[16] Now that the church has expanded into all accessible national, ethnic, and religious communities worldwide, the consciousness of The Church of Jesus Christ of Latter-day Saints as a world religion instead of a sect of Christianity bound to Western history or Western culture has begun fully to serve the needs of the operational church, which today is global in scope.

Joseph Smith held a magnanimous view of the church's destiny:

> The Standard of Truth has been erected; no unhallowed hand can stop the work from progressing; persecutions may rage, mobs may combine, armies may assemble, calumny may defame, but the truth of God will go forth boldly, nobly, and independent, till it has penetrated every continent, visited every clime, swept every country, and sounded in every ear, till the purposes of God shall be accomplished, and the Great Jehovah shall say the work is done.[17]

In March 1833 the Lord commanded the people of the church to "study and learn, and become acquainted with all good books, and with languages, tongues, and people" (D&C 90:15). In May of the same year the Lord explained that Latter-day Saints were also expected "to obtain a knowledge of history, and of countries, and of kingdoms . . . for the salvation of Zion" (D&C 93:53). And, as mentioned at the beginning of this chapter, Joseph Smith and his associates were admonished in December of 1832 to obtain "a knowledge . . . of countries and of kingdoms" (D&C 88:79). Why? "That ye may be prepared in all things when I shall send you . . . that you may be perfected in your ministry to go forth among the Gentiles for the last time" (D&C 88:80, 84). In other words, Latter-day Saints are expected to study the history, the peoples, the cultures, and the nations of the world in preparation for successful worldwide missionary work.

In pondering the question of why Latter-day Saints should study the religions of the world, we need to reconsider seriously the purposes for which the Lord commanded that a school of the prophets be organized in March of 1833:

> That thereby they may be perfected in their ministry for the salvation of Zion . . . [t]hat . . . through their administration the word may go forth unto the ends of the earth . . . in convincing the nations . . . of the gospel of their salvation. For it shall come to pass in that day, that every man shall hear the fulness of the gospel in his own tongue, and in his own language. (D&C 90:8–11)

There may be a key here that draws a distinction between a "tongue" (language) and a "language" (way of thinking, religion). The non-Christian nations of the earth are to be taught in their own tongues in the context of their own ways of expression and thought. But in order to be fully prepared to carry the gospel message effectively to all nations, we must first "study and learn" both the "tongues" and religions of these peoples.

Continually, nations previously closed to missionaries are extending a welcome, and these new associations—especially in the Middle East, Asia, and Africa—have been the most challenging of any the church has faced in history. Many of the old theological categories and comparisons used in the past to discuss Catholicism, Protestantism, and Judaism have little or no clear relevance in countries where Buddhism, Taoism, or Hinduism prevail. It is becoming more evident now than before that, if we intend to communicate effectively with people in these countries, it is not sufficient just to be conversant in their language and familiar with church doctrine; we must also know the assumptions which comprise their lives. We must be aware not only of what *we* say, but also of what *they* hear.

PURSUIT OF TRUTH

Latter-day Saints are expected to seek truth wherever it may be found. We are expected to seek learning by study as well as by faith (D&C 88:118). We are commanded to pursue truth, which is the "knowledge of things as they are, and as they were, and as they are to come" (D&C 93:24), not only that we may share more effectively with others, but also that we may grow and develop personally.

This is not a limited assignment, confined only to what has been revealed in the scriptures. As indicated at the beginning of this chapter, the Lord has commanded that we must be instructed more perfectly "in all things" that pertain to the kingdom of God, including "things both in heaven and in the earth, and under the earth [physical, natural, and mathematical sciences]; things which have been, things which are, things which must shortly come to pass [history and other social sciences]; things which are at home, things which are abroad; the wars and perplexities of the nations, and the judgments which are on the land [political science and international relations], and a knowledge also of countries and of kingdoms [geography, humanities, the arts, languages, and cultural studies of all kinds, including comparative religions]" (D&C 88:78–79). And in this search, even small and seemingly unrelated customs and traditions can offer considerable understanding. For instance, asks James Toronto, what can the clothing worn by a member of another religious sect reveal? What special attire is required in a given religious community, and what functions does it have? Which aspects of dress are specifically prescribed by religious dogma, and which are merely reflections of cultural norms? Are the mores and strictures governing dress exactly the same for both men and women? If not, why not? Modesty is valued in all religions, but how does the definition of modesty and its expression in personal attire change from culture to culture, and from time to time within the same culture? All these observations can give insight into the faith of the people so clothed.

Or, continues Toronto, consideration of the role ritual plays in religious life can prove a fascinating and stimulating topic. For his purposes, he defines ritual as the frequently repeated use of words, actions, or objects that represent abstract spiritual truths. It is revealing for students of comparative religion to ask themselves questions like these: What rituals do I participate in within my religious milieu? What purposes and meanings are reflected in these rites? Is there a healthy balance between physical form and spiritual content in the religious life of the community? Is individual commitment and status within the community determined more by observance of external forms or by demonstration of internal spiritual qualities? Most of the answers to these questions will, he admits, be subjective and tentative unless based on in-depth research, observation, and interviewing. But discussing and thinking about these issues can yield vital insights about the nature of individual and communal religious experience.

In our search for knowledge, humility and integrity should prevail. As Hugh Nibley has cautioned, we must resist both the historic danger of underestimating our ignorance and the danger of complacency:

Having been given great knowledge the Saints were in constant danger of underestimating their own ignorance. It was necessary to remind them again and again that if God's gifts are treated lightly they will be lightly withdrawn. The Latter-day Saints have constantly slipped into the dangerous complacency of the student who feels superior because he has the only answerbook in the class. Had they been given too much light? Since when would they be ready for more?[18]

Latter-day Saints do not claim to have a monopoly on knowledge, refinement, or civilization. Brigham Young said: "This is the belief and doctrine of the Latter-day Saints. Learn everything that the children of men know, and be prepared for the most refined society upon the face of the earth, then improve upon this until we are prepared and permitted to enter the society of the blessed—the holy angels that dwell in the presence of God."[19] Hugh Nibley comments on this quote:

What could be more foolish than to reject such gifts because they are found outside the Church? Just as the King James version of the Bible is worthy of our reverent attention until the day when we can excel it, so it is no disgrace that the Church has not produced a Bach,

Michelangelo, or Shakespeare—the whole world has hardly produced a handful of such men in a thousand years. We should receive their gifts with gratefulness before we presume to supplant them with our own poor talents.[20]

For Latter-day Saints, the pursuit of knowledge is a religious quest. We are committed to research and scholarship that lead to the discovery of true principles, to the enrichment of our lives, and to the blessings of others. For us, as Nibley suggests,

[i]ntelligence, the glory of God, is a moral quality [see D&C 93:36, 42]. It is "problem-solving ability." And how do [we] solve any problem? The first step for me is to discover what I do *not* know . . . —I must search out the weak and defective spots in my knowledge. . . . The next step is to find out [what it is] that I do *not* know but should; and thus I move forward in my quest, progressively laying bare dark new areas of ignorance. . . . It is a humiliating experience, and checks, corrections, revisions, deletions, weary retracing and new beginnings never end. There is no terminal degree. Only the truly humble can [walk this path].[21]

Latter-day Saints should rejoice in all discoveries and revelations of truth, whether directly from God or from the ponderings and experiences of humankind. In the words of Orson F. Whitney:

[The gospel] embraces all truth, whether known or unknown, it incorporates all intelligence, both past and prospective. No righteous principle will ever be revealed, no truth can possibly be discovered, either in time or in eternity, that does not in some manner, directly or indirectly, pertain to the Gospel of Jesus Christ.[22]

Our prophet-leaders have long maintained that all religions of the world teach important truths which have blessed God's children through the centuries in every continent and nation of the earth. John A. Widtsoe, for instance, taught that "spiritual outreachings are not peculiar to one country. [People] have arisen in every land, who have tried to formulate the way . . . to happiness for the benefit of themselves and their fellow [human beings]."[23]

The perspectives of Orson F. Whitney also apply: God has been using not merely his covenant people, but other peoples of the world as well, to carry out a work that is too demanding for the limited numbers of Latter-day Saints to accomplish by themselves. This has been true down through the ages. Prophets and apostles and patriarchs holding the authority of God's priesthood have done what the Lord has required at their hands; but other good and great men and women, who have not borne the priesthood or been fully aware of God's ultimate designs, but who have thought profoundly, accumulated great wisdom, led exemplary moral lives, and unselfishly desired to uplift their fellow beings, have been inspired by God under many circumstances to deliver dimensions of light and truth that the people were able to understand and use wisely. This includes many teachers, reformers, and founders of the religions of the world, such as Zarathustra, Gautama Buddha, Lao Tzu, Muhammad, and Guru Nanak.[24]

Thus, Latter-day Saints should study the religions of the world not only to improve our effectiveness in sharing the gospel with others, but also for what we can learn from them—their views, their values and their spiritual experiences. They can teach us things about themselves, about the world in which we live, about the dealings of God with all his children, and even about ourselves and the meanings of our own faith as viewed from a variety of religious persuasions. If we accept Alma's teachings in the Book of Mormon that God has granted wisdom to all people "of their own nation and tongue" (Alma 29:8), or Nephi's word that God has spoken to his children according to his own pleasure—to the Jews in Palestine, to the Nephites on the American continent, to all the scattered remnants of the house of Israel, and to "all nations of the earth" (see 2 Ne. 29:7–12)—then there is much of significance and worth beyond our own experience for us to investigate and cherish.

Thus, it should be an adventure for us to be exposed to the religious literature of the Eastern world, to be able to draw comparisons between our writings and theirs, and to be enriched by the experience. Paradoxically, in such a study we can learn much about our own faith. One of the best ways to clarify our own thinking is to set our beliefs over against other systems of thought or to see ourselves from afar. We can gain fresh insights into the gospel through observing how others seek to apply many of its principles and ordinances in new settings.

Upon becoming familiar with the religious world as it is, other vital questions arise. What about the many messiah figures of the religions of the world? How do they compare with our own understanding of Jesus as the Savior and Messiah of the world? Is Jesus different, or is he unique? In what ways? If one carefully examines the religions of the world with some sense of objectivity, what remains in Latter-day Saint doctrine that is absolutely unique? What specifically do we have to offer that other great religions do not already provide? These are timely, relevant, and provocative questions that affect the faith of converts to The Church of Jesus Christ of Latter-day Saints from Hindu, Sikh, Zoroastrian, Jewish, Muslim, and Buddhist backgrounds.

The Samaritan woman at the well of Sychar asked Jesus a searching question: "Art thou greater than our father Jacob . . . ?" (John 4:12). It is a serious query that will likely be posed by members either privately or in public church meetings more often in the future than it has in the past. What do we find in the gospel we have received? How does it fit into the world at large? What is the relationship between the message of The Church of Jesus Christ of Latter-day Saints and the traditional beliefs in the religions of the world? These questions are examined in this book.

Some might fear that the gospel will be diluted or that personal testimonies are at risk of being seriously jeopardized through study of the religions of the world. Experience shows that the opposite is the case. By examining ourselves and our religion within a global rather than a regional or sectarian frame, we find a message that we never before realized. We find that The Church of Jesus Christ of Latter-day Saints measures up well as a world religion. The restored gospel is compelling when compared with other religions. There need be no reason for reticence or apology. Studies of world religions open exciting new mental and spiritual horizons. As never before, we can realize the condescension of God and his universal love for humankind; we can gain greater appreciation for the marvelous ways in which Latter-day Saints are bound to their brothers and sisters of other faiths—not just Christians and Jews, but other communities as well—while more clearly understanding the significant differences that exist. Perhaps most spiritually satisfying, we can learn to understand better the global viability of the gospel of Jesus Christ in meeting individual needs, and its capacity for unique and powerful contributions in today's world. Ultimately, in a world context, the restored gospel will be seen for what it is: the crown and capstone of all religious experience. It is to the Restoration fulness that all other religious experience points.

Notes

1. Roger R. Keller, *Reformed Christians and Mormon Christians: Let's Talk* (Ann Arbor, Mich.: Pryor Pettengill, 1986), xv, xvi.

2. Spencer W. Kimball, "The Evil of Intolerance," *Improvement Era* 57, no. 6 (June 1954): 425.

3. Richard P. Lindsay, "A Mormon View of Religious Tolerance" (address given to the Board of Directors of the Anti-Defamation League of B'nai B'rith, Central Pacific Chapter, San Francisco, February 6, 1984).

4. This is based on my personal observation of the event; I was present at the mission home as a missionary.

5. Joseph Smith, *History of the Church of Jesus Christ of Latter-day Saints*, 7 vols. (1949; reprint, Salt Lake City: Deseret Book, 1970), 4:227. See also the Book of Mormon: "Behold, the Lord esteemeth all flesh in one" (1 Ne. 17:35); "the Lord . . . inviteth all to come unto him and partake of his goodness; . . . and all are alike unto God, both Jew and Gentile" (2 Ne. 26:33); "for thus saith the Lord: Ye shall not esteem one flesh above another" (Mosiah 23:7).

6. News interview with Phil Riesen, held in Salt Lake City on May 12, 1995; reprinted in Sheri L. Dew, *Go Forward with Faith: The Biography of Gordon B. Hinckley* (Salt Lake City: Deseret Book, 1996), 576.

7. Gerald E. Jones, "Respect for Other People's Beliefs," *Ensign*, October 1977, 70–71.

8. Joseph Smith, "Counsel against Secrecies," in Joseph Fielding Smith, comp., *Teachings of the Prophet Joseph Smith* (Salt Lake City: Deseret Book, 1979), 146–47.

9. Wayne Ham, *Man's Living Religions* (Independence, Mo.: Herald, 1966), 17–19.

10. Paul Hutchinson, "How Mankind Worships," in Sam Welles, ed., *The World's Great Religions* (New York: Time, 1957), 1.

11. Ibid.

12. Robert S. Ellwood, Jr., *Alternative Altars: Unconventional and Eastern Spirituality in America* (Chicago: University of Chicago Press, 1979), esp. 4–19; Ellwood, *Many Peoples, Many Faiths: An Introduction to the Religious Life of Mankind* (Englewood Cliffs, N.J.: Prentice-Hall, 1976), 7–10; Ellwood and Harry B. Partin, *Religious and Spiritual Groups in Modern America*, 2d ed. (Englewood Cliffs, N.J.: Prentice-Hall, 1973), esp. 11–16.

13. Hutchinson, "How Mankind Worships," 2.

14. As quoted in Ham, *Man's Living Religions,* 12–13.

15. E. L. Allen, *Christianity among the Religions* (Boston: Beacon Press, 1961), 133–36.

16. See Spencer J. Palmer, *The Expanding Church* (Salt Lake City: Deseret Book, 1979), 1–14.

17. Smith, *History of the Church,* 4:540.

18. Hugh Nibley, "More Brigham Young on Education" (address given at the Sidney B. Sperry Symposium, Brigham Young University, Provo, Ut., March 11, 1976), 11.

19. Brigham Young, "Ignorance of the World . . . ," May 25, 1873, in Brigham Young et al., *Journal of Discourses,* 26 vols. (1842–96; reprint, Salt Lake City: n.p., 1967), 16:77.

20. Nibley, "More Brigham Young," 15.

21. Ibid., 8.

22. Orson Whitney, "The Gospel of Jesus Christ," *Elder's Journal* [Southern States Mission] 4, no. 2 (October 15, 1906): 26.

23. John A. Widtsoe, *Gospel Interpretations: Aids to Faith in a Modern Day* (Salt Lake City: Bookcraft, 1947), 216.

24. Orson F. Whitney, untitled address, in *Ninety-First Annual Conference of The Church of Jesus Christ of Latter-day Saints* (Salt Lake City: The Church of Jesus Christ of Latter-day Saints, 1921), 32–33; see also the statement of the First Presidency, February 15, 1978, in Palmer, *Expanding Church,* frontispiece.

Part Two
South Asian Religions

The religions of south Asia—Hinduism, Jainism, Buddhism, and Sikhism—all have their origins in India, and thus they share basic precepts. All believe in seeking identification with the ultimate—which may be thought of as an internal essence, spirit, or mind. This includes renouncing the finite in order to gain recognition of the infinite, and renouncing ego's claims (individuality) to conclusiveness. All believe in karma, or the law of cause and effect. Coupled with this is a belief in the doctrine of reincarnation, and consequently the goal for all is to gain release from the rounds of rebirths. The amount of karma an individual accrues over numerous lifetimes determines the situation into which he or she will enter in the next lifetime. Most also believe that all life is integrated and all beings are dependent upon one another. Thus, a sense of nonviolence or noninjury is prevalent in Hinduism, Jainism, and Buddhism. Since all life is related, no life should be harmed or injured.

Here the similarities end, however. How persons gain release from the wheel of rebirths differs from religion to religion. Adherents to some religions—Jains, Theravada Buddhists, and Hindus of some traditions—believe that no gods exist who can assist them off the wheel, that all persons have to work out their own salvation. Others—Mahayana and Vajrayana Buddhists, Hindus of some traditions, and Sikhs—hold that there are helping beings or gods who assist in the salvation process. One tradition, Sikhism, believes in one all-powerful, inclusive God, who is both monotheistic and monistic. Some of the traditions are highly egalitarian—notably Svetambara Jainism, Buddhism, and Sikhism. Others are either very structured, with a caste system—as in some forms of Hinduism—or are exclusive, particularly in relation to the place of women—such as Digambara Jainism.

Some of the world's oldest and newest religious traditions have arisen in south Asia. These religions are rich in their answers about the meaning of life and the inequities found within the human situation, and in their attempts to help persons understand their proper relationships with one another. Those answers are sometimes different from the ones Latter-day Saints might give, and as such they offer valuable possibilities to expand Latter-day Saints' understanding of what motivates the faith of millions of their brothers and sisters in south Asia.

Hinduism

Spencer J. Palmer

T is extremely difficult to form a comprehensive definition of Hinduism. Actually, *Hindu* was the term used by persons living outside India to designate those persons who lived "beyond the Indus." It was a geographical designation initially and had virtually nothing to do with religion. A more correct term for the religious traditions practiced by the majority of persons living in India would be *dharma,* meaning "the way." Each person has his or her own individual way to follow, and one way may be very different from some other way.

It is precisely this diversity that makes Hinduism so difficult to define. There is no one body of belief common to all practitioners of the faith, with the exception that most persons on the Indian subcontinent believe in the concepts of reincarnation, *karma,* and the possibility of ultimate release from the round of rebirths. There is, however, no central authority, no universal moral code, and no founder. As one observer has stated the situation, "Starting from the Veda, Hinduism has ended in embracing something from all religions, and in presenting phases suited to all minds. It is all-tolerant, all-compliant, all-comprehensive, all-absorbing."[1]

A person may be a virtual monotheist, a thoroughgoing polytheist, or even a functional atheist and still fall under the umbrella of Hinduism. Hinduism may consist of the most primitive types of animism and animal worship or may embrace the highest of philosophical systems. Thus, any attempt to define Hinduism is fated to be only a partial description. The present discussion seeks to describe some of the basic streams within the faith.

The roots of Hinduism are lost in the mists of time, but it is probably a composite of traditions indigenous to India, as well as religious ideas brought to India by invading peoples. Hinduism is complex, but to one willing to devote the time to its study it has some profound and interesting answers to the problems of human life.

ARYAN BACKGROUND

To fully understand the foundations of Hinduism—as well as Zoroastrianism—one must be aware of the common legacy of these faiths. In the mists of antiquity, some of the ancestors of today's Iranians and Indians formed one people. They were Caucasians and were known as *Aryans.* Their original homeland is uncertain. It may have been on the south Russian steppes, to the east of the Volga River, on the Pamir Plateau of central Asia, in central or alpine Europe, or even in the extreme Arctic region. Whatever the case, it is clear that the peoples comprising two main branches of the Aryan race—who later intermingled with the native Iranians and Indians—originally lived together in one place for a long time and, practically speaking, had the same language, the same religious beliefs, the same manners and customs, and the same divinities and myths. They were a branch of the Indo-Europeans, and they lived a pastoral, semimigratory life, herding cattle, sheep, and goats.[2]

After centuries of close association, at some time perhaps in the third millennium B.C.E., these people divided into at least two groups. One of these migrated to the Iranian tableland and drove out the indigenous inhabitants or absorbed them. Eventually, under the guidance of Zarathustra, these people originated Zoroastrianism in Iran. The other group settled in the valley of the Indus River in India. The people with whom they came in contact were called *Dravidians.* The *Rig Veda,* the earliest religious text of Hinduism, indicates that the Aryans were divided into several tribes. At first they were concentrated in the Indus Valley, but later they spread into the Ganges Plain and then throughout

India. India became known as Hindustan, and by the sixth century C.E. the people became known as Hindus.

BASIC BELIEFS

The Gods

The gods of Hinduism are many and varied. Some individuals count 96,000 gods, while others suggest there are 330,000 gods or more. It should be understood, however, that the gods of Hinduism are a product of the interaction between the religion the Aryan invaders brought with them and the religion that was already present in India among the Dravidian natives.

Very little is known about the Dravidian culture. Most of what is known is derived from archaeological evidence and not from texts, since those few samples of writing from the Indus Valley centers of Dravidian culture, Mohenjo-Daro and Harappa, have not yet been deciphered. Archaeological evidence, however, indicates that the Dravidians were predominantly worshipers of fertility gods and goddesses. Nude female figures, as well as images of bulls, tigers, buffalo, and elephants, have been found. In the context of a culture which was predominantly agricultural, these all suggest a fertility cult. The fertility aspect of the Hindu god *Shiva* is thus very probably derived from the Dravidian religion.

Because the Aryans were a nomadic herding people, the religion that they brought with them was predominantly nature-centered. The Aryan gods were personifications of the natural world which affected the people's lives—sky, rain, sun, moon, storms, and wind. Reference to these gods may be found in the most ancient of Hindu texts, the Vedas, which are in many parts Aryan in origin. Thus, one finds hymns, particularly in the Rig Veda, to *Indra* (the atmospheric god), *Soma* (god of drink), *Agni* (god of fire), and *Varuna* (god of the sky), as well as many other gods. To these gods, the Aryans sacrificed food, drink, and animals.

As they entered India, the Aryans brought not only their gods but also a social structure which developed into the caste system. The upper three divisions became the castes which could be "twice born," or initiated into full social responsibility at adulthood. These were the priests (*Brahmins*), the nobles and warriors (*Kshatriyas*), and the commoners

and merchants (*Vaishyas*). Below this was the servant or slave caste (*Sudras*), who were predominantly of the Dravidian race and who could not be "twice born." Today, there is an additional major stratum composed of people who are rejected ("out-caste"), or who hold socially despicable jobs. To elevate them in society, Mahatma Gandhi gave them the name *Harijan*—children of God.

Nature Deities: Earliest of the Aryan Deities

INDRA. The patron god of the Aryans, Indra, is precisely the sort of god that would have appealed to a nomadic, semiwarlike people. He is fond of the hallucinogenic drink soma and many times used his thunderbolt to battle the enemies of the Aryan people. He is predominantly an atmospheric god who controls the thunder and the lightning (known as *vajra*), but he is also seen as a creator god. This latter role is explained through Indra's mythical battle with the evil serpent, *Vritra,* who had swallowed the sun and all water. The world could not be created until these essential elements were released. This Indra did by slashing open the belly of Vritra, thereby liberating the sun and water.

SOMA. Soma is both a god and a drink. At times it is difficult to determine which is intended in the literature, as one notes in the following: "We have drunk the Soma; we have become immortal; we have gone to the light; we have found the gods. . . . [A]s a friend to a friend[.] [F]ar-famed soma, stretch out our life-span so that we may live" (Rig Veda 8.48.3–4).[3] The drink, which is made by pressing juice from the leaves of the soma plant and mixing it with milk, has powerful hallucinatory properties which give the worshiper a sense of immortality, the characteristic of the god Soma. Thus, by imbibing soma, one takes on the quality of the god and can thereby face danger or life itself with great self-assurance. The god Soma became identified with the moon, and it bears his name.

AGNI. The god of fire, Agni, takes many forms. He is found in terrestrial fires, in the sun, and in lightning and is therefore omnipresent. Agni is principally the mediator between heaven and earth, for he bears the offerings of men to the gods.

VARUNA. The sky god, whose eye is the sun and whose garment is the universe, is Varuna. Like Agni, he is seen as everywhere present. He has a thousand eyes, and thus no one may escape his examination. He knows the hearts of all. He dwells, however, in a house of a thousand doors, indicating his complete accessibility. In addition to being associated with the sun, Varuna is also attached to the moon and is understood as the ruler of the night. Thus, there is a certain capriciousness about him; but he is normally benevolent. He also controls *maya* (illusion).

The Hindu Trimurti: An Expanded Understanding of God

By the last half of the first millennium B.C.E., Hinduism as it is known today began to emerge from the interaction between Aryan and Dravidian thought. With its emergence came the three high gods, *Brahma,* Shiva, and Vishnu, who form a trinity of gods known as the *Trimurti,* a threefold manifestation of the ultimate reality called *Brahman-Atman.*

BRAHMA. Brahma, while a major god, is without a significant following in Hinduism. This is because he is the creator god. In essence, he is viewed as having completed his work and being thus withdrawn from active involvement in the created order. Hindu art often portrays him with four bearded faces and four arms, studying the Vedas, and riding on a white goose. He lives on Mount Meru with his wife *Sarasvati,* the goddess of the creative arts. From this exalted place he surveys the earth without being active in its affairs.

SHIVA. Shiva is the best Hindu example of the wedding of Aryan and Dravidian traditions. Shiva's precursor appears to have been *Rudra,* the dread mountain god of the Aryans. He was the god of winter storms. To a pastoral people, the winter storms of the Himalayas could be fearful, destroying vast numbers of animals and taking human lives as well. Thus one reads: "Do not slaughter the great one among us or the small one among us, nor the growing or the grown. Rudra, do not kill our father or our mother, nor harm the bodies dear to us" (Rig Veda 1.114.7). Consequently, a dominant feature of Rudra was his destructive side, a side which included death and disease. However, there was a duality to Rudra. He was also the god of healing, an apparent contradiction until one realizes that healing herbs are to be found in the mountains.

Shiva is similarly a god of duality. Like Rudra, his Aryan predecessor, he is a god of destruction. He will destroy the world at the end of this current age (*kalpa*). He brings death. As *Nataraja,* Lord of the Dance, he destroys ignorance and is often portrayed dancing upon the prostrate demon of ignorance in a ring of fire. His second function—derived from Dravidian roots—is that of fertility, a role which replaces Rudra's healing function. In this role Shiva brings new life out of death. A symbol specifically associated with Shiva's fertility aspect is the *lingam,* a phallic symbol through which he is worshiped. Another symbol associated with Shiva is the bull *Nandi,* upon which he rides. Nandi is perhaps derived from the Dravidian fertility cult.

The power by which Shiva both creates and destroys is known as *shakti,* and the worship of that power is called *shaktism.* This power is personified in four female consorts or wives of Shiva—*Uma, Parvati, Durga,* and *Kali.* Uma and Parvati are kind and benevolent, while Kali and Durga are fierce and dreadful. In Hindu art, Kali is portrayed holding a knife and drinking blood from a human skull while dancing on the prone form of Shiva. However, both Kali and Durga protect those who worship them. Their violence is directed at evildoers.

Shiva is also the god of meditation and is the patron of ascetics. He is often portrayed as an ascetic clad in an elephant-skin loincloth, with matted hair and with his body smeared in ashes. According to legend, the god of love once tried to tempt Shiva while he was meditating, and the intruder was turned into a heap of ashes by a ray from Shiva's third eye.

Shiva has two sons, both significant gods within Hinduism. The first, named *Ganesha,* is a friendly, elephant-headed god who removes obstacles from the paths of people who call on him. The second son, Karttikeya, is a great warrior and the commander of the army of the gods.

VISHNU. Vishnu, derived from the sun god of the Vedas, is the preserver of the universe. He exhibits a constant concern and compassion for the world and its inhabitants. The legend which explains Vishnu's role indicates that the universe came into existence when Vishnu awoke from his long cosmic night of sleep. Just prior to the dawn of this kalpa, Vishnu, who had been reclining on the great serpent *Sesha,* awoke. From his navel grew a lotus, from which Brahma arose. Then from Vishnu's head Shiva was born, and with the presence of the three gods this current kalpa began. It will end when Vishnu goes back to sleep.

As mentioned, Vishnu is close to the world and is directly involved in it. This involvement manifests itself in nine incarnations (*avatars*) through which

Vishnu has come to earth to preserve the world and its people, with one avatar that is yet to come. The avatars have been both animal and human and are as follows:

1. *Matsya:* A fish who rescued *Manu,* the first man, from the flood. Manu is sometimes considered to be the Hindu equivalent of Noah as well as Adam.

2. *Kurma:* A tortoise who, by swimming around a mountain in an ocean of milk, churned the nectar of immortality.

3. *Varaha:* A boar who rescued the earth, which had sunk into the ocean, by lifting it with his tusks.

4. *Narasimha:* A man-lion who saved a boy whose father wanted to kill him for worshiping Vishnu. This is the only avatar that is not solely animal or solely human.

5. *Vamana:* A dwarf who reclaimed heaven and earth from the clutches of Bali, the king of the demons. As Vamana, Vishnu appeared before Bali and requested that he be given as much territory as he could cover in three steps. Bali, amused, agreed. Vishnu then changed into his glorified form and in two steps encompassed heaven and earth, but did not take the third step, leaving hell in the possession of Bali.

6. *Parasurama:* A Brahmin warrior who preserved the supremacy of the Brahmin caste by defeating rival Kshatriyas twenty-one times in battle.

7. *Rama:* A prince who lost his kingdom and retreated to the forest. When his wife Sita was kidnaped by the evil Ravana, Lord of Sri Lanka, Rama battled against and defeated him to rescue Sita. During her captivity, Sita retained her purity and virtue. Rama is the Hindu ideal of manhood, and Sita is the ideal woman. Their story is found in the *Ramayana.*

8. *Krishna:* Either a warrior or a merry youth. As a warrior and the hero of the *Bhagavad Gita,* Krishna taught the warrior Arjuna that devotion is the highest form of religious life and should always be directed to Vishnu. As a youth, Krishna was attractive to young ladies and was at times impish. He portrayed the ideal of love. As the young ladies sought him and clung to him, so should all seek and cling to Vishnu in love.

9. *Siddhartha Gautama:* A prince who founded Buddhism, which Hindus see as a part of Hinduism.

10. *Kalki:* In the abundant lore of Hinduism there is a heroic god who will yet descend to earth and deliver humankind from darkness and evil. His name is Kalki, and he is the future incarnation of the god Vishnu. Like all other solar deities, Vishnu is likened to a white horse. In the *Mahabharata* and the *Puranas,* Kalki is either a hero, mounted on a white horse and bearing a blazing sword, or a giant with a white horse's head. He is sometimes portrayed as a universal ruler called Parasraya, mounted on a white horse. Compare this to a portion of the Revelation of John in the New Testament:

And I saw heaven opened, and behold a white horse; and he that sat upon him was called Faithful and True, and in righteousness he doth judge and make war. His eyes were as a flame of fire, and on his head were many crowns; and he had a name written, that no man knew, but he himself. (Rev. 19:11–12)

The historical Buddha is sometimes quoted as having said that at the end of the current æon another divine manifestation will appear. Some argue that this is a prophecy regarding Kalki; others assert that it refers to Maitreya, a Buddhist messiah figure. In either case, a messiah will appear at the end of the present age of darkness in which irreligion has proliferated, dharma has disappeared, and people have sunk to wickedness and debauchery. Kalki's return is for the purpose of restoring law, justice, and right.

As one views the above avatars, one gets a sense of the deep concern that Vishnu has for the world and its inhabitants. It is little wonder that Vishnu is the most popular of the divine figures and that there are very many people devoted to him.

In the art of India, Vishnu is often represented as a young man wearing a crown and either lying on the serpent Sesha or riding on the giant eagle *Garuda.* He is usually depicted with blue skin and lotus eyes, which are considered marks of beauty, and sitting on a lotus flower. In his hands he may be holding a mace and a discus, symbols of power, or a conch shell and a lotus, symbols of magic and purity.

Achieving Salvation

Hindus attain salvation from the dilatory constraints of this world by following one of three paths. First, there is *karma,* the Way of Works. Karma involves the inexorable law of the harvest—one will reap precisely as one sows—and has had a profound impact on Indian society. It has led to caste exclusions and inequalities, as well as to the belief in reincarnation. Second, there is *jyana,* the Way of

Knowledge, which emphasizes mystical experience leading to union with the One Supreme Reality as a profound key to the attainment of *nirvana*. Third, there is *bhakti,* the Way of Worship. This is the path of devotion and faith in a god or gods whose mercy and grace are able to save.

Salvation through Works (Karma)

One of the challenges of any religion is explaining the apparent injustices of life. Why, for instance, are some people born into favorable circumstances while others are forced to undergo terrible and seemingly undeserved ordeals? The inability to rationalize such inequality with the notion of a benevolent, supervisory God has driven many modern thinkers to what has been termed "existential despair." In India, however, the explanation for this inequality offered centuries ago is still the basic principle in a world view professed by millions. Their answer, found in "the law of karma," has many parallels with an idea that is fundamental to Latter-day Saint theology—the concept that persons must bear responsibility for their actions.

THE TERMS. Karma, the Hindu doctrine that is widely diffused among the religions of Asia, literally means "deeds" or "actions," and the "law of karma" is a system of cause and effect whereby people's actions determine the circumstances of their lives. Inequalities in life can be explained by the doctrine of karma. Social distinctions, caste, racial differences, poverty, and wealth are all products of one's karma created over numerous lifetimes. Social and economic status, according to this view, are not matters of random fortune, or the whim of the gods, but consequences of personal actions. By their actions all beings determine their own fates, build their characters, make their destiny, and work out their salvation. It is the Christian "law of the harvest" vigorously applied. "[W]hatsoever a man soweth, that shall he also reap" (Gal. 6:7). The effects of karma are inescapable, following persons even beyond death and into their next lives. Where can one fly from one's karma? The answer, of course, is nowhere. It is not limited by time or space and is not strictly individual; there is group karma. Once earned, karma will stay with an individual through endless rebirths (reincarnations) until it is burned up by virtuous living. In the effort to live virtuously, however, the individual risks generating new karma and perpetuating the cycle.

The neutralization of karma must be complete if the individual is to gain emancipation. Marcus Bach writes, "Nothing [one] does is ever lost, nothing is unaccounted for, nothing is forgotten, discarded, or irrelevant. Karma is an eternally moving wheel that, like the mills of the gods, grinds out men's destinies."[4] As long as a person's karma is stifling his or her soul, the wheel is indeed eternal.

The law of karma works in connection with the principle of reincarnation (*samsara*—the cycle of rebirths). As a result of karma, the individual comes into physical life with a character and in an environment that are the result of all his or her actions in all past lives. Character, family, circumstance, and destiny are all, therefore, one's karma, and according to one's reaction to present "destiny" he or she modifies and builds a future. The day of karmic reckoning, then, is the time of rebirth into a new life, the circumstances and status of which are dictated by the karma amassed over all previous lives. Those who have been of pleasant conduct will enter a pleasant womb—either the womb of a Brahmin, or the womb of a Kshatriya, or the womb of a Vaishya. But those who have been evil will enter the womb of a dog, a swine, or an outcast.

The lack of a clear distinction between the status of animals and lower-caste humans in the hierarchical continuum of life is a reflection of the kind of karma-oriented thinking that maintains the caste system in India. If life circumstances are a just consequence of past deeds, those in the upper castes can assert that they deserved their births into favorable circumstances. Indeed, they might even consider the idea of sharing their wealth with those of lower castes to be an affront to the just law of fate. The law of karma brings the same fatalistic acceptance of social immobility in the lower classes as well. Their frustration is abated by the belief that the next life will be better, if they endure their present situation well. It is in this light that one must understand the remark by Mahatma Gandhi that the class system "is not based on inequality; there is no question of inferiority."[5]

Bach describes an enlightening encounter with the karmic mentality that took place while he rode in a taxi with a Hindu. They spotted a man lying at the side of the road, Bach says, and upon stopping to help they found he was dying. "'It is karma,' said my friend. And I thought to myself, 'That is how Hindus explain everything in the world—suffering, blessings, sorrow, joy, low caste, high caste, pauper and priest, poor man, rich man. Karma covers all of life and assures the individual that what he is at any given moment is the consequence of what he has done at some previous moment.'"[6] You get only what you earn. You are exactly what you deserve.

THE METHOD. The Way of Works builds on the concepts of karma and reincarnation. It makes the basic assumption that persons must work their way up the ladder of existence. Whatever forms their incarnations may take, individuals must live them to the best of their ability. If one is reincarnated as a dog, then one should be a good dog. If one returns as a Brahmin, then one should be a good Brahmin, and so on. The concept of *ahimsa,* of doing no harm to other life, is an important principle in the formation of a positive karma leading to better conditions in succeeding lives and eventual escape from the round of rebirths. In this method, one would rarely move rapidly through the chain of existence, especially from the lower to the higher levels.

The basic guide for proper conduct lies in the laws of one's caste, which means that in the Way of Works not everybody is required to live in the same way. Each lives his or her own way, or dharma. Thus, the dharma for a Brahmin (a member of the priestly caste) would be different from that of a Kshatriya (a member of the noble or warrior caste) or Sudra (a member of the slave or servant caste). It is assumed that persons must move through the caste structure and ultimately become Brahmins before they finally have the disposition to get off the wheel of reincarnation. This emphasis on actions appropriate to a person's situation in life, which was the product of the accrued deeds of all his or her previous existences, led, as noted above, to a highly stratified and highly segregated society. People were precisely where they belonged in life.

The Way of Works is a path persons walk by themselves. No gods help them. They simply live their dharmas, and if they do this well, they will gradually progress up the spectrum of life until such time as they have freed themselves sufficiently of karma to gain release from the round of rebirths.

Salvation through the Way of Knowledge (Jyana)

Religious people seem to recognize the weakness of language in describing things not subject to empirical study—that is, those events and concepts which are of a profoundly spiritual nature. Moses, in the Bible, in relating his encounter with God,

described a burning bush. Joseph Smith's experience with God the Father and Jesus Christ the Son in the sacred grove said their "brightness and glory defy all description" (JS–H 1:17).[7] Some of the words spoken by Jesus when he visited the American continent were words which "no tongue can speak, neither can there be written by any man, neither can the hearts of men conceive so great and marvelous things" (3 Ne. 17:17).

Fondness for experiences beyond words seems always to have been characteristic of Hindus. This trait manifests itself in the *Upanishads.*[8] Looking "outward," the student of the Upanishads comes to a realization that this world is merely a bundle of fleeting names and forms, that there is only one permanent reality underlying the manifold phenomenal world, and that, in the ultimate analysis, that one reality, Brahman, is identical with the human personality, namely Atman. Thus, individual life is essentially universal life, the world soul. Atman equals Brahman.

This is not easy to describe. The Chandogya Upanishad (6:12–14) reports one effort to do so.

There, verily, was Shvetaketu, the son of Uddalaka Aruni. To him his father said: . . . "Bring hither a fig from there." "Here it is, sir." "Break it." "It is broken, sir." "What do you see there?" "These extremely fine seeds, sir." "Of these, please break one." "It is broken, sir." "What do you see there?" "Nothing at all, sir." Then he said to Shvetaketu: "Verily, my dear, that subtle essence which you do not perceive—from that very essence, indeed, my dear, does this great fig tree thus arise. Believe me, my dear, that which is the subtle essence—this whole world has that essence for its Self; that is the Real . . . ; that is the Self; that (subtle essence) art thou, Shvetaketu."[9]

This leads to the second way in Hinduism that a person may gain release from the wheel—that is, the Way of Knowledge.

THE METHOD. The premise of the Way of Knowledge is that while people may finally gain release from the wheel through works, it is the way of the spiritually less mature. Knowledge is the way of the male who has the inner disposition to follow this higher way. Like the Way of Works, it has no belief in helping deities. An individual is still on his own to gain release from the wheel.

Just as one is expected to attain the spiritual purity of a Brahmin before embarking on this path, it is also assumed that one will, either in this life or some other, be disposed to pass through all four stages of life. These are student, householder, hermit, and holy man. Normally a person will become a student at a young age, when ceremonially invested with the sacred thread indicative of caste, the attainment of manhood, and spiritual rebirth. He will later move on to the stage of husband and father. He who has his eyes set on higher things, however, will eventually leave the comfort of home and family and become a hermit, seeking to lose all attachments to worldly things. Having achieved this goal, the individual will then become a holy man, desiring only to achieve *moksha,* meaning release from the round of rebirths. This results from the experience of oneness with the one universal reality.

This experience of oneness is enlightenment, or *samadhi.* Samadhi will guarantee moksha and, upon death, entrance into nirvana, in which all sense of individuality is extinguished. The route to this goal is a study of the Upanishads, immersion in the concepts of *monism* and Brahman-Atman, and meditation. The following definitions of the terms just used will help in understanding this complex pathway.

THE TERMS. The Upanishads are philosophical and mystical treatises appearing at the end of each of the Vedas. A person on the path of knowledge will immerse himself in these writings as he seeks a correct understanding of ultimate reality within himself and within the universe. However, understanding is more than the mere intellectual grasp of a concept. Ultimately, to understand is to experience reality as it is, and thus meditation is the method to comprehend that course toward which the philosophies of the Upanishads point.

Monism is the fundamental concept toward which the Upanishads move. It is the belief that all things are one. To hold to a dualistic view of the world, in which it is believed that some things act against other things, is maya (illusion). Ultimately, people themselves are only illusions, for they are no more than waves on the ocean of existence. They have no independent identity of their own; because of illusions born of the five senses, they only believe that they do. Until that illusion is broken and they understand their true identity, they will continue to be reborn.

Brahman (the world spirit) is the ocean and Atman (the individual spirit) is the wave. Brahman is the reality that constitutes all things and Atman merely the extension of that reality. Atman does not exist apart from Brahman, for they are one, just as the ocean and its wave are one.

When taken together, the above concepts define the Way of Knowledge, the mystical way in which one realizes the oneness of all things and the oneness of Brahman-Atman through intense meditation. This is exemplified by one of the most common phrases in the Upanishads, "Tat twam asi," meaning, "That art thou," or, "That person yonder and I are one, or, "I and god (that subtle essence within all) are one." There is only one Reality. Gaining a consciousness of union with this ineffable Divine is the aim of jyana—salvation through an experiential understanding of the oneness of all things.

Salvation through Devotion (Bhakti)

The third way off the wheel of existence is the Way of Devotion, or bhakti. This is the way followed by the majority of Hindus today, for it is a path open to all persons regardless of caste or sex. Bhakti means devotion to one or more of the numberless gods in the belief that prayers to them will be answered and assistance gained in the quest to find release from the wheel of rebirths. No longer does one dwell in a functionally atheistic world. No longer is there the need to expect an interminable round of rebirths, even for the lowliest Sudra.

Normally a worshiper's devotion is directed to one of two major gods: Shiva or Vishnu. Those who worship and call on Vishnu seek the support of the preserver, who is held to be the personal expression of Brahman-Atman. Vishnu is often worshiped through his two avatars, Krishna and Rama. The Bhagavad Gita, a portion of the epic poem Mahabharata, recounts the adventures of Arjuna and his charioteer, who is Krishna (Vishnu) in disguise. Krishna teaches Arjuna his reflections on the three ways of salvation, and while he does not discount either the Way of Works or the Way of Knowledge, he states that devotion to him is the highest of all ways. Ultimately, Krishna reveals himself in his splendor to Arjuna, underscoring the message that devotion to his glorious person is the ultimate path to salvation.

Around Rama, as well, there is an extensive literature that has become scripture to the devotees of this way. The Ramayana, a counterpart to the Bhagavad Gita, details the exploits of Rama. It is of interest to note that Gandhi's dying words were "O Ram," a cry directed to Vishnu as Rama. Similar devotion is given by many to Shiva.

SCRIPTURES

Robert E. Van Voorst cites several interesting examples of the substantial impact of Hindu scriptural traditions in India.

1. After the monsoon season, people in cities and villages all over northern India gather to celebrate Rama-Lilas, a dramatic reading and reenactment of the *Ramayana,* the epic Hindu scripture. At its decisive point, wood and straw effigies of the demon Ravana are made and stuffed with fireworks. When night falls, the fireworks are set off and the demon is destroyed. Rama and the forces of good have prevailed.

2. In 1981, South India is experiencing a severe drought. As part of the response, Brahmin priests gather to chant Sanskrit verses from the three-thousand-year-old *Rig Veda.* While well-drilling crews work nearby, the priests invoke Indra, the god of the sky, for rain.

3. At a popular pilgrimage site, people gather at a booth to hear a holy man cite the *Bhagavad-Gita.* Even though the *Gita* is familiar to them, they are still attracted to its telling. Of special interest is the end of the text, which promises them a blessing. The person who listens in true faith will win release from suffering and rebirth.

4. Before dawn breaks in India, a householder rises and purifies himself with water. He then stirs back to life the embers of the sacred household fire while chanting sacred verses. Raising his arms to the rising sun, he recites a prayer to the sun-god from the most ancient scripture, the *Rig Veda.* This ritual . . . has been performed continually in India for more than three thousand years.[10]

Van Voorst observes that the scriptures of Hinduism mirror the diversity of this religion, its numerous gods, and its various means of salvation. Although "vast in size, varied in usage, and profound in influence," the Hindu scriptures can, he concludes, be reliably classified in two groups, known as *shruti* and *smriti*. Shruti, the body of primary revelation, consists of the four Vedas, the Brahmanas, the Aranyakas, and the Upanishads; this canon is "basically fixed." The smriti corpus comprehends all other scripture and is vast in size. It includes "the myths and legends of the Puranas, the epic stories of the Mahabharata and the Ramayana, and law codes" such as the Laws (or Code, or Ordinances) of Manu. Many of these have been translated into English from their original Sanskrit renderings.[11] The most widely used of these scriptures are discussed below.

The four Vedas (or "books of knowledge") are the fundamental scriptures of Hinduism. The Rig Veda, the first, contains 1,028 hymns in ten books,

each hymn being directed to a particular god or goddess. Indra, the atmospheric or sky god, and Agni, the god of fire, appear most prominently in the Rig Veda, as does Soma, the god of the hallucinogenic drug or drink which is consumed during a sacrificial ceremony. In the Yajur Veda are collected a number of formulas, mostly in prose, which are recited by priests during sacrificial ceremonies. The Sama Veda is a compilation of songs used in sacrificial ceremonies. The Atharva Veda, which is considerably different from the others, includes twenty books of 731 hymns containing spells, charms, and cures, for the most part.

As mentioned previously, the Upanishads (literally, "sittings near a teacher") are philosophical and mystical in nature and deal with topics such as cosmic reality. They often take the form of monologues or, occasionally, of debates between teachers of opposing points of view. Their primary emphasis is on self-denial as one searches for the one absolute primal reality, called Brahman. The Upanishads tend to deemphasize the ritualism that characterizes the Vedas and the Brahmanas.

The Mahabharata and the Ramayana are the two main epics of Hindu literature. The Ramayana ("story of Rama") was written in the third century B.C.E., possibly by a poet named Valkimi. Rama, a prince and avatar of the god Vishnu, is forced from his kingdom in exile; Sita, his wife and avatar of Vishnu's consort, Lakshmi, is kidnaped by the many-headed demon Ravana. With the assistance of the monkey god, Rama is able to rescue his faithful wife and regain his kingdom. Four times the length of the Bible, the Mahabharata is considered the longest epic poem in the world.

The famous Bhagavad Gita ("song celestial"), a small section or segment of the Mahabharata, is perhaps the most famous and influential text of Hinduism and is important for understanding the devotional, or Bhakti, aspect of Hinduism, which has flourished from about 400 C.E. until today. The Gita features the rivalry between the Kaurava brothers and the Pandava brothers for the rule of India. For thirteen years the Pandavas were forced into exile, leading to civil war. As preparation for war begins, Krishna, another avatar of Vishnu, becomes a charioteer for Arjuna, a Kshatriya, who is about to engage a major battle. Arjuna asks his charioteer to drive him between the lines so he may see the armies more clearly. As he looks on both sides, he sees that the battle will pit relative against relative, and he becomes horrified at what he is about to do. His charioteer, however, advises him to follow the dharma of a Kshatriya, a warrior, and points out that death is not final, but that all things return. In the context of this discussion, the charioteer—the god Krishna—teaches Arjuna the several ways to salvation, with devotion to the saving grace of Krishna being the transcendent key. The Gita contains seven thousand verses grouped into eighteen chapters.

The Puranas, traditionally eighteen in number, are also concerned with myth, lore, and legend. Emerging some time between 400 to 1000 C.E., they stress devotion to a specific divinity as a way of release.

The Laws of Manu, composed about 200 C.E. in twelve books, encompass the codification and operations of the four-caste system, societal roles, life stages, diet, government, and other matters. Hindu social life has in large measure been formed and justified by the Laws of Manu down to the present day.

DENOMINATIONS

Hinduism encompasses a vast number of deities and forms of worship, a huge body of scriptural writings, and several divergent methods of achieving moksha. In addition, it has no central authority and no founder. Consequently, its precepts tend to be broad and flexible rather than strict and precisely defined. The idea of religious "denominations" in the Western sense of the term is, therefore, not really applicable. There are, of course, various groups with leaders and codes of law, but none of these necessarily excludes other sources of spiritual guidance. A Hindu may simultaneously follow several different gurus in pursuit of several different courses to salvation, in effect tailoring his or her form of worship to meet his or her individual spiritual needs. It is a religion well suited to the diverse range of adherents it serves: Brahmin, Kshatriya, Vaishya, Sudra, and Harijan, whether male or female.

WOMEN AND FAMILY LIFE IN HINDUISM

The status of women among Hindus is paradoxical. Hindu society is decidedly patriarchal. Its defining structure relates males to males, and women find their place in society by associations with men in their lives.

The intense emphasis on marriage and family can be a source of anxiety and anguish for women. Historically, parents married their children off at an early age to insure theirs and their children's security. According to the Laws of Manu, when women do not bear children or simply fail to bear sons, this can be grounds for annulment of marriage and/or polygamy for the husband. When only daughters are born, infanticide has sometimes been practiced. In the Hindu caste system, women are regarded as Sudras, the lowest caste of the four social castes. Traditionally, educational opportunities and religious rites such as fasting and the reciting of prayers were denied to women.[12] According to Manu, the duties of women are as follows:

In childhood, a female must be subject to her father, in youth to her husband, when her lord is dead, to her sons; a woman must never be independent.

The husband who wedded her with sacred texts, always gives happiness to his wife, both in season and out of season, in this world and in the next.

Though destitute of virtue, or seeking pleasure elsewhere, or devoid of good qualities, yet a husband must be constantly worshiped as a god by a faithful wife.

No sacrifice, no vow, no fast must be performed by women apart from their husbands; if a wife obeys her husband, she will for that reason alone, be exalted in heaven. (Manu 5.148, 153–55)[13]

Yet, it is an amazing and compelling religious paradox that women are also often eulogized and given great deference and honor in Hindu texts and in Hindu mythology. High praise for the devoted wife is found in the Mahabharata and the Ramayana, and even in the Laws of Manu, which says: "A man is only half his self. Till he takes a wife he is incomplete and so not fully born." Furthermore, a father "through a son conquers the worlds, through a son's son he obtains immortality" (Manu 9.137)— but not without a wife to bear him such sons. In India, it is recognized that women play an essential role in bringing honor and happiness to men and to society. Without women, men could not be. Hence, marriage is highly anticipated and celebrated in Hinduism.

Yes, the overarching structures in Indian mythology have tended to be conceived in male terms. The traditional scheme that has emerged encompasses three major forms of divinity (trimurti): Brahma, Vishnu, and Shiva—who have vied with one another for supremacy. However, this formula, or

Bathing in the Ganges, the sacred river of Shiva,
one of the two fundamental acts of pilgrimage to Kashi
(Banaras), India, the object being to "feel" the presence
of the divine. *(Photo courtesy of Diana Eck)*

this stereotype so often projected in classrooms, glaringly omits and ignores the tremendous status and power of shakti in Hindu lore and Hindu thought. Shakti power can be expressed as predominant divine power, manifest in the many female goddesses of Hindu religion.

The female goddess is permanently present in the mythology and worship of Hindus from ancient times.[14] Goddesses have great power and are greatly admired and praised. And they are absolutely essential to the work of the male deities. The rich folklore and the myriad cults associated with Radha, the divine consort of Krishna, and of Kali, one of Shiva's wives, are prime examples. There are no Hindu male deities independent of their female counterparts. Both male and female are absolutely essential. The female aspect of Hindu thought and practice cannot

be overemphasized and, in this sense, cannot fail to demonstrate the great importance of women in the tapestry of Indian religion.

HINDUISM TODAY

Hinduism may be of greater vitality inside India today than ever before. The resurgence of religious fundamentalism in the world in recent history is not confined to Christianity in Europe and North America or to Islam in the countries of the Middle East; it has also become a phenomenon within Hinduism in India as well. This emergence of militant Hinduism (a paradox, considering that Hinduism is normally celebrated for its philosophical passivity) is perhaps best illustrated by the Rashtriya Swayamsevak Sangh movement (RSS).[15] This organization has become a motivation factor in radical political activity in India.

According to RSS, India is sacred land. Indians must return to Hinduism, the soul of India, in order to transcend all political affiliation and activity. The answer to India's ills is the reemergence of India's native faith, which will once again give a national identity and focus to the Indian people. In this climate of neo-religious nationalism, Indians must actively resist the encroaching influences of Christianity, Islam, Sikhism, or any other non-Hindu religious influence.

But the contemporary influence is also marked by the expansion of Hinduism into other countries, and particularly into countries of the Western world. A number of Hindu denominations or movements are now also expanding within the United States. Perhaps best known is the *International Society of Krishna Consciousness,* sometimes known as *Hare Krishna* ("praise to Krishna"), or ISKCON.

As its name implies, society members are devoted to the worship of the Hindu divinity Krishna. They practice vegetarianism and live in ashrams adjacent to Krishna temples. One such temple is planned for construction near Spanish Fork, Utah. Unlike some Hindu traditions, ISKCON is a theistic tradition in which Krishna is the supreme lord. A characteristic of Krishna consciousness is the congregation's recitation and repetition of the maha-mantra: "Hare Krishna, hare Krishna, Krishna Krishna, hare hare; hare Rama, hare Rama, Rama Rama, hare hare."

ISKCON teaches that the spirit is eternal—that it rebounds, or reincarnates. Because of bondage within the physical world, including the demands and limitations of the body, the spirit forgets its eternal identity and identifies with the material and the gross. It can be liberated only through revival of one's original consciousness of Krishna. The function of the individual is to render service to Lord Krishna.

The Krishna movement in India numbers in the millions, but in the United States only in the tens of thousands. The Hare Krishna society was founded in the United States in 1966 by A. C. Bhaktivedanta Swami Prabhupada. At first Americans were surprised and amused to see young Hare Krishna members at airports and other public places, dressed in Indian clothing with dots of white paint on their foreheads, dancing and chanting. The movement made its first significant inroads among New York's bohemians. It rapidly spread to San Francisco and then to other major metropolitan cities in the United States. Krishna followers today are busily engaged in proselyting through the ownership and operation of radio stations.

LATTER-DAY SAINT REFLECTIONS

The Way of Works

Karma

Latter-day Saints recognize both the law of the harvest and the intercessory power of a merciful God. "[Latter-day Saints] stand in between the Oriental faiths and much of the Christian world. . . . For us, the immutable law of infinite consequence sustains nature and critically influences [humanity]. . . . [We] believe in a cosmic law of justice, that cause and effect are intrinsic to the human condition—that [people] are blessed or disadvantaged according to their willingness to comply with divine law."[16]

The salience of law in the eternal progression of mankind is clearly pointed out in the Doctrine and Covenants:

There is a law, irrevocably decreed in heaven before the foundations of this world, upon which all blessings are predicated—And when we obtain any blessing from God, it is by obedience to that law upon which it is predicated. (D&C 130:20–21)

It appears from this and other revelations that the Latter-day Saint "law of the harvest" is more specific and personal in its cause-and-effect relationships than the karma of Eastern philosophy. The violation of specific commandments brings specific punishments, just as obedience to a law entitles an individual to a personal blessing. Hindu karma, on the other hand, tends to respond to evil deeds indirectly. For example, one of the Hare Krishna faithful might maintain that people who eat meat are doomed to violent death in war. According to the Laws of Manu, "The slayer of a Brahman [sic] enters the womb of dogs, boars, asses," or some other animal (12:55), and "A Brahman [sic] (who is) a thief (would pass) thousands of times (into the womb) of spiders, snakes, chameleons," or the like (12:56).[17] None of these embodiments is clearly related to the sin that occasions them; but these low rebirths nonetheless represent punishments which, though indirect, are causally linked to the evil deeds. In contrast, Christian scriptures teach that the "law of the harvest" is not the sole cause of earthly misfortune. Besides the classic tale of Job, there is this account from the book of John:

And as Jesus passed by, he saw a man which was blind from his birth. And his disciples asked him, saying, Master, who did sin, this man, or his parents, that he was born blind? Jesus answered, Neither hath this man sinned, nor his parents: but that the works of God should be made manifest in him. (John 9:1–3)

Hence, Christian theology provides for the possibility that God may afflict people (or allow them to be afflicted) with poverty, sickness, and sorrow in this world for reasons other than their own unrighteousness. Moroni writes that the Lord "give[s] unto men weakness that they may be humble" (Ether 12:27), not necessarily as a punishment for sin. Christ told his followers that, as a result of their faith and righteousness, "[in] the world ye shall have tribulation" (John 16:33). A corollary idea is that sinners sometimes find themselves among favorable worldly circumstances. Job, a "perfect and upright" man (Job 1:1) in the midst of terrible afflictions given him as a test, lamented to his friends,

Wherefore do the wicked live, become old, yea, are mighty in power? Their seed is established in their sight with them, and their offspring before their eyes. Their houses are safe from fear, neither is the rod of God upon them. . . . Therefore they say unto God, Depart from us; for we desire not the knowledge of thy ways. (Job 21:7–9, 14)

The Eastern doctrine of karma does not recognize this phenomenon of deferred justice. The typical Hindu insights would reject the unfairness of forcing a person who led a righteous premortal existence, as Job undoubtedly did, to suffer undeserved torments in mortality. In the Eastern view, a person's karma—not the intervention of deity—is the principal factor in determining his happiness in life.

The flexibility of the Latter-day Saint "law of the harvest" stems from its subjection to the will of God. It is not the law that deals with mankind in Latter-day Saint theology, but the Lawgiver acting in accordance with the law. The Lord metes out the blessings and the afflictions, and he may choose to withhold either as a test of faith. The Eastern law of karma can operate independent of deity. A person

gets in life what he is fated to get. Not even a god can make it otherwise.

Reincarnation

Over 1.5 billion people—more than one-third of the world's population—believe in reincarnation. It is today a commonly accepted doctrine in the countries of Asia, especially among Hindus, Buddhists, Sikhs, and Jains. Faced with the biblical question, "If a man die, shall he live again?" (Job 14:14), the proponents of reincarnation might well respond, "Yes, many times!—and in various forms and circumstances." Belief in reincarnation, however, is not confined to the Eastern world. A 1982 Gallup poll showed that 23 percent of Americans believe in reincarnation.

Henry David Thoreau not only expressed belief in reincarnation, but, judging from his letters, he also believed he had a recollection of past lives. In a letter to Emerson, Thoreau wrote: "And Hawthorne, too, I remember as one with whom I sauntered, in old heroic times, along the banks of the Scamander, amid the ruins of chariots and heroes."[18] Some of the great Western poets, such as Walt Whitman in his *Leaves of Grass*, also reflect a belief in reincarnation.

Among Hindu texts, none is more forceful than the Bhagavad Gita in expressing the Hindu belief that the spirit is subject to an indefinite series of existences, in various material forms, and that the spirit must ultimately escape this round of rebirths. It says that one existence follows another just as different stages of life—childhood, young manhood, and old age—follow one another (2:13). Or again, just as one lays off old garments and dons new ones, so the spirit lays off an old, worn-out body and puts on a new one (2:22). The Gita affirms that from the highest plane in the material world down to the lowest, all are places of misery and impermanence. Rebirth is a mark of sorrow (8:15).[19]

Latter-day Saints agree with the Eastern faiths that life does not begin with birth nor end with death. They teach that each human being lived in a spiritual estate before he or she was born on earth. As individual spirit children of Heavenly Father, humans were born into mortality, and each spirit inhabits his or her own physical body. According to the restored gospel, this process also extends to animals and plants as the Lord's creations (see Moses 3:5–7).

The scriptures, as well as the prophets of the church, repeatedly affirm that righteousness—compliance with the irrevocable laws of God in the premortal existence and in this life—influences a person's worthiness now, as well as in the life to come. How he or she behaves in mortality is of crucial importance in determining future, eternal livelihood and happiness.

Latter-day Saints do not generally accept the doctrine of reincarnation, regarding it as basically contrary to revealed truth. Joseph Smith made a strong statement on the matter when he taught that reincarnation is a false doctrine originating with the devil.[20] In the Latter-day Saint view, the doctrine of reincarnation may be thought of as a reminder of the divinely conceived plan of eternal progression that perfection cannot be achieved in the short span of a mortal lifetime. However, there are special aspects of reincarnation that are contrary to Latter-day Saint teachings. First, reincarnation denies the reality of one death and of the goodness of the body. Latter-day Saints believe that death is a separation of the spirit and the body. Resurrection is a reuniting of the same spirit with the essential elements of that same physical body. In the Resurrection, all will have the privilege of regaining their mortal bodies, which are in God's image. The spirit bodies of animals and plants will also, after death, reinhabit the material bodies they had in mortality. In the Resurrection the body and the spirit of individual souls will be united, never to be separated again. The doctrine of the Resurrection negates the belief that the body is merely a casual abode of the spirit, or a tabernacle that is either repeatedly changed or terminated (see Alma 11:45).

For Latter-day Saints, physical bodies are sacred. The elements of these bodies are eternal, and the spirits that inhabit them have been assigned to remain with them forever. In elaborating on the question of what happens to material bodies after death and in the Resurrection, the prophet Joseph Smith indicated:

There is no fundamental principle belonging to a human system that ever goes into another in this world or in the world to come. . . . If any one supposes that any part of our bodies, that is, the fundamental parts thereof, ever goes into another body, he is mistaken.[21]

Secondly, Latter-day Saints believe that the children of Heavenly Father were sent to the earth, to this life, this one time, to be tested and to mature, and that all who came agreed to this plan of salvation.

And we will prove them herewith, to see if they will do all things whatsoever the Lord their God shall command them; And they who keep their first estate [the pre-existent spiritual estate] shall be added upon [will have the opportunity to gain a physical body and new experience in a physical world]; and they who keep not their first estate shall not have glory in the same kingdom with those who keep their first estate; and they who keep their second estate [our mortal lives here and now] shall have glory added upon their heads for ever and ever. (Abr. 3:25–26)

The doctrine of reincarnation, on the other hand, promotes the idea that a human being is given many opportunities, many future lives, in which to work out his or her salvation. Latter-day Saints feel that this is consistent with Satan's strategy to relieve people of any feeling of urgent need to repent of their sins, obey the gospel, and work out their salvation here and now. It disputes the admonition of Alma: "This life is the time for men to prepare to meet God" (Alma 34:32).

Finally, for Latter-day Saints, the status of Jesus is compromised in the doctrine of reincarnation. Those who accept the multiple reincarnations (avatars) of gods, so basic to the religious outlook of the Eastern world, imply a relativity in which Jesus would become one of many incarnated deities. His unique and special mission as the one incarnation of a member of the Godhead is thereby denied. Christ is forced to yield his rightful position as the "King of kings, and Lord of lords" (1 Tim. 6:15), the "[only] name under heaven . . . whereby we must be saved" (Acts 4:12). The Savior's crucifixion becomes just one more event in the life of a temporarily embodied savior. To accept this premise would involve the repudiation of the act of redemption, perhaps the most fundamental feature of the religion of the Latter-day Saints. Reincarnation denies the unique atonement of Jesus Christ, and thus his mercy and love.

The Way of Knowledge

Hindus indicate that they have discovered heightened dimensions of spirituality and have sometimes reached expanded states of spiritual awareness. These states have included a sense of identity with an undergirding ultimate spirit in the universe, sometimes called the world soul. This is a familiar concept to Latter-day Saints, who have studied the 88th section of the Doctrine and Covenants and its descriptions of the pervasiveness of the Spirit of Christ in providing underlying light to the entire universe.

In Latter-day Saint doctrine, the Spirit of Christ "fill[s] the immensity of space" (D&C 88:12) and "lighteth every [person] that cometh into the world" (D&C 93:2). This sounds similar to descriptions of Brahman in the Upanishads. Brahman is unlimited and pervasive; so is the Light of Christ. Brahman is incomprehensible and unthinkable; the Light of Christ also sometimes seems to impact in that way, giving assurances and insights that are beyond human capacity to fully communicate or understand.

There are two differences that must be noted, however. First, unlike Brahman, the Light of Christ teaches, entices, and reveals. It leads respondents to greater light, to the power of the Holy Ghost, whose calling is to testify of God the Father and his Son Jesus Christ. The Light of Christ is not God or Ultimate Reality; it is an influence from God and of God. Second, the universal radiance of the Light of Christ must not be regarded as a definition of God or of ultimate reality. In Hindu thought, Brahman is ultimate, the highest single fact of the universe. In Latter-day Saint thought, ultimate reality consists of three personal deities: God the Father, His Son Jesus Christ, and the Holy Ghost. Although they are cosmic and are unified in principle and power, they are still three distinct, tangible individuals.

The Way of Devotion

There is a familiar ring to bhakti for Latter-day Saints, who worship Heavenly Father through devotion to him and by seeking his guidance in all aspects of life. There is also a superficial similarity between Hindu bhakti, particularly in the avatars of Vishnu, and the incarnation of Jehovah/Jesus. However, the similarity breaks down quickly, for Jesus is not an avatar. He is the one and only incarnation of the Son, and he has come to work what no other corresponding savior figure in any other religion works: an atonement through the sacrifice of his own life.

THUS, in the wide-ranging scope of Hinduism there are a number of interesting points of comparison to the gospel of Jesus Christ as accepted and practiced by Latter-day Saints, as well as many points of contrast. In spite of the numerous differences between their traditions, this means common ground on which adherents of the two faiths can meet in understanding. Not the least of these points of commonality is the term by which Hinduism is more accurately known: dharma. As Hindus come to know their duty to deity, others, and self through their beliefs, so do Latter-day Saints come to know their duty to God, others, and self through their religion. Fulfillment of this duty is perceived by both peoples as the course to salvation.

Glossary of Hindu Names and Terms

AGNI. The Vedic god of fire; personification of fire in its various forms; the mediator or priest to men and gods.

AHIMSA. Noninjury, nonviolence, noncoercion; a reverence for all life.

ARYANS. A nomadic group that migrated into India in 1800–1500 B.C.E., conquered the Dravidians, and began the caste system.

ASHRAM. A community adjacent to an ISKCON temple in which members live.

ATMAN. The eternal self or soul, identical to Brahman; the self or inner essence of the universe and of man.

AVATAR. The "descent" of the divine; the incarnation of Vishnu in different animal and human forms.

Traditionally there are ten such avatars: Matsya (the fish), Kurma (the tortoise), Varaha (the boar), Narasimha (the man-lion), Vamana (the dwarf), Parasurama (Rama with ax), Rama, Krishna, the Buddha, and Kalki at the end of time.

BHAGAVAD GITA. "Song celestial"; a scriptural text from the Mahabharata concerning Krishna, who, as an avatar of the god Vishnu, teaches the ways of salvation, particularly through devotion. This is perhaps the most influential of all Hindu scriptures.

BRAHMA. The creator god, who is one of the Hindu Trimurti.

BRAHMAN. The absolute; the ultimate ground underlying everything; the reality that is the source of all being and all knowing.

BRAHMIN. The priests of Hinduism; the highest of the social castes.

DRAVIDIANS. Prehistoric inhabitants of India who initially lived in the Indus Valley and were later conquered by Indo-Aryans.

DURGA. One of the names of the Devi as consort of Shiva; both a mother and warrior.

GANESHA. "Lord of Ganas," the elephant-headed son of Shiva and Parvati and the keeper of the thresholds of space and time. He is honored at the doorway and at the outset of any venture.

GARUDA. Mythical sunbird and the vehicle of Vishnu.

HARE KRISHNA. The popular name of ISKCON (defined below) and its adherents.

HARIJAN. "Children of God"; the "out-castes" of India, who were given this name by Gandhi; also known as "untouchables."

INDRA. The Vedic warrior god, wielder of the lightning bolt (vajra). He is the liberator from obstructive forces. He set free water and light by killing Vritra, the gigantic and evil snake.

INTERNATIONAL SOCIETY FOR KRISHNA CONSCIOUSNESS (ISKCON). A movement centered in devotion to Krishna, who is regarded as the supreme lord and is worshiped through service, study, meditation, and chanting.

KALI. Divine Mother; the goddess of destruction who was both mother of life and destroyer; also a consort of Shiva.

KALKI. The tenth and last avatar of Vishnu; a messianic figure who will come to restore the dharma and destroy the wicked at the end of the fourth world period, the current kalpa.

KALPA. An age or æon; a period in cosmic time equaling one day of Brahma or 1,000 "great yugas"—a total of 4,320 million years. Shiva will administer destruction to the world at the close of the present kalpa.

KARMA. The moral law of cause and effect by which one reaps what one sows. In Hinduism it becomes a law by which all of one's deeds, from all of one's lives, are balanced against each other to determine the nature of one's next incarnation.

KRISHNA. The eighth avatar of Vishnu. Vishnu, the cosmic force of goodness, comes to earth as Krishna to reestablish dharma, or law. Krishna is the friend and advisor of the Pandava brothers, especially Arjuna, to whom he reveals the teachings found in the Bhagavad Gita. He is the inner Lord, who personifies spiritual love and lives in the hearts of all beings.

KSHATRIYA. A member of the warrior caste; the second caste of the Hindu social structure whose natural work is heroism, high spirit, resolution, ability, not fleeing in battle, giving, lordship.

KURMA. The second avatar of Vishnu; the tortoise.

LINGAM. A phallic symbol through which Shiva is worshiped as a god of fertility.

MAHA-MANTRA. The "great mantra" chanted by adherents of ISKCON.

MANU. The father of humanity; the Hindu equivalent of Adam, the first man, and Noah. He is also the reputed author of the Laws of Manu, a classic text of Indian juridical theory.

MATSYA. The first avatar of Vishnu; the fish.

MAYA. The illusion that there is a reality apart from the one reality of Brahman-Atman.

MOKSHA. A technique of transcending the senses to bring one to release; also, release itself. It is the name of the fourth permissible goal of life.

NANDI. The white bull Shiva sometimes rides upon, who also makes music to which his master dances.

NARASIMHA. The fourth avatar of Vishnu; the man-lion.

NATARAJA. "Lord of the Dance"; an incarnation of Shiva who will appear at the end of the present age to destroy ignorance through dancing.

NIRVANA. The oneness with Brahman-Atman which extinguishes any sense of individuality and is attained when one is released from the cycle of reincarnation.

PARASURAMA. The sixth avatar of Vishnu; often depicted as Rama with ax.

PARVATI. One of the consorts of Shiva.

RADHA. The wife of Krishna. The love between Krishna and the milkmaid Radha sometimes represents the union of the individual soul (Atman) with the world soul (Brahman).

RAMA. The seventh avatar of Vishnu; one of the most popular Hindu gods, the model of righteousness. As son of Dasaratha and husband of Sita, he is the great hero of the Ramayana.

RAMAYANA. Hindu scripture telling the story of the heroic exploits of Rama, an avatar of the god Vishnu.

RIG VEDA. India's first religious text, and one of the four Vedas; essentially a product of Indo-Aryan thought.

RUDRAS. Vedic gods; the terrible gods of storms. Sometimes Rudras are mentioned as a group; at other times they are thought of as a single god, Rudra.

SAMADHI. The experience of oneness with Brahman-Atman attainable in this life; the experience of enlightenment which guarantees release from the round of rebirths at death.

SAMSARA. The cycle of rebirths.

SARASVATI. Name of a sacred river; later the wife of Brahma and goddess of knowledge, learning, holy speech, and music.

SESHA. The serpent on whom Vishnu is often depicted as reclining.

SHAKTI. Power or energy; the female, active power of a god, which assumes the creative function; personified as the goddess Shakti, wife of Shiva.

SHAKTISM. The worship of Shakti as the wife of Shiva.

SHIVA. "The Destroyer," the third member of the Trimurti.

SHRUTI. The body of primary revelation in the Hindu scriptural canon, consisting of the four Vedas, the Upanishads, the Aranyakas, and the Brahmanas.

SIDDHARTHA GAUTAMA. The Indian prince who founded Buddhism; considered by Hindus as the ninth avatar of Vishnu.

SMRITI. All Hindu scripture not comprised in the shruti, such as the Puranas, the Mahabharata, the Ramayana, and law codes such as that of Manu.

SOMA. A drink used in Vedic ritual; the drink of the gods.

SUDRA. The fourth Hindu caste, consisting of slaves, servants, or menial workers.

TRIMURTI. The Hindu trinity of gods: Brahma, Vishnu, and Shiva.

UMA. A consort of Shiva.

UPANISHADS. Ancient mystical documents found at the end of each of the four Vedas.

VAISHYA. A member of the third Hindu caste; a merchant. The Vaishya is related to the soil; agriculture and trade are his professions.

VAJRA. The lightning bolt controlled by Indra, the atmospheric god.

VAMANA. The fifth avatar of Vishnu; the dwarf.

VARAHA. The third avatar of Vishnu; the boar.

VARUNA. The Vedic god of natural and moral law; probably the sky god in earliest times.

VEDAS. Scriptural books of hymns, charms, and formulas used in Hindu worship; these constitute some of the oldest of the Hindu scriptures.

VISHNU. The second deity of the Hindu Trimurti; the preserver. He is held to be the personal expression of Brahman-Atman and is often worshiped through his two avatars, Krishna and Rama.

VRITRA. The dragon or snake who retained the waters and was slain by Indra.

Notes

1. Monier Monier-Williams, *Hinduism,* Non-Christian Religious Systems, vol. 1 (New York: Macmillan, 1919), 12.

2. Mary Boyce, *Zoroastrians: Their Religious Beliefs and Practices* (London: Routledge and Kegan Paul, 1979), 2.

3. The translation of the Rig Veda used here and elsewhere is Wendy Doniger O'Flaherty's, published in 1981 by Penguin Books, Harmondsworth, England.

4. Marcus Bach, *Major Religions of the World* (New York: Abingdon, 1959), 24–25.

5. Mahatma Gandhi, *Young India, 1919–1922,* 2d ed. (New York: B. W. Huebsch, 1924), 480. For an expanded analysis of Gandhi's views on this subject, see also Gandhi, *Young India, 1924–1926* (New York: Viking Press, 1927), 648–53.

6. Bach, *Major Religions,* 24.

7. See also Joseph Smith, *History of the Church of Jesus Christ of Latter-day Saints,* 7 vols. (1949; reprint, Salt Lake City: Deseret Book, 1970), 1:5.

8. Robert Ernest Hume, *The World's Living Religions . . . ,* rev. ed. (New York: Charles Scribner's Sons, 1959), 25.

9. As translated in William Theodore de Bary, ed., *Sources of Indian Tradition,* 2 vols. (New York: Columbia University Press, 1958), 1:33.

10. Robert E. Van Voorst, *Anthology of World Scriptures* (Belmont, Calif.: Wadsworth, 1994), 23.

11. Information in this paragraph and the remainder of this section is drawn from ibid., 23–30.

12. Mildreth Worth Pinkham, *Woman in the Sacred Scriptures of Hinduism* (New York: AMS Press, 1967), 187–89.

13. Quoted in Pundita Ramabai Sarasvati, *The High-Caste Hindu Woman* (Philadelphia: Jas. B. Rodgers, 1888), 59.

14. This theme is thoroughly elaborated in John Stratton Hawley and Donna Marie Wulff, eds., *The Divine Consort: Radha and the Goddesses of India* (Berkeley, Calif.: Asian Humanities Series, 1982). This book clearly posits the conclusions that have been drawn here.

15. Walter J. Anderson and Shridahar Damie, *The Brotherhood in Saffron: The Rashtriya Swayamsevak Sangh and Hindu Revivalism* (Boulder, Colo.: Westview Press, 1987).

16. Spencer Palmer, "Gurus, Buddhas, and Messiahs: A Mormon View" (address given at the Brigham Young University Devotional Assembly, Provo, Ut., July 25, 1978), 16–17.

17. The translation used is Arthur Coke Burnell's, edited by Edward W. Hopkins, in its second edition (New Delhi, India: Oriental Books Reprint Corp., 1971).

18. "To R. W. Emerson (at Concord). Staten Island, July 8, 1843," in F. B. Sanborn, ed., *Familiar Letters,* vol. 6 of *The Writings of Henry David Thoreau,* 20 vols. (Boston: Houghton Mifflin, 1894), 6:110.

19. Franklin Edgerton, trans., *Bhagavad Gita* (Cambridge, Mass.: Harvard University Press, 1972); Juan Mascaro, trans., *Bhagavad Gita* (Baltimore: Penguin Books, 1962), 2:13, 22; 8:15.

20. Joseph Smith, "Transmigration a Doctrine of the Devil," in Joseph Fielding Smith, comp., *Teachings of the Prophet Joseph Smith* (Salt Lake City: Deseret Book, 1979), 105.

21. Smith, *History of the Church,* 5:339. Compare Alma 41:23 and 42:2, in which it is promised that all parts of the body will be "restored."

Vardhamana Mahavira

Jainism

Spencer J. Palmer

3

AINISM constitutes a small but influential community in India. Jains can be recognized in some areas by an orange vertical streak of sandalwood paste and saffron worn on their foreheads when paying homage in their temples. Although they number only about four million members, they are a significant force in the economic and social life of India. They are generally traders and businessmen and are strict pacifists.

Their monks and nuns wear simple white clothing, sometimes with a white cloth covering over their mouths, and they follow daily practices of extreme asceticism (self-denial). Members of this faith are scattered all over the country, but most are concentrated in the southern states of Mysore and Madras; in the northern states of Rajasthan, Gujarat, and Maharashtra; and in central India.

THE BEGINNINGS OF JAINISM

The period between the seventh and fifth centuries B.C.E. was a turning point in the religious and philosophical development of the entire world. This was an unprecedented age of intellectual ferment. More of the now-extant great religions began during this period, affecting a greater number and variety of people throughout the earth, than during any other period in human history. H. G. Wells has written:

This sixth century B.C.E. was indeed one of the most remarkable in all history. Everywhere . . . men's minds were displaying a new boldness. Everywhere they were waking up out of the traditions of kingships and priests and blood sacrifices and asking the most penetrating questions. It is as if the race had reached a stage of adolescence—after a childhood of twenty thousand years.[1]

This was the time of the earliest philosophers of Greece, of the great Hebrew prophets Jeremiah and Ezekiel, of the pilgrimage of Lehi and other Book of Mormon prophets, and of Lao Tzu and Confucius

in China. During this period in India there arose the Upanishadic sages, inspired by the ancient Vedas, as well as less orthodox teachers who completely rejected the Vedas. It was at this inquiring and creative time that the two most successful of a number of unorthodox systems began—that is, Jainism and Buddhism, founded respectively by Vardhamana *Mahavira* ("Great Hero") and Siddhartha Gautama, the Buddha.

As India's material culture advanced and spread, these new religious ideas accompanied it. For example, in the Vedas the doctrine of transmigration is never explicitly treated, and it does not seem likely that the Aryans of Vedic times believed in it. However, the early Upanishads do present it as a new doctrine, rare and profoundly mysterious. In the Buddhist scriptures that arose out of the religious atmosphere of the period, the doctrine of transmigration is treated as a matter of course; thus, in time it was accepted throughout the Eastern world.

The Buddhist scriptures also refer to six unorthodox teachers, or "heretics," each of whom led an important group of followers, including both ascetics and laymen. The fifth of these, called *Nigantha Nataputta,* was none other than Vardhamana Mahavira, the founder of Jainism.[2] Historically speaking, Jainism, unlike Buddhism, has not spread beyond the boundaries of the Indian subcontinent. On the other hand, it has not disappeared in the land of its birth, as has Buddhism.

THE FOUNDER: VARDHAMANA MAHAVIRA

There is considerable debate concerning Mahavira's birth and death dates, and there are many legends which surround his life. However, the traditional accounts place his birth in present-day Basadha in north Bihar in the year 599 B.C.E. Mahavira's father was a rich Kshatriya by the name of Siddhartha. His mother, Trisala, was a princess who reportedly had fourteen auspicious dreams which indicated that her son would be either a great king or a great saint.

One of the difficulties in gaining knowledge about Mahavira's life is that one is dependent upon traditions preserved in the two dominant schools of Jainism. One account is found among the conservative *Digambaras,* and another among the slightly less conservative *Svetambaras.* Of these two schools, more will be said later. Because of certain unique emphases within each group, specific details of Mahavira's life may have been corrected or omitted to support prevailing practices. The Digambaras, for example, deny that Mahavira was ever married, believing it unthinkable that he should have indulged in the pleasures of the flesh in such a manner.

To Mahavira (as to the Buddha), tradition ascribes a long account of previous births, which number thirty-three in some accounts. In one incarnation he earned merit by offering food and drink to hungry monks; in another, as a son of a king and queen he conquered six portions of the world. In yet another there is an impressive account of his life as a lion with sharp teeth and claws who lived in the tops of the Himalayas. This tale in particular reflects values important to Jains; for in this incarnation Mahavira-to-be was going to eat a deer, but two monks dissuaded him. The hungry beast vowed not to take further food until death.[3]

> His body looked picture-like,
> His mind too was calm,
> Never generating fear in others, . . .
>
> Died the lion, fixed in vow,
> With concentration of his mind,
> To be born in heaven. . . .[4]

There is general agreement that Mahavira spent his youth in palatial luxury. Following the death of his parents, he left his home at age thirty in order to seek salvation through self-denial. "He cast aside his fine clothes, gave away all his property, plucked out his hair in five handfuls, and vowed absolute holiness. . . . He [became] a naked ascetic."[5] He wandered far and wide in the Ganges Valley until, at the age of forty-two, he found full enlightenment and became a "conqueror," a *jina.* This took place precisely twelve years, six months, and fifteen days after the beginning of his mendicant journey. Attaining this state of *kevala-jñana* (infinite knowledge, knowledge involving

awareness of every existence in all its qualities and modes) made him the twenty-fourth and final jina of the present cosmic cycle. He became a *tirthankara* ("ford-finder"), completely free from defects of human existence such as hunger, thirst, need for sleep, need to sweat, fear, disease, and aging. According to legend, Mahavira's body "shone like a crystal on all sides. Above his head was hoisted the royal insignia of a white umbrella, signifying that nothing could be higher or holier than he."[6] He founded a disciplined order of four thousand monks, by the highest count; his women followers, some thirty-six thousand, renounced the world and became nuns.

At age seventy-two Mahavira died in the village of Pava, not far from *Patna.* It has become one of the most sacred places of pilgrimage in India and is visited by thousands of Jains each year. If Mahavira were born in 599 B.C.E., the date of his death would then be 527 B.C.E. However, many authorities believe that these dates are too early and that his actual death date may be 468 B.C.E.[7]

BASIC BELIEFS

Karma

As noted above, Mahavira was understood to be the twenty-fourth and final tirthankara of this age. He has shown others the path to follow if they wish to gain release from the cycle of birth, death, and rebirth. Thus, reincarnation plays its part in Jain thought, just as it does in Hinduism. Similarly, karma controls a person's rebirth; but there are some significant differences between Jainism and Hinduism on this point.

The Jains do not hold the monistic view of life that is exemplified in the Upanishads. A person has a soul (*monad* or *jiva*) and exists as an identifiable entity in a universe shaped in the form of a man and composed of all existing souls or monads. A person's soul "floats" in this universe and moves up and down the scale of existence dependent upon the amount of *karma-matter* the soul bears.

In Hinduism, karma is a law that balances all one's good deeds against all one's bad deeds from all one's prior existences. Dependent upon the result of this weighing, the individual's soul enters a new life at the level determined by the impersonal law of karma. In Jainism the basic idea of cause and effect is present, but now karma is not a law but a substance:

karma-matter. As evil deeds are done, karma-matter builds up on or permeates the soul. The more karma-matter contaminating the soul, the further the soul sinks in the universe and the lower it falls on the scale of existence.

The way off the wheel is to free the soul of the collected karma-matter, thereby permitting it to rise to the top of the universe, where it enters a heavenly realm and finds peace and rest. It is important to note that there is no extinction of the soul in this view, but the continuation of some form of individual life.

To find release ultimately, one must free oneself from all attachments in the world that can generate karma-matter. Desire for fleshly things only adds to the karma-matter. Thus, extreme asceticism or self-denial is a fundamental pillar of Jainism. Likewise, respect for all life—*ahimsa*—is central, for all life is sacred and interrelated. The taking of life adds significantly to one's karma-matter. Therefore, the second pillar of Jain theology and practice is the absolute respect for and preservation of all life. Coupled with these two pillars—extreme asceticism and ahimsa—is the practice of meditation, through which one hopes to gain enlightenment, or infinite knowledge of all existences in all their qualities and modes. The process is completely one of self-salvation, for in Jainism there are no gods to assist one off the wheel. Lay Jains begin to approach the difficult path of self-denial, while the *sadhus,* or monks, seek to implement it fully.

Monastic Vows

Monks and nuns take five vows when they enter the ascetic life. These vows stress the two central pillars of Jainism and are as follows:

1. Never to take life. To be sure that life is not taken, sadhus often carry small brooms to sweep the path in front of them as they walk, wear gauze masks to prevent the inhalation of insects or the damaging of the air, and strain water through cloth before drinking it to remove insect life. However, ahimsa is much broader than simply not taking life. It includes the concept of noninjury in both the physical and psychological sense. Thus, to speak angry words to another would be a violation of ahimsa, for a person's spirit would be harmed.

2. Never to be untruthful. Often, lies are told to make people appear better than they are. Because it is a form of self-denial, this vow therefore reflects the value of asceticism. It also involves ahimsa, since lying can hurt others.

3. Never to take what is not given. Once again, this vow reflects asceticism. A sadhu will not eat unless offered food which has not been prepared specifically for him or her. But the vow extends beyond this to not picking fruit from a tree or even off the ground. The essence of Jain life is to proclaim to a materialistic world that all the things people believe to be essential to life are not. Even food is not essential. Thus, if no one offers the sadhu anything to eat, he or she gets along perfectly well. Even clothing is nonessential, as the Digambaras demonstrate. The sadhus serve as a model for a non-attached life in a materially oriented world.

4. Never to be unchaste. For the sadhu this is a vow of celibacy. There are numerous secondary laws around this basic vow which forbid monks from talking about women, looking at women, staying in the same dwelling as a woman or female animal, or eating highly spiced food (which is supposed to increase carnal tendencies). All this also holds true for nuns as far as males may be concerned.

5. Never to be attached to anything. This last vow is a summary of the others. Persons must become detached from all things material if they are finally to become Siddhas, or persons who have found *moksha.* Any attachments to persons, places, or things prolong the round of rebirths.[8]

Clearly, the ascetic life is stringent and extreme. Yet, it is the goal of all Jains in some lifetime. It is the path all must walk if they are to find release from the round of rebirths which are a product of attachment to the material world.

The Vows of the Laity

Lay Jains order their lives by vows similar to those of the monks and nuns, but there are differences which permit the layperson to live in the world while slowly moving toward the ascetic life in its fulness. The lay Jain lives by twelve vows. Note the less stringent nature of these vows, but also the progression toward fuller asceticism and ahimsa.

1. Never *knowingly* to take life. This vow limits the vocations that a Jain may hold. For example, a Jain cannot farm, since the act of plowing would kill various life forms in the earth. Consequently, Jains tend to be involved in business and banking and other commercial enterprises.

2. Never to lie.

3. Never to take what is not given. This injunction is aimed particularly at stealing and certainly does not prevent one from making purchases in the market or other shops.

4. Never to be unchaste. This is essentially the same as the Latter-day Saint vow of chastity: one is not to have sexual intercourse with any but one's spouse and is to be clean in thought and word.

5. To limit one's possessions. This is a clear step in the direction of asceticism and seems to refer to major possessions such as land and houses.

6. Not to travel far from home. The idea is to limit the temptation to violate one's vows.

7. To limit personal possessions. Again, this moves toward asceticism but, unlike vow number five above, it is oriented more toward personal items such as towels, soap, clothing, perfume, and so forth.

8. To guard against unnecessary evils. This means that one should avoid situations that could lead to the breaking of the vows.

9. To perform meditation daily. The point here is to remove all evil thoughts from the mind and to come to a harmony with the world.

10. To be involved in special periods of self-denial. During these times participants may fast, stay in their home village, eat sparingly, or perform other practices which might turn their minds from the material world.

11. To spend occasional periods as an ascetic.

12. To assist ascetics. If people have not yet embarked fully on the ascetic life, they can reduce their own karma by assisting those who have.[9]

These vows present the ideal pattern for Jain laypersons. Not all live these values, but many do. Accordingly, Jains are noted for their philanthropy; for their compassion for the sick and the injured, both human and animal; and for their involvement in antiwar and antinuclear movements.

Ahimsa: Reverence for Life

All of the religions of India advocate the doctrine of ahimsa, but Jainism has been more fervently supportive of this teaching than the others. Therefore, despite the fact that Jainism is numerically one of the smallest of the major religions discussed in this book, and ahimsa is an important doctrine of both Hinduism and Buddhism, it is within the context of Jain ideology that ahimsa should be fully examined.

Ahimsa literally means "noninjury," but in effect it connotes respect or reverence for life. It is the basis of Indian views and values on war, nonviolence, vegetarianism, and the treatment of animal life. The doctrine of ahimsa raises critical theological and moral issues for religious people everywhere. At the end of this chapter these issues are examined within the framework of the religion of the Latter-day Saints.

As a general principle, all cultures respect life, or at least human life. How this principle is put into practice, however, varies greatly among different peoples. If respect for all living things is flouted by big-game hunters and voracious meat-eaters of the West, there are religionists in Asia who seem to go to the other extreme. In any event, the strict application of the idea of respect for life in the East is consistent with Asian philosophical emphases on passivity, tolerance, and harmony with nature.

Ahimsa means that man should not injure any living creature. Such an act is considered not only an offense against nature, but an indication of character weakness, as well as a diminishing of the individual who takes life. Reverence for life goes beyond the mere avoidance of cruelty. Ahimsa is not a fruit of Asian religion; it *is* religion.

Ahimsa suggests a common fraternity of all living things, a point that distinguishes Eastern from Western thought. The monotheistic faiths (Judaism, Christianity, Islam, and Zoroastrianism) stress belief in a God who is personal, worthy of worship, the creator of an almost endless variety of individual creatures, and separate from the natural world, though continuously active in directing it. In the monism of India the divine, or "god," is undifferentiated from the human mind or spirit, or from the spiritual life within all nature, including animals and the smallest insects. In monotheism, God the creator is transcendent. He is outside nature. However, in the religions of India (which have been transmitted to the far reaches of the Asian world), the divine is the sacred, pervasive, absolute, universal power that is within all phenomenal forms. Ahimsa emphasizes this common bond, this underlying life force that is found within the simplest forms of life as well as within human beings. Thus, with the distinctions of species removed, injuring animals is tantamount to fratricide. And this is true even of animal sacrifice to the gods. To most, the offering to the deities of meat obtained by killing animate beings is like offering a mother the flesh of her own child. However, the cult of Kali within Hinduism still makes such sacrifices. Except for uncommon instances such as this, the growth of Jainism and Buddhism, with their strong emphasis on ahimsa, brought to an end the Vedic sacrifices within Hinduism.

Still, even among the different sects of the East, there is room for divergence on how strictly to apply the doctrine of ahimsa. Gandhi took a moderate approach that allows for compromise between the conflicting demands of society and religion:

We are helpless mortals caught in the conflagration of *himsa* [violence]. . . . Man cannot for a moment live without consciously or unconsciously committing outward *himsa*. The very fact of his living—eating, drinking and moving about necessarily involves some *himsa,* destruction of life, be it ever so minute. . . .

Hence man cannot be wholly free from *himsa*. So long as he continues to be a social being, he cannot but participate in the *himsa* that the very existence of society involves.[10]

Even if society cannot exist without the commission of himsa, the Jains are apparently willing to make the trial. Mahavira must be history's greatest champion of noninjury. As Lewis M. Hopfe relates, Jain legend recounts that

during the rainy season [Mahavira] stayed off the roads to avoid walking where he might inadvertently step upon an insect. During the dry season he swept the road before him as he walked to avoid crushing insects. He strained all the water that he drank in order to prevent swallowing any creature that might be in it. . . . He refused to eat raw food and preferred to eat only that which had been left over from the meal of some other person, in order that he might not be the cause of death.[11]

Following the legacy of Mahavira, Jain monks pledge noninjury as one of their five monastic vows, and they may emulate him in their use of brooms, straining cloths, and masks, as noted above.[12]

Though not as extreme as the sadhus in their practice of noninjury, Jain lay adherents are strict even by Indian standards in their precautions against himsa. They are forbidden to hold any occupation that realizes profit from killing. Therefore, Jains cannot be butchers, soldiers, fishermen, leather workers, exterminators, or even farmers.[13] To the Jains, himsa is himsa, regardless of what seems necessary for the operation of society.

The traditional Indian view of ahimsa is more moderate. Gandhi's idea of a balance between reverence for life and respect for society reflects the same compromise reached by many Indian kings and theologians of ancient times. The great Buddhist king Asoka, who reigned from 274 B.C.E., ordered his palace cooks to refrain from killing animals and discontinued the royal hunting outings after he became repulsed by the idea of taking animal life.[14] But Asoka's reverence for life evidently was not unconditional, because he maintained capital punishment for those who committed serious crimes and continued his military campaign against the rural tribesmen who frequently raided his cities.[15]

Gandhi, who used ahimsa as the philosophical basis for his nonviolent civil disobedience to the British government during India's fight for independence, explains how his view reconciles ahimsa and participation in war:

When two nations are fighting, the duty of a votary of ahimsa is to stop the war. He who is not equal to that duty, he who has no power of resisting war, he who is not qualified to resist war, may take part in war, and yet wholeheartedly try to free himself, his nation and the world from war.[16]

The restrictions of ahimsa apply to all breathing, existing, living sentient creatures. Of particular sanctity is the cow. Legend states that *Surabhi,* the first cow, was one of the original treasures that appeared on the earth from the cosmos, and from antiquity cows have been considered living temples that graciously provide milk for man.[17] The theology of the Hindus and of many Buddhist sects teaches that eating meat is not only immoral but unnatural for humans. "Human beings are meant to eat vegetarian food," Swami Prabhupada says flatly. "The tiger does not come to eat your fruits. His prescribed food is animal flesh. But man's food is vegetables, fruits, grains, and milk products."[18] The feeling of kinship between man and "sentient creatures" is again apparent.

This philosophy has not stopped people in all parts of Asia from eating animal flesh, but it has generated social sanctions against butchers and fishermen, even in some areas where the consumption of meat is accepted. This situation apparently arose from a conflict between the need or desire of some societies to use animal flesh as food and the Buddhist teaching of noninjury. The Japanese and Koreans resolve the conflict by eating meat while holding in contempt those who kill and prepare it. A. L. Basham states that popular interpretations of the first of the Buddhist Ten Precepts—that is, "refrain from harming living beings"—does not forbid Buddhists from eating meat but does prevent them from working as hunters or butchers.[19] The Paekchong class of Korea, made up of butchers and their families, was traditionally discriminated against. Deprived groups, like the Eta of Japan and certain low castes in India, have been ostracized because their occupations are associated with disrespect, injury, and irreverence toward living things.

There is, then, some variation across Asia in the way in which ahimsa is practiced from one faith to another. However, it is fair to say that adherents of Jainism are among its most devout practicants. Certainly, if nothing else, the image of a sadhu sweeping the path before him as he walks and straining the water he drinks and even the air he breathes tends to call forth a respect for one who is willing, at great personal sacrifice, to adhere so strictly to a very demanding principle.

SCRIPTURES AND DENOMINATIONS

In Jainism, the nearest word to "scriptures" is the Sanskrit term *agamas.* The Jain view of what constitutes the agamas is at the same time precise and vague, in that the term can be taken as denoting not just a canonical body of scriptural texts, but also any text which has a degree of antiquity and is accepted as having been written by an illustrious teacher. Scripture, then, is a concept which has to be treated carefully when studying Jainism. The notion of a totally fixed canon of sacred writings is not so compelling as it is in many other religious traditions.[20]

Knowledge derived from the scriptures counts for nothing in Jainism if it is not accompanied by the practice of austerities. In other words, the study of scriptures is not recommended for those who have not already entered the path. Moreover, because there is no unitary attitude toward scriptural texts within Jainism, there has been a general tendency throughout this religion's history to regard the study of scriptures by the unqualified, whether lay or ascetic, as a dangerous and unwarranted activity.[21]

As mentioned, there are two main sects of Jains in India. The very conservative *Digambaras,* or "sky-clads," are so called because their sadhus wander about India nude as a sign of complete renunciation of worldly goods and all other pleasures of the flesh. Among the slightly less conservative *Svetambaras,* or "white-clads," ascetics wear white robes and permit women to participate fully in all aspects of Jain life.

These two sects of Jainism have differing attitudes toward the scriptures. The Digambaras think that the transmission of the original teachings has been hopelessly corrupted. Therefore, they do not recognize the canonical writings which the Svetambaras revere. Their only canonical material, known as *Siddhanta,* is difficult and has attracted large commentary treatments. The Svetambaras, though they lost some of the early sources, did retain various works called *Angas,* or "limbs," plus a subsidiary canon known as *Angabahya.* The Angas are the featured scriptures of Jainism. The Angabahya includes various commentaries and eulogistic works in praise of Jain leaders and saints, including the Great Renunciation and Enlightenment of Mahavira.[22]

WOMEN AND FAMILY LIFE

Another point of divergence between Digambara and Svetambara thought is in the status of women and the family. As has already been indicated in the discussion of women in Hindu society (where they have been traditionally restrained and regarded as inferior) and mythology (in which they are often eulogized as preeminent and powerful), texts of traditional India provide a wealth of material on questions of gender and sexuality, projecting a generally ambivalent attitude toward the status and role of women.

The Jains have been significantly influenced by the unfavorable Brahmanical milieu as it relates to the nature and functions of women. Yet, as Padmanabh Jaini observes, Jains have struggled with the problem raised by their monastic communities, who place great stress upon the avoidance of family ties, emotional bonds, and, most particularly, sexuality and the pleasures of the senses—all of which are associated with women. Jaini explains:

The problem is then constructed in terms of the degree to which women can make the same sort of renunciatory commitment and spiritual progress as men. It is a problem precipitated by the somewhat reformist tendency of the heterodoxies that derives naturally from their attack on Brahmanical privilege and pretensions. Yet, although Buddhist and Jain thinkers are willing to reject the notion of a hierarchical social order, the power of the patriarchal doctrine of male supremacy in all matters, proved harder for them to escape. Indeed, with their obsessive concern with renunciation, withdrawal from the secular social universe, and avoidance of the sensual life, the texts and sermons of Buddhism and Jainism often stress a virulently negative view of women.[23]

The question of the possibility of a woman's living the life of a renunciant, which the Jains believe is the only path to spiritual liberation, is open to dispute among the two major sects of Jainism. Arguments are brought forth by the Digambara authors to support their position that there can be no spiritual liberation for women. The inferiority of women is demonstrated by their alleged fickleness, their lack of intellectual and supernatural powers, by the fact that nuns have to show deference even to monks who may be far junior to them, and even by the fact that they are subject to sexual harassment and assault by men.[24]

But the Svetambara are radically opposed to this view of women. Svetambaras believe that, regardless of their social and political status relative to that of men, women are as capable as men of achieving spiritual liberation. They point out that the Kalpasutra is quite clear that upon Mahavira's death the community which he had founded contained a body of female ascetics two and a half times as large as the number of male ascetics. More strikingly still, the Svetambaras claim that the nineteenth ford-finder (tirthankara), Malli, was a woman.

Although Digambaras have little to say about nuns, there are charismatic Svetambara nuns in India today whose preaching can attract large audiences.

Latter-day Saint Reflections

Jiva and the Material World

As already noted, there is a distinct tension between matter and the essence or spirit of an individual. Jains believe that the material world binds and limits humanity and, consequently, that people must be freed from the material to attain moksha. What the Latter-day Saint calls a person's spirit, the Jain calls a jiva or monad. This is the life force within many entities, not just sentient creatures; and thus, the jiva approaches the Latter-day Saint idea that even the earth itself possesses a spirit (Moses 7:48–49). It should be noted that the monism of Hinduism with its concept of an all-pervasive Brahman-Atman is lacking in Jainism, for the jiva has an individuality which remains when one is released from the reincarnational cycle.

William Theodore de Bary cites a famous Jain parable, told by a sadhu to a prince in order to explain the basic Jain view of the evils of the physical world and the need to gain freedom from it. Latter-day

Saints familiar with the many metaphors expressed in Lehi's dream in the Book of Mormon should be intrigued by the philosophy of this grim little story.

A certain man, much oppressed by the woes of poverty,
Left his own home, and set out for another country.
He passed through the land, with its villages, cities, and
      harbors,
And after a few days he lost his way.

And he came to a forest, thick with trees . . . and full of wild beasts. There, while he was stumbling over the rugged paths, . . . a prey to thirst and hunger, he saw a mad elephant, fiercely trumpeting, charging him with upraised trunk. At the same time there appeared before him a most evil demoness, holding a sharp sword, dreadful in face and form, and laughing with loud and shrill laughter. Seeing them he trembled in all his limbs with deathly fear, and looked in all directions. There, to the east of him, he saw a great banyan tree. . . .

And he ran quickly, and reached the mighty tree.
But his spirits fell, for it was so high that even the birds
      could not fly over it,
And he could not climb its high unscalable trunk. . . .
Until, looking round, he saw nearby an old well
      covered with grass.
Afraid of death, craving to live if only a moment longer,
He flung himself into the well at the foot of the
      banyan tree.
A clump of reeds grew from its deep wall, and to
      this he clung,
while below him he saw terrible snakes, enraged at the
      sound of his falling;
And at the very bottom, known from the hiss of
      its breath, was a black and mighty python
With mouth agape, its body thick as the trunk of
      a heavenly elephant, with terrible red eyes.
He thought, "My life will only last as long as these reeds
      hold fast,"
And he raised his head; and there, on the clump of reeds,
      he saw two large mice,
One white, one black, their sharp teeth ever gnawing at
      the roots of the reed-clump.
Then up came the wild elephant, and, enraged the
      more at not catching him,
Charged time and again at the trunk of the banyan tree.
At the shock of his charge a honeycomb on a large branch
Which hung over the old well, shook loose and fell.
The man's whole body was stung by a swarm of
      angry bees,
But, just by chance, a drop of honey fell on his head,
Rolled down his brow, and somehow reached his lips,
And gave him a moment's sweetness. He longed for
      other drops,
And he thought nothing of the python, the snakes,
      the elephant, the mice, the well, or the bees,
In his excited craving for yet more drops of honey.

This parable is powerful to clear the minds of those
    on the way to freedom.
Now hear its sure interpretation.
The man is the soul, his wandering in the forest the
    four types of existence.
The wild elephant is death, the demoness old age.
The banyan tree is salvation, where there is no fear
    of death, the elephant,
But which no sensual man can climb.
The well is human life, the snakes are passions,
Which so overcome a man that he does not know
    what he should do.
The tuft of reed is man's allotted span, during which
    the soul exists embodied;
The mice which steadily gnaw it are the dark and
    bright fortnights.
The stinging bees are manifold diseases,
Which torment a man until he has not a moment's joy.
The awful python is hell, seizing the man bemused
    by sensual pleasure,
Fallen in which the soul suffers pains by the thousand.
The drops of honey are trivial pleasures, terrible at
    the last.
How can a wise man want them, in the midst of such
    peril and hardship? [25]

Reflections on Ahimsa

Ahimsa in Mainstream Christianity

The Western counterpart to ahimsa is relatively weak. In the Judeo-Christian mentality, man is a creation separate from and superior to the brute animal kingdom. A key biblical verse is in the book of Genesis, wherein God tells Adam, "[R]eplenish the earth, and subdue it: and have dominion over the fish of the sea, and over the fowl of the air, and over every living thing that moveth upon the earth" (Gen. 1:28). From this position of "dominion," traditional Christians of the West have viewed the animal world with condescension. Humans and animals have little in common besides their Maker, and only humans have the special distinction of having been made in the image of God. The Lord has concern for all of his creatures, but humans often do not. The New Testament quotes Christ as saying of the sparrows, "[O]ne of them shall not fall on the ground without your Father," but he adds that "ye are of more value than many sparrows" (Matt. 10:29, 31). Another biblical contributor to the Western attitude toward animals may be the Old Testament heritage of animal sacrifice. To the practical Western mind only superficially familiar with the cultural context, method, and symbolism involved, this seemingly wasteful activity could be narrowly

interpreted as a statement by God to the effect that animals are relatively unimportant.

There is not a strong scriptural basis for ahimsa in traditional Christianity; and though many Christian theologians promote kindness to animals, this is usually a secondary precept that is supported only by its consistency with the more fundamental doctrines of the church. One Christian commentator writes, "Man is bound to treat dumb animals kindly and to abstain from unnecessary cruelty, not because these animals possess any real rights (for only intelligent beings can have real rights) but because they are creatures of God." [26]

If there is a counterpart to Mahavira in Christianity, it must be Saint Francis of Assisi. Born in 1182 C.E., Francis matched Mahavira's concern for even lowly creatures when he reportedly picked up worms from the road and moved them to a safe place so passing pedestrians would not step on them. Francis's legendary sympathy for animals is illustrated in this account related by Arnaldo Fortini:

Francis [was] passing through a village of the Marches. He met a man on his way to market, carrying over his shoulder two little lambs, bound together. They bleated so pitifully that Francis was filled with pity, and he went to them and touched them with the compassion that a mother would show to her weeping child.

Francis said to the man: "Why are you torturing my brother lambs, tied up and hanging like this?"

The man replied: "I am taking them to the market to sell them, because I need the money."

Francis asked: "What will happen to them then?"

And the man answered: "Those who buy them will kill them and eat them."

"This must not happen," Francis said. "Take this mantle I am wearing as their price and give the lambs to me." [27]

Legend also states that Francis made friends with animals, including birds, wolves, and insects, which faithfully obeyed his instructions and craved his company.

Latter-day Saint Views on Ahimsa

Somewhere between the Eastern and traditional Christian concepts of reverence for life falls the Latter-day Saint position. The Latter-day Saint attitude toward animal life is founded on the belief that animals are subjects of salvation, an idea that goes well beyond the mainstream Christian position that animals have no "real rights." Animals do have rights in Latter-day Saint theology, but these rights are limited. Thus, the Latter-day Saint view of the animal kingdom is not as egalitarian as the Eastern philosophy, which downplays the distinctions between higher and lower species to allow for the cross-species mobility required by reincarnation. Latter-day Saints see humans and animals not as coequal, but rather as coeternal.

According to the restored gospel, just as people have had a spiritual premortal existence, so did the lower forms of life. A revelation concerning this premortal existence of both human beings and other forms of life is recorded in the book of Moses:

I, the Lord God, made the heaven and the earth, And every plant of the field before it was in the earth, and every herb of the field before it grew. For I, the Lord God, created all things, of which I have spoken, spiritually, before they were naturally upon the face of the earth. . . . [F]or in heaven created I them; and there was not yet flesh upon the earth, neither in the water, neither in the air; . . . but spiritually were they created and made according to my word. (Moses 3:4–5, 7)

Gerald Jones writes that The Church of Jesus Christ of Latter-day Saints is distinct among Christian churches in its approach to "ahimsa" because of its belief in the eternal existence of animal spirits. "Animals are given an eternal existence," says Jones, who has compared Latter-day Saint doctrine toward animals with that of four other American Christian denominations. "In Latter-day Saint terminology this means animals have always existed in the past as spiritual beings in heaven before their existence on earth and will continue to exist after this mortal life."[28]

However, gospel teachings indicate that human beings and beasts are eternally unequal. A statement by former church president John Taylor suggests that the premortally existent spirits of living things were begotten as distinct species in the pre-earth existence:

The animal and vegetable creations are governed by certain laws . . . each having an organism and faculties governed by prescribed laws to perpetuate its own kind. . . .

These principles do not change, as represented by evolutionists of the Darwinian school, but the primitive organisms of all living beings exist in the same form as when they first received their impress from their Maker. . . . As the horse, the ox, the sheep, and every living creature, including man, propagates its own species and perpetuates its own kind, so does God perpetuate His.[29]

This inequality, which apparently began with the organization of spirits in the antemortal world, continues during mortality. A major distinction is

intelligence. There is a difference, at least in the mortal state, between the limited mental powers of animals and the relatively advanced intellect of man. Former member of the Quorum of the Twelve Orson Pratt writes that humanity "is advanced far beyond the apparent manifestations of knowledge that exist among the lower orders of beings," which exhibit only "small glimmerings of light."[30] Perhaps the close connection between intelligence and agency qualified humans for their earthly position of "dominion." As Joseph F. Smith wrote, "Animal life [is] entrusted to our care. . . . To [God] all life is a sacred creation for the use of His children."[31]

The superior status and intellect of humans in mortality does not preclude the enjoyment of blessings in the hereafter by animals. Animal spirits are by nature eternal—meaning that they must endure beyond mortality—and the gospel provides for them the opportunity to attain a state of joy appropriate to their station. The agency of animals may be limited in the world; but to the extent that they fulfill their appointed roles, they are as deserving of an eternal reward as are their more intelligent caretakers. Heber C. Kimball used the idea of fulfillment within a particular "sphere of action" as the basis for a rebuke of Latter-day Saints who, he said, were whipping their horses excessively. "Let them rest," he said. "They are as good as we are in their sphere of action; they honour their calling, and we do not, when we abuse them."[32]

Honoring their calling qualifies animals for eternal life, and Joseph Fielding Smith speculates that resurrected animals may inherit the same kingdoms of glory as men:

Animals do have spirits and . . . through the redemption made by our Savior they will come forth in the resurrection to enjoy the blessing of immortal life. . . . It is very probable that they, like mankind, will be distributed in the various kingdoms, celestial, terrestrial, and telestial. We may well believe that in each of these kingdoms such creatures will be assigned.[33]

The scriptures further indicate that some of the changes humans will enjoy in the hereafter, such as increased knowledge and communion with God, will also be enjoyed by celestialized animals. The ancient apostle John recorded in his revelation a vision of four beasts that surrounded the throne of God, praising their Maker. Joseph Smith's request for an interpretation of this vision is recorded in Doctrine and

Covenants 77:2–4. Referring to this revelation, an official statement by the First Presidency said, "The whole animal creation will be perfected and perpetuated in the Hereafter, each class in its 'distinct order or sphere,' and will enjoy 'eternal felicity.' That fact has been made plain in this dispensation."[34]

HUNTING. Those who do not respect the lives of beasts are and will be held accountable for the abuse of their stewardship, according to Latter-day Saint belief. Such abuse is constituted by needlessly hurting or killing animals. George Q. Cannon, a counselor to three church presidents, writes, "No man or woman, no boy or girl, who has any kind feelings will inflict unnecessary pain upon any creature. . . . [God] will condemn and punish them for so doing."[35] A modern revelation gravely warns, "[W]o be unto man that sheddeth blood or that wasteth flesh and hath no need" (D&C 49:21). Does this "wo" apply to the thousands of Latter-day Saint hunters who stalk deer each autumn? This is one of many practical questions that could and perhaps should be asked.

President Lorenzo Snow gave up hunting after such an evaluation. At age twenty-four, he experienced a sudden revulsion toward the activity while stalking game in a Missouri wood:

While moving slowly forward in pursuit of something to kill, my mind was arrested with the reflection on the nature of my pursuit—that of amusing myself by giving pain and death to harmless, innocent creatures that perhaps had as much right to life and enjoyment as myself. I realized that such indulgence was without any justification, and feeling condemned, I laid my gun on my shoulder, returned home, and from that time to this have felt no inclination for that murderous amusement.[36]

Similarly, President Spencer W. Kimball said during the October 1978 general conference:

It is not only wicked to destroy [innocent little birds], it is a shame. . . . I think that this principle should extend not only to the bird life but to the life of all animals.
. . . They were to be used only, as I understand, for food and to supply the needs of men. It is quite a different matter when a pioneer crossing the plains would kill a buffalo to bring food to his children and his family.[37]

President Kimball's remarks brought so many questions from hunters in the church that he approved a press release clarifying his position on hunting:

To my knowledge, Church leaders have not released any statements concerning whether or not members should engage in hunting or fishing activities. The decision to hunt and fish, under appropriate regulations, is left to the discretion of the individual.

However, many clear guidelines have been supplied to assist those who may be involved in such activities. These guidelines are designed to stop the unnecessary and wasteful slaughter of animals and birds, not to define public policy on predator control and game management.[38]

Thus, a categorical condemnation of hunting on the basis of official Latter-day Saint teachings is unjustified. Deer hunters argue that shooting deer each fall within the constraints of the hunting regulations prevents the agonizing starvation of thousands of animals in the overpopulated intermountain wilderness, and that in the process they can enjoy the outdoors and obtain some venison for their families. Ultimately, only the individual hunter can judge his own motivations and can determine what to him is "wasteful or unnecessary" slaughter. The gospel allows people to use animals for their own needs but requires all to answer for the blood of every animal and strongly denounces killing that is motivated by a thirst for the shedding of animal blood. The Lord pronounces woe for such.

Finally, Joseph Smith taught that animals will not lose their antagonism toward humans until the Saints cease to "make war" against the lower creation. He vividly demonstrated his commitment to this belief while leading a group of Latter-day Saint men and boys on a trek (known as Zion's Camp) from Kirtland, Ohio, to Missouri in 1834. While some of the men were pitching their tents, they found three rattlesnakes. The men were about to kill the snakes when the prophet interceded, saying,

Let them alone—don't hurt them! How will the serpent ever lose its venom, while the servants of God possess the same disposition, and continue to make war upon it? Men must become harmless before the brute creation, and when men lose their vicious dispositions and cease to destroy the animal race, the lion and the lamb can dwell together, and the sucking child can play with the serpent in safety.[39]

Peace with nature will be required of the Saints before the Second Coming. Joseph clearly wanted his people to begin the truce immediately. If this is the case, mistreating animals has ramifications in Latter-day Saint theology that go beyond the sins of the individual offender. All this is consistent with the concept of ahimsa in Eastern faiths, especially as found in Jainism.

VEGETARIANISM. The Indian doctrine shuns not only the killing of animals, but also the eating of meat. What do the scriptures and the leaders of the church have to say to Latter-day Saints regarding vegetarianism?

The scriptures state that "[t]he beasts of the field and the fowls of the air, and that which cometh of the earth, is ordained for the use of man for food and for raiment" (D&C 49:19), making total abstinence from meat an apparently unhallowed doctrine. The apostle Paul looked upon vegetarianism as detrimental to faith. "[I]n the latter times[,]" he wrote, "some shall depart from the faith, . . . commanding to abstain from meats, which God hath created to be received with thanksgiving of them which believe and know the truth" (1 Tim. 4:1, 3). Having said that, however, the Lord by revelation has encouraged the Saints to eat meat sparingly, and prominent church leaders have limited their consumption of animal flesh as a matter of religious principle.

The heart of the dietary code of the church, found in the Doctrine and Covenants, attaches conditions to the proper use of meat:

Yea, flesh also of beasts and of the fowls of the air, I, the Lord, have ordained for the use of man with thanksgiving; nevertheless they are to be used sparingly; And it is pleasing unto me that they should not be used, only in times of winter, or of cold, or famine. All grain is ordained for the use of man and of beasts, to be the staff of life, not only for man but for the beasts of the field, and the fowls of heaven, and all wild animals that run or creep on the earth; And these hath God made for the use of man only in times of famine and excess of hunger. (D&C 89:12–15)

That grains and vegetables are the proper food of human beings and beasts is a precept that is consistent with the Latter-day Saint view of the Millennium, when "the lion shall eat straw like the bullock: and dust shall be the serpent's meat" (Isa. 65:25). The *Times and Seasons* concurred in 1842 that, during this tranquil era, "the enmity between beast and beast shall be taken away, and they will eat vegetable food, and no more devour the inferior beast to satisfy their appetite."[40]

Heber J. Grant, at age eighty, gave partial credit for his good health to an almost meatless diet:

I think that another reason why I have very splendid strength for an old man is that during the years we have had a cafeteria in the Utah Hotel, I have not, with the exception of not more than a dozen times, ordered meat

of any kind. On these special occasions I have mentioned I have perhaps had a small, tender lamb chop. I have endeavored to live the Word of Wisdom, and that, in my opinion, is one reason for my good health.[41]

In summary, Latter-day Saint doctrine stops short of commanding the complete vegetarianism that is the case in Jainism, Buddhism, and Hinduism, but with respect to personal practice some Latter-day Saints seem to have been convinced that the Lord is more pleased with it than with the wanton consumption of meat.

VIOLENCE AND WAR. Latter-day Saints believe that Jesus Christ of the New Testament and of the restoration scriptures was the God of the Old Testament who dealt with the Israelites. This means that the same being who commanded his people to annihilate the inhabitants of Canaan has also told his disciples to "renounce war and proclaim peace" (D&C 98:16), for "all they that take the sword shall perish with the sword" (Matt. 26:52). The scriptures are replete with examples of both militarism and pacifism. In them, there are both "hawks" and "doves." The Book of Mormon quotes a revelation to the Nephites that commands them to defend their land by force (Alma 43:47), but the same book also contains the account of the Anti-Nephi-Lehies, who covenanted not to fight their enemies and instead allowed themselves to be slaughtered (Alma 24). Moses, who quoted the Lord's commandment of "Thou shalt not kill" to the Israelites (Deut. 5:17) also said, "The Lord is a man of war," after God destroyed the pursuing Egyptian army (Exod. 15:3).

The ideal, of course, is noninjury based on love. Indeed, pure love is the first great commandment of life. The gospel indicates that God discourages any type of thinking or behavior that would create contention or violence among his children. During the test of mortality, however, human beings are free to express their most base desires. War, it seems, is an inevitable by-product of this free agency. John A. Widtsoe wrote during World War II, "The Lord abhors war or contention. . . . The responsibility for war rests upon man, the free agent, not upon the Lord. . . . It would be a violation of His own plan, should He step in, and, by His undoubted power, stop warfare among the children of men."[42] When people kill each other, whether it be on the interpersonal or the international level, it is always the result of sin.

In the face of this wicked desire to kill, it can be argued that the righteous might be in danger of extermination if they did not collectively fight back. Joseph Fielding Smith has observed that if all people acted like the Anti-Nephi-Lehies, who refused at the cost of their lives to fight their enemies, "there could be no war."[43] In this instance, the individual's right to life is sacrificed for the higher goal of building up the kingdom of God. This is possible because the Latter-day Saint belief in a glorious afterlife makes death more of a change in station than a tragedy. Death is not an ultimately important event. This is reiterated in the scriptures.

Like hunting animals, killing people is a temporal matter; it occurs in mortality because the free agency of people is not restrained. Latter-day Saint scriptures indicate that the kingdom of God, to be fully established during the millennial reign of Christ, will be free of contention, death, and killing among both

humans and beasts. Meanwhile, the conflicts between higher and lower principles of righteousness allow for some ambiguity that ultimately requires the individual to appeal to his or her own conscience.

On a number of points dealing with the sanctity of life, then, Jain and Latter-day Saint teachings share common ground. Obviously, the doctrinal bases from which these teachings spring are vastly different, but it is interesting to note the similarities in results. Latter-day Saints who understand the motivations behind the strict observances of Jain monks can respect the determination they show to go through life causing as little harm to other beings as possible. Their actions recall the instructions of the Savior to his apostles: "[B]e ye therefore wise as serpents, and harmless as doves" (Matt. 10:16).

Glossary of Jain Names and Terms

AHIMSA. The principle of noninjury, nonviolence, and respect for all life.

ANGABAHYA. Subsidiary scriptural writings containing commentaries and eulogistic works praising Jain leaders and saints, as well as the Great Renunciation and Enlightenment of Mahavira; accepted by Svetambara Jains.

ANGAS. Literally, "limbs"; the central scriptures of Svetambara Jainism.

DIGAMBARA. Means "sky-clad" and refers to those Jain monks who wander naked.

HIMSA. Violence or injury to life.

JINA. A "conqueror" or victor; one who has attained enlightenment or infinite insight. This word is the root from which the word Jainism is derived. It may also be used as a synonym for tirthankara.

JIVA. The spirit contained within all living things, be they human, animal, or plant.

KARMA-MATTER. The substance that contaminates a person's soul as the consequence of evil deeds, causing the soul to sink in the universe and on the scale of existence.

KEVALA-JÑANA. Enlightenment which involves the gaining of infinite knowledge.

MAHAVIRA (ca. 599?–527? B.C.E.). The title (and name) of the founder of Jainism, meaning "great one"; also known as Vardhamana.

MONAD. A human soul.

NIGANTHA NATAPUTTA. Another name for Mahavira found in Buddhist literature.

PATNA. A village near the site of Mahavira's death; one of the most holy places to Jains and hence the goal of pilgrimages.

SADHU. A Jain monk.

SIDDHANTA. The sole body of Digambara Jain scripture.

SURABHI. In Jain mythology, the first cow; considered to be one of the original treasures to appear on earth.

SVETAMBARA. Means "white-clad" and refers to those Jain monks who wear a white robe or loincloth.

TIRTHANKARA. Means "ford-finder." Mahavira is considered the twenty-fourth and last "ford-finder" of this æon. He, like the previous ones, found the way to gain release from the wheel and has shown this way to others.

Notes

1. H. G. Wells, *A Short History of the World* (New York: Macmillan, 1922), 156.

2. These details on the background of Jainism and Buddhism are drawn from William Theodore de Bary,

   Sources of Indian Tradition, 2 vols. (New York: Columbia University Press, 1958), 1:35–41.

3. K. C. Lalwani, *Sramana Bhagavan Mahavira: Life and Doctrine* (Calcutta: Minerva Associates, 1975), 23–28.

4. Quoted in ibid., 28.

5. Robert Ernest Hume, *The World's Living Religions . . .*, rev. ed. (New York: Charles Scribner's Sons, 1959), 46–47.

6. Padmanabh S. Jaini, *The Jaina Path of Purification* (Berkeley: University of California Press, 1979), 27–28, 34–35.

7. See de Bary, *Sources of Indian Tradition*, 1:43.

8. See Mrs. Sinclair Stevenson, *The Heart of Jainism* (New Delhi, India: Munshiram Manoharlal, 1970), 234–38.

9. Ibid., 205–19.

10. Mohandas K. Gandhi, *An Autobiography: The Story of My Experiments with Truth* (Boston: Beacon Press, 1957), 349.

11. Lewis M. Hopfe, *Religions of the World*, 6th ed. (New York: Macmillan College Publishing, 1994), 125.

12. Ninian Smart, *The Religious Experience of Mankind*, 3d ed. (New York: Charles Scribner's Sons, 1969), 93.

13. Hopfe, *Religions of the World*, 131.

14. T. Walter Wallbank, *A Short History of India and Pakistan* (New York: Mentor Books, New American Library, 1958), 40.

15. A. L. Basham, *The Wonder That Was India: A Survey of the Culture of the Indian Sub-Continent before the Coming of the Muslims* (1954; reprint, New York: Grove Press, 1959), 54–55.

16. Gandhi, *An Autobiography*, 349.

17. Basham, *Wonder That Was India*, 319.

18. A. C. Bhaktivedanta Swami Prabhupada, *The Science of Self-Realization* (New York: Bhaktivedanta Book Trust, 1977), 122.

19. Basham, *Wonder That Was India*, 281, 285.

20. Paul Dundas, *The Jains* (London and New York: Routledge, 1992), 55.

21. Ibid., 54, 55.

22. Ninian Smart and Richard D. Hecht, *Sacred Texts of the World: A Universal Anthology* (New York: Crossroad, 1982), 277.

23. Padmanabh S. Jaini, *Gender and Salvation: Jaina Debates on the Spiritual Liberation of Women* (Berkeley: University of California Press, 1991), xi.

24. Ibid., xvi–xix.

25. Quoted in de Bary, *Sources of Indian Tradition*, 1:53–55.

26. Francis J. Connell, "Answers to Questions," *American Ecclesiastical Review* 146 (April 1962): 270.

27. Helen Moak, trans., *Francis of Assisi: A Translation of Nova Vita di San Francesco by Arnaldo Fortini* (New York: Crossroad, 1981), 539.

28. Gerald E. Jones, "Concern for Animals as Manifest in Five American Churches: Bible Christian, Shaker, Latter-day Saint, Christian Scientist and Seventh-day Adventist" (Ph.D. diss., Brigham Young University, 1972), 55.

29. John Taylor, . . . *The Mediation and Atonement of . . . Jesus Christ* (Salt Lake City: Deseret News, 1882), 164–65.

30. Orson Pratt, "Language . . . ," October 22, 1854, in Brigham Young et al., *Journal of Discourses*, 26 vols. (1842–96; reprint, Salt Lake City: n.p., 1967), 3:98 [hereafter cited as *JD*].

31. Joseph F. Smith, "Editorial Thoughts," *Juvenile Instructor* 53, no. 4 (April 1918): 182.

32. Heber C. Kimball, "Organization . . . ," August 2, 1857, in *JD*, 5:137.

33. Joseph Fielding Smith, "Your Question," *Improvement Era* 61, no. 1 (January 1958): 16, 17.

34. The First Presidency, "The Origin of Man," *Improvement Era* 13, no. 1 (November 1909): 81.

35. George Q. Cannon, "Editorial Thoughts," *Juvenile Instructor*, no. 17 (September 1, 1868): 132.

36. Quoted in Thomas C. Romney, *The Life of Lorenzo Snow* (Salt Lake City: Sons of the Utah Pioneers Memorial Foundation, 1955), 23.

37. Spencer W. Kimball, "Fundamental Principles to Ponder and Live," *Ensign*, November 1978, 45.

38. Quoted in *Church News* section of *Deseret News* [Salt Lake City], October 7, 1978.

39. Joseph Smith, "Kindness to Animals Required of Man," in Joseph Fielding Smith, comp., *Teachings of the Prophet Joseph Smith* (Salt Lake City: Deseret Book, 1979), 71.

40. "The Millennium," *Times and Seasons* 3, no. 7 (February 1, 1842): 674.

41. Heber J. Grant, untitled address, in *One Hundred Seventh Annual Conference of The Church of Jesus Christ of Latter-day Saints* (Salt Lake City: The Church of Jesus Christ of Latter-day Saints, 1937), 15.

42. John A. Widtsoe, "Why Does the Lord Permit War?" *Improvement Era* 45, no. 2 (February 1942): 97.

43. Joseph Fielding Smith, *Church History and Modern Revelation*, 2 vols. (Salt Lake City: The Council of the Twelve Apostles of The Church of Jesus Christ of Latter-day Saints, 1953), 1:435.

Siddhartha Gautama

Buddhism

Spencer J. Palmer

4

BUDDHISM has been one of the most important religious forces in Asia for nearly two thousand years. No other religion has affected the thought, culture, and politics of so many people. In æsthetics, architecture, dance, drama, handicrafts, literary arts, and music, Buddhism has also been the single most important civilizing influence in the Eastern world.

The founder of Buddhism, *Siddhartha Gautama,*[1] rejected all the Hindu gods and objected to the Hindu/Brahmin prejudice that hereditary bloodlines should determine social positions. In this he advocated a doctrine of enlightened equality. Huston Smith suggests that when people questioned him they did not ask, "Who are you?" with respect to his name, origin, or ancestry. Rather, they asked, "What are you?"—meaning, to what order of being did he belong, or what species did he represent? The Buddha answered, "I am neither a god, an angel, or a saint. I am awake." His answer became his title, for "Buddha" means "the Awakened One."[2] A study of Buddhism in its various forms will demonstrate that the historical Buddha suggested a profound philosophy concerning the nature of humanity and the world. He discovered a path which he felt helped people deal with the deepest questions of life—issues such as human suffering, the importance of compassion, the meaning of life, and the nature of ultimate reality. These are the issues that will be explored in this chapter.

However, one must also recognize that there is probably no such thing as "pure" Buddhism in the world today. The highest official Buddhist teachings have been interlaced in practice with many of the superstitions, folk deities, charms, legends, amulets, and magic of the people. Thus, there may be a wide gap between the Buddhism of the classroom and the Buddhism practiced by people in the various cultures influenced by Buddhism.

Buddhism has found adherents in almost all parts of the world. It is ironic, however, that Buddhism has all but vanished in the land of its origin, India, where the faith became virtually extinct during the thirteenth century C.E.

Buddhism spread to all the countries surrounding India at an early date. It found an enduring home among the Tibetans, gained acceptance in China, flourished among Mongol peoples in northern Asia, permeated large areas of Korea and Japan, and thrived in several countries of southeast Asia and on the island of Sri Lanka. More recently, Buddhism has also reached the United States and other Western countries.

One cannot, however, refer to a "world" of Buddhism in the same way that one may speak of the world of Christianity or of Islam. Although its doctrines extend to all persons, its primary purpose in the beginning was not to teach its followers how to live while in the world, but to instruct them in how to attain release from the cycle of rebirths that bind them to the world. The Buddha's intent, therefore, was not to found a new world order in the sense that Jesus or Muhammad did.[3]

In the sixth century B.C.E., Siddhartha Gautama achieved enlightenment and thereby became the Buddha. In his enlightenment he learned of the suffering that permeates all life and to which all persons are subject, as long as they continue in the cycle of rebirths. Coupled with this insight, he learned that all things are transient and temporary. Both the transience and suffering can be overcome as one finds release from the wheel into the complete ego-free peace of *nirvana*. The path to this freedom which the Buddha taught to his disciples and his view of life have now penetrated many corners of the world.

49

THE FOUNDER: SIDDHARTHA GAUTAMA

According to poetic legends, Siddhartha Gautama was destined for enlightenment in the premortal spirit world long before he was born into his last existence. This Buddha-to-be passed through 550 existences as animal, man, and god before he was qualified to carry out his ultimate mission. In a "spirit" state he surveyed the world, and when he found that conditions were ripe for his last descent to earth he changed himself into a white elephant and entered the womb of his mother Maha Maya while the latter was sleeping. He was born in a grove of trees at the foot of the Nepal hills near Lumbini in 563 B.C.E., to the accompaniment of flowers blooming out of season and happiness pervading the world.

On the day of Siddhartha's birth a sage named Asita, dwelling in the Himalayas, saw the gods dancing in glee; and when he asked them the reason for their delight, he learned that a future Buddha had been born in a grove in the town of Kapilavastu. When Asita saw the child endowed with the thirty-two major and eighty minor marks of a great man, he immediately realized that this child, when grown, would either become a universal monarch ruling over the whole Indian realm or an enlightened one, the Buddha. And he so prophesied.

The child's father, Suddhodana, was an aristocratic chieftain of a small kingdom. He belonged to the traditional warrior caste, the Kshatriya, and he brought his son up in the princely splendor and luxury of the palace. The following is a description found in one of the *sutras* of the Buddha's early life:

I was delicately nurtured, exceedingly delicately nurtured. . . . For instance, in my father's house lotus-pools were made thus: one of blue lotuses, one of red, another of white lotuses, just for my benefit. . . . By day and night a white canopy was held over me, lest cold or heat, dust or chaff or dew, should touch me. Moreover . . . I had three palaces: one for winter, one for summer, and one for the rainy season. In the four months of the rains I was waited on by minstrels, women all of them. I came not down from my palace in those months.[4]

Later commentaries say that Hindu priests were invited by Suddhodana to foretell the future of his son. They prophesied that the youth would leave the household life and the shelter of the palace when he saw four signs: an old man, a sick man, a corpse, and a mendicant. In order to prevent Siddhartha from seeing these signs, his father initiated elaborate precautions to keep the boy in seclusion and pleasure so that he would be satisfied to become a great monarch rather than to seek a religious life.

At age sixteen Siddhartha married Yasodhara. She later gave birth to a son, Rahula. According to a legend widely known and fully accepted among Buddhists of whatever tradition, at age twenty-nine, after a life of carefully sheltered comfort, Siddhartha became dissatisfied with the meaningless luxury surrounding him. With his father's reluctant approval, he determined to go outside the confines of the palace and see the world as it was. His father was concerned that he see nothing that would trouble his serenity. The city was decorated with garlands and streamers; a magnificent chariot was prepared; and the cripples, the aged, and the beggars were ordered off the streets where the prince would pass.

Yet, for all the precautions, Siddhartha had not traveled far before he came upon an old man beside the road. He was stunned by what he saw. The man had white hair, no teeth, deeply sunken cheeks, wrinkled skin, a bent back, and ribs which protruded. Siddhartha asked his charioteer what he was seeing, for the figure before him looked like a man but was totally unlike anyone he had previously experienced. From his charioteer he learned about the reality of old age.

Next Siddhartha encountered a sick man. This person was so weak that he could not stand up but rolled and writhed on the ground. His eyes were bloodshot, his mouth was frothing, and he groaned and beat his breast in agony. As before, the charioteer explained the phenomenon, and once more the prince was overcome with anxiety.

Siddhartha then confronted the spectacle of death—a lifeless body carried along on a rack—and learned about the reality of life's end. Finally, he encountered a group of mendicant monks who appeared content and who were seeking enlightenment through extreme self-denial.

This graphic spectacle of human suffering became the catalyst for Siddhartha's introspective discovery of the *Four Noble Truths*. Profoundly shocked by the sights of old age, sickness, and death, he determined to leave secretly at night from his father's palace, while his wife and young son lay sleeping, to become a wandering ascetic in search of an answer to the misery of earthly life.

Following his departure from the pleasures of the palace, he practiced the extreme austerity of the Hindu monks for six years, once reportedly reminiscing:

To such a pitch of asceticism have I gone that naked was I, flouting life's decencies, licking my hands after meals, never heeding when folk called to me to come or to stop, never accepting food brought to me before my rounds or cooked expressly for me. . . . I have visited only one house a day and there taken only one morsel; . . . or [have had] one [meal] every two days, or [one] every seven days, or only once a fortnight. . . . In fulfillment of my vows, I have plucked out the hair of my head and the hair of my beard, have never quitted the upright for the sitting posture, have squatted and never risen up, . . . have couched on thorns, have gone down to the water punctually thrice before nightfall to wash (away the evil within). After this wise, in divers fashions, have I lived to torment and to torture my body;—to such a length in asceticism have I gone.[5]

Siddhartha claimed that, during the last broiling month of the summer and before the rains, he dwelt in the open. Cowherd boys spat upon him, pelted him with dirt, and stuck bits of wood into his ears. He claimed to have lived on a single bean a day, on a single sesame seed a day, or a single grain of rice a day. But all this failed to bring to him the ennobling gifts of superhuman knowledge and spiritual insight that he expected would come from extreme self-denial.

Finally, realizing that his very desire for enlightenment was preventing the attainment of his goal, Siddhartha stepped back from his extreme asceticism, ate a bowl of rice, and shed his final desire. He then sat down in a cross-legged position under a *bodhi* (fig) tree at Gaya with his face toward the east and made a vow: "Even if my skin should parch, even if my hand should wither, even if my bones should crumble into dust, until I have attained supreme knowledge I shall not move from this seat." Thereupon he was attacked by the demonic spirit Mara, and also by wind, rain, rocks, and weapons. But Siddhartha withstood. He meditated on *karma,* the cosmic law of justice; and, before the end of that night, Siddhartha had realized "the path of deliverance" known as the Four Noble Truths. "The rafters are broken," he exclaimed. "The old walls are down. The ancient mountain crumbles; the mind attains to nirvana; birth is no more for desire is no more."[6]

At age thirty-five Siddhartha had reached enlightenment. He was now a Buddha, "one who is awake." He could now be called Tathagata, "he who has gone thus," "he who has passed beyond all bounds."

After remaining in meditation for many days, the Buddha arose and went to Banaras. On its outskirts, in Sarnath, the "Deer Park," he met five ascetics with whom he had been associated before. He preached to them and they were converted. They became his first disciples. As he wandered about, teaching, other disciples joined him, until there was a band of sixty accompanying him. The Buddha's ministry lasted forty-five years and was widely successful. Thousands came to him or his disciples seeking lay or monastic initiation, many from the highest ranks of society. In time an order of nuns was also established.

But there was opposition. Certain Hindu Brahmin priests murmured against the Buddha's doctrine. One of his disciples, Devadatta, encouraged by a hostile king, became a "Judas" and tried to kill the Buddha; but his plots were foiled. The Buddha's end finally came from eating spoiled food; he died under a tree at Kushinara in 483 B.C.E. at eighty years of age, reportedly passing away surrounded by his disciples.

The Buddha never claimed to be a supernatural being, a mysterious person, or a god. In fact, the *Theravada* Buddhism founded by him rejected all individualities, including all deities of any kind. In the earliest Buddhist scriptures, especially in the poem sections, the Buddha was regarded merely as an outstanding or exemplary man. In later times Buddhists called him *Sakyamuni* (the prince of the Sakya clan), but in the earliest days his disciples addressed him only as Sakya without using any honorific title. In these older poems also, Brahmin youths addressed him as if talking to an intimate friend, not a divine person.[7]

DIVISIONS WITHIN BUDDHISM

Before beginning a discussion of the basic doctrines taught by the Buddha, it is appropriate to state that over the span of time since he taught there have occurred major divisions within Buddhism that have established significantly different interpretations of his initial teachings. Although all present "schools" of Buddhism hold to some of the same basic tenets taught by the Buddha, other concepts—for example, those involving deity, the individual's role in life, and the interpretation of nirvana—are dramatically different. Thus, a brief introduction to the various schools here will set the context for all that follows.

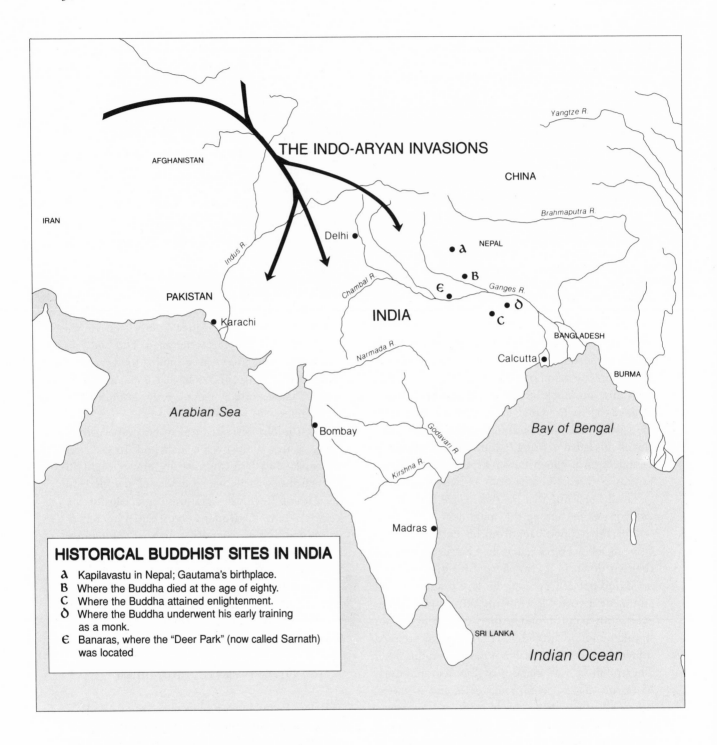

THE INDO-ARYAN INVASIONS

HISTORICAL BUDDHIST SITES IN INDIA

ॲ Kapilavastu in Nepal; Gautama's birthplace.
B Where the Buddha died at the age of eighty.
C Where the Buddha attained enlightenment.
ठ Where the Buddha underwent his early training
   as a monk.
Є Banaras, where the "Deer Park" (now called Sarnath)
   was located

There are three principal schools of Buddhism in the world today. The first and earliest is called Theravada, the Way of the Monks. It was founded by the Buddha. This school is sometimes known as *Hinayana,* the Lesser Vehicle, perhaps a pejorative designation applied by members of the Mahayana community. Theravada is dominant today in the countries of southern and southeastern Asia (Sri Lanka, Thailand, Burma, Cambodia, and others) and provides the foundational doctrines and monastic traditions of Buddhism.

The second major school is *Mahayana,* the Great or Greater Vehicle, with many deities and a vast pantheon of buddhas and savior beings. Mahayana flourishes in northern Asia in the countries of China, Korea, Japan, and Taiwan.

Another school of Buddhism, which can be treated as an aspect of Mahayana, is called *Vajrayana,* the Vehicle of the Thunderbolt. Vajrayana emphasizes a bold theology which mingles traditional thought with magic. It is known under several names: Lamaism, because of the predominance of *lamas* (priests or monks) in it; Mantrayana, Vehicle of the Mantras or Holy Words; and Tantrayana, which emphasizes the use of magical manuals or texts. Vajrayana is practiced primarily in Tibet.

THERAVADA BUDDHISM

The Four Noble Truths

The fundamental content of the Buddha's enlightenment consisted of insights into the nature of life known as the Four Noble Truths. These truths charted a course between the extremes of indulgence and asceticism, thus causing Buddhism to be known as the "middle way." The teachings of the Buddha are best preserved within Theravada Buddhism. The Four Noble Truths are fundamental to this school. They are:

1. Life is painful. Birth, disease, old age, and death are painful. Sorrow, lamentation, and grief are painful. Not to get what one wants is painful.

2. Selfish desire is the origin of pain and suffering. Craving bound up with pleasure and lust is the source of suffering. Selfish desire has its root in the senses—the eyes, ears, nose, tongue, and body. Visual objects, sounds, smells, tastes, bodily impressions, and mental objects are delightful and pleasurable; yet from them comes attachment to the things of mortality, which cannot be permanently held since they are by nature temporary and elusive.

3. Craving, the origin of suffering, can be eliminated. Whoever regards the things of this world—its delights and physical pleasures—as impermanent and miserable, as a disease and a cancer, can overcome selfish craving. The extinction of attachment, the elimination of egotistical love, the elimination of anger and of delusions of enduring health, life, and death—this brings nirvana, a heightened state of peace. He who has considered all the contrasts of the world and freed himself from the painful frustrations that derive from desiring to cling permanently to the transient human condition is he who reaches enlightenment.

4. The *Eightfold Middle Path* leads to the extinction of suffering. As noted above, the Buddha concluded at Gaya that the path of freedom lies between the extremes of self-indulgence and self-denial. The steps on that path can be followed, at least at first, by the lay people; but ultimately in *some* life a person will reach the point of desiring enlightenment. At that point he or she will take up a monastic existence in order to complete the steps to enlightenment. These are known as the Eightfold Middle Path. The steps must be followed sequentially through one's various existences. The first two steps involve right understanding, the next three involve correct morals, and the final three involve right concentration. According to the Buddha, this is the way off the wheel of existence.

The Eightfold Middle Path

The path of moderation is based upon right views, right thought, right speech, right action, right livelihood, right effort, right mindfulness, and right concentration. Right views means understanding the Four Noble Truths. Right thought is thought that is free from ill will and cruelty. Right speech means abstaining from lying, talebearing, harsh language, and vain talk. Right action means abstaining from violence, killing, stealing, and unlawful sexual relations. Right livelihood is a way of earning a living that causes no harm to any living thing. This affects especially the butcher or the fisherman, but it goes further than that. For example, selling alcohol would not be considered a right livelihood because the seller lives on the proceeds of a commodity that harms other people. Thus, *ahimsa* is a part of the Buddhist lifestyle, just as it is part of Hinduism and Jainism.

The first five steps in the Eightfold Middle Path are attainable by lay people. Thus far it is a down-to-earth path. But the final three steps approach the mystical techniques of the Hindu ascetics and require withdrawal from the world.

Right effort includes four great efforts: to avoid, to overcome, to develop, and to maintain, meaning that one should avoid morally incorrect activities while cultivating those which are correct. Right mindfulness is to be fully conscious of one's movements and acts so that nothing that goes on inside one's mind escapes attention. Right concentration is concentration on a single object and is associated with wholeness of consciousness.

In these last three steps, which include successive trances and the teaching of a state of perfect purity of balance and equanimity, the Buddha was clearly going beyond that which is possible for the average layperson; he was advocating that which was appropriate only to a special order of monks or nuns known as the *Sangha*. Thus, he called those on the first five steps disciples, while those on the last three he called brothers. Only those who forsook the common life and gave themselves up wholly to the pursuit of liberation in the monastery (nunneries were established later) truly approached the ideal laid down by the Buddha. The life of the monks was and is strictly governed by rules, of which the basic ten are prohibitions against taking life; taking that which is not given; sexual misconduct; lying; drinking liquor; eating in the afternoon; watching dancing, singing, and shows; adorning oneself with garlands, perfumes, and jewelry; sleeping in a high bed; and receiving gold and silver.

It should also be noted that the Eightfold Middle Path is a path of self-salvation. Even though gods may exist, they cannot help others gain release from the wheel of rebirth, since they themselves are subject to death and rebirth. Thus, Theravada Buddhism is functionally nontheistic. Each person works out his or her own salvation.

Nirvana

The ultimate goal in the world of Buddhism is nirvana. In Buddhist beginnings, nirvana was a form of annihilation or extinction of individuality, described in Buddhist texts as a state of exaltation and freedom. The word is derived from a root meaning "extinguished through lack of fuel." Freedom from rebirth is attained by the extinguishing of all desires. One who has attained to this state is called a saint (or *arhat*) and at the death of his physical body attains complete or final nirvana, in which all attributes relating to phenomenal existence cease. This is cessation of existence as known and experienced by human beings; the attainment of Being (as distinct from becoming); union with Ultimate Reality. The Buddha speaks of it as "an unborn, unoriginated, uncreated, unformed" state, contrasting it with the born, originated, created, and formed phenomenal world.

A Western mind, considering this concept in isolation, would likely perceive it as a negative outcome of existence; however, when considered in the context of the culture it awakens some chords of human understanding, especially among those who

have visited India or east Asia. It is part of the universal human condition to experience some degree of discomfort at some point in time. In fact, as is made evident in the story of the Buddha's early life, near-superhuman measures must be taken to keep a person physically comfortable at all times in certain climates and social conditions, and even then mental or emotional comfort may not be assured. Granted, discomfort with the existing situation can and does lead to much in the way of human growth and progress, both on individual and collective levels. Still, poverty, disease, hunger, warfare, suppression of the human spirit, and other such conditions have made life chronically difficult and painful in some areas of the world, including India and many areas of central and east Asia. The idea that these conditions must be borne again and again through successive lifetimes over many ages can be daunting. For a person of spiritual sensitivity, the prospect of all humankind laboring repeatedly through the same set of difficult circumstances with no hope of breaking the cycle cannot be anything short of universally depressing. Nirvana represents an end to this horrific fate. Westerners tend to think of nirvana as primarily the annihilation of individual volition and the possibilities and pleasures associated with it, but to Buddhists it also represents the annihilation of physical and spiritual pain, incessant labor, weariness, inequity, and crushing challenges. In that light, nirvana can to some extent be compared to Western concepts of heaven and "rest eternal."

Scripture: The Tripitaka[8]

The *Tripitaka* is the scriptural foundation of Buddhism, particularly Theravada Buddhism. According to tradition, shortly after the Buddha's death five hundred monks gathered at Rajagaha during the rainy season and chanted the entirety of the Tripitaka, a name which means "three baskets." Traditionally, the gathering is referred to as the First Council and was purported to be under the direction of Kashyapa, a close disciple of the Buddha.

The "three baskets" of the Tripitaka are the Vinaya Pitaka, the Sutta Pitaka, and the Abhidhamma Pitaka. The Vinaya Pitaka contains the monastic rules for the Sangha, the Buddhist order. The Sutta Pitaka, the discourses, contains the teachings of the Buddha, thus making it the most important part of the canon. Two portions of the Sutta Pitaka are often cited. The

was a sandalwood statue carved in the Buddha's lifetime for a king known as Udayana. However, the first historically verifiable images of the Buddha were carved in Gandhara (located in what is today Afghanistan and part of Pakistan) as early as the first century C.E. It is certain that the first representations of the Buddha in human form were created centuries after his death, when a special need was felt for anthropomorphic representations of him—even though the representation of the Buddha was prohibited in several passages of the Buddhist canon.

Mahayana Buddhism did not appear overnight. It took time for it to develop. For example, as the Buddha began to be worshiped, prayer (*puja*) to him began to replace the contemplation and practice (*yajna*) of his message. Devotion replaced the hard road of Theravada Buddhism. Buddhist devotionalism was probably affected by the bhakti movement within Hinduism, in which Shiva and Vishnu (and Vishnu's avatars) were able to assist their adherents in finding release from the wheel. The way of devotion was wide and open to all, as one can see in Krishna's comment to Arjuna in the Bhagavad Gita.

> For if they take refuge in Me, son of Prtha,
> Even those who may be of base origin,
> Women, men of the artisan caste, and serfs too,
> Even they go to the highest goal.[17]

In response, the devotional movement within Buddhism also grew and, as the faith entered the countries of northeast Asia (Tibet, Mongolia, China, Korea, Taiwan, and Japan), it gained many new deities and legendary heroes drawn from the mythologies of the new environments. While the deification of the Buddha was a product of Indian influence, the expansion of the Mahayana pantheon had influences not only from the countries it entered but even perhaps from Greek mythology, Christian beliefs about salvation, and Zoroastrian views of Ahura Mazda and his associates.

Mahayana Savior Beings

The best known helping beings in Mahayana Buddhism, other than the deified Buddha himself, are the buddhas *Vairocana* and Amitabha and the bodhisattvas *Maitreya* and *Avalokitesvara,* whose characteristics will be discussed below. Another well-known figure is *Bhaisajyaguru,* the bodhisattva of medicine. Before speaking more of them, though, it

may be helpful to look at the types of savior beings represented in the Mahayana tradition, so as to enable a student to identify some order in the Mahayana pantheon of helping beings. There are two broad, general categories of divine beings in Buddhism—bodhisattvas and buddhas.

Buddhas

Although the title "Buddha" was first applied to a single individual, the enlightened Gautama, it has over time accumulated different meanings and applications in the various schools of Buddhism. As indicated earlier, Gautama never claimed to be a supernatural being, a mysterious personage, or a god. In the earliest Buddhist scriptures he was regarded simply as an outstanding person and a great inspirational teacher. However, as Buddhism spread into northern Asia, where mythical and legendary figures abound, Gautama himself in time was deified and has become one of a vast plethora of divine beings and saviors. These "enlightened ones," or buddhas, in the Mahayana Buddhism of China, Korea, and Japan, are gods of wide-ranging power. They are worshiped and invoked through prayer and public chants and are credited with blessing their devotees not only with salvation and ultimate rebirth into heavenly places, but with fulfillment of routine physical and social needs. They include, principally, Amitabha (Amida), the Buddha of Boundless Light; Maitreya, the messiah figure of Mahayana Buddhism; Bhaisajyaguru, the buddha of medicine, who is the light of the realm of the Eastern Paradise; and Vairocana, the cosmic buddha, who is a personification of essential enlightenment. More will be said below of the former two figures.

Although Vajrayana Buddhism in Tibet and Mongolia is generally considered to be a part of the Mahayana tradition, it does contain a dogma unique to it that involves the recognition of "living Buddhas." In this doctrine, certain priests and monks (lamas) are perceived as incarnations of saints and deities, including buddhas. When an incarnate lama dies, his "spiritual being," or his soul, goes first to a celestial abode, then—at the end of a period somewhere between forty-six days and four years—is reborn in the body of a child who, from his birth, shows signs of supernatural character. This belief has, of course, meant that lamas have great spiritual influence in Vajrayana. In the latter half of the fifteenth century, this doctrine resulted in the ascendancy of a "Grand Lama" and, later, of the Dalai Lama, who has come to be honored as an incarnation of Avalokitesvara.[18] Thus, the head lama of Vajrayana Buddhism is considered to be a living buddha, or god.

Bodhisattvas

The term bodhisattva refers to one who is a buddha-to-be. Siddhartha Gautama, both in his previous lives and in his last life until he received enlightenment at Gaya, was a bodhisattva. In the Mahayana view, he had at some time taken a vow before a living buddha that he too would become a buddha—that is, he committed to perfect himself to the degree that he would become an earthly buddha (sometimes referred to as a manushi buddha) who could teach others the way to salvation. According to Buddhist lore widely accepted in various parts of Asia, only one buddha at a time may be on earth; and thus, after numerous incarnations, Siddhartha had to wait in Tushita-heaven for the appropriate time for his advent. That time came when the teachings of the previous buddha had completely disappeared.[19] In essence, he initiated the next "dispensation" of Buddhism by his birth into the world and his attainment of supreme enlightenment. When he entered this life he was a bodhisattva, and when he left it he was a buddha, or "one who is awake."

Bodhisattvas are the paradigm for all Mahayana Buddhists who seek to release or unlock the buddha-nature which lies within every person. The bodhisattva has reached the point of being totally free from birth and death and shares his or her merit with those who call upon him or her. The bodhisattva lives on the edge between existence and non-existence, never taking the step to nirvana because of compassion for and desire to help all who are still subject to death and rebirth.

[In] the Mahayana tradition the term [bodhisattva] designates those sublimely indifferent, compassionate beings who remain at the threshold of nirvana for the comfort and salvation of the world. Out of perfect indifference (egolessness) and perfect compassion (which is also egolessness) the Mahayana Bodhisattva does not experience the "real or true enlightenment". . . of the Buddha and then pass to final extinction . . . but stops at the brink—the brink of time and eternity—and thus transcends that pair of opposites: for the world will never end; the round of cosmic eons will go on and on without ceasing; the vow of the Bodhisattva, to remain at the brink till all shall go in before him, amounts to a vow to remain as

he is forever. . . . In popular worship the Bodhisattva is invoked because he is possessed of an inexhaustible power to save. . . .

The supreme and especial test of the Bodhisattva is that of his readiness and power to expand, time and time again, in boundless giving. . . . This requires of him a continuous abdication—or rather, non-experience—of ego.[20]

Five bodhisattvas are often named together: Samantabhadra, Vajrapani, Ratnapani, Visvapani, and Avalokitesvara. The latter is the most popular and best known.[21]

Buddhas and bodhisattvas are viewed by Mahayana Buddhists as savior beings who, through their powers and personal goodness, can help seekers to attain nirvana. Following is a discussion of three of the most popular of these helping beings.

Amitabha, Lord of the Western Paradise

Amitabha is a widely revered and worshiped buddha. He is Lord of the Western Land, to which his adherents hope to be taken at death. He dwells in Sukhavati-heaven, and he exerts himself for all humankind through meditation. He is a savior figure in whom many Mahayana Buddhists have deep faith.

Known in China as Omit'ofu and in Korea and Japan as Amida, this deity has had a strong appeal to the common persons in Asia. In Amidism (the worship of Amitabha, or Amida), believers seek enlightenment through rebirth in the land of the pure realm where Amitabha lives. Therefore, the more frequently his name is recited ("Hail to the name of Amida!"—a popular *mantra* or chant in Mahayana Buddhism), the greater the spiritual benefit. In this religion there are no austerities, no secret teachings, and no complicated rituals—nothing except saving merit from faith in Amitabha manifested through recitation or thought of his name.

It is difficult to trace Amitabha's origins. His name does not appear in the early documents of Theravada Buddhism, and he is not worshiped in Sri Lanka, Burma, or Thailand. It was not until the second century C.E. that texts dealing with Amitabha's western realm began to appear. He is a dominant figure among Chinese, Koreans, and Japanese today.

Several scholars believe that Amitabha did not originate in India; but if this is the case, from whence might he have come? Alice Getty, following views of Paul Pelliot and Sir Charles Eliot, suggests that Amitabha has certain characteristics which may reflect a Zoroastrian origin and that all the features of his western paradise may be traced to Zoroastrian theology, including the idea of multiple paradises, with the highest of them being called the "Land of Endless Light."[22]

Some Christian and Greek influences may also be present in the Amidist school of Buddhism. That a connection existed between the Western Buddha and the Christian idea of a Heavenly Father is suggested in the notion that Amitabha often presides over a trinity, usually consisting of himself, Avalokitesvara, and Maitreya. The Amidist trinity is a good example of a divine power acting through two agents or representatives.[23]

Buddhist descriptions of Amitabha's heavenly realm involve three degrees of glory. It is only in the highest degree that the faithful will fully enjoy the presence of the divine. The first degree is described as being reserved for "those who have lived steadfast in purity." Amitabha "will *come in welcome* with His host of Bodhisattvas and Arhats, to fill their eyes at the end with an ineffable glory." The second degree is for "others who have led devout lives as laymen." To them Amitabha "will grant a dying *vision* of the welcome, identical in appearance with the real one." And the lowest or third degree is for "those whose good impulses have been offset by backsliding or unbelief"; the buddha "will permit [them] to *dream* of Him at the last." And finally, "all these three grades [of glory] will share equally in the bliss of the Western Land, in the end; only the last group will have to pass through a purgatorial period of five hundred years. . . . The souls on probation will be isolated, unable to see the Buddha or hear Him preach until their term has run out."[24]

Amitabha is the ethereal form of the buddha. In the most common artistic representations, he sits with his legs locked in the lotus position and his hands in his lap in the meditation or *dhyana* hand position. He is artistically portrayed with a topknot (*ushnisha*), a third eye representing wisdom (*urna*), and long-lobed ears. He is known only in Mahayana Buddhism. Neither of the two famous Buddhist pilgrims, Fa-hsien, in the account of his travels to India (399–414 C.E.), and Hsuan-tsang on his journey (629–645 C.E.), mentions him, although they do refer to Avalokitesvara and others.

Mahayana Buddhists hold that before entering into nirvana the Buddha communicated to one of his disciples the knowledge of Sukhavati, the Western Paradise. Descriptions of it differ, with the imaginations of the authors contributing greatly to the varying accounts. All, however, describe a wondrous, joyous realm. The Saddharmapundarika, or *Lotus Sutra*, records that no women may enter therein unless, by performing acts of merit on earth, they earn the right to masculinity in the hereafter.[25]

It was only after the Amitabha Sutra was translated into Chinese by Kumarajiva in the fifth century C.E. that the cult of Amitabha began to spread rapidly into China. Amidism caused alarm among some Confucianists in China and raised a lively dispute between the two sides. The Chinese were slow to understand and appreciate the Indian concept of nirvana because ancestor veneration was a universal practice in China, even in Buddhist monasteries, where the monks honored deceased members of the community. The great Chinese teachers, moralists, and philosophers therefore rejected the idea of complete annihilation after death; but they also disapproved of the doctrine of immortality in paradise. They compromised by avoiding the question of the hereafter, instead concentrating on how to live here and now. Of course, the common people understood none of the controversy.[26]

In Japan, Amida was often looked upon as incarnate in the great sun goddess Amaterasu, although some preferred to identify the buddha Vairocana with the primal kami or god of the sun. Actual worship of Amida in Japan goes back no further than the twelfth century. Through the Amida *Jodo Shu* and *Jodo Shinshu* (Pure Land and True Pure Land) sects of Japan, founded in the thirteenth century, belief in the Western Paradise and in salvation through faith in Amida has become widely popular. Amida in Japan is artistically represented wearing the usual monastic garments, but both shoulders are covered.[27] His pose of crossing the legs with both soles of the feet turned upward symbolizes that his whole body, including his feet that touch the ground, has become illumined. Celestial powers are thus streaming through his feet, bringing about a harmony of conflicting energies in the universe. The white *lotus* flower upon which Amida sits symbolizes the process of purification through which this buddha has gone successfully. The ambrosia vessel which he may hold represents the mendicant's bowl into which heaven now places its bread (ambrosia) for the nourishment of humanity.

Avalokitesvara

In Buddhist lore, Avalokitesvara was created from a ray of light which emanated from the third eye (eye of enlightenment) of his father, Amitabha. He dwells near his father and is usually one of the figures seen with Amitabha in artistic representations of the trinity which rules the Western Land. Out of compassion for humankind, Avalokitesvara postpones his own nirvana to assist others off the wheel. He is believed to protect people from shipwreck, robbers, and beasts of prey, and he hurries to help anyone who calls on his name. He is the personification of the Buddhist ideal of compassion.

The Mani Kambun, a Tibetan historical work attributed to a Tibetan king, states that

"once upon a time, Amitabha, after giving himself up to earnest meditation, caused a white ray of light to issue from his right eye, which brought Padmapani [Avalokitesvara] Bodhisattva into existence." . . . [Then] Amitabha blessed him, whereupon the Bodhisattva brought forth the prayer: *"Om, mani padme, hum!"* "Oh! the jewel (of creation) is in the lotus!"[28]

How early the worship of Avalokitesvara began in India is unknown. Worship of him came into Tibet in the middle of the seventh century, when the prince sRong-Tsan-Gam-Po was proclaimed by Buddhist priests to be an incarnation of him. As a representative of the Buddha and guardian of the faith until the coming of Maitreya, the Buddhist messianic figure, he has become the most popular among all the Mahayana Buddhist gods. According to legend, Avalokitesvara has manifested himself on earth 333 times. It should be emphasized that he is not only supposed to have become incarnate in the Tibetan prince sRong-Tsan-Gam-Po but in every Dalai Lama of Tibetan Buddhism since that time, including the one currently living in exile in India. Each has been looked upon as a living Avalokitesvara. He is still the principal living buddha in the Tibetan tradition.

Worship of Avalokitesvara spread into China near the close of the first century C.E. Originally a male figure in southwest Asia, in time Avalokitesvara was feminized. Known in China as Kuan Yin, this deity practically became a national divinity. The Lotus Sutra affirms that all her many earthly incarnations were in human form except one. This was when the bodhisattva was incarnated as a horse who rescued an incarnation of Maitreya from a horde of demons in female guises who were besetting the buddha-to-be.

The Lotus Sutra credits this deity with the ability to change from male to female but does not confirm any such changes.[29]

Kuan Yin is often portrayed as a multi-armed or even multi-eyed deity in India, China, Korea, and Japan. Most often this deity is portrayed as a gentle madonna, and this is her vow: "Should any being recite and cleave to the sacred Dharani of Great Compassion and yet not be reborn in my Buddhaland, I vow not to enter upon Supreme Enlightenment."[30]

In Japan Kuan Yin is known as Kannon, and in Korea as Kwuan Um. In Japan, by the end of the thirteenth century C.E., she was believed to exhibit the ideal virtues of womanhood. Today, in conjunction with the concept of the feminine ideal, she represents motherly love, humility, endurance in suffering, and nobility of character.

Maitreya

In Buddhist tradition, Maitreya can be manifest as either a bodhisattva or a savior buddha of the future. He has been preparing himself in Tushita-heaven for the past five thousand six hundred and seventy million years to descend to this world to rescue humanity. He is waiting. He sits in a relaxed but pensive posture. Unlike other Buddhist divinities, he is seated in Western fashion, with pendant legs sometimes crossed at the ankles and usually resting an elbow on a knee and a hand on his chin. Maitreya is the bodhisattva that the Buddha prophesied would return to earth as another buddha to redeem an iniquitous world at the last day. The hour of his advent is not known, but it is believed that at his return there will be a great dislocation in nature—that is, mountains will be laid low and the human life span will increase to as much as eighty thousand years.

According to Tibetan and Chinese translations of the now-lost Divyavadana, when Maitreya returns many disciples and saintly monks will accompany him. One such is Kobo Daishi, a Japanese Buddhist priest who studied in China and founded the Shingon sect. He was a man of humility and devotion. After receiving permission from the emperor, Kobo Daishi built a temple on Mount Koya. He died there in 835 C.E. while in a state of fasting and prayer. Kobo Daishi's followers believe that he is today in his tomb awaiting the advent of Maitreya. When Maitreya comes, Kobo Daishi is expected to rise and join in the glory of his victory.

It is also believed that when Maitreya comes he will visit Mount Kukkutapada, in the environs of Gaya, India, where Siddhartha Gautama reached spiritual enlightenment. At that time the mountain will open of its own accord and Maitreya will revive Mahakasyapa, the venerable friend of the historical Buddha, who has been slumbering there since the time of the death of the Buddha. The Buddha entrusted his own priesthood robe, which was woven of gold, to Mahakasyapa and bade him present it to the messiah (Maitreya) when the latter achieved glorification. When Mahakasyapa was nearing his own death he went to the top of Mount Kukkutapada, wrapped himself in the robe of his master, and recited a prayer. As the mountain opened, Mahakasyapa died; and the mountain closed over him.

All this is background to the belief that when Maitreya descends to earth at the last day the mountain will split apart and Mahakasyapa will emerge; deliver the sacred robe of investiture to Maitreya; and, after performing various prodigious feats, sacred symbols, and signs, enter into his own nirvana.[31]

In Mahayana Buddhism the impact of the bodhisattva concept is immense, not only because it provides divine assistance to a devotee to get off the wheel of life but because it inspires serious Buddhists to become bodhisattvas themselves. John Noss expresses this well when he says:

Just as the Bodhisattvas, who are now divine but once were human, vowed in a distant past to become Buddhas and then from pure altruism postponed their entrance into Nirvana by transferring their merit to others in order to help the needy, so any human being of the present, man or woman, can, if he or she wishes, make a similar vow with regard to the future. Everyone is potentially a Buddha and should now take the vow to be a Bodhisattva. The length of time necessary to fulfill the destiny thus undertaken may be almost beyond reckoning, but true benevolence needs no urging and waits for nothing. The time to begin is now.[32]

The Schools of Mahayana Buddhism[33]

Having viewed the diversity of the deities in Mahayana Buddhism, it should not be surprising that the faith contains numerous schools of thought. These are sometimes associated with one of the principal Buddhist divinities and sometimes with a discipline or concept which is emphasized as a means of reaching spiritual fulfillment. The most important of these schools follow.

Amitabha or Pure Land School

As explained earlier in this chapter, the widely popular Amitabha Pure Land school seeks rebirth into the merciful presence of Amitabha, the Lord of the Western Paradise, through the recitation of his name as a manifestation of pure faith in him.

The founder of the *Jodo* or Pure Land school of Buddhism in Japan was *Shinran Shonin,* who was born near Kyoto in 1173. He spent over fifty years teaching an enlightened way of life through the wisdom and compassion of Amida Buddha. Shinran was a humble man who claimed no disciples of his own. All were the children of Amida Buddha. However, so influential were his teachings that his followers organized Hompa Hongwanji, the most widespread school of Buddhism in Japan today.

Jodo Buddhism was the first Japanese Buddhism to reach America. The Jodo Shinshu movement began in San Francisco with the arrival of two priests from the Hompa Hongwanji in 1898, who came to explore the possibility of establishing Buddhist congregations in this country. Today, the Buddhist Churches of America is an autonomous organization governed by American Buddhists; its ties to the Hongwanji in Kyoto are spiritual only.

Nichiren: The Sociopolitical School

Nichiren Shoshu is called the orthodox school of Buddhism by its adherents and was founded in Japan by a young monk named *Nichiren Daishonin* (1222–1282). He was an aggressive and dogmatic teacher who is widely credited with having said, "I am the pillar of Japan and Japan is the pillar of the world." After studying all the Buddhist scriptures left by the Buddha, Nichiren proclaimed that the truth of the Buddha's enlightenment lay only in his ultimate teaching, the Lotus Sutra. The Lotus Sutra taught that life is eternal, alternating between the stages of life and death, and that all people innately share what is known as the buddha-nature, or the highest state of life. The point of Nichiren Daishonin's Buddhism is to achieve this highest condition in this lifetime. Due to the eternity of life, this condition can thereafter be carried over and activated in subsequent incarnations.

To make this possible, Nichiren Daishonin embodied the truth of the Buddhist teachings in a *mandala,* or scroll, known as the *Dai-Gohonzon*. This prototype scroll is enshrined in the *Sho-Hondo* (Grand Main Temple) at the Nichiren Shoshu Head

Stupa, Gaya, India. According to tradition, the bodhi tree
under which Siddhartha Gautama received enlightenment stands
in front of this monument. *(Photo by Roger R. Keller)*

Temple, Taisekiji, situated at the foot of Mount Fuji in Japan. Down the center of this Dai-Gohonzon is the inscription "Nam-myoho-renge-kyo" ("Hail to the Marvelous Law of the Lotus Sutra"), which signifies the oneness of the Mystic Law of Life (Nam-myoho-renge-kyo) with one's own life as symbolized by Nichiren Daishonin himself.

Upon joining Nichiren Shoshu, each member receives a Gohonzon, a scroll modeled exactly after the Dai-Gohonzon. Practitioners of Nichiren Shoshu Buddhism therefore chant "Nam-myoho-renge-kyo" to the Gohonzon to achieve their own enlightenment by drawing out their buddha-nature. The Mystic Law of Nam-myoho-renge-kyo, Nichiren Daishonin said, is the key to all believers' enlightenment which lay hidden in the Buddha's highest teaching, the Lotus Sutra. The repetition of this chant is also a means of gaining reward and benefits.

A key tenet of Buddhism is that one's destiny, or karma, is formed by one's actions throughout the three existences of past, present, and future. According to Nichiren Shoshu, to change negative karma one invokes the Law of Nam-myoho-renge-kyo, thereby activating one's buddha-nature and unlocking the necessary wisdom, power, and decision-making ability to bring about absolute happiness in this lifetime. As a result of fusing with the Mystic Law of Life through chanting to the Gohonzon, believers also form a harmonious relationship with other people and nature in general. This in turn leads to improvements in family life, community life, global relations, and environmental harmony, resulting ultimately in what is called *kosen-rufu*—loosely translated as world peace, but much broader in meaning than the mere absence of hostility.

The only true scripture for followers of Nichiren is the Lotus Sutra, and gaining merit through chanting the Lotus Sutra is a cardinal feature of public services.

Zen: The Meditative School

Zen Buddhism is a form of Mahayana Buddhism that seeks access to truth or reality through meditation. Also known as the meditative school, Zen has as its goal enlightenment through disciplined meditation, such as the historical Buddha received under the bodhi tree at Gaya. Zen Buddhists do not hold a concept of God, soul, or salvation; in fact, they deny the necessity of vows, scriptures, or rituals. Zen has been described as a religion with a unique method of mind-body training with the aim of *satori*

(enlightenment) or self-realization. Attainment of satori comes entirely from self-effort (*jiriki*) rather than from some outside power. A Zen Buddhist does not need faith in any buddha; rather, he needs faith in his own buddha-nature and the determination to continue in self-effort until he experiences satori.

According to Zen practitioners, Zen is as old as the Buddha himself. The legend states that the Buddha was once approached by a Brahmin raja who gave him a golden flower and then asked him to preach the Dharma. The Buddha took the flower and held it, gazing at it in silence. After a while he gave it to one of his disciples, Kashyapa, who smiled but uttered not a word. This is said to be the ideological beginning of Zen, and Kashyapa is said to be the first Zen patriarch. His smile was handed down to twenty-eight other patriarchs, the final one being Bodhidharma, an Indian prince who arrived in China in 520 C.E. Bodhidharma taught the principles and techniques of what was called the *Dhyana* (Meditative) school of Buddhism in China. As Dhyana practice spread throughout northern Asia, the Chinese transliterated its name to Ch'an, the Koreans to Son, and the Japanese to Zen.

The practice most central to Zen is zazen. Zazen consists of both oral instruction from a teacher (*roshi*) and meditation. Technically, the meditation is "sitting meditation." The meditator usually sits cross-legged on a thick round cushion and meditates, preferably in the full-lotus or half-lotus position. The back must be straight, and the eyes must be directed toward the floor a short distance from the body. The optimal area upon which to center one's inner attention is just below the navel.

There are several schools of Zen Buddhism, including *Rinzai* and *Soto*. Rinzai Zen considers satori to be a sudden illumination or epiphany. It is attained by hard, concentrated work on *koans* (riddles) which are insoluble by the processes of reason, such as, "What was your original face before your parents were born?" or, "What is the sound of one hand clapping?" A Zen student who solves the koan must reject logical reasoning and find an answer through the use of a deeper level of the mind beyond the rational intellect. Soto Zen believes in a more gradual process of enlightenment.

The Rationalist Schools

The Zen intuitionist's utter purging of the mind in hope of obtaining enlightenment was based on feeling rather than reason. Perhaps as a reaction to this anti-intellectualism, a countervailing rationalist tradition emerged within Buddhism in northern Asia. The best known sect is called T'ien-t'ai in Chinese and Tendai in Japanese. Its emphasis is that meditation should be balanced with concentrated study of Buddhist texts.

"The Mystery School"

Known as Chen Yen in China and Shingon in Japan, the mystery school emphasizes magical hand formulas and mystical ceremonies that owe much to the Tantric Buddhism of Tibet. Practitioners of this school of Buddhism view all phenomena of the universe as manifestations of the buddha Vairocana.

Mahayana Scriptures

The Buddhists of northern Asia have never reduced their scriptures to a comprehensive system such as that found in the canon of the Theravada school. Mahayana scriptures must be sought in at least four languages—Sanskrit, Tibetan, Chinese, and Japanese. The most complete records of the Mahayana canon are today contained in the collections of the Tibetan, Chinese, and Korean Tripitaka. Only a few of these have been translated into English. Listed below are the more important of the Mahayana scriptures.

Perfect Wisdom (Prajnaparamita)

The Prajnaparamita contains two very sacred texts known as the Diamond Sutra and the Heart Sutra. Both have been translated into English.

The Lotus Sutra (Saddharmapundarika)

The Lotus Sutra is supposedly the final sermon of the Buddha and focuses on religious rather than philosophical issues. It is used extensively by the Nichiren, Tendai, and Zen schools in Japan.

Kegon Sutra (Avatansaka)

The Kegon Sutra is believed to have been transmitted by the Buddha three weeks after his enlightenment while he was still in the state of meditation. It therefore focuses on enlightenment.

The Lankavatara Sutra

Supposedly Bodhidharma, the founder of Zen Buddhism, gave the Lankavatara Sutra to a disciple.

It focuses on complete spiritual regeneration as a step toward buddhahood.

VAJRAYANA BUDDHISM IN TIBET

The Buddhism one encounters in central Asia is a product of the interaction between various faiths. It retains elements of the pre-Buddhist religion of Tibet, known as Bon, which was a shamanistic, nature-oriented faith. Secondly, it draws elements from the Tripitaka, the Pali-language scriptures of Theravada Buddhism. Thirdly, it contains many elements and divinities of the popular Mahayana traditions. Lastly, it is composed of tantric elements drawn from the Vajrayana scriptures.

Buddhism came to Tibet relatively late, having first entered China, Korea, and Japan, as well as southeast Asia. About 630 C.E. the Tibetan prince sRong-Tsan-Gam-Po sent persons to northern India to learn about Buddhism, but little came of the trip. It was not until almost a century later that *Padma Sambhava* brought to the mountain kingdom a form of Buddhism that caught the interest of the inhabitants. Padma Sambhava was a wandering ascetic who impressed people with his exotic yogic skills and his shamanistic possessions. His Buddhism was from Bengal, India, and it consisted of sex symbolism, magic, demonology, and exorcism.

Padma Sambhava's Buddhism became known as Red Hat Lamaism, because its adherents wore red robes instead of the yellow robes and hats worn by earlier Buddhists. The oldest sect of the Red Hats was the *Nyingmapa* sect, whose clergy were married and who believed that spiritual growth came through being *in* the world rather than separated from it. It was this type of Buddhism that became accepted in Mongolia in the thirteenth and fourteenth centuries, after the Mongols conquered Tibet. Tibetan Buddhism was much more compatible with the pre-Buddhism religious heritage of the Mongols than any other form of Buddhism.[34] Vajrayana is still the prevalent form of Buddhism in Tibet and Mongolia today.

Tantric Buddhism[35]

Vajrayana Buddhism in its more mystical aspect is also known as Tantric Buddhism. Within tantric thought, male and female energies become the focal point of spiritual development. Male and female represent external and internal energies, and there are many esoteric rituals and rites which an adherent may use both to release and to integrate these energies. Tantras, or manuals, are used in the process because of their magical nature and thereby give their name to this form of Buddhism. There is a similar strain of thought in Hinduism.

Tantric Buddhism is very much a religion of the world. It is to be carried out in the midst of daily life, and consequently one need not depart from daily activities to rise above them, as monks and nuns in other traditions do. In fact, the union of male and female is viewed as a source of great natural power, and in tantric theology all deities and saints have spouses to maximize this power. These many gods and goddesses assist people in their spiritual development. One important aspect of tantric practice is the process of visualization, in which a graphic figure of a deity is brought before the practitioners. As the figure appears, practitioners visualize themselves merging with it, thereby taking upon themselves the characteristics of the god or goddess. Associated with this practice are often many prayers and chants, which invoke the powers available through the deity.

Mantras and Mandalas

Within both Hinduism and Buddhism there is a stress on certain syllables and sounds (mantras) which are believed to be the sound and embodiment of the eternal. "Om" and "hum" are both believed to contain the essence of the universe in sound. Therefore, they are used as part of meditation and other spiritual disciplines to bring the devotee ever closer to ultimate oneness with the universal. Mantras may also be of much greater length, and the recitation of them is believed to have some magical effect.

Mandalas are circles, created either by having worshipers stand in a circle or by drawing circles on the ground or on paper, painting them on a wall, or weaving them into a tapestry. The mandalas may include images of buddhas, bodhisattvas, humans, and animals. It is believed that through the mandalas, often coupled with mantras, a person may become identified with heavenly beings. An extension of this is the Lamaist belief that various of the heavenly beings are incarnated in earthly persons and that just prior to death they convey to their

followers clues regarding their next incarnation. The Dalai Lamas, all considered to be successive incarnations of the bodhisattva Avalokitesvara, have each been identified by their followers through clues of this kind.

WOMEN IN BUDDHISM

The traditional Buddhist monastic attitude toward women is prejudicial. Women are regarded as obstacles to spiritual realization. In general, however, especially in Mahayana texts, an ambivalent atttitude toward women is apparent. "On the one hand, woman was regarded as a danger, potential and actual, to a man's . . . progress" toward nirvana. Women have been "viewed as the cause of mental anguish and pain, as competitors to the Buddhist monastic [discipline, which requires celibacy], and as threats to [social and] familial stability."[36] Several Mahayana texts declare that women cannot enter the path without rebirth as men.

On the other hand, in a number of Mahayana sutras women are shown as nothing less than men, and indeed as personifications of beautiful bodhisattva ideals. The image of the feminine is exalted through the association of feminine qualities with certain Buddhist deities, especially to the celestial bodhisattva Kuan Yin. Still, at the most fundamental level, in most Buddhist traditions both men and women are expected to nullify all lust and sexual desire through meditation and thus to acquire a beautiful and fresh body. The single major exception to this view of sexuality is the Tantric tradition, in which the union of male and female is considered a source of creative spiritual power and both genders consequently bear equal importance. In general, though, Buddhism is considered to be asexual rather than androgynous (prejudiced in favor of men and against women) in nature. The most evident indication of this is the regular concealment of the male sexual organ in Buddhist images.[37] Consistent with this, in Buddhist art one can hardly tell whether any depiction of a human being is male or female in gender. All references to sexuality of any kind must be removed. Ultimately, then, there can be no justified denigration of women in one who is truly seeking enlightenment. The following anecdote illustrates both the humor and inconsistency of maintaining misogynous monastic attitudes:

On one occasion Tanzan [a Zen monk] was travelling with another monk, Ekido, down a muddy road, where they met a beautiful girl in a fine silk kimono, unable to cross the intersection. Lifting her in his arms, Tanzan carried her across the road. Ekido did not speak to Tanzan until they reached a lodging temple that night, when he finally exploded angrily: "Monks do not go near females, especially young and lovely ones!" "I left the girl there at the crossroads," replied Tanzan simply. "Are you still carrying her?"[38]

FAMILY LIFE

In the majority of Buddhist traditions, enlightenment is an individual matter. Whether one believes that nirvana comes solely through adherence to the Eightfold Middle Path, as Theravadins do, or whether one can draw upon the help of buddhas and bodhisattvas in the quest, as many of the Mahayana schools teach, ultimately one will receive enlightenment or enter into nirvana alone. Among Theravadins, family connections are generally seen as impediments in the way to enlightenment, for they encourage attachment to this world. It is expected that serious seekers in this tradition will in time leave family members, as Siddhartha did, so as to devote full attention to the search for enlightenment.

In Mahayana Buddhism, however, the influences of Confucianism have tempered the view of family and social connections. Buddhists in China, Japan, and Korea maintain strong family ties, practice filial piety, and observe the rituals honoring ancestors; and the monastic life, though embraced by many, is not held to be the only means of achieving enlightenment and nirvana. Among some orders of Mahayana monks, in fact, it is customary to honor deceased members of the community in the same manner as departed ancestors, indicating that social ties are not seen as a hindrance to spiritual progress.

Finally, in Vajrayana Buddhism, the belief is that one may achieve enlightenment in the midst of the world. While there are many monks in this tradition, some of these are married, and neither they nor lay practitioners need leave their families in order to fulfill their spiritual goals. On the contrary, the relationship between man and woman is seen as a source of spiritual power that may help achieve these goals. This is symbolized in Vajrayana art by the representation of the *vajra* (thunderbolt) in conjunction with the lotus, or the union of masculine knowledge with feminine principles.

LATTER-DAY SAINT REFLECTIONS

To better understand both similarities and contrasts between The Church of Jesus Christ of Latter-day Saints and Buddhism, it may be useful to compare the teachings of their founders: the historical Buddha and Jesus Christ. In general, Christ and the Buddha believed that covetousness and lust were at the root of human suffering and that men must shake the dust (the cares of this world) from the mirror of their minds and seek to nourish the spirit of the inner man. Both declared that freedom lies in following a way of life that is devoid of cruelty, falsehood, killing, stealing, and unlawful sexual relations. Parallels between the life stories and reported sayings of Jesus and the Buddha have intrigued the followers of these two religious leaders, as well as secular scholars at large. Leaving aside for now the credibility of the narratives and comparing only commonly accepted beliefs, the following resemblances are worthy of note.[39]

1. Both Jesus and the Buddha were foreordained in a premortal spirit world to come forth at a particular time, after examination and selection of the most favorable family, country, race, and mother to which to be physically born.

2. Both entered the womb of their mother in a miraculous manner, having no mortal father.

3. Both were born into a world whose inhabitants' primordial spiritual bodies had become coarse and gross and who had lost much of their original brilliance.

4. The births of both were accompanied by special heavenly illuminations.

5. Both were recognized in infancy by religious leaders as persons of great promise with special missions to perform among mankind.

6. Both visited holy temples in their youth and displayed unusual precocity and wisdom before their elders: Siddhartha with Asita and Jesus with the scribes and Pharisees.

7. Both launched their ministries early in their thirtieth year following periods of fasting and solitude.

8. Both gained disciples under a fig tree.

9. Both were severely tempted by an evil being (Mara in the one case and Satan in the other).

10. Both selected a council of special disciples and joined with them in carrying out their religious ideals through the way of example.

In addition to these "historical" similarities, agreements in thought and phraseology between the gospels of the New Testament and the Dhammapada of Theravada Buddhism include the following:[40]

1. *From Christ:* "Now do ye Pharisees make clean the outside of the cup and the platter; but your inward part is full of ravening and wickedness. Ye fools, did not he that made that which is without make that which is within also?" (Luke 11:39–40).

From the Buddha: "What is the use of platted hair, O fool! what of the raiment of goat-skins? Within thee there is ravening, but the outside thou makest clean" (Dhammapada 26:394, The Brahmana).[41]

2. *Christ:* "[S]trait is the gate, and narrow is the way, which leadeth unto life, and few there be that find it" (Matt. 7:14). "Our soul is escaped as a bird out of the snare of the fowlers: the snare is broken, and we are escaped" (Ps. 124:7).

Buddha: "This world is dark, few only can see here; a few only go to heaven, like birds escaped from the net" (Dhammapada 13:174).

3. *Christ:* "Let them alone: they be blind leaders of the blind. And if the blind lead the blind, both shall fall into the ditch" (Matt. 15:14).

Buddha: "As when a string of blind men are clinging one to the other, neither can the foremost see, nor can the middle one see, nor can the hindmost see, just so, methinks, Vasettha, is the talk of the Brahmans [*sic*] versed in the three *Vedas*" (Tevijja Sutta 1:15).[42]

4. Jesus said to the woman of Samaria that his salvation is as "living water" (John 4:10–14). In the Lotus Sutra, the Buddha compares salvation to water for all (Saddharmapundarika 5).

Besides the founders, other figures in these two religious faiths resemble each other in certain ways. The bodhisattvas of Mahayana Buddhism, in particular, strike a familiar chord. Kuan Yin's saintly vow of compassion to tarry on the earth in order to uplift those who are burdened by darkness and evil is not something unknown to Christians, who are familiar with episodes in the scriptures of saints, disciples, and prophets who have yearned to remain on earth in order to bring the blessings of salvation to wayward men and women. John, the beloved apostle of Jesus, was one such. His compassion was far-reaching and Christlike. He implored the Lord to allow him to be spared from death, to tarry on the earth until the Second Coming, so that he might bring souls to him (see John 21:21–23). John's desire

was commended by Christ as superior to the aspiration of the apostle Peter, who prayed that he might speedily enter the kingdom of heaven. Among Latter-day Saints it is believed that John was literally granted his desire, and in modern scripture he is designated by the Lord "as flaming fire and a ministering angel" (D&C 7:6).

Latter-day Saints also believe that, on the American continent, the prophet Moroni observed that there was no one who really understood the true God in his day except selected disciples of Jesus who tarried in the land seeking to prevail against the wickedness of their day. And no one knew what had become of them (Morm. 8:10). These are known as the Three Nephites, disciples chosen by Jesus during his ministry in the New World who had been granted their desire to tarry on earth until Christ's second coming. According to the promises of the Lord, they will endure persecution but will have a fulness of joy as they seek to minister to all of God's people—that is, the gentiles, the Jews, the lost and scattered tribes of Israel, and all nations. In Latter-day Saint belief, they are still performing this marvelous work (see 3 Ne. 28:1–12).

Thus, in Latter-day Saint lore there are many stories of persons who continue on earth in compassionate service to others. Likewise, among Mahayana Buddhists there are many stories of the ministrations of Kuan Yin. Chinese Buddhists believe that, as the patron goddess of fisherman, she is guarding the entrance to Keelung Harbor in Taiwan today.

But in spite of these similarities in teachings and beliefs, there are also significant differences between Buddhism and Latter-day Saint beliefs. In the Buddhism founded by the Buddha, in order to follow the way one must become an arhat, a monk, who has renounced the world and any social or sensual attatchments and who adheres to the philosophical dogma inherent in the Four Noble Truths; that is, that which is called the individual soul is only a complex of incongruous, transitory elements, a stream of consciousness. Thus, nirvana is the only permanent reality, a reality of nonexistence. Latter-day Saints, however, accept a world of external realities. The spirit and body of a person are considered both real and good before God, and at the Resurrection they will be reunited to experience judgment and, most likely, some degree of salvation and joy.

While Latter-day Saints appeal to a God who is Creator and Lord of all and to Jesus Christ who redeems men from sin, in Theravada Buddhism there is no god and no savior. There is no future life, but only the bliss—or extinction—of nirvana. Supreme power is not individualized. The human body and all other things material are transitory, as are human activity and the individual human soul. In sharp contrast, Latter-day Saint doctrines teach that the body is not to be despised, that it is a sacred tabernacle of the human spirit. They seek to sharpen one's understanding of the individual and one's relationship to God, teaching that the ultimate aim is not to escape life but to continually enlarge and perfect it.

In any variety of Buddhism there is law (intrinsic dharma), but there is no divine Lawgiver and no Father-Creator-God. Although there are humanitarian principles and moral values on an interim basis, there are no divine moral imperatives and no ultimate creedal pronouncements such as the Ten Commandments that God gave to Moses on Mount Sinai.

In Theravada Buddhism, loving self or loving other individuals is a hindrance to the attainment or the realization of nirvana. Benevolence can be emphasized, but not individualized love. All attachments are to be shed. Latter-day Saints, on the other hand, are expected to show both benevolence and individualized love toward friends and enemies alike and, in particular, to be strongly attached to family members, nurturing, sustaining, and loving them throughout life and beyond. Those who do not stand in danger of the judgment of God.

For Latter-day Saints, the restored gospel teaches that God and man are self-conscious, self-determining beings who know how to make plans and execute them. This means that God can make things other than himself (such as the physical world, plants, animals, and humans) and allow events and forces other than himself to occur that are out of harmony with his divine will. He distinguishes between good and evil, and he is able to act in favor of that which he approves and to oppose persuasively what he disapproves.

Philosophically speaking, the Buddhist goal transcends all opposites, including good and evil. It refutes both theism and the idea that reality consists of two distinct and eternal aspects (dualism), so that ethical concepts of truth and error, of right and wrong, are largely irrelevant. So also is the idea of historical actuality. There is no phenomenal world; there is only the passing illusion of such.

Obviously, there are conflicting presuppositions in Latter-day Saint and Buddhist doctrine that cannot be reconciled. If the universe has been formed out of the mind and hand of a personal, loving God, it cannot be a complex of consciousness in one inclusive buddha-mind. If the restored gospel is true, then "the worth of souls is great in the sight of God" (D&C 18:10). For this reason, it is not possible for a conscientious Latter-day Saint also to be a Buddhist. Still, in Latter-day Saint belief Buddhists, like everyone else, are the children of God. They are entitled to receive the blessings attendant on all of his commandments that they keep, and they are eligible to receive more knowledge and blessings at any time they seek them. And Buddhists, while they might not agree with all of Latter-day Saint doctrine, are likely to appreciate the ideals of losing oneself, of doing no harm, and of leaving behind worldly desires in seeking for the kingdom of God.

Glossary of Buddhist Names and Terms

In Buddhist studies, names and terms are usually given in Sanskrit (S)—or Pali (P), Chinese (C), Japanese (J), Korean (K), or English translations and equivalents. The resultant plurality of variant names for the same thing is often very confusing. In the following list of some key names and terms in the history of Buddhism, Sanskrit and Pali forms are given first, Chinese second, Japanese third, and Korean fourth. It should also be noted that some of the terms below are only treated briefly in the text. A selection had to be made concerning those topics most in need of textual treatment. However, a student who wishes to study Buddhism further should be aware of other terms, and a few of those are included in the glossary.

NAMES OF THE HISTORICAL BUDDHA (563–483 B.C.E.)

1. Gautama (S); Gotama (P): The Buddha's family name, meaning "on earth the most victorious." It is a Brahmin name, although the clan was of the Kshatriya (warrior) caste.

2. Siddhartha: The Buddha's given name; a shortened form of Sarvartthassiddha, meaning the "realization of all desires."

3. Sakyamuni (S), Shih-chia-mu-ni (C), Shaka [muni] (J), Sokka [muni] (K): Means "the Sage of the Sakyas." It is a title applied to the Buddha by those outside the clan. Sakya is the name of the clan to which the Buddha

belonged. The Sakyas were not ruled by kings, as were the majority of the Aryan states, but were republicans led by chieftains called rajas, the Buddha's father (whose name was Suddhodana) being such a ruler. They made their own laws in meetings for this purpose. They were monogamous and did not recognize the caste rules of the Hindus.

OTHER BUDDHAS OR BODHISATTVAS

1. Vairocana (S), P'i-lu-che-na (C); Ta-jih-Ju-lai (C); Bruishana (J); Dainichi Nyorai (J): The personification of the essential bodhi, or enlightenment.

2. Maitreya (S); Mi-lo-fo (C); Miroku (J); Miruk (K): A bodhisattva and the buddha of the future.

3. Amitabha (S); Omit'ofu (C); Amida (J); Amida (K): The buddha of infinite light; best known as the Lord of the Western Land.

4. Avalokitesvara (S); Kuan-Yin (C); Kannon (J); Kwanum (K): The bodhisattva of mercy. Symbols associated with this figure are the vase of water, the willow branch, and the lotus.

5. Bhaisajyaguru (S); Pindola (S); Yao Shih Liu-li-kuang (C); Yakushi-ruriko (J): The buddha of medicine, and the light of the Paradise of the East. His symbols are the patra (alms bowl) and the fruit known as "Buddha fingers."

SCHOOLS OF BUDDHISM

1. Theravada: Means "Way of the Elders." Another term applied to this school is Hinayana, meaning "Lesser Vehicle." Theravada Buddhism most closely approximates the teachings of the Buddha. Its doctrine is one of "self-help." Thus, no deities provide assistance in gaining release from the wheel. Theravada spread chiefly, but not exclusively, into southeast Asia.

2. Mahayana: Means "Greater Vehicle." It differs from Theravada principally in that it contains a multitude of helping beings who assist their worshipers off the wheel and into a heavenly realm. The concept of nirvana, which originally meant extinction, refers now to a "place" or heavenly home.

3. Vajrayana: Means "Vehicle of the Thunderbolt" (vajra means thunderbolt or diamond). Its adherents expect to attain enlightenment through magical power. The school arose in northeast India in the eighth century C.E. and spread to Tibet in the eleventh century. It includes the Lamaism of Tibet, Mongolia, and other areas of central Asia.

4. Hinayana: Another name for Theravada Buddhism.

OTHER TERMS AND FIGURES

AHIMSA. Refraining from destroying life.

ARHAT (S); LOHAN (C); RAKAN (J). A disciple of the Buddha; a saint or monk; may also have the narrower meaning of one who is close to enlightenment, or even one who is enlightened.

BODHI. Fig tree; in Buddhism, symbolic of enlightenment, because that is where the Buddha was enlightened.

BODHISATTVA. A buddha-to-be.

DAI-GOHONZON. A mandala upon which is written a mantra embodying the central place of the Lotus Sutra in the Nichiren tradition.

DHYANA (S); JHANA (P); CH'AN (C); ZEN (J); SON (K). A meditation sect that spread to China in the sixth century C.E. with Bodhidharma.

EIGHTFOLD MIDDLE PATH. The method taught by the Buddha for moral and intellectual self-development leading to enlightenment. The eight constituent parts are: (1) right views; (2) right thought; (3) right speech; (4) right action; (5) right livelihood; (6) right effort; (7) right mindfulness; and (8) right concentration.

FOUR NOBLE TRUTHS. The basic content of the Buddha's enlightenment that he set forth in his first sermon. The four truths are: (1) life is painful; (2) the cause of suffering is egoistic desire; (3) the elimination of desire brings the cessation of suffering; and (4) the way to the elimination of desire is the Eightfold Middle Path.

JATAKA TALES. "Other lives" or "birth stories"; tales purportedly told by the Buddha of his previous lives as bird, animal, and human being. They were remembered and recorded by his followers not long after his death and are 547 in number. The theme throughout the stories is the line of life that possesses the spiritual qualities that will blossom into buddhahood.

JODO SHINSHU. The form of Japanese Buddhism, known as "True Pure Land," that teaches devotion to Amida (Amitabha) as a compassionate lord.

KARMA. The law of cause and effect. The root meaning is "action," and the derived meaning thus becomes "action and the appropriate result of action." Applied to the moral sphere, karma is the Law of Ethical Causation through the operation of which a man "reaps what he sows." Karma does not, in itself, bind to the wheel of rebirth. The binding element is personal desire for the fruit of action. Liberation is therefore achieved by elimination of desire for self.

KOANS. Riddles, unsolvable by rational thought, designed to promote enlightenment in Soto Zen students.

KOSEN-RUFU. In Nichiren thought, world peace in the broad sense of universal harmony in nature and human relations.

LOTUS. Flower symbolizing the female principle and self-creation, because out of the procreative powers of water it vegetates from its own matrix or womb without being fostered in earth. Every buddha or bodhisattva is supported by a lotus flower to indicate divine birth.

LOTUS SUTRA. The central scripture of the Nichiren tradition, among other Buddhist sects.

MAITREYA. The buddha-to-be prophesied in Mahayana Buddhism.

MANDALA. A ritual or magic circle; in Tibet, a diagram used in invocations, meditation, and temple services.

MANTRA. Chant used in meditation and other spiritual disciplines to draw the worshiper closer to the ultimate.

NICHIREN DAISHONIN (1222–1282). Founder of Nichiren Shoshu Buddhism, known as Nichiren Shoshu of America in the United States.

NICHIREN SHOSHU. A Buddhist movement dedicated to helping its adherents achieve the highest state of life, or buddha-nature, through chanting the Lotus Sutra.

NIRVANA. Release from the limitations of existence and of reincarnation; the supreme goal of the Buddhist endeavor, attainable in this life by right aspiration, purity of life, and the elimination of egoism. The Theravada school tends to view nirvana as an escape from life by overcoming its attractions; the Mahayana views it as the fruition of life, the unfolding of the infinite possibilities of the innate buddha-nature, and exalts the saint who remains in touch with life rather than the saint who relinquishes all connection with it.

NYINGMAPA. A form of Tibetan Buddhism teaching that human beings are energy and through meditation, yoga, and prayer can learn how to expend energy wisely. Their monks are known as Red Hat lamas.

PADMA SAMBHAVA (8th century C.E.). The founder of Nyingmapa Tibetan Buddhism.

RINZAI. The Zen Buddhist school that regards enlightenment as a sudden epiphany.

ROSHI. A teacher of Zen Buddhism.

SANGHA. The Buddhist order of monks founded by the Buddha himself.

SATORI. Enlightenment.

SHINRAN SHONIN (1175–1262). The founder of Jodo Shinshu Buddhism.

SHO-HONDO. The Grand Main Temple of Nichiren Shoshu, where the Dai-Gohonzon is housed.

SOTO. The Zen Buddhist school that believes enlightenment to be a gradual acquirement.

STUPA. A mound of earth or brick in which the bodies or ashes of prominent persons were deposited. The name stupa was usually reserved for those structures containing relics of the Buddha or of arhats; otherwise they were called dagobas.

SUTRA (S); CHING (C); KYO (J); KYONG (K). A thread or string on which jewels are strung; applied to that part of the Pali canon containing the dialogues or discourses of the Buddha.

TRIPITAKA (S); DA-TSANG-CHING (C); DAIZOKYO (J); DAECHANG-KYONG (K). The foundational scriptures of Theravada Buddhism. The word Tripitaka means "three baskets" and reflects the three major divisions of the Pali canon. The first division contains the rules for the Sangha, the second the teachings of the Buddha, and the third esoteric knowledge.

VAJRA. Means "vehicle of the thunderbolt." Especially in the tantric form of Buddhism, which is found in conjunction with Vajrayana, the thunderbolt becomes the symbol of the male sexual member. The representation of the vajra on the lotus symbolizes the union of masculine and feminine, or knowledge and principles.

ZEN BUDDHISM. A form of Mahayana Buddhism that seeks enlightenment through meditation. Two of several schools are Rinzai and Soto.

Notes

Portions of this chapter were originally published in the June 1972 issue of the *Ensign* (in the article by Spencer J. Palmer entitled "Buddhism") and in *BYU Studies* 16, no. 4 (Summer 1976): 660–62 (in the article by Spencer J. Palmer entitled "Mormon Views of Religious Resemblances"); they are reprinted here by permission.

1. The Buddha's name was Siddhartha Gautama. In this text he is referred to before his enlightenment as Siddhartha. However, after his enlightenment he is referred to as "the Buddha."

2. Huston Smith, *The Religions of Man* (New York: Harper and Row, Harper Colophon Books, 1964), 80.

3. Heinz Bechert and Richard Gombrich, eds., *The World of Buddhism: Buddhist Monks and Nuns in Society and Culture* (London: Thames and Hudson, 1984), 7.

4. F. L. Woodward and E. M. Hare, trans., *The Book of the Gradual Sayings . . .* , 5 vols., Pali Text Society Translation Series, no. 22 (London: Luzac and Co., 1960), 1:128.

5. Lord Chalmers, trans., *Further Dialogues of the Buddha*, 2 vols. (London: Oxford University Press, 1926), 1:53, 54. (The two volumes of this work comprise vols. 5 and 6 of *Sacred Books of the Buddhists*, ed. Mrs. Rhys Davids.)

6. A. Ferdinand Herold, *The Life of Buddha: According to the Legends of Ancient India*, trans. Paul C. Blum (Rutland, Vt.: Charles E. Tuttle, 1954), 88–98.

7. Spencer J. Palmer, "Buddhism," *Ensign*, June 1972, 69.

8. David S. Noss and John B. Noss, *Man's Religions*, 7th ed. (New York: Macmillan, 1984), 126–28;

W. Woodville Rockhill, trans., *The Life of the Buddha and the Early History of His Order . . .* , popular ed., Trübners Oriental Series (London: Kegan Paul, Trench, Trübner, 1884), 148–61. This work is derived from Tibetan works in the Bkah-Hgyur and Bstan-Hgyur, the Tibetan Tripitaka.

9. Daisetz T. Suzuki, *Outlines of Mahayana Buddhism* (1907; reprint, New York: Schocken Books, 1963), 1–2.

10. Ibid., 2–3.

11. Ibid., 11.

12. Information within this section is drawn largely from Noss, *Man's Religions,* 138–43.

13. Asvaghosha, *Discourse on the Awakening of Faith in the Mahayana,* trans. Daisetz T. Suzuki (Chicago: Open Court, 1900).

14. Suzuki, *Outlines of Mahayana Buddhism,* 7, 21, and 99.

15. Noss, *Man's Religions,* 138–39.

16. Ibid., 139.

17. Franklin Edgerton, trans., *Bhagavad Gita* (Cambridge, Mass.: Harvard University Press, 1972), 9:32.

18. Alice Getty, *The Gods of Northern Buddhism: Their History, Iconography, and Progressive Evolution through the Northern Buddhist Countries,* 2d ed. rev. (Rutland, Vt.: Charles E. Tuttle, 1962), xxxiii.

19. Frank E. Reynolds and Charles Hallisey, "Buddha," in Mircea Eliade et al., eds., *The Encyclopedia of Religion,* 16 vols. (New York: Macmillan, 1987), 2:327.

20. Heinrich Zimmer, *Philosophies of India,* ed. Joseph Campbell, Bollingen Series, no. 26 (New York: Meridian Books, 1957), 535, 539.

21. Getty, *Gods of Northern Buddhism,* 45.

22. Ibid., 38; Alexander Coburn Soper, *Literary Evidence for Early Buddhist Art in China,* Artibus Asiae, vol. 19 (Ascona, Switz.: Artibus Asiae, 1959), 147.

23. Soper, *Literary Evidence,* 147–48.

24. Ibid., 141–42; emphasis in original.

25. Getty, *Gods of Northern Buddhism,* 38.

26. Ibid., 40.

27. Ibid., 41–42.

28. Ibid., 57.

29. John Blofeld, *Bodhisattva of Compassion: The Mystical Tradition of Kuan Yin* (Boston: Shambhala, 1988), 40.

30. Quoted in ibid., 84.

31. See Joseph Hackin et al., *Asiatic Mythology: A Detailed Description and Explanation of the Mythologies of All the Great Nations of Asia* (London: George G. Harrap, 1932), 96.

32. Noss, *Man's Religions,* 146–47.

33. The following summary is based on ibid., 152–64.

34. See Sechin Jagchid, "Why the Mongolian Khans Adopted Tibetan Buddhism as Their Faith," in *Essays in Mongolian Studies* (Provo, Ut.: David M. Kennedy Center for International Studies, Brigham Young University, 1988), 83–93.

35. The discussion of Tantric Buddhism is based on Noss, *Man's Religions,* 150–51.

36. Diana Y. Paul, *Women in Buddhism* (Berkeley, Calif.: Asian Humanities Press, 1979), ix, 304.

37. Ibid., ix–x, 307–8.

38. M. Conrad Hyers, *Zen and the Comic Spirit* (London: Rider and Co., 1973), 176–77.

39. The parallels in life events are drawn from S. H. Kellogg, *The Light of Asia and the Light of the World . . .* (London: Macmillan, 1885), 82–165.

40. The parallels in teachings are drawn from ibid., 135–36.

41. The translation used is F. Max Müller's, in F. Max Müller, ed., *The Sacred Books of the East,* American ed., 14 vols. (New York: Charles Scribner's Sons, 1901), vol. 12.

42. As quoted in Kellogg, *Light of Asia,* 136.

Guru Nanak

Sikhism

Spencer J. Palmer

5

UPERFICIALLY, a *Sikh* is one who wears a beard and a turban, drives taxis and buses in New Delhi, India, handles the limousine traffic in front of the posh hotels of Hong Kong, mans police patrols in cities such as Penang and Singapore, and has a reputation for remarkable physical prowess in the Indian military establishment and in the Indian sports world. Supposedly, Sikhism is also easily defined: it is a religious community based in the *Punjab* of northwest India and defined as a simple synthesis of Hinduism and Islam.

This is the prevalent stereotype, and it should be dispelled. W. H. McLeod's studies of Sikhism, which form the basis for much of this chapter, show how much this incomplete stereotype "misrepresent[s] both the pattern of Sikh history and the nature of modern Sikh society."[1]

HISTORICAL BACKGROUND

It is a mistake to interpret Sikhism as a conscious effort to reconcile Hindu and Islamic beliefs by means of a synthesis of the two religions. It is a synthesis, but one in which Islamic elements are relatively unimportant. The pattern evolved by its founder, *Guru Nanak,* has its own originalities; but it is also a reworking of a prior synthesis. This synthesis is known as the *Sant* tradition of northern India.

Many of the ideas found in Sikhism were not original with Guru Nanak. Some could be found in the Sant tradition, which, much like the bhakti cult of Vishnu, held that devotion was essential to the realization of *mukti,* or release from the round of rebirths. However, they differed from the Vaishnavites in holding that God is without form

or qualities and cannot become incarnate or be represented in graphic form. Thus, God could have no avatars—nor could there be statues or pictures of him as found of Vishnu/Krishna/Rama in the Hindu tradition.

Among the Sants, devotional orientation was coupled with the *Nath* tradition, which focused on the internal search for God. Religion was interior, and through hatha yoga one's spirit could ascend to mystical bliss. While the Sants substituted meditation for hatha yoga, they retained the sense of interior mystical ascent. Thus, the fundamentals of Sant, by which Nanak was strongly influenced prior to his call to be a guru, included the element of devotion, the transcendence of God without form or qualities, meditation, an inward search for God, and the mystical ascent to bliss. As will be seen, these are all elements found in Sikh theology, but it is erroneous to hold that Nanak was the first to create these ideas without prior antecedents. However, to deemphasize his revelatory experience and his influence upon what became known as Sikhism would be equally incorrect.

Sikhism is a product of Nanak's personal search for truth. Religion, as revealed to Nanak, was not the repetition of empty rituals or participation in multiple pilgrimages. Religion was not something defined by institutions. Instead, true religion was to focus on the moral and spiritual aspects of life and to enable oneself to be remade by God. The power of this simple teaching attracted many who became followers of the way which Nanak preached. These men and women became known as "Sikhs," meaning disciples. The religious movement now known as Sikhism began with Nanak and continued through a line of nine successors, also known as gurus, who looked upon him as the greatest of all inspired teachers.

GURU NANAK[2]

Childhood

Guru Nanak was born in 1469 in the village of Talwandi, not far from present-day Lahore, Pakistan. Today the birthplace is named Nankana Sahib, out of respect for its most famous inhabitant. Nanak was born in the peaceful hours of the last watch of the night. Sikh accounts assert that heavenly music sounded as a host of deities announced the birth, proclaiming that "God has saved the world!"

As a child Nanak played with other children, but from a very early age he differed from them in that he was concerned about spiritual matters. At the age of five he began to express profound and mysterious ideas. Two years later he was sent to school, but his studies lasted only one day. On the second day he told his teacher, "These subjects which you have studied are all useless." He returned home and sat down and there he stayed for many days. After this period of withdrawal he began to associate with ascetic holy men.

At the age of nine Nanak was invested with the sacred Hindu thread and began to learn Persian. Soon, however, he went back to sitting silently at home. Nanak's father became increasingly disquieted by his son's behavior. His family belonged to the local Katri caste which had established ancestral vocations concentrating on commerce and farming. He felt that Nanak needed to become responsible in a worldly sense. A marriage was arranged for him, and when he was twelve he was duly married. But he showed no interest in family and household life and still would not speak to anyone.

Call

Nanak's parents continued their attempt to involve him in the affairs of the world, and Nanak continued to resist. A solution was finally produced by Nanak's brother-in-law, *Jai Ram,* husband of his sister Nanaki. Jai Ram persuaded Nanak to seek work in the town of Sultanpur. He found employment and, according to the *janam-sakhis* (accounts of the life of Nanak), it was during this period that Nanak received his call from God to preach the message of the divine Name.

After returning home from work Nanak spent his nights singing hymns, and in the final watch of the night went to the river to bathe. According to legend, one morning he entered the stream but did not emerge. His servant searched for him until the middle of the morning, then returned home to tell Jai Ram, who instituted a thorough but fruitless search. Finally, after three days and nights, Nanak came up out of the river. Quoting from the janam-sakhi, Harbans Singh describes the interval as a crucial mystical experience:

As the Lord willed, Nanak the devotee, was escorted to His Presence. Then a cup filled with amrit (nectar) was given him with the command, "Nanak, this is the cup of Name-adoration. Drink it. . . . I am with thee and I do bless and exalt thee. Whoever remembers thee will have My favour. Go, rejoice in My name and teach others to do so. . . . I have bestowed upon thee the gift of My name. Let this be thy calling." Nanak made the salutation and stood up.[3]

Nanak's first reported declaration upon his return was to have an enormous impact on all those who were to follow him. Simply, he stated: "There is neither Hindu nor Muslim."

Whatever the precise nature of the experience, it profoundly changed Nanak. He took even less interest in the things of the world. With *Mardana* the Bard as a companion, he left Sultanpur and assumed the ascetic life for a time.

Ministry

Between 1499 and 1521 Guru Nanak spent much of his time preaching the message which had been entrusted to him. Sikh sources describe journeys to Sri Lanka, Tibet, Assam, Baghdad, Mecca, and Medina. There are many anecdotes and legends associated with each of these experiences. The visit to Mecca is of special interest.

There seems to be no serious doubt that Nanak visited Mecca, and Sikh tradition ascribes miraculous events to that visit. These include an instantaneous journey thence, a cloud which followed Nanak on his way, the springing forth of fresh water from the wells of Mecca, and a moving *mihrab* (niche in a mosque which indicates the direction of the Ka'aba). The last instance illustrates a basic theme in Guru Nanak's teachings. According to the story, on his first night in Mecca the guru lay down to sleep in a mosque with his feet pointing toward the mihrab. Observing him thus, a Muslim judge became incensed, kicked him, and accused him of blasphemy. Nanak answered by suggesting that the judge move his feet to point in a direction where God and the Ka'aba were not. This he did, only to find that the mihrab moved as well, remaining at the guru's feet. Overwhelmed, the judge prostrated himself.[4]

Death

Nanak made his home in Kartupur (a city northeast of Lahore on the India-Pakistan border) and died there in 1539 at seventy years of age. Once again according to legend, Nanak, realizing that his end was near, sat under a withered acacia tree, which immediately flowered and became green again. *Angad,* his chosen successor, prostrated himself; Nanak's wife and family began to mourn and weep. As his followers sang hymns of praise, Nanak went into an ecstatic trance.

Converted Hindu and Muslim followers began to discuss whether the guru's body should be buried according to Muslim tradition or cremated according to Hindu custom. Nanak instructed them to place flowers around him, with those from the Hindus on the right side and those from the Muslims on the left. He would be burned or buried depending on which set of flowers was still fresh the next day. He then bade the assembly to sing, covered himself with a sheet, and died. The flowers from both parties remained fresh, and when his followers removed the sheet they discovered that his body was no longer there.

SIKHISM AFTER NANAK

Leadership of the Gurus

The generally accepted interpretation of the development of Sikhism is that it has evolved in three stages. First, Guru Nanak founded an original religion and gathered around himself a following drawn from both Hindus and Muslims. This first stage took place during the first half of the sixteenth century. Under the leadership of Guru Nanak, Sikhism was a faith that sought to reconcile differences between peoples, and particularly the differences between Hindus and Muslims. The fundamental premise was that there was only one God, True Name, and that all faiths worshiped him, albeit in many instances under different names. Some of those names might be Allah, Vishnu, Shiva, or Brahma, but the end result was the same: True Name was being worshiped. Consequently, it was a violation of all faiths to indulge in interfaith rivalry and strife. This basic

vision of reconciliation was maintained through the time of the first four gurus.

It was Guru *Arjun,* the fifth guru, who compiled the *Adi Granth,* the scriptures of Sikhism, of which more will be said later. He lived in a region of India governed by a Mughal (Muslim) ruler, who read the Granth and saw no harm in it. However, this Mughal was succeeded by his less tolerant son, who feared Arjun's growing power as a religious leader. Guru Arjun was arrested on charges of insurrection and was tortured. In 1606, while still in custody, he died from this mistreatment; but before he died he commanded his son, *Hargobind,* the sixth guru, to rule fully armed, prepared to defend the faith. This he did, and thus began the second stage of Sikh development, occupying the first half of the seventeenth century. Guru Hargobind, persuaded by the martyr's death his father had suffered that, for the defense of the faith, he must resort to arms, gathered around himself an army and built fortresses. The religious teachings of Guru Nanak were kept intact, but his followers would now be prepared to defend by military means their right to adhere to these teachings. From this point on, the fortunes of Sikhism varied. Sometimes its followers were able to defend themselves, and at other times they were in danger of being destroyed. However, with the coming of the tenth guru, *Gobind Singh* (Gobind the Lion), Sikhism became firmly established.

The solidly established leadership of the first stage and the difficulties and threats to the community from outside during the second stage had resulted in a strongly unified faith with virtually no dissenting sects or denominations within it. Events of the final traditional stage of Sikh development, which involved further response to the hostile intentions of the Mughal overlords, assured the continuance of this unity by prompting a new refinement. The tenth guru, Gobind Singh, having reflected upon the weakness of his followers in meeting the military power of the Mughals, reached the momentous decision to establish the Khalsa, an order or society with a religious foundation and a military discipline that would enable the Sikh community to defend righteousness by force with an invincible army.

The Khalsa

Realizing that the Sikh community needed to be strengthened in order to survive, in April of 1699

Guru Gobind Singh appeared at a spring festival called Baisakhi. He set up his tent and remained withdrawn from the festivities until the celebration was well underway. He then emerged suddenly and demanded from among his followers a Sikh who would be willing to give his head for the faith. From among the hushed multitude a volunteer finally came forward and was taken into the tent; a thud was heard, and Gobind Singh emerged with a bloody sword, demanding another person willing to die. The people were horrified as the same events occurred again and yet again. Finally, after five men had been taken into the tent, Gobind Singh threw back the curtain, revealing all five men alive, along with five decapitated goats.

Gobind Singh then delivered a powerful sermon in which he declared that the five men, who had exhibited such courage in the face of what they assumed was certain death, would be the foundation of the Sikh order called the *Khalsa* ("The Pure Ones"). The Khalsa would have no castes, and members could not use ancient scriptures from either Hinduism or Islam, nor could they worship various lesser gods. All must worship True Name, or *Sarab-loh* (the name for God used by Gobind Singh, meaning "all-steel").[5] Gobind Singh then made *amrit,* a sweetened nectar, by stirring sugar into water with a two-edged sword, and had the five drink it from a common cup. Since the five were apparently of different castes, this one act destroyed the caste system within Sikhism, for it was forbidden for persons of different castes to sit at the same table, much less drink from a common vessel. In addition, they were baptized with the water by having it splashed on them. Male members of the Khalsa took the name Singh (lion) and female members the name Kaur (princess). These have become heredi-tary family names and appear in the names of virtually all Sikhs today. In a way, this name pattern reflects the direct influence the Khalsa has had on the thought, faith, and lifestyle of every Sikh, for essentially every Sikh family has an ancestor, relative, or connection of some kind who was or is a mem-ber of the Khalsa.

Over time, rules for the Khalsa were developed. The essential elements are as follows:

1. Baptism should be performed using amrit stirred with a two-edged sword.

2. Wherever five members of the Khalsa are gathered, there is the whole Khalsa.

3. Khalsa members should believe in the one true God and wear the five marks of the Khalsa: uncut hair and beard (*kesh*), the comb (*kangha*), short underdrawers (*kachh*), the steel bracelet (*kara*), and a short dagger (*kirpan*). Each of the "K's" has symbolic significance to Sikhs. The kesh symbolizes spirituality and respect for natural laws. The kangha represents the controlling of one's mind and body. The kachh reminds one to be moral and controlled. The kara symbolizes the oneness of God and the unity of the individual with both God and all humankind. Finally, the kirpan represents dignity, self-defense, and the just use of power.

4. There are to be no distinctions within the Khalsa based on social prejudices or economic status.

5. Members of the Khalsa are to revere the Granth and travel to *Amritsar* to dip themselves in the Pool of Immortality surrounding the *Golden Temple.*

6. Khalsa members are to be ready for war in defense of the faith, if no other means of settling differences can be found.

7. Wealth should be honestly earned and a tenth should be given to causes dear to Nanak, especially to those who are poor or hungry.

8. Sikhs are distinct from both Muslims and Hindus and should therefore not practice the rites and rituals of these faiths.

9. One should regard the relatives of others as one's own family and treat them as such. There should be no gambling, theft, or use of tobacco or alcohol.

10. Sikhs are free to marry Sikhs, since there are no caste distinctions, but should not marry those who break the laws of the Khalsa.

11. Salutations upon meeting a Khalsa member are "The Khalsa is the Lord's" and "Victory is the Lord's."

12. Persons who violate the rules of the Khalsa—particularly those against the use of tobacco, the cutting of hair, the eating of meat killed according to Semitic custom, and sexual intercourse outside marriage—must repent, pay a fine, promise not to in-dulge in the activity in the future, and be rebaptized.[6]

OTHER BASIC BELIEFS[7]

Although not all Sikhs are members of the Khalsa, all share essentially the same set of basic beliefs regarding life, God, and the relationship human beings bear to him, which are examined below. The study of these beliefs cannot be better enhanced than by the reflections of a devout Sikh, explaining thoughtfully why he adheres to that faith. Karandeep Singh, the first Sikh to graduate from Brigham Young University, prepared upon invitation an essay on his religion as he knows it, and portions of that insightful personal essay appear in semibold type through this section of the chapter. They offer from a first-hand perspective the motivations behind the faith and practice of Sikhism.

Purpose of Life

From the excesses of the tangible Seen to the serenity of the intangible Unseen. From the worries and tensions of the temporal to the ecstatic bliss of the spiritual. From the meretricious flares of the external to the quiet, subtle delights of the internal. From individuality to submission, mightiness to meekness. From "I," "me," and "mine" to "thee," "thou," and "thine." From death to a God-intoxicated, eternal life. In other words, from without to within, for that is where Truth resides. Such is the quest of the Sikh, that manifestation of the Divine that, with long, flowing, vibrant tresses, has been commanded to live in the presence of God twenty-four hours a day, in this very lifetime.

The basic purposes of Sikhism are twofold. The first goal, as with all other religions whose roots lie in India, is to achieve release (mukti) from the round of rebirths. However, life is not viewed as negatively in Sikhism as it is in Hinduism, Jainism, or Buddhism. The second goal is to achieve union with God, who is infinite, eternal, immaterial, and inexpressible, yet personal. He can hear prayer. He cares about all his children.

Thus, the purpose of this existence, as defined by the Sikh gurus—God-realized masters revered as role-models of the spiritual endeavor—is to reunite with Deity. But why must one attempt to reunite? After all, it's a wonderful life, and there is so much to do besides losing one's self in God. The answer to that cynical but legitimate question holds the key to the Sikh understanding of the nature of the soul. In Sikhism, the soul is considered a spark of the Divine Flame. The central injunction, then, is to recognize our true origin, which is God. But this recognition is not intellectual, for the intellect does not have the

capacity to go further than the outer courtyard of divinity. The recognition is intuitive—revelatory, or as a Franciscan or a Sufi might say, rapturous— and it entails complete and unequivocal merging of the spark back into the Flame. Here is the revolution that Nanak set afoot. One doesn't have to undergo physical death to attain perfection. God is attainable in this lifetime; perfection can be achieved here and now. In fact, that is why we are here, for the human form is the only opportunity for the soul to return to its Source.

Nanak was the agent of this God. God, or True Name (*Ik Oankar*), spoke through Nanak and his successors. True Name is the eternal Guru, but since Nanak and his successors were the spokesmen for God, they too became known as gurus. The meaning, however, is much deeper than simply that of being a teacher. They bear the word of the one true Guru to the people. With the death of the tenth guru, Gobind Singh, there have been no further successors; instead, the Adi Granth, the scriptures of Sikhism, have become the guru. Thus, the scriptures are often referred to as the Guru *Granth Sahib.*

God

A Relational Being

Guru Nanak's teachings were often terse, and there is no better illustration of this than the opening statement of the Granth:

This Being is One. He is eternal. He is immanent in all things and the Sustainer of all things. He is the Creator of all things. He is immanent in His creation. He is without fear and without enmity. His Being is not subject to time. He is beyond birth and death. He is Himself responsible for His own manifestation. He is known by the Guru's grace.[8]

But, as McLeod inquires, is the affirmation of the unity of God the one of monotheism or the one of monism? Guru Nanak's approach here is

essentially . . . mystic. "Duality" is to be destroyed, but it is to be a swallowing up in mystical union [with God]. The creation does indeed provide a vital revelation of God, but the physical phenomena which impart this revelation are to be regarded as expressions of a God of grace who dwells not only in creation but also beyond. The ultimate essence of God is beyond all human categories, . . . transcending all powers of human expression. Only in [personal] experience can He be truly known.

The One of whom [Guru Nanak] speaks is conceived as a personal God, a God of grace to whom man responds in love.[9]

God is both immanent and transcendent. Although he is formless, he is personal. Yet, God is not wholly beyond human comprehension, for he possesses attributes which human beings can understand. They can worship him and can come into a relationship of oneness with him.[10]

It is imperative to realize that God in Sikhism is not anthropomorphic; He (the masculine pronoun is more conventional than theological, although there are references in the scriptures to God as the Bridegroom) is a being of love, or, in other words, God is the epitome of love. Here comes the challenge: God is neither a "he" nor a "she," but is not an "it" either. As mentioned earlier, it is this accessibility of Deity that makes Sikhism unique in many ways. Since He is a being of love, He incessantly attracts all beings in the cosmos towards Him. The fact that some of us don't feel those "messages of love" is due to the nonreceptive states of our consciousness. Receptivity is directly contingent upon our willingness to do His will; or, as a Taoist might say, to flow harmoniously with the current. Latter-day Saints might refer to this state as being "in tune" with the Spirit.

The Way to God

MEDITATION. This harmony is attained by *simran*, continuous meditation by the recitation of the *Gurumantra*, which for Sikhs is "Vaheguru" (Praise the Lord). The Gurumantra is significant for the Sikhs because it is bestowed upon a new initiate by the Five Beloved Ones during the Amrit ceremony (the Sikh equivalent of baptism). It is the first rung in the ladder of spiritual progress, for the Gurus say that this mantra is not mere letters; it takes the consciousness to that universal realm of love and brotherhood where there is eternal peace. Lest the reader misunderstand, this "realm of love" is not an external place or the Sikh equivalent of heaven. It is a state of mind that is found only when one travels the infinite distance within; the Gurumantra is but a vehicle with which that distance is traversed. Heaven and hell, therefore, are not understood as a reward or reprimand in the hereafter; if one enjoys the presence of the Bridegroom here and now, then this life itself is heaven; if not, it's hell.

SERVICE. Simran is the first part of the tripartite Sikh way of life—the "way of the three S's."

The second "S" is *seva,* or service. The disciple serves the Master with unquestioning obedience, and since the Master in this case is the Creator (who is manifest in his creation), the injunction to serve one's fellow creatures becomes natural. One serves to get closer to God, because by serving others one chisels away that which keeps us from God: our ego. It is not uncommon to see Sikhs cleaning bathrooms at a temple, or polishing shoes, or doing manual labor or some such similar chore. This is worth noticing because, in the caste-ridden society of India, only "lower" castes do menial jobs. But since Sikhs reject the caste system at the outset, any kind of legal labor is dignified, especially if it is done with a reverent attitude. The giving of one-tenth of one's income for charitable purposes (tithing) is also included in this practice of seva.

THE GUIDANCE OF ADVANCED TEACHERS. The third, and perhaps most important "S" is *sangat,* or the company of illuminated and enlightened souls. This can be understood as the guidance of advanced disciples; or, to use a Frostian image, sangat is the ægis of those who are further along the road less traveled. It is considered a non-negotiable component of spirituality, primarily because a novice needs a master, a teacher, a guide to trigger the journey. Even Theravada Buddhists, who have no room in their tradition for any kind of deity, cannot circumvent this compelling need for a teacher. When the monk chants *Buddham Sranam Gacchami* ("I seek the Buddha as my refuge"), he acknowledges the Buddha as a master. This is also why congregational worship is of utmost importance in Sikhism. But a congregation is not a mere collection of people; it is the concentrated presence of sincere seekers who are willing to walk the arduous strait and narrow. Such a seeker can be compared to a red-hot, burning coal. It does not matter how many lifeless, unlit coals may surround it; one burning coal can ignite all of them. Similarly, Sikhs believe that one true disciple can ignite the hearts of hundreds of people; he or she, by strength of his or her conviction, can set the consciousness of an entire congregation ablaze.

As with everything else in Sikh thought, these three S's are also ultimately directed toward a unity. For there comes a time when simran, seva, and sangat are not three disparate practices, but one united way of life. To be in sangat becomes synonymous with simran and seva. Says Nanak (as I recall it): "Without sangat, love [for the Beloved] does not get ignited; without love, it is impossible to worship Him [by doing simran and seva]."

The Names of God

The Sikh name for God is Ik Oankar (One True Name). Other names for God are *Satnam* (The True Name) and *Akal Purakh* (The Eternal One). This Ultimate Reality, forever existent in the Guru Granth, is a metaphysical one. He has been characterized as a dynamic and reverberating concept. He is also Creator, sovereign, and permanent, but without form.

Human Beings

The Sikh term for man transcends the physical, bodily entity so often assumed to be the person. "Man" means something closer to the English word "mind," or perhaps it is not too far distant from the Latter-day Saint understanding of the human spirit. The nature of a human being is determined by the orientation of the mind. The "natural" man or woman, tied to worldly desires and concerns, exhibits *haumai*. This term denotes a self-centered person who is prideful, ego-filled, and subject to continual deaths and rebirths until that attitude or orientation changes.

Haumai gives rise to lust, anger, covetousness, and attachment, all of which are *maya* (illusion), but illusion in a sense different from that found in Hinduism. For the Hindus, maya means that one lives under the mistaken delusion of being an individual, someone separate and distinct from Brahman-Atman. For the Sikhs, however, maya means to be attached to something other than the ultimate True Name and thus living an illusion in that sense. A Latter-day Saint term for this type of illusion might be idolatry.

Gunindar Kaur explains this further when she says that "when man does not live to the utmost and forfeits his time and energies to joys mundane and ephemeral, his life, precious like a diamond, becomes totally worthless." The critical alternative, Kaur emphasizes, is to realize that "existence is important and man acquires freedom while existing" on this earth, as indicated in these words of Guru Arjun: "One can achieve liberation Even as participating in life, laughing, playing, wearing finery and eating delicacies" (Guru Granth 5:522).[11] To bring this about, one must exhibit the opposite attitude to haumai—that of humility, in which one focuses on True Name, becomes dependent upon God, and subdues the self—so that the spirit may gain liberation and ultimate union with God.

Worship

As indicated above, Sikhism is not a religion of externals. Nanak had little use for rituals and rites. These were not the things that determined one's relationship to God. Idolatry, ritual baths, pilgrimages, and asceticism were of no value to the person, in his view. Rather, true religion was characterized by faith in God, love for fellow humans, mercy, humility, compassion, and righteousness. If one's life exhibited these qualities, then mukti was not far off. Mukti, however, was not solely self-attained; ultimately it was granted through the grace of God.

As originally noted, the devotionalism of Sikhism, along with the Sant tradition, owes much to the bhakti movement within Hinduism, especially that which focuses on Vishnu. One finds the imagery of a bride longing for her beloved among the Sikhs much as one might expect to find it among devotees of Krishna. The devotionalism in Sikhism, however, is to a formless, although personal, Lord. Faith is demonstrated through the hymns one sings, the prayers one utters, and the use of the *mala* (similar to the Catholic rosary), which assists one in the prayers.

Discipleship

The journey of a disciple—"Sikh" is the Punjabi word for disciple—is not that facile, though. Discipleship is acknowledged as a strenuous pilgrimage in Sikhism. It demands a lifelong commitment and an inclination to sever one's head without hesitation for the sake of fellow pilgrims, should such a need arise. It calls the pilgrims to bear their own crosses and to walk, barefoot, on a bed of burning embers. It requires one to wear a crown of thorns and to seek solace in the fire of a burning stake. It calls for a willingness to be buried alive and a desire to be incinerated in the passion of the cause. The death that one must suffer, even though not physical, is perhaps more excruciating than the physical one: one must annihilate one's ego, lose one's self in God, and die to the world. Only after such a death is a disciple born, for only in this crucible of fire, where all worldly attachments are extinguished, can a God-oriented consciousness be molded.

Thus, the paradox starts to unfold. Unlike Buddhist monks, Hindu ascetics, or Benedictine friars, renunciation in Sikhism is not external. Sikhs have been commanded to be householders and to earn an honest livelihood by the sweat of their brow. All but one of the Sikh gurus were householders (the eighth guru, Guru Hari Krishan, passed away at the tender age of eight). The abnegation is internal; it is the desire to be worldly that is to be given up. The recurrent metaphor in the Sikh scriptures to explain this idea is that of a lotus. Just like the lotus grows in muddy water, the Sikh gurus say, but remains aloof from its squalor, so must a disciple be in the world, but with a heart that is always detached. Again, detachment in Sikhism is not an attempt to attain any kind of *samadhi*, or a state of no thoughts. Instead, detachment is more of an uprooting, where one's roots are disinterred from this world and embedded, by the firm hand of love, in God. So all attachments must be consumed in the attachment to God. One is not to go away to the mountains or the woods to meditate. In fact, the Sikhs are the woods, with their unshorn hair providing deep comfort in shade to anyone who might seek it. They are the mountains, firm and majestic; dazzling reminders of the heights to which the soul can ascend.

Notice how thorough and unequivocal is Nanak's renunciation of external ritual. What difference does it make, echoes his question even today, whether one addresses God as Allah or Ram? Who cares if one goes to the Ganges or to Mecca, or whether one wears ocher robes or nothing at all? Irrespective of what one is doing on the outside, the only thing of supreme importance in Sikhism is a loving relationship with God—a celestial romance, if you will. It's like closing one's eyes and chanting "London, London," repeatedly. Nanak's question: are we getting to London? Or is it mere chanting? Mere ritual? In other words, the spiritual quest, according to Nanak, takes one beyond the mundane into the magical. If it is fired by the pure love of God, then even the most trivial act can assume cosmological significance. There is the case of

Dhanna, one of the bards enshrined in the Guru Granth Sahib, who, with his unflinching devotion and childlike sincerity, found God in a piece of rock. Nanak is almost ascerbic in his denunciation of idolatry, and yet Dhanna is at par with Nanak in the holy book. The reason? The latter's faith and passion for God was so intense that he found him even in a rock. The journey, then, even though it begins in this world with our egoistic consciousness, culminates in a divine, universal love-consciousness which is expressed by Nanak thus: "There remain no foes and no strangers: the connection of love with all beings has been established."

Scripture: The Guru Granth Sahib

As mentioned above, the eleventh guru is not a person, but scripture itself. The Guru Granth is the eternal Guru, True Name, because it is the pure word of God. Thus, the Guru Granth and the ten human gurus are properly called "Guru" only because they are the pure conduit for the word of the one and only Guru, God, or True Name.

Thus, the Adi Granth (the First Book) or Guru Granth is the very embodiment of God. It is his living word. In the *gurdwara*—the Sikh places of worship—the Granth is enthroned daily. Early in the morning the Granth is brought out, opened with great ceremony, draped in silk, and placed on a high pedestal. At the Golden Temple in Amritsar, the most holy of Sikh temples, a person reads the Granth aloud throughout the day. For the faithful, who consult the Granth each morning, it is part of every important life event—birth, the naming of children, marriage, trouble, and death. At many of these events, the worshipers circumambulate the Granth. For example, circumambulation is a component of the marriage ceremony.

The content of the Granth is predominantly hymns written by various of the gurus, although some hymns and poetry by other authors are also included. The earliest and most sacred portion is that which was written by Nanak and is known as the *Japji*. It consists of 974 hymns. Guru Arjun, the fifth guru and the compiler of most of the Granth, included 2,218 hymns of his own. He also incorporated 62 slokas (verses) of Angad, the second guru; 907 hymns of *Amar Das,* the third guru; and 679 hymns of *Ram Das,* the fourth guru. Ram Das was the composer of the Sikh marriage hymn. Further, Arjun included 209 hymns of *Kabir,* a forerunner of Nanak whom Nanak greatly admired, as well as 3 slokas by Nanak's traveling companion, Mardana. Included after Guru Arjun were 59 hymns and 56 slokas of *Tegh Bahadur,* the ninth guru.

THE GOLDEN TEMPLE

Besides the compilation of the Guru Granth, Guru Arjun, the fifth guru, was responsible for the construction of the Sikhs' most sacred temple, the Golden Temple at Amritsar. The temple is exceptionally beautiful, having its ornate cupolas and domes gilded with gold. It sits in the middle of the Pool of Immortality, which is said to have miraculous powers of healing, and is reached by a marble causeway that extends across the water.

A visit to the Golden Temple to hear the scriptures sung and to partake of *langar,* a free meal eaten in common with other pilgrims and guests, is an unforgettable experience. As McLeod suggests, the best time to visit is early morning or late evening. The most interesting activity at the temple takes place when it opens at 3:00 A.M., when the installation of the Guru Granth Sahib takes place. No one can witness this event without recognizing the great reverence with which this book is regarded.[12] The strong feelings Sikhs hold for this central place of the faith have in recent years led some to adopt a defensive stance toward the Golden Temple in the face what they feel is encroachment by negative outside influences. Even so, it is not a center of war, but of peace, contemplation, and worship of True Name.

WOMEN, FAMILY, AND WAY OF LIFE[13]

Sikh Social Relations

The imposition of castes, which has had the sanction of Hindu texts and doctrines, does not exist in Sikh society. The Sikh gurus attempted to bring about a total fundamental revolution in the societal structure of India by challenging the Brahmin claims to superiority and sounding a message of mutual respect and egalitarianism within society and family. The gurus also condemned social injustices against women; and thus religious congregations are open to women, who are permitted to participate freely in all aspects of religious and social life. After

journeying in other parts of India, a visitor is likely to find it unusual to come to Amritsar and see a man freely associating with his wife and their children in public.

Marriage

The marriage ceremony, called *anand karaj* (the ceremony of bliss), differs markedly from that of the Hindus. The Hindu marriage ceremony is elaborate. In order to please the gods, Hindus choose the day and time of a wedding in accordance with omens and signs. Sikhs do not concern themselves with this. The ceremony can be held on any day at any time, but it is usually conducted at dawn. In Hinduism, the bride and groom circumambulate the sacred fire; Sikh couples circumambulate the Guru Granth Sahib, which must be present. The hymns sung are, of course, from the Granth.

Death and Funerals

At death, hymns are recited. The one strict injunction is that forbidding the lamentation and beating of the breast so prevalent among Hindus and Muslims on funeral occasions. Whereas Hindus cremate their dead, and Muslims bury their dead, in keeping with Guru Nanak's general teaching of nonadherence to the practices of either faith (enunciated both at the beginning of his ministry and at his death), Sikhs may either bury or cremate their dead.

LATTER-DAY SAINT REFLECTIONS

As Latter-day Saints and Sikhs examine each other's beliefs, they find some disparity in their conception of the nature of God. For Latter-day Saints, the members of the Godhead are tangible beings. They are not one, but three, and are not without form. And yet, descriptions of the attributes, functions, and personal influence of God in the Sikh community are not far distant from what Latter-day Saints believe. The reciprocity of love between adoring humans and the pervasive interior peacefulness that comes from the power of realizing God in one's life are consonant with Latter-day Saint doctrine and experience. In addition, both Sikhs and Latter-day Saints subscribe to brotherhood and sisterhood among members of the faith, purity and righteous behavior, respect for the body, the importance of family, a strong work ethic, service (seva) through donation of time and a tenth of one's income for the benefit of others, and a devotional life involving love and praise of God. Other points of comparison include the spare and simple nature of ritual and symbolism, the central importance of scripture, and the staunch determination to defend the faith and witness to the truth "at all times and in all things, and in all places that ye may be in, even until death" (Mosiah 18:9). Finally, there is a sense of robust freedom and joyousness in Sikhism that should positively reverberate in the hearts and minds of Latter-day Saints, who believe in the equality of humankind, that "all are alike unto God" (2 Nephi 26:33), and who also believe that "men are, that they might have joy" (2 Nephi 2:25).

Glossary of Sikh Names and Terms

ADI GRANTH. One of the names for Sikh scripture, meaning "first book."

AKAL PURAKH. A Sikh name for God meaning "The Eternal One."

AMAR DAS (1479–1574). The third guru; author of parts of the Granth.

AMRITSAR. The location of the Golden Temple in the Punjab region of northwest India.

ANAND KARAJ. The Sikh marriage ceremony or the "ceremony of bliss."

ANGAD (1504–1552). Nanak's successor and thus the second guru.

ARJUN (1563–1606). The fifth guru, the compiler of the Adi Granth, who died a martyr for the faith.

GOBIND SINGH (1666–1708). The tenth guru and the one who established the Khalsa.

GOLDEN TEMPLE. The temple in Amritsar which is especially sacred to Sikhs.

GRANTH SAHIB. "The revered book"; the original name for the Sikh scriptures.

GURDWARA. Any place where the scriptures have been installed, but in the wider sense also a community center of Sikh life.

GURU. Spiritual leader. There is only one Guru—God, the inner voice; but earthly gurus represent the divine presence and are thus human vehicles of the divine Guru.

GURU GRANTH. The "eleventh guru." Gobind Singh, the tenth guru, declared that he would have no successor but the Adi Granth. Thus, the scripture is understood to be the embodiment of the divine Guru.

HARGOBIND (1595–1644). The son of Arjun and the sixth guru. He began to strengthen the Sikhs militarily after his father's martyrdom.

HARI KRISHAN (1656–1664). The eighth Guru.

HARI RAI (1630–1661). The seventh Guru.

HAUMAI. Pride, or innate self.

IK OANKAR. The Sikh name for God which means "One True Name."

JAI RAM. Nanak's brother-in-law.

JANAM-SAKHIS. Accounts of the life of Nanak.

JAPJI. Early hymns contained in the Granth and written by Nanak.

KABIR (ca. 1440–1518). An early representative of the Sant tradition.

KACHH. Short underdrawers; symbolize moral behavior and self-control; one of the five marks of the Khalsa.

KANGHA. Comb; symbolizes the controlling of mind and body; one of the five marks of the Khalsa.

KARA. Steel bracelet; symbolizes the oneness of God and the unity of man with God and with man; one of the five marks of the Khalsa.

KESH. Uncut hair and beard; symbolizes spirituality and respect for natural laws; one of the five marks of the Khalsa.

KHALSA. The Sikh order; "The Purified Ones."

KIRPAN. Short dagger; symbolizes dignity, self-defense, and the just use of power; one of the five marks of the Khalsa.

MALA. Beads similar to the rosary of a Catholic and used by Sikhs in the saying of prayers.

MARDANA. The minstrel who was Nanak's companion during his preaching tours.

MAYA. In Sikhism, delusion as opposed to unreality as connoted in the monism of Hinduism. It is a delusion to believe that anything in the impermanent world has ultimate reality.

MUKTI. Release from the round of rebirths; same as Sanskrit moksha.

NANAK (1469–1539). The founder of Sikhism and first guru.

NATH. A Hindu tradition focusing on the interior search for God through the practice of hatha yoga and other disciplines so that the spirit may ascend to mystical bliss.

PUNJAB. The region in northwest India which is the home of the Sikhs.

RAM DAS (1534–1581). The fourth guru; author of parts of the Granth.

SANGAT. The company of illuminated and enlightened souls.

SANT. A Hindu tradition believing in a devotional relationship to deity but denying that God has form. This tradition deeply influenced Nanak.

SARAB-LOH. "All-steel"; the name for God used by Gobind Singh and identified with the sword.

SATNAM. A Sikh name for God meaning "The True Name."

SEVA. Service.

SIKH. A follower of Nanak and a word meaning "disciple."

SIMRAN. Meditation.

TEGH BAHADUR (1621–1675). The ninth guru.

Notes

1. W. H. McLeod, *The Evolution of the Sikh Community: Five Essays* (London: Oxford University Press, 1976), 1.

2. This biographical sketch is based primarily on W. H. McLeod, trans. and ed., *Textual Sources for the Study of Sikhism* (Manchester, Engl.: Manchester University Press, 1984), 19–25; McLeod, *Guru Nanak and the Sikh Religion* (London: Oxford University Press, 1968), 34–147; Harbans Singh, *Guru Nanak and Origins of the Sikh Faith* (Bombay: Asia, 1969); W. Owen Cole, *Sikhism and Its Indian Context, 1469–1708* . . . (London: Darton, Longman, and Todd, 1984).

   Biographical studies of Guru Nanak do not rely on the scriptures of Sikhism nor on the writings of Nanak, but on a fund of popular anecdotes supplied by a number of "janam-sakhis," hagiographic accounts of the life of Guru Nanak.

3. Quoted in Singh, *Guru Nanak and Origins,* 95.

4. This famous incident is elaborated in McLeod, *Guru Nanak and the Sikh Religion,* 123.

5. W. Owen Cole, *The Guru in Sikhism* (London: Darton, Longman, and Todd, 1982), 67–72.

6. Ibid., 70–71.

7. In the preparation of this section, I have drawn generally from McLeod, *Guru Nanak and the Sikh Religion,* 163–89, 208–14, as well as on the excerpts from the essay by Karandeep Singh. Originally from New Delhi, India, Singh graduated with University Honors in humanities/philosophy and anthropology. He taught anthropology at BYU before entering a Ph.D. program in American studies at Brandeis University in the fall of 1996. I appreciate his insights and the permission he kindly granted to use his essay in this chapter.

8. Quoted in ibid., 163–64.

9. Ibid., 164–65.

10. Ibid., 167.

11. See Gundindar Kaur, *The Guru Granth Sahib: Its Physics and Metaphysics* (New Delhi, India: Sterling, 1981), 48–49.

12. McLeod, *Evolution of the Sikh Community,* 63–64.

13. The comments in this section are drawn from discussions in Gurmit Singh, *A Critique of Sikhism* (New Delhi, India: Ishar Singh Satnam Singh, 1964), 47–51, 56–62.

Part Three
East Asian Religions

Confucianism, Taoism, and Shinto are the religions of east Asia. The former two have their origins in China, while Shinto originated in Japan. In their original forms, none of these religions evidenced much interest in an afterlife. They were primarily concerned with the present. Confucianism sought to state how persons should live together in a productive, wholesome society. While there are religious overtones that can be sensed behind traditional Confucianism, they are very much in the background when one studies the social philosophy of Confucius.

Taoism in its original, philosophical form was mystical, and yet it addressed the same issues as Confucianism: how should people live in peace? Its methodologies were those of quietism and non-aggression, and its followers sought unity and harmony with the natural forces of the universe. But it was difficult to live in this mystical realm; and over time, religious Taoism developed into an active search for gods, methods, and potions to prolong life and secure immortality.

The last of the three, Shinto, is a religion that makes sense only in Japan, because it is about the Japanese people, the land of Japan, and the sacred powers that are found throughout the natural world there. These powers may be personalized, may be sought in prayer, and may assist in daily life—especially if that life relates worshipers to the natural world. Over time, Shinto became a state religion and served to undergird the Japanese expansionist policies in the late nineteenth and early twentieth centuries. Following the Second World War, Shinto was removed from the realm of the state and returned to the private domain. Even so, it is still a religion about Japan and the Japanese, with strong overtones of patriotism and cultural purity, and the emperor still stands at its head.

Thus, the religions originating in east Asia dealt fundamentally with structure and order in everyday life. In the case of Confucianism and Shinto, that still holds true; and although religious Taoism has overshadowed philosophical Taoism in popular practice and seeks goals that it would not have sought, the philosophy behind the faith was very much an understanding of the natural world and one's place in it.

Lao Tzu

Taoism

6

Dong Sull Choi

TAOISM and Confucianism are the two major native religions of China. Confucianism is primarily concerned with people—with human behavior in a structured social environment, including conformity to specific moral principles that define social relationships and appropriate ritual performances. Taoism, on the other hand, is concerned with ineffable powers within nature. It is relatively subjective, intuitive, and mystical.

HISTORICAL BACKGROUND

While Taoism and Confucianism represent contrasting philosophies in many ways, they sprang from a common historical and cultural context which influenced their development. An understanding of this context is essential to a comprehension of the similarities and differences between the two faiths, as well as points of comparison and contrast with other world religions.

Religious Considerations

Worldly Orientation

First and foremost, the Chinese version of religion is very much oriented to this existence. Belief in an afterlife may be of personal concern to individuals, but it is not a primary focal point of faith. There is no tradition of an eschatological end of the world or final judgment or union with deity in a state of eternal bliss, as in Western faiths; and doctrines and practices regarding death and the afterlife tend to a great extent to be borrowed from Buddhism or even from Western religions. Chinese religion has had a materialistic, practical, and this-worldly outlook from its early beginnings, and even its mythology is more likely to be based on history than on tales of the supernatural. It is more concerned with the

operation of natural law than with a supreme being as lawgiver.[1]

Gods and Spirits

In spite of this here-and-now orientation, the ancient Chinese believed in numerous gods and spirits who were to be recognized, propitiated, or exorcised as needed. To the gods of the sky and earth, who were in a position to influence the growth of crops, emperors made elaborate sacrifices regularly each spring and autumn. On a local level, the people practiced rituals and made sacrifices to the *shen* (beneficial spirit beings associated with lighted areas), in order to remain on good terms with them. Other sacrifices and rituals were intended to keep the *kuei* (evil or troublesome spirits associated with dark and gloomy spots) at a distance so that life could go on as it should.[2]

Filial Piety

While attention and respect was due to these deities and supernatural beings, greater attention and respect amounting to veneration was due to the elderly members of the family. Parents and grandparents were governing forces within the home, and children were to honor them, obey them, and consider their comfort in all things for as long as they lived. When they died, children were to provide proper burial, maintain the grave site, perform ritual sacrifice there each year (sometimes at great personal expense), and hold them and their accomplishments in remembrance from generation to generation.[3] This sense of filial obligation may justly be called one of the most distinguishing aspects of Chinese culture.

Yin and Yang

Another unique dimension of the traditional Chinese world view was the anciently held concept that the universe operates through the interaction of the two opposite yet complementary natural forces of *yin* and *yang*. The yang force is associated with positivity, masculinity, paternity, intellect, light, warmth, heaven, strength, and life. The yin force is associated with all the opposites of these: negativity, femininity, maternity, intuition, darkness, coolness, earth, weakness, and death. No value judgment is implied by these classifications; one is not held to be more necessary or of more value than the other. Rather, they are viewed as necessary components of the same harmonious whole, like opposite ends of the same stick. Both are considered vital for the balanced functioning of the world from moment to moment, day to day, and year to year. In other words, to the ancient Chinese the constant interaction of yin and yang represented the essence of life.[4]

Wu-hsing: The Five Elements Theory[5]

Closely related to the concept of yin and yang was the *wu-hsing* theory, which conveyed the belief that constituted reality and constituted change in nature come about through the relationships of the five basic elements: fire, earth, metal, water, and wood. These were considered dynamic, interacting, and successive forces inherent in nature. The earliest mention of wu-hsing occurs in an inscription on a jade sword-handle dating to nearly 400 B.C.E. The *Shu Ching,* or Book of History (later one of the five Confucian classics), expounds upon it in detail. Over time, the wu-hsing theory became the basis for a cyclical (repetitive) view of nature; of a dynastic, rather than a lineal, view of history; and of every conceivable category of things in the universe, including the five tastes, five smells, five musical notes, five heavenly bodies, five colors, five styles of government, five classes, five animals, five grains, five sense organs, and eventually the five social relationships of Confucianism. The wu-hsing theory has become the basis of rather wide-ranging religious and social practices in Japan and Korea relating to marriage, birth, the naming of children, and even childhood games.[6] Peter Occhiogrosso concludes that the bipolarity of yin and yang and "the cyclical interplay of the Five Elements"—forces that "relate the inner microcosm of the human body to the outer macrocosm of the [universe]"—have given birth to "the essence of Chinese spirituality."[7]

Divination

The Chinese sages also believed that the unified universe governed by the balanced operations of yin

and yang and the cyclical successions of wu-hsing could be interpreted through signs in nature, and those who read the signs well could use them to predict coming events. A skilled individual could divine the future through patterns formed by randomly scattered objects—such as stalks of wheat or yarrow, dice, or coins—the patterns on the shell of a tortoise, or the cracks that appeared when the shoulder bone of a sheep was heated over a fire. Solid lines were interpreted as yang lines, meaning yes, and broken lines as yin lines, meaning no. The reading of these patterns resulted in the development of a series of trigrams and hexagrams, which in turn formed the basis for the *I Ching,* or Book of Changes, one of the Five Classics of Confucianism and still one of China's most provocative and influential books.[8]

Wu-wei

Implicit in the ancient Chinese world view and beliefs as outlined was a plan of action for human beings to follow in living within the world. Known as *wu-wei,* it meant essentially inaction of a kind that allowed the universe to take its natural course. Because the principle of wu-wei became so fundamental a part of Taoist thought in particular, it is discussed in more detail in the section describing philosophical Taoism below.

Political Considerations

In addition to the cultural background from which Chinese religion has emerged, a long political history has had its effect on the founding of both Taoism and Confucianism. The 390-year span known as the Spring and Autumn period (771–481 B.C.E.) was a time of great turmoil; numerous wars, battles, invasions, besiegements, and conquests reduced some eight hundred vassal states to a set of seven great powers with a few weaker ones acting as buffers between them. Then came the time known as the Warring States period (481–221 B.C.E.), in which these larger powers fought each other. During this latter period—the same era in which the Buddha, Mahavira, and the Greek philosophers were active—there arose throughout China a large number of schools of political and social thought, each offering different solutions for the mayhem surrounding them. It is within this context, and as a part of this intellectual outburst, that Taoism and Confucianism developed.

THE FOUNDER: LAO TZU[9]

Taoism as a distinctive religion can be said to begin with *Lao Tzu,* a historical figure who, according to tradition, became disillusioned with social and political solutions and relished individual introspective spontaneity in the pursuit of the mysterious *Tao,* the ethereal flow within nature. According to a Chinese legend, on the fourteenth of September, 604 B.C.E., a woman gave birth to a child as she leaned against a plum tree. He was called Lao Tzu, or Old Boy.

Little is known of his youth. However, it is said that in later life he worked in government circles in the Chinese imperial capital, where he became keeper of the archives for the court of Chou. It also appears that he married and had a son named Tsung, who became a successful soldier and through whom emperors of the T'ang dynasty traced their lineage to Lao Tzu.

Less is known of Lao Tzu than of the founding figure of any other major world religion. But there is one famous apocryphal story based on a report of the ancient illustrious Chinese historian Ssu-ma Ch'ien, who speaks of a meeting between Lao Tzu and *Confucius* that sheds light on their disparate philosophies. The meeting allegedly took place in 517 B.C.E., when Confucius was thirty-four and Lao Tzu over half a century older. The elder sage apparently

advised the younger . . . to abandon his arrogant ways, suave demeanor, and unbridled ambition. [Confucius], perhaps overawed, later admitted to his students, "Roaming animals may be caught in a pit or cage, fish with a net or rod, and birds can be shot down with an arrow. The dragon, however, cannot be caught by such cleverness. It soars towards heaven riding upon the wind and clouds. Today I have seen Lao-tzu, and he is like a dragon."[10]

According to legend, Lao Tzu lived to the venerable age of 160 years and ultimately became disgusted with society and governmental service, vowing to leave the realm. Thus, mounted on a black ox, he left China through the Han-ku Pass, west of Loyang. However, before opening the gate and allowing him to depart, the keeper of the pass asked him to write down his thoughts. This Lao Tzu agreed to do. What he recorded has become the basis for the most important Taoist text, the *Tao Te Ching,* the Book of the Way and Its Power.

FOUNDATIONAL SCRIPTURES: THE TAO TE CHING

The full Taoist canon as known today is the assemblage of what Lawrence Thompson calls "an enormous 'Bible' of esoteric texts comprehensible only to those with special competence."[11] But from among the whole, two rather brief classic texts are the most widely known and used—the *Chuang Tzu* (Master Chuang) and the Tao Te Ching, which is preeminent in its importance. It consists of about five thousand characters comprising eighty-one brief chapters in verse on the meaning of the Tao, *wu-wei,* and related themes. According to Welch, the Tao Te Ching is the most translated book in the English language after the Bible.[12] Lewis Hopfe concludes that "the Tao Te Ching has become the most influential book in Chinese literature, except for the Analects of Confucius."[13] Because no personal or place names occur within it, it cannot be dated internally. Its language, while superficially quite simple, proves on closer examination to express profound concepts in terms that may have multiple layers of meaning.[14] At least a thousand commentaries have been written on it, one of the earliest being that of Chuang Tzu.

BASIC BELIEFS AND PRACTICES

Although Lao Tzu is generally regarded as the founder of Taoism, since his time the religion has developed in very divergent directions. The teachings recorded in the Tao Te Ching form the foundation for what is known as philosophical Taoism (*tao chia*), which may be considered as an expression of the pure theory behind the faith. However, early Chinese religion has infused into the theory a wide variety of practices whose basis in the Tao Te Ching is nominal at best. This may be described as religious Taoism. Since belief and practice are intertwined parts of the same whole, one might think of philosophical Taoism as the yin, or passive, side and religious Taoism as the yang, or aggressive, side of the religion.

Philosophical Taoism

Philosophically, Taoism holds the same here-and-now naturalistic world view as existed in early Chinese religion. The most important factor is awareness in this world of the continuing flow of the inherent impersonal Tao, rather than future salvation in the presence of a personal deity. As Laurence Thompson explains, Taoist themes are concerned with features of regularity within nature—cyclical processes (wu-hsing), processes of growth and decline, and the bipolarity of yin and yang—which affect human beings on earth in the immediate present. In fact, he adds, all other principles in Taoist philosophy hinge on the operation of yin and yang.[15]

Tao

The ancient theory of yin and yang asserts that the universe is in a constant state of flux. This does not refer simply to the Book of Mormon doctrine of categorical opposition, as expressed by Lehi in 2 Nephi 2:11. Rather, yin and yang are *correlative* opposites, and neither can exist independent of the other. It is their ambivalence, their simultaneous repulsion and attraction, that precludes stagnation or even settled balance. Rather, it produces continuing viability, infusing the universe with life and moving within the flow of nature—the Way, or the Tao.

Wu-wei: A Call to Inaction

As mentioned above, wu-wei means submission to the natural order of things or, literally, "non-action" or "not doing." But actually, wu-wei as explicated in the Tao Te Ching is a call to passive action: doing nothing in such a way that all is accomplished. One should not resist, confront, or defy. One should not lay down nostrums, rules, or requirements which others are expected to obey. To use Wayne Ham's metaphor, "just as no amount of stirring can clear a pool of muddy water—the pond must be left alone to clear itself—so men and nations must be free to follow the natural course of events without excitement or undue agitation."[16] Ambition, excessive desire, and pride always produce the opposite of what is expected. If one is greedy or otherwise egoistical in an effort to amass wealth and possessions, these things will ultimately possess him or her. One must give up the world in order to possess it. One must abandon self-interest and ambition in order to find spiritual fulfillment. To put a Latter-day Saint application to the idea, one cannot get to the celestial kingdom by selfish, egoistic grasping for it. One does not attempt to force his will on others. Only sincere humility, minimal desires, and pure spontaneity can enable one to find the Way.

Don Herold, in his simplistic and semihumorous article "Don't Jump Out of the Frying Pan," explores an important aspect of wu-wei: the importance of resisting the temptation to foist betterments onto others. He argues that remedies are often worse than the diseases they claim to cure:

Air-conditioners give us pneumonia in August. Vacations produce fatigue. Exercise to limber us up makes us stiff. And I'm convinced that get-well cards make me sicker.
   Marriage counselors cause unhappy marriages by writing articles entitled "Is Yours a Happy Marriage?" . . .
   After years of observation of hundreds of devices and gadgets designed to alleviate life's little distresses I've decided that they usually *add* to the distress. . . .
   So beware of betterments! . . .
   Internationally, wars to end wars cause wars. . . . Censorship starts people reading dirty books. "Wet Paint" signs make people touch wet paint. And telling children not to put beans up their noses causes children to put beans up their noses.
   All these things suggest to me that a lot of the time the best idea is to sit still and not rock the boat![17]

Lao Tzu's doctrine of wu-wei, then, indicates a particular form of inaction—one that Holmes Welch characterizes as "difficult to practice." Four statements from the Tao Te Ching, quoted by Welch and translated by Arthur Waley, help illustrate this.

The more laws are promulgated, The more thieves
   and bandits there will be. (chap. 57)
[S]uch things [as weapons of war] are wont to rebound.
   (30)
[The Sage] does not boast . . . , therefore he succeeds. (22)
He who acts, harms; he who grabs, lets slip. (64)[18]

The capstone message is simply that "in human relations force defeats itself."[19] He that is not grasping will receive most. He that is not grasping can be in tune with the movement of the Tao.

In Search of the Tao

Lao Tzu's main concern was to search for and to submit to the mysterious Tao. Although the Chinese word for Tao may quite literally mean the Way—the road or the path to follow—this term has come to refer to the inexplicable and eternal underlying principle that establishes order and harmony within the universe. It is absolute, ineffable power. Tao is not an ethical principle, but it is the fountainhead of all ethics and all physical forms.

A person can attain ultimate peace, human happiness, and wisdom by adjusting himself or herself to the motion and movement of the universe. Adepts of the Tao allow themselves to move freely without conventional social and moral constraints, or conventional morality. But this does not mean that they live without ethics. Their ethics are those of the Tao—of the underlying principle of the universe. Thus, their philosophy is not "Do your own thing," but "Live in harmony with that which gives ultimate order and ultimate ethics to the universe." Like birds who use the drafts and currents of air to support them as they glide, instead of fighting against them, Taoists seek to find their own niche in the scheme of things. The characteristics of the Tao are expressed in these selected passages from the Tao Te Ching:

The Tao that can be told is not the eternal Tao.
The name that can be named is not the eternal name.
The nameless is the beginning of heaven and earth.
The named is the mother of ten thousand things.
Ever desireless, one can see the mystery.
Ever desiring, one can see the manifestations.
These two spring from the same source but differ
    in name; this appears as darkness.
Darkness within darkness.
The gate to all mystery. (chap. 1)

The Tao is an empty vessel; it is used, but never filled.
Oh, unfathomable source of ten thousand things!
Blunt the sharpness,
Untangle the knot,
Soften the glare,
Merge with dust.
Oh, hidden deep but ever present!
I do not know from whence it comes.
It is the forefather of the emperors. (4)

Something mysteriously formed,
Born before heaven and earth.
In the silence and the void,
Standing alone and unchanging,
Ever present and in motion.
Perhaps it is the mother of ten thousand things.
I do not know its name.
Call it Tao.
For lack of a better word, I call it great.

Being great, it flows.
It flows far away.
Having gone far, it returns.

Therefore, "Tao is great;
Heaven is great;
Earth is great;
The king is also great."

These are the four great powers of the universe,
And the king is one of them.

Man follows the earth.
Earth follows heaven.
Heaven follows the Tao.
Tao follows what is natural. (25)[20]

Water was one of Lao Tzu's favorite images in the Tao Te Ching, and it remains the quintessential symbol of Tao. The implications of this are summarized by Lewis Hopfe as follows:

Tao . . . is most often compared to a stream or a moving body of water as it progresses endlessly and inexorably. As water wears away the hardest stone or metal and carries off buildings in its path, [likewise] it is useless to struggle against the Tao. Therefore, the ancient Taoist philosophers believed that all humankind's accomplishments and monuments will sooner or later be destroyed by the Tao. The greatest buildings will fall into decay, hard-won knowledge will be superseded, wealth will fail, and even the sharpest sword will become dull. For this reason, it behooved people not to struggle against the Tao but to seek to blend with it and be guided by it. True Taoists live quiet and simple lives. They avoid any achievement except that of seeking to understand the Tao.[21]

In an assessment of Taoist principles, Taoism may sometimes seem to Westerners to justify anarchy and amorality; but in fact it does offer advice in important areas of education and society. For example, in government a nonaggressive and "stand-back" leader is the ideal; he who governs least governs best. In education, a permissive approach is favored—one that enables teacher and learner to share with each other as values are transmitted. In pursuing a natural process, the growth of an individual cannot be forced.[22]

Religious Taoism

There is an enormous difference between the abstract precepts of philosophical Taoism as presented in the classical texts and, on the other hand, the beliefs of religious Taoism as practiced by the Chinese people at large. At the widest level of its influence, by the first century of the common era, Taoism became characterized as a popular cult whose members practiced divination, geomancy, exorcism, healing, sorcery, and magic. This religious Taoism fostered polytheism—belief in multiple gods and spirits. Religious Taoists sought happiness and physical immortality through the use of rituals, pills, magical potions, physical exercises, and dietary practices. They also worshiped dragons, rats, weasels, foxes, and snakes, alongside other higher spirits such as the Jade Emperor, the god Shang Ti, and other shen and kuei.

Applications of Divination

Divination, the practice of attempting to tell the future or explain the unknown through mystic or mysterious means, became an important part of Taoist practice, as it had been in ancient Chinese religion. Thompson categorizes two major motivations for the practice of divination among the Chinese, one being to gain understanding of supernatural operations in nature so as to bring one's life into harmony with them. The other motivation is to discharge the filial obligation to honor and communicate with departed ancestors so as to ascertain how best to serve them, wherever they might be.[23] This second use of divination is not confined to Taoists, but has great appeal among Confucianists as well. Fortune telling through a variety of occult practices is a well-known feature of religious Taoism still practiced today. Taoist diviners and even Confucian moral philosophers have produced handbooks of oracular judgments that have become widely consulted.[24]

Exorcism

Taoist priests also practiced exorcism on an ongoing basis, since the kuei were abundant everywhere. These were appeased or banished through the means of loud noises and fire in any of numerous forms: bonfires, fireworks, candles, torches, or lanterns. Priests sometimes scorched their own skin to produce the desired result.[25]

Ko Hung and the Quest for Immortality

It is probable that China has had more people intently involved in the search for long life and immortality than any other country in history. What this meant for many Taoists is that they turned away from the concepts of wu-wei and orderly living. Instead of seeking natural harmony with the universal principle of the Tao, the religious Taoists moved to find an unnatural way to immortality. Instead of practicing inaction, they sought to force open the path to long life and immortality through their own acts.

A dominant figure in the development of the immortality school of religious Taoism was *Ko Hung* (283–343 or 363 C.E.), "an encyclopedic Taoist scholar," as described by Liu Xiaogan. Among the

methods he favored to achieve immortality was alchemy. Just as Western medieval alchemists sought ways of turning lead into gold, so the Taoist alchemists tried to turn herbs into an elixir of immortality, and wu-hsing became the backdrop in this search. The interaction of the five elements—earth, wood, metal, fire, and water—produced the balanced universe, and, as Liu explains, the alchemists endeavored to reproduce that same balance within human beings through their potions and pills.[26] A positive result of this search was the development of the practice of herbal medicine, which was a precursor to modern pharmacology. On the negative side, trial-and-error experimentation undoubtedly hastened the end of life for many.

It was believed that those who became *hsien,* or immortals, dwelt on a paradisiacal island called *P'eng-lai.* In time it was speculated that it might be possible by some special means to resurrect an entombed body; but best of all was during life to become a hsien, forever deathless and ageless. To this end, Ko Hung promoted and Taoists adopted complicated systems of breath control and gymnastics similar in some respects to Hindu yoga practices. Sexual practices received varying emphases in a curious combination of license and austerity. Of course, such deliberate and sustained effort to achieve immortality, even through strictly physiological means, also runs counter to wu-wei, the doctrine of inaction.[27]

The Hygiene School[28]

Another expression of religious Taoism's concern for perpetuating the vitality of the physical body was the hygiene school, and particularly one of its offshoots, the interior gods hygiene school. This group believed that within the body there were thirty-six thousand gods who mirrored the thirty-six thousand gods in the heavens. The body was a microcosm of the universe; and thus the left eye was the sun, the right eye the moon, and so forth. These gods were necessary for life; if they left, the person died. Consequently, it was important to stay in touch with the gods. This was done through a meditative or trancelike state which permitted one to review all the internal gods sequentially. Since these gods detested wine and meat, one had to avoid these foods.

Another aspect of the hygiene school was the belief that the body contained three regions known as the *Fields of Cinnabar.* These were located in the head, the chest, and the abdomen. Each of these was inhabited by a worm which caused old age, disease, and death. These worms lived on the five grains; this, coupled with the belief that the gods could not stand meat and wine, made it difficult to find a satisfactory diet for many Taoists. Some were reduced to surviving on jujubes. Advanced Taoists never ate solid food, for it produced excrement which prevented the proper circulation of the breath. Thus, they lived on liquids only. The hygiene school also developed techniques of gymnastics and breathing to complement diets and meditation.

The Primacy of Goodness

Alchemy, diet, exercise, and all other forms of discipline contributed to the attainment of immortality, taught Ko Hung, but of equal importance was the accumulation of goodness through kindness to others in a vein reminiscent of the Golden Rule. As Liu explains, this idea derived from Confucianist philosophy came to be

used as a means of practicing longevity. Like other Taoist thinkers, Ko also connected morality and life span. He said that according to the Taoist classics, doing good stands in first place; eschewing one's faults comes next. . . . Those who wish to seek immortality should treat loyalty, filial piety, friendliness, obedience, benevolence, and trustworthiness as basic principles. If they do not perform meritorious acts but solely pursue esoteric techniques, they will never attain longevity.[29]

Although used for a self-interested purpose, this principle brings an element of familiarity into a faith that might otherwise seem totally foreign and mystical to outsiders. For in virtually all the major religions of the world, personal goodness and kindly concern for one's fellow beings pave the way to a satisfactory life here and a desirable existence hereafter.

Women in Taoist Tradition

By virtue of its understanding of the universe, Taoism should be the most open of all religious traditions to the full participation of women. It understands the female principle of yin and the male principle of yang to be complementary opposites, not contradictory or competing opposites. The concept of wu-wei carries with it the yin characteristics, as opposed to the yang, male-dominated, activist stance of Confucianism. Given this, there should be no question that women would be equal

partners with men in a Taoist society; and it is true that one of the Taoist immortals is a woman. However, theory and practice are often not at one in any religious society. Ancient Chinese literature seems to indicate that patriarchal values were well entrenched in China before the time of Confucius or Lao Tzu, meaning that the role of women, in the words of Stewart McFarlane, was already "strictly defined and delimited" at the time these religions were developing. Although "women have long occupied important roles as mediums, shamans, divination experts and fortune tellers in Chinese popular religion," including religious Taoism, the reality of the Taoist world is that men control the priesthood and their sons succeed them.[30]

In purely philosophical Taoism, the Tao Te Ching elevates yin/female/maternal qualities and promotes their emulation—chapters 10 and 28 recommend a yin stance in one's actions in order to conserve energy and to assume a nonaggressive, nonintrusive role. Ellen Marie Chen sees "the elevation of the feminine" in this prime Taoist text as "a genuine expression of an authentic tradition within early Chinese culture"; she goes so far as to conclude that "a more matriarchal value system . . . may actually have existed in ancient China" preceding the Confucianist elevation of the patriarchal system.[31]

However this may be, the patriarchal values reflected in Confucianism were never generally overcome in Chinese society at large, and the philosophical Taoist vision of the elevation of the feminine principle was not generally realized in traditional Chinese society. Women were generally subordinated and devalued. Today women still influentially participate in Taoist cult activities as shamans—intermediaries between the living and the dead—but outside that they do not have a generally high status in Chinese society.

Taoist Family Life

Although women may not be highly revered for their own sakes, their value is confirmed as mothers of children. Posterity is a necessity in all forms of Chinese culture, for it is the role of children and grandchildren to care and provide for their elderly parents and grandparents in life and in death. Just as in the most ancient times in China, for as long as elderly Taoists live, their descendants are expected to show concern for their well-being, deference to their wisdom, and obedience to their wishes. Upon their death, the children of the deceased tend their grave sites and perform ritual ceremonies there each year. Religious Taoists also communicate with them through shamans to see that their needs are still being met in the afterlife.

TAOISM TODAY

It is difficult to calculate the number of Taoists there are today, since many of them also worship at Confucian and Buddhist temples. By combining the figures for Buddhists and Taoists, the Religious Affairs Bureau of the People's Republic of China estimates between 60 to 70 million adherents in that nation, spanning every ethnic group except Tibetans; more practice on Taiwan and in other east Asian nations with Chinese populations. The number of recognized sects stands at eighty-six.[32]

In the West, Taoism has also made its influence felt. Philosophical Taoism appeals popularly to a generation tired of fighting an intractable world, and many of the health practices of religious Taoism are gaining a following. Still, as a religion it is primarily Chinese in its appeal and orientation and cannot be said to be practiced in its "purity" by Westerners.

LATTER-DAY SAINT REFLECTIONS

As different as Taoism may seem on the surface from anything that Latter-day Saints believe, there are some significant points of contact. In the realm of philosophical Taoism, there are resemblances between the impersonal Tao and the personal Latter-day Saint God. The Tao is that which gives rise to all else. It benefits all, and all are to be in total harmony with it. Were one to personalize the Tao, it would begin to appear much like the God Latter-day Saints worship. Behind all things stands the Supreme Being, with whom all persons are to be in perfect harmony. Their minds are to be in accord with his mind and their spirits are to be in harmony with his Spirit, very much as the Taoist is to be in mystical harmony with the Tao. One begins to feel, rather than to understand in intellectual terms, what it means to be in harmony with the pervasive Tao, much as one can only feel what it finally means to be in spiritual oneness with God and with Jesus Christ, or at least to be in tune with the Light of Christ, which "fill[s] the immensity of space" (D&C 88:12).

Wu-wei also has parallels in Latter-day Saint thought. Wu-wei is a way of life. It requires persons to live in an unselfish, nonegoistic way. Nothing in life is forced; everything is done in absolute harmony with that which gives order and meaning to the universe—the Tao. Likewise, Latter-day Saints are called to a nonegoistic life; but rather than being in mystical harmony with an impersonal entity, they are to be in perfect harmony with the Father through the Spirit. Latter-day Saints are to walk by the Spirit, submitting their lives and their egos to God, not always knowing where God may be leading them. Further, persons in leadership positions are to practice wu-wei. Force is not appropriate.

No power or influence can or ought to be maintained by virtue of the priesthood, only by persuasion, by long-suffering, by gentleness and meekness, and by love unfeigned; By kindness, and pure knowledge, which shall greatly enlarge the soul without hypocrisy, and without guile—Reproving betimes with sharpness, when moved upon by the Holy Ghost; and then showing forth afterwards an increase of love toward him whom thou hast reproved, lest he esteem thee to be his enemy; That he may know that thy faithfulness is stronger than the cords of death. (D & C 121:41–44)

Also, in accordance with the philosophical ideals expressed in the Tao Te Ching, women occupy a central place in Latter-day Saint life and leadership, participating in an equal partnership with men among the Saints and sharing in the burdens and joys of church life and leadership. Roles are different, but men and women stand before God on an equal footing in theory and practice. Just as no ward can function without a bishop, no ward can function without a Relief Society president. Male and female complement and complete one another, fulfilling the interrelationship anciently defined in China by the words yin and yang.

Connections between religious Taoism and the restored gospel may be harder to see. Certainly, health codes come to mind; but the austerity of the hygiene school and Latter-day Saint thought are in reality distant from one another. The Word of Wisdom (D&C 89) clearly spells out a health code that limits the intake of those things which harm the body. In this there are similarities to the hygiene school's limitations on wine and meat, for alcohol is prohibited in the Word of Wisdom and meat is to be eaten sparingly. By contrast, however, all grains are good among Latter-day Saints (D&C 89:12, 14), while even grains are prohibited within the hygiene school. Thus, there are superficial similarities, but Latter-day Saints avoid the extremes reflected among the religious Taoists.

Returning again to the Tao Te Ching, Latter-day Saint students of comparative religion can readily identify passages in Lao Tzu's book that closely parallel admonitions in the Book of Mormon. One such is King Benjamin's teaching in Mosiah 3:19 that Saints must become "as a child, submissive, meek, humble, patient, [and] full of love," emulating what the Taoists call the yin aspects. Thomas Romney, a pioneer Latter-day Saint writer, for example, has compiled a number of such important parallels between the teachings of Lao Tzu and Jesus.[33]

As mentioned, the Bible is the only book that has been translated into English as frequently as Lao Tzu's Tao Te Ching. One reason, no doubt, for the many Western versions of this book lies in the parallels between the two. A graphic illustration of this is the comparative list prepared by Holmes Welch, using the translations by Lin Yutang and Arthur Waley (Figure 1).[34]

Finally, in spite of the impersonality of the Tao, it is impossible to overlook the obvious comparison of the Savior's description of himself as "*the way,* the truth, and the life" (John 14:6; emphasis added). Just as Taoist philosophy calls upon humanity to submit humbly to the intrinsic virtue of the Tao, the essence of life, so Latter-day Saints are commanded, in King Benjamin's words, to become "submissive, meek, humble, patient," and willing to live in harmony with the sustaining principles of truth as Jesus Christ taught and practiced them. In both faiths, "the way . . . which leadeth unto life" (Matt. 7:14) is the central concept.

New Testament	Tao Te Ching
[D]o good to them which hate you. (Luke 6:27)	Requite hatred with virtue. (chap. 63)
[R]esist not evil. (Matt. 5:39)	It is because [the sage] does not contend that no one in the world can contend against him. (22)
[T]hey that take the sword shall perish with the sword. (Matt. 26:52)	The violent man shall die a violent death. (42)
Except ye . . . become as little children, ye shall not enter into the kingdom of heaven. (Matt. 18:3)	In controlling your vital force to achieve gentleness, Can you become like the new-born child? (10)
Behold the Lamb of God which taketh away the sin of the world. (John 1:29)	Who bears himself the sins of the world Is the king of the world. (78)
If any man desire to be first, the same shall be last of all. (Mark 9:35)	. . . [T]he Sage puts himself last, And finds himself in the foremost place. (7)
For whosoever will save his life shall lose it. (Matt. 16:25)	He who aims at life achieves death. (50)
Lay not up for yourselves treasures upon earth . . . where thieves break through and steal. (Matt. 6:19)	When gold and jade fill your hall, You will not be able to keep them safe. (9)
For what is a man profited, if he shall gain the whole world, and lose his own soul? (Matt. 6:26)	One's own self or material goods, which has more worth? (44)
[W]hosoever shall exalt himself shall be abased. (Matt. 23:12)	He who is to be laid low Must first be exalted to power. (36)
Parable of the lost sheep (Matt. 18:12)	Did [the Ancients] not say, "to search for the guilty ones and pardon them?" (62)
Consider the lilies of the field, how they grow; they toil not, neither do they spin. (Matt. 6:28)	[Tao] clothes and feeds the myriad things. (34)

FIGURE I

Glossary of Taoist Names and Terms

CHUANG TZU. Lao Tzu's disciple, who lived some two hundred years after him and wrote numerous treatises on the Tao. He is still considered the best interpreter of the Tao Te Ching; and his collected writings, named after him, stand second in importance only to the Tao Te Ching in the Taoist canon.

CONFUCIUS. The founder of Confucianism and the philosophical "opponent" of Lao Tzu.

FIELDS OF CINNABAR. The three regions of the body which, according to religious Taoists, are located in the head, chest, and abdomen.

HSIEN. Those who become immortal.

I CHING. "Book of Changes," containing explanations of systems of divination; also accepted as one of the five Classics of Confucianism.

KO HUNG (283–343 or 363 C.E.). Taoist scholar and proponent of the immortality school of religious Taoism, including alchemy, many of the hygiene practices, and the accumulation of goodness as a means to attaining immortality.

KUEI. Bad and unpredictable spirits.

LAO TZU (b. 604 B.C.E.). The most familiar name of the founder of Taoism, meaning "old boy."

P'ENG-LAI. The paradisiacal island upon which the hsien were believed to dwell.

SHEN. Beneficial spirits, associated with the sun and the spring, who protected people from the kuei.

SHU CHING. "Book of History"; one of the five Classics of Confucianism.

TAO. Literally means "way" or "order," but in Taoism refers to the ordering principle of the universe. For things to be in their natural and proper state, they must be in harmony with the Tao.

TAO CHIA. Philosophical Taoism.

TAO TE CHING. Translates as "The Book of the Tao," "The Wisdom of Lao Tzu," or "The Book of Tao"; the basic text of Taoism composed by Lao Tzu.

WU-HSING. The five elements: earth, wood, metal, fire, and water.

WU-WEI. "Non-action," "not doing," or "inaction"; the Taoist form of action, meaning to do nothing in such a way that all things are accomplished and the world is brought into subjection to the Tao.

YANG. The male principle of the universe, characterized by light, heat, strength, positivity, intellect, aggressiveness, dryness, sky, heaven, sun, and south.

YIN. The female principle of the universe, characterized by darkness, cold, weakness, negativity, intuition, sluggishness, wetness, earth, moon, and north.

Notes

Various portions of this chapter are based on coverage which appeared in the chapter on Taoism in the previous edition of this text.

1. Lawrence G. Thompson, *Chinese Religion: An Introduction,* 4th ed. (Belmont, Calif.: Wadsworth Publishing, 1989), 3, 5.

2. Lewis M. Hopfe, *Religions of the World,* 6th ed. (New York: Macmillan College Publishing, 1994), 186.

3. Ibid., 188.

4. Ibid., 229–30; Hopfe, *Religions of the World,* 3d ed. (New York: Macmillan, 1983), 229–30; Peter Occhiogrosso, *The Joys of Sects: A Spirited Guide to the World's Religious Traditions* (New York: Doubleday, 1994), 148.

5. This section is drawn largely from Spencer J. Palmer, "Uses of the Five Elements in East Asia," *BYU Studies* 4, nos. 3–4 (Spring–Summer 1965): 123–34.

6. Compare the symbolic correlation charts in ibid., 133–34.

7. Occhiogrosso, *Joys of Sects,* 148.

8. Hopfe, *Religions of the World,* 6th ed., 188.

9. The biographical information on Lao Tzu comprising this section is drawn from Holmes Welch, *Taoism: The Parting of the Way,* rev. ed. (Boston: Beacon Press, 1966), 1–2.

10. As quoted in Occhiogrosso, *Joy of Sects,* 158–59.

11. Thompson, *Chinese Religion,* 90.

12. Welch, *Taoism: Parting,* 4.

13. Hopfe, *Religions of the World,* 6th ed., 192.

14. David G. Bradley, *A Guide to the World's Religions* (Englewood Cliffs, N.J.: Prentice-Hall, 1963), 134–35.

15. Thompson, *Chinese Religion,* 3.

16. Wayne Ham, *Man's Living Religions* (Independence, Mo.: Herald, 1966), 129.

17. Don Herold, "Don't Jump Out of the Frying Pan," *Reader's Digest,* February 1962, 85–86. Condensed from *Contemporary,* December 17, 1961.

18. Quoted in Welch, *Taoism: Parting,* 20. The translation used is that of Arthur Waley: *The Way and Its Power:*

A Study of the Tao Te Ching and Its Place in Chinese Thought (New York: Grove Press, 1958).

19. Ibid.

20. The translations used here are those of Gia-fu Feng and Jane English: *Tao Te Ching* (New York: Vintage Books, 1972).

21. Hopfe, *Religions of the World,* 6th ed., 193.

22. Ham, *Man's Living Religions,* 130.

23. Thompson, *Chinese Religion,* 20.

24. Hopfe, *Religions of the World,* 6th ed., 188.

25. Ham, *Man's Living Religions,* 131.

26. Liu Xiaogan, "Taoism," in Arvind Sharma, ed., *Our Religions* (San Francisco: HarperCollins, 1993), 263, 265.

27. Herrlee G. Creel, *What Is Taoism? And Other Studies in Chinese Cultural History* (Chicago: University of Chicago Press, 1970), 7–9. See also Liu, "Taoism," 261–64.

28. This section is drawn largely from Welch, *Taoism: Parting,* 106–8.

29. Liu, "Taoism," 263.

30. Stewart McFarlane, "Chinese Religions," in Jean Holm with John Bowker, eds., *Women in Religion,* Themes in Religious Studies Series (London: Pinter, 1994), 159, 164–65.

31. As paraphrased in ibid., 165.

32. Occhigrosso, *Joy of Sects,* 190; Foster Stockwell, *Religion in China Today* (Beijing: New World Press, 1993), 57, 61. Stockwell, noting that there are fewer Taoist temples than Buddhist ones and that they tend to be less well attended, estimates much more conservatively at 1.5 million Taoist adherents.

33. Thomas Cottam Romney, *World Religions in the Light of Mormonism* (Independence, Mo.: Press of Zion's Printing and Publishing Co., 1946), 366–97.

34. Welch, *Taoism: Parting,* 5–6; Lin Yutang, ed., *The Wisdom of China and India* (New York: Random House, 1942), 583–624; Waley, *Way and Its Power,* 203.

Confucius

Confucianism

7

Dong Sull Choi

OR the student of just about any aspect of Chinese life, the importance of understanding *Confucius,* the credited founder of Confucianism, can scarcely be overemphasized. In the words of Chen Jingpan, he has been a "national ideal of the Chinese people" and has defined the character of human relations within Chinese society for more than two thousand five hundred years.[1]

The ultimate goal implicit in all that Confucius taught is the realization of a peaceful world. According to the *Great Learning,* one of the Four Books of Confucianism, the pursuit of personal virtue—or moral self-realization—is the foundational step toward the attainment of universal peace. The worthy behavior of the ancient sage-kings is a model for humankind in modern times:

Their hearts being rectified, their persons were cultivated. Their persons being cultivated, their families were regulated. Their families being regulated, their States were rightly governed. Their States being rightly governed, the whole kingdom was made tranquil and happy. From the Son of Heaven [the emperor] down to the mass of the people, all must consider the cultivation of the person the root of everything besides.[2]

A RELIGION OR NOT?

There is some equivocation among both Chinese and Western scholars about whether Confucianism should be called a religion. Although Confucius became China's first professional teacher and is known today as Asia's greatest moral and social thinker, he was not a theologian and he did not foster belief in deities and spirits. He seemed to sidestep this issue. In the *Analects,* it is recorded that

Tzu Lu [one of his disciples] asked how one should serve ghosts and spirits. The Master said, Till you have learnt to serve men, how can you serve ghosts? Tzu Lu then

ventured upon a question about the dead. The Master said, Till you know about the living, how are you to know about the dead? (11:11)[3]

Neither did Confucius deal with metaphysical or philosophical speculation, and he refused to discuss afterlife or ultimate reality. Thus Lin Yutang says: "Confucianism, . . . unlike Christianity, is of the earth, earth-born. . . . [S]trictly speaking, [it] was not a religion: it had certain feelings towards life and the universe that bordered on the religious feeling, but it was not a religion."[4]

We have very few statements from Confucius about spiritual beings or divine powers. It is said specifically that "the Master never talked of prodigies, feats of strength, disorders or spirits" (Analects 7:20). As Lewis Hopfe expresses it,

Confucius seems to have believed that, while the gods existed and worship and rituals were of value in bringing people together, these things were of secondary importance when compared to an equitable social order. . . . His attitude seems to have been that ideally one should respect the spirits but keep them at a distance.[5]

And yet, Confucius's firmest and most frankly stated convictions related to heaven, or *t'ien.* He obtained a conviction that his was a heaven-sent mission. He looked upon heaven as the source of his power—a heaven that had entrusted him with a sacred mission as a champion of the good and the true in China's culture. In danger, Confucius dismissed his enemies as powerless against him in the face of heaven (Analects 9:5). In despondency, he took comfort in the fact that heaven, at least, understood him. When accused of wrongdoing, he called upon heaven to witness his innocence.[6]

Although Confucius often spoke of heaven in impersonal terms, from time to time he also seems to have regarded heaven in personalized religious terms, as the lord of human affairs. According to Unokichi Hatori's studies, Confucius became convinced of divine direction from heaven in his life.[7] This perspective is somewhat consistent with Herrlee Glessner Creel's finding that the Chinese character for heaven in its original form was clearly the figure of a man. Creel's theory is that the original meaning of t'ien was "simply 'a great man,' that is, a man of power, prestige, and importance." Thus, it is easy to think of heaven being originally conceived by the Chinese as an overruling power of a single or of multiple powerful spiritual persons and, by extension, as the place where such spiritual beings may have dwelt; but whether this is what Confucius himself believed is uncertain.[8]

Whether Confucianism is a religion in the teachings of Confucius is questionable; but with the rise of the Neo-Confucian school of principle and reason during the Sung dynasty in the twelfth century, under the leadership of the philosopher Ch'u Hsi and others, a new synthesis arose which clearly borrowed from both Taoism and Buddhism. Confucianism was redirected from a primarily moral and social tradition to a philosophy which included cosmological and metaphysical answers to questions regarding humankind in a universal setting. The "new" Confucianism now addressed human origins, the workings of natural forces, and explanations of the Great Ultimate.[9]

Finally, there are the religious implications of the cult of Confucius, which must not be ignored. In his examination of Confucian temple rites still carried out in Korea, Japan, and Taiwan, Spencer Palmer notes that scholars of Confucianism have tended to neglect these ritual and religious aspects of Confucian tradition and to examine "the old question [of] whether Confucianism is a religion . . . by an analysis of the Confucian texts; but the answer may ultimately rest on the impact of Confucius and his disciples on individual lives."[10] He points to the "great energy" that has gone into the study of Confucianism's historical aspect but notes that little attention has been directed toward the everyday Confucian practices of Koreans, Japanese, Chinese, and other inhabitants of southeast Asia as they visit shrines, tombs, and temples; bow before statues, spirit tablets, and paintings of Confucius and other Confucian saints; offer invocations to the spirits of these worthies; offer food and drink sacrifices to the worthy dead; and participate in ceremonies—all

activities based on religious assumptions and values. The enactment of elaborate biannual Chosen dynasty (1392–1910 c.e.) rituals still carried out in Seoul, Korea, are probably the most historic surviving example of pious religious devotion to the Chinese sage in the world today.[11] All these aspects of Confucianism indicate that, whatever its philosophical beginnings, it assumes the place and the function of a religion in the lives of millions of people and thus deserves study in a book about world religions.

THE FOUNDER: CONFUCIUS[12]

The dates traditionally ascribed to Confucius are 551–479 b.c.e. His Chinese name was K'ung Ch'iu and, as a respected teacher, he was called by his disciples K'ung the Master—K'ung Fu-tzu. It was later Western religionists and scholars, notably sixteenth-century Jesuit monks, who Latinized the name and title to "Confucius."

Confucius was born in the principality of Lu, located within the present-day province of Shantung. Although his lineage was aristocratic, his immediate family was impoverished; Confucius was only three when his father died, leaving his mother to raise him in poverty and hardship. Nevertheless, he determined at the age of fifteen to become a scholar. He married at nineteen; although the marriage eventually ended in divorce, he had by it a son, who lived to maturity but preceded him in death. Little else is known about his wife or family, although historian Ssu-ma Chien's *Shih Chi* includes a lengthy chapter featuring his biography. According to some traditions, his mother died when he was twenty-three years old and he, as a devoted son, mourned her passing for three years.

It was at some point during his twenties that Confucius embarked upon his true vocation of teaching. The reputation his scholarship had brought him quickly built respect, and young people seeking learning were rapidly attracted to him—according to some traditions, as many as three thousand young men were his pupils by the time he had reached the age of thirty-four.

Confucius's career, according to Ch'u Chai and Winberg Chai, centered on three main goals: "to serve government, to teach youth, and to transmit the ancient culture to posterity." In his primary aspiration to politics, they continue, his success was limited; his greatest achievements lay in the field of education.

In legend, Confucius was the first man in Chinese history to support himself by teaching.

He was a teacher of great skill and reputation, [gathering] a group of aspiring young disciples . . . from the lowest as well as the highest social strata. Bearing as little as "a bundle of meat" for tuition, they came to be instructed in various branches of knowledge based upon the "Six Arts," more commonly known as the "Six Classics." These are the *I* (Changes), the *Shih* (Poetry), the *Shu* (History), the *Li* (Rituals), the *Yueh* (Music), and the *Ch'un Ch'iu* (Spring and Autumn Annals), which had existed before the time of Confucius and constituted the cultural legacy of the past. Prior to the time of Confucius, all branches of learning had been in the official custody of hereditary aristocrats. Confucius was the first . . . to instruct the private individual and to set up a sort of school for all young men, irrespective of their status and means. He believed that "in education, there should be no class distinction." ([Analects] 15:38)[13]

Still, education for education's sake was not the motivation behind the instruction Confucius gave. His aim was to provide, through education, the means to become a *chun tzu*—a superior, cultured man, or what has become known as the Confucian gentleman. Such men were to take their places as government officials and, through living the ethical principles he taught, bring order and peace to the communities they served. In fact, it is recorded that at least half those disciples named in the Analects did ultimately serve in governmental posts, some achieving quite high rank.

When Confucius was fifty, according to legend, he received an appointment as the Duke of Lu's prime minister and was finally able to put into practice the principles of good government that he had taught for so long. They were, reportedly, highly effective: the crime rate plummeted to the extent that people felt no need to lock their doors; lost money and goods lay untouched until their owners claimed them. However, jealous enemies forced him from office after only five years, and he retired to wander in exile with a handful of followers. After some twelve years, he was able to return to Lu by invitation of a former student, but his days of government service were over. Instead, he taught and made compilations of some classical texts until his death in 479 B.C.E. He was buried at Ch'u-fu, in his home state of Lu, where his grave is still maintained. Tradition has it that his most faithful disciple lived in a hut beside the grave, mourning for three years as if for a parent.

The life and teachings of Confucius have been the subject of an enormous amount of writing, much of it highly fanciful. Arthur Waley concludes that "one could construct half a dozen other Confuciuses by tapping the legend at different stages of its evolution."[14] Still, no one doubts the extent of his influence on Chinese culture and thought. In his assessment of the place of Confucius in Chinese civilization, Chen sees Confucius as both preserving and creating Chinese civilization, concluding that he sought to preserve what he perceived as "the best of the original Chinese culture" as it had come down from antiquity.[15] Although Confucius himself felt that he was a transmitter rather than a creator (Analects 7:1), he was not blindly traditionalistic, for he is reported to have said: "He who by reanimating the Old can gain knowledge of the New is fit to be a teacher" (Analects 2:11).

Confucian Thought

Moral Teachings

Confucius's teachings on the subject of morality cluster around four principal themes: *jen, li, hsiao,* and *chung yung.*[16] Following his death, faithful disciples such as *Mencius* (372–289 B.C.E.) and Hsun Tzu (298–238 B.C.E.) continued teaching adherence to these four cardinal virtues, and they still characterize Confucian philosophy as understood today.

Jen

Jen (pronounced "ren") is so central a concept in Confucius's thought that Confucianism is sometimes called the philosophy of jen. The term recurs 108 times in the Analects, and scholars still argue over its various etymologies and translations of the term into English.[17] In Chinese writing, the character for jen is composed of "person" and "two," signifying the relationship between man and man, man and woman, or humans and the divine. Lin Yutang rendered it in English as "true manhood" and occasionally as "kindness." Waley interpreted it as "good" or "goodness."[18] Other scholars have translated it as "humanheartedness," "benevolence," "goodness," "humaneness," or "love"—even meaning sexual love, though this sense almost never appears in Confucian literature.[19] In sum, jen is regarded as the most important attribute of the chun tzu, the superior man; its attainment is, therefore, the object of education.

Li

Jen is realized, according to Analects 12:1, through the practice of li.[20] The term is used 71 times in the Analects and 489 times in the *Tso Chuan* in contexts that identify it as "the standard for political, social, and individual affairs"; but, like jen, it has no exact equivalent in English.[21] Attempts at translation have included "rites," "rituals," "propriety," "courtesy," "ceremonies," "good manners," and "politeness." Taken in the broadest sense, the term encompasses all moral codes, ethics, and social behavior. More narrowly, it means the forms of socially acceptable conduct, or the way things should be done.[22] In general, li is the blueprint for a well-conducted life.

Confucius taught that five basic social relationships existed in life and that the presence of li in these relationships would ensure an ideal society. These relationships illustrate the importance of the family in Confucianism. As listed by Lewis Hopfe, they are:

1. Father to son. There should be kindness in the father and filial piety in the son.
2. Elder brother to younger brother. There should be gentility in the elder brother and humility in the younger.
3. Husband to wife. There should be righteous behavior in the husband and obedience in the wife.
4. Elder to junior. There should be consideration among the elders and deference among the juniors.
5. Ruler to subject. There should be benevolence among the rulers and loyalty among the subjects.[23]

As this list makes clear, Confucius did not perceive the individual as an isolated entity, but rather as one surrounded by human relationships. In essence, there is no individual; each living being is defined by his or her relationships with other beings. The purpose of li is to set parameters for those relationships. As Confucius said in Analects 6:28, "[T]o turn your own merits to account . . . help others to turn theirs to account." In other words, the reciprocal give-and-take required by living in human society is a necessary factor in individual development; correct adherence to li leads, therefore, to the attainment of jen.[24]

Hsiao

From the earliest beginnings of their long history, the Chinese have valued the virtue Confucius described as hsiao—usually rendered in English as "filial piety" or "filiality." Chen describes it as "the root of all virtues, [which] serves as the moving force for action in accordance with moral standards. It permeates all virtues, and gives life and strength for their translation into actions."[25]

Laurence Thompson notes that the written character for hsiao is the character for "old" supported from underneath by the character for "son," in a succinct yet eloquent summary of its meaning. He further suggests that this concept forms the basis for Chinese belief in the hierarchy of all human relationships. As he explains, the son is inferior to his father and owes hsiao—respect and obedience—to him. So, too, the wife is inferior to her husband and owes him corresponding hsiao. Younger brother, servant, and citizen owe hsiao to elder brother, master, and emperor. Thompson cites both Mencius, the Confucian authority second only to Confucius, and Confucius himself to confirm the essential importance of hsiao in Chinese thought. "[Mencius] said, 'Which is the greatest duty? Duty to parents is the greatest. . . . Among our many duties, the duty of serving the parents is fundamental.'" Then, in this famous passage from the Hsiao Ching, attributed to Confucius:

Filiality is the root of virtue, and that from which civilization derives. . . . The body, the hair and skin are received from our parents, and we dare not injure them: this is the beginning of filiality. (We should) establish ourselves in the practice of the true Way [Tao], making a name for ourselves for future generations, and thereby bringing glory to our parents: this is the end of filiality. Filiality begins with the serving of our parents, continues with the serving of our prince, and is completed with the establishing of our own character.

Thus, Thompson concludes, hsiao forms the basis of family unity, is the primary quality of the ideal person, and acts as the most influential force in maintaining the orderliness of the state.[26]

As mentioned previously, Confucius is said to have mourned the death of his mother for three years. This practice is an expression of hsiao dating far back into Chinese antiquity. The Shu Ching reports that upon the death of the sage-king Yao (traditionally ca. 2358–2357 B.C.E.) "people mourned for him three years, as if for the death of their own parents."[27] An Old Testament story reminiscent of hsiao is that of Joseph, the son of Jacob, whose jealous older brothers sold him into Egypt as a slave. Although he passed the remainder of his life in this land among a foreign people with foreign ways, and although he rose high in their esteem, he always remembered with love and concern the parents and family he had lost. When his brothers came to Egypt for food during a great famine, he wept for joy at seeing them again, though he did not at once make himself known to them. When at last reunited with his father, Joseph "fell on his neck, and wept on his neck a good while" (Gen. 46:29); this tenderness very much impressed the pharaoh and the Egyptian people. Upon Jacob's death, Joseph entreated the pharaoh: "My father made me swear, saying, Lo, I die: in my grave which I have digged for me in the land of Canaan, there shalt thou bury me. Now therefore let me go up, I pray thee, and bury my father, and I will come again" (Gen. 50:5). Impressed with this desire Joseph showed to honor his father's last request, the pharaoh agreed; and Joseph traveled with his family to Jacob's grave site in Canaan. There, after conducting the customary funeral rites, "they mourned with a great and very sore lamentation: and he made a mourning for his father seven days" (Gen. 50:10).

Since the 1911 revolution, the traditional acceptance and practice of hsiao has been increasingly criticized in mainland China. However, its efficacy in strengthening peaceful societal relations is still defended by many Confucian scholars today. In the words of one of them:

The logical result of the doctrine of filial piety should be that "all [humankind] is but one large family," and if rightly understood, such a doctrine should be a strong moving force towards the realization of the universal [kinship] of [humanity].[28]

Chung Yung

The fourth main topic of Confucian moral teachings was chung yung, which has sometimes been translated as "central harmony" but usually as "golden mean" or "doctrine of the mean," resembling as it does the Greek philosopher Aristotle's doctrine of the mean. Confucius felt that many of the troubles of his day stemmed from the fact that this virtue had been neglected; it therefore held a central place in his moral instruction. In accordance with it, he himself rejected extremes of any kind, keeping instead to a course of moderation. For instance, his social theory endorsed neither communal primacy nor individualism. Instead, he taught—and exemplified—balance in life through jen, li, and hsiao, with emphasis on both individual and social responsibilities as well as on the

interrelationships between thoughts and actions, motives and consequences, or innate tendencies and acquired experiences.[29]

Political Philosophy

As previously stated, the projected end of a Confucian education was service in a political office. The moral teachings of Confucius, therefore, constitute the direct source of the political philosophy he taught; the applications were simply made specific to the business of promoting a harmonious society. In accordance with the concept of chung yung, his philosophy may be examined in two contexts: the role of the individual toward the society, and that of the society toward the individual.

Cheng Ming

The role of the individual in society has first to do with semantics, or the principle of *cheng ming,* which translates literally as "rectification of names." Confucius taught that there must be an accurate correspondence between words, thoughts, and objective reality:

If language is incorrect, then what is said does not concord with what was meant; and if what is said does not concord with what is meant, what is to be done cannot be effected. . . . Therefore the gentleman uses only such language as is proper for speech, and only speaks of what it would be proper to carry into effect. The gentleman, in what he says, leaves nothing to mere chance. (Analects 13:3)

Let the prince be a prince, the minister a minister; the father a father and the son a son. (Analects 12:11)

In these words Confucius counsels people to behave according to the titles they hold—to find out what their responsibilities and duties are and then live by them. They accord well with the admonition in Doctrine and Covenants 107:99 that all persons should "learn [their] duty, and . . . act in the office in which [they are] appointed"; for this is the key to harmony and peace in the community.

The political principle implied in the rectification of names is specified in Analects 12:17: "Ruling [governing] is straightening. If you lead along a straight way, who will dare go by a crooked one?" Confucius believed, then, that government was formed to sustain its people in the societal roles in which they belonged.

Governance

Confucius had no interest in representative government through a legislative body and little patience with repressive law enforcement. Order should be maintained by these aggressive means only, he felt, when all else had failed. Instead, he taught that "[h]e who rules by moral force is like the pole-star, which remains in its place while all the lesser stars do homage to it" (Analects 2:1), suggesting, first, that government should rule through morality rather than through law or force, and second, that a good leader acts as an exemplar for those being led by fulfilling the requirements of the position with rectitude.[30]

The book of Chung Yung quotes Confucius at length on the qualities that constitute a good leader. Not surprisingly, the moral qualities of jen, li, hsiao, and chung yung figure prominently in his description:

> When the ruler pays attention to the cultivation of his personal conduct, there will be respect for the moral law. When the ruler honors worthy men, he will not be deceived (by the crafty officials). When the ruler cherishes affection for his kindred, there will be no disaffection among the members of his family. When the ruler shows respect to the high ministers of state, he will not make mistakes. When the ruler identifies himself with the interest and welfare of the body of public officers, there will be a strong spirit of loyalty among the gentlemen of the country. When the ruler becomes a father to the common people, the mass of the people will exert themselves for the good of the state. When the ruler encourages the introduction of all useful arts, there will be sufficiency of wealth and revenue in the country. When the ruler shows kindness to the strangers from far countries, people from all quarters of the world will flock to the country. When the ruler takes interest in the condition and welfare of the princes of the empire, he will inspire awe and respect for his authority throughout the whole world.[31]

Neo-Confucianism

Any discussion of Confucianism today must include ideas and principles that were not taught by Confucius or Mencius but are the legacy of the great synthesis which was put in place by the philosopher *Chu Hsi* (1130–1200 C.E.). Under his leadership, the Confucian revival during the Sung period achieved great distinction in bringing into the traditional Confucian concerns for social humanism new metaphysical ideas and philosophical answers to profound problems faced by many generations of

Chinese—problems of being and ultimate reality which previously had been addressed only by Taoism, Buddhism, or other schools of thought.

In his examination of the cosmos, Chu Hsi was led to view all things as having been brought into being by two elements: the physical, known as *ch'i*, and the rational principle, known as *li* (not to be confused with the Chinese character for ritual, discussed above, which is also pronounced li). Li, the rational principle, impels the vital physical force toward movement or generation. Every object in nature exhibits some aspect of this principle, this Great Ultimate, that works within it.

This kind of metaphysical speculation or analysis was a significant departure from traditional Confucian discussions. In ancient Confucianism the stress was upon perfecting one's moral qualities to become a chun tzu, or true gentleman. In Neo-Confucianism, beyond the idea of the chun tzu lay an even loftier goal: to embody a profound metaphysical and ontological reality. That is, an ideal person was not only one who possessed moral and social virtues, but one who had reached the ultimate potential of complete identification with all creation, whose thought and action flowed in effortless harmony with the cosmic Tao. Such an idea was influenced not only by Taoism but also by the Buddhist concept of the bodhisattva.

FOUNDATIONAL WRITINGS

The orthodox canon of Confucianism that has survived until modern times is comprised of nine works: the Five Classics and the Four Books. The Four Books have been paramount in Confucian pedagogy since the time of Chu Hsi, the father of Neo-Confucianism, who has done more than anyone to formulate the canon as it is known and used today.

The Five Classics

Shu Ching (Book of History)

The Shu Ching, a collection of documents dating from antiquity, contains the sayings and acts of the ancient sage-kings.

Shih Ching (Book of Poetry)

The *Shih Ching,* a collection of songs dating back to the Chou dynasty, is regarded as one of the great works of Chinese literature.

I Ching (Book of Changes)

Originally a handbook of divination, in the hands of Confucius the I Ching became a source book of wisdom. Thompson regards it not only as a "core" book in the Confucian canon but also as "one of the most influential books ever written," if for no other reason than its illumination of the naturalistic, "proto scientific world view of the Chinese."[32] It is highly regarded for oracular judgments in the use of trigrams and hexagrams.

Ch'un Ch'iu (Spring and Autumn Annals)

The Spring and Autumn Annals comprise a terse chronicle of Confucius's native feudal state of Lu. The Tso Chuan, one of three commentaries on the Annals, was required memorization in the classical Confucian education.

Li Chi (Book of Ritual)

The Li Chi contains an illuminating discussion of the meaning of the various rituals. It contains two of the Four Books of Confucianism, as listed below.

The Four Books

Lun Yu (Analects)

The Analects are the most important single source of the life and verbatim sayings of Confucius and his immediate disciples. Numerous references from it are cited in this chapter and in other writings about Confucian thought.

Chung Yung (Doctrine of the Mean)

Originally a chapter in the Li Chi, the Chung Yung, as described previously, deals with the relationship between human nature and the underlying moral order of the universe, prescribing moderation in all courses of action.

Ta Hsueh (Great Learning)

The Ta Hsueh was also originally in the Li Chi before it was extracted by Chu Hsi. It seems to have been designed as a basis for ordering society through the self-cultivation of the individual. In classical Chinese education, the Great Learning was the first text studied by schoolboys.

Meng Tzu (Book of Mencius)

Dating from the time of Mencius, the Meng Tzu is a collection of writings, sayings, and thoughts of Confucius's most famous and influential orthodox disciple. Mencius is usually credited with having finalized the doctrine of the Mandate of Heaven, holding that a ruler in China could legitimately continue in power as long as his behavior followed the will of heaven.

WOMEN AND CONFUCIANISM

One of the elemental relationships governed by the Confucian concepts of li and hsiao and specifically mentioned in Confucian writings is that between man and woman. Traditionally, the fundamental role of a woman in Confucian society is that of wife and mother. According to Confucius, a husband should exhibit righteous behavior toward his wife, and the wife, being inferior, should obey the husband. The result is that women who follow the traditional Confucian ways, even in modern Asian countries, are still private figures whose role is to serve the men in their families. Age ultimately gains a woman a certain amount of deference, but she still stands in the shadow of her husband. Many Asian women are breaking this stereotype as they gain education and as they interact with values that come from other traditions, such as Christianity or the West in general; but a submissive and obedient wife is still considered a prize by many Confucian-oriented males.

In fairness, however, to Confucius and his teachings, it must be pointed out that, in his time, his mention of women as worthy of notice and righteous treatment by their husbands may have been considered quite benevolent. In early China it had been a common practice for kings and emperors to be buried along with the best of their possessions, sometimes including their still-living wives. Confucianism elevated the status of women above that of mere property and dignified them with a place in society upheld by custom and law, and in these respects it has improved their lot.

THE ROLE OF THE FAMILY

The importance of family relations in Confucianism is difficult to overstate. The first three of the five basic social relationships as taught by Confucius directly concern relations within the family unit, and many of his teachings emphasize the role of careful nurturing of children in order to produce individuals of quality who can influence society for the better. The classical Confucian education was designed to reinforce the orderly peace and security of home life as well as external social relations.

The concept of filial piety, which had long been entrenched in Chinese tradition, was institutionalized as Confucianism became the operating policy of the nation-states within China. Parents were responsible for the care and education of their children, enabling them to attain a productive adulthood. This in turn resulted in a sort of natural social security for the elderly, who were assured of care, support, and respect from their children and grandchildren. The extended period of ritual mourning following a parent's death, the care taken of the grave site, and the ceremonial activities to assure that needs of those in the afterlife were still being met all assured that the importance of the family would remain in the forefront of its younger members' everyday concerns. This view of family has become a part of Chinese culture to such an extent that even sweeping changes in government and Chinese society have made little impact on it.

CONFUCIANISM'S INFLUENCE TODAY: EDUCATION

China is generally believed to have developed the first formalized educational system; this came about as a result of the standardized civil service examinations for prospective government officials, which were instituted during the Sui dynasty in the sixth century C.E. Central to this educational system was its required curriculum: the Confucian classics. Up until the abolition of civil service examinations in 1905 under the Ch'ing dynasty, boys would begin study of these classics at age seven or eight, learning seven complete works by heart by the age of fifteen—the Analects, the Meng Tzu, the Li Chi (which contains the Chung Yung and Ta Hsueh), the I Ching, the Shih Ching, the Shu Ching, and the Tso Chuan. Thus, all of the Five Classics and the Four Books were represented. This required the memorization of a total of 431,286 characters in sequence; at a rate of two hundred characters a day, it took exactly six years.[33]

The passing centuries have not diminished the importance of education in China, nor in other Asian nations with a tradition of Sinic influence. Japan and South Korea are noted for their long school year of 245 classroom days, with only five

weeks of vacation in the summer, as well as for their low rate of absenteeism and long hours of study time at home. At school, children learn social responsibility alongside their academic subjects by keeping the schools clean, weeding the grounds, serving and cleaning up after lunches, and working quietly on assignments without supervision when the teacher is absent. Japanese parents typically spend more on education, both proportionately and in actual figures, than American parents. Literacy rates are extremely high, and competition for admission into the "best" high schools and universities is rigorous. Correspondingly, teachers are in high demand and are greatly valued. Annual polls taken in Japan and South Korea consistently place education as the national top priority.[34] This stress on education can be traced directly to the great importance Confucianism has traditionally placed on the quest for knowledge, though Confucius himself emphasized education for the sake of self-cultivation and eventual governmental service in the greater society rather than for the sake of personal prestige or self-aggrandizement.[35]

LATTER-DAY SAINT REFLECTIONS

Latter-day Saints often feel much at home in the Confucian environment. They appreciate the emphases on moral values, on the family, and on a society that is ordered for the well-being of all its citizens. There is, however, a major difference between Latter-day Saint thought and that of Confucianists. Confucius, as a student of history, basically held that ethics and morals derived from the golden age of Chinese life—the early Chou dynasty—while Latter-day Saints hold that all ethics and morality derive from God's will for his children. Confucianism, then, is the best of humanism, while Latter-day Saint Christianity stands solidly within the Judeo-Christian heritage of ethical monotheism in the belief that right and wrong are ultimately determined by God the Father.

This does not denigrate the validity, however, of much that Confucius taught; for regardless of how he may have viewed the origins of his teachings, Latter-day Saints can see God's hand in the good that he brought to his day and time. Mormon said, "But behold, that which is of God inviteth and enticeth to do good continually" (Moro. 7:13). Certainly, Confucius's teachings meet that criterion.

Further examination makes apparent other similarities and differences between Confucian thought and that of the Latter-day Saints. For instance, li, the ordering social system of Confucianism, defines appropriate ways for people to relate to one another, in large measure depending upon the position or status that they hold in society, as determined by cheng ming (rectification of names). Latter-day Saints, while not too concerned about this on the social or political level, are quite concerned about it in the context of church life. There is a hierarchy within the church where the persons holding offices are respected and followed because of those offices. This is particularly true in relation to General Authorities, stake presidents, and bishops. Unless persons hold those offices, they do not have the right to make decisions related to those areas of responsibility. Deference is shown to these people. There are appropriate ways of relating to them because of the offices which they hold.

Jen is the humanizing influence within Confucianism. Without it, li, with its ritual relationships, could become sterile and cold. However, jen injects into relationships the dimension of love and human-heartedness toward other human beings. While it has elements of the "pure love of Christ"—a universal compassion for all—the Confucian love has a stronger element of enlightened self-interest and specifically directed love.

In Confucianism, jen is found most clearly in the concept of filial piety. Here, deference is shown particularly to elderly parents, recognizing that from them have come life and wisdom. They are to be shown respect in life and in death. In the latter case, respect is shown through the performance of proper rituals of remembrance. This may be compared with the love shown by Latter-day Saints as they go to the temple to do ordinances for deceased ancestors which enable those ancestors to progress in the afterlife toward the Father. This concern for "salvation for the dead" shows decided parallels between Confucianism and the restored gospel of Jesus Christ.

In the area of governance, there are again some similarities and differences. Confucius advocated governance by the chun tzu, saintly and ideal human beings trained in Confucian values and practices. The person who governs should ideally be like Plato's philosopher-king. In fact, the idea of virtue being a necessity in government leaders bears a marked resemblance to the views of the Founding Fathers of the United States, as expressed in the *Federalist* papers—views drawn largely from classical Greek philosophical ideals and approved by the Lord in Doctrine and Covenants 101:76–80. Likewise, members of The Church of Jesus Christ of Latter-day Saints are expected to put off vulgar and worldly things and become purified, saintly people, filled with the powers of moral example and moral suasion, as King Benjamin taught in Mosiah 3:19. Unfortunately, few persons of this caliber exist on earth. And in the Latter-day Saint view, truly righteous leadership requires the sustaining influence of the Spirit of God.

Both Confucianism and the restored gospel place great emphasis on the importance of the family and on parental concern for nurturing children in the things of righteousness. In both, men usually have greater visibility than women. However, Latter-day Saints understand that women can and should be much more visible in religious functions and in society than the average Confucian woman would be. Latter-day Saint women are expected to obey their husbands only when the husbands are in harmony with the will of God. Both leadership and obedience are limited by self-sacrificing love (D&C 121:34–44). Among Latter-day Saints, males and females are partners in life, companions, joint participants in decisions, and coparticipants in the leadership of the family. Some roles are different, but men and women do not differ in their relationship with their Heavenly Father. There is an equality between males and females among Latter-day Saints that is circumscribed by the pure love of Christ.

Although Confucius never claimed to be a prophet, he did point the way to ideals that God would have all people pursue. In his teachings he laid a wonderful foundation for truths to come. For Latter-day Saints, it may be said that the completion of the Confucian way of life awaited the coming of Christianity and finally the fulness of the restored gospel of Jesus Christ.

Glossary of Confucian Names and Terms

ANALECTS (LUN YU). A collection of sayings of Confucius compiled by his disciples; one of the Four Books.

CHENG MING. Literally, "rectification of names"; accurate correspondence of words with objective reality.

CH'I. The physical element of being.

CHU HSI (1130–1200 C.E.). Chinese philosopher who formulated the Confucian canon and established Neo-Confucianist thought.

CH'UN CH'IU. "Spring and Autumn Annals," chronicling the history of the state of Lu; one of the Five Classics.

CHUNG YUNG. Principle of the "golden mean," similar to Aristotle's doctrine of the mean. It is described in one of the Four Books, which bears the same title.

CHUN TZU. The Confucian gentleman.

CONFUCIUS (551–479 B.C.E.). The founder of Confucianism. His name in Chinese is K'ung Ch'iu, but he was called K'ung Fu-tzu (Master K'ung); hence the Latinized version Confucius.

HSIAO. Filial piety; the respect due to parents, elders, and superiors.

I CHING. "Book of Changes," containing keys to divination and the identification of materials and objects with their associated yin and yang properties; one of the Five Classics.

JEN. "Human-heartedness" or "true manhood"; the ideal attribute and goal of a Confucian education.

LI (rational principle in Neo-Confucianism). Impels the vital physical force in every object toward movement or generation.

LI (ritual). The proper way in which relationships between people should be managed.

LI CHI. "Book of Ritual," discussing the meanings of rituals; one of the Five Classics, incorporating as chapters two of the Four Books.

MENCIUS (MENG TZU) (390–305 B.C.E.). Disciple of Confucius and influential interpreter of his doctrines.

MENG TZU. "Book of Mencius"; one of the Four Books, representing a compilation of Mencius's sayings and writings.

SHIH CHING. "Book of Poetry," containing song lyrics; one of the Five Classics and the seminal work of early Chinese poetry.

SHU CHING. "Book of History," featuring sayings and doings of the ancient sage-kings; one of the Five Classics.

TA HSUEH. "Great Learning"; discourse on promoting order in society through self-cultivation of individuals. It is one of the Four Books and was the "primer" text in a classical Confucian education.

T'IEN. "Heaven"; the supreme "deity" through much of Chinese history.

TSO CHUAN. One of three commentaries on the Spring and Autumn Annals, and required memorization for the classical Confucian student.

Notes

The discussions of Neo-Confucianism and foundational writings in this chapter, as well as various other small portions, are based on coverage which appeared in the chapter on Confucianism in the previous edition of this text.

1. Chen Jingpan, *Confucius as a Teacher: Philosophy of Confucius with Special Reference to Its Educational Implications* (Beijing: Foreign Languages Press, 1990), 5.

2. James Legge, trans., *Confucian Analects, The Great Learning, and The Doctrine of the Mean,* vol. 1 of *The Chinese Classics,* 5 vols. (Hong Kong: Hong Kong University Press, 1960), 1:358–59. The Great Learning (*Ta Hsueh*) represents a concise resume of Confucian ethical and political philosophy, with emphasis on the importance of personal virtue. As the passage from the Great Learning (1:5–6) indicates, social harmony and world peace begin with moral self-cultivation.

3. Unless otherwise indicated, quotations from the Analects in this chapter rely on the translations of Arthur Waley: *The Analects of Confucius* (New York: Vintage Books, 1938).

4. Lin Yutang, *My Country and My People,* enlarged ed. (New York: John Day and Co., 1939), 104–5.

5. Lewis M. Hopfe, *Religions of the World,* 6th ed. (New York: Macmillan College Publishing, 1994), 202.

6. See Huston Smith, *The Religions of Man* (New York: Harper and Row, Colophon Books, 1964), 169.

7. Unokichi Hatori, "Confucius's Conviction of His Heavenly Mission," *Harvard Journal of Asiatic Studies* 1 (April 1936): 105–6.

8. Herrlee Glessner Creel, *The Birth of China: A Study of the Formative Period of Chinese Civilization* (New York: Frederick Ungar, 1937), 342–43.

9. Compare William Theodore de Bary et al., *Sources of Chinese Tradition,* Introduction to Oriental Civilizations Series (New York: Columbia University Press, 1961), 510–57.

10. Spencer J. Palmer, *Confucian Rituals in Korea,* Religions of Asia Series, no. 3 (Berkeley, Calif.: Asian Humanities Press, [1980]), 16.

11. Ibid., passim.

12. In the preparation of this biographical sketch I have drawn upon John E. Wills, Jr., *Mountain of Fame: Portraits in Chinese History* (Princeton, N.J.: Princeton University Press, 1994), 11–32; Hopfe, *Religions of the World,* 200; and Ch'u Chai and Winberg Chai, *Confucianism* (Woodbury, N.Y.: Barron's Educational Series, 1973), 31.

13. Chai and Chai, *Confucianism,* 31; the translation from the Analects is theirs rather than Waley's.

14. Waley, *Analects of Confucius,* 13.

15. Chen, *Confucius as a Teacher,* 7.

16. Ibid., 247.

17. Joseph S. Wu, "Confucius," in Ian P. McGreal, ed., *Great Thinkers of the Eastern World . . .* (New York: HarperCollins, 1995), 4.

18. Waley, *The Analects of Confucius,* 28.

19. Chen, *Confucius as a Teacher,* 248–49.

20. Wu, "Confucius," 4.

21. Chen, *Confucius as a Teacher,* 249–50, 266.

22. Wu, "Confucius," 4–5.

23. Hopfe, *Religions of the World,* 203.

24. Wu, "Confucius," 5.

25. Chen, *Confucius as a Teacher,* 275–76.

26. Laurence G. Thompson, *Chinese Religion: An Introduction,* 4th ed. (Belmont, Calif.: Wadsworth Publishing, 1989), 41–43; quotations appear as he cited them.

27. Quoted in Chen, *Confucius as a Teacher,* 282.

28. Liang Ch'i-ch'ao, as cited in ibid., 284.

29. Ibid., 288–89.

30. Wu, "Confucius," 6.

31. Lin Yutang, ed. and trans., *The Wisdom of Confucius* (New York: Modern Library, Random House, 1938), 118–19.

32. Thompson, *Chinese Religion,* 20.

33. Ichisada Miyazaki, *China's Examination Hell* (New York: Weatherhill, 1976), 22.

34. William T. Ziemba and Sandra L. Schwartz, *Power Japan: How and Why the Japanese Economy Works* (Chicago: Probus, 1992), 65–68, 103; Boye Lafayette De Mente, *Japan Encyclopedia* (Lincolnwood, Ill.: Passport Books, 1995), 116–17, 127, 403–4. I add to these sources my personal observations as a former resident and student in South Korea.

35. Tu Wei-ming, *Confucian Thought: Selfhood as Creative Transformation* (Albany: State University of New York Press, 1985), 75–77.

Shinto 8

Dong Sull Choi

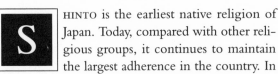HINTO is the earliest native religion of Japan. Today, compared with other religious groups, it continues to maintain the largest adherence in the country. In 1995, according to the *Japan Almanac,* followers of Shinto exceeded 118 million, or nearly 54 percent of all Japanese claiming a religious affiliation. Buddhists comprised almost 90 million, or 40 percent; Christians numbered about 1.5 million, or .7 percent; and others figured at a little more than 5 percent. But since the total number of those claiming a religious affiliation according to these figures amounted to nearly twice the total population of Japan in 1995, it is clear that these are not mutually exclusive categories and that many Japanese practice more than one religion concurrently.[1] For instance, Masayoshi Ohira, the only Christian prime minister in Japanese history, was known to conduct prayer at the renowned Shinto shrine at *Ise,* celebrate the Buddhist Festival of the Dead, and meditate at Zen temples. Taking an eclectic or syncretistic approach toward religion, the Japanese generally feel no self-consciousness or inconsistency in this sort of mixed religious practice.[2]

It was not until the infusion of Chinese thought and culture through Taoism, Buddhism, and Confucianism that Shinto was formally born. When these religions made their influence felt, some began to ask what it meant to be uniquely Japanese. The very name Shinto is in fact a Chinese term meaning "Way of the Gods," derived from a Japanese pronunciation and use of two Chinese characters, *shen* (gods) and *tao* (way). The native Japanese language expression, *kami no michi,* came into being only after the sixth century C.E. Before that time, though, the elements of Shinto had existed among the people, coexisting with nature worship, fertility cults, shamanism, and divination. Originating as a religion of military groups who lived by Spartan standards

and ideals that included sensitivity to spiritual forces within nature, Shinto drew together into a more complete whole the stories about the native gods, the land, and the people of Japan.[3]

Even today, Shinto's primary function is to celebrate the land and people of Japan. Rather than a systematic set of doctrinal beliefs or a prescribed moral code of laws, it is still a diverse set of unstructured traditional beliefs, sentiments, rituals, ceremonies, and approaches to living which have been shaped and conditioned by the historical experience of the Japanese people. It has no founder, no official canonical scriptures, and no organized theology. Over the centuries it has influenced or been influenced by Confucianism, Taoism, Buddhism, and, in modern times, Christianity; in spite of this, long-standing and unique—though sometimes nebulous—customs and life-ways of ancient Japan have been maintained through it.[4]

HISTORICAL DEVELOPMENT

In the historical development of Japanese religion from the earliest neolithic times until the end of the Heian period in 1185 B.C.E., six fundamental religious themes can be identified: animism (a belief in spirits within natural phenomena), nature worship, ancestral reverence, shamanism (the shaman votaries were often females), agricultural rites, and purification ceremonies.[5]

From the time of its introduction from Korea to Japan during the sixth century B.C.E., Buddhism has coexisted with Shinto in an uneasily symbiotic relationship. Prince Shotoku (574–622 C.E.) attempted to further this relationship by establishing a multireligious policy intended to bring indigenous Shinto and imported Buddhism into harmony. Part of the resultant amalgamation of beliefs included the idea that Japan's nature deities, the *kami,* were actually manifestations of the Buddha. Variations of this perception continued until the mid–nineteenth century.[6]

The medieval period (1185–1868) was distinguished not only by the rise of the *samurai,* or warrior class, but also by the rule of a military government led by *shoguns.* The famous Code of Warriors (*bushido*), associated with Shinto, was also formulated during this time period. During the last of the feudal regimes, that of the Tokugawa clan (1603–1867), Neo-Confucianism was promoted and popularized, and concentrated efforts were made to bring about a synthesis of Confucian values and Shinto devotion.[7]

The eighteenth century was marked by a revival of Shinto studies, and the nineteenth century featured efforts to purify and restore "true Shinto" in Japan. Those involved in this movement found fault with the long-standing synthesis of Shinto, Confucianism, and Buddhism and favored a return to the "Ancient Way," or Shinto as it was before these foreign faiths entered Japan.[8] This endeavor contributed at least in part to the end of the feudal regimes and the inauguration of Emperor Meiji in 1868. In the belief that a version of Shinto that glorified the emperor would grant symbolic status and strength to the new regime, as well as a renewal of Japanese cultural identity, his advisors created state Shinto. It was a government institution, and its priests were government officials. It recognized the emperor as the direct descendant of *Amaterasu,* the kami of the sun, and hence a divine and sacred personage to whom all Japanese owed allegiance, including the descendants of the shoguns who had formerly ruled the land under feudalism.

As state Shinto gained ascendancy, Buddhism was suppressed. It was blamed for the ills of past years, instigating a purging of Buddhist elements from Shinto worship. It was pronounced illegal to teach that the kami were Buddhist manifestations, shrines were revamped to eliminate all Buddhist influences, and Buddhist priests were defrocked unless they chose to be reinvested as Shinto priests. The religio-patriotic fervor engendered by state Shinto effectively harnessed traditional beliefs and loyalties for the political benefit of the government. This brand of Japanese religious nationalism flourished until state Shinto was disbanded by the occupying American forces following World War II. At that time, government-maintained shrines became independently operated institutions, state Shinto was renamed shrine Shinto, and Japan ceased to have an official state religion.[9]

BASIC SHINTO BELIEFS

According to Edwin Reischauer, Shinto's fundamental essence is "joyful acceptance of life and a feeling of closeness to nature. Life and death [are] seen as part of the normal processes of nature." Adherents worship the superior objects of nature—the kami—and concern themselves with ritual purity in the presence of these beings.[10]

The Kami

In speaking of the term kami, D. C. Holtom observes, "No other word in the entire range of Japanese vocabulary has a richer or more varied content and no other has presented greater difficulties to the philologist."[11] Depending on the scholar doing the translating, it is usually defined as "gods," "spirits," or "mana"; but, if not inexact, all these translations are at least inadequate. In Japanese literature, the classic discourse on the meaning of kami was given by the scholar Motoori Norinaga (1730–1801):

I do not yet understand the meaning of the term, *kami.* Speaking in general, however, it may be said that *kami* signifies, in the first place, the deities of heaven and earth that appear in the ancient records and also the spirits of the shrines where they are worshipped.

It is hardly necessary to say that it includes human beings. It also includes such objects as birds, beasts, trees, plants, seas, mountains and so forth. In ancient usage, anything whatsoever which was outside the ordinary, which possessed superior power or which was awe-inspiring was called *kami.* Eminence here does not refer merely to the superiority of nobility, goodness or meritous [*sic*] deeds. Evil and mysterious things, if they are extraordinary and dreadful, are called *kami.* It is needless to say that among human beings who are called *kami* the successive generations of sacred emperors are all included.[12]

In general, according to John Fenton and his associates, kami may be classed in three types: deified powers of nature, clan ancestors, and souls of the dead.

1. Deified powers of nature. The ancient Japanese venerated the natural world surrounding them and the forces behind its operation, which they held to be superhuman or supernatural and therefore deities. The majority of kami are thus associated with nature and natural phenomena: sun, moon, the earth, mountains, fields, seas, rivers, rain, clouds, plants, animals, minerals, the underworld, and so forth.

2. Clan ancestors. The *ujigami,* or clan kami, might be a force of nature but was also considered to be the clan's ancestral founder. Members of the clan and their affiliates (through marriage or other ties) worshiped the clan kami as the deity whose existence and protection were vital for the clan's physical maintenance, political influence, and social status.

3. Souls of the celebrated dead. Human beings who in life had achieved prominent standing, committed notable deeds, or simply manifested strong traits of character could be worshiped as kami after death. People so honored include emperors and war heroes, and their tombs are treated as shrines. A well-known example in Tokyo is the Yasukuni Shrine to the war dead. During the period of state Shinto, it ranked as one of the nation's most important shrines and played a key role in the military-oriented affairs of government.[13]

Purity

The second central feature of all Shinto worship is ritual purity. One must be pure in order to worship the kami, and the land must be pure in order to be blessed by the kami for the benefit of its inhabitants. The beautiful and well-kept gardens all over Japan are a result of this emphasis on purity, as well as respect for the kami of nature and the land itself. Since basically all Shinto ritual is an outgrowth of the quest for purity before the kami, more will be said of it in conjunction with ritual and worship practices below.

SHINTO MYTHOLOGY

To speak of scriptures in conjunction with Shinto is misleading. The two most prominent volumes of sacred writings, the *Kojiki* (Record of Ancient Matters) and the *Nihongi* (Chronicles of Japan), both dating from the eighth century C.E., cannot be called scripture in a strict sense because they do not contain any dogmas, philosophy, metaphysical thought, eschatology, or other forms of theological discussion. They are not referred to for answers to life's problems by followers of Shinto. Instead, their importance rests in the mythological record they contain of the kami and of the origins of the Japanese islands and people. It is from this mythology that a great deal of Shinto ritual and worship—and, indeed, the entire Shinto world

view—is derived. Portions of it are frequently reenacted at shrines on festival days.

The story begins with a council of gods who conclude that it is time that the Japanese islands be formed. To this end they sent the primal male, *Izanagi,* who is the kami of the sky, and *Izanami,* the primal female and kami of the earth, to create the islands. Izanagi dips his jeweled spear into the watery chaos and, as he lifts it out, the foam which drips from its tip forms the great island of Japan. Izanami subsequently gives birth to eight more islands and thirty-five kami. However, in giving birth to the last, she dies and goes to the underworld.

Izanagi, heartbroken, determines that he will follow her into the underworld and bring her back. Ultimately he finds Izanami and, despite her objections, looks upon her. Corruption has begun, and he flees in horror. Izanami, furious that Izanagi would see her in such a condition, chases him with the help of other inhabitants of the underworld. Finally, finding his way out of the underworld, Izanagi slams a rock over the entrance to stop the pursuers and goes immediately to the ocean to cleanse himself of the impurity he incurred while in the underworld. As Izanagi washes his left eye, the sun goddess, Amaterasu, is born. Then, as he washes his right eye, the moon god, *Tsuki-yomi,* appears. With the washing of his nose, *Susano,* the storm god, comes into being. Izanagi assigns Amaterasu to rule the heavens, Tsuki-yomi to govern the night, and Susano to reign over the ocean (Kojiki 1.4; 1.6; 1.9; 1.11.22–24).[14]

The relationship between Amaterasu and Susano is not a good one. They have children; but the more children they have, the more obnoxious Susano becomes. He tramples the dikes in Amaterasu's rice paddies. He defecates in the sacred hall of the First Fruits. He skins the dappled heavenly pony from its tail to its head, a heavenly sin, and tosses it into the weaving hall, causing Amaterasu to injure herself on the spindle (Kojiki 1.16–18). Finally, Amaterasu is no longer able to bear the insults and locks herself in a cave, from which she refuses to emerge. With the disappearance of the sun goddess, the world is plunged into darkness. The Kojiki reports that "the cries of the myriad deities were everywhere abundant, like summer flies; and all manner of calamities arose" (1.17.1–3).

As many as eight hundred kami attempt to lure Amaterasu from her hiding place. They bring birds, which sing beautifully, to the cave. They make long strands of jewels. They bring beads and mirrors. They practice divination rituals, bring sprigs from the sacred *sakaki* tree, and stamp on an overturned bucket. In a word, they have a marvelous party.

Amaterasu begins to wonder how everyone can be having such a wonderful time without her, and then one of the kami has an idea. He suggests that they say they no longer need Amaterasu because they have found someone more beautiful than she. Upon being told this, Amaterasu's feminine curiosity is piqued. She cracks the door to look out, and an enterprising kami holds up a mirror, apparently astounding her with her own beauty. She pushes the door open further, the kami grab her and drag her out, and the world returns to normal.

As punishment for his bad behavior, Susano has his beard clipped and his fingernails and toenails cut, and then he is banished (see Kojiki 1.17.4–25). Among his legendary exploits which follow, he plants seeds widely over the earth and with his powerful sword hews down enemies in battle.

After these events, Amaterasu, deciding that order needs to come to the islands, sends her grandson, *Ninigi,* to become their first ruler. Subsequently, according to legend, Ninigi's grandson, *Jimmu,* becomes the first emperor of Japan in 660 B.C.E. Thus, not only are the islands of Japan considered unique and divine creations of the gods in Japanese mythology, but the members of the royal family are recognized as direct descendants of the sun goddess. Likewise, the Japanese people as a whole are, mythologically, descendants either of Amaterasu or of other kami, thereby giving all the people of Japan a sacred legacy. It was no accident that part of the armistice at the end of World War II required Emperor Hirohito (1901–1989) to renounce the claim that he was a divine descendant of the gods. Also, one may better understand why the symbol on the Japanese flag is the rising sun, and why the three royal regalia of the Japanese imperial family today are the mirror, the jewel, and the sword.

There are many Shinto shrines in Japan today—at one estimate, over a hundred thousand, many of which are major ones[15]—but the best known is the shrine at Ise, which is dedicated to the sun goddess. The shrine is relatively simple, but it is the one most closely connected with the destiny of the nation. In its center is a building housing the relics of Amaterasu. In Japanese lore, it was the rise of the Yamato clan to supremacy in pre-Buddhist Japan that brought Amaterasu into prominence, for she was the Yamato clan kami.

SHINTO WORSHIP AND FESTIVALS

As is the case in many religions outside the ethical monotheistic tradition, the focus in Shinto is less on strictly adhering to certain beliefs than it is on participating in specific rituals on the prescribed occasions. As one observer notes: "In Japan religion is a tool for petitioning for business profits, the safety of the household, success on school entrance exams, painless childbirth, and numerous other concrete rewards now." In other words, the expression *kurushii toki no kami danomi* ("turning to the gods in times of distress") is indeed a living reality in Japan.[16]

Elements of Worship

Clark Offner notes that "Shinto worship consists of four basic elements: purification, offering, prayer, and a sacred meal."[17]

Purification

The purpose of purification (*harai*) is to cleanse the worshiper of pollutions, defilements, and impurities that might bar him or her from communion with the kami. The process precedes both individual worship before the household's *kami-dana* (family altar) and a visit to a shrine. At home one might bathe, wash hands and face, or simply rinse the mouth with water. At a shrine, the first place a worshiper visits after entering through the *torii* (entrance gate) is the ablution pavilion (*omizuya*), in order to rinse the mouth and fingertips with water before proceeding toward the sanctuary itself. Those who are ill, who have an open wound or a flow of blood, or who are in mourning cannot be ritually cleansed and traditionally should not participate in worship while their condition persists. Sakaki sprigs, ropes of rice straw hung with cut paper, and bamboo rods with streamers of paper or flax, symbolic of purification, also adorn the shrines.

Offerings

Both in home worship and at shrines, offerings (*shinsen*) are made to the kami. Those made at the family kami-dana usually consist of food or drink, such as rice (cooked or raw), fish, vegetables, salt, rice wine, or water placed on a shelf before the shrine. The offerings are to be made once or twice a day, and faithfulness in fulfilling this obligation is believed to please the kami and bring continued good fortune. Food and drink may be offered at communal shrines too, as well as goods in kind and symbolic offerings such as flowers. However, the most common offering is money.

Prayer

Prayers (*norito*) are also a part of home and shrine worship. Usually not spoken aloud, they generally convey thanks, request favors, or report on promises made to the kami. Bows and hand-clapping accompany them. At a shrine, a supplicant may pray silently, pay a priest to offer a prayer, or pay ceremonial dancers to perform in conjunction with a prayer in order to increase the effectiveness of the petition.

Sacred Meal

At the conclusion of any ceremony, at home or at a shrine—other than the simple daily offering or prayer—worshipers partake of a sacred meal (*naorai*) as a symbol of communion with the kami. For most of the participants, this usually consists merely of a sip of rice wine presented to them by the priest or an assistant; but after a large ceremony it can mean an actual festive meal shared by the priests and their guests.

Matsuri

Popular festivals called *matsuri* are described by Stuart Picken as "the heart of all Shinto activities and of every shrine" in Japan. "Thousands are held nationwide every year, ranging in scale and size from the great festivals such as the Chichibu Yo Matsuri in Saitama, which attracts over a quarter of a million people every year, to tiny village festivals that attract only a few hundred local parishioners."[18] As Fenton and his associates explain,

Matsuri at shrines are usually scheduled according to a regular ritual calendar of yearly and monthly rites. Priests preside at the services, which seek basically to ensure continued order in the cosmos. Humans wish to influence the sacred powers so as to keep the world favorable to human life and prosperity. Matsuri are basically rites of hospitality, analogous to inviting honored guests to one's home. Kami are to be entertained, offered food and drink, and praised or flattered, and promises are made to them.[19]

Matsuri have retained their religious significance through many centuries of Japanese history, but a major reason for their popularity has always been the fun and enjoyment they involve.

Although some of the numerous matsuri held each year across Japan are regional festivals, others are celebrated nationally. Two of the most important on the national level are the Harvest Festival (*Niiname Matsuri*) and the Grand Purification Ceremony (*Oharai*). Because the first of these is performed by the emperor himself, acting as a priest and as a direct descendant of Amaterasu, and the second features a prayer confirming his divine heritage, they were of great importance during the period of state Shinto; now, although still popular, they are practiced more for tradition's sake. The Niiname Matsuri is performed each autumn after the harvest, on November 23; the national holiday on which it occurs is known as Labor-Thanksgiving Day. It is celebrated at midnight by torchlight, giving it an aura of mystery and solemnity unlike the lively character of many other matsuri. In giving thanks for the harvest, the emperor offers its first fruits to the kami and, as an act of communion with them, samples them himself as naorai. The ceremony of Oharai, which occurs twice annually on the last days of June and December, consists of a long ritual prayer, dating from ancient times, which asks forgiveness for a specific list of impure practices; this is accompanied by the sprinkling of water and the waving of a *haraiguishi,* a wand with streamers, in order to cleanse the entire land and all the people of Japan.[20]

BUSHIDO: THE CODE OF CHIVALRY

Personal characteristics which the Japanese have traditionally considered to be virtues worthy of emulation include several that, in Western culture, have been associated with the concept of chivalry. These include courage and forms of honor such as courtesy, loyalty to leaders, gratitude, and patriotism. Just as Shinto religious tradition teaches respect for the land and its kami, including the emperor, so the military tradition of bushido, the code of the samurai, paralleled these teachings with a code demanding a high degree of loyalty and honor to the emperor and the feudal lords under him. The samurai, who may be regarded as the equivalent of knights in the Western chivalric tradition, were warriors and were not necessarily religious, but they esteemed the emperor and the land of Japan as devoutly as any Shinto priest.

As previously noted, military clans dominated the islands of Japan before Chinese influence entered the country. These groups were spiritually close to nature, and each had its own patron kami. Martial values were prized, and the military class ruled the country. In contrast, the top of the social ladder in China and Korea was held by the Confucian civilian scholarly officials, and one progressed in society through the study of the Confucian classics and by developing the social graces of the court. Confucian officials ruled under the "mandate of heaven," which could be withdrawn if a ruler failed in his moral responsibilities. In the society of Japan, the emperor ruled by his right of birth and by his descent from the kami of the sun, Amaterasu.

The bushido code, in alliance with Confucian ethics, has profoundly influenced Japanese religious life. The first duty of all has been loyalty to one's divinely established lord, the emperor, and, after him, to the lord whom one immediately serves. And in the words of a well-known Japanese proverb, "A loyal retainer does not serve two lords." In *Chushingura,* the popular Japanese story in which forty-seven unemployed samurai avenge the death of their former overlord, the principal disciple explains that his loyalty to his military superior must take precedence over his loyalty to his family. This is in sharp contrast to the Confucian value system of China and Korea, where the integrative commitment of loyalty to the family takes precedence over any other lineal consideration. Other basic elements of the bushido code are the following:

1. Gratitude and courage: Life was surrendered gladly in the service of the lord. To die honorably was considered a great blessing. For a warrior to die in bed before having the chance to sacrifice his life for his master was a great shame.

2. Justice: Selfishness must not be allowed to interfere with duty.

3. Truthfulness: A samurai would never lie in order to avoid harm.

4. Politeness: To be polite in every circumstance, even toward a foe, was an indication of a strong and worthy man.

5. Reserve: Feelings were never to be openly shown, no matter how profoundly one was moved.

6. Honor: The samurai knight always carried two swords: the long one to fight enemies and the short one to take his own life in case of defeat or some other disgrace.[21]

DENOMINATIONS

As noted, currents of Buddhist and Confucian thought have exercised some influence over the development of Shinto through the centuries. However, it was not until the Meiji regime's designation of state Shinto as a patriotic rather than a religious institution that Shinto began to divide into distinct denominations in a more Western sense. Under state Shinto, observances that were deemed strictly religious could not be practiced by the state's priests, and those who wished to practice them formed their own groups in order to do so, finding private support alongside all the other religions then in Japan. As Joseph Kitagawa explains:

The Meiji regime, which was compelled to take into account the religious aspirations of the masses as well as the internal disunity of the historic Shinto tradition, decided to create a category of "Sect Shinto" (Kyoha Shinto) in contradistinction to State Shinto. It was decreed that only State Shinto could apply the title *jinja* to its shrines and receive direct and indirect support from the government. Sect Shinto was ordered to use the title *kyokai* (church) for its establishments, which of course did not receive any government support. Between 1882 and 1908, the government recognized thirteen Sect Shinto denominations.[22]

The names of these sects and their founders, listed in order of the year of government recognition, are as follows:

Name	Founder	Recognition
1. Kurozumi-kyo	Kurozumi Munetada	1876
2. Shinto Shusei-ha	Nitta Kuniteru	1876
3. Izumo Taisha-kyo	Senge Takatomi	1882
4. Fuso-kyo	Shishino Nakaba	1882
5. Jikkyo-kyo	Shibata Hanamori	1882
6. Taisei-kyo	Hirayama Sosai	1882
7. Shinshu-kyo	Yoshimura Masamochi	1882
8. Ontake-kyo	Shimoyama Osuke	1882
9. Shinto Tai-kyo		1886
10. Shinri-kyo	Sano Tsunehiko	1894
11. Misogi-kyo	Inoue Kasakane	1894
12. Konko-kyo	Kawate Bunjiro	1900
13. Tenri-kyo	Nakayama Miki	1908

Of these sects, all but Shinto Tai-kyo have charismatic persons as founders. Except for Konko-kyo and Tenri-kyo, all worship the three kami traditionally most honored in Shinto: Izanagi, Izanami, and Amaterasu. Kitagawa classifies them under five headings: the "Shintoistic" sects (including Izumo Taisha-kyo, Shinto Tai-kyo, and Shinri-kyo), the "Confucian-inspired" sects (Shinto Shusei-ha and Taisei-kyo), the "mountain-related" sects (Jikkyo-kyo, Fuso-kyo, and Ontake-kyo), the "purification" sects (Shinshu-kyo and Misogi-kyo), and the "utopian or faith-healing" sects (Kurozumi-kyo, Konko-kyo, and Tenri-kyo).[23] For the most part, the promises extended by most of these sects are of a worldly nature: healing, protection, success, and the like.

Perhaps the most well-known of these sects is Tenri-kyo (literally, "divine reason"), whose founder, a peasant woman named Nakayama Miki (1798–1887), experienced a healing that she considered miraculous and, feeling possessed by the kami of divine reason, accepted this as a call to preach. Along with faith healing, her teachings centered on mantic principles long engrained in Shinto, such as shamanism, use of oracles, and ecstatic dance. Today it emphasizes volunteer labor and public charity work, but faith healing still holds a prominent place. Superficial resemblances have led some to refer to Tenri-kyo as "the Christian Science of Japan."[24]

SHINTO TODAY

From its very unified beginnings and development, Shinto has become today a varied and fragmented religion. The abolition of state Shinto after World War II and the subsequent expansion of religious liberty led to the growth of denominations of sect Shinto far beyond the original thirteen—by 1949 there were seventy-five officially recognized groups. Still other groups have formed that, though they may have sprung from Shinto roots, now depart from its basic principles in dramatic ways. Known collectively as "the new religions" (shinko shukyo), they include five categories, as outlined by Kitagawa:

(1) those which stemmed from Buddhism, e.g., Soka Gakkai ("Society for the Creation of Values") and Rissho Koseikai ("Society for the Establishment of Righteousness and Friendly Relations"); (2) those which profess a monotheistic or, to be more technical, monolatristic belief, e.g., Tensho-kotai-jingu-kyo, commonly referred to as the "dancing religion," and Sekai Kyusei-kyo ("Church of World Messianity"); (3) those which follow a pantheistic belief, even though one kami or Buddha among them may be chosen as the center of worship, e.g., Ananai-kyo, which claims to be the synthesis of all major world religions; (4) those which are utopian and messianic, e.g., Reiyu-kai ("Association of the Friends of the Spirit"); and (5) those which are primarily concerned with practical aspects of life, e.g., PL Kyodan ("Religion of Perfect Liberty").[25]

As with the "religions of the marketplace" described by Robert Ellwood, it is largely the personality and charisma of the founder that lends each of these groups its distinctive flavor. Mantic spiritual powers such as divination, incantations, oracular pronouncements, and healing are prominent in many of them.[26]

THE ROLE OF WOMEN

As already indicated in this chapter, women were highly important figures in the early religious history of Japan. Amaterasu, kami of the sun, from whom the emperors were said to have descended, was one of the primary deities worshiped in Japan from the earliest days to the present. She is a paradigm of feminine religious expression in Shinto. Women have also served from ancient times as shamans, or mediators for the kami, whether dancing at shrines or communicating with the dead. Another significant instance of female importance emerges in the seventh century C.E., when an imperial princess was installed to serve at Shinto shrines. Duties of the virgin princess included worship of the kami, but she was not called upon to perform divination as a shaman. Princesses served in this capacity until the fourteenth century.[27]

From time to time in Japanese history, women have also dominated the literature of their day. The Heian period is the best example of this. The world's first enormously impressive novel, The Tale of Genji, was produced in the eleventh century by a woman known today only by her pen name, Murasaki Shikibu. She recorded that her father appreciated her talents but wished that she had been born a boy. The author of the contemporaneous work The Pillow Book was Sei Shonagon, daughter of a provincial governor.[28]

Although they apparently did not rule politically, women enjoyed higher status in every other sphere in Japan before the feudal era (twelfth through seventeenth centuries C.E.), when the bushido code exalted military values. Perhaps even more damaging to their status, however, were the influences of Buddhism and Confucianism entering the country. Both had deeply entrenched ideas about women's inferiority, and these supported laws which curtailed women's rights to divorce or inherit property. Menstrual blood, already considered a pollutant in Shinto belief, was in Buddhism a symbol of the overall impurity of women. Buddhist women—even nuns—were not permitted to visit Japan's sacred sites and holy mountains; and the prestige of Shinto women suffered likewise, as their shamanic role dwindled to become basically a symbolic one.[29]

In recent history, women's status in Shinto has begun to increase again. During World War II, some women were allowed to act as priests at the shrines as men were called into military service. A number of the Shinto denominations and the "new religions" have women as founders, and women form the majority of their followers. But Confucian and Buddhist ideas of women's inferior nature persist, and these "new religions" and sects often tend to reinforce them. Still, women acting as healers and prophetic votaries for the faithful in these groups gain a sense of personal value as well as social importance. Also, it is traditionally the women who prepare the offerings placed on the kami-dana and pay regular visits to the shrines as part of their expected familial and social role.[30]

LATTER–DAY SAINT REFLECTIONS

Differences

It is axiomatic among Latter-day Saints that it is the "work and . . . glory of God to bring to pass the immortality and eternal life of man" (Moses 1:39). The message of the gospel is hope for the future. People are to live in faith and righteousness so that they will come forth in the first resurrection to be exalted in the celestial kingdom, to live with the Father, the Son, and the Holy Ghost. These are the glad tidings of the gospel of Jesus Christ, the "glorious . . . voice we hear from heaven, proclaiming in our ears, glory, and salvation, and honor, and immortality, and eternal life; kingdoms, principalities, and powers!" (D&C 128:23).

Unlike The Church of Jesus Christ of Latter-day Saints, Shinto is a religion of the present only. It has a this-world orientation. Surrounded by fertile seas and dwelling in a beautiful and abundant land, natives of early Japan had no reason to look elsewhere for joy—their present existence supplied it all. Wayne Ham comments that "there is little concern here for personal immortality and no systematic doctrine of [life after death]. If a Shintoist becomes concerned about any aspect of the next life, he [or she] may turn to Buddhism for answers without violating [the] Shinto faith." While Shinto priests often perform weddings in Japan, Buddhist priests usually handle funeral ceremonies.[31] Not only are the doctrines of eschatology, resurrection, and spiritual exaltation absent in Shinto, but concepts of a cosmic atonement and a messiah figure are lacking as well.

There is a second major difference between Shinto and the beliefs of Latter-day Saints which focuses on the number and character of the gods. In Shinto, the innumerable kami are not superhuman beings who live in a distant heaven. They are neither transcendent nor omnipotent. Instead, they exist within nature, being found in rocks, trees, mountains, and waterfalls. As Picken explains, "A kami is understood to mean anything that can inspire in human beings a feeling of awe, reverence, or mystery."[32] Even the kami of electricity is now recognized and has a shrine dedicated to him. Overall, the kami are legion, do not give moral mandates for living, are essentially carefree, and are unencumbered by spiritual laws.

In contrast, Latter-day Saints worship only the three personages comprising the Godhead: the Father, the Son, and the Holy Ghost. They govern natural phenomena on this earth, but they live apart from it, in some actual distant location (see Abr. 3:9). These are perfect beings, free from all vices, unbridled passions, and inconsistencies of behavior; they are the exemplars after which mortal beings are to pattern their lives. All Latter-day Saint instruction—in personal study materials, church, and temple alike—conveys that the Godhead has issued divine commandments that must be obeyed in order to obtain eternal joy and avoid eternal punishment in the judgment to come. The significance of these directives extends far beyond the here and now; it reaches into infinity.

The members of the Godhead of the restored gospel are also creator Gods. The Son, through the endowment of the Father and the interfacing influence of the Holy Ghost, has brought into being all creatures, and through the Son all creation will be redeemed from sin. The power of the Godhead is universal. By comparison, the functions and powers of the kami are selective and particular. Each kami is limited to specific aspects of nature—the sun, the moon, the wind, a mountain, a stream, the sea. Since the kami do not deal in divine laws affecting human life after death, which people are thereby required to obey, there is no sin as Latter-day Saints understand it. The only thing to shun is pollution. Therefore, in Shinto there is no need for divine expiation from guilt that may come from committing sin.

Third, because of the above, and as Paul Watt explains, in Shinto,

the tensions . . . in Western religion between the Creator and the created, and the human and natural realms, are conspicuously absent. In the Shinto view, the natural state of the cosmos is one of harmony in which divine, natural, and human elements are all intimately related. Moreover, human nature is seen as inherently good.[33]

In the scriptures of the restored gospel there is a reiterated theme of tension and duality between God and the natural or fallen man (see Mosiah 3:19).

Affinities

It has been argued that there exists a special link between the peoples of the Old Testament and ancient Japan.[34] Jews and Judaism are popular Japanese themes. The remarkable resemblances between Jews and Japanese have caught the attention of foreigners as well,[35] and claims that the Japanese have historical roots among the peoples of the Bible and that Japanese culture has retained elements of this Hebrew past are often made. A surprising and incredible fable of a Christian-Japanese connection claims that Jesus once lived, ministered, and married in Japan, after having first visited the American continent.

This is the so-called Herai Mura myth. It raises a wide range of theological and religious questions.[36]

Another interesting instance of affirming ancient Japanese gospel connections is found in Elder Heber J. Grant's prayer when he dedicated Japan for missionary work in 1901. According to Alma Taylor's reminiscences of the event, Elder Grant

spoke of those who, because of iniquity, had been cut off from among the Nephites . . . and said we felt that through the lineage of those rebellious Nephites who joined with the Lamanites, that the blood of Lehi and Nephi [and of all Israel] had been transmitted unto the people of this land, many of whom have the features and manners of the American Indians, [and he] asked the Lord that if this were true that He would not forget the integrity of His servants Lehi and Nephi and would verify the promises made unto them concerning their descendants in the last days upon this [the Japanese] people for we felt that they were a worthy nation.[37]

In perhaps the only essay written by a General Authority of The Church of Jesus Christ of Latter-day Saints regarding Shinto and the Japanese, Elder James E. Talmage of the Council of the Twelve Apostles has offered this salute:

You who cherish the ancient Shinto faith claim descent from divine parentage.

My brothers of *Shinto,* or *Kami-no-michi,* you profess to follow the "Way of the Gods" as your name declares. Your holy *Kami* were the creators of the heavens and the earth, the sea and all things that in them are. We [Latter-day Saints] hold that the Godhead is a Trinity comprising the Eternal Father, Jesus Christ the Son, and the Holy Ghost; that by the power of the Godhead were the worlds made; and that man is the child of Deity.

Shintoism enjoins toleration of the beliefs of others; freedom of thought and action; love for fellow men; kindness toward all. We as Latter-day Saints profess that without these virtues we cannot please God; that if we love not our brother, we cannot truthfully say we love God; that we must live in virtue and chastity, sobriety and honesty, and obey the law made plain by the Lord Jesus Christ, if we would finally reach the abode of the blessed in the house of our Father.[38]

Glossary of Shinto Names and Terms

AMATERASU. The sun goddess, who was born when Izanagi washed his left eye.

BUSHIDO. The code of the warrior, comparable to the code of medieval chivalry; "the Warrior-Knight Way."

HARAI. Ritual purification made preparatory to communion with the kami.

HARAIGUISHI. Traditional purification wands used by the Shinto priests.

ISE. The location of the Grand Shrine of Ise dedicated to Amaterasu.

IZANAGI. Primeval kami of the sky. He and his wife, Izanami, created the Japanese islands.

IZANAMI. Primeval kami of the earth. She gave birth to a number of the islands of Japan and thirty-five deities.

JIMMU. The grandson of Ninigi and first emperor of Japan.

KAMI. Powers or divine beings which reside in all things; they can bless or, if not appropriately treated, can cause unhappiness in life.

KAMI-DANA. Household shrine where prayers and daily offerings to the kami are made.

KAMI NO MICHI. Literally, "way of the gods"; native Japanese term for Shinto.

KOJIKI. "Record of Ancient Matters"; contains the basic story of the Shinto myth.

MATSURI. Festivals at Shinto shrines.

NAORAI. Sacred meal "shared" with the kami as a symbol of communion; often consists of a sip of rice wine, but may be a full banquet on certain occasions.

NIHONGI. "Chronicles of Japan"; also known as the Nihon Shoki. Like the Kojiki, it contains the basic myth about the creation of Japan.

NIINAME MATSURI. Harvest festival at which the emperor offers first fruits to the kami.

NINIGI. The grandson of Amaterasu and the first ruler of Japan.

NORITO. Prayers offered at home or communal shrines; accompanied by ritual bowing and hand-clapping.

OHARAI. "Great Purification," a twice-yearly festival in which the whole of Japan and her people are purified.

OMIZUYA. Ablution pavilion at the entrance of a shrine.

SAKAKI. An evergreen tree whose foliage is symbolic of purification.

SAMURAI. The military class of the Japanese feudal tradition; comparable to knights in Western feudal culture.

SHINSEN. Offerings made to the kami at home (usually food or drink) or at a shrine (usually money, but may be goods, food, drink, or symbolic offerings).

SHINTO. Name of the religion, meaning "way of the gods"; derived from the Chinese "shen" (gods) and "tao" (way).

SHOGUNS. Military leaders of Japan during its feudal era and the actual powers behind the emperor until the Meiji restoration.

SUSANO. The storm god and mischievous brother of Amaterasu; created when Izanagi washed his nose.

TORII. The gate before a shrine which separates the mundane world from the sacred enclosure.

TSUKI–YOMI. The moon god, who was created when Izanagi washed his right eye.

Notes

Various portions of this chapter, including the sections on mythology, the bushido code, and Latter-day Saint reflections, are based on coverage which appeared in the chapter on Shinto in the previous edition of this text.

1. *Japan Almanac 1995* (Tokyo: Asahi Shimbun, 1994), 255; *Japan as It Is: A Bilingual Guide,* rev. ed. (Tokyo: Gakken, 1990), 29.

2. Taichi Sakaiya, *What Is Japan? Contradictions and Transformations,* trans. Steven Karpa (Tokyo: Kodansha International, 1995), 104.

3. Paul Watt, "Shinto and Buddhism: Wellsprings of Japanese Spirituality," *Focus on Asian Studies* 2, no. 1 (Fall 1982): 21; Wayne Ham, *Man's Living Religions* (Independence, Mo.: Herald, 1966), 151–52.

4. Sakaiya, *What Is Japan?,* 106–7; Clark B. Offner, "Shinto," in Norman Anderson, ed., *The World's Religions,* 4th ed. (London: Inter-Varsity Press, 1975), 191; Joseph M. Kitagawa, *On Understanding Japanese Religion* (Princeton, N.J.: Princeton University Press, 1987), 139.

5. Stuart D. B. Picken, *Essentials of Shinto: An Analytical Guide to Principal Teachings* (Westport, Conn.: Greenwood Press, 1994), 8–10.

6. Kitagawa, *On Understanding Japanese Religion,* 155–59.

7. Ibid., 160–64.

8. Ibid., 164–65.

9. Ibid., 166–68.

10. Edwin O. Reischauer, from his introduction to Stuart D. B. Picken, *Shinto: Japan's Spiritual Roots* (Tokyo: Kodansha International, 1980), 6.

11. D. C. Holtom, *The National Faith of Japan: A Study in Modern Shinto* (New York: Paragon, 1965); reprinted in Byron Earhart, *Religion in the Japanese Experience* (Encino, Calif.: Dickinson Publishing, 1974), 10.

12. Quoted in ibid., 10–11.

13. John Y. Fenton et al., *Religions of Asia* (New York: St. Martin's Press, 1993), 200; Picken, *Essentials of Shinto*, 43–47.

14. Citations from the Kojiki in this chapter rely on the translation by Donald L. Philippi: *Kojiki* (Tokyo: University of Tokyo Press), 1968.

15. Boye Lafeyette De Mente, *Japan Encyclopedia* (Lincolnwood, Ill.: Passport Books, 1995), 446.

16. *Japan as It Is,* 29.

17. This quotation and what follows regarding the four basic elements of worship are drawn from Offner, "Shinto," 203–4, and Sokyo Ono with William P. Woodward, *Shinto: The Kami Way* (Rutland, Vt.: Charles E. Tuttle, 1962), 51–62.

18. Picken, *Essentials of Shinto,* 176.

19. Fenton et al., *Religions of Asia,* 202–3.

20. Offner, "Shinto," 205–6.

21. Paraphrased from Christopher Noss, *Tohoku: The Scotland of Japan* (Philadelphia: Board of Foreign Missions of the Reformed Church in the United States, 1918), 87–88, as quoted in David S. Noss and John B. Noss, *Man's Religions,* 7th ed. (New York: Macmillan, 1984), 318–19.

22. Kitagawa, *On Understanding Japanese Religion,* 168–69.

23. Ibid., 169–70.

24. Lewis M. Hopfe, *Religions of the World,* 6th ed. (New York: Macmillan College Publishing, 1994), 233–34.

25. Kitagawa, *On Understanding Japanese Religion,* 172–73.

26. Ibid., 173; see also n. 12 in chapter 1 of this book.

27. D. P. Martinez, "Japanese Religions," in Jean Holm with John Bowker, eds., *Women in Religion,* Themes in Religious Studies Series (London: Pinter, 1994), 169, 170.

28. Sharon L. Sievers, "Women in China, Japan, and Korea," in the "Asia" packet of *Restoring Women to History: Teaching Packets . . .* (Bloomington, Ind.: Organization of American Historians, 1988), 76–77.

29. Martinez, "Japanese Religions," 170, 171.

30. Ibid., 172–74.

31. Ham, *Man's Living Religions,* 155.

32. Picken, *Shinto: Japan's Spiritual Roots,* 10.

33. Watt, "Shinto and Buddhism," 22.

34. Compare, for example, Kiuro Teshima, "Uzumasa no Kami," *Seimei no Hikari* 250 (July 1971): 1–24, and Marvin Tokayer and Hakozaki Souichi, *Yudaya to Nippon: Nazo no Kodaishi* (Judah and Japan: A Puzzle of Ancient History) (Tokyo: Sangyounouritsu Daigaku Shuppanbu, 1975).

35. Spencer J. Palmer, "Jews and Japanese: Two Peoples Who Have Surprised the World" (paper delivered for the David M. Kennedy Center Lectures Series, Brigham Young University, Provo, Ut., 1987).

36. A full overview of this subject is covered in Spencer J. Palmer, "Did Christ Visit Japan?" *BYU Studies* 10, no. 2 (Winter 1970): 135–50.

37. Alma Taylor to his father, September 1, 1901, in Andrew Jensen et al., comps., *Journal History of The Church of Jesus Christ of Latter-day Saints* (Harold B. Lee Library, Brigham Young University, Provo, Ut.; Salt Lake City: Historical Department, The Church of Jesus Christ of Latter-day Saints, 1906–), microform, box 19, reel 101.

38. James E. Talmage, "In the Lineage of the Gods," *Improvement Era* 8, no. 10 (August 1905): 728.

Gallery of Photographs

Hindu boy selling sweets and flowers as offerings for Durga at the festival of Shravna Durga Mela, Banaras, India. *(Photo by Diana Eck)*

Vishnu and his consort, Lakshmi, in the avatars of Krishna and Radha, the Hindu ideals of love. *(Photo by Spencer J. Palmer)*

Hindu temple of Shiva, Banaras Hindu University, Banaras, India. *(Photo by Roger R. Keller)*

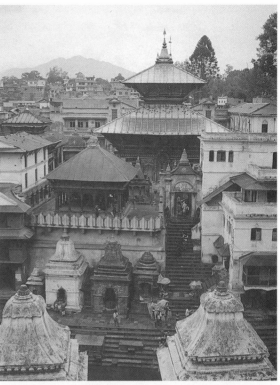

Stone image of Ganesha, Hindu god in charge of removing obstacles and son of the god Shiva. *(Photo by Roger R. Keller)*

Shiva temple complex, Katmandu, Nepal. *(Photo by Roger R. Keller)*

The Hindu Trimurti. A stylized and symbolic representation of (from left to right) Shiva, Vishnu, and Brahma, the threefold manifestation of the Ultimate Reality, Brahman-Atman. *(Photo by Spencer J. Palmer)*

Jain caves, Gwalior, India. *(Photo by Mark Juergensmeyer)*

Jain temple, Sarnath, India. *(Photo by Roger R. Keller)*

Statue of one of the twenty-four Jain tirthankaras, or "ford-finders," in the temple at Sarnath, India. *(Photo by Roger R. Keller)*

Massive bronze statue of Amida, Kamakura, Japan.
(Photo by Roger R. Keller)

Maitreya, Popjusa Temple complex, Korea. This thirty-three-foot-high Buddha-of-the-future is believed to be the world's tallest Buddhist statue constructed of metal. It was dedicated in April 1990. *(Photo courtesy of Popjusa Temple)*

Young Buddhist monks in yellow robes, Bangkok, Thailand. *(Photo by Spencer J. Palmer)*

Stupa in Sarnath, India, marking the traditional spot where the newly enlightened Buddha preached his first sermon. *(Photo by Roger R. Keller)*

The Amida Triad, as pictured on a silk scroll at the Zenrin Temple, Kyoto, Japan. Here Amida (Amitabha) is flanked by Kannon (Avalokitesvara) on his right and Maitreya on his left. *(Photo courtesy of Zenrin Temple)*

Offerings made in front of the Temple of the Emerald Buddha, Bangkok, Thailand. *(Photo by Roger R. Keller)*

Golden Temple, Amritsar, Punjab, India. The temple, the most holy place in Sikhism, is surrounded by the sacred Pool of Immortality. The family group in the foreground with the husband and wife holding hands in public represents an unusual sight in India. *(Photo by David Shuler)*

Interior of Gurdwara Rakabganj, New Delhi, India. The Granth is being read aloud from the archway in the center of the picture. *(Photo by Roger R. Keller)*

Sikhs in traditional costume. Each is wearing the five emblems of membership in the Khalsa: uncut hair and beard, steel bracelet, comb, short underdrawers, and dagger. *(Photo by David Shuler)*

Sikhs at a langar meal open to all in the Gurdwara Bangla Sahib, New Delhi, India. *(Photo by Roger R. Keller)*

Lungshan Temple, Taipei, Taiwan. Although primarily Buddhist, this temple represents a mix of Buddhism, Taoism, and folk religions. *(Photo by Roger R. Keller)*

Spirit medium in preparation for a ceremony in religious Taoism. *(Photo by Gary S. Williams)*

Chinan Monastery, Taipei, Taiwan. Vertical wooden members of the building are painted a vivid red. *(Photo by Roger R. Keller)*

Entrance to the Chinan (Taoist) Monastery compound, Taipei, Taiwan. The statues at the peak of the gate portray the Three Immortals. *(Photo by Roger R. Keller)*

Temple of Confucius, Qufu, Shantung Province, People's Republic of China. This is the prototype Confucian temple for all others. *(Photo by Spencer J. Palmer)*

High-ranking Confucian officials entering the Temple of Confucius, Seoul, Korea. *(Photo by Spencer J. Palmer)*

Lavender-robed musicians of the Terrace Orchestra performing during the national semiannual Sokchon (Confucian) ceremony, Seoul, Korea. *(Photo by Spencer J. Palmer)*

Red-robed Confucian dancers performing the ritual line dance, Seoul, Korea. *(Photo by Spencer J. Palmer)*

Tomb of Confucius, Qufu, Shantung Province, People's Republic of China. *(Photo by Roger R. Keller)*

Statue of Confucius, Yushima Shrine, Tokyo, Japan. In at least one area of Japan, Confucius is honored as if he were a Shinto kami in an interesting integration of two religious traditions. *(Photo by Spencer J. Palmer)*

Shinto torii, Inland Sea at Miyajima, Japan. The photo was taken at low tide; normally this large torii is surrounded by water. *(Photo by Spencer J. Palmer)*

Shinto faithful carrying a portable shrine (mikoshi) during a festival, Kyoto, Japan. *(Photo by Spencer J. Palmer)*

Shinto priests exiting a shrine for a festival occasion, Kyoto, Japan. *(Photo by Spencer J. Palmer)*

Inner torii gate, Meiji, Japan. *(Photo by Roger R. Keller)*

Farohar, the symbol of Zoroastrianism. *(Photo by Spencer J. Palmer)*

Zoroastrian fire temple. *(Photo by Spencer J. Palmer)*

White-robed Zoroastrian priests carrying out a Jashan ceremony in the fire temple. A powdered substance is burning in plates atop the two polished metal vessels in front of the priests. Each veiled priest is holding a flower in his hand. *(Photo courtesy of Rohinton Rivetna)*

Ancient Zoroastrian "tower of silence" (dakhma) at Rei, Iran. Here the dead are laid to rest. *(Photo from A. V. Williams Jackson,* Persia Past and Present *[New York: Macmillan, 1906], opposite p. 440; in the public domain)*

Yeshiva (Rabbinic) students, Temple Mount, Jerusalem. *(Photo by D. Kelly Ogden)*

The Western Wall of the Second Temple (destroyed), which was in turn built on the ruins of the Temple of Solomon. The wall is often regarded as the most holy place in Judaism. Above it is the Mosque of Omar, or Dome of the Rock, the third most holy place in Islam. Jerusalem is a holy city for Christians as well as for Jews and Muslims. *(Photo courtesy of Sara K. Lush)*

Torah scroll held high during a bar mitzvah ceremony
in the courtyard near the Western Wall, Temple Mount,
Jerusalem. *(Photo by D. Kelly Ogden)*

Orthodox Jew worshiping at the Western Wall,
Jerusalem. The bits of paper in the cracks of the wall
contain prayers. *(Photo by D. Kelly Ogden)*

Jewish boy at his bar mitzvah, near the Western Wall, Temple Mount, Jerusalem. The man at the left is wearing on his
forehead a phylactery, which contains short excerpts from the Torah. *(Photo by D. Kelly Ogden)*

The Sea of Galilee, at or near where Jesus, a Galilean (from Nazareth), called most of his disciples, carried out the miracle of the loaves and fishes, delivered the Sermon on the Mount, and walked upon the surface of the sea. *(Photo by Caroline Christy Otto)*

Church of the Nativity, Bethlehem. The star at the center of the niche's floor marks the traditional spot of the birth of Jesus. Hanging above it are censers for the burning of incense. The church is shared by several different Christian traditions. *(Photo by Sara K. Lush)*

Golgotha, outside Jerusalem, is regarded by some as the traditional site of the crucifixion of Jesus. The name, which means "place of a skull," is said to derive from the configuration of the small caverns in its rock face. Graves at the top are those of Christians from all over the world who requested burial at this holy site. *(Photo by Sara K. Lush)*

Crucifix above the altar of the Church of the Holy Sepulchre, Jerusalem. According to some traditions, the church is located at Calvary, where Jesus was crucified and from where he ascended into heaven. This is the most holy place for many Christians. *(Photo by Caroline Christy Otto)*

The Garden Tomb, outside the walls of Jerusalem. Many Christians believe this to be the burial place from which Jesus of Nazareth was resurrected. *(Photo by Sara K. Lush)*

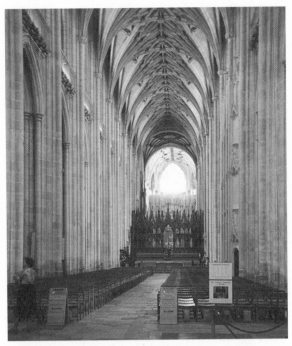

Cathedral nave, Winchester, England. Romanesque and Gothic Christian cathedrals represent a form of architecture unique to Christianity and are still renowned for both their beauty and their technical workmanship. *(Photo by Roger R. Keller)*

Seoul Korea Temple, The Church of Jesus Christ of Latter-day Saints. As of January 1997 there were sixty-four Latter-day Saint temples and temple sites worldwide. The Seoul Korea Temple was dedicated in 1985. *(Photo by Jae Koo Shin)*

Blue Mosque, Istanbul, Turkey. *(Photo by D. Kelly Ogden)*

Minaret of the Muhammad Ali Mosque, Cairo, Egypt. Traditionally, a muezzin climbed into this minaret to call faithful Muslims to prayer five times daily. *(Photo by D. Kelly Ogden)*

Muezzin issuing the call to evening prayer, Jerusalem. Nowadays the call to prayer may be issued through loudspeakers installed in many minarets, although the traditional Qur'anic forms of the calls are still used. *(Photo by Sara K. Lush)*

The Grand Mosque and the Ka'aba, Mecca, the most sacred site in Islam. *(Photo courtesy of Saudi Arabian Embassy, Washington, D.C.)*

Veiled young woman in Yemen. While many Islamic women wear the veil, many do not. Those who do see it as a spiritual commitment to be taken voluntarily. *(Photo by Arnold Green)*

Hajj painting on the exterior of a home, Gurna, Egypt. When a family member makes the pilgrimage to Mecca (hajj), the journey is documented by wall paintings depicting the method of travel and other details of the event. *(Photo by Arnold Green)*

Part Four
Southwest Asian Religions

The religions of southwest Asia are all monotheistic, meaning that they focus on one God. These are the religions of Zoroastrianism, Judaism, Christianity, and Islam. Each has an identifiable founder who experienced a special relationship with the one God whom he worshiped and served. These religions accept the reality of human history and see God directly involved in that history. All of them hold that God is the creator of all things—although Zoroastrianism would add the caveat that he is the creator of all good things. God gives laws by which he expects people to live, for their own good. Thus, these four religions are often referred to as being representatives of ethical monotheism—a tradition in which there is one God who gives ethical directions to his adherents. Because there is a concept of creation—a beginning to linear history—there is also an understanding that history comes to an end. Ultimately, God's purposes will be fulfilled, despite human sin or cosmic opposition. God will reign supreme, and his adherents will dwell with him. Following some sort of final judgment, there will be a life after death. Ultimately, dwelling with God is what gives meaning to human history and religious exertion.

Unique among these religions is Christianity, for only Christians hold that God has actually entered human history as a human being. This gracious act on the part of God the Son, Jesus Christ, is for the purpose of freeing human beings from their sins. He offers himself as a substitutionary sacrifice in the place of sinful human beings. Those persons who turn to Christ in faith and repentance may rely on his sacrifice to cover their sins, thereby opening the way for them to the presence of God the Father. However, ethical living is still required; otherwise, one does not demonstrate that he or she is a true lover of God.

Unquestionably, Latter-day Saints find their greatest affinities with the monotheistic faiths, because the central doctrines are generally familiar. An understanding of these religions becomes especially important for Latter-day Saints who live in the United States, since Judaism, Christianity, and Islam are the religions whose followers they are most likely to meet. And as they encounter and come to know their beliefs, Latter-day Saints can expect to find that they hold vital truths in common with the adherents of these faiths.

Zarathustra

Zoroastrianism

9

Spencer J. Palmer

RIGINATING in the geographical area known today as Iran, Zoroastrianism is one of the historically great religions. And yet, it is practically unknown in the world today outside India. Its importance far outweighs its present small numbers, however, for almost no other religion has so deeply influenced other religious traditions. It was Zoroastrians who inhabited the land of Babylon during the Jewish exilic period and who, according to many scholars, provided the Jews with the concepts of angels, resurrection, Satan, and afterlife. These concepts were later reaffirmed and deepened by Christianity. Other scholars believe that Islam was similarly influenced by its contacts with Zoroastrianism. Zoroastrianism should also hold special interest for Latter-day Saints, for there are some amazing doctrinal parallels to examine. For these reasons, Zoroastrianism will be explored more extensively than one might expect given its small numbers.

Zoroastrianism asserts that there is one God (monotheism) who gives guidance and direction to his people through laws and commands (ethics). *Zarathustra,* the religion's founder, is thus considered one of the world's great ethical monotheists. Zoroastrianism is a practical faith and deals with the reality of everyday life, for God is concerned about and interested in his people. He expects them to live by the ideals he conveys to them. Within Zoroastrianism, history has a beginning and an end, and at the end people will be judged against the laws which God gave. In addition, the faith has an eternal view which spans a possible premortal life, mortality, and an afterlife with some very interesting aspects from a Latter-day Saint perspective.

Zoroastrianism is one of the oldest "revealed" religions. Mary Boyce feels that it has done more "[to] influence . . . mankind, directly and indirectly, than any other single faith. In its own right it was

the state religion of three great Iranian empires, which flourished almost continually from the sixth century [B.C.E.] to the seventh century [C.E.], and dominated much of the Near and Middle East."[1] Through the centuries of its somewhat embattled history, Zoroastrianism has maintained a surprising degree of cohesion—there are no institutional cleavages or denominations, although communities may be widely separated geographically—but today it is confronted with something of a crisis. Numbers are dwindling, for there is a tension between the desire to maintain the pure faith while at the same time meeting the needs of a modern world. This issue will be addressed more fully later in the chapter.

BACKGROUND[2]

Like Hinduism, Zoroastrianism has its roots in the ancient *Aryan* pastoral culture of eastern Europe or central Asia. General background on this culture has been presented in the chapter on Hinduism and will not be repeated here. However, a number of specific elements of that culture have influenced the form and practice of Zoroastrianism in unique ways, and these are discussed below.

Aryan Roots and Cultic Practices

Two elements essential for life among the Aryan peoples were fire and water. Water gave life to the Aryans in the arid regions in which they lived. Goddesses personified water and were worshiped. Thus, it is not surprising to see water as fundamental to the religion of the Zoroastrians. Modern Zoroastrians still pour out liquid libations, but these now consist of milk mixed with the sap of two plants, thereby constituting the *haoma* sacrifice. Originally this haoma (Persian) or *soma* (Indian) libation was also drunk by the warriors, giving them a sense of invincibility in battle, since the drink was hallucinogenic.

Fire was the element which provided warmth under severe climatic conditions and which cooked the nomads' food. Because of its utility, ancient Aryans sacrificed to the fire clean dry fuel, incense, and animal fat. Due to the difficulty of lighting fires, a fire was tended almost constantly and never permitted to go out. It was even carried with the travelers as they moved from one location to another. In Zoroastrianism today, fires in the fire temples are maintained constantly by the priests and never permitted to be extinguished.

Fire and water were essential ingredients of the broader Aryan sacrificial rites, including the blood sacrifices which provided, for example, the fat for the sacrifice to the fire. The taking of life was a serious act for the Aryans, and it was always carried out with solemnity and awe. Such sacred acts had to be done in sacred precincts, but these were quite simple. They were no more than a rectangular piece of ground surrounded by a furrow to separate the sacred from the profane. The area was sprinkled with water to purify it, and then the priest, sitting cross-legged, would attend the sacred fire within the confines of the now-sanctified area. Purity seems to have been essential to the Aryans, for it was a way of protecting themselves against demonic forces. For cleansing, they used the source of ammonia they had at hand: cattle urine (*nirang*). Once again, the purification rites of both the Zoroastrians and the Hindus probably have their roots in these ancient rituals.

Aryan Nature Gods

Most of the deities of the Aryans were associated with nature, for nature was that which had direct impact on the daily lives of a nomadic, herding people. Thus, gods personified the wind, the sky, the storms, the mountains, the sun, the moon, and the earth. Coupled with this was a belief in natural law—known as *asha* among the *Avestan* peoples and *rita* among the early Indians—which regulated life. This sense of order on the cosmic level was then translated into the ethical realm, indicating that truth, loyalty, virtue, and courage were all appropriate to the natural order of humanity.

Intrinsic to Aryan faith was the belief in the high God who rules over all other gods. He is the greatest of the lords and is called in the Avestan language

Ahura (Mazda), the Lord (of Wisdom). In the Rig Veda, which reflects an Aryan background similar to that found in Persia, he is known as Asura, "The Lord." He directs the actions of all gods and lesser beings and is universally in control.

Aryan Views of Death and Afterlife

Early Aryans held a belief in life after death, but it was not a particularly happy view. They held that the soul of the deceased remained near the body for three days, a concept still held by Zoroastrians, and that it then went to a shadowy underworld existence, much like the Old Testament *sheol*. There the dead were dependent upon their living relatives, especially the eldest son, to provide them with food and clothing for a period of thirty years.

Before the Aryan people began the migration which took them to areas to the south and west of Russia, there developed a concept of paradise, a place of bliss where the deceased went after death to await a resurrection in which bodies and souls would be reunited. It was believed that this resurrection would take place within the first year after death, and this may have led to the Indian practice of cremation, whereby the body was quickly destroyed so as not to be in a state of decay at the time of its reunion with the soul. The bone fragments remaining after cremation were then gathered and buried in expectation of this resurrection.

The Persian practice differed, however, from that of the Indians. Because fire was deemed to be sacred, they felt they could not pollute it with dead bodies. This, therefore, led to the practice of exposure of the body on a rocky outcrop, where the wild animals and birds would quickly remove the flesh from the bones. Then, as with the Indian tradition, the bones were gathered and buried. This practice is the probable precursor to the Zoroastrian ritual of exposing the dead in "towers of silence" (*dakhmas*).

THE FOUNDER: ZARATHUSTRA

While Aryan influences account for some of the elements distinctive in Zoroastrianism, by far the greatest influence in the formation of this faith was wielded by its founder, a prominent and well-recognized figure within the world's religious history. In fact, the term Zoroastrianism, by which the Western world knows this faith, comes from the ancient Greek name Zoroaster, referring to this first leader. Zarathustra is the form of his name drawn from the ancient Persian language which he spoke.[3] His followers revere him as the most outstanding figure in human history—one who received revelation, reformed the ancient religions of Persia, and contributed extensively to the understanding of humanity's place before God. Dastur Framroze A. Bode states that

Zarathustra was the fore-runner and perhaps the major inspiration behind the later remarkable outburst of spiritual, religious and philosophical activities which took place in the sixth and fifth centuries before Christ, in Iran, India, China and Greece. Great teachers like Solon, Thales, Laotze, Pythagorus [sic], Buddha, Mahavira, Confucius, Socrates and Plato all flourished in a span of a hundred and fifty years. It may be that this great awakening of thought in a galaxy of highly gifted seers and thinkers was independent. If, however, we take into consideration the subtle intellectual communication which had been going on from the earliest times between the seers and thinkers of different races, we may be justified in assuming that the commercial intercourse between the great empires of antiquity carried with it an interchange of a great variety of cultures, philosophies, ideas, arts and legends. The teachings of Zarathustra and the culture of ancient Iran have exerted significant influence on world cultures.[4]

His Life

Zarathustra was born[5] and raised within Indo-Aryan religious traditions, which owed much of their conservatism to the existence of a powerful hereditary priesthood. In pre-Zoroastrian times, the priests were called *magi,* and their calling was from father to son. The traditional priesthood was a major factor in resistance to Zoroastrian proselytizing.[6]

Zoroastrian documents report many marvelous incidents in Zarathustra's life. Legend states that when he was a young boy the wizards and priests in his town discovered by their magic that he would become the founder of a great religion that would put an end to their lucrative and influential careers. On several occasions they attempted to kill him, but each time he was miraculously preserved.[7]

Iranian custom dictated that fifteen was the age at which maturity was reached, and it was at that age that Zarathustra was selected to receive the sacred girdle as a symbol of his devotion, and he became a priest. Apparently, like so many other religious leaders, he felt a dissatisfaction with the current religious traditions and their answers to life's dilemmas.

Consequently, according to tradition, at about age twenty he began to wander, seeking answers to his deepest religious questions. His hymns seem to indicate that he observed a great deal of suffering and destruction during his search. Finally, at about age thirty, he was called into Ahura Mazda's presence and commissioned as a prophet to preach the true and final religion.[8] This experience is alluded to in one of the scriptural *Gathas,* found in Yasna 43, and in the *Pahlavi* work Zadspram 20–21.

Zarathustra's Initial Vision

According to this latter source, Zarathustra received his initial vision during a spring festival. He had gone to the river to draw water for the haoma sacrifice; and as he was coming out of the water in a purified state, he was met by a brilliant figure who identified himself as Vohu Manah (Good Thoughts). Vohu Manah led Zarathustra into the presence of the supreme God, Ahura Mazda. Also present were five other beings like Vohu Manah, all of whom radiated such brilliance that Zarathustra could not see his own shadow because of the light surrounding him. From Ahura Mazda Zarathustra received his first commission, which was made complete over time by further visitations by these heavenly beings.[9]

Over the next ten years Zarathustra had further associations with Ahura Mazda and became firmly convinced that he had been called to be his prophet and to preach a universal message for the benefit of all mankind. But in ten years of preaching he converted only his cousin Maidhyoimanha. Eventually, however, he was able to bring about the conversion of Vistaspa, king of Persia. During the final twenty years of his life, between ages fifty-seven and seventy-seven, he seems to have been involved in giving religious support to the king in his policies of militaristic nationalism.

Traditions vary regarding Zarathustra's family. He may have had as many as three wives, one of whom was the daughter of the counselor to the king. He is said to have had three sons and three daughters.[10]

His Death

The death of Zarathustra is not reported in the main body of scripture, the *Avesta*. However, it is reported in contemporaneous documents that he was killed by an invading army at the age of seventy-seven.

According to the story commonly held as truth by Zoroastrians, King Vistaspa's conversion angered King Arjasp of Turan, who wrote to demand that he abandon the new faith and resume worship in the Iranians' traditional cult. Vistaspa's refusal brought the two to war, in which Arjasp suffered defeat. About twenty years later, seeking revenge, Arjasp ordered the invasion and destruction of a fire temple and the slaughter of numerous priests. Reportedly, one of Arjasp's confederates slipped into a fire temple where Zarathustra was and struck him down with his sword. However, as he began to succumb to this mortal injury, the prophet flung his rosary at the invading soldier. The power of the beads was so potent that the assailant fell dead at the feet of Zarathustra.[11]

BASIC BELIEFS AND PRACTICES

Zarathustra's original religious outlook can be summarized in several key doctrines: there is one God, who has six lesser immortal beings working in concert with him; fire is of central importance in worship; and people have the freedom to choose between good and evil. In addition, surviving Zoroastrian literature indicates that there is a predetermined course for human beings to follow in life that may extend from before their mortal birth to well after their death.

The Nature of Deity

One God: Ahura Mazda

The faith Zarathustra taught was a radical departure from much of what preceded it. He rejected the sacrificial system of the Aryans and declared the traditional Aryan gods to be demons masquerading as divine beings. Above all supposed divine figures, he taught, was the one Lord, Ahura Mazda.

He felt conscious of his presence, or heard his words calling him to his service, a summons which he wholeheartedly obeyed. "For this (he declares) I was set apart as yours from the beginning" (Yasna 44:11). "While I have power and strength, I shall teach men the right" (Yasna 28:4). In a startling departure from [traditional] beliefs, he proclaimed Ahura Mazda to be the one uncreated God, existing eternally, and Creator of all else that is good, including all other beneficent divinities.[12]

In creating human beings and the earth, Ahura Mazda was not just the artisan or technician, but the master planner and engineer whose mind conceived

it all and brought it to fruition. Yasna 44 may be Zarathustra's finest hymn or psalm describing this aspect of the God he worshiped:

This I ask Thee. Tell me truly, Lord. Which man in the beginning was the father of truth during the creation? Which man did fix the course of the sun and of the stars? Through whom does the moon wax (now), wane later? These things indeed and others I wish to know, Wise One. . . . Which man has upheld the earth below and the heavens (above) from falling? Who the waters and the plants? Who yoked the pairs of swift (steeds) to the wind and to the clouds? Which man, Wise One, is the creator of good thinking?. . . Which craftsman created the luminous bodies and the dark spaces? Which craftsman created both sleep and activity? Through whom does dawn exist, along with midday and evening, (all of) which remind the worshiper of his purpose?. . . Who fashioned esteemed piety in addition to rule? Who made a son respectful in his attentiveness to his father? By these (questions), Wise One, I am helping to discern thee to be the creator of everything by reason of Thy virtuous spirit. (3–5, 7)[13]

The Amesha Spentas: The Six Holy Entities

The traditional mythology and polytheism of the Indo-Aryans was made by the genius of Zarathustra into a theology. In Zarathustra's view, Ahura Mazda works in concert with six lesser immortal beings (or divine emanations) known as the *Amesha Spentas*. These are as follows: Vohu Manah (Good Thoughts), who leads the way and who first appeared to Zarathustra and led him into the presence of God; Asha (Righteousness and Order), who personifies the powerful principle of order and truth; Armaiti (Love), who embodies devotion, piety, and love; Kshathhra (Desirable Dominion), who represents each person's power to bring about righteousness in life, as well as the power of God's kingdom on the earth; Haurvatat (Health), who confers well-being and the power of healing in life; and Ameretat (Long Life), who embodies the power of the resurrection and of eternal life.[14] The first three immortal beings appear to be superior to the remaining three and form a triad of their own. The importance of these six immortals is that they represent qualities of God and can thus bestow these same qualities upon his worshipers. It is through them that God interacts closely with the faithful. These immortals act in many ways like the Holy Ghost of Christian belief.

Benevolence and Justice

In the dominant Abrahamic religions (Judaism, Christianity, and Islam) the term creation is used generically. God created the universe and everyone and everything in it, and apparently he did so out of nothing—from a formless, matterless void. However, Ahura Mazda, the Zoroastrian creator, differs in that he created good phenomena only. Also, unlike the God described by the Abrahamic religions, the God of Zarathustra does not exact revenge. In Judeo-Christian belief, Jehovah can be made angry and may act in fury, jealousy, or wrath (see Ezek. 20; Exod. 20:5); he can plan destruction or evil and then repent of it (see Exod. 32:9–14). In Islam, Allah's punishment is described as grievous punishment (Qur'an 15, "Al-Hijr"), and he takes vengeance on the unrighteous (Qur'an 75, "The Rising of the Dead"). But Ahura Mazda does none of this. Having laid down the law of asha—the law of consequences and justice—he lets it take its course; happiness or suffering are thus the results of one's own actions. He is neither vengeful nor merciful, but perfectly benevolent and just. He neither forgives nor punishes sins, and therefore not even his prophet, Zarathustra, can mediate or intercede for sinners. This absence of angry or vengeful tendencies does not in the least undermine the benevolent omnipotence which is one of Ahura Mazda's six cardinal attributes. Such spiritual and benevolent power as he possesses simply does not lend itself to destruction and evil doings. This absolute goodness of Ahura Mazda is a firmly fixed article of Zoroastrian faith.

Fire and the Fire Temple

As mentioned above, fire—Agni—was an important deity within the ancient Aryan faith. Thus, the symbolism of fire was well known to Zarathustra, who was probably an Aryan priest. As he molded the Zoroastrian faith and redefined elements within the Aryan tradition, fire was likewise redefined and given new life. Fire was a universal element, and it was the earthly manifestation of the light and power found in the sun. For many Zoroastrians, fire is the symbol of Ahura Mazda, while for others fire is divine in itself—a manifestation of Righteousness, one of the immortal beings in the Godhead. Through meditation before the fire and through personal righteousness, the worshiper can cause this immortal being to dwell within him or her.

Fire is thus the central symbol of Zoroastrianism. Zoroastrians pray before sacred fires in fire temples, usually very small buildings designed to attract

no particular notice. The most noted temples today are in India, but there are also temples in Iran and the United States. Zoroastrians have often been accused of being fire worshipers, but such is clearly not the case.[15]

The traditional haoma sacrifice is another central act within Zoroastrian worship and is performed by the priests. It is carried out in the fire temple, but in a room separate from that in which the sacred fire is located. The haoma drink is made by crushing a special plant with certain hallucinatory properties. This preparation is done during a highly complex ritual; at its culmination the priest drinks the haoma, which has been mixed with milk. The result is an ecstatic state which is understood to be a heightened communion with God. The ritual is often performed on behalf of lay worshipers, with the priest functioning in a mediational capacity between them and God.

Agency of Human Beings

Dualism

Zarathustra was essentially a monotheist who also believed in duality or dualism—the idea that there are two basic principles or powers in the world: Truth versus the Lie. In vision he beheld an adversary that coexisted with Ahura Mazda before the creation of the world: the "Hostile Spirit," whose name was *Angra Mainyu*, or Ahriman. With a prophet's eye, Zarathustra beheld these two in a great battle before the world was physically created.[16]

Angra Mainyu is an ignorant and totally evil being. He seeks to lead persons away from Ahura Mazda and to bring disorder and destruction to the world. The last thing Angra Mainyu wants is for people to find immortality in the presence of God. In many ways, he is an evil god acting in opposition to the good God, Ahura Mazda. He functions, however, only by the permission of Ahura Mazda. Thus, monotheism and dualism are brought together by Zarathustra. As Ilya Gershevitch says,

In the Gathas Zoroaster reveals himself as a monotheist in that he worships one god only, Ahura Mazdah. He is, however, also a dualist, because he assumes the existence of two aboriginal principles, Truth and Falsehood. . . . Two religions, therefore, appear to have been syncretized by the prophet: a monotheism centered in a god of whom Truth is an emanation, and a dualism in which Truth is primordial.[17]

Freedom of Choice

In the words of Mary Boyce, "in offering the hope of heaven to everyone who would follow him and seek righteousness, [Zarathustra] was breaking [old] aristocratic and priestly tradition[s]."[18] The doctrine he taught was one of free will: all people were created good, but life in this world obligated them to choose between good and evil. This principle of choice is clearly delineated in Yasna 30:

Listen with your ears to the best things. Reflect with a clear mind—man by man for himself—upon the two choices of decision, being aware to declare yourselves to Him before the great retribution. . . . Men, when ye learn those commandments which the Wise One has posed, when ye learn (there is) both a way of easy access and one with no access, as well as long destruction for the deceitful but salvation for the truthful, then each one (of you) shall abide by (all) these commandments. . . . (2, 11)

Humanity's Eternal Path

Pre-earth Existence

As much as two-thirds of the Zoroastrian literature has been lost or destroyed. In addition, there have been many changes made in Zoroastrian theology over the years. Thus, it is somewhat difficult to be absolutely precise about all Zoroastrian beliefs. The extant Avesta and Pahlavi literature, however, gives us a broad picture which extends back to a pre-earth time, gives meaning and direction to mortality, and then draws back the curtains on the final scenes at the end of time.

Essentially, human beings are both spiritual and physical creations of Ahura Mazda. According to some Zoroastrian thought, the spiritual portion of a person may have existed in a premortal life prior to its union with the physical body. Mortality is a time to choose between good and evil, and there is a constant war in the soul between these opposing forces. One must choose the right as directed by Ahura Mazda in order to attain the highest of the heavenly abodes.

Fravashi

The concept of the *fravashi* in Zoroastrianism is not totally clear. Originally it seems to have been a guardian angel which watched over a person. Over time, the concept developed to the degree that it could be construed as a premortally existent human essence or spirit which enters mortality with a person

and exists after death. In a word, its later form could be compared to the Latter-day Saint understanding of a person's eternal spirit, which lived a pre-earth life, lives in mortality, and enters a spirit life to await the time of resurrection.

The fravashi may be represented artistically in the *farohar,* the universal symbol of Zoroastrianism. This composite creature has a man's head and face, two wings, a bird's tail, and two hands. The right hand is raised in blessing and the left hand holds a ring representing authority. The head represents the fact that each soul has free will and can make choices, while the wings are symbolic of the soul's ability to progress.

Mortal Creation

Only the spiritual creation of man is dealt with in the Zoroastrian literature (Yasna 30–31). In the Gathas, there is only a passing reference to the corporeal body being given special shape by God. Similarly, there is no account of a garden of Eden or of a fall through the breaking of divine commandments. In contrast to the biblical account, knowledge of good and evil is never withheld but is required of humanity, so that they may be able to choose the righteous path (see Yasna 30:2, quoted above). As explained in the Gathas, ignorance was the cause of humanity's fall, not the desire for knowledge.

GAYOMART, THE PRIMAL MAN. *Gayomart* is the first father or prototype of the human race. He is the son of Ahura Mazda and the Earth, but he is not the first man in the sense of being the first recognizably corporeal human being with arms and legs and other distinctively human features. He gives life to the first human couple, the lineal parents of mankind.

MASHYE AND MASHYANE, THE FIRST MORTAL PARENTS. The seed of the dying Gayomart fell into his mother, the Earth, and in due course the first human couple, *Mashye* and *Mashyane,* arose from her in the form of a rhubarb plant. Later they separated and assumed fully human form.

It was intended that Mashye and Mashyane live on the earth without eating food, and they remained on earth for thirty days without taking nourishment of any kind. Only then did they succumb to the temptations of Az, the demon of greed, and venture to try a little goat's milk; but after drinking it they complained that they felt ill. Next they slaughtered an animal (either an ox or a sheep) and roasted it on a fire. They made clothing of skins, then wove a rug and other cloth in order to fabricate more clothing.[19]

From the time of Mashye and Mashyane, humanity has been intended to choose the good over the evil and thus combat the influence of Angra Mainyu in the world while worshiping and serving Ahura Mazda. These purposes form the basis for the important ceremonies in the lives of Zoroastrians, as well as their day-to-day practice of the faith.

Death and the Disposal of the Body

Death is the realm of Angra Mainyu, and therefore anything that bears the character of death is polluting and is to be avoided. The Zoroastrian mode of dealing with the dead is unique among the major world religions and is deeply rooted in the view of the sanctity of God's good creations. Since death is a result of Angra Mainyu's activity, a corpse is unclean. That impurity should not contaminate earth, fire, or water, all of which are good creations of Ahura Mazda. Consequently, cremation, burial, or submersion of a body are not possibilities for the Zoroastrians, and another method has been developed.

When Zoroastrians near death, a priest is called to hear their confessions, for Zoroastrians should die with a prayer on their lips. Once death occurs, the corpse is washed and dressed in clean but old clothing and then carried to the funeral grounds. The body is placed in a special house in which a fire burns and a dog is present to ward off evil spirits. When funeral preparations are complete, the body is taken to a nearby tower of silence (dakhma). The face of the deceased is uncovered to give the family a final look before the body is carried into the dakhma, which is open to the sky. The shroud over the body is then opened, the pallbearers leave, and the relatives pray nearby while vultures remove all flesh from the body, a process that takes about thirty minutes. Later, after the bones have dried in the sun, they are placed in a central hollow in the dakhma to deteriorate further.

Since the Zoroastrian community is diminishing in size and its members are sometimes widely dispersed, a dakhma is not always readily available, and other forms of dealing with the dead have had to be found. Burial is now an alternative, but the body must be placed in a lead-lined coffin to prevent contamination of the earth.

Dead matter may include a number of things besides a corpse, including some which result from the processes of the living body—for instance, spittle,

urine, feces, cut nails and hair, and blood. All of these are potentially polluting and must be disposed of properly. Because spent breath is also considered to be dead matter, a priest in a fire temple will wear a mask over his nose and mouth while ministering at the fire altar to prevent contamination of the sacred fire.

Life after Death[20]

The Gathas, or earliest scriptures of Zoroastrianism, do not provide a clear picture of life after death, but the Later Avesta contains passages explicitly describing how the spirit (urvan) of a departed person "is believed to hover near its earthly tenement, in confidence or in fear, for three days and three nights before it passes [on the fourth day] to the individual judgment."[21] After the spirit of a righteous person departs its body, it takes its place at the head of the body, chanting sacred hymns and anticipating the happiness that Ahura Mazda will give the blessed. The spirit of a wicked person crouches in dread of the approaching judgment.

From Sassanian times (226–541 C.E.), it has been customary to keep a bright fire constantly burning during these three days near the place where the body of the deceased is laid. The spirit of the righteous, while seeing the body inert and devoid of feeling, is nonetheless filled with great joy, being confident of attaining to the Best Existence. The spirit is certain of the Final Renovation, when life shall once more be united with the flesh, when the body and the spirit shall be joined at the time of the Resurrection. The spirit of a wicked individual has no such unqualified assurance.

The Gathas emphasize the fact that the deceased's conscience will decide the destiny of the spirit. At the end of the third night after death, when the dawn appears, the spirit of a righteous person seems to be in a luxuriant garden with beautiful plants, breathing the pleasant fragrances of a breeze from the south, when a beautiful maiden appears. In the case of a wicked person, a hag arrives on a chill north wind laden with sickening smells. The maiden and the hag are manifestations of the conscience of the deceased, whether it be good or evil.

The Gathas indicate that the beautiful maiden conducts the spirit of the righteous to the Judgment Seat at the *Chinvat* Bridge—that is, the Bridge of Judgment (or Separation)—which has been created by Ahura Mazda as the reckoning place where both the righteous and the wicked must cross on the way either to felicity or to damnation. Pavry concludes that the Judge or Separator at the bridge is Ahura Mazda, assisted by the Amesha Spentas.[21] According to the Later Avesta writings, the spirits of the wicked are dragged to the Chinvat Bridge by the demon Vizaresha, where they are judged by a triad of heavenly judges: *Mithra* (the most important), Sraosha, and Rashnu. (In the Later Avesta, Mithra, a pre-Zarathustrian Indo-Iranian deity, personifies the sun's light and is described as the angel of truth.) This is the first judgment, or the first separation of the righteous from the wicked; the ultimate great general judgment takes place later. Zarathustra also plays a role, both at this interim judgment and at the last judgment.

Saoshyant

Zoroastrianism has a strong doctrine of the resurrection of the dead, in which body and spirit are literally reunited. The figure who will usher in the Resurrection is known as *Saoshyant,* which name may be translated as "redeemer" or "savior." Saoshyant is a literal offspring of Zarathustra who will be miraculously conceived and born of a virgin three thousand years after Zarathustra's death. His mission will be to conquer Angra Mainyu and all his evil forces, raise the dead and summon them to be judged, and institute a reign of peace under Ahura Mazda.

One Zoroastrian teaching relative to the coming of Saoshyant that is of some special interest to Jews and Christians is that, at his coming, the earth will again be made flat and become one great plain. This belief is paralleled by the teachings of the prophet Isaiah, who wrote concerning the coming of the biblical Messiah:

> Prepare ye the way of the Lord, make straight in the desert a highway for our God. Every valley shall be exalted, and every mountain and hill shall be made low: and the crooked shall be made straight, and the rough places plain: And the glory of the Lord shall be revealed, and all flesh shall see it together. (Isa. 40:3–5)

The Final Judgment

The Zoroastrian view of the final judgment holds that there will ultimately be universal salvation. Once the dead are raised, they will be subjected to a bath of molten metal which will feel like warm milk to the righteous but will be excruciatingly painful to the wicked. However, after all evil is burned from the wicked, they, along with the righteous, will inherit some degree of salvation. Only Angra Mainyu and his angels, who are totally evil, will be completely eradicated in the sea of molten metal and thus be destroyed.

Scriptures

The surviving sacred books of Zoroastrianism are known as the Avesta. They comprise (1) the Yasna, containing the Gathas, the songs or hymns, which are ascribed to Zarathustra himself; (2) the *Yashts,* or sacrificial hymns, addressed to various deities (in the Yashts is found a polytheism which is very similar to the Rig Veda—a polytheism against which Zarathustra rebelled); and (3) the *Vendidad,* the law against demons, which is a treatise dealing mainly with ritual impurity and in which the dualism initiated by Zarathustra is carried to great lengths in the sphere of practical life.

The Gathas were the earliest part of the Avesta. They are hymns or psalms similar to the verses of the Hindu Vedas. There are seventeen of them in all. The style of expression is very lofty and the ideas are abstract in character, so that interpretation of some of the passages is difficult.

Books added to the Avesta in periods after Zarathustra—known as the Later Avesta—are preponderantly concerned with the end of time. They deal much more with principles than with details. The books of the Later Avesta differ greatly in themes and style. They may be regarded as contemporaneous with the Achaemenian rule (651–558 B.C.E.) in Persia. Still later writings, the Pahlavi books, belong mainly to the Sassanian period (226–541 C.E.), when Zoroastrianism enjoyed both material prosperity and a spiritual revival.

Women and Family Life

Although Zoroastrian society is patriarchal and patrilineal, women, children, and family life are highly valued and very important in the faith. Both men and women may enter freely into the practice of the religion, though in different roles; for example, while only men officiate as priests at the fire temples, women may assist them in the ceremonies in various capacities. Children are to be taught and prepared to take part in the battle against Angra Mainyu and his forces of evil on the earth.

Navjote

Navjote is the public ceremony of initiation into the Zoroastrian faith and fills a role much like that of the bar or bat mitzvah within Judaism. Young persons, at some time between ages seven and fifteen, pass through this ceremony. As they sit barefoot before a bowl of fire, clothed in white, priests chant sacred texts and then present them with a sleeveless undershirt known as a *sudre*. In the front of the sudre is a pocket to be filled symbolically throughout life with good thoughts, good words, and good deeds. At the Final Judgment, the content of a person's life will be judged based on these three values. In addition, the initiates receive a woven woolen hollow cord called a *kusti* which is tied around the waist, symbolic of being girded with faith. A Christian, learning of this ritual, cannot help recalling Paul's admonition in Ephesians 6:11 to "[p]ut on the whole armour of God[.]" The sudre and the kusti are to be worn day and night throughout the initiate's life. After receiving the two sacred emblems, the initiate is washed and then recites the principles of the faith, thus being endowed to face life as a full member of the community.

Marriage

Marriage is a sacred act in Zoroastrianism.[23] Couples are united for life, and only one wife at a time is permitted. A good wife is considered indispensable:

A woman who is willing to give happiness to her husband and who likes to walk on the path of gladness, who takes care of the household and keeps her body pure, such a woman makes a good wife.[24]

A practice of close-kinship marriages has developed, particularly as numbers dwindle and there are fears that permitting people to convert to Zoroastrianism might contaminate an already threatened faith. Thus, cousins and even brothers and sisters may marry.

Traditionally, it was proper for a girl to marry at age fifteen, but one as young as twelve might select her own husband and tell her parents about her choice. Today girls may marry much later, but they are still expected to have a dominant role in the selection of a husband. Parents participate in the process as guides and go-betweens, carrying out conversations with prospective in-laws. The marriage ceremony may occur in any of a variety of places—a courtyard, a large room in a fire temple, a

hotel, or the bride's home. It takes place on a raised platform, with the bride and groom sitting on two chairs facing one another. A cord is passed around them, binding them together, and a curtain is raised between them, which when dropped is the signal for them to throw rice at each other. The ceremony concludes with a priest's blessing.

Sexuality

Sexual expression is to occur within the bonds of marriage and is a sacred act preceded and followed by prayers and ablutions. The primary way of fighting Angra Mainyu is through bringing righteous children into the world. Consequently, anything that thwarts this purpose is forbidden. Any sexual expression in which semen is wasted is abhorrent, and thus homosexuality and adultery are considered gross sins. Relations with a prostitute are entirely forbidden, for such acts would involve a mingling of a believer and an unbeliever.

As in many other religious cultures, a woman during her menstrual period is considered a source of impurity because of the flow of blood. This does not imply anything immoral about her condition; she is simply the unfortunate victim of an attack by Angra Mainyu and is therefore required to separate herself temporarily from people, including her family. During this period of time, she lives in a separate room and uses separate clothing and utensils. She is not permitted to go to the temple, approach the fire altar, or come into contact with priests during her period.

Prayer

The single most powerful weapon in defeating the evil influence of Angra Mainyu is prayer. Zoroastrians are expected to pray five times a day to fulfill their mission of opposing evil with good. Before praying, a Zoroastrian will perform a ritual washing, for physical and spiritual purity are connected. Besides the five daily prayers, prayer is said before all important events in life, including worship at the fire temple.

CHALLENGES WITHIN ZOROASTRIANISM TODAY[25]

As mentioned at the beginning of this chapter, Zoroastrianism has remained an essentially unified religion in spite of a history of oppression and geographical division of the community. Thousands of Zoroastrians were living in Persia when Muslim Arabs conquered that country in the seventh century. They were persecuted and some were forced to convert; even today, Zoroastrians in Iran are sometimes known by the Muslim pejorative term *Gabar*. But others emigrated to the Indian subcontinent, where they became known as the *Parsis* ("Persians"), these eventually becoming the largest group of Zoroastrians in the world.

Those Zoroastrians who moved to Bombay eventually established a comfortable working relationship with the British, serving as a bridge between the British rulers and the local population. Several were knighted, and others became excellent business people who made large fortunes and served their communities well. Inevitably, North America became an enticement to Zoroastrians with its offer of technological advancements, as well as its economic and artistic opportunities. For example, Zubin Mehta, the well-known conductor, and Persis Khambatta, the actress, are Zoroastrians. But it is such talented and educated people as these, removed from the homeland of their religion, who have begun to create tensions within the religious community. The Zoroastrians "in exile" have begun to question the authority of the older community.

But unlike the insular communities in Iran and India, where each generation could absorb the faith by osmosis, in the United States families are isolated in suburban homes and are facing the same dilemma other minority ethnic or religious groups have encountered here—how not to lose their unique identity in the solvent of American mass culture.

Zoroastrianism today seems to be surviving in a twilight zone. The current internal battle among members over identity—whether one can be counted among the faithful only through birth, bloodline, and tradition, or whether one can be so numbered through conversion from outside communities—has become the bellwether of a number of large issues now facing the membership.

The controversy in part centers around navjote, the ritual initiation to the faith. Who may receive the navjote ceremony in today's changing world? Who is admissible for membership? It is precisely these questions that were debated at the Fifth North American Zoroastrian Congress meetings in Los Angeles in the early fall of 1985 and that have continued to grip the attention of Zoroastrians worldwide.

Traditionally, Zoroastrianism was a patrilineal religion, and one had to be the child of a Zoroastrian father in order to receive navjote. But then a so-called liberal group of Zoroastrian priests performed the ceremony in New York for Joseph Peterson, a native Minnesotan who is well versed in Zoroastrianism. This sparked widespread disagreement not only among members in the United States, but in Iran and India as well, and at a time when Zoroastrianism was already in decline.

There are 115,000 Zoroastrians remaining in the world today; 7,000 of them live in North America. With low population replacement rates and with intermarriage and singleness on the rise, one would think new blood would be welcomed. But Zoroastrian traditionalists evidently are convinced that it is precisely because the community is so fragile that they must draw the line. Conversions, they feel, would only dilute the religion's traditional ethnic-cultural strength at a time when it can least afford it. The opposition maintains that Zoroastrianism began as a creedal religion, preached to all who would listen, and only later evolved into an exclusively ethnic faith.

This debate is being watched carefully by those interested in religion. Phillip Lopate observes that

the West has long had a subterranean crush on Zoroastrianism, from the classical period onward. Zarathustra . . . was viewed romantically if misguidedly as a great magus; the Enlightenment philosophes Diderot and Voltaire sought out Zoroastrianism as an alternative to Christianity; later, the romantic poets Wordsworth, Byron and Goethe praised the prophet's animistic reverence for all living things.[26]

Such opinions have caused a faith that is relatively small in numbers to maintain a visible presence among the religions familiar in today's world.

LATTER-DAY SAINT REFLECTIONS

According to Ellis Rasmussen, a specialist on ancient Near Eastern religions and former dean of religious education at Brigham Young University, those who know the restored gospel of Jesus Christ can see significant commonalities between the Zoroastrian and Latter-day Saint faiths.[27] Others have also said as much. But finding parallels has been easier than finding explanations for the parallels. James Whitehurst of Illinois Wesleyan University, for example, has identified an interesting and useful list of similarities—similarities remarkable enough to lead him to speculate that the ancient Jewish mystical movement, the Kabbalah, might have preserved "those unique Zoroastrian thought forms that were forced underground during the earliest Christian centuries."[28]

While the above perhaps does not address the root of similarities adequately, Zoroastrianism's historic connections with the Bible are real and have not escaped the general attention of scholars of religion, nor of those who find inspiration in the scriptures and joy in considering God's dealings with his children. Robert Hume states that, of all the nonbiblical religions, Zoroastrianism has the closest connections with the world view of the Bible. Although Zoroastrianism is not mentioned by name in the Bible, Hume notes that the kings of Persia (Artaxerxes, Darius, Cyrus, Ahasuerus), most if not all of whom were Zoroastrians, are mentioned in eight books of the Old Testament (see 2 Chron. 36:22–23; Ezra 1:1, 8:1; Neh. 2:1; Esther 1:2, 10:2; Isa. 44:28, 45:1; Dan. 9:1, 10:1, 11:1; Hag. 1:1; and Zech. 1:1). In addition, the book of Matthew in the New Testament reports that "[among] the very first persons who came to see the newborn Jesus were certain wise men from the East, Magi, who may be identified as priests of Zoroastrianism."[29] Rasmussen observes that "it may have been the Magi of Zoroastrianism who perceived by some manner of revelation from the heavens that a miracle child was born in Judea to be a king and who came to worship him."[30]

Zoroastrians are also unique in being the only members of other religions mentioned in the Bible that are commended rather than condemned by the Lord. Cyrus is referred to by Jehovah as his "anointed" and "my shepherd," an instrument in his hands for performing his will (Isa. 45:1; 44:28).[31] Zoroastrian leaders repeatedly influenced the course of Old Testament events. The beautiful and faithful Esther, after whom a book of the Bible is named, married the Zoroastrian king Ahasuerus. This king saved Mordecai and all the Jews from the vengeful actions of Haman and his confederates. In the Jewish faith, this blessing is still celebrated each year in the feast of Purim, one of the major festivals of the Jewish calendar.

As noted above, there are many scholars who see historical contacts between Zoroastrianism and biblical Judaism. This view extends not only to cultural elements, but also to a postulated Zoroastrian impact on the Jewish world view. It is claimed, for example, that had it not been for Zoroastrian contacts, the Jews would not have had conceptions of life after death, resurrection, the duality of good and evil, the devil, angels, and so on. As support for this view, 2 Samuel 24:1 and 1 Chronicles 21:1 are cited. Both these texts deal with an experience of King David, but the 2 Samuel text is preexilic while the 1 Chronicles text is postexilic. In the first we read, "And again the anger of *the Lord* was kindled against Israel, and he moved David against them to say, Go, number Israel and Judah" (emphasis added). In 1 Chronicles, however, "Satan" is substituted for "the Lord." It is argued that there was not a clear distinction in the preexilic period between God as the agent of good and Satan as the agent of evil. Such a dualism supposedly arose out of the Jewish contact with Zoroastrianism in the Babylonian exile and during the Persian period.[32]

Latter-day Saints, however, are not at all surprised that there would be knowledge within Judaism of all these items. Every one of them is part of the plan of salvation which was known prior to this earth life. Every one of them was made known to Adam and then to Noah, from whence they undoubtedly were assimilated by various peoples of the world, albeit somewhat inaccurately at times. Thus, we see that Lehi knew of the opposition in all things (2 Ne. 2:11) and that immortality was known to Moses (Moses 1:39). These are eternal principles. Satan was in the garden of Eden, and from there he was cast out to wander the earth attempting to thwart God's purposes. From the days of Adam it has been known that humanity was that for which Satan and God vied, as they opposed one another. In the end, God will win; but in the meantime a tension exists between good and evil that challenges and stretches humankind. Although all persons must die, they will be resurrected into immortality. Through the interaction of Christ's atonement, the workings of the Holy Ghost, and their own volition, they will enter the realms of either light or darkness. This is Latter-day Saint doctrine, but it is also God's doctrine. It is not derived from cultural contacts but through revelation from the beginning.

However, it cannot be simply assumed that because the plan of salvation with all its attendant parts was revealed in the beginning it was still commonly known and taught in the Old Testament Jewish world. The prophets undoubtedly knew those things mentioned above, but Israel in general may not have been ready to hear or able to heed the higher things of God. It is possible that the Zoroastrians did teach the Jewish exiles something which they should have learned from their own traditions, if they had not ignored or abolished them.

Zoroastrian–Latter-day Saint Resemblances

In the study of world religions, parallels are everywhere and may mean little or nothing. But similarities between the Zoroastrian and Latter-day Saint faiths are wide-ranging. Here are a representative few.

God's Adversary

There was a pre-Zoroastrian figure known as a daeva, which originally indicated "a brightly shining One." He became reidentified in Zoroastrianism as one opposed to God. Zarathustra recast many an ancient divinity as a demonic figure, thereby permitting them to continue to exist in the minds of the people but with a radically redefined role. The obvious counterpart to this Zoroastrian figure in Latter-day Saint thought is Lucifer, whose Hebrew name as given in Isaiah 14:12–15 means "shining son of the dawn." The parallel is clear, but how closely linked the actual figures are will always be open to discussion.[33]

Premortal Existence

In the book of Abraham (3:22–28), there is first a spiritual creation of man, animals, and plants. To mankind in this premortal state God explained his plan for organizing and redeeming the world soon to be physically created. The spiritual beings who were in attendance at this council in heaven included Abraham, a "noble and great one," chosen for leadership even before he was physically born on earth. Another leading spirit, Lucifer, rebelled against the plan and was cast out with his hosts to plague the earth.

The Avesta describes first a spiritual creation, followed by a physical creation. In Zoroastrian doctrine, human beings existed as intelligent spirit persons before being born into this physical world. According to one account, God agreed to give Angra Mainyu—Satan—nine thousand years to persuade the human race to hate the God who had created them and to worship Satan instead. If he and

his followers did not succeed in this aim, they would be destroyed.[34] Hints of this spiritual premortal life are seen in the Bible (Gen. 2:4–5; John 17:5). The doctrine is plainly taught in Moses 3:4–5.

Zoroastrian thought is permeated with the idea that life is a battlefield where humans are called upon to choose sides between good and evil, between Truth and the Lie (note, for example, Yasna 30:3). So, too, among Latter-day Saints dualism is axiomatic: "For it must needs be, that there is an opposition in all things" (2 Ne. 2:11).

When one contrasts Zoroastrian with Latter-day Saint thought on the issue of dualism, there are both similarities and differences. In Zoroastrianism, Ahura Mazda and Angra Mainyu become almost equals in opposition to each other. There is no question of any such equality between God and Satan among Latter-day Saints, for Satan acts only by the permission of God. Satan deludes himself into believing that he has the power to thwart God's ultimate purposes. In Zoroastrianism, Angra Mainyu is the creator of "evil" things such as scorpions, spiders, and cacti. In Latter-day Saint theology, God creates all things, both good and "evil," because some things are in this world for human beings to overcome in order to grow. There is truly a creative opposition in all things for Latter-day Saints. Thus, while there may be superficial similarities between the concepts of good and evil in Zoroastrianism and among Latter-day Saints, a deeper examination reveals that they differ significantly.

Sacred Garments

Zoroastrians, both men and women, traditionally wear the sudre, a white cotton undershirt, with the kusti, a woolen cord tied at the waist. Their purpose, as Whitehurst explains, is

to aid them in their struggle against evil and to symbolize their obedience to the faith. . . . These are put on with prayers and worn constantly, except in times of bathing. They bear no symbolic designs; but there is a pocket for storing good deeds . . . , and the knots used in tying the kusti have accumulated much symbolism.[35]

Such garments are also thought to protect the body from demonic attacks on the occasion of a funeral.[36] Faithful Latter-day Saints also wear sacred undergarments which are believed to bring divine protection and help the wearers to recall commitments and covenants made with God. Both Zoroastrian and

Latter-day Saint members receive these garments in special services at the hands of religious leaders.

Monasticism and Asceticism

Both Latter-day Saints and Zoroastrians disavow monasticism and asceticism. Both groups believe that the body and this physical world are basically good and that humans need active and healthy bodies to struggle against evil.[37] Sexual union, children, and family life are regarded as great blessings. They are among the highest spiritual values, to be thoroughly enjoyed. Latter-day Saints believe that "men are, that they might have joy" (2 Ne. 2:25). In the Zoroastrian view:

Asceticism on the one hand and pure hedonism on the other are extremes and therefore to be avoided. If anything, the former is the worse of the two for it implies an insult to God who made the world and made it good, and who put Man into it to combat evil which can only be achieved by making the world to prosper.[38]

Degrees of Glory

Since there are varying degrees of obedience to the ethical principles and laws given by Heavenly Father or by Ahura Mazda, humans in the life after death do not all receive the same heavenly rewards. But all humanity survives death and in the hereafter will be raised in a physical resurrection. In both Zoroastrian and Latter-day Saint thought the spirit and the body will be reunited, for the body is the garment of the spirit and is necessary for one to experience full personhood.

But what kind of body shall be prepared? For both religions, heaven is a place of individuality, variety, and gradation. Just as there are different levels of

worthiness, there will be different degrees of heavenly light and glory. According to the Avesta, the spirits of the dead attain paradise through the three intermediate stages of good thoughts, good words, and good deeds. In a later tradition (the Sad Dar),

each of these stages is respectively identified with the place of the stars (the nearest to earth!), the moon, and the sun.

What is the reason for this order? It is obvious that the stars, moon, and sun follow each other in the order of increasing light [and increasing glory], and this progression is completed in a . . . final stage, which is the destination point of the soul's journey: one of the names of Paradise is, in fact, Infinite Lights.[39]

For Latter-day Saints, the resurrection from the dead is the salvation of the soul—the inseparable reunion of body and spirit. All humans will be so raised into the state of immortality. There will be three general categories or degrees of glory in the hereafter—the glory of the stars, the telestial; the glory of the moon, the terrestrial; and the glory of the sun, the celestial. Those whose obedience and worthiness entitle them to the highest of the degrees of glory will dwell in endless light; they shall be entitled to dwell with God (D&C 76).

ZOROASTRIANISM, then, has a history, a moral stance, and a body of doctrine that Latter-day Saints can understand and, in large measure, appreciate. In particular, the Zoroastrian view of life as a battle between the forces of good and evil in which all human beings are expected to participate rings true to Latter-day Saints. And the idea that good will triumph at the last is both a rallying cry and a source of comfort for members of both faiths.

Glossary of Zoroastrian Names and Terms

AHURA. Lord.

AHURA MAZDA. Zarathustra's name for God, meaning "Lord of Wisdom"; the supreme deity, the power of good, the creator of the world, the guardian of humankind; also known as Ohrmazd.

AMESHA SPENTAS. "Holy Immortals"; six divine attributes, archangels, or lesser immortal beings who, along with Ahura Mazda, make up the Holy Heptad, the sacred seven. In some Zoroastrian thought, the Amesha Spentas are heavenly beings created by Ahura Mazda and, combined, represent the sevenfold character of God.

ANGRA MAINYU. Zarathustra's name for the destructive spirit, the devil; also known as Ahriman.

ARYANS. A caucasoid branch of the Indo-European family that historically separated into at least two groups, one migrating into Iran and another into India. Some of the Aryans of Iran originated Zoroastrianism, and the intrusive Aryans of India originated Vedic Hinduism.

ASHA. "Order, truth, justice"; the governing principle of the world.

AVESTA. The sacred book of ancient Zoroastrianism. Only a quarter of the original has survived.

AVESTAN. The language of Zarathustra and the Avesta.

CHINVAT. The bridge of judgment which connects this world with the unseen afterlife. After death, it is a means by which people cross between the two. Humans are judged before they cross this bridge.

DAKHMA. Originally, "grave"; later, a walled tower open to the sky where Zoroastrians expose the dead to vultures and crows for disposal of the flesh; sometimes called tower of silence.

FAROHAR. The winged symbol or emblem of Zoroastrianism, the precise meaning of which is open to some question. It is the most commonly used Zoroastrian symbol. The central figure is popularly believed to be either Ahura Mazda or the fravashi.

FRAVASHI. Possibly a guardian spirit, but may also be a spirit which enters this life with a person and continues with him or her beyond death.

GABARS. A pejorative term used by Muslims in Iran for members of the Zoroastrian faith.

GATHAS. Hymns or poems written by Zarathustra; considered to be the most authoritative expressions of the Zoroastrian religion.

GAYOMART. The Primal Man; first progenitor of the human race and father of Mashye and Mashyane.

HAOMA. The sacred plant whose juice is used as an offering in the Yasna.

KUSTI. Literally, "sacred cord"; girdle received by Zoroastrians at navjote and worn at all times. It is untied and retied several times a day to the accompaniment of prayers.

MAGI. The priestly caste of ancient Persia, in time associated with the Zoroastrian priesthood. The singular form, "magus," is the Greek version of the Old Persian word "magu," meaning priest.

MASHYE AND MASHYANE. The first human couple, male and female; the Adam and Eve of Zoroastrian tradition.

MITHRA. A "high god" of pre-Zoroastrian Iran that survived the advent of Zoroastrianism and also continues to have a presence in the Vedas of Hindu literature in India.

NAVJOTE. The public ceremony of initiation into the Zoroastrian faith.

NIRANG. Urine of an ox or bull which has been consecrated by prayer and is used externally for cleansing and drunk for internal purification.

PAHLAVI. Also called Middle Persian; the language of Sassanian and early Islamic times in which later Zoroastrian books are written.

PARSIS. The "Persians" who settled in India in 936 C.E. to seek a land of religious freedom away from oppression in Muslim Iran. Parsis today make up the largest community of Zoroastrians in the world.

SAOSHYANT. The coming Savior; the messiah figure of Zoroastrianism.

SUDRE. A white cotton undershirt worn next to the skin at all times (except when bathing) as a religious symbol of commitment and protection.

URVAN. The spirit or soul of man.

VENDIDAD. "Code against the demons"; a book of purification in the Avesta, read at night in a lengthy ritual.

YASHT. A hymn to Ahura Mazda or some other immortal being. The yashts form an important part of the Avesta.

ZARATHUSTRA. The name of the founder of Zoroastrianism in its original Avestan language form. The Greek form of the name is Zoroaster.

Notes

1. Mary Boyce, *Zoroastrians: Their Religious Beliefs and Practices* (London: Routledge and Kegan Paul, 1979), 1.

2. For this section I have relied almost entirely on ibid., 3–15.

3. See Noel King's foreword to P. D. Mehta, *Zarathushtra: The Transcendental Vision* (Longmead, Engl.: Element Books, 1985), xiii n; Boyce, *Zoroastrians*, 18.

4. Dastur Framroze A. Bode, *Man, Soul, Immortality in Zoroastrianism* (Bombay: n.p., 1960), 7.

5. It is impossible to establish fixed years for Zarathustra's life. The date of his birth is still highly controversial among scholars, who argue that he lived anywhere between 1500 and 583 B.C.E. The conventionally accepted years are from 660 to 583. The traditional date of Zarathustra was fixed in the sixth century B.C.E. so as to correspond with the time of Cyrus the Great and is based upon a stipulation that "the date of Zoroaster" meant the year in which, at the age of forty-two, he converted a king named Vistaspa. The argument hinges upon an acceptance of the idea that Vistaspa, the convert-king who befriended Zarathustra, is the same person as the father of King Darius, whose name was also Vistaspa. See Robert C. Zaehner, *The Teachings of the Magi: A Compendium of Zoroastrian Beliefs*, Ethical and Religious Classics of East and West, no. 14 (London: George Allen and Unwin, 1956), 10–11; T. R. Sethna, *A Review of the Date of Zoroaster . . .* (n.d., n.p.), esp. 2. Other scholars (I have

been influenced here by personal discussions and interviews with Professor Michael Simmons) maintain that there is no historical basis for this conclusion. They posit that the antiquity of the Gatha hymns, authored by Zarathustra, and the structure of their language argue for an earlier date. In addition, they point out that the society pictured by these earliest Zoroastrian writings is pastoral and unsophisticated, not organized and settled as was the case in the later times of Cyrus the Great.

6. Boyce, *Zoroastrians,* 46, 48.

7. Ali A. Jafarey, *The Passing Away of Asho Zarathustra: A Treatise Based on Available Sources in Avesta, Pahlavi, Arabic, and Persian Scriptures* (Teheran: n.p., 1980), 4.

8. James Darmesteter, trans., in F. Max Müller, ed., *The Sacred Books of the East,* 50 vols. (1879–1910; reprint, New Delhi, India: n.p., 1965), 47:153; Robert Ernest Hume, *The World's Living Religions . . . ,* rev. ed. (New York: Charles Scribner's Sons, 1959), 202.

9. Boyce, *Zoroastrians,* 19.

10. Ibid., 31; Hume, *World's Living Religions,* 203–6.

11. Jafarey, *Passing Away,* 5.

12. Boyce, *Zoroastrians,* 19–20.

13. The translations of the Zoroastrian scriptures used herein are those of S. Insler, in *The Gathas of Zarathustra,* vol. 1 of Textes et mémoires, 3d series of *Acta Iranica: Encyclopédie permanente des études iraniennes . . .* (Teheran: Bibliothèque Pahlavi, 1975).

14. Boyce, *Zoroastrians,* 22–23.

15. Mary Boyce, A *Persian Stronghold of Zoroastrianism* (Oxford, Engl.: At the Clarendon Press, 1977), 61.

16. Boyce, *Zoroastrians,* 20.

17. Ilya Gershevitch, "Zoroaster's Own Contribution," *Journal of Near Eastern Studies* 23, no. 1 (January 1964): 12.

18. Boyce, *Zoroastrians,* 30.

19. Zaehner, *Teachings of the Magi,* 77.

20. This section is based primarily upon Jal Dastur Cursetji Pavry, *The Zoroastrian Doctrine of a Future Life: From Death to the Individual Judgment,* 2d ed., Columbia University Indo-Iranian Series, vol. 11 (New York: AMS Press, 1965).

21. Ibid., 9.

22. Pavry, *Zoroastrian Doctrine,* 56.

23. Comments here on marriage are based on John R. Hinnells, *Zoroastrianism and the Parsis* (London: Ward Lock Educational, 1981), 44–48.

24. Firoze M. Kotwal and James W. Boyd, eds. and trans., *A Guide to the Zoroastrian Religion: A Nineteenth-Century Catechism with Modern Commentary* (Chico, Calif.: Scholars Press, 1982), 127. For more on the many restrictions and taboos associated with marriage, childbirth, widowhood, and remarriage, see 125–37.

25. In preparing this section I have generally drawn upon Phillip Lopate's article, "Zoroaster in the New World," *New York Times Magazine,* October 19, 1986, pp. 82–85, 100–101.

26. Ibid., 84.

27. Ellis T. Rasmussen, "Zoroastrianism," *Ensign,* November 1971, 37.

28. James Whitehurst, "The Zoroastrian Connection: Mormon Theology's Persian Roots" (paper delivered at the annual Sunstone Conference, Salt Lake City, 1987; typescript in the possession of Spencer J. Palmer), 15.

29. See Hume, *World's Living Religions,* 199.

30. Rasmussen, "Zoroastrianism," 38.

31. Hume, *World's Living Religions,* 199–200.

32. Ibid., 200; Lewis M. Hopfe, *Religions of the World,* 6th ed. (New York: Macmillan College Publishing, 1994), 259.

33. Rasmussen, "Zoroastrianism," 37.

34. Robert C. Zaehner, *Zurvan: A Zoroastrian Dilemma* (Oxford, Engl.: Oxford University Press, 1955), 132.

35. Whitehurst, "Zoroastrian Connection," 4. See also Boyce, *Zoroastrians,* 31–32; Jacques Duchesne-Guillemin, *Symbols and Values in Zoroastrianism: Their Survival and Renewal* (New York: Harper and Row, Harper Torch Books, 1970), 50.

36. Whitehurst, "Zoroastrian Connection," 18n.

37. Ibid., 5.

38. Zaehner, *Teachings of the Magi,* 99.

39. Duchesne-Guillemin, *Symbols and Values,* 139.

Moses

Judaism

10

Roger R. Keller

O this point, it has been relatively easy for students to take an objective view of the religions under examination in this text because they have few Latter-day Saint presuppositions about the content of the religions, some of which may have been totally new to them. However, Judaism—or at least the Old Testament as it is used within Judaism—evokes numerous preconceived notions among Latter-day Saints. Those notions must be laid aside, permitting Jewish people to speak without interruption for themselves and for their beliefs. At the end of this chapter, as in all the other chapters, the time will come to reflect on the similarities and differences between traditional Jewish views on the issues of life and those held by Latter-day Saints. Until that time, however, all prior understandings of Jewish beliefs must be held in abeyance as students seek to hear what Jews themselves believe.

HISTORICAL BACKGROUND

Judaism is one of the oldest religions on the face of the earth, originating in the area which runs from Mesopotamia in the east to Egypt in the west. It arose in a region fraught with polytheistic religions. The Sumerians had their nature deities: Anu, the sky; Enlil, the air; Enki, water; and Ninhursag, the earth.[1] Among the Canaanites were found the chief god El, a distant father figure and creator; Baal, his son, strong and involved in a constant battle with chaos; and Astarte, Baal's consort and the goddess of love and fertility. There were also many other Canaanite gods.[2] To the west the Egyptians worshiped over time a number of divine figures: Atum, chief of the gods, as well as Shu, Tefnut, Geb, and Nut, who were associated with the elements of the natural world. In addition were Osiris, god of the dead; Isis, associated with fertility; and Horus, the

god of upper and lower Egypt. As with the Canaanites, there were also many other gods.[3] It is within this milieu of multiple deities, many of whom were associated with nature and fertility, that the fathers of Judaism wandered. It is into this context that they injected the concept that there is one God—not many.

FOUNDING AND INFLUENTIAL FIGURES

Abraham

Numerous historical figures have contributed to Jewish life and thought, but the story begins with the patriarch Abraham. Upon this all Jews agree. Abraham, whose name is given initially as Abram, was from Ur, a city located on the Euphrates River in the south of the area known as Mesopotamia. Probably early in the second millennium B.C.E., he moved with his family far to the north to Haran and was then called by God to leave Haran with its pagan worship and journey to a land which God would show him (Gen. 12:1). Abram responded, because he recognized behind this call the voice of the true Creator. He had found the God who expected moral behavior from his people, the God who in himself was just, righteous, and loving.

Along with the promise of a land, God also promised Abram that he would be the father of a great people and that through them he would be a blessing to many nations (Gen. 12:2–3). The mark of that covenant was circumcision. In obedience to God, Abram instituted this practice and, as a result, his name was changed to Abraham ("Father of many people"). To signify her participation in the covenant also, his wife Sarai's name was changed to Sarah. Unfortunately, however, Sarah was barren and it appeared that she would never have children. As a consequence, she gave her maid, Hagar, to Abraham, so that they might have offspring (Gen. 16:1–16). From that union came Ishmael, the father of the Arab peoples.

Ultimately, Sarah did conceive and bore Isaac; but God tested Abraham and commanded him to sacrifice his son to him. Abraham prepared to comply, even though to all outward appearances this would mean the end of the covenant. As Abraham was about to kill Isaac, the Lord stopped him and provided a ram as a substitutionary sacrifice. As a result of Abraham's faithfulness, Jews understand that the covenant promises of posterity and of being a blessing to the nations were renewed (Gen. 22:17–18). The covenant was then carried through Abraham's son Isaac, through Isaac's son Jacob (Israel), and finally through Jacob's twelve sons.

According to later Jewish traditions found in the *Talmud,* Abraham observed all God's commandments, lived in harmony with God's oral law before it was given at Sinai, was the father of all proselytes because he converted so many persons himself, and received the priesthood in the tradition of Melchizedek.[4] It was this man who is the father of the Jewish people.

Moses, the Lawgiver

The descendants of Abraham lived in Canaan and its environs, finally settling in Egypt following the great famine at the time of Joseph, son of Jacob. After many years in Egypt, Abraham's descendants were enslaved, and their deliverance from slavery begins the next stage of the Jewish covenantal history, for the covenant made with Abraham and his descendants would be ratified by God at Mount Sinai.

It was in the exodus from Egypt and at Sinai that Israel was constituted as a people before God. God's agent in that covenant ratification was Moses. Through Moses the loosely knit tribes of Israel were hammered into a free people who were servants to no one but the one God, Jehovah. In that relationship they were called to live a higher moral law than their neighbors, as defined in the laws given to Moses by God at Sinai. The laws— 613 in all—are complex, encompassing not only all aspects of daily life but also the ritual life of God's covenant people.

As a result of receiving the law, the people of Israel were not to be like other people. Their lives were to testify to God's presence in the world. They were to be a holy nation and a kingdom of priests (Exod. 19:6)—examples of holiness. This holiness would be reflected as they lived the commandments of God both in the cultic realm and in the realm of human relations.[5]

Because he was the one who received the *Torah* from God, Moses' stature within Judaism is great. However, he was human and not to be confused with the divine. Even after all that he did in leading the people out of Egypt and establishing the covenant law, he did not enter the promised land. Yet, to the *rabbis,* Moses was generally seen as "Moses our Master," meaning *the* teacher of the Torah.[6] Jews understand Moses to have received at Mount Sinai not only the written Torah but also the oral Torah, which includes the *Mishnah,* the *Talmud,* the *Aggadah* (traditions), and all interpretations that any future student of these might have revealed to him.[7] Jews hold that, for all his greatness, Moses was not nearly as important as that which he delivered: the laws of God which defined the lives of the people of God from his day to the present.

As a summary to the Jewish position on the place of the law in religious life, the novelist Herman Wouk states, "Tradition says the Creator gave our folk the task of bearing witness to the moral law on earth."[8] In the end, it is the way a Jew lives his or her life that really counts. Orthodoxy, or right belief, is not nearly as important as orthopraxy, or right practice, which extends to and includes "right living."

The Prophets

The prophets are not founders within Judaism. They are the persons who applied and extended the revelation at Sinai into the new historical situations which the people of Israel encountered in their historical wanderings. Men like Isaiah, Jeremiah, and Ezekiel spoke God's word to their contemporaries, but it was not a new word. It was the same word spoken at Sinai. That word in every generation called people to remember who they were, and it explained God's continuing historical acts, often in the face of Israelite disobedience to and desertion of God. The messages of the prophets helped Israel make sense out of what appeared to be historical disasters. Through the prophets, God's hand was seen in the Assyrian and Babylonian invasions. Through a prophet like Ezra, God reestablished his covenant with the people after the exile in Babylon.

In reality, the prophets set the pattern for Jewish survival across the centuries, for they taught Israel that the revelation at Sinai could be applied to any new situation—be it the dispersion in 70 C.E., the ghettoes of Europe, the *pogroms* of Russia, the Holocaust of the twentieth century, or the building of a third commonwealth in the land of Israel.

The Rabbis

Since both the written and oral Torah are believed to have been given to Moses at Sinai, and since the prophets were not speaking a new word not found in the original revelation, the role of the rabbis is simply an extension of the prophetic role. With the exile to Babylon, the Jews faced a new life without the temple or the land of Israel. Under the guidance of Ezekiel, study of the law and prayer replaced the temple services. The synagogue was instituted, becoming primarily a place of study. The commandments found in Deuteronomy 6:6–7 became institutionalized in the synagogue in Babylon and were reemphasized by Ezra following the return to the land:

And these words, which I command thee this day, shall be in thine heart: And thou shalt teach them diligently unto thy children, and shalt talk of them when thou sittest in thine house, and when thou walkest by the way, and when thou liest down, and when thou risest up. (Deut. 6:6–7)

Thus, as Judaism came out of the exile and moved closer to the common era, the responsibility for learning about the faith, particularly among the Pharisees, became an individual act of piety which was not dependent upon the priestly class. Consequently, when the temple was destroyed in 70 C.E. and the Jews were banned from Jerusalem following the Bar Kochba rebellion (132–135 C.E.), the structures were already in place to meet the crises. The carriers of the traditions were the rabbis, who studied the written and oral law and who filled a role similar to that of the prophets of old by interpreting for the people the once-for-all revelation of Sinai in a new environment. Consequently, the rabbis of today bring the revelation of Sinai into the present day, just as Isaiah, Jeremiah, Ezekiel, and Ezra brought it into their days.[9] In this sense, the rabbis too must be considered foundational to the Jewish faith.

BASIC BELIEFS

God

"Hear, O Israel: The Lord our God is one Lord" (Deut. 6:4). So states what is known as the *Shema*, the basic confession of faith of Judaism. The God of Abraham, Isaac, and Jacob, who met Moses in the burning bush, who led Israel out of Egypt, is the one and only God, and it is this God alone whom Israel worships.

Israel's God is a personal God—a God who hears and answers prayer, who calls and elects a people, who loves by giving his revelation to them on Sinai, and who is constantly active in the history of his elect people. He is not a God above history and separated from people. He is, in fact, a God who moves in history and guides his people through both his judgments and his mercy. His personality is expressed by biblical authors either by stating his roles—King, Judge, Father, Shepherd, Healer, Redeemer—or by stating his attributes.[10] Exodus 34:6–7 says:

And the Lord passed by before him, and proclaimed, The Lord, The Lord God, [is] merciful and gracious, longsuffering, and abundant in goodness and truth, Keeping mercy for thousands, forgiving iniquity and transgression and sin, and that will by no means clear the guilty; visiting the iniquity of the fathers upon the children, and upon the children's children, unto the third and to the fourth generation.

While God is incomparable, omniscient (all-knowing), omnipotent (all-powerful), omnipresent (everywhere present), and invisible, he may still be recognized through his works of creation and his works in history. Isaiah, for example, ties these two themes together when he says:

Have ye not known? have ye not heard? hath it not been told you from the beginning? have ye not understood from the foundations of the earth? It is he that sitteth upon the circle of the earth, and the inhabitants thereof are as grasshoppers; that stretcheth out the heavens as a curtain, and spreadeth them out as a tent to dwell in: That bringeth the princes to nothing; he maketh the judges of the earth as vanity (Isa. 40:21–23).

It is this God of creation that brought about Israel's destruction in 722 B.C.E. and Judah's in 586 B.C.E., both at the hands of foreign and pagan armies who worked at his command. He could do this because he has a unique and special relationship with his people—a relationship of election and covenant that, when broken, brings heightened culpability to these same people (Amos 3:1–2). Sin they may, and punished they will be; but in the end the promise to Abraham that his descendants would bless the nations will be fulfilled through the people whom God has chosen to be his light in the world (Jer. 3:17–18).

Thus, in Jewish faith, God stands above all the things he has created, including humans, who are relational beings like himself. The human being is the crown of all God's creative activity. It is even on account of this human creature that God willingly limits himself by providing freedom of will to humanity. They can turn from God; but even in the face of disobedience, God's purposes for creation and human history will come to fruition and completion. He will bring about a new heaven and a new earth (Isa. 66:22), and human beings will ultimately be given a new heart (Ezek. 36:26–27). In the end, God is in control. Humanity may have finite understanding, but all that occurs fits into a divine scheme which is wholly known to God.

Human Beings

Human beings are the crown of God's creation, as noted above. They are created in the image of God—not in resemblance of a physical image, but rather bearing the traits of the divine. They are capable of reasoning, of creativity, and of relationships. It is this last that most clearly distinguishes humans from the beasts. Humans can commune with God and enjoy their relationship with him (Gen. 2–3). As relational beings, they are co-participants with him in his activity in the world.[11] In addition, Jewish tradition holds that only humans were formed directly by God. Their likeness to God is further emphasized by their lordship over the earth and its creatures, a role that is similar to God's lordship over the universe.

Humanity is composed of males and females. In many ways they are the same: they each have free will, and each is a moral being, but each stands in a tension between what the rabbis called the good inclinations and the evil inclinations.[12] Jews hold that, as a result of free will, the first persons of the race, Adam and Eve, rebelled against God, and their original virtue was lost. However, their descendants still stand before God at the crossroads between good and evil. They must choose between the law of God and the law of the world.

For all their commonalities, there are differences between men and women. According to some rabbis, women, because they are made from the durable substance of Adam's rib, are better able to deal with difficulties and pain than are men. In addition, they are more innately intelligent and thus mature more quickly in their ability to arrive at opinions. On the other hand, women are more prone to tears and have a propensity for lesser traits of character, such as arrogance, eavesdropping, meddling, and flitting about. Men tend to be more hospitable than women and more ready to be reconciled when differences occur.[13] Be that as it may, men and women stand equally before God and are incomplete without one another.

The Torah

The Torah is often misunderstood by those outside Judaism, largely because the word has been translated as "law." In reality, the Torah is dynamic and living, not static and cold. A better translation of the word Torah would be "teaching" or "instruction." Generally, the Torah is identified with the Pentateuch, or the first five books of what Christians call the Old Testament. It is believed that God gave the Torah to Israel to make her a kingdom of priests and a holy nation (Exod. 19:6). The Torah was, however, in two parts—a written portion and an oral portion.[14] Both were received by Moses at Mount Sinai. The oral Torah was for the purpose of explaining the written Torah. For example, what does it mean to keep the Sabbath day holy? The answers to that question were contained in the oral Torah, which was passed down in conjunction with the written Torah.

Contained within the oral Torah was the information which would enable Israel to adapt to new historical situations as they occurred. Thus, the living character of the Torah becomes evident. It was this adaptability of the Torah that enabled the Jews to survive the exile in 586 B.C.E., the destruction of the temple in 70 C.E., and the various other challenges they have faced over the centuries.

While there has been much rabbinic thought related to the Torah, Hillel probably best summed up its essence: "What is hateful to you, do not to your fellow."[15] The Torah, therefore, deals not only with humanity's relationship to God, but of equal import is humanity's relationship to itself. Consequently, while there are numerous laws dealing with ritual issues which concern the Jews' relationship to God, much of the Torah is concerned with interpersonal relationships between people. It is concerned with civil issues, criminal issues, health problems, marital issues, and dietary rules. These became expanded as discussions among the rabbis ensued. Thus, from the Torah has sprung all of Jewish life and practice. The following of the guidelines found within the Torah creates within a Jew a disciplined life, oriented toward both God and humanity.

The Messiah

The Jewish concept of the Messiah ("anointed one") has always been that of a human being reigning over an earthly kingdom. It has been suggested that it arose in three stages. The first grew out of God's promise to David that there would be an unbroken line of his descendants who would rule Israel. The second was to look for a ruler who would reunite a divided Israel and extend Israel's control over the neighboring lands. The third stage was to move from a stress on a Davidic dynasty to one which highlighted the qualities of the king, particularly the quality of justice. However the Messiah was defined, he was always God's agent.[16] Rabbinic thought further defined the Messiah's role:

The Messiah was expected to attain for Israel the idyllic blessings of the prophets; he was to defeat the enemies of Israel, restore the people to the Land, reconcile them with God, and introduce a period of spiritual and physical bliss. He was to be prophet, warrior, judge, king, and teacher of the Torah.[17]

The Jewish understanding of the Messiah, therefore, is that of a human being who participates in human life and existence. He will establish God's reign on earth.

A Chosen People

The mystery of divine election defines Israel's chosenness. There was nothing inherently superior about the Jewish people; to all outward appearances they were the least of the peoples of the earth. Despite this, God in his grace summoned them to be his witnesses in the world. They are to bear witness

to the one God and his presence in the world, and they are to do it through living disciplined and obedient lives. As Israel continues to exist through all the vicissitudes of its history, its very existence bears witness to God's presence in the world. In living a life different from their neighbors, a life directed and commanded by God, the people of Israel also bear witness to God's presence. It is precisely this that has led to their suffering over the millennia. Where God is present, evil will gather in abundance. Of such the Jewish people can testify. Thus, chosenness is a vocation, not a status. It is a role required of Israel—a role that can never be shed, for God has chosen his people in perpetuity.[18]

FESTIVALS AND PRACTICES

Jewish ritual life is the way that Jews remember and re-participate in their history with God. Remembrance is not done from a distance; rather, it is accomplished through rituals and festivals which draw worshipers into the very events commemorated. The God of history thus becomes present through commemorative acts. God is present in words, acts, and drama, and for any Latter-day Saint who has experienced the temple endowment there should be immediate empathy for this mode of encountering and worshiping God.

Thus, Jewish life is structured around the festivals. God is held in constant remembrance throughout the week and throughout the year. Each week the Sabbath gives new life to the Jewish people, just as each year the High Holy Days draw the people to an annual self-examination and repentance before God. Religious life needs structure of some sort, and Judaism finds this structure in their festivals and rituals. In this way, the remembrance of God and humanity's dependence upon him is kept ever before the Jewish people.

Major Festivals

Sabbath

"More than Israel has kept the Sabbath, it is the Sabbath that has kept Israel."[19] This statement reflects the centrality of the Sabbath in Jewish life. The Sabbath celebration requires no temples, no priests, no synagogues, and no rabbis. It only requires a family gathered in their home around a table, two candles, two loaves of bread, and, if available, a cup of wine. The Sabbath has been celebrated by Jews in good times and in bad, in Jerusalem and in concentration camps, in times of peace and in the midst of pogroms. Each week the religious Jew looks forward to the coming Sabbath and in the new week looks back to the spiritual strength derived from it. Jews who may be paupers are spiritually elevated on the Sabbath to the status of kings or queens, assuming their natural positions before God for one day each week. The heights of the Sabbath have enabled Jews throughout the centuries to endure the depths of life the remaining six days of the week.

While there are synagogue services on the Sabbath—both on Friday evenings and Saturdays—the heart of the Sabbath lies in the home. According to Jewish tradition, two angels, one evil and one good, accompany a Jew home from the synagogue on Friday night. If the house is bright and cheerful, with the candles lighted and the table laid, the good angel leaves a blessing of happiness on the house, and the evil angel is required to grant a grudging "amen." If, however, the home is not prepared, the evil angel curses the house with a lack of Sabbath joy, and the good angel must give a sorrowful "amen."[20]

The Sabbath is a day of joy, and all work ceases in the household. Since God is encountered through both creation and his historical acts, the Sabbath is a testimony to the presence of God in his world. Consequently, as God rested on the seventh day from his creative activity (Gen. 2:1–3), so the family ceases to labor, as do all servants, visitors, or animals associated with them (Exod. 20:8–11; 23:12; 34:21). Rest was commanded particularly for slaves, for those who had been in bondage themselves should know the need for a day of rest (Deut. 5:14–15).[21] Thus, the Sabbath ties together in the community's remembrance two divine creative events: the creation of the world, and the creation of the Jewish people through the Exodus.[22] Its main effect is to produce release from the world, peace and gaiety in the home, and the lifting of the spirits of those involved in its celebration. In the event of an emergency, however, all restrictive laws are removed until the emergency is past.

The rituals of the Sabbath are simple. First, with the table set, two loaves of Sabbath bread on the table and covered, and a cup of wine at the head of the table, the mistress of the house lights the two Sabbath candles. In her words of blessing, the meaning of the Sabbath is captured.

> Blessed art Thou, O Lord our God, King of the universe, who hast sanctified us by Thy commandments, and commanded us to kindle the Sabbath lights.[23]

A voluntary prayer may be added which gives added explanation of the Sabbath's significance:

> May the Sabbath-light which illumines our dwelling cause peace and happiness to shine in our home. Bless us, O God, on this holy Sabbath, and cause Thy divine glory to shine upon us. Enlighten our darkness and guide us and all mankind, Thy children, towards truth and eternal light. Amen.[24]

After the lighting of the candles, hymns are sung which welcome the Sabbath angels and which praise the mistress of the house in the words of Proverbs 31:10ff. Following this, the father may bless his children. For boys, the initial blessing is "May God make thee as Ephraim and Manasseh." For the girls, it is "May God make thee as Sarah, Rebekah, Rachel, and Leah." Each blessing concludes with:

> May the Lord bless thee and keep thee: May the Lord cause His countenance to shine upon thee, and be gracious unto thee: May the Lord lift up His countenance towards thee and give thee peace.[25]

After the blessings, the head of the house raises a cup of wine and recites Kiddush, which recalls God's acts as creator and as deliverer. During the meal, more hymns may be sung, and at the close of the meal an extended grace is said.[26]

The Sabbath is ushered out with the Havdalah service (the service of separation). Present are three elements—wine, spices, and light. Blessings are said over each in thanksgiving for the fruit of the vine, for different kinds of spices, and for the light of the fire. Havdalah concludes with the following:

> Blessed art Thou, O Lord our God, King of the universe, who makest a distinction between holy and profane, between light and darkness, between Israel and other nations, between the seventh day and the six working days. Blessed art Thou, O Lord, who makest a distinction between holy and profane.[27]

Thus, the sweet savor of the spice of the Sabbath lingers into the following week, and a longing for the Sabbath bride's return enlivens the week's enterprises.

Rosh Hashanah

Rosh Hashanah means "head of the year." It is the first day of the Jewish new year, falling in September or October depending on the synchronization of the Hebrew lunar calendar with the solar. It is the day in which God remembers a person's deeds, and it is the day on which God sits in judgment. Rosh Hashanah begins the High Holy Days, or the Days of Awe, which culminate ten days later in *Yom Kippur*, the Day of Atonement. The Days of Awe are a period of introspection and repentance before God. According to Jewish tradition, on Rosh Hashanah God metaphorically enters his heavenly palace and is seated on the throne of mercy. He reviews the thoughts, words, and deeds of all human beings over the preceding year and makes judgments concerning who will live, who will die, who will prosper, and who will sorrow. These judgments, however, are not unchangeable. Persons have a ten-day period in which to rectify their lives and alter those judgments through their repentance and through God's readiness to accept their repentance.[28]

The *shofar* is the central symbol of Rosh Hashanah. It was originally the trumpet that warned Israel of an impending threat or called her together for peaceful assemblies. Consequently, it is the shofar, blown one hundred times on Rosh Hashanah, that calls the Jews to self-examination and repentance over the next ten days, during which wrongs to others are to be rectified; restitution is to be made, if possible; and forgiveness for wrongs committed against one's neighbors, friends, and acquaintances is to be sought. As one author said of the shofar, "Its purpose is to shake up the worshipers in time for the heavenly judgment."[29] On the tenth day at sundown, at the close of Yom Kippur, the heavenly books will be sealed and the fates of humans decided for the coming year. Repentance cannot be postponed.

The services in the synagogues stress the ability of persons to repent, God's desire for such, and the guarantee of God's forgiveness, when contrition is sincere. The Torah reading is Genesis 21–22, which is the story of Abraham's willingness to offer his son Isaac in obedience to God's command. An additional custom performed by Orthodox Jews is known as *tashlich,* a tradition based on Micah 7:19, in which persons symbolically cast their sins into the sea, a spring, or a river, thereby symbolizing the cleansing of themselves of past wrongdoing.[30]

Yom Kippur

Yom Kippur, the Day of Atonement, is the culmination of the Days of Awe. It is the most solemn day in the Jewish calendar. Beginning before sundown, Jews engage in a twenty-five-hour fast which prohibits all food. In addition, one is forbidden to drink, to bathe, to anoint oneself, to have sexual relations, or to wear leather shoes. All work is prohibited. Persons are to focus on repentance. As noted above, amends should be made for all wrong done to others, since these need to be forgiven by the persons so wronged. It is customary to change the cloths in the synagogue to white, and many Jews will wear white, a color which indicates purity and equality.

The evening service begins with the *Kol Nidre,* a prayer which asks God to forgive the people for breaking any vows they made during the year. This refers only to those vows made between humans and God and not to commitments to others, which require their release and forgiveness. The Torah reading is drawn from the texts which deal with the high priest's role on Yom Kippur. This is followed by a passage from Isaiah 58:6–9, which summons the congregation away from empty ritualism to a life of justice and mercy. As a result, God promises to be with them.

Yom Kippur ends with a service in which confidence in God's goodness and mercy is the central theme. Because the worshipers have come before God in repentance, he will forgive. The final plea, given in humility and confidence, is:

Our Father, our King, seal us in the book of a happy life.
Our Father, our King, seal us in the book of redemption and salvation.
Our Father, our King, seal us in the book of maintenance and sustenance.
Our Father, our King, seal us in the book of merit.
Our Father, our King, seal us in the book of pardon and forgiveness.[31]

The service ends with a blast of the shofar, and the congregation returns home to break the fast.

Succoth

Succoth, the Feast of Tabernacles, begins five days after Yom Kippur. It is a holiday of joy. Its roots lie in the remembrance of the wilderness wanderings of Israel and God's providential care of his people.

Ye shall dwell in booths seven days; all that are Israelites born shall dwell in booths: That your generations may know that I made the children of Israel to dwell in booths, when I brought them out of the land of Egypt: I am the Lord your God. (Lev. 23:42–43)

The central symbol of Succoth is the *sukkah* (booth or tabernacle), which families are to construct outside their homes directly under the heavens. It is to have a minimum of three sides and is to be roofed with vegetation in such a way that there is more shade than sunlight. However, one should be able to see the stars through the cover. The sukkah is usually decorated, and meals are to be eaten in it. Ideally, persons are meant to sleep in it as well; but this is not compulsory, especially if the weather is inclement. Even eating in the sukkah under such circumstances is not required. Where families are unable to build their own sukkah, they share one with another family for meals or take them in a communal sukkah built, for example, by a congregation for the use of its members.

The second central commandment is the use of the four species—citron, myrtle twigs, palm branches, and willows (in keeping with Lev. 23:40), all of which are carried and waved during the festival services. Some rabbis suggested that the four species taught a lesson about the diversity of the community: each member, though different, is necessary to the community as a whole and can in his or her own way bear witness to God.

A custom amongst certain Jewish communities is to "invite" one of seven biblical figures for each day of the festival—Abraham, Isaac, Jacob, Moses, Aaron, Joseph, and David. In the Kabbalistic (mystical) tradition they are identified with seven characteristics—loving kindness, power, beauty, victory, splendor, foundations, and sovereignty.

On the seventh day, *Hoshana Rabba* (the Great Hosanna) is celebrated. Prayers are said for God's blessing on the people, Jerusalem, the land, and its harvest. All the scrolls are removed from the ark that holds them. The reader, followed by persons bearing the scrolls and congregants carrying the four species, walks around the synagogue seven times chanting hymns that conclude with the refrain "Hoshanah" (oh, deliver). At the conclusion of these circuits, branches of willow twigs are beaten so that the leaves drop, mimicking nature and affirming nature's dependence upon the divine blessing of water. These ceremonies in the synagogue were conducted in the temple while it was standing. Because it is believed that God established a special grace period between Yom Kippur and Hoshana Rabba, solemn prayers from the Days of Awe are intertwined with these prayers on the last day of Succoth. The eighth day is a separate and full holy day known as *Shemini Atzeret* (Eighth Day of Solemn Assembly), in which prayers for rain are said.

The eighth day in Israel (the ninth day in the *diaspora*) is also *Simhat Torah* (Rejoicing of the Torah), a festival which celebrates the final reading of the annual Torah cycle and the first reading of the new cycle. Both at evening and morning services, the Torah scrolls are carried around the synagogue to the accompaniment of joyous singing and dancing which lasts well into the night.[32] In the morning, the last portion of Deuteronomy is read, and the one called up for the final passage is known as the Bridegroom of the Torah. The individual who is called up for the reading of the first passage of the new cycle is known as the Bridegroom of Genesis. It is customary for the two to invite the synagogue congregation to a party in honor of the Torah and the day.

Passover

While the festivals of Rosh Hashanah, Yom Kippur, and Succoth are fall festivals, *Passover* is a seven-day festival celebrated in the spring, beginning on the fifteenth day of the month Nisan. Passover celebrates the Exodus from Egypt. As the Festival of Unleavened Bread (remembering that the ancient Israelites fled Egypt at midnight before their dough could rise), it reflects the Bible's command that no leaven be eaten or even be present in the home for the duration of the festival. This requires not only the complete change of an observant Jew's pantry for the Passover, but the cleansing of all utensils as well. As a result, in traditional Jewish homes a veritable "spring cleaning" takes place in preparation for the Passover. On the night before Passover, there is a special ceremony to search and eliminate the last remnants of leaven before the Passover.

The first night of the Passover commemorates Israel's last night in Egypt when the angel of death passed over Israel's firstborn while causing the deaths of the firstborn among the Egyptians. It is upon this act of deliverance and the events surrounding it that the ritual meal on the first night of Passover focuses. The Passover meal is a teaching tool which draws all persons into the past event of deliverance and makes them contemporary coparticipants with those whom God brought out of Egypt "with a mighty hand, and with an outstretched arm, and with great terribleness, and with signs, and with wonders" (Deut. 26:8).

During the second temple period, each family took a lamb on the eve of Passover (the fourteenth day of Nisan) to the forecourt of the temple to be slaughtered. It was then roasted whole and eaten before morning by the group (usually the family) who had brought it originally to the temple. Whatever was left over was burned. With the destruction of the temple, the sacrifice could no longer be made in the temple. However, the Passover meal continued, in keeping with the rest of the commandments found in Exodus 12 and 13 and in Jewish tradition.[33]

The Passover meal is known as the *seder* (meaning "order"), and the order of events is the same year after year. Certain symbolic elements are essential. The three obligatory foods are bitter herbs, unleavened bread, and four cups of wine.

Three pieces of *mazzah* (unleavened bread) are present, which represent the two normal Sabbath loaves of leavened bread plus "the bread of affliction," which reminds the family of the bondage in Egypt and the haste in which Israel left Egypt. They are stacked on top of each other. Early in the service, the middle piece, the bread of affliction, is broken in two, and the larger half is set aside for later use. This half is known as the *afikomen,* and during the meal the children try to steal and the leader tries to hide it. The game is an inducement for the children to remain awake during the seder. The afikomen is the last thing eaten, as a final reminder of Israel's bondage.

Secondly, bitter herbs in the form of lettuce or horseradish are present to remind the participants of the bitterness of Jewish suffering. Four cups of wine must be drunk at the seder to toast divine redemption, in keeping with the "four terms of redemption" mentioned in Exodus 6:6–7:

Wherefore say unto the children of Israel, I am the Lord, and I will *[1] bring you out* from under the burdens of the Egyptians, and I will *[2] rid [deliver] you* out of their bondage, and I will *[3] redeem you* with a stretched out arm, and with great judgments: And I will *[4] take you to me* for a people, and I will be to you a God: and ye shall know that I am the Lord your God, which bringeth you out from under the burdens of the Egyptians. (emphasis added)

In addition, on the seder plate are a shank bone, which symbolizes the paschal lamb, and a burnt egg, which symbolizes the temple festival offering. Before commencing the seder meal, it is traditional to eat an egg (not the burnt egg) dipped in salt water, which commemorates the destruction of the temple. Hence, a sobering note is introduced into an otherwise joyous occasion.

Finally, on the seder plate there is a paste made of a mixture of fruit, spices, wine, and mazzah meal. It reminds persons of the mortar the Jews were forced to make in Egypt. In addition, there are some vegetables such as potatoes, radishes, celery, or parsley that serve as an appetizer—something only the wealthy would have normally enjoyed. A bowl of salt water is reminiscent of the Jewish tears shed while in bondage. The egg and the appetizers are dipped in this.[34]

Since the Passover meal is a teaching tool, central to it is the *hagaddah*—the telling of the story of the Passover. This section commences with the four questions that the youngest child asks in keeping with the commandment in the Torah, "And you shall tell your son on that day, saying . . ." This phrase appears four times in the Torah, and thus the hagaddah represents the four questions as reflecting four sons: one who is wise, another wicked, another simple, and one who cannot ask questions. The four questions are:

a. Why is this night different from all other nights, for on all other nights we may eat hametz [leaven] and mazzah: on this night only mazzah?

b. Why is this night different from all other nights, for on all other nights we eat other kinds of vegetables: on this night we eat bitter herbs?

c. Why is this night different from all other nights, for on all other nights we do not dip (our vegetables) even once: on this night we dip twice (the appetizer into salt water and the bitter herbs into the mixture of fruits)?

d. Why is this night different from all other nights, for on all other nights we may eat either sitting up straight or reclining: on this night we all recline?[35]

Obviously, as these questions are asked and answered, the story of God's deliverance from Egyptian bondage is told.

Included in the symbols of the Passover is an additional cup of wine which is known as Elijah's cup. There are clear messianic hopes tied to the festival, which recalls redemption past while looking forward to redemption future. Since Elijah is to be the herald of the Messiah, his cup reflects these hopes. Also, after the meal, the door is opened briefly to welcome Elijah and to demonstrate that the Passover is a night of divine protection in which Israel exhibits no fears.[36] God is the liberator and the remover of all fear.

The order (seder) of events is fixed. Some events are part of a regular Sabbath meal, while others are unique to the Passover seder. The complete order is as follows:

1. The benediction over the first cup of wine.
2. Ritual washing of the hands without an accompanying benediction.
3. Dipping of the appetizer in the salt water.
4. Breaking and hiding of the afikomen.
5. The hagaddah and drinking of the second cup of wine.
6. Ritual washing of the hands with a benediction.
7. The usual Sabbath benediction over the bread. The upper mazzah and the unhidden half of the middle mazzah are eaten.
8. Eating of the bitter herbs which are dipped in the fruit mixtures.
9. Eating of a sandwich made from the bottom mazzah, bitter herbs, and the fruit mixture.
10. The meal.
11. Eating of the afikomen.
12. The grace after the meal over the third cup of wine.
13. Songs of praise and the drinking of the fourth cup of wine.
14. Recognition of God's acceptance of the actions and hymns of praise.[37]

Minor Festivals

The minor festivals—those not prescribed in the Torah—extend the opportunities for the Jewish people to recognize God's hand at various times in their history or to recall events, such as the Holocaust, which can never be forgotten.

Purim

The festival of *Purim* is rooted in the book of Esther, the Jewish wife of King Ahasuerus of Persia. When Haman, the archvillain of the book, masterminded an edict for the extermination of the Jews, Mordecai, the uncle of Esther, persuaded her to intercede on behalf of her people. This she did at the risk of her own life. When Haman's wickedness was revealed, he and his sons were executed. Mordecai was elevated to his place, and the Jewish people were empowered to protect themselves against the extermination order (see the Book of Esther).

Purim celebrates the preservation of the Jewish people, not only in ancient Persia, but in all those circumstances in which anti-Semitism has and does flourish. Consequently, Purim is one of the happiest holidays in the Jewish calendar. Like *Hanukkah,* it is a minor holiday, so work is permitted. However, both women and men are commanded to hear the reading of the scroll of Esther in the synagogue. Because of the festive nature of the day, many may come dressed in costumes, while the children bring noisemakers to the reading of Esther. Every time the name Haman is mentioned in the reading—and it appears over fifty times—the synagogue explodes into noise, with boos, hisses, and other forms of racket. Since Jewish tradition forbids the reading of a text when it cannot be heard, the reader has to stop until the noise subsides. However, upon the next mention of Haman's name, the room erupts in noise once again. There is a traditional festive meal which is celebrated as part of Purim.[38]

In addition to hearing the reading of the scroll (*megillah*) and the festive meal, it is a commandment on Purim to give at least two gifts to the poor and at least one gift of two kinds of prepared foods to a friend. Most observant Jews give many of the latter to many friends. These commandments reflect the idea that it is through compassion and friendship that one may fight evil and hatred.

Hanukkah

Hanukkah is a relatively new festival in comparison to the festivals discussed above. Its roots lie in the second century B.C.E. during a time when *Antiochus IV* of Syria was persecuting the Jews. Antiochus sought to remove Jewish resistance by forcing them to assume Hellenistic customs and eliminating the traditional Jewish ones. To this end, he polluted the temple, ordered the destruction of Torah scrolls, banned Sabbath observance, forbade the circumcision of children, and suspended the festivals. Violation of any of these edicts carried the punishment of death.[39] The result was precisely the opposite of that for which he hoped. In 167 B.C.E. a revolt erupted under the leadership of Mattathias of the Hasmonean family and his son Judah. By 165 the Syrians had been driven out of Jerusalem, and on the twenty-fifth day of Kislev of that year, the temple was cleansed and the lights relighted. However, according to tradition, there was only enough oil for the lights to burn for one day. Miraculously, they burned for eight days until appropriate oil could be provided. Thus, the eight-day winter festival of Hanukkah is known as the feast of lights and celebrates the victory of Judaism over its Hellenistic persecutors.

The central element in Hanukkah today is the lighting of the nine-branched Hanukkah *menorah,* the ninth candle being used to light the other eight.

On each day of Hanukkah, a new candle is added to the menorah. In some communities (primarily in Christian lands where the Christmas season parallels Hanukkah) it is customary to give children Hanukkah gifts or small sums of "Hanukkah" money. For Jews in the United States particularly, Hanukkah can provide a Jewish alternative to the Christmas season. It is also customary to eat foods that have to do with oil, reflecting the oil that burned for eight days.[40] Hanukkah serves as a reminder of the need to retain the Jewish faith in the face of persecution or assimilation.

Fast Days

There are five fast days, two major and three minor, in the Jewish liturgical calendar. The major fast days are Yom Kippur, discussed above, and Tisha Be'av, which falls on the ninth day of Av (late June to mid-August). It was on this date that the Babylonians destroyed the first temple, the Romans burned the second temple, King Ferdinand and Queen Isabella expelled the Jews from Spain, and the Nazis took special pleasure in persecuting Jews. Thus, it is a day of mourning and a full fast day lasting from one evening to the next. As with Yom Kippur, food, drink, bathing, leather shoes, anointing, and sexual relations are forbidden. However, unlike Yom Kippur, one may smoke and work, unless it distracts from mourning.

On the minor fast days, food is forbidden only from dawn until sundown. Bathing and work are permitted. The minor fasts relate to the destruction of the two temples. The tenth day of Tevet (usually in January) remembers the beginning of the Babylonian siege against Jerusalem. The seventh day of Tammuz in the summer commemorates the first breaching of Jerusalem's walls by the Romans in 70 C.E. The fast of Gedaliah falls on the day after Rosh Hashanah. Gedaliah was the Jewish governor installed by the Babylonians following the destruction of the temple in 586 B.C.E. However, radical Jews assassinated him, thereby placing Judah under direct Babylonian control and causing the Jews to lose any semblance of national sovereignty until it was restored briefly under the Maccabees in 165 B.C.E.[41]

Modern Days of Remembrance

Four modern days of remembrance need to be mentioned. The first is Yom ha-Shoa (Holocaust Memorial Day). No real rituals have been established, with the exception of two minutes of silence initiated by the sounding of a siren. Yom ha-Shoa occurs on the twenty-seventh day of Nisan between mid-April and early May.

Yom ha-Zikaron is Israel's Memorial Day, in remembrance of those who have fallen in battle; it occurs on May 14. Yom ha-Atzma'ut is Independence Day, celebrating the Israeli declaration of independence on May 15, 1948. Thus, these two days are interlaced, with the solemnity of Memorial Day coming first and the joyousness of Independence Day following. Finally, Yom Yerushalayim (Jerusalem Day) is the newest holiday. It commemorates the return of the old city of Jerusalem to Jewish control as a result of the 1967 war.[42]

Rites of Passage

In all religions there are rituals which mark major transitions in human life. Hindus initiate a boy into adult responsibilities through the ceremony of the sacred thread. A Buddhist monk's head is shaved and he dons the saffron robe, indicating his new station in life as an ascetic. So also, life's transitions are commemorated in Judaism through rites of passage. These rites occur at birth, religious maturity, marriage, and death.

Circumcision

Circumcision is a ritual performed on a male child when he is eight days old, if he is healthy. It is the ancient mark of the covenant given to Abraham in which the foreskin of the penis is removed by a ritual specialist known as a *mohel*. At the circumcision, the boy's name is announced. Converts to Judaism must also be circumcised.

At the birth of a girl, the only ceremony is the announcement of her name, usually at the first reading of the Torah after her birth. Such readings occur on Monday, Thursday, and Saturday, but many parents wait until the Sabbath for the announcement. The father is called up to read the Torah selection for the day, and this is followed by a special prayer. The girl's name is then announced.[43]

Redemption of the Firstborn

On the thirty-first day after the birth of a firstborn son, the rite of the redemption of the firstborn takes place. Historically, the firstborn male was dedicated to the Lord for religious service (Exod. 13:1–2), and at that time it was required that he be redeemed by the payment of five silver shekels (Num. 18:16) in order to remain with his natural family unit. The practice continues today, using the currency of the various countries in which Jews live in lieu of shekels.

Bar Mitzvah / Bat Mitzvah

A boy becomes a "son of the commandment" at age thirteen and a girl a "daughter of the command-ment" at age twelve. This reflects the natural onset of puberty. Traditionally, a boy was called up at this time to read from the Torah or from the prophetic portion of scriptures to mark the occasion. In many Jewish households, especially in America, this event is then celebrated with an elaborate party. In theory, a boy studies in Hebrew school prior to his thirteenth birthday and then continues his studies following his *bar mitzvah*. Unfortunately, what is supposed to be the real beginning of study in the Jewish traditions, especially in the Talmud, becomes the end of Jewish education for many non-Orthodox Jews, most par-ticularly in the diaspora.

In Orthodox circles, a girl's attainment of adult-hood is not marked by being called up to the Torah to read, since women may not participate publicly in the leading of synagogue services, which is an office reserved to men. However, among Conservative and Reformed Jews, a *bat mitzvah* ceremony in which the girl is called up to the Torah has become common.[44]

Marriage

Marriage is an expected part of human life among Jews (Gen. 2:24). In Talmudic times there was a year's time between the engagement (betrothal—see Matt. 1:18–25) and the marriage itself. Were the engagement to be broken, a formal divorce had to be granted. Today, however, the formal engagement and marriage essentially take place at the same time.

On the Sabbath before the wedding, the groom is usually called up to read from the Torah. The wed-ding day is sacred, and because of its serious nature the couple should fast and offer penitential prayers which are drawn from the liturgy of Yom Kippur.

The wedding ceremony itself is simple. In many Orthodox communities, it is traditional for the bride to walk around the groom seven times under the wedding canopy. Two blessings extolling the joyous nature of marriage are made (usually by a

rabbi), and the bride and groom drink from the cup of wine. A ring is placed by the groom on the bride's forefinger, and he says, "You are hereby sanctified unto me with this ring according to the laws of Moses and Israel."[45] The marriage contract is then read. It states the responsibilities of the groom to provide for the bride's material and conjugal rights.[46] Following the reading of the marriage con-tract, the rabbi pronounces seven blessings over a second cup of wine, giving thanks for creation, man and woman, and the love that brings them together. In addition, hope is expressed for the restoration of and return to Zion, in which the voices of brides and grooms will be heard once more in keeping with Isaiah's prophecy (Isa. 61:10). The bride and groom are given to drink from this second cup. Finally, a glass is broken under the heel of the groom to remind the people, in this moment of joy, that the temple is still destroyed and that this is still a bro-ken and imperfect world. After the ceremony, the couple is permitted to be alone together for some minutes of privacy, indicating that it is proper for them as a married couple to be alone. Prior to the marriage, especially in Ultra-Orthodox communi-ties, this would be utterly improper. Following the wedding, it is customary for family and friends to hold celebratory meals every evening for the couple for seven days, always including one person who had not been at the wedding, so that there may be new joy at the union of the couple.[47]

Death

Death is real and is not to be denied. The rituals surrounding death emphasize that reality, while at the same time bringing the mourner through the experience to a psychologically adequate conclu-sion. Thus, it is appropriate to show emotion and to feel the loss.

At the time of death, the mourner is to make a small tear in his or her clothing signifying the sepa-ration which is caused by the death. Immediately upon returning from the cemetery, the family sits *shiva,* meaning that for seven days they sit on low stools receiving visitors. Visitors are to enter quietly, sit near the mourner, and wait for the mourner to address them. Such mourning is required upon the death of a father, mother, sister, brother, son, daughter, or spouse. Daily prayer services (normally held in the synagogue) are held in the home where the shiva takes place, during which *kaddish,* the "mourner's prayer," is said, which reflects on the greatness of God and his future redemption of the world. In effect, these prayers acknowledge God's gift of life and his dominion over life's commencement and termination. In addition, these prayers force the mourners to be with others, rather than isolating themselves. Shiva is discontinued during the Sabbath.

During shiva, shaving, bathing, the wearing of leather shoes, sexual relations, or the laundering of clothes is prohibited. Persons also do not go to work, unless it is absolutely essential economically, and then only after the third day. The mourning period, to a lesser degree, continues up to thirty days for all but parents. In their case, the mourning period is one year. During these extended mourning periods, attending joyous events such as weddings is prohibited unless it involves one's livelihood. Thus, musicians or caterers might need to break this prohibition.[48]

Ritual Practices

As with the festivals or rites of passage, regular ritual practices keep Jewish worshipers ever mindful of God's claim on their lives. Rituals, when performed with an eye toward God, remind persons of what is important in life.

Purity

Ritual purity is central to Jewish life, especially within the context of the home. The central ritual associated with purity is immersion in a ritual bath of pure natural waters, known as a *mikveh*. This purity relates especially to women and the effects that it has upon marital relations between a husband and wife. During the menstrual period and for seven days after it, women in Orthodox circles are considered to be ritually impure. During this period sexual relations between husband and wife are forbidden. At the end of this time, Orthodox women will immerse themselves fully in a mikveh, once again becoming ritually pure, and relations with their husbands may then recommence. Many Jews feel that the restraint required during the periods of impurity lead to healthier sexual relations between husband and wife, because abstinence creates a renewed sense of desire for each other that is missing in other traditions without the periods of separation.

The mikveh fills another function in Jewish ritual life. If persons convert to Judaism, they must be immersed in a mikveh as a sign of their entry into the community and as an indication of the transition from the old to the new.[49]

Prayer

As with all monotheistic faiths, prayer plays a prominent role in the life of the Jewish people. Community prayers are very much a part of synagogue worship, and it is necessary for a *minyan* (quorum) to be present before the prayers can be said. Among Orthodox Jews, a minyan consists of ten adult males—males over the age of thirteen. In Conservative and Reformed synagogues, women may be included in the minyan.

During the morning prayer services a *tallit* (prayer shawl) is worn (in some communities only by adult males). On it are four tassels known as *tzitzit,* which are to remind the worshiper of God's commands (Num. 15:37–41), and thus the tzitzit give the shawl its meaning. The shawl is worn over the shoulders after pronouncing the blessing, "Blessed be Thou, Lord our God, King of the universe, who sanctified us with His commandments, and commanded us to wrap ourselves in the tzitzit."[50] Some worshipers may bring the shawl over their heads to aid in concentration. The tzitzit may also be worn on the four corners of an undergarment.

Also worn at prayer are the *tefillin*—two leather boxes which contain scriptural texts, handwritten on parchment, which command their use (Exod. 13:1–10, 11–16; Deut. 6:4–9; 11:13–21). One is worn on the left arm, if the worshiper is right-handed (or on the right, if he is left-handed), and the other is worn on the forehead. They symbolically represent keeping the Lord's commands ever before the worshiper's mind and near his heart. The wearing of the tefillin is the first command fulfilled by a boy following his bar mitzvah, and they are to be worn during prayer each weekday morning of the year, with the exceptions of Sabbaths and holy days.[51]

Head Coverings

The covering of one's head indicates respect before God. Orthodox men wear the skullcap known as the *kippah* (Hebrew) or *yarmulka* (Yiddish) throughout the day. Jews of the Conservative or Reformed traditions may or may not wear them, although Conservative Jews will normally wear them in the synagogue. There are a variety of head coverings among men. Ultra-Orthodox men prefer a hat, because it covers more of the head than the kippah, although they will normally wear both. Adult Ultra-Orthodox Jewish men of Hasidic background wear fur hats and caftans on Sabbaths and festivals. Married Ultra-Orthodox women will wear head coverings, since only their husbands are permitted to see their hair.[52]

Mezuzah

Deuteronomy 6:9 commands the people of Israel to write the commands of the Lord "upon the posts of thy house, and on thy gates," and *mezuzah* is the Hebrew word for doorpost. Ritually, the mezuzah is a small parchment on which the first two paragraphs of the Shema (Deut. 6:4–9, 13–31) are written. The mezuzah is to be affixed to the upper third of the exterior doorpost, normally in a small oblong box, as well as to all internal doors except the bathroom door. As people see it, they are to remember how to act within the home. As they leave the home, they are to remember how to act within the world as people of God. Some Jews may kiss the mezuzah upon entering a dwelling or room, or touch it and then kiss their finger.[53]

Kosher Diet

The word *kosher* means "fit" and is used primarily in relation to foods, although its meaning may be used in a broader sense. As part of his commandments to the people of Israel, God gave laws regarding foods that could and could not be eaten. While many persons try to rationalize why certain foods are permitted and why others are not, that is not the concern of the biblical laws. The dietary laws relate to discipline and are obeyed because God gave the commands.

Animals which have cloven hooves and chew the cud are permitted. Thus, beef and mutton are the two most commonly eaten meats among Jews. However, the animals must be slaughtered in such a way that there is no pain—their throats are slit with one stroke of a knife. The meat is then prepared so that the blood is removed from it. Animals or birds which eat meat or carrion are not permitted. Thus, among the fowl, the most commonly used birds are chickens, turkeys, and ducks. Fish with scales and fins are permitted, but shellfish are not. Consequently, shrimp and lobster are forbidden.

Milk and meat products may not be mixed due to the threefold injunction in the Torah that a young goat cannot be cooked in its mother's milk (Exod.

23:19; 34:26; Deut. 14:21). Thus, a truly kosher kitchen will keep separate sets of pans and utensils for the preparation of meat or milk products. After eating a meat meal, persons must wait a certain length of time (which varies according to their tradition) before eating a milk meal. Some foods are neutral and may be eaten with either milk or meat. These are fish, fruits, and vegetables.

Dietary rules are followed with varying degrees of strictness depending upon the tradition which individual Jews follow. Some Jews try to follow the dietary regulations fully and will eat almost wholly within their own homes or in the homes of others who hold the same dietary rules as they hold. Among others, the rules are modified to be more dependent upon the degree of adjustment to the surrounding world that the persons are prepared to make. Reformed Jews, for example, may observe almost none of the dietary rules, with the possible exception of not eating pork.[54]

GROUPS WITHIN JUDAISM

As indicated, the degree to which Jews practice the rituals within the faith depends greatly upon which tradition within Judaism they follow. Initially, adherents to Judaism can be divided into two large traditional groupings known as the *Ashkenazim* and the *Sephardim*. The designations relate to the area of the world from which Jews have come. Loosely, Ashkenazim come from Europe (particularly eastern Europe) and Sephardim come from Spain or the Arab world. One finds both of these groups represented in Israel and the United States.

Of greater theological importance are the groups that have formed over the question of the relationship between tradition and modernity. In practice, there is a spectrum of Jewish life oriented around these twin poles, as Figure 1 illustrates.[55]

On the two extremes are Jews who either have separated themselves from the modern world (Ultra-Orthodox) or who have given up their Jewish identity to it (assimilated). In contrast, the majority of Jews have tried to come to some kind of balance between tradition and modernity.[56]

Modern Orthodox Jews try to adhere strictly to the traditional Jewish commandments, such as the Sabbath and dietary laws, while at the same time working in the world and trying to improve it. However, they do not abandon the traditions to

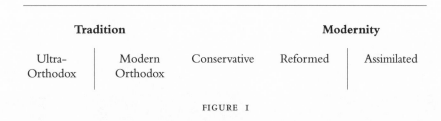

Tradition   Modernity

Ultra-   Modern   Conservative   Reformed   Assimilated
Orthodox   Orthodox

FIGURE I

accommodate the world's views. They bring their traditions into the world. Thus, modern Orthodox Jews insist on a minyan of ten males for prayers. They do not drive to synagogue on Sabbath. Only men are called up to read the Torah. Only men are permitted to be cantors and rabbis, and men and women sit separately in the synagogue.

Conservative Jews, like modern Orthodox, believe they are bound by the rituals and laws of the Torah. However, they believe it is possible to introduce modern innovations into Jewish life. Thus, they hold that, while a minyan is essential for prayers, it can be composed of both males and females. They may drive to the synagogue, especially if it is distant or the weather is inclement. Women, as well as men, may be called up to read the Torah, and women may be cantors or rabbis. In this same vein, men and women sit together in a Conservative synagogue.

The Reformed movement feels that many of the traditions that are important to modern Orthodox and Conservative Jews are not binding in the modern world. Thus, they deny the necessity of a minyan for prayer, and most consider the dietary laws flexible. Women and men have equal roles within the Reformed life. Synagogue services include organ music and often appear much like a Protestant service. In the United States the services are conducted wholly in English. Many Reformed congregations have abolished the essential nature of circumcision and the mikveh for converts. In the Reformed view, individuals are Jewish if their father is Jewish; the mother need not be. Traditionally, however, for a person to be Jewish, the mother had to be Jewish. Thus, the gap between the Reformed Jews and the modern Orthodox and Conservative Jews is large. While the Reformed Jews see themselves along with Orthodox and Conservative as fully Jewish, Orthodox tend to see Reformed Jews as truncated in their Judaism.

What defines the Ultra-Orthodox is their attempt to separate themselves as completely as possible

from the modern society. The males are readily recognizable with their black coats and hats, patterned after the clothing of the seventeenth and eighteenth centuries. Often they also wear long side curls and untrimmed beards. The women are dressed very modestly with long sleeves, long dresses, and stockings. Married women will normally either cover their hair or wear a wig and may shave their heads. The Ultra-Orthodox separation is stimulated by the recognition that modern society contains many enticements that could lead the young people astray. In Israel, one finds a large number of Ultra-Orthodox in Jerusalem, with lesser numbers in Tel Aviv and Haifa. In the United States the Ultra-Orthodox are also present, but in very small numbers.

There are two main groupings within the present-day Ultra-Orthodox community—the *Hasidim* and the *Mitnagdim*. The Hasidim base their lives in the traditions which flowed from Israel ben Eliezer, who became known as the Ba'al Shem Tov (Master of the Good Name), or the Besht. His message was that God loved humanity and wanted their hearts. Thus, mystical, emotional elements are an important part of the Hasidic tradition. The movement centers around *rebbes,* charismatic leaders who serve as the bridge between their followers and God. They way the rebbes live their lives is almost more important to their followers than their teachings. In contrast, the Mitnagdim represent a strand that opposed the emotionalism of the Hasidim and based their lives and behavior solidly in the received traditions of Judaism.

Initially, the Mitnagdim were radically opposed to the Hasidim. However, as the Hasidim have stressed more the study of the Talmud, the gap between the two has lessened and the animosities have disappeared. Both stood together in opposition to the Enlightenment, and both stand together today in their basic opposition to any accommodation with the modern world.

Jews of various traditions worshiping at the Western Wall, Jerusalem.
(Photo courtesy of D. Kelly Ogden)

SCRIPTURES

Jewish life of whatever tradition does not spring from a vacuum. The festivals, practices, rituals, and ethics that characterize the faith are all found in the revelation given through Moses at Mount Sinai: the Torah, in both its written and oral forms. Hence, all the writings which guide Jewish life have their roots in the Torah. The written Torah is found in the Pentateuch—the first five books of what the Jews call the *Tanak* and what Christians call the Old Testament. The word Tanak is actually a manufactured word derived from the first letters of the names of the entities of which it is composed—the Torah, the *Nevi'im* (Prophets), and the *Ketuvim* (Writings).

The Torah contains Genesis, Exodus, Leviticus, Numbers, and Deuteronomy. The Nevi'im writings are comprised of two groups, the first being the "former prophets"—whose stories are found in Joshua, Judges, 1 and 2 Samuel, and 1 and 2 Kings—and the second being the "latter prophets," meaning Isaiah, Jeremiah, Ezekiel, and the "twelve prophets" (Hosea, Joel, Amos, Obadiah, Jonah, Micah, Nahum, Habakkuk, Zephaniah, Haggai, Zechariah, and Malachi). The Ketuvim contains Psalms, Job, Proverbs, Ruth, Song of Solomon, Ecclesiastes, Lamentations, Esther, Daniel, Ezra, Nehemiah, and 1 and 2 Chronicles. Since the entirety of God's revelation was given at Sinai, the Prophets and the Writings are considered commentary or expansion on the original revelation, making the Torah the most sacred and foundational portion of all Jewish writings.

The second part of what was given at Sinai is known as the oral Torah. God gave much more than was written down, and the oral Torah was fundamentally an expansion and explanation of that which was in the written Torah. Thus, whatever precepts the rabbis prescribed through discussion as norms for Jewish life were viewed as part of the oral Torah. Finally, the volume of oral traditions became so great that they had to be written down. While this preserved the oral Torah, it also limited its flexibility.

The oral Torah actually had two components—the *Halacha,* containing legal discussions (law), and the Aggadah, containing philosophy, theology, legends, and traditions (lore). It was the Halacha which was written down first, in about 200 C.E., and recorded as the Mishnah. The Mishnah contained the legal discussions of the rabbis up to that time concerning the way Jews should live. However, this was followed by much discussion from later rabbis, both in Palestine and Babylon. These discussions, in conjunction with some of the Aggadah, were put in written form about 500 C.E. and became known respectively as the Palestinian and Babylonian *Gemaras.* Thus, when the Mishnah is added to the Palestinian Gemara, the Palestinian Talmud is formed. When the Mishnah and the Babylonian Gemara are brought together, the Babylonian Talmud is the end product. It is the latter upon which Jewish discussion is based today. Portions of the Aggadah that did not find their way into the Gemara were eventually recorded in the Midrash. Figure 2 defines in graphic form these relationships.

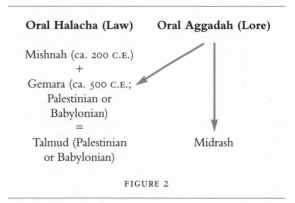

Oral Halacha (Law)   **Oral Aggadah (Lore)**

Mishnah (ca. 200 C.E.)
+
Gemara (ca. 500 C.E.;
Palestinian or
Babylonian)
=
Talmud (Palestinian   Midrash
or Babylonian)

FIGURE 2

In addition to the above materials, Jewish rabbis and laypersons may turn to other bodies of literature. The first group consists of the commentaries, which may be written with relation to the material in the Tanak or in the Talmudic material. The second group is known as Responsa, in which the authors attempt to relate the traditional materials to new issues arising within the community. The third group of materials is known as codes, and these are attempts by Jewish scholars to place before the Jewish community the essence of Jewish life in a manner accessible to all.

Thus, the resources to which the Jewish community can turn for guidance in daily life are rich and deep. It is these resources which have given meaning to Jewish life for hundreds of years and which will continue to guide the Jewish community into the next millennium.[57]

SPECIAL FOCUS AND CHALLENGES

As shown above, the Jewish people are a peculiar people among the nations. Their purpose is to bear witness to the presence of God in the world. Their dietary laws, their festivals, and the mode of dress for some separate the religious Jews from their neighbors and identify them as a distinct entity that is at variance with many of the world's values and customs. Because of that uniqueness, they have often been a people upon whom others have chosen to vent their anger and frustration. As a consequence, suffering has been a constant portion in Jewish life through the centuries. As Rabbi Rosen has said, wherever there is evil it must try to rid itself of that which bears witness of God. If, in fact, the Jews are God's chosen people, then evil will always find them.[58]

The most awful manifestation of that evil appeared in modern times in Adolf Hitler's Third Reich. Jews became the object of German hatred and of Germany's need for a scapegoat for unrealistic demands placed on them by the Allies at the end of the First World War. Anti-Semitism, the irrational hatred of Jews, gradually grew in its intensity in Germany and culminated in the "final solution"—the program to exterminate the Jewish race. Thus were born the death camps of Auschwitz, Bergen-Belsen, Dachau, and many others. Six million Jews—men, women, and children—lost their lives to Nazi rifles, machine guns, and gas chambers. Their bodies were thrown into mass graves or incinerated in specially built crematoria. Those who survived bore the deep scars of their own suffering, as well as the death and suffering of so many others.

Theologically, the Holocaust created questions about the justice and mercy of God. How could a God who is professed to be involved in history let so many innocent people die? The answer for some Jews has been that God could not have been involved and therefore must have withdrawn from the world. However, to take this stance invalidates the historical Jewish claim that God is a God who involves himself in history. He does not merely exist above it. The more universally accepted answer is Rabbi Rosen's—evil cannot pass by those who witness of God. The Holocaust, then, is in itself an affirmation that the Jews are God's witnesses among the nations.[59]

While the Holocaust was a malignant, vile challenge to Jewish life, a more insidious and perhaps more dangerous threat today comes from a very different problem—assimilation. The strength of Judaism has always been its uniqueness in the face of the world's values. However, as Jews live in the comfort of the West, where few people ask questions about religious affiliation, more and more Jews are leaving their heritage and beginning to disappear into the surrounding culture. Sometimes assimilation comes through marriage with a non-Jewish partner. Sometimes it comes because keeping dietary laws or Sabbath regulations is inconvenient. Whatever the reason, Jewish identity is being threatened by the very openness and pluralism of Western society, particularly that which is found in the United States.

In the face of the twin challenges of persecution and assimilation, the state of Israel may provide a counterpoint for those who wish to control their own political destinies as well as maintain a Jewish religious lifestyle. Any Jews anywhere in the world will be received in Israel, thus placing them in a position of political autonomy. In addition, there are groups within Israel pressing people to assume a more authentic Jewish way of life than that which they may have experienced elsewhere. Judaism may wane in other countries, but it has the possibility to grow in its ancient and modern homeland.

WOMEN AND FAMILIES

As can be seen from the above summary of the groups within Judaism, women play different roles in the various communities. Regardless of the tradition, however, marriage and family life have always been central to Jewish life. Male and female were meant for each other as companions and mates. Thus, bearing and rearing children are very much a part of a Jewish woman's life, especially in the Ultra-Orthodox community. There, families are often quite large, and a great deal of the woman's time is devoted to family maintenance. It is also a great honor for Ultra-Orthodox women to marry scholars, and the wives of these scholars will go to great lengths to provide their husbands with the time they need to study. Thus, the wives run the home, as well as working outside the home, so that their husbands may be freed for their studies. However, one sees many Ultra-Orthodox fathers pushing baby carriages and strolling with their children.

The roles of women become progressively broader as one moves across the spectrum between tradition and modernity. In addition to family concerns, the wives of modern Orthodox Jews may have their own professions and make substantial contributions to the broader community, just as do their husbands. They are limited, however, in the roles they may play in public worship. In the Conservative and Reformed traditions, women's roles are extended into the public religious arena. Girls receive bat mitzvah; women may be counted in the minyan, may be called up to read from the Torah, and may be ordained rabbis.

The place in which a Jewish woman has the least to say about her life is in the attainment of a divorce. In Jewish tradition, a civil divorce is insufficient, and without a religious divorce (*get*) a woman who remarries is considered to be living in adultery. In the Orthodox tradition it is the man's privilege to issue the get. Mutual consent between estranged partners is generally all that is required for a religious divorce. However, some men have withheld the get out of bitterness or in order to elicit money from wives and their families. In such instances, it is permissible for the courts and community to effect sanctions against the husband, in order to persuade him to provide a get. Reformed Judaism has eliminated the need for the get, while Conservative Judaism has included in the marriage contract a requirement to issue a get in the event of a divorce.[60]

JEWISH INFLUENCE TODAY

The influence of the Jewish community has always exceeded its numbers. The reason probably lies in the emphasis that Judaism has placed on education and hard work. Education provides a legitimate way to rise above the poverty in which many Jews have had to live. Consequently, those Jews who have been fortunate enough to have access to education have made the best of the opportunities. Judaism has produced scientists, musicians, writers, physicians, politicians, and researchers in various fields.

With the rise of the state of Israel, the Jews now have a place to call their own. Any Jew may enter Israel and gain immediate citizenship. Because Israel is a Jewish state, Judaism as a religion can remain vital, for there is a significant community of religious Jews who support one another. By contrast, the diaspora presents some great challenges for the religious Jew. There, the religious support structures are too often disappearing before the pressures of modernity. More and more diaspora Jews are marrying non-Jews, which leads to a breakdown of the traditions in the home and a minimizing of the impact of Judaism on the children. Thus, even though the largest Jewish community in the world is in the United States,

the future of Judaism does not lie there. Rather, it lies in the state of Israel, where Judaism, in all its various forms, is the lifeblood of the nation.

The modern Jewish movement that led to the establishment of the Jewish state is known as *Zionism,* and its founding father was Theodore Herzl. In the late nineteenth century he articulated the dream of a Jewish state. He did not live, however, to see the birth of the state of Israel on May 15, 1948.

It may be surprising to know that not all Jews supported the idea of an independent state. This was true of assimilated and Reformed Jews, as well as the Ultra-Orthodox. The liberal Jews believed that a state of Israel was an archaic dream. They saw themselves as citizens of the countries where they were living. They were British, French, and German citizens who followed the Mosaic faith. In contrast, the Ultra-Orthodox believed that the restoration of Israel was to be brought about by God and not through political means. However, after the Holocaust, it became evident that if there was to be any safety for Jews, it would have to be in their own land. Thus, Jews of many different persuasions support the Zionist cause, although they may look at the relation between religion and the land differently than do their neighbors.

LATTER-DAY SAINT REFLECTIONS

The major difference between Latter-day Saints and persons who hold the Jewish faith is that Latter-day Saints, like all other Christians, believe that Jesus of Nazareth was the Messiah and that he was God incarnate. Jews do not accept these assertions, in part because the Messiah is expected to bring an era of peace, something which has certainly not happened since Jesus' day. Also, were Jesus the Messiah, in Jewish eyes his followers could never have treated God's chosen people as they have over the centuries. The most brutal treatment of Jews has come at the hands of professed Christians—brutality that culminated in the "final solution," which was accepted by some Christians and overlooked by many others.

However, as Christians, Latter-day Saints find a common heritage with Judaism. Abraham is the father of the Christian faith. The God who called Moses, who delivered Israel from Egypt, who gave the Law at Sinai, who led the people in the wilderness, and who gave them the land of Canaan is also the God of the Latter-day Saints. Likewise, Latter-day

Saints hear the prophets Amos, Hosea, Isaiah, Jeremiah, and Ezekiel speaking to them. What they hear is different from what Jews hear, in view of Latter-day Saint beliefs about Jesus and latter-day revelation.

Persons of the Jewish faith would be uncomfortable with Latter-day Saint understandings about God. Within Judaism, God is one, but for Latter-day Saints there is a Godhead composed of the Father and the Son (both of whom have bodies of flesh and bones) and the Holy Ghost. Each member is divine, and people may stand in relation to each. Jews, as do Latter-day Saints, believe that God is involved in human history. However, Latter-day Saints believe that the ultimate demonstration of God's involvement in history comes in the incarnation in which God the Son *enters* human history, a position with which no Jew can totally agree.

Jews believe that they belong to the chosen people of Israel. Latter-day Saints believe that they are, either by blood or by adoption, members of God's chosen people, Israel; and they acknowledge that all Jews are also among the chosen people. If God's promises to the Jews are not still valid, then the Latter-day Saints have no basis upon which to trust in God's promises to them. However, Latter-day Saints do not see membership in Israel as committing them to live the Law of Moses, as do the Jews. Latter-day Saints would say that, although the moral mandates are still binding, the ritual portions of the Law no longer are, because they pointed to Christ's atoning sacrifice. Judaism cannot separate the ritual from the moral, for both are divinely given, and people have no right to pick and choose what commandments they will or will not keep.

The idea among Latter-day Saints that a portion of the Law has been abrogated in Jesus Christ leads to a difference in the understanding of revelation between the two communities. For Orthodox Jews, the revelation at Sinai contains in its written and oral forms all that God needs to say to his people. Anything beyond the Torah is commentary, whether it be the writings of the prophets or the deliberations of the rabbis. No new revelation is forthcoming. In contrast, for Latter-day Saints the canon is always open. God may indeed have more to say, providing new knowledge that was not contained in previous revelations.

On two other fronts, there are commonalities between Latter-day Saints and Jews. The first concerns the role of women and the centrality of the family. Latter-day Saints stand closest to modern Orthodox Jews on the importance of marriage and family. The woman's first role is within the home as wife and mother. However, she may also fulfill other roles in the secular world provided the primary role is not neglected.

The other realm of commonality is that of persecution. Latter-day Saints should have some small sense of what Jewish suffering has entailed, for because of their faith they had to flee for their lives from the midst of a supposedly tolerant society in order to find freedom of worship. Like the Jews, Latter-day Saints are a peculiar people who have set themselves apart from the societies in which they live by their stress on the Word of Wisdom and their moral standards. Like some Jews, they dreamed of a theocratic state; but when that did not come about, they immersed themselves in American society, becoming its leaders in many instances. Like the Jews, Latter-day Saints have become successful—and therein lies the danger to Latter-day Saints, just as surely as it is a danger to American Jewry. Both communities run the risk of being assimilated slowly and quietly into the fabric of Americanism. As several Latter-day Saint prophets have said, the church will be tested far more by success and prosperity than it ever was by persecution. Ultimately, the danger for the future of Latter-day Saints and Jews alike is to become too much like the nations and not to be what God has called them to be. If, however, they follow the revelations God has given them, they each in their own ways may become great witnesses of the God who involves himself in human history.

Glossary of Jewish Names and Terms

AFIKOMEN. The broken piece of the unleavened bread set aside (or hidden) to be eaten at the end of the Passover meal.

AGGADAH. Jewish "lore"; that part of the oral Torah which contains expositions of biblical texts, theologies, philosophies, and stories related to Jewish life.

ANTIOCHUS IV. Ruler of Syria (175–163 B.C.E.) who tried to force Jews to assume Hellenistic ways.

ASHKENAZIM. Those Jews who come from Europe, especially eastern Europe.

BAR MITZVAH. Literally, "son of the commandment"; refers to a boy's attainment of adulthood at age thirteen and his obligation to keep the Jewish law. In his Bar Mitzvah, a boy is called up in the synagogue to read from the Torah.

BAT MITZVAH. Literally, "daughter of the commandment"; a ritual for twelve-year-old girls of the Conservative and Reformed Jewish traditions similar to the Bar Mitzvah for boys.

DIASPORA. The world outside Israel.

GEMARA. Commentary by later rabbis on issues raised in the Mishnah.

GET. Religious divorce obtainable only at the request of the husband.

HAGADDAH. The ritual retelling of the story of Passover during the seder meal.

HALACHA. That part of the oral Torah which is law.

HANUKKAH. The festival of lights which celebrates the Jewish victory over the Hellenization program of Antiochus IV.

HASIDIM. Members of a mystical Jewish movement that emerged in eastern Europe in the eighteenth century which focuses on the love of and a personal relationship with God.

HOSHANA RABBA. "The great Hosanna"; the seventh day of Succoth, on which prayers are said for a good harvest cycle.

KADDISH. Prayer which reflects on the greatness of God and his ultimate triumph; also recited by mourners at prayer services during the period of their mourning.

KETUVIM. Hebrew word meaning "writings"; refers to the third portion of the Jewish Bible.

KIPPAH. Hebrew word for the circular head covering worn by many Jewish males.

KOL NIDRE. A prayer said on the eve of Yom Kippur which asks God to forgive a person for the breaking of any vows which were made to God.

KOSHER. Means "fit"; used primarily in relation to food which Jews are permitted to eat.

MAZZAH. Unleavened bread.

MEGILLAH. The scroll read during the celebration of Purim, retelling the story of Esther.

MENORAH. Candelabrum. The seven-branched version was one of the temple furnishings and today symbolizes Israel on its national seal; the nine-branched version is specifically used to commemorate Hanukkah, eight of the candles symbolizing the eight days of the festival and the ninth traditionally being used to light the others.

MEZUZAH. Literally, "doorpost." Ritually, it is a small parchment containing the first two paragraphs of the Shema (Deut. 6:4–9, 13–31) which is usually placed in a small box or container and affixed to the doorpost.

MIDRASH. Literally, "search" for meaning; indicates the portion of the oral traditions not incorporated into the Gemara and later recorded separately.

MIKVEH. Ritual bath.

MINYAN. Ten males (Orthodox) or males and females (Conservative or Reformed) required for certain prayers.

MISHNAH. The written compilation of what had been oral halacha (law). It was set down in written form about 200 C.E.

MITNAGDIM. Opponents of the Hasidim who placed emphasis on learning the tradition rather than emotion.

MOHEL. The person who performs the ritual of circumcision.

NEVI'IM. Hebrew word meaning "prophets"; refers to the second part of the Jewish Bible.

PASSOVER. Spring festival celebrating the salvation of the people of Israel when the angel of death passed over Israel's firstborn in Egypt, as well as Israel's ultimate deliverance from bondage.

POGROM. Organized riots which resulted in the murder of Jews and the pillaging of their homes and possessions.

PURIM. Spring festival celebrating the deliverance of the Jews in the days of Queen Esther.

RABBI. Means "my master"; an authorized teacher.

REBBE. The spiritual head of a Hasidic community.

ROSH HASHANAH. Festival celebrating the new year.

SEDER. The order of the ritual of the Passover meal.

SEPHARDIM. Jews who have come from Spain or Arab lands.

SHEMA. Literally, "hear"; the name for Israel's fundamental confession of faith found in Deuteronomy 6:4.

SHEMINI ATZERET. The eighth day of assembly following Succoth, on which the prayers for rain are said.

SHIVA. Seven-day period of mourning deceased relatives in the home, during which the family sits on low stools and receives guests.

SHOFAR. The ram's horn sounded one hundred times on Rosh Hashanah and again to end Yom Kippur.

SIMHAT TORAH. "Rejoicing of the Torah"; the celebration of the conclusion and recommencement of the Torah reading cycle which takes place on Shemini Atzeret (or the second day of Shemini Atzeret in the diaspora).

SUCCOTH. The Feast of Tabernacles, commemorating divine protection of Israel during her wanderings in the wilderness.

SUKKAH. Literally, "tabernacle"; a booth constructed of three walls and a partial roof in which Jewish families should partake of meals and may sleep during the celebration of Succoth.

TALLIT. Prayer shawl.

TALMUD. The Mishnah plus the Gemara; the foundational writings of Orthodox Jewish life.

TANAK. The made-up name for the Jewish Bible (the Christian Old Testament) based on its three parts—Torah, Nevi'im, and Ketuvim.

TASHLICH. The custom of symbolically casting one's sins into flowing water; performed on Rosh Hashanah.

TEFILLIN. Two leather boxes which are worn on the arm and on the forehead at weekday morning prayers.

TORAH. The Pentateuch, or the first five books of the Tanak.

TZITZIT. The fringes on the prayer shawl or on an undershirt which remind one of the commandments in the law.

YARMULKA. Yiddish word for the round head covering often worn by Jewish males.

YOM KIPPUR. The Day of Atonement.

ZIONISM. The movement to establish a Jewish state in the land of Israel.

Notes

1. Chaim Potok, *Wanderings* (New York: Fawcett Crest, 1978), 26.

2. Ibid., 47–48.

3. Ibid., 64.

4. "Abraham," Cecil Roth et al., eds., *Encyclopædia Judaica*, corrected ed., 17 vols. (Jerusalem: Keter, [1974?]), 2:115–16.

5. From lectures given by Rabbi David Rosen in the fall semester, 1995, at the Brigham Young University Center for Near Eastern Studies, Jerusalem.

6. "Moses," *Encyclopædia Judaica*, 12:394.

7. Ibid., 397.

8. Herman Wouk, *This Is My God: The Jewish Way of Life*, rev. ed. (New York: Simon and Schuster, 1986), 15.

9. Rosen lectures.

10. "God," *Encyclopædia Judaica*, 7:650.

11. "Man," *Encyclopædia Judaica*, 11:844.

12. Ibid., 846.

13. Ibid., 847–48.

14. "Torah," *Encyclopædia Judaica*, 15:1235–36, 1238–39.

15. Ibid., 1239.

16. "Messiah," *Encyclopædia Judaica*, 11:1408–10.

17. Ibid., 11:1411.

18. Rosen Lectures.

19. Ahad Ha-'Am, quoted in Abraham E. Millgram, *Sabbath: The Day of Delight* (Philadelphia: Jewish Publication Society of America, 1944), 1.

20. Ibid., 1–2.

21. "Sabbath," *Encyclopædia Judaica*, 14:558.

22. Wouk, *This Is My God*, 42–43.

23. Millgram, *Sabbath*, 24.

24. Ibid., 24.

25. Ibid., 25.

26. Ibid., 26–35.

27. Ibid., 91.

28. Wouk, *This Is My God*, 62.

29. Ernest Stock, *Discovering Israel through Its Traditions, Customs, and Concepts* (Jerusalem: Rubin Mass, 1994), 92.

30. Rosen handout on the Days of Awe.

31. Ibid.; "Sukkot," *Encyclopædia Judaica*, 15:495–502.

32. Ibid.

33. Mordell Klein, ed., *Passover*, Popular Judaica Library Series (Jerusalem: Keter, 1973), 26–30.

34. Ibid., 57–61.

35. Ibid., 68–69.

36. "Passover," *Encyclopædia Judaica*, 13:168.

37. Klein, *Passover*, 51.

38. Joseph Telushkin, *Jewish Literacy: The Most Important Things to Know about the Jewish Religion, Its People, and Its History* (New York: William Morrow, 1991), 578.

39. John Bright, *A History of Israel,* 3d ed. (Philadelphia: Westminster Press, 1981), 422.

40. Stock, *Discovering Israel,* 39–40.

41. Telushkin, *Jewish Literacy,* 594–97.

42. Ibid., 587–88, 589, 591.

43. Ibid., 609–11.

44. Ibid., 611–13.

45. Ibid., 614.

46. Ibid., 615–16.

47. Ibid., 616.

48. Ibid., 627–32.

49. Ibid., 617–19.

50. Hayim Halevy Donin, *To Pray as a Jew: A Guide to the Prayer Book and the Synagogue Service* (New York: Basic Books, HarperCollins, 1980), 31.

51. Telushkin, *Jewish Literacy,* 661–62.

52. Ibid., 662–64.

53. Ibid., 633.

54. Ibid., 634–37.

55. Rosen lectures.

56. The following material is based on ibid. and on Telushkin, *Jewish Literacy,* 230–32, 396–98, 436–38.

57. Rosen lectures.

58. Ibid.

59. Ibid.

60. Telushkin, *Jewish Literacy,* 621–24.

Jesus Christ

Christianity

11

Roger R. Keller

I N a text written primarily to inform Latter-day Saints about the religious beliefs of non-Christians, it may seem superfluous to include a chapter on Christianity. However, Christians in general have little understanding of the historical high points in their own traditions. Latter-day Saint Christians have had even less exposure to the major issues in historical Catholicism and Protestantism, since their experience is with restored Christianity following 1830. Thus, to complete the circle, it is appropriate to provide a chapter from which Christians of all traditions may reflect upon their historical roots, regardless of whether those roots are Catholic, Orthodox, Protestant, or Latter-day Saint. This chapter, then, briefly sketches major issues within historical Christianity.[1]

Christianity has within it three broad divisions: Roman Catholic, Eastern Orthodox, and Protestant. Juxtaposing these traditions allows examination of points of divergence in the flow of their histories, thus enabling a better understanding of how Christians within these traditions resemble each other, as well as how they differ. In many instances, the starting point will be Roman Catholicism, where the issues, be they theological, liturgical, or practical, are often found in their historical forms. Since Eastern Orthodox thought agrees with Roman Catholicism in so many instances, in this chapter the term *Catholic* will be used to comprehend both traditions, unless specific distinction is made otherwise.

HISTORICAL BACKGROUND

Christianity arose from the midst of Judaism; it was initially a Jewish sect composed of persons who believed that the Messiah had come in the person of Jesus Christ. Early Christians continued to go to the temple (Acts 3:1) and to worship there. There were even persons in the church who argued that true Christians needed to take upon themselves the practices of the Jewish law. Thus, Christians today must look for their roots among the Jews of the first centuries B.C.E. and C.E.—centuries that were politically turbulent.

Palestine was a land of many competing currents. At the end of the Babylonian captivity, Cyrus of Persia permitted any Jews who wished to return to their homeland to do so in 538 B.C.E. They remained, however, under Persian domination until Alexander the Great conquered the Persians. With Alexander's death, his empire was divided between the Ptolemies in Egypt and the Seleucids in the Fertile Crescent; Palestine was, for the most part, under Seleucid domination. A major effort to eradicate Judaism was mounted by Antiochus IV in 167 B.C.E., when he polluted the temple and outlawed all Jewish religious practice. In response, the Jews rose in revolt under the Maccabees and purified the temple in 165 B.C.E. after evicting Antiochus's forces. Following these events, the Jews enjoyed a measure of independence under the leadership of the Hasmoneans (142–63 B.C.E.), which ended when the Roman general Pompey took Jerusalem in 63 B.C.E. From that point, Palestine functioned as a vassal state of Rome. One ruler, Herod the Great, did much to beautify the country with his building projects, even rebuilding the temple of Zerubbabel, a project which began in 20 B.C.E. and was completed just before the outbreak of the Jewish Revolt in 66 C.E. However, Herod was hated by most of the Jewish population because he was an Idumean. He was brutal in his rule and only marginally Jewish in his practice.

Judaism in this period was anything but cohesive. The more that is learned about this period, the greater the diversity appears. There were Sadducees, Pharisees, Scribes, Essenes, and Zealots, all at variance with each other and with the Romans. Intermingled with party views was an expectation among many persons that the Messiah, the anointed deliverer, would appear and free the Jews from the Roman stranglehold. Tensions ran high, and messianic characteristics and expectations were ascribed to various leaders, both temporal and spiritual. One such leader was Jesus of Nazareth.

JESUS CHRIST: THE FOUNDATION OF CHRISTIANITY

"The book of the generation of Jesus Christ, the son of David, the son of Abraham" (Matt. 1:1). In this statement beginning his Gospel, Matthew is stressing the dual nature of Jesus' role and ministry. On the one hand, Jesus fulfills Jewish hopes. He is indeed the son of David, the Messiah expected by the Jews. On the other hand, his mission and ministry extend beyond the Jewish nation to fulfill the promise to Abraham that he and his descendants would be a blessing to the nations of the world (see Gen. 12:3). Thus, Jesus came to and for all the people of the family of God. His was not a parochial mission, but rather a universal one. His was not a mission only to the great, but also to the small and insignificant of the earth. His was not to be a reign which was exercised in marble palaces, but rather was one which would encompass eternity. His was not a leadership that would place him at the head of an army of Zealots seeking to rid their land of the hated Romans. Instead, he stood at the forefront of the hosts of heaven and could, if he wished, summon legions of angels to do his bidding.

His birth was in a stable. Much of his life was lived within the walls of a carpenter shop. His ministry was singularly unsuccessful by worldly standards, though large numbers of the "little people" of the world found hope in his teachings and in his presence. In death, he shared his place of execution with thieves, and he died the death of a common criminal. Thus ended his story, so some thought; and for three days it seemed that this was indeed the case. Then the impossible happened. His tomb was found empty. People began to say that they had seen him, talked with him, shared a meal with him. Frightened men who had fled back to homes, families, and vocations suddenly became giants of spiritual strength, no longer fearing anyone or anything. They claimed to be empowered by

the risen King of heaven and earth as they preached a message of faith, repentance, *baptism*, and the empowering strength of the Holy Ghost. They claimed that this carpenter of Nazareth was God who became human in order that he might work out an *atonement* for the sins of all people and thus open the way for them to their Heavenly Father's presence.

Even the death of these early followers could not stamp out the work they began, for the message of this common man of Nazareth, this man named Jesus, has spread over the face of the earth so effectively that approximately a quarter of the world's population professes adherence to his person and teachings. Thus began the story of The Church of Jesus Christ in the meridian of time. Following the course of this story from its beginnings to the time of the restoration of the gospel in this last dispensation is vital in gaining a better understanding of the faith of those who profess many things in common with those Christians who call themselves Latter-day Saints.

BASIC BELIEFS

The Doctrine of God

The Knowledge of God

A major question within Christian theology has always been "How does one come to know God?" Two basic answers have surfaced within the history of Christian thought and are expressed in the two Latin phrases *analogia entis* (analogy of being) and *analogia fidei* (analogy of faith). Analogia entis assumes that one can learn about God and reason one's way to God through observation of the natural order. Saint Thomas Aquinas (ca. 1225–74) is normally associated most closely with this mode of thought. Analogia fidei means that one comes to know God only as God makes himself known through revelation. The center point of this knowledge is faith in Jesus Christ, and it is in him that the faithful learn about the world, humanity, and God as they really are. Apart from God's self-revelation to people, there can be no knowledge of God. In Protestant circles, this path to a knowledge of God would be associated with persons like *John Calvin* (1509–1564), the great Reformer, and Karl Barth (1886–1968), the twentieth-century Reformed theologian.

The Trinity

In traditional Christian thought, Christians learn some unique lessons as they are confronted with Jesus Christ. First, they learn that the Father has a Son. Second, they learn that the Son is God. Third, they learn that the Holy Spirit or Holy Ghost is one with the Father and the Son and is thus God also. Fourth, they believe that God is one.

As the gospel moved from the Jewish world into the Hellenistic (Greek) world, a transition took place in Christian thought. The God who had been described in active terms by early Jewish Christians was now described in static *neo-Platonic* terms by Hellenistic Christians. Hence, there developed a desire to understand and explain how God could be one and three at the same time. It was noted by expositors of scripture that there was a thoroughgoing monotheism throughout the Bible, while at the same time both the Son and the Holy Ghost were spoken of in ways that ascribed deity to them. How could this be? The answer was given that the Father, the Son, and the Holy Ghost must all be of one essence (*homoousios*) but were simultaneously three. Many attempts have been made to clarify and explain this concept, but none has ever been wholly adequate. Ultimately, one had to bow before the mystery of the divine and affirm that God's ways were not humanity's ways, that the finite human mind could not fully comprehend the infinite God. Thus, the trinitarian understanding, while purportedly explaining the biblical texts, also remained a mystery incomprehensible to finite human beings.

Protestants hold the same position on the doctrine of the *Trinity* as do Catholics. Eastern Orthodox theology states, like Catholic theology, that the members of the Godhead are of one substance (homoousios), as opposed to the belief, held by Arius of Alexandria and his followers in 325 C.E., that the three persons were of "like substance" (*homoiousios*). This trinitarian controversy led to the denunciation of the Arians as heretics and the formulation of the first Nicene Creed, which used the term homoousios. There is, however, among Eastern Orthodox, a tendency toward subordinationism within the Godhead, in which the Son and the Holy Ghost operate under the direction of God the Father, and passages such as 1 Corinthians 15:28 appear to support this idea. Further, for the Orthodox, the Holy Spirit proceeds from the Father only, not from both the Father and the Son as in Roman Catholic thought, thereby further emphasizing the primacy of the Father in the Godhead.

For all the mystery surrounding it, the doctrine of the Trinity is the very doctrine which brings God into personal, close contact with human beings. The doctrine clearly states that God is not distant, but personal. He is so personal that he relates to individuals as a personal Creator and Father, as a personal Savior and Redeemer in the person of the Son, and as Sanctifier in the person of the Holy Ghost. While one may not understand all the mysteries of the Trinity, one can still have a close, personal experience of the presence of God, who is Father, Son, and Holy Ghost and who relates directly to his people through each of the three persons.

Eternity and the Inner-Trinitarian Decree

In both Catholic and Protestant thought, God has existed from all eternity. He has always existed as Father, Son, and Holy Ghost. However, nothing else is eternal. Everything else in the universe is a creation of this trinitarian God. Out of his graciousness and love, he chose to create beings to have a relationship with him. It was not out of any need on God's part that this decision was made, for he was already a being who had the perfect relationship within himself—that of the Father and Son bound together in the love of the Holy Ghost. But his decision went beyond the mere creation of people, for his deepest intent was to have a relationship with people as a human being himself through the incarnation of the Son. Thus, in one strain of Christian thinking, the incarnation was the center of the entire plan of God. Whether people had sinned or not, Jesus would have come. However, people did sin, even to the degree that they tried to crucify their God and to rid the universe of him. Out of love for his creatures, the Lord of heaven and earth submitted to this humiliation, taking upon himself the sins of all people for all time. For three days the plan to rid the universe of God seemed to have worked. However, on the third day Jesus was raised from the dead and in him God's plan to be eternally with humans as a human was realized; for the exalted man, Jesus Christ, stood at the right hand of the Father, and all humankind could be saved through him.

Such is the understanding of some Christians. Others modify this conception, saying that God wished to have fellowship with persons outside of himself but, knowing that humanity would fall, provided the plan of salvation, which focused less on the incarnation and more on the cross and the resurrection. Thus, Christ's coming into the world was for the purpose of atoning for humanity's sins more than for fellowship with people. In either case, the universe, the world, the vegetation, and the animals were all created to provide humanity with a residence and the means for survival. All of these, including people, were created out of nothing, and nothing existed prior to them—not intelligences, spirits, matter, or energy. All were creations of God and God alone. Only God in his triune character was preexistent.

The Atonement

No theologian has ever been able to explain adequately how the sufferings and death of Jesus Christ could atone for the sins of all humanity. Explanations give only partial answers. In some unknown way, Christ's sacrifice cleansed people of their sins, and Christ's acceptance in himself of God's judgments upon human beings satisfied the demands of justice against them. The principal concern of theological discussions has been, however, more on the way that one appropriates the results of the Atonement into one's own life and less on how the Atonement itself was effected. Within Catholicism the Atonement is appropriated primarily through sacramental means. It becomes real through the avenues of confession, *penance*, baptism, the *eucharist*, and the mass. Faith plays a role in the reception of the external sacraments, which are essential for the salvation of members of the church. Chiefly through the sacraments, the church and its priesthood mediate salvation to the believer.

The Protestant Reformers reacted against this system of mediated grace and claimed that each person had direct access to the atonement of Christ through the avenue of faith. The phrase so often associated with *Martin Luther* (1482–1546) is "by faith alone are ye saved." Salvation was not dependent upon ecclesiastical structures, priesthoods, or sacraments but came directly to the individual through faith. Faith, however, gave rise to the desire in the individual to avail himself or herself of baptism and the Lord's Supper and to do good works. But none of these was a prerequisite to receiving release from one's sins. Faith alone was sufficient. Thus, persons could come to Christ in the last

moments of their lives, die never having been baptized, and still be accepted into the presence of God based on their confession of faith. Therefore, Christendom has not been united in its understanding of how the vital event of the Atonement affects individuals.

The Doctrine of Humanity

Humanity's Reason for Being

"Question—What is the chief end of man? Answer—Man's chief end is to glorify God, and to enjoy him forever."[2]

According to both Catholic and Protestant belief, human life is to be directed to God. When people stand in an open relationship with their Creator, they are what God created them to be. As they recognize their dependence upon God for all things in life, as well as for life itself, people can give praise and direct glory to their God by magnifying their place in the created order. Thus, from the moment of their creation and through all eternity, they could have stood in companionship with God. They could have enjoyed the radiance of the divine presence. It was for this that people were created.

Fall, Free Will, and Procreation

Men and women were not, however, to be automatons. They were created to bow freely before their God, and to do this they had to have free will. Forced worship was no worship at all. Therefore, Adam and Eve were placed in the Garden of Eden with full freedom of choice, as well as the power to procreate. In Catholic and Protestant belief, Adam and Eve could have lived forever in the garden with their offspring. They chose, however, to usurp God's rightful place and sought to become like him through disobedience to his commands. Thus, they were cast out of his presence, and only through the atonement of Jesus Christ could they ever again reside in the divine presence. Ever since this time, all the family of Adam has been tainted by the desire to take God's place. Thus, Adam passed on to his children the seed of willfulness which has come to be known as "original sin," the idea that there is something basically evil in human beings which can only be corrected by the grace of God. Apart from that grace, humanity has no hope. Perhaps the most concise and famous text used to support this thought is found in Paul's letter to the Romans:

Now we know that what things soever the law saith, it saith to them who are under the law: that every mouth may be stopped, and all the world may become guilty before God. Therefore by the deeds of the law there shall no flesh be justified in his sight: for by the law is the knowledge of sin. But now the righteousness of God without the law is manifested, being witnessed by the law and the prophets; Even the righteousness of God which is by faith of Jesus Christ unto all and upon all them that believe: for there is no difference: For all have sinned, and come short of the glory of God[.] (Rom. 3:19–23)

Thus, Catholics and many Protestants believe that natural human beings find themselves helpless before God. They cannot will themselves into fellowship with their Creator, fundamentally because they will not recognize that God is God and that they are creatures of that God. Humans prefer the illusion of personal godhood to the reality of expressing their humanity before a gracious and loving Creator. Humans are sunk in an inescapable morass of self-pride, error, and sin. Only God can free them, but people have done nothing to earn or deserve freedom. If God chooses to offer them freedom, it will be an act of total love and grace.

Salvation History

As already stated, within the inner-trinitarian life of God subscribed to in Protestant and Catholic theology, before any creative acts, God had already chosen humans as the beings outside himself with whom he would have fellowship. Humanity's puny disobedience could not short-circuit that divine plan. Therefore, what had been planned and proposed on the cosmic level had to become a reality in human history. Having permitted humankind to fall, God chose not to inject the Son immediately into history; rather, he chose to prepare his people to receive the Son. Thus, he chose a special people to bear the unique vocation of blessing all the peoples of the world with a knowledge of the true and living God. Most Catholic and Protestant theologians find the historical roots of this covenant in Genesis 12:1–3, when God calls Abraham.

Now the Lord had said unto Abram, Get thee out of thy country, and from thy kindred, and from thy father's house, unto a land that I will shew thee: *And I will make of thee a great nation*, and I will bless thee, and make thy name great; and thou shalt be a blessing: And I will bless them that bless thee, and curse him that curseth thee: *and in thee shall all families of the earth be blessed*. (emphasis added)

There are two basic promises made to Abraham, which are emphasized above. The first promise is that from Abraham will come a great nation. From his grandson, Jacob, arose the nation of Israel. Its greatness lay not in the territories and the peoples it conquered, but rather in its unique priestly vocation. Not all the men of Israel wanted to be priests, and so the Lord called only the sons of Aaron to that role, with the remainder of the Levites to assist them. Even so, the whole of Israel had the obligation to live the covenant and to witness to the world of the God who created all things. This many Jews have tried to do over the centuries, often being willing to sacrifice life itself rather than to deny their special faith and vocation.

The second promise to Abraham was that he would be a blessing to the nations. Israel has not always understood this mission. There were times when the Jews actively sought converts; but as the pressures of foreign nations and peoples caused hardship and persecution among them, they tended to band together by necessity and to reach out less and less. A people can only endure so many deportations, inquisitions, and holocausts before they decide they need no one but themselves. After the Romans destroyed Jerusalem in 70 C.E. and the Jews were scattered in the diaspora, most of Christendom came to the conclusion that the church was now the true Israel, that old Israel was gone and no longer held any covenantal rights. Thus, great purges of the Jews, "those who had crucified the Lord," were periodically held. These purges stand in harsh contrast to the Christian concept of God as a loving Father who created all humankind as his children. But since the Second World War, all the mainstream Christian traditions have developed greater understanding toward the Jewish people and have abandoned any institutionalized persecutions of them.

Human Destiny

God created people to live with him, and through the Atonement he made that possible. Christian theologians, however, do not agree completely on the scope of the Atonement. Some claim that it is effective only for those who profess that Jesus is Lord and Savior. Others see it as universally effective, since Christ took "the sins of the world" upon himself. Nevertheless, there is no disagreement that God wishes to have eternal fellowship with at least some of his children. Thus, the question of the nature of that fellowship is pressed to the fore.

Clearly, the doctrine of the Resurrection as found in the scriptures states that body and spirit will one day be united and the "whole person" will dwell in the presence of God. However, some recent Christian theological thinking questions the reality of the resurrection of the body. Some Christian theologians hold that the resurrection is only spiritual in nature. To them the binding of the material and the spiritual into a whole seems inconsistent with the nature of a trinitarian God and with the neo-Platonic belief that matter is evil. The majority of Christian laypersons, however, believe in the literal resurrection of the body. They feel that one must stand as a whole person before the Father, just as does Jesus, and that cannot be done without the body. It is an integral part of one's personhood.

Following death and resurrection, traditional Christianity maintains that there is judgment for all. The judgment, however, focuses less on "deeds" than it does on one's acceptance of Christ's atonement. If Christ has been accepted, then his atonement covers the person's sins and the person is welcomed fully into the presence of the Lord. If Christ has not been accepted, then there is no atonement for the person's sins and he or she is banished to hell, outer darkness, or extinction. Thus, humanity's chief end is, indeed, "to glorify God and to enjoy him forever," if people are willing to accept that blessing.

PRACTICES

When Jesus came into the coasts of Caesarea Philippi, he asked his disciples, saying, Whom do men say that I the Son of man am? And they said, Some say that thou art John the Baptist: some, Elias; and others, Jeremias, or one of the prophets. He saith unto them, But whom say ye that I am? And Simon Peter answered and said, Thou art the Christ, the Son of the living God. And Jesus answered and said unto him, Blessed art thou, Simon Barjona: for flesh and blood hath not revealed it unto thee, but my Father which is in heaven. And I say also unto thee, That thou art Peter, and upon this rock I will build my church; and the gates of hell shall not prevail against it. And I will give unto thee the keys of the kingdom of heaven: and whatsoever thou shalt bind on earth shall be bound in heaven: and whatsoever thou shalt loose on earth shall be loosed in heaven. (Matt. 16:13–19)

If the history of the Christian community were to be a history of the interpretation of scripture, the above passage from Matthew would stand as the centerpiece of that history. Few passages have had greater effect on Christendom than has this one, for numerous people and traditions have tried to determine to what the word rock refers. Is it Peter, as Catholics believe? Is it his confession of faith, as Protestants interpret it? Is it revelation, as Latter-day Saints assert? The way one answers these questions to a great degree determines how one views Christianity and understands its organization.

Authority

The Roman Catholic church has always understood Matthew 16:13–19 to describe the setting apart of Peter as head of the church, or its first pope. Peter is given the keys of the kingdom. Peter is given authority, based on the faith and knowledge that are given to him. It is his successors who bear those same keys. Thus, Catholicism has always understood the structure of the church which Christ founded to be *episcopal* in nature, meaning that it is founded upon a hierarchical structure consisting of bishops and priests. It is through the bishops of the church that direction is given by Christ to his followers.

Therefore, authority within the Catholic tradition lies in and is mediated by the priesthood, beginning with the pope, who is the direct successor of Peter. There has been some discussion among Catholics asking whether councils have authority greater than the pope, but in 1870 Pope Pius IX issued a declaration asserting the infallibility of the pope under certain conditions. It states:

The Roman pontiff, when he speaks ex cathedra, that is, when in discharge of the office of pastor and doctor of all Christians, by virtue of his supreme apostolic authority, he defines a doctrine regarding faith or morals to be held by the universal church, by the divine assistance promised to him in blessed Peter, is possessed of that infallibility with which the divine Redeemer willed that His church should be endowed.[3]

Thus, the Catholic church claims direct apostolic authority through an unbroken chain of bishops in Rome who stand in the shoes of Peter. Christ's authoritative priesthood continues to exist upon the earth today because of that succession.

In the Eastern Orthodox tradition, the patriarch of Constantinople is generally viewed as the leader of the Orthodox community. However, he is not held to be superior in authority to other bishops within the church. All the apostles held equal authority and power, although Peter was their "prince." Similarly, all bishops within the Orthodox communion hold equal authority in their areas of responsibility. Since the basic Orthodox organizations are associated with the countries within which they exist, authority resides primarily in the patriarchs who head the national churches—for example, the Russian Orthodox patriarch, the Bulgarian Orthodox patriarch, and several others.

Protestants do not have a belief in a strong, central human authority. As a result, and because of the belief that Christ alone is head of the church and that all persons have direct access to him, it is very difficult to define where authority lies among Protestants, as the presence of numerous denominations attests. All, however, would agree that the scriptures are central to this question, and it is in them that prophetic and apostolic authority may be found. Yet, since all persons have the right and obligation to interpret scripture for themselves, many hold that they themselves are the final authority under the guidance of the Holy Spirit. Some Protestants attempt to define how these individual interpretations may be checked, thereby creating some harmony among believers by stating that councils of bishops, general conferences, general assemblies, synods, and other like organizations supersede individual interpretations of believers. In the end, however, one can never be sure where and when God speaks, for so many hear his voice in so many different places, hear him in so many different ways, and hear him saying so many different things.

Ministry

Clergy

In Catholicism, it is through bishops and priests that the sacramental life of the church is carried out, meaning that work which is composed of the sacraments of baptism, confirmation, eucharist, penance, *unction* (anointing with oil), *holy orders*, and marriage. Catholic clergy bear great responsibility for the maintenance of the church's spiritual life, for they are those called by God to mediate the saving ordinances to the people.

In Roman Catholicism the clergy are males who receive the sacrament of holy orders and promise poverty and celibacy at the time of their ordination

to the diaconate, the last step before priesthood. Upon being ordained a priest, the man becomes a representative of Christ on the earth who is given the authority through his bishop to act as an agent of God in the sacramental work of the church. Thus, he can baptize members into the church, consecrate the elements of the sacrament, hear confessions, prescribe acts of penance, forgive sins in Christ's name, anoint the ill, and stand as a witness to marriages. Essentially, he is ordained to an office in which he acts as an authoritative conduit between God and the congregation.

Eastern Orthodox clergy perform the same functions as Roman Catholic priests, but they are not all required to be celibate. They may marry, but those who choose to do so must remain among the "lower" clergy.

Among Protestants in the Episcopalian denomination, the first function of the clergy, much as with the Catholic tradition, is to provide the sacraments of baptism and *Holy Communion* to the people. However, episcopal priests share a strong tradition of preaching with other Protestants. The range of responsibilities among all Protestant clergy, who may be married, is immense. They are expected to be preachers, teachers, counselors, crisis ministers, public figures, mentors for youth, and comforters of the aged. Many congregations have come to depend upon the clergy to do the full work of the ministry, although the priesthood of all believers, the shared ministry of the people of God, is the very essence of the Protestant tradition.

Baptism

Among all Christians, baptism is the initiatory rite through which a person, infant or adult, is ushered into the church. In the Catholic church, infant baptism is the norm, but adults may be baptized either by pouring or by immersion. Catholics believe that "baptism is not merely a sign of grace, but actually contains and confers [grace] on those who put no obstacle . . . in its way."[4] Thus, baptism has historically been viewed as necessary and essential to salvation—even for the salvation of infants, since even infants bear the mark of original sin inherited from Adam and Eve. It is now believed, however, that infants who die without baptism are not excluded from entrance into heaven. The vows taken by parents at the baptism of their child are to be confirmed by the child when he or she is somewhat older. At this time, children undertake a course of instruction, are confirmed, and from then on take responsibility for their own faith and life.

Eastern Orthodox Christians retain infant baptism. The infant is not sprinkled but may be either soaked thoroughly by pouring or fully immersed three times. The child is then anointed with oil and consecrated by a bishop.

Among Protestants, some believe that baptism by sprinkling is adequate and others call for complete immersion. Some hold baptism to be essential to salvation, although most would probably claim that God can and does save without it. Baptism is, however, understood to signify one's entry into the church either as an infant or as an adult. When administered to infants, it is understood as a visible sign of God's pure grace in accepting the child before the child knows God or can call on him. If baptized as infants, persons are expected to make their own confessions of faith in their youth and to accept fully the responsibilities of church membership. This process of instruction and admission into the full fellowship of the church is also known among Protestants as confirmation.

Preparation for Worship

A Christian worship service is not designed to entertain. It is for those who have prepared themselves spiritually to encounter the Word of God, Jesus Christ, in the context of the music, the prayers, the sacraments, and the sermon. Among Roman Catholics, confession, or the sacrament of penance, is a traditional prerequisite to participation in worship. In confession, one of the *seven sacraments,* Catholics confess their sins to a priest, who is authorized to forgive sins on behalf of Christ. He must prescribe certain penitential acts which the one confessing is expected to fulfill. To the worshiper who understands the role of confession, the act can be a new beginning in that person's life. Confession is not merely a ritual, but a profound request for forgiveness from God and thus a new beginning in life.

The Eastern Orthodox tradition retains confession as part of the preparation for worship and for the taking of the eucharist; but it is not private confession, as in the Roman tradition, with the one confessing and the one hearing the confession being separated and invisible to one another. Instead, the person confessing sits with the priest, thereby enabling the priest to perform an extended pastoral or counseling role in addition to hearing the confession. Confession is effective only after reconciliation with those who were wronged or estranged.

Among Protestants, the practice of formal confession to a priest has essentially vanished. This is due, in large measure, to the basic doctrine of Protestantism that a worshiper needs no intercessor with God other than Christ. Persons can confess directly to God. Any formal confession takes place in the context of worship, where the congregation joins together in voicing through printed prayers of confession their corporate guilt before God for things both done and not done. Even so, there is a recognition that there can be no encounter with the divine without eliciting a confession of sin from those being drawn to the worship of God.

Congregational Worship

Among Roman Catholics, the mass forms the center of Catholic worship. Some non-Catholics have mistakenly held that Catholics believe Christ to be resacrificed each time the mass is said. In reality, the mass is a re-presentation of Christ's atonement before both the Father and the faithful. Just as the sacrament among Latter-day Saints recalls Christ's suffering and death, as well as his resurrection and victory, so also does the mass. The contemporary reform of the mass divides it into two parts: the Liturgy of the Word (ordinary, proper, scripture reading, and preaching) and the Liturgy of the Eucharist (consecration of the bread and wine and the communion of the faithful). Within these two parts are said or sung the basic elements of the mass. The first element, the *Kyrie,* is a request for mercy ("Lord have mercy"). This is followed by an ascription of glory (the *Gloria*) to God the Father and his Son, who are to be praised, worshiped, and glorified, for the Son has taken the sins of the world upon himself. Next comes the *Credo,* or creed. This is the worshipers' confession of faith in the God who has acted on their behalf. This is followed by the *Sanctus* ("Holy, holy, holy, Lord God of Hosts"). Finally comes the *Agnus Dei,* which says, "Lamb of God, grant us peace." Thus, the mass leads the worshiper from a cry for mercy, through praise and confession, to ultimate peace with God because of the sacrifice of the Lamb. The service then culminates with the gathered church sharing in the eucharist, dedicating themselves anew to Christ, and receiving once again the benefits of his sacrifice for them.

Among the Eastern Orthodox, the reality of the life-giving incarnation of the Son is conveyed through the mass, just as that reality is conveyed through all other sacraments of the church. A difference between Eastern Orthodoxy and Roman Catholicism is that music has historically been a more vital part of Eastern Orthodoxy than it has been in Roman Catholicism. Until recent years there has been a distrust among Catholics of the sensual nature of music. However, among the Orthodox it is considered one of the best vehicles to express the mystical union which takes place between God and the worshiper.

Among Protestants, worship may be quite formal and follow a structure almost identical to the Catholic mass (Episcopal and some Lutheran congregations), or be very free in form (some Baptist communions and Pentecostal groups), or fall somewhere in between (Presbyterians and Methodists). While those communions which grew out of Catholicism or the Church of England still have a strong focus on the sacramental means of mediating grace to the worshiper, most of the worship among the Protestant traditions has a central stress on the scriptural and preached word. Thus, for example, the "high point" of Presbyterian or Lutheran services is the reading of the biblical word and its exposition through the sermon. The word of God is life-giving and life-changing when preached and is available to all within the pages of scripture. In a very real sense, the reading of scripture and the hearing of the preached word have almost become "sacraments" within Protestantism.

Eucharist

The taking of the eucharist, or what Latter-day Saints term "the sacrament," is the culminating point of the mass. It is in the taking of the bread and wine that the worshiper ultimately encounters the crucified and risen Christ. But how is that union brought about? How is Christ present in the elements of bread and wine? Since the thirteenth century, the doctrine of *transubstantiation* has been used by Roman Catholics in an attempt to explain this mystery. Technically, the doctrine states that the elements of bread and wine become the "substance" of the body and blood of Christ, while only the "accidents" (the appearance of the bread and wine) remain. The bread and wine actually are changed through the words of institution into the body and blood of the

Lord. Thus, there is a special sacredness attached to the elements once they have been consecrated by a priest. Any remaining consecrated wine is consumed by the priest, and any remaining bread is locked away on the altar so that it may not be desecrated. The one who partakes of the eucharist is participating in the sacrifice of Jesus Christ. In essence, the worshiper is taking Christ's sacrifice upon himself or herself and accepting the effects of that sacrifice.

For the Eastern Orthodox, the eucharist is also the culmination or high point of the mass. However, they do not concern themselves with the subtleties of the doctrine of transubstantiation. Instead, Christ is felt to be present in the sacrament due to the operation of the Holy Ghost.

Among Protestants, the eucharist or Holy Communion is the sign of Christ's real presence with his people—people who participate in his life, death, and resurrection spiritually as they partake of the sacrament. It is also an opportunity for them to recommit themselves to the Lord, to become clean, and to renew their covenants to lead a Christian life.

Accessories to Worship

LITURGICAL CALENDAR. As an aid to worship and as a way of directing people's thoughts to the critical events of God's plan of salvation, there is present in Catholic as well as Protestant traditions what is known as the *liturgical calendar*. It leads the worshiper through the Christian year, and each season of the year is represented by a special color to assist in recalling the importance of that particular season.

The calendar begins with *Advent*, which consists of the four Sundays prior to Christmas. It is a season of preparation for the coming of Christ and involves introspection. It is a contemplative season and is thus represented by the somber color of purple. Advent is followed by the season of Christmas, a time of joy because of God's entry into the world. Its color is therefore white. Following Christmas is the season of *Epiphany*, celebrating the coming of the wise men, who symbolize the world coming to Christ. Its color is green. Next comes the season of *Lent*, a forty-day period (exclusive of the Sundays) of contemplation and preparation for the passion of Jesus Christ. Thus, as with Advent, its color is purple. Often small sacrifices are made during Lent to remind worshipers that Christ died for their sins and that the things of the world have no significant meaning in the light of that one terrible yet wonderful event.

Lent culminates with Good Friday and the remembrance of Golgotha and the cross.

Following Lent is the season of Easter, a season of joy and celebration—for God, not humans, has conquered, rules, and reigns even over death itself. As with Christmas, the color is white. Easter season ends with the coming of *Pentecost*, which celebrates the arrival of the Holy Ghost and the beginnings of the worldwide church. Since the Holy Ghost is seen as tongues of fire, red is the liturgical color. Finally, the last five months of the year are known as the season of *Trinity*. This is the period in which the church contemplates the implications of the gospel for daily life in every corner of the world. Just as green is the color of Epiphany, so also it is the color of Trinity.

If one follows the liturgical seasons, both in personal and public worship, at the end of a year he or she will have contemplated seriously every major aspect of the Christian gospel.

CROSS. The *crucifix* (the dead Christ hanging on the cross) is ever present in Catholic churches and is often worn around the necks of Catholics as a symbol of their faith. Often misunderstood by non-Catholics, the crucifix is a profound symbol of the extent to which Christ went to free us from our sins. He gave his life that we might live. What more graphic way is there to stress Christ's ultimate sacrifice and love for us, Catholics would explain, than the image of him hanging in death on the cross? For Catholic Christians, the crucifix points to the centrality and absolute necessity of the Atonement.

Eastern Orthodox churches are rich in scriptural art, with the two-dimensional representations known as *icons* being especially important. Through them divine grace is conveyed to the believer, and they are thus similar to sacraments. One of the more frequently portrayed subjects is Jesus on the cross; but there is a significant difference between Orthodox and Catholic crucifixes. In some Orthodox representations Christ is not portrayed as dead, but instead he is shown in full glory. He is radiant, with his head up. It is the crucified *and* risen Christ who is on the Orthodox cross; and thus his death, resurrection, and exaltation are bound together in one complete symbol. The Jesus of Orthodox iconography represents the Jesus shown us in the Gospel of John, who attains his full glory on the cross and in resurrection.

Usually in Protestant sanctuaries one will observe a cross, often a very large one. It differs from the Catholic and Orthodox crosses in that it is an empty cross. The cross itself draws the worshipers' attention to the Atonement, while the fact that it is empty conveys to believers that Christ is no longer dead but risen.

Thus, in all of the traditions considered, there is a rich symbolism surrounding the cross, whether Christ hangs on it or whether it is empty.

MARY AND THE SAINTS. Roman Catholics believe that there is a direct and active relationship between the living and the dead and that the dead can assist the living. As one writer explains it:

In the [New Testament] the gift of special privileges to certain persons in the next world is indicated in Christ's promises to the Apostles (Matt. 19:28). Support for the intercession of the dead on behalf of the living is found in the parable of Dives and Lazarus (Luke 16:19–31). Other [New Testament] references are the description of the saints of the Old Covenant as a "cloud of witnesses" (Heb. 12:1), which Christians are to imitate (13:7), and the martyrs who pray before the throne of God (Rev. 6:9f.) and receive white robes (7:14–17) as a reward of their martyrdom. But the principal theological basis of the practice is Saint Paul's doctrine of the Mystical Body of Christ, in which all members have their particular office (Rom. 12:4–8) as "fellow citizens with the saints, and of the household of God" (Eph. 2:19).[5]

Fundamentally, the saints may intercede on behalf of the believer, so that the believer may gain the favors of God and Christ. Principal among the saints is the Blessed Virgin *Mary*. Just as Eve caused our death, Catholics believe, so also Mary is the cause of our salvation in that she is the mother of God. Being the mother of the Author of all grace, she can obtain grace for us by her maternal intercession. Catholics revere her deeply, but they still realize that Jesus, not Mary, is the Savior.

In Eastern Orthodoxy, saints are venerated through the use of icons. However, the emphasis is less on their intercessory power and more on the examples they present of the power that flows into persons' lives when they are in union with Christ. Among Protestants the veneration of saints has vanished, although there are days on which saints are remembered in the Anglican tradition.

Spirituality

The aim of Roman Catholicism is to promote a deep, abiding spirituality in the lives of its adherents. Many will attend mass daily, not because they must but because it places the events of the day in their proper context—that is, within an eternal context. That spirituality has led to the founding of numerous orders for both men and women. These orders are composed of priests, monks, or nuns and focus on a variety of ministries, including preaching, medical service, teaching, prayer, and meditation. Likewise, there is great emphasis on spirituality in the Eastern Orthodox tradition, but the emphasis is for all persons, be they clergy or laity.

Individual piety is stressed within Protestantism. Because the monastic life is not generally a part of Protestant thought, the spirituality is quite personal and individual and works itself out in the midst of life in the world.

SCRIPTURES

Formation of the Canon

Jews, Muslims, and Christians are all "people of the book." This means that they each have a literary "canon," or "measuring rod or rule" by which they gauge their life and their faith. Muslims turn to the Qur'an and understand it to be Allah's final and complete word to the faithful. Jews turn to the Torah, Prophets, and Writings—to what Christians call the Old Testament—to hear God's will for his people. And Christians turn to both the Old and the New Testaments to hear the word of God as the testaments bear witness to it. None of these scriptural canons came into existence all at once. Each has a history of "additions" before its final stage of completion.

It should therefore not be surprising to learn that the Christian canon is still in flux today. A continuing debate within Christendom has been whether to include the Old Testament *Apocrypha* in the canon. This is an issue between Protestants, who reject the Apocrypha, and Catholics, who accept it. Latter-day Saints have had to consider this issue also, and we read the following in the Doctrine and Covenants:

Verily, thus saith the Lord unto you concerning the Apocrypha—There are many things contained therein that are true, and it is mostly translated correctly; There are many things contained therein that are not true, which are interpolations by the hands of men. Verily, I say unto you, that it is not needful that the Apocrypha should be translated. Therefore, whoso readeth it, let him understand, for the Spirit manifesteth truth; And whoso is

enlightened by the Spirit shall obtain benefit therefrom; And whoso receiveth not by the Spirit, cannot be benefitted. Therefore it is not needful that it should be translated. Amen. (D&C 91:1–6)

The formation of the New Testament has also had its problems. By about 130 C.E., the four Gospels and the thirteen letters of Paul were established as canonical. There were some who questioned the inclusion of the Gospel of John, feeling that it did not take seriously enough Jesus' humanity. However, between 170 and 220 C.E., all of these writings were considered to be of the same inspired nature as the Old Testament. Doubts persisted about Hebrews, Jude, 2 Peter, 2 and 3 John, and Revelation. There were some who would have included the Epistle of Barnabas or the Shepherd of Hermas in the canon. The earliest witness to the present canonical form is found in a writing of Saint Athanasius in 369 C.E. A council held in Rome in 382 affirmed the canon as it is now constituted.[6]

Open or Closed Canon?

Catholic and Protestant Christians generally affirm that the canon of scripture is "closed." What this means is that they do not believe that new writings should be added to the existing scriptures. They feel that God has said all he needed to say through his prophets and his apostles; that the canonical scriptures are sufficient to lead the believer to right faith, morals, and practice in daily life; that God has made himself known in Jesus Christ; and that the scriptures of the Old and New Testaments provide abundant evidence of God's love, mercy, and justice and state all that humankind needs to know at this time. When studied and searched, they will lead the faithful into the presence of God.

Using the Scriptures

It may seem strange to those who have always had ready access to the scriptures that there was once a time when only a few persons could read them. Initially, the biblical writings appeared in the language of the people who wrote them, the Old Testament being mostly in Hebrew, with a few portions in Aramaic, and the New Testament appearing entirely in Greek. As Jews began to move into the Greek-speaking world, well before the time of Christ, there was a need for their scriptures to be translated into the language of the people. For the most part this language was Greek, and thus the *Septuagint* (LXX) was produced. It is this version of the Old Testament that comprised the scriptures of the early church. However, as the church spread into the Roman world, there was a need for a Bible in Latin, the language which many people used. Saint Jerome produced the Latin version of the Bible known as the *Vulgate*, completing the translation of the Gospels in 384 C.E., the New Testament in approximately 386, and the total Bible by 404. It was this basic translation of the scriptures that was used by the Catholic church from Jerome's time until relatively recently.

While many Christians originally spoke and understood Latin, with the fall of the Roman Empire it became a continually less-used language, except in the church. Consequently, many people never were able to hear the scriptures read in a language that was familiar to them and were thus dependent upon their priests to tell them what was in the scriptures. Needless to say, this led to a good deal of biblical illiteracy on the part of the average Christian and an ever-increasing role for the priest. One of the responses to this dilemma was the creation of the medieval morality play, which was generally performed on the steps of a cathedral. The play normally portrayed biblical stories or focused on moral dilemmas. Through this means, much of the biblical story became known to the average person, but it still could not substitute for the actual hearing of the text in a person's own language.

This reality was recognized by various persons in the late Middle Ages. John Wycliffe (ca. 1329–1384) was a principal driving force behind the first English translation of the Bible. In reality, Wycliffe was a reformer before the Reformers of the sixteenth century. He questioned many of the doctrines of the Catholic church, and his desire to see the scriptures in the vernacular was merely an extension of his wish that the people have an understanding for themselves of the Christian faith. After his death his writings were ordered burned, and his bones were dug up in 1428. However, the light that he brought to the Christian world could not be extinguished; two of his followers, Nicholas of Hereford and J. Purvey, completed the translation which he had begun.[7]

The desire to place the scriptures in the hands of all persons in their own language was a major rallying point of the Reformation. By translating from Hebrew and Greek texts, Martin Luther produced a Bible that made the gospel message available to the German people. The following statement captures the impact of this great work.

The first version in German from the original text, it is remarkable for its power and warmth. In its successful use of popular speech, it brought the Bible to life in the German language, and made it henceforward a dominant influence in German religion. It also contributed largely to the formation of the modern German tongue.[8]

With the availability of the Bible in German and other languages, people were no longer so dependent upon Roman Catholic priests for the interpretation of the scriptures. The Holy Spirit came to be regarded as the principal agent of interpretation, and each Christian became a student of the Bible with the right to receive direct revelation through its pages. Hence, the knowledge of God, his ways, and his works was available to all his people without mediation. Each person was capable of his or her own interpretation, but this too had its dangers, for there was no authoritative source of interpretation. Consequently, the Reformation and the period following it saw the genesis of many denominational groups, each claiming that its interpretations of various scriptural passages were the correct ones.

Sola Scriptura (Scripture Alone)?

Theology

The word theology is a composite of two Greek words—*theos* (God) and *logos* (reason or word). Thus, theology is the discipline whereby the person of faith seeks to reason within the various Christian communions. Theology seeks to understand, in rational and explainable terms, the mysteries God has revealed. Hence, it is not enough for theologians merely to repeat the words of scripture when asked a question. Instead, they try to bring their knowledge of the scriptures into contact with the people to whom they speak, so that the religious message is placed in terms and categories their hearers can understand.

Latter-day Saints understand this process, for they know that few of the doctrines of their church are fully articulated in any one place in the scriptures. Instead, as a doctrine is explained, the speaker may cite various scriptural texts, each of which is probably incomplete in itself. When all are brought together, however, they create the doctrine's complete tapestry. This is the process of "theology" in Protestant and Catholic thought. Scripture or other sources, such as tradition, are brought into contact with the needs and problems of people at given historical moments. The word of God should address the real needs of real people in real historical circumstances. Thus, a theological discussion in the fourth century focused on the nature of God, culminating in the Council of Nicaea (325 C.E.), while one in the sixteenth century focused on the nature of the church and led to the Reformation (1517) and the Council of Trent (1545–63). As an example of developing theological thought, Latter-day Saints are very familiar with the phrase found in the Westminster Confession of Faith which says that God is "without body, parts or passions."[9] This phrase is a summation of the developing thought about God over the centuries which was influenced both by neo-Platonic thought and by the popular ideas of the nature of God. Because of the neo-Platonic belief that spirit was superior to matter, over time God was conceived as being more and more distant and humans less and less like God—although the human spirit, freed of the body, could be prepared to enter the spiritual realm in which God lived. This was a radical departure from the basic message of the Old and New Testaments, which stated that God created all things good, including the material world.

This neo-Platonic direction in the "reasoning about God" was coupled with another concern which led to a further separation between God and human beings. The "gods" within the cultural tradition which surrounded the birth of the church were not particularly exemplary in their behavior. Either they were the gods of the Roman pantheon, with all the frailties and appetites of their earthly counterparts magnified to god-sized proportions, or they were the Roman emperors. In both instances, sensuality and sexuality were dominant characteristics. In seeking to distance God from such conceptions of divinity, the early church defined him as "without body, parts or passions." In effect, he was without a physical body, without sexual parts, and without lust. He was different from the gods the people had been used to worshiping. When placed in historical context, it is a little easier to understand why postbiblical Christians might seek to deny the corporeality of God.

Still, the point is that there was a vibrant theological process taking place in this debate. Church leaders took the scriptures, read their statements about God, and tried to use this understanding to relate God to the lives of faithful people. Errors may have been made, but the intent was to state doctrines which clarified and defined proper relations in the everyday lives that all must live. No one, of whatever religious tradition, can read scripture without simultaneously "doing theology," for scripture deals with real people and real life.

Creeds

The above discussion should also help explain the role of "creeds" or "confessions of faith" in Protestant and Catholic thought. Among Latter-day Saints there has been a great deal of misunderstanding about what a creed is and how it is to function. In large measure, this may be due to a misunderstanding of what the Lord meant when he told Joseph Smith that he

must join none of them [the sects or denominations], for they were all wrong; and the Personage who addressed me said that all their creeds were an abomination in his sight; that those professors were all corrupt; that: "they draw near to me with their lips, but their hearts are far from me, they teach for doctrines the commandments of men, having a form of godliness, but they deny the power thereof." (Joseph Smith—History 1:19)

There is a tendency to understand the word creed here as a *confession* of faith, such as the *Apostles' Creed* or the Nicene Creed. The whole context negates this interpretation, however, for that which precedes and follows this passage deals entirely with the religious people of Joseph's day. Thus, their creeds were their *professions* of faith, which had few outward manifestations of love. Thus, a closer and less jaundiced look at the historic confessions of faith within the Christian tradition is in order.

Fundamentally, a creed is the Christian community's attempt at a particular time in history to address in relatively short compass the vital issues affecting the church at that time. Usually, it addresses certain misunderstandings among some church members. Creeds may focus on the nature of God, the nature of Christ's atoning work, the relationship between the two natures in Christ, the role of scripture, the relationship between the church and the world, and many other topics. However, creeds as understood by Protestants were never intended to be equivalent to scripture; they were always to be checked against the scriptural word. Creeds could theoretically be altered or added to as new knowledge was given, but scripture could not be. Among Catholics, creeds were another witness with the scriptures. Creeds formed the broad boundaries within which Christians moved theologically, and they sought to capture the heart of scripture. Most of the current creeds and confessions used within Christendom are profound religious signposts. Two creeds of particular importance in Christian theological history are the Apostles' Creed and the Nicene Creed. As a comparative reading of these two creeds shows, the Nicene is concerned with clarifying the nature of Christ, which is only partially defined in the Apostles' Creed. The form of language is that used today in the Catholic church.

Apostles' Creed: I believe in God the Father Almighty, Creator of heaven and earth; and in Jesus Christ, His only Son, our Lord; who was conceived by the Holy Spirit, born of the Virgin Mary, suffered under Pontius Pilate, was crucified, died, and was buried. He descended into hell; the third day He rose again from the dead; He ascended into heaven; sits at the right hand of God, the Father Almighty; from thence He shall come to judge the living and the dead. I believe in the Holy Spirit, the holy Catholic Church, the communion of saints, the forgiveness of sins, the resurrection of the body, and life everlasting. Amen.

Nicene Creed: We believe in one God, the Father Almighty, maker of all things, both visible and invisible; and in one Lord, Jesus Christ, the Son of God, Only begotten of the Father, that is to say, of the substance of the Father, God of God and Light of light, very God of very God, begotten, not made, being of one substance with the Father, by whom all things were made, both things in heaven and things on earth; who, for us men and for our salvation, came down and was made flesh, was made man, suffered, and rose again on the third day, went up into the heavens, and is to come again to judge both the quick and the dead; and in the Holy Ghost.

Additional creeds within the Protestant tradition which students of Christian religious history may want to examine are the Augsburg Confession, the Heidelberg Catechism, the Westminster Confession of Faith, the Shorter Catechism, and the Theological Declaration of Barmen.[10]

Tradition

In addition to creedal statements and theological reflection, scripture is augmented, particularly in Catholicism, by what is known as "tradition." This assumes that not all of the Lord's words or commandments were preserved in scripture. In addition, it is the Catholic answer to continuing revelation; for tradition can have additions made to it, much as Latter-day Saints add to their "tradition" through the Doctrine and Covenants. In Catholicism, tradition stands on an equal footing with scripture and, since scripture is usually interpreted in the light of tradition, can actually become normative and superior to scripture.

Thus, while scripture is important in all Christian traditions, neither Protestants nor Catholics permit it to stand entirely by itself. Protestants would claim that they live by the rule of scripture solely, yet in practice they have their own traditions, which are captured in their creedal statements. Hence, Christians of divergent theologies have much in common, for it can be argued that Latter-day Saints, too, have traditions through which they read the scriptures.

Denominations

Catholicism

The Catholic world is divided into two major branches: Eastern Orthodoxy and Roman Catholicism. Initially the Christian world was unified, but over time tensions began to develop between western Christianity, with its center in Rome, and eastern Christianity, with its center in Constantinople. Both branches of Catholicism were united through the first seven ecumenical (worldwide) councils, which dealt with the issues related to the Godhead, the divinity of Christ, the two natures of Christ, and the two natural energies and the two wills of Christ. They differed, however, over certain theological and structural issues. For example, structurally, they differed over whether the pope had supreme jurisdiction over the church or merely had a primacy of honor. Theologically, they differed over whether the Holy Ghost was sent by the Father *and* the Son (western Catholics), or whether the Holy Ghost was sent only by the Father (eastern Catholics). In the first instance, there is clear equality between members of the Godhead, while in the second case there appears to be a subordination of the Son and the Holy Ghost to the Father.

Often 1054 C.E. is considered to be the dividing point between eastern and western Christianity, for in that year a delegate from the pope to Constantinople excommunicated the patriarch of

Constantinople, who in turn excommunicated the delegate. In reality, it was a rather local disagreement. The real separation came in 1204 when the knights of the Fourth Crusade sacked Constantinople. The eastern Christians have never forgiven the West for this act, and attempts to reconcile differences have not been fruitful. Since that time, there have been two clearly identifiable traditions in the Catholic world: Eastern Orthodox and Roman Catholic.

Eastern Orthodox

As can be seen from the discussions above, Eastern Orthodox Christians have their own unique contributions to make in many areas of Christian life. Probably the greatest difference between eastern and western Christianity lies in the deep concern the East expresses for the spiritual dimensions of life, as opposed to the structural or theological concerns of the West. The East seeks the mystical union between the worshiper and the divine in this life. They seek the light that shone in the transfiguration of Jesus.

The Eastern Orthodox tradition has found its way into many of the eastern European countries. Saint Cyril and his brother, Methodius, were the early missionaries to the Slavic countries. They were the ones who put the Bible into the Russian language, using an alphabet which Cyril created from Greek, Hebrew, and created letters. Thus, the basic belief that the scriptures and service books should be in the language of the people was realized when they were translated into Russian and other Slavic languages. The church's main strength lies in the countries of Russia, Bulgaria, Romania, and Greece. Administratively, each country in which the church resides is independent, usually administered by a patriarch. The patriarch of Constantinople (Istanbul, Turkey) is viewed as the first among equals, and he does not have the authority over Orthodox Christians that the pope does over Roman Catholics.

The prime concern of the Eastern Orthodox communions, as suggested above, is with the spiritual dimension of life and its influence on daily living. They feel that the Spirit may be found *in* the material world, not just above it. Thus, icons (two-dimensional artistic representations of sacred subjects) are viewed as channels through which grace may be received. The icons draw one into the spiritual reality they represent. They are a door to the spiritual world, and many Eastern Orthodox Christians will venerate the icons by kissing them or bowing before them. Thus, there is a profound spiritual character to the Eastern Orthodox tradition.[11]

Roman Catholicism

The distinctive character of Roman Catholicism stems from its claim for the primacy of Peter. The Roman Catholic roots clearly go back to Peter, and it is felt that he continues to speak to the whole church through the bishop of Rome, the pope, who is the pastor of the universal church on the earth. This tie between Peter and the bishop of Rome was articulated under Pope Leo I, who presided from 440 to 461 C.E. The papal hierarchy developed its full scope during the Middle Ages, when the popes were crowned like secular emperors and kings, with all the attendant pomp and circumstance. This practice was discontinued by Pope John Paul I (1912–1978) in 1978, but it was actually Pope *John XXIII* (1881–1963) who laid the foundation for the removal of the excessive pageantry when he declared that he did not wish to be referred to as the Supreme Pontiff (Supreme Head of the Church) but as the Supreme Pastor to the people.

At the time of the Reformation, of which more will be said below, there were unquestionably excesses in the Roman Catholic church that needed correction. As a response to the Reformation movement, the Council of Trent was called to deal with the issues raised by Luther and others. It established a middle way between faith and works, trying not to bend to either extreme. For centuries, the normative directions for Roman Catholics were derived from the Council of Trent.[12]

Some changes, however, have occurred in recent years in the Roman Catholic church, and most are a direct result of the Second Vatican Council (1962–66), popularly known as "Vatican II." This was a worldwide council of the Catholic church which came together in 1962 under the leadership of Pope John XXIII and was continued after his death by his successor, Pope *Paul VI* (1897–1978). The major changes that came from it were a proposal for liturgical reform which led to dramatic shifts in liturgical rites, including mass in the local language of the people rather than in Latin; the development of a more collegial and less hierarchical arrangement among the bishops and priests; greater lay participation in the life of the church; permission for Catholics to worship with non-Catholics;

recognition that persons of traditions other than the Catholic could receive salvation; and a declaration that the Jews should not be held collectively responsible for the death of Christ. These decisions have markedly changed the Roman Catholic church.

Protestantism

The beginnings of Protestantism are found in the Reformation. Martin Luther is normally considered the father of the Reformation, although the ideas which came to the fore with Luther were present long before the division between Catholics and Protestants. The usual date for the beginning of the Reformation is 1517, when Luther, an ordained Catholic priest, nailed ninety-five theses to the door of the church in Wittenberg, Germany, challenging the sale of "indulgences," which promised release from a certain number of years in purgatory if the purchaser would contribute to various papal projects. The real problem was that, in questioning the validity of indulgences, Luther challenged the authority of the papacy; and in expressing the belief that priests were not necessary for the salvation of the people, he had gone too far to back down.

Among Protestants there are a myriad of denominations. To identify all of these would be impossible, given the scope of this chapter. However, it is possible to class them in three categories—episcopal, *reformed*, and independent movements—and elaborate on a few of the major denominations within each area.

Episcopal

The episcopal category classes the denominations by their structure. These have bishops and priests who stand in a mediatorial way between God and the lay members of the congregations and "mediate" grace to them through the sacraments, much as in Catholicism. The clergy in these traditions are ordained to an "office" that separates them to some degree from the general congregation. The two denominations that are most representative of this form of government are the Church of England (Episcopalian in the United States) and the Methodists.

EPISCOPALIAN.[13] The Episcopal church is the American manifestation of the Church of England and is properly known as the "Protestant Episcopal Church." The Church of England traces its roots back to the very earliest of times in the British Isles. The precise entry of Christianity into England is not known, but the fact that British bishops were in attendance at the Council of Arles in 314 C.E. attests to the existence of an organized church. Throughout English history there was a continual tension between the English crown, which traditionally claimed leadership of the British church, and Rome, whose influence became dominant with the Norman conquest of England in 1066. With Henry VIII (1491–1547) the Tudor Reformation took place, occasioned by Henry's divorce from Catherine of Aragon. In actuality, Henry was returning to the older precedent of the king being head of the English church. Little was changed under Henry. The church remained episcopal (led by bishops) in nature, and doctrine remained essentially the same. The major change involved the break with Rome and the leadership exercised by the crown.

The first Anglican church was established in America at Jamestown, Virginia, in 1607, but it was after the War of Independence that the Protestant Episcopal Church became an autonomous organization. The clergy of Connecticut elected Reverend Samuel Seabury as their bishop. Legal difficulties prevented his consecration in England, but in 1784 he received the episcopal succession from the bishops of the Anglican church in Scotland. The laity are involved in much of the work and administration of the church; but the priests still exercise an authoritative role, since the sacrament of Holy Communion over which they officiate is the center of Christian life. Although distinctly separate from the Church of England, the Episcopal church nonetheless manifests a strong affinity with the English church. Much of the liturgy is identical, and both share a magnificent musical tradition.

METHODIST.[14] The Methodist church arose from within the Church of England. Originally, Methodism (the origin of the name is obscure) was promoted at Oxford in 1729 by John Wesley, his brother Charles, and their followers. It was fundamentally an attempt to recapture some of the essential spiritual dimensions of the gospel in the face of what John Wesley felt was a rather sterile scholasticism within the Church of England. Wesley himself was never a "Methodist"; he remained a priest in the Church of England until his death. However, as the movement spread, and particularly when Wesley set apart Thomas Coke and others for the North American ministry in 1784, it became recognized as a separate denomination.

The Methodist church considers itself to be part of the Church Universal but claims no divine authority for its particular form of order. Laity are much involved, but there is still an episcopal structure present. Annual conferences representing geographical areas make many decisions for the church and are designed to be balanced in their membership between laity and clergy. Traditionally, Methodism is actively concerned with both evangelism and social welfare, and its centralized organization enables coordinated efforts in these directions.

Reformed

The second group—Reformed—are those who were influenced by the German and Swiss reformations under Martin Luther, John Calvin, and others. The unifying characteristics of this tradition are the absolute certainty that God has come to humanity in Jesus Christ, that all persons are called to be priests of God, and that God's word is present for all in the scriptures. Thus, all that people receive is a gift of God, and there is no hierarchy of priests, for all people are called to the vocation of priesthood. Therefore, clergy are viewed differently in the reformed tradition than they are in the episcopal tradition. Ministers are called to a Christian vocation, as are all believers, and not to an office that separates them from the congregation. All believers have specific vocations within the congregation; and though they may be different and require differing degrees of preparation, they are all vocations given by God and thus essential to the well-being of the church. All are equal, for a vocation given by God is of infinite worth and thus of equal value before God to any other.

LUTHERAN.[15] There are numerous Lutheran fellowships around the world. Generally, they function much as do the Orthodox communions in that they are administered within the national boundaries of the countries in which they exist. Thus, there are Lutheran churches in Germany, Denmark, Norway, the United States, and several other nations, all essentially organized separately from one another but sharing the same basic theological principles and insights. In the United States, the major Lutheran communions are the Evangelical Lutheran Church in America (the result of the recent uniting of the Lutheran Church in America and the American Lutheran Church), Missouri Synod Lutheran, Wisconsin Synod Lutheran, and other smaller Lutheran

bodies. Lutherans generally hold that the scriptures are the sole rule of faith and that creeds and other traditional statements of belief are subordinated to them. The primary tenet of Lutheranism is justification by faith alone. Redemption results from a person's justification by faith in Christ, at which point—though in fact as much a sinner as before—he or she is found to be righteous in the sight of God without further action on his or her part. The omnipotent action of God is thus the point of strongest emphasis.

PRESBYTERIAN.[16] The Presbyterian church has its most immediate ecclesiastical roots in Scotland, being founded there by John Knox in 1557. Its theological heritage goes back to John Calvin. The denomination takes its name from the Greek word *presbyteros,* which means "elder." The name points to the form of government used in the church, which is representative in nature, with elders elected by individual congregations to administer both the spiritual and material work of the congregation. The Presbyterian form of government was the model used for the representative form of government which citizens of the United States enjoy. The only clergyman to sign the Declaration of Independence was John Witherspoon, a Presbyterian minister from New Jersey.

Governing bodies in the Presbyterian church are derived from areas encompassing progressively larger numbers of congregations. Ministers are called and elected by the people. Above the congregational level are the presbytery, then the synod, and finally the General Assembly. Each of these bodies is composed of elected delegates, with an equal balance between clergy and laity. Presbyterians, like Lutherans, live under the word of God found in scripture as it points toward Jesus Christ. Presbyterians have often been associated with the doctrine of predestination, but there is today a good deal of reassessment of the doctrine taking place. In its most powerful form, the doctrine asserts the absolute primacy of God in all matters. Calvin called predestination a comforting doctrine,[17] for it affirms that all things lie in the hands of a good and gracious God. Major Presbyterian denominations in the United States are the Presbyterian Church (USA), the Cumberland Presbyterian Church, and the Presbyterian Church in America.

CONGREGATIONAL/UNITED CHURCH OF CHRIST.[18] Like the Presbyterian and Lutheran traditions, the

Congregationalists had their roots in the Reformation. Luther believed in the priesthood of all believers, and this was the foundation of the congregational movement which became most visible in England. One of the most articulate early proponents of the "congregational" principles was Robert Browne (ca. 1550–1633), a Puritan separatist. Browne maintained that the church began with groups of worthy Christians gathering together to exercise their covenantal obligations without denominational ties. The movement spread to the Continent and to the Americas, where independent congregations, governed by the whole congregation, became prominent. The Congregational church was dominant in New England until well into the nineteenth century; in Connecticut it was the constitutionally established religion—in early years, to the nearly total exclusion of all others—until 1818, and in Massachusetts until 1833.

Various denominations were formed over time, but all denominational ties were loose, being more confederacies than denominations. In 1957, two of the largest bodies sharing Congregational principles—The Congregational Christian Churches and the Evangelical and Reformed Church—united to form The United Church of Christ. This latter body has had a history of ecumenism and of deep involvement in social issues.

Independent Movements

This third group encompasses a number of denominations which have their roots in the "radical" reformation. Many of these groups sought a return to first-century Christianity with adult baptism by immersion, pacifism, anticlericalism, and a scorning of ornate houses of worship. These attitudes were normally coupled with a strong sense of the presence of the Holy Ghost and its individual workings on believers. From these came the Mennonites, Unitarians, and tangentially the Baptists.

MENNONITE.[19] Mennonites had their origins in Switzerland and derive their name from Menno Simons (1496–1561), a Dutch reformer. Congregations are independent and, although they may vary somewhat in belief and practice, all reject church organization, infant baptism, and the real presence in the eucharist. Both men and women may preach, and the Lord's Supper is administered by elders chosen by the community. Most Mennonites refuse military service, the taking of oaths, and public office.

UNITARIAN.[20] Historically, Unitarianism had its beginnings in the Reformation era, its earliest exponent probably being Martin Cellarius (1499–1564). Unitarianism rejects the doctrines of the Trinity and of the divinity of Christ, preaching instead the unipersonality of God. The criteria of belief and practice among today's Unitarians are reason and conscience. The first definitely Unitarian congregation in America, King's Chapel in Boston, dates from 1785.

BAPTIST.[21] Baptists trace their origins in modern times to 1609, when John Smyth, a Separatist exile in Amsterdam, reinstituted the baptism of conscious believers as the basis for fellowship in a gathered church. The beginning of American Baptist history dates to the settlement of Roger Williams at Providence, Rhode Island, and the church he formed there on Baptist principles in 1639. Baptists are evangelical in their approach to the gospel and believe in preaching the good news of Jesus Christ to all peoples. They generally stress a moral life as well as a spiritual one. The congregations are essentially independent, and thus they call and ordain their own pastors. In the United States there are two major Baptist communions: the American Baptist Church and the Southern Baptist Convention. The latter is the larger of the two. There are also other Baptist communions, such as the Old Regular Baptists, the Primitive Baptists, and the Free-Will Baptists. For all the differences that may exist, they are all united in their belief that only persons who can profess Jesus as Lord should be baptized—which, of course, excludes infants and very young children. They also hold that the only appropriate form of baptism is immersion, because that is the mode found in scripture. Laypersons are deeply involved in the life and ministry of Baptist churches.

The Ecumenical Movement

In the twentieth century, persons of many denominations have concluded that Christ never intended his church to be fragmented and divided. Thus, there have been various attempts to bridge some of the divisions that exist, even within the same denomination. For example, the Presbyterian church in the United States was divided at the time of the Civil War. Only in the early 1980s was that rift finally healed, with the two major groups of American Presbyterians being reunited as the Presbyterian Church (USA). The Lutherans experienced a similar reunion when the Lutheran Church in America and the American Lutheran Church came together in one body.

Beyond these intradenominational efforts, there was also an attempt to bring nine denominations together into one large denomination of some twenty-five million members. This movement was called the *Council on Church Union (CCU)*, and it sought to bring Episcopalians, Methodists, Presbyterians, Lutherans, and others into one unified church. Issues of authority, doctrine, and structure have been constant stumbling blocks, but the desire for closer cooperation and sharing among all Christians is a laudable goal.

CHALLENGES AND OPPORTUNITIES

Evangelism

Proclamation or Social Action

Historically, Christianity has been a missionary faith. What this has meant is that Christians, believing that their religion enabled them to understand God's purposes more fully than members of other religious traditions can, have felt an obligation to proclaim the good news of Jesus Christ to all persons of all religions who would listen to their message. The saving message of the gospel of Jesus Christ was that which brought salvation to all humankind. The book of Acts and Paul's letters are biblical testimonies to this missionary movement, as is the history of the church up to the present day. Because of that missionary emphasis, Christianity is today the largest religion on the face of the earth, with over one billion adherents who live in every country of the world.

But success and a heightened appreciation for what God has done through other religious traditions has blunted the missionary fervor of much of the Christian world. In the first instance, there are many countries of the world in which almost the entire population is Christian, at least in name. Whom does one evangelize? The answer for many Christians, especially those of a conservative bent, is that churches should be reactivating the thousands of Christians who are Christians in name only. Thus, there are innumerable programs among the various denominations which focus on church renewal and membership reactivation, both of which are legitimate forms of missionary work.

Even the mainstream denominations participate in this sort of evangelism.

In the second instance—that of interface with other religions—there are a number of Christians who have lost the vision of the uniqueness of the Christian message. These persons have come to feel that, while Christianity may be the way *they* can best worship and serve God, others may be just as able to worship and serve him as Hindus, Muslims, or Buddhists. If this is the stance one takes, then Christianity simply becomes one good way among many good ways to God. Thus, the primary missionary effort of the churches becomes one in which the social well-being of peoples is enhanced but the need for active proselyting work ceases. Plainly, this represents a departure from the fervor that the early apostles so clearly felt which impelled them to risk their lives in the proclamation of the one true way.

Christianity and Culture

Another challenge Christianity has had to face, precisely because it has become a world religion, is that of the relationship between the gospel and the culture in which it is preached. What is essential to Christianity, and what can be retained of the culture? Do persons have to assume the clothing, foods, music, language, and marriage customs of the West, if they become Christians, or can the native customs serve to further the expansion of the gospel? Catholics have often tried to blend Christianity with the culture to which it has come—so much so that sometimes the Christianity becomes diminished. Many Protestants have moved in the other direction, exporting Western culture with the gospel. Neither extreme has had fully desirable results, and there needs to be an ongoing effort to find the proper balance.

This-Worldly or Other-Worldly

A continuing question among Christians has concerned the relationship between Christians and the world. Has the Christian been called to live in the world or to be separated from it physically? Within Catholicism the answer has been that both modes of life may be appropriate, dependent upon the Christian vocation to which God calls persons. The majority of church members are called to live Christian values within the world as they marry, raise families, make livings, and enjoy recreation.

But a small portion of the church God calls to special vocations of service; some, as priests and nuns, live in parishes and work with the people, while other priests, monks, and nuns may be called to live a life fully separated from the world in monasteries. These latter persons have vocations of prayer, study, and worship that bring spiritual depth to the whole church. Thus, living in the midst of the world and being separated from it have historically been valid possibilities within the Catholic world.

Among Protestants, however, separation from the world has been a rare occurrence. Generally, Protestantism has seen the separated and celibate life as not congruent with the will of God. Persons, including clergy, are intended to marry, have families, and support them. While one may withdraw briefly to a retreat center, the withdrawal is for the purpose of renewing one's spirituality for reentry into the world.

Church and State

The proper relationship between the state and the church has been an issue ever since Constantine declared the Christian church to be legal and gave preferential treatment to certain Christian persons and groups. Initially, following Constantine, the church and state were often closely interlaced, especially through the institution of the Holy Roman Empire, the high point of which was the crowning of Charlemagne as Holy Roman Emperor in 800 C.E. However, as the church began to realize the need for ecclesiastical discipline unrestricted by monarchs, there came a separation in which the Roman Catholic church particularly demanded its independence from secular oversight. This was the issue between Henry II of England and Archbishop Thomas à Becket that led to the latter's assassination in 1170. Some three and a half centuries later, the same issue in reverse—the independence of secular government from the political influence of the Catholic church—motivated Henry VIII of England to declare himself the head of the church in England and lead his nation into Protestantism, as discussed above. Protestants, obviously, would initially have agreed with this separation of powers. However, neither Protestantism nor Catholicism has been able to stay fully separate from the state at various points in history. For example, some Catholic and Protestant clergy supported the Third Reich, while others opposed it. The Russian Orthodox church did not openly challenge Communism but tried instead to live alongside it.

In the main, it is necessary, if the church is to be the church, for it to stand apart from secular powers, so that it may always speak God's undiluted word to those powers when necessary. To do so may cost the lives of Christians, but that has always been the fate of some faithful persons who dare to call the world and its values into question in the name of God.

Clergy and Laity

The role of the clergy versus the role of the laity has been much debated within the church. Within the episcopal traditions (Catholic, Episcopal, Methodist), clergy are ordained to an office. They are different, by dint of their ordination, from the laypersons. They have certain prerogatives, such as consecrating the eucharist, that laypersons do not.

In the nonepiscopal traditions, generally clergy are viewed as being ordained to a vocation—a special role within the Christian community—but that role is just one vocation among many. Much of what the pastor does, the laypersons can and should do also. In many traditions, even the eucharist may be blessed by a layperson if an ordained person is not present. Often, the pastor is viewed as a teacher who prepares the members of his or her congregation for their own ministries. Thus, the distinction between clergy and laity in many Protestant traditions is generally not as great as that within Catholicism or within the episcopal traditions of Protestantism.

THE ROLES OF WOMEN

To determine the place of women in the Christian faith, one must first look at the way in which Christ treated women. For his day and time, his attitudes toward the women who surrounded him were revolutionary. He permitted them in his retinue and taught them, elevating women by his public recognition of them. It was to a woman that he first appeared following his resurrection. Thus, the biblical accounts are clear that Jesus established different norms for the treatment of women from those prevalent in the Judea of his day.

Not every person in the early church appears to have appreciated Jesus' openness toward women, and Paul is usually cited as one who did not understand what Jesus had intended. However, it is Paul who proclaims, "There is neither Jew nor Greek, there is neither bond nor free, there is neither male nor female: for ye are all one in Christ Jesus" (Gal. 3:28). Any statement of Paul's needs to be seen in the light of this broad principle, thus recognizing that some of his apparently less-than-sympathetic statements about women may have been the products of particular problems in specific settings, rather than attitudes to be universalized. He is certainly grateful for a number of women who share in his work, several of whom are mentioned in Romans 16: Phebe, Priscilla, Mary, Tryphena, and Tryphosa.

As Christianity spread, however, social pressures and customs seem to have overcome the attitudes that Jesus exhibited, and women became less respected by some. By the best theologians, however, women were far from denigrated. A look at the way Eve was treated gives some insight into the place of women among Christians through the centuries. For example, Saint Augustine says that Eve, by virtue of being created from Adam's rib, represents the unity of society and the harmony which should exist among all Adam's progeny. Eve is indispensable, for without her there could be no generation of humankind.[22] According to Saint Thomas Aquinas, woman is subject to man by nature, since the power of rational discernment is stronger in man than in woman. Even so, by creating Eve from Adam's rib God assured that Adam would love Eve and indicated that man and woman were essentially equal in their relationship. Eve was neither Adam's superior nor his slave.[23] For Martin Luther, Eve was similar to Adam in justice, wisdom, and happiness, but she was not equal in glory or prestige. She was the companion of Adam—a thought which repudiates Catholic celibacy—and at her creation the family was brought into existence.[24] Finally, John Calvin held that Eve completed Adam, and he thus saw her role in the context of marriage.[25]

Within the Catholic tradition, women have always occupied a special place as they participated in the religious orders, where they exercised a great deal of control over their own lives. They staffed hospitals and schools and even served in missionary roles. For example, Marie Guyart (1599–1672) was the first woman missionary in the New World.[26] She was not alone, however, because the first Quaker missionaries to arrive in the New World were Ann Austin and Mary Fisher.[27] With the evangelical movement of the Second Great Awakening in the United States (from 1795 to the Civil War), women began to become more and more public in their religious activities. Women like Ellen White (1827–1915), the founder of the Seventh-Day Adventists; Elizabeth Ann Seton (1774–1821), the founder of the Sisters of Charity; and Frances Willard (1839–1898), a leader in the Women's Christian Temperance Union, all left their mark on nineteenth-century America. With the coming of the twentieth century, the role of women in all churches grew significantly.

Today, most of the major Protestant denominations ordain women to the ministry. If ordination is not available to them, then significant leadership roles within the congregation or the broader community are. Roman Catholics still depend heavily upon women in the religious orders; but with Vatican II other opportunities were presented for laywomen, including service in roles such as eucharistic ministers, readers, and parish council members. Essentially, any woman who wants to find meaningful roles within her church can find them today. Women within Christian churches are generally held to be coequal with men, and the reality is that there are many more women active in Christian churches today than there are men. Without them, many churches would have few persons to minister to the needs of the many.

CHRISTIAN INFLUENCE

The Christian churches have had immense influence on the world's attitudes, morals, and concerns over the centuries. The Catholic traditions have permeated every corner of the world, and they have done much good, especially in the social realm. Much the same holds true for the Protestant traditions, and they too exercise great influence, especially in the spheres of social justice and the alleviation of human suffering. Christendom has created a united voice in the World Council of Churches with its headquarters in Geneva, Switzerland. From there, the churches carry on dialogue with governments, heads of state, and secular decision-making bodies.

For all the good they have done, however, many major Christian traditions have lost their missionary zeal. They have slipped into seeking to improve people's physical lots in life, while diminishing the effort to improve their souls. In addition, there has been a move away from the clear moral mandates that have previously characterized Christianity to an attitude of open acceptance of virtually all lifestyles. Thus, nothing seems to be a "sin" anymore. Christians are often no longer a peculiar people. The standards and faith for which their parents died have been lost in the cultural assimilation of this generation. Too many Christians today are merely cultural Christians. If that trend continues, Christianity will cease to be a moral force in today's world.

LATTER-DAY SAINT REFLECTIONS

Latter-day Saint Christians share much in common with their brothers and sisters of other Christian denominations. Virtually all Christians believe that there are three members within the Godhead. Latter-day Saints do as well, but they differ from their neighbors in understanding the Father to have physical form, as well as the Son, and in believing that the two are one not in essence, but in purpose and love.

Most Christians believe that human beings are created by God and that the spirit enters the child's body while it is still in the mother's womb. Life, then, begins with this life. However, Latter-day Saints are virtually alone in the Christian world in claiming that human beings had an existence in the presence of God before birth into mortality. Given that premortal existence, mortal life takes on greater meaning as a period of growth and development, as part of an eternal progression which extends from premortality through mortality and into a postmortal life. Likewise, Latter-day Saints understand that their goal is to return to live in fellowship with their Father and their family members, something which requires certain ordinances. No other Christian community stresses the essential nature of ordinances to the degree found among Latter-day Saints.

While other Christians believe in heaven, Latter-day Saints believe that there are degrees of glory in the hereafter and that not all persons will live in the Father's presence. Only those who have had faith in Christ and repented, but who have moreover fulfilled the ordinances and who have sought to live as Christ would have them live, will enjoy that privilege. There are moral and ethical standards which God expects his sons and daughters to exhibit, if they truly love him. In the end, Latter-day Saints are called not merely to live in the presence of God, but

to be like God, as is God's Son, Jesus Christ. This can be accomplished only in the highest degree of heaven, known as the celestial kingdom.

The restoration of the fulness of the gospel under Joseph Smith also promoted an understanding of the Jews that departed from the mainstream Christian viewpoint of the time. He recognized that, if the Lord were to be trusted in the latter days, his covenants made with Israel still had to be in force. This meant that Israel—including the tribes of Judah, Simeon, and Benjamin (today's Jews)—were to be gathered together, to be returned to their lands of inheritance, and to have their worship reestablished. The Lord's plan is that Christians and others will become part of Israel, not replace it as the covenant people. It is through this ingrafting of all the peoples of the world into Israel, the offspring of Abraham, that the nations will be blessed.

Throughout history, assert Latter-day Saints, the Lord has always had a covenant people on the earth to point to the Lord Jesus Christ. That people has been Israel, although various tribes may become the torchbearers at different points in history. Israel was the herald of the coming Christ in the years preceding Christ's birth, primarily through Judah, Simeon, and Benjamin (in the Old World), just as Israel (or its adopted children) is the herald of the returning Christ today, primarily through the tribes of Ephraim and Manasseh. Ultimately all tribes will be drawn to Zion, and the nations of the world will be grafted into them, forming a united people of God. Although a sense of covenant responsibility has historically been strong among Christians of all traditions, no other Christian group has viewed itself as part of the fulfillment of the Abrahamic covenant in so specific a sense as Latter-day Saints have.

In structure, The Church of Jesus Christ of Latter-day Saints is episcopal in nature. Its membership believes that there is one head, the living prophet, and that the prophet administers the church through a clear structure of General Authorities, stake presidents, and bishops. Thus, The Church of Jesus Christ of Latter-day Saints is much closer to the Roman Catholic church than to any Protestant denomination. The prophet and the pope occupy similar positions of authority in their respective communions.

A major difference, however, between Latter-day Saints and most other Christians is the lay ministry exercised among Latter-day Saints. While most other traditions have seminary-trained ministers, called and set apart by appropriate authorities, to lead the congregations, Latter-day Saints call laypersons to lead in the church. These laypersons are not compensated financially for their time, and they hold regular jobs during the week. Like Roman Catholics, the ordinance and administrative roles are held by men; but the women fulfill supporting roles in the auxiliaries, without which no local unit could survive. Some Protestant denominations emphasize a lay ministry, but in reality they normally expect their ministers to do the bulk of the work.

As far as the sacramental ministry is concerned, Latter-day Saints are once again more like Roman Catholics than Protestants. Catholics have seven sacraments through which persons encounter God's grace. Similarly, Latter-day Saints have a number of ordinances through which God is met, and those that parallel the Catholic sacraments are baptism, the sacrament, ordination, sealing, anointing, and confirmation as a member of the church. The seventh sacrament in the Catholic church, penance, is not a formal ordinance among Latter-day Saints. It is comparable, however, to confession to the bishop in the process of repentance. In summary, Latter-day Saints and Roman Catholics actually have much more in common than do Latter-day Saints and Protestants.

Concerning the scriptural canon, however, Latter-day Saints hold a position unique in Christendom. They believe that the canon should always be "open." This is a product of their belief in continuing, direct revelation to the church through Christ's latter-day prophets. According to them, God has not said all that he has to say to his people, and thus the canon must always be open to enable the inclusion of further revelations. The addition of sections 137 and 138 and Official Declaration 2 to the Doctrine and Covenants in recent years are evidence of this. The question of an open or closed canon of scripture is, therefore, directly tied to the understanding of revelation and its continuance or lack thereof in the present day.

IN conclusion, regardless of the Christian tradition to which Latter-day Saints may be compared, they have a voice which can add greatly to the understanding of the Christian message, if they are but permitted to be part of the broader Christian conversation. Latter-day Saints have a well-developed theology touching every one of the issues raised and addressed in this summary of Christian beliefs. They are firmly committed Christians in every sense of the term, and their vigor and vibrant belief in the mission of Christianity can and does add vitality and conviction to the religion today.

Glossary of Christian Names and Terms

ADVENT. The liturgical season of the Christian year consisting of the four Sundays preceding Christmas. Its liturgical color is purple.

AGNUS DEI. The formula beginning with the words "O Lamb of God" recited three times by the priest in the Latin mass shortly before the Communion.

ANALOGIA ENTIS. Literally, "analogy of being"; the process of gaining knowledge about God through rational thought or the observation of the natural world.

ANALOGIA FIDEI. Literally, "analogy of faith"; the process of gaining knowledge about God through revelation given by God himself.

APOCRYPHA. The biblical books received by the early church as part of the Greek version of the Old Testament but not included in the Hebrew Bible. Catholics include these books in their canon, while Protestants normally exclude them.

APOSTLES' CREED. A statement used only in the western Catholic church (not in the Orthodox churches). It falls into three sections concerned with the Father, Jesus Christ,

and the Holy Ghost. Its precise origins are unknown, but it was probably in use by the fourth century C.E.

ATONEMENT. Humanity's reconciliation with God through the sacrificial suffering and death of Christ.

BAPTISM. The sacramental rite, either through sprinkling or immersion, which admits a candidate to the Christian church.

CALVIN, JOHN (1509–1564). French reformer and theologian.

COUNCIL ON CHURCH UNION (CCU). A movement in the United States, particularly during the 1960s and early 1970s, which sought to bring together nine of the major Protestant communions into one large cohesive denomination.

CREDO. Literally, "I believe"; the title of the portion of the Latin mass which contains the Nicene confession of faith.

CRUCIFIX. A model of the cross bearing an image of the crucified Lord.

ECUMENICAL MOVEMENT. The movement among Christians concerned with the recovery of the unity of all believers in Christ, transcending differences of creed, ritual, and polity.

EPIPHANY. The season in the Christian liturgical calendar beginning on January 6 which either celebrates the baptism of Christ (Orthodox) or Christ's manifestation to the non-Jewish world in the persons of the Magi (Catholic). The liturgical color is green.

EPISCOPAL. Refers to the system of church government which is overseen by bishops.

EUCHARIST. From the Greek word meaning "thanksgiving"; another name for Holy Communion, the Lord's Supper, or, in Latter-day Saint terms, the sacrament.

GLORIA. A portion of the Latin mass which gives praise to God in the words "Glory to God in the highest."

HOLY COMMUNION. The eucharist, or the Lord's Supper. It is the equivalent of the Latter-day Saint term sacrament.

HOLY ORDERS. The higher grades of the Christian ministry—bishop, priest, and deacon.

HOMOIOUSIOS. The term preferred by Arian Christians to express the relation of the members of the Godhead. It means "of like substance." Arianism is a heresy in both Catholic and Orthodox thought.

HOMOOUSIOS. The term used in early Christian creedal statements to express the relation of the members of the Godhead. It means "of one substance."

ICONS. Flat pictures—usually painted on wood, but sometimes made from mosaic, ivory, and other materials—representing the Lord, the Blessed Virgin Mary, or other saints; used and venerated among the Orthodox communions.

INNER-TRINITARIAN DECREE. The concept that God, within himself as a triune God composed of Father, Son, and Holy Ghost, determined the plan of salvation long before the creation of anything outside himself.

JOHN XXIII (1881–1963). Became pope in 1958. He is best known for calling the Second Vatican Council (Vatican II), which reviewed Catholic doctrines relating to the laity, interfaith attitudes, the role of clergy, etc.

KYRIE. Refers to a portion of the Latin mass which contains the words "Lord have mercy."

LENT. The forty days before Easter, exclusive of the Sundays. Lent is normally observed as a time of penance by abstaining from festivities, by almsgiving, and by devoting more than the usual time to religious exercises. The liturgical color for this season of the Christian year is purple.

LITURGICAL CALENDAR. Sets out certain periods within the Christian year for special observance and thereby highlights the major acts of Christ's redeeming work.

LUTHER, MARTIN (1482–1546). The founder of the German Reformation, a Catholic priest, and a professor of moral philosophy and scripture at the University of Wittenberg.

MARY. The virgin mother of Jesus. She is an object of veneration in Catholic theology and, because of her position as the mother of Jesus, is chief among the saints.

NEO-PLATONIC THOUGHT. The philosophical system of Plotinus (ca. 205–260 C.E.) and his successors. It drew its ideas from Plato, but its purposes were more religious. The main purpose of the neo-Platonists was to provide an intellectual basis for life: in God the distinction between Thought and Reality was to be overcome.

PAUL VI (1897–1978). Became pope in 1963 and carried through much of the work of Vatican II.

PENANCE. Originally a long and difficult process of public confession of sin with accompanying works to allow a return to the church. Today, penance is a private act between priest and parishioner consisting of confession, absolution, and formal penance.

PENTECOST. The day in the church calendar fifty days after Easter which celebrates the coming of the Holy Ghost to the church. The liturgical color is red.

REFORMED. Used in this chapter to designate those denominations and traditions which generally arose from the teachings of Luther and Calvin. Denominations technically considered "reformed" are Presbyterian, Lutheran, Congregational, and Dutch Reformed.

SANCTUS. That portion of the mass which contains the words "Holy, holy, holy, Lord God of Hosts."

SEPTUAGINT. The most influential of the Greek versions of the Old Testament; often abbreviated LXX.

SEVEN SACRAMENTS. The sacraments of the church celebrated by Catholic Christians: baptism, confirmation, the eucharist, penance, unction, holy orders, and matrimony.

TRANSUBSTANTIATION. The Catholic doctrine that the bread and wine of the eucharist actually become the body of Christ in their essence, but in their accidents (appearances) appear still to be bread and wine. The doctrine is an attempt to explain how the believer may actually participate through the eucharist in the life and death of the Lord.

TRINITY. The doctrine of the Father, the Son, and the Holy Ghost as one God of the same substance, yet in three manifestations, in a manner that cannot be explained by mortals. The term also refers to the last five months of the Christian year, in which the implications of the worldwide gospel in daily life are contemplated. The liturgical color is green.

UNCTION. The process of anointing with oil, which may be used at baptism or confirmation or in blessing the sick.

VULGATE. The Latin version of the Bible most widely used in the West. It was the work of Saint Jerome, who compiled it at the command of Pope Damasus (382 C.E.).

Notes

1. Excellent and concise articles on Christian history are contained in F. L. Cross, ed., *The Oxford Dictionary of the Christian Church* (London: Oxford University Press, 1971), hereafter cited as *Oxford Dictionary*. Some of that material is cited here, as indicated below, and students may want to examine this source for additional information. Much of the material in the glossary definitions is also drawn from this highly authoritative source.

2. "The Shorter Catechism," in *Book of Confessions* (New York: Office of the General Assembly of the Presbyterian Church [USA], 1983), 7.001.

3. Quoted in David S. Noss and John B. Noss, *Man's Religions*, 7th ed. (New York: Macmillan, 1984), 484.

4. "Baptism," *Oxford Dictionary*, 126.

5. "Saints, Devotion to the," *Oxford Dictionary*, 1207.

6. "Canon of Scripture," *Oxford Dictionary*, 229–30.

7. "Wycliffe, John," *Oxford Dictionary*, 1480–81.

8. "Luther, Martin," *Oxford Dictionary*, 832.

9. *Book of Confessions*, 6.011.

10. All of these except the Augsburg Confession may be found in ibid.

11. Kallistos Ware, "Eastern Christianity," in Mircea Eliade et al., eds., *The Encyclopedia of Religion*, 16 vols. (New York: Macmillan, 1987), 4:558–76; hereafter cited as *Encyclopedia of Religion*.

12. Richard P. McBrien, "Roman Catholicism," *Encyclopedia of Religion*, 12:429–45.

13. "Church of England" and "Protestant Episcopal Church," *Oxford Dictionary*, 287–90, 1115–16.

14. "Methodism" and "Methodist Churches," *Oxford Dictionary*, 892–94.

15. "Lutheranism," *Oxford Dictionary*, 833–34.

16. The section on Presbyterianism is based on my personal knowledge; I grew up in the tradition and served for fifteen years as an ordained Presbyterian minister.

17. From a lecture given by Edward A. Dowey at Princeton Theological Seminary, Princeton, New Jersey, in the fall term of 1968. See also John Calvin, *Institutes of the Christian Religion*, ed. John T. McNeill, trans. Ford Lewis Battles, 2 vols. (Philadelphia: Westminster Press, 1960), bk. 3, ch. 24, sec. 6.

18. Again, most of this comes from my own theological background; but see also Milton V. Backman and Spencer J. Palmer, unpublished manuscript on religions of the world, in possession of Milton V. Backman, Provo, Ut.

19. "Mennonites," *Oxford Dictionary*, 886.

20. "Unitarianism," *Oxford Dictionary*, 1390–91.

21. "Baptists," *Oxford Dictionary*, 127–29.

22. Roger R. Keller, "Adam: As Understood by Four Men Who Shaped Western Christianity," in Joseph Fielding McConkie and Robert L. Millet, eds., *The Man Adam* (Salt Lake City: Bookcraft, 1990), 154–55.

23. Ibid., 161.

24. Ibid., 168.

25. Ibid., 176–77.

26. Mark A. Noll, *A History of Christianity in the United States and Canada* (Grand Rapids, Mich.: William B. Eerdmans, 1992), 21.

27. Ibid., 65.

Muhammad

The design of this angular Kufic inscription
consists of three words: Allah (God)—in the center;
Muhammad (the Prophet of Islam)—the bordering
inscriptions repeated four times; and Ali (devoted
son-in-law)—the lighter interior inscriptions.

Islam

12

James A. Toronto

ISLAM is one of the world's largest and fastest-growing religions. With more than one billion adherents (almost one-fifth of the world's population) and with high annual rates of birth and conversion to bolster its ranks, Islam, according to some demographers, could surpass Christianity in the first half of the twenty-first century as the most populous religion in the world. The geographic expanse of the Islamic world, those areas in which *Muslims* are the majority population, is also vast, reaching from Morocco to Indonesia and from the Muslim republics of central Asia to Sudan and Nigeria in sub-Saharan Africa (see map). But beyond its impressive demography and geography, Islam is a religion that deserves attention because of its important contributions to civilization, its prominent role in contemporary international politics, and, above all, its profound influence in the spiritual lives of millions throughout the world.

The Arabic word islam means, literally, submission or surrender, and a muslim, therefore, is a person who submits or surrenders. The etymological root of islam (s-l-m) is associated with ideas of peace (*salaam*) and well-being (*salaama*), and the implication in a religious context is that a person who submits his or her will completely to the worship of the one God, *Allah,* finds peace, safety, and salvation. For both etymological and theological reasons, then, Muslims commonly speak of Islam as "the religion of peace."

It is a source of great consternation and bewilderment to Muslims, therefore, to learn that in the minds of many throughout the world Islam has come to represent the antithesis of peace. Misconceptions and stereotypes are widespread and have contributed to a spirit of "Islamophobia" among Westerners. Surveys in many different countries indicate that historic attitudes of hostility, suspicion, and prejudice between the Christian West and the

Islamic nations of the East still linger and that Muslims are widely regarded as violent, greedy, malevolent, oppressive to women, rich, and dishonest. Recent events such as revolutions, death sentences, warfare, and terrorist activities carried out by Muslim extremist groups in the Middle East, Europe, and the United States have reinforced in the public's mind these associations. The media often perpetuate such misinformation and stereotypes: movies, cartoon strips, and print media typically portray Islamic religion and culture as menacing and alien, thus contributing to a climate of distrust that has characterized Christian-Muslim relations for centuries. In short, while Islam is one of the world's most dynamic religions in terms of geographic coverage and rapid growth, it is also one of the most misunderstood and maligned.

Western students typically have had little exposure to religions like Buddhism, Hinduism, Jainism, or Taoism and therefore have little knowledge and few opinions about these more obscure philosophies. But virtually all students have been exposed to Islam and carry with them the psychological baggage of preconceived ideas. The challenge for students and teachers of Islamic religion, then, is to seek open-mindedly to address questions such as these: Which picture of Islam is accurate—the religion of violence and terrorism, or the religion of peace and harmony? If Islam is a malicious religious ideology that promotes violence and oppression, why does it continue to be so dynamic and popular throughout the world, including the West? What are we to think of visions, miracles, and teachings of Muhammad, and in particular the sacred text, the *Qur'an,* revealed to him? What is the meaning and purpose of veiling in Islam: is it merely a symbol of repression of women's rights and status in Muslim society? Is Islam essentially tolerant or intolerant in its relations with other religious groups?

This chapter approaches the study of Islam on the basis of three ground rules. The first is to present Islam from a Muslim point of view, from Muslim sources, through the eyes of those who believe in it, practice it, and find spiritual fulfillment in it. The second is to make fair comparisons which are neither superficial nor invidious in nature by examining all religious traditions, including one's own, through the same analytical lens. The third is to leave room in the study for humility and integrity—what some have referred to as "holy envy," or the idea that one's own religious understanding and experience can be greatly enriched by open-minded consideration of others' relationship with deity.

Pre-Islamic Arabia

On the eve of the birth of Islam—in the late sixth and early seventh centuries c.e.—the Arabian peninsula was a place far removed from the major centers of culture and political power. A vast and desolate area, it was for the most part sparsely populated by Bedouin nomads and punctuated by small oasis towns. The two great powers of the day were the Byzantine Empire (the Greek-speaking, Christian continuation of the old Roman Empire), with its capital at Constantinople, and the Persian empire of the Sassanians, composed of Zoroastrians. Each empire was militantly dedicated to its own religion and to the destruction of the other. Perso-Roman hostilities were centuries old. However, as the seventh century dawned, the two empires were about to embark on a long war which would eventually leave each of them exhausted and vulnerable.

The pre-Islamic Arabians were for the most part animists and polytheists. Somewhere up above the *jinn* and other subordinate demigods to whom they paid marginal attention was the distant and mysterious high God, *Allah.* His name, a contraction of the Arabic words *al* and *ilah,* which together mean "the god," is the Arabic form of the old Semitic name for the high God and is closely related to the word *Elohim,* formed from the Hebrew word *eloh,* "god," and the masculine plural suffix *-im.* To most of the pre-Islamic Arabs, though, this Allah was too remote to pray to or even to think about.

Arabia had long derived much of what wealth it had from the trade routes which ran its length, bringing frankincense and myrrh from Yemen, Ethiopia, Somalia, and even India. It was probably along the most important of these trade routes that Lehi of the Book of Mormon led his family six hundred years b.c.e. Not far from Lehi's postulated route of travel was the ancient oasis of *Mecca,* established around a well called Zamzam. Mecca was a historic city; Ishmael, the firstborn son of Abraham, was thought to be the first person to dwell there permanently. As the sixth century c.e. opened, Mecca was beginning to acquire great wealth. It had managed to gain a major share of the caravan profits and had also turned itself into a major center of pilgrimage, with its shrine called the *Ka'aba* (cube-shaped shrine). Each year hundreds of pilgrims would gather in Mecca to pray and perform sacrifices to the myriad gods represented by statues and other icons inside the Ka'aba. Mecca thus became an island of affluence and a thriving center of trade, commerce, and religious pilgrimage for the inhabitants of the Arabian peninsula.

The prosperity of Mecca brought economic and social changes that fostered new problems in society. The old values of family and tribe, which performed the functions of a "government" in the modern sense, fell victim to a new economic order that emphasized the acquisition of wealth and material comforts. Widows and orphans, who had been secure and cared for under the old tribal system, were now left largely on their own. Some people seem to have been sensitive to these problems and began to look for something better. They sought higher values than wealth and a higher religion than the vague and primitive polytheistic paganism around them. But where could they turn for a higher religious experience? The Jews of pre-Islamic Arabia were not interested in converts. There were Christians, but to align oneself with Christianity was, willingly or not, to make a political statement and join the Byzantine party. The same was true if one decided to become a Zoroastrian. So these seekers and prophetic figures—or, as they were known in Arabic, these *hunafa'*—seem to have held to a nonaligned and simple monotheism, praying and fasting and hoping for something better. Muhammad was one of these.

The Life of Muhammad

Born in 570 c.e. and orphaned in early childhood, Muhammad was cared for first by his grandfather, 'Abd al-Mutallib, and then by his uncle, Abu Talib. As an orphan, he was exposed to many of the

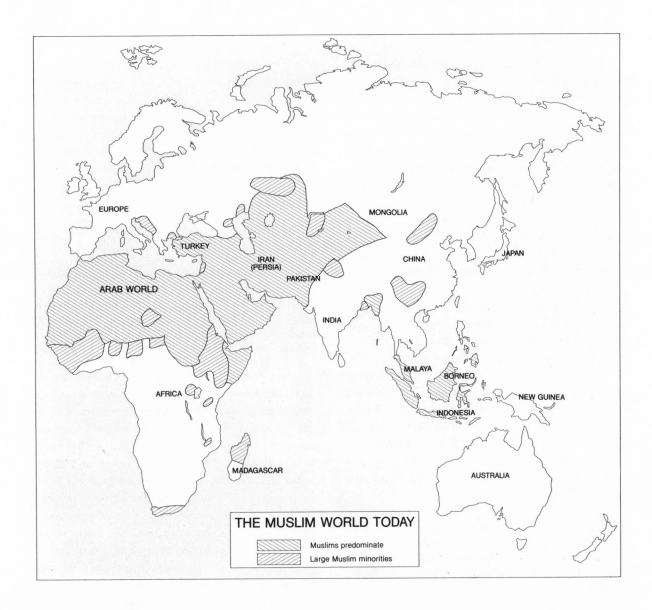

THE MUSLIM WORLD TODAY

Muslims predominate

Large Muslim minorities

hardships of life in Mecca. Even though he triumphed over his disadvantages by virtue of character and ability, and even though he went on to a life of prosperity and renown, he seems not to have forgotten his childhood. He remained always sensitive to children, widows, orphans, and the poor and disenfranchised in society.

Popular Muslim literature is replete with stories of Muhammad's childhood in Mecca, describing the exemplary conduct and the extraordinary signs that portended the advent of a great religious figure.[1] The year of his birth is known as the Year of the Elephant because it was during that time that an army from Yemen, using an elephant as part of their attack strategy, advanced toward Mecca. Miraculously, flocks of birds carrying stones in their beaks and

claws flew over the invading army who, when pelted with the stones from above, fled in disarray back to Yemen. It is said that light emanated from the womb of Muhammad's mother, Amina, in the months before his birth. His wet nurse, Halima, noticed that when Muhammad was with her, her goats gave more milk, the rains came after a long drought, and her lame donkey was healed. He was an obedient, intelligent, and disciplined young man who never indulged in the mischievous activities of other children or, as a young man, in the vice and immorality found in abundance in Mecca. He gained a reputation at an early age for being dependable, honest, and hard-working, acquiring the nicknames *Sadiq* ("true") and *Amin* ("trustworthy"). He lived a life of poverty as a youth, working as a herdsman for his family and neighbors—an occupation that gave him ample time and solitude to contemplate the deeper questions of life.

At the age of twenty-five Muhammad married a widow, Khadija, who was fifteen years his senior and a prosperous caravan merchant. She knew of his reputation for honesty and hard work, and she made the proposal of marriage. The union turned out to be a successful and happy one, producing four daughters and two sons. For the next fifteen years Muhammad was engaged with Khadija in running the family business and raising their family. It was during this period also that he intensified the practice of *tahannuth,* the Arab tradition of retreat into the solitude of the desert to pray, meditate, and worship. He continued to be dissatisfied with the corruption, idolatry, and social inequities that plagued Mecca; he sought for a higher truth that would provide peace, justice, and spiritual fulfillment for him and his people.

In the year 610 C.E., at the age of forty, his spiritual seeking and preparation reached a culmination. On the night known to Muslims as *Laylat al-Qadr* ("Night of Power"), while Muhammad was engaged in prayer and meditation in a cave on Mount Hira near Mecca, the angel Gabriel suddenly appeared to him to deliver a message from God. Three times the angel commanded that Muhammad

> Proclaim! In the name of the Lord and Cherisher Who created, Created man out of a leech-like clot: Proclaim! And thy Lord is Most Bountiful, He who taught the use of the Pen, Taught man that which he knew not (Qur'an 96:1–5).[2]

When the vision was ended and the words of the divine injunction were indelibly impressed in his mind, he left the cave wondering about the validity of the manifestation. On the road back to Mecca, now in bright sunlight, the angel appeared a fourth time and reiterated the message so that there could be no mistake about the reality of the experience. When he arrived home he was shivering from fright and begged Khadija to cover him with blankets. When he told her of his experience in the cave at Mount Hira and expressed his fears about what had happened, she reassured him:

> Joy to my cousin! Be firm. I pray and hope that you will be the Prophet of this nation. By God, He will not let you down. You will be kind to your kin; your speech will all be true; you will rescue the weary, entertain the guest, and help the truth to prevail.[3]

Khadija, who was the first to embrace Muhammad's teaching of Islam, continued to support and encourage Muhammad during the ensuing period of silence when the angelic visitor did not reappear. Muhammad, like other religious figures who have reported an epiphany of this nature, was left feeling abandoned and doubtful of his status, concerned that he had incurred the wrath of God. But after a time, the revelations continued with these comforting words:

> By the glorious morning light, And by the night when it is still, Thy Guardian Lord hath not forsaken thee, nor is He displeased. And verily the Hereafter will be better for thee than the present. And soon will thy Guardian-Lord give thee (that wherewith) thou shalt be well-pleased. Did He not find thee an orphan and give thee shelter (and care)? And He found thee wandering, and He gave thee guidance. And he found thee in need, and made thee independent. (Qur'an 93:1–8)

For a period of twenty-two years, from 610 C.E. to his death in 632, Muhammad received revelations on a regular basis—divine communications that he recognized as being from a source beyond himself and that he memorized verbatim and recited orally to his disciples. These oral recitations of Allah's mind and will, collectively referred to as *al-Qur'an* by Muslims, were in turn memorized by his companions and written down on pieces of parchment, bone, palm leaves, and other materials, but were not compiled into a book of scripture until after Muhammad's death. As a result of these revelatory experiences, Muhammad gained the courage, knowledge, and stature to go forth as a prophet (*nabi*) and apostle (*rasul*), boldly proclaiming the true religion of the one absolute God, Allah.

However, Muhammad's preaching of *tawheed* (the oneness of God) and his unrelenting denunciation of idolatry, polytheism, female infanticide, and other religious and social corruptions met stiff resistance in Mecca. His views were considered a threat to the social and economic status quo because the community's commercial life depended largely on the worship of idols in the Ka'aba. His message, therefore, was rejected in this early period in Mecca, and he and his fledgling community of converts—mostly a few family members and close friends—were shunned, persecuted, and even tortured. To escape the unbearable conditions in Mecca, some of the Muslim converts emigrated to Abyssinia (Ethiopia) to seek refuge.

It was during this bleak period of adversity that Muhammad's "Night Journey and Ascension" (al-Isra' wal-Mi'raj) took place. Muslim views and accounts of this event differ to some degree, but the basic story is that Muhammad was awakened one night by the angel Gabriel, who accompanied him on the back of the legendary creature Buraq from the Ka'aba in Mecca to Jerusalem. There he met several of the ancient prophets—Abraham, Moses, Jesus, and others—who gathered behind him in prayer on the holy mount. Then he ascended through the seven heavens into the presence of Allah.

During the course of his ascent and descent, Muhammad received instructions concerning his mission and the nature of God's teachings. Among other things, he was told that wine and other intoxicants are forbidden and that Muslims should pray fifty times each day. However, as described in one of the most delightful accounts in Muslim tradition, Muhammad (with encouragement from Moses) pleaded with Allah, who mercifully reduced the number to five. These miraculous events happened in the course of one night, Muhammad returning to Mecca before sunrise. When he recounted his experience to the people of Mecca, they scoffed at him and ridiculed the Muslims further. But as proof, Muhammad described meticulously the caravans he had passed while traversing from Jerusalem to Mecca, and when the caravans arrived during the next few days, his detractors were astonished—and his followers overjoyed—to see that his descriptions were accurate in every detail.

Muhammad's Night Journey and Ascent was a formative event in early Islamic history for several reasons. It came at a time of severe trial in the Muslim community, providing confirmation to the converts of Muhammad's prophetic calling and further evidence of his preeminent spiritual stature. It also established Jerusalem, already the holy city for Jews and Christians, as a sacred place for Muslims, who ever afterward have regarded it as a site of pilgrimage, calling it simply al-Quds, the Holy. Because Muhammad's ascent is said to have commenced from the very spot which marked the Holy of Holies in Solomon's Temple, this rock outcropping is now enclosed by the splendid Dome of the Rock mosque. Thus, the same piece of real estate is claimed as a holy site by three major world religions; and this fact, ironically, has laid the foundation for centuries of sectarian conflict in the City of Peace.

When a group of men came on a pilgrimage from a town called Yathrib and asked Muhammad to come and act as an arbitrator in the squabbles which were ruining their town, Muhammad saw an opportunity to alleviate the suffering of the Muslims and agreed to leave Mecca. First he sent his followers, and then he himself went to the town which would thereafter be known as Madinat al-Nabi, "City of the Prophet"—or, simply, Medina. This emigration, called in Arabic the Hijra, took place in 622 C.E., a year that is commemorated as the starting point of the Muslim Hijri calendar. Muslims saw in the Hijra a fundamental turning point in the life of the prophet and in the nature of the Muslim community. From being a rejected preacher, Muhammad became a statesman, legislator, judge, educator, and military leader. In contrast to their status as a persecuted, marginal religious minority in Mecca, the Muslims in Medina had the freedom to establish themselves securely, develop their institutions for governance and education, and become a thriving, prosperous religious community of expanding influence. In short, the Hijra was the transition point that provided Islam the conditions and resources to surpass its local Arabian origins and achieve status as a world religion of global scope and impact.

Within a few years after the Hijra, Muhammad was able to return to and take over the city of Mecca without bloodshed. Prior to this, he had already made the Ka'aba the goal of Muslim pilgrimage. Today, Mecca is considered by Muslims the center of the universe and the holiest of cities, with Medina as the second and Jerusalem the third holiest cities.

In 632 C.E., at the age of sixty-two, Muhammad died unexpectedly after a short fever. By any measure, Muhammad was phenomenally successful during his career, even though his name and achievements have been the subject of intense controversy over the centuries. Many Western writers have portrayed him as a false prophet, a demagogue, and an implacable enemy of all Christians. Some Western historians have been more objective and complimentary, pointing out that Muhammad's achievements in both the political and religious realms assure him a place as one of the most influential figures in history. One such writer, a Frenchman named Lamartine, summed up Muhammad's accomplishments and influence in a book entitled A History of Turkey:

If a man's genius is measured according to the greatness of his design, the limited nature of the means at his disposal, and the immensity of the results achieved, then Muhammad was great in a way that no modern figure can hope to emulate. The most celebrated among them have done no more than win a few victories, pass a few laws, or create an empire. When and if they actually accomplished something, it was usually swept away after their death. Muhammad's ideas set whole armies in motion, affected legislation, empires, peoples, dynasties, millions of people in an area covering one-third of the inhabited surface of the globe. But he accomplished more than that: he also stirred up new ideas, beliefs, and souls. On the basis of one book, whose every word has become a law, he created a spiritual nationality that embraces people of every color and language. The indelible character of this Muslim faith resides in a hatred of false idols and a passion for the one and only, immaterial deity. . . . Philosopher, orator, apostle, legislator, warrior, conqueror of ideas, restorer of rational dogma, of a cult without images, founder of twenty worldly empires and one spiritual empire, such is Muhammad.[4]

ISLAM AFTER MUHAMMAD'S DEATH: EXPANSION AND CONSOLIDATION

After Muhammad's death, Islam continued to expand rapidly beyond the borders of the Arabian peninsula. The ancient and mighty Persian empire, weakened and demoralized by its long war with Constantinople, fell quickly to the Muslim armies that came from the south. The Byzantines also offered little resistance, yielding to the Muslims large sections of territory, including their "breadbasket," the fertile province of Egypt. Within a hundred years the Muslim advance had reached west across north Africa and into the Iberian peninsula and east as far as Pakistan and India. Over the next few centuries, Islam gradually but steadily extended its influence until it became the dominant religion and culture in much of the Indian subcontinent and southeast Asia.

How does one account for Islam's phenomenal success in propagating its faith and way of life? This question has been a persistent point of controversy between Muslim and non-Muslim historians for centuries and continues to present fertile ground for polemical discussion in the interfaith setting. One cannot possibly do justice to a many-faceted issue like this in a brief chapter; there is space only to summarize the debate and offer some perspective that will inform further exploration by students.

Western scholars have frequently explained the rapid expansion of the Islamic empire in terms of Islam's perceived fanaticism, militancy, and intolerance. These sources portray marauding Bedouin warriors, imbued with a new spirit of religious zealotry, swarming out of the Arabian desert, proclaiming, "Islam or the sword," massacring those who refuse to convert, and relentlessly pursuing their quest for spiritual domination and material gain. Students often wonder how Muhammad and his religious community could rationalize their involvement in raiding and waging war against neighboring communities and nations.

A balanced assessment of the issue takes into account a complex interplay of historical, economic, and sociopolitical factors. First, it is helpful to bear in mind that Islam's military expansion was not incongruous with the prevailing historical norms. International laws governing relations between nations and stipulating respect for human rights—basic civil and religious liberties taken for granted today—are a relatively modern development, not widely codified and observed until the nineteenth and twentieth centuries. Principles such as separation of church and state, freedom of expression, humane treatment of captive belligerents, and respect for national or imperial boundaries (which were, in any case, ill-defined or nonexistent) were virtually unknown. Nearly every sociopolitical community in history has resorted to warfare, whether defensive or aggressive (and indeed, the line between the two varieties is often obscure), in order to protect and promote its interests; and it was commonly the case that political, military, and religious leadership of the community centered in one powerful individual whose role was to mobilize the support and loyalty of the people. The history of religions is replete with examples of this statesman/warrior/prophet motif: besides Muhammad and the *caliphs* from Islamic tradition, these include the Buddhist emperor Asoka, the Old Testament prophets Moses and Joshua, and the Christian emperor Charlemagne. To the assertion by a Christian scholar that Islam was propagated and "enforced at the point of a sword," Ameer 'Ali provides a candid, historically defensible response:

Every religion, in some stage of its career, has, from the tendencies of its professors, been aggressive. Such also has been the case with Islam; but that it ever aims at proselytism by force, or that it has been more aggressive than other religions, must be entirely denied.[5]

In a similar vein, Elder Dallin H. Oaks of the Quorum of the Twelve has called for caution and fairness in passing judgment from our twentieth-century perspective on individuals who lived long ago and under much different circumstances. Referring to the controversy in Latter-day Saint history when Joseph Smith ordered the destruction of the opposition newspaper in Nauvoo, Elder Oaks observed that what critics have labeled a tyrannical violation of law and civil rights was not, in fact, an illegal or unprecedented action during that early period in the evolution of America's legal system. His perceptive conclusion provides a guideline for the study of any historical personality, regardless of the time period or religious tradition in question: "We should judge the actions of our predecessors on the basis of the laws and commandments and circumstances of their day, not ours."[6]

Social, economic, and political conditions must also be considered in order to understand why Muslim political control flourished and Islamic religion gradually took root in conquered territories. Those who did convert to Islam were often drawn (as is the case with converts to Islam today) by the simple appeal of the new religion's doctrine of theological and social unity. In India, for example, we find that "Hindu workers and artisans were exposed to caste-free Islam and were in part attracted by the ideal of 'social oneness'; for the Islamic *shari'a* gave them more possibilities for development than the Hindu tradition. . . . Hence we hear of conversions on a larger scale, of the weavers, for instance."[7] Others converted, no doubt, when they perceived that there were political and economic advantages to being a Muslim in a Muslim-dominated state. Those who chose to remain non-Muslims (*dhimmis*, "protected citizens") were second-class citizens within the Islamic empire: they were required to pay special taxes and act deferentially toward Muslims and were forbidden to serve in the military, ride horses, or propagate their own religion. But they were also given opportunities not usually enjoyed by conquered peoples at that time, including the right to practice their religion and hold high office in the Muslim government. Frederick Denny points out that

[a]lthough the letter of Islamic law regarding the *dhimmis* was somewhat harsh, the application of it varied greatly from place to place and period to period. For the greater part, the People of the Book have been treated tolerantly and respectfully by the Muslims, far more so than could be said of non-Christians in predominantly Christian lands over the same centuries. . . . The Jews, especially, flourished under Muslim rule in such places as Iraq, Egypt, and the Maghrib (especially Spain). Though there there were periods of persecution and tragedy, they were rare.[8]

He goes on to say that in some areas like Syria, Palestine, and Iraq, the transformation to Islamic rule caused little upheaval because "the Arabs brought a new version of a basically familiar religious and ethical system to peoples whose native language was also in the Semitic family and closely related to the language of the Qur'an."[9]

Regardless of the controversy surrounding this issue, it is clear that the rise of the Islamic empire and the subsequent development and contributions of Islamic civilization remains one of the most extraordinary sagas in world history. Unfortunately, the intellectual and æsthetic achievements of Islam and their influence on Western civilization, though well documented, have remained relatively unknown outside the sphere of Islam. For more than five hundred years, beginning in the eight century C.E. while Europe was struggling through internecine warfare, intellectual stagnation, and spiritual decline, the Islamic world was a major center of educational, scientific, and cultural advancement. Major centers of Islamic learning thrived, and one of them—Al-Azhar in Cairo, Egypt—is one of the oldest universities in the world today (dating from 960 C.E.). Muslim scientists, mathematicians, and explorers made significant contributions to world civilization. Al-Razi and Ibn Sina (known, respectively, as Rhazes and Avicenna in Europe) wrote medical treatises that became standard textbooks for centuries in European universities. Al-Biruni calculated the circumference of the earth with a remarkable degree of accuracy and theorized that the earth rotated on an axis. Muslim mathematicians developed algebra (*al-jabr*) and influenced the development of Western science with the replacement of Roman numerals by Arabic numerals and with the introduction to Europe of the Hindu concept of zero. Geographers like Ibn Battuta traveled widely throughout the world and left detailed written accounts and maps, and Muslim navigators used the astrolabe they developed and their knowledge of astronomy to chart sea routes that helped prepare the way for later generations of European explorers. Ibn Khaldun devised a theory of social and political change in nations that continues to provide intellectual challenge and historical insight in academic circles. Artisans, architects, and craftsmen across the Islamic world produced stunning tapestries, pottery, and metal work and constructed exquisitely designed and decorated mosques, palaces, and private dwellings. Urban planning among Muslims was highly developed: cities like Cordoba, Spain, were models of cleanliness, efficiency, and symmetry during their time and included parks, public baths and fountains, water drainage and sewage, mosques and churches, and even an elaborate system of street lights. The influence of Muslim science, technology, and literature on pre-Renaissance Europe can be seen in many words that eventually made their way from Arabic into English: sherbet, alcohol, syrup, admiral, giraffe, gazelle, nadir, zenith, apricot, cotton, genie, minaret, algebra, cipher, elixir, and lute.

DENOMINATIONS AND POLITICAL HISTORY

One result of the spread of Islam outside the heartlands of Arabia and the Middle East can be seen today in the cultural, linguistic, and ethnic diversity that characterizes the Islamic community. This fact means that the terms Arab and Muslim are not equivalent, as many Westerners suppose. While most Arabs are Muslims, not all are: the Arab world has always included significant Jewish and Christian minorities. An Arab is defined today as one who speaks Arabic as a native language: it is not a question of religious affiliation or ethnicity. It is also true that the vast majority of Muslims—more than 75 percent—are not Arabs, including the inhabitants of some Middle Eastern Muslim countries like Turkey and Iran. Although the spiritual and educational center of Islam is still the Middle East—in cities such as Mecca, Medina, Jerusalem, Cairo, Istanbul, and Teheran—the population centers are located primarily in southern and southeastern Asia. The largest Muslim country in the world is Indonesia (with nearly two hundred million people), and dominant or prominent Muslim populations are present in such varied places as Pakistan, India, Afghanistan, Bangladesh, Malaysia, China, Azerbaijan, Tajikistan, and Nigeria. Over the centuries, what has become known as Islamic culture has drawn upon Turks, Iranians, Mongols, and Africans and has developed a rich diversity. It has tapped Jewish legends, Greek philosophy, Indian mathematics, and Persian manners. It has produced lawyers, mystics, skeptics,

poets, and scientists. We must be careful, then, when we talk about "Islam." Although Westerners like to speak of the monolith of Islam, there are very few generalizations that would be true of, say, both a tenth-century surgeon in Baghdad and a twentieth-century Indonesian peasant. In fact, there are nearly as many "denominations" and points of view in Islam as there are in Christianity, and Islamic history is equally complex.

The Caliphate

Because Muhammad died suddenly, he had not officially and publicly named a successor or given instructions on transfer of leadership and authority in the *umma* (Muslim community) after his death. His closest companions were left to decide who this should be and whether the principle governing succession should be hereditary, with rights of leadership descending to members of the prophet's family, or electoral, with the successor (Arabic *khalifa*, English "caliph") being chosen by consensus from among a particular qualified body of men.

Sunnis and Shi'ites

Opinions diverged from the start as to who the first caliph would be and how he should be chosen. Some supported Abu Bakr, reputed to be the prophet's closest companion and most pious disciple. Others favored 'Ali, who was also an early and close disciple and, perhaps more importantly, had joined Muhammad's family by marrying his daughter Fatima. Those who supported Abu Bakr held that succession should be elective, with the caliph to be chosen from among those who had been close to the prophet and who were thereby more spiritually prepared to direct the affairs of the community according to the prophet's example, or *sunna*. 'Ali's faction (*shi'a*, "party" or "sect") claimed that Muhammad had specifically named 'Ali as his successor and had privately passed on to him esoteric spiritual knowledge. In any case, they argued, succession should be hereditary ('Ali was the prophet's closest surviving male relative, Muhammad's two sons having died before him).

Both issues of sunna and heredity are interesting ones. Arguably, 'Ali as well as Abu Bakr could have claimed succession on the basis of sunna, as both stood out over all the others as being exemplary in their devotions to God and as close companions to the prophet. And both Abu Bakr and 'Ali were connected to Muhammad by marriage, the former being his father-in-law—father of his wife A'ishah—and the latter his son-in-law.

But whatever the merits of these two claims to succession, Abu Bakr became the first caliph. The caliphate remained in *Sunni* hands (the term came into use somewhat later, but the ideological tendency was already apparent at an early date) over the next twenty-two years and through two more successions: those of 'Umar and 'Uthman, both members of the powerful and influential Umayyad clan (to which Muhammad had also belonged). Rebellion and civil war broke out in 656 C.E. 'Uthman was killed and 'Ali finally succeeded to the caliphate. But his reign lasted only five years; he was assassinated in 661. Although his son Hasan was named his successor, the Sunnis immediately forced Hasan to abdicate in favor of Mu'awiyah, one of Muhammad's former scribes and also a member of the Umayyad clan. Mu'awiyah ruled Islam from 661 until his death in 680. His son Yazid was elected to succeed him.

In the meantime, Hasan, following his forced abdication of the caliphate, retired to Medina, where he died in 680—the same year as did Mu'awiyah. Immediately upon Mu'awiyah's death, the *Shi'ites* once again rose in revolt, this time under Hasan's brother Husayn. The uprising was crushed, Husayn was killed, and the Sunnis remained in power under a series of Umayyad caliphs in their capital city, Damascus. The Umayyad dynasty was finally overthrown by the Abbasids in 750. Hereditary succession of the caliphate had taken root in Islam, but not in the manner the Shi'ites had hoped for.

The death of Husayn is still commemorated by Shi'ite Muslims in annual passion plays which hold a central place in their religious life. The memory perennially fans the flame of their antagonism toward the Sunnis, whom Shi'ites view as corruptors of the correct Islamic tradition and usurpers of its leadership.

Although other parties and schisms have emerged within Islam, the two dominant groups today remain the Sunnis and the Shi'ites. The former comprise approximately 85 percent of the Islamic world and the latter about 15 percent. The Sunnis have historically approached governance and decision-making on the basis of community consultation and consensus. Among the Sunnis there is no centralized, worldwide leadership, since any semblance of that disappeared finally with Ataturk's abolition of the caliphate in Turkey following World War I.

The Shi'ites, on the other hand, view Muhammad as the prophet of Islam and his son-in-law, 'Ali, as the divinely designated successor, the commander of the faithful, and the one who reveals truth. Thus, there developed a doctrine of succession among the Shi'ites—a succession of *imams*, or spiritual leaders, like 'Ali. This led to the concept of the "hidden imam," who instead of dying went into occultation, or hiding. The Sevener Shi'ites (commonly called Isma'ilis, whose leader is the Aga Khan) consider the seventh imam to be the Hidden Imam, while the Twelver Shi'ites (adherents of the largest sect in Shi'ism, who are centered in Iran and whose supreme leaders are called Ayatullah, "Sign of God") consider the twelfth imam to be this mysterious figure. The hidden imam's influence is still present today through persons who remain in touch with him. In Shi'ite tradition, it is he who will return at the end of history as the messiah figure, or *Mahdi,* to prepare the world for God's judgment day.

SOURCES OF ISLAMIC EPISTEMOLOGY: QUR'AN AND SUNNA

Nature and Role of the Qur'an in Muslim Society

According to Islamic tradition, the process of *wahy,* or direct revelation, that produced the Qur'an (sometimes anglicized as Koran) did not involve, as in Latter-day Saint and other religious traditions, any translation of ancient lost records or any writing down of Muhammad's own thoughts, however inspired they might be. The Qur'an is totally "other than" Muhammad, a perfect replication of God's literal speech that reflects nothing of the prophet's life or thought processes:

[The Qur'an] is the actual Word of Allah; not created but revealed for the benefit of all mankind. . . . It is complete and comprehensive. . . . So well has it been preserved, both in memory and in writing, that the Arabic text we have today is identical to the text as it was revealed to the Prophet. Not even a single letter has yielded to corruption during the passage of the centuries.[10]

The Qur'an is first and foremost an oral tradition, not a written one. It is primarily the sound of the

Qur'an—oral recitation rather than textual exegesis—which has become a distinguishing characteristic of Islam. It permeates all aspects of Muslim life. One hears the sound of recitation constantly at the market, in taxis, in government offices, in public schools, before and after television broadcasts, and in private homes. In addition, Qur'anic verses executed in exquisite Arabic calligraphy adorn the walls of mosques, apartment buildings, schools, public offices, and stores.

In order to understand fully the centrality of the Qur'an's role in Islamic society, one can compare the relationship between Muhammad and the Qur'an in Islam and Jesus and the Bible in Christianity. For Christians, Christ is the Word of God incarnate, the message to humanity, the object of devotional worship. The Bible—the sacred text—is then the messenger, that which reveals the message and brings one to Christ. The sacramental rite in Christian worship services, during which the believer partakes of the emblems of Christ's flesh and blood, is a powerful reminder of Christ's centrality in reconciling mankind with God. For Muslims, the Qur'an is the vital message, the Word of God inlibriate, revealing the literal mind and will of Allah, who is the sole object of worship. Muhammad is merely the messenger through whom Allah revealed his message: the holy Qur'an, which proclaims the oneness of God. The Islamic equivalent to the Christian sacrament, then, is the act of imbibing the word of God through seeing, hearing, or reciting the Qur'an.

In Muslim belief, the Qur'an is taken from the great Book which was with God from all eternity, uncreated, as God's everlasting and unchanging utterance. The Torah, the Psalms, and the Gospels of the New Testament come likewise from the "Heavenly Tablet," but Muslims believe that they have been corrupted over time and contain theological inaccuracies in their present form.

Muslims often speak of the miraculous nature—the inimitability—of the Qur'an. They believe that Jesus performed many wonderful miracles but that none can compare to Muhammad's one miracle—having brought forth, though untutored and illiterate, a divine book of incomparable beauty, truth, power, and majesty. In two verses that will have the ring of familiarity to Latter-day Saints (compare D&C 67:4–9), Allah challenges critics and doubters to try to create anything like the Qur'an and warns them of the consequences:

And if ye are in doubt as to what We have revealed from time to time to Our servant, then produce a Sura like thereunto; and call your witnesses or helpers (if there are any) besides Allah, if ye are truthful. But if ye cannot—and of a surety ye cannot—then fear the Fire whose fuel is Men and Stones—which is prepared for those who reject Faith. (Qur'an 2:23–24)

With this in mind, it is little wonder that the Qur'an is the focus of Muslim worship and the backdrop for everyday life in Islamic society. The desire of Muslims, in the early years of Islam, to comprehend and explicate the word of God gave rise to the development of Arabic grammar and prompted the zealous pursuit of knowledge, culminating in the marvelous literary and artistic achievements of Islamic civilization. Through the centuries since the rise of Islam, study of the Qur'an has formed the basis for the curriculum of Islamic schools. It is still considered a great honor, which many young Muslim students work assiduously for years to attain, to become a *hafiz,* or one who has memorized the entire Qur'an and can recite it correctly by heart.

A devout Muslim, because of his or her respect and reverence for God's word, will not open a volume of the Qur'an or recite from it without first performing the ritual of cleansing and saying the words, "In the name of Allah, Most Gracious, Most Merciful." Muslims worldwide perform the prescribed ritual acts of worship in Arabic, whether they understand them completely or not (and the vast majority are not Arabic-speaking), because that is the language of God. To use another language would diminish the spiritual power and meaning of the ritual. A Chinese Muslim, for example, might read from a Qur'an written in Chinese characters; but the characters represent a transliteration of the actual words and sounds of the Arabic text and not a translation of the text into Chinese. Many Qur'anic words and phrases have been adopted as everyday usage in the Arabic language, even by the millions of Arabs who are not Muslim. The Qur'an is believed to possess great *baraka* (spiritual power). Therefore, Muslims commonly decorate their homes, automobiles, offices, schools, and commercial establishments with verses and copies of the Holy Book as a safeguard against evil. One of the favorite pastimes in Muslim communities is attending performances by famous Qur'an reciters and sponsoring competitions in the art of recitation among young aspirants.

For Latter-day Saints, although the Qur'an has often been compared with the Book of Mormon, it is more accurate to compare it with the Doctrine and Covenants. Unlike the Old Testament and the Book of Mormon, the Qur'an is not a narrative or a history. Like the Doctrine and Covenants, it is a collection of revelations and statements on many different subjects.

The organization of the Qur'an is somewhat unique. Essentially, it is arranged from longest to shortest chapter (*sura*). The exception to this is the first sura, a short invocation known as *al-Fatihah*, "The Opening." It can rightly be called "The Lord's Prayer of Islam" in the sense that it forms a central part of the liturgy that is recited by Muslims throughout the world during ritual prayer five times a day. Muslims say that the Fatihah contains in its few brief, sublime lines the essence of Islam. It reads:

In the name of Allah, Most Gracious, Most Merciful. Praise be to Allah, the Cherisher and Sustainer of the Worlds: Most Gracious, Most Merciful; Master of the Day of Judgment. Thee do we worship, and Thine aid we seek. Show us the straight way, the way of those on whom Thou hast bestowed Thy Grace, those whose portion is not wrath and who go not astray.

There are 114 suras in the Qur'an. Beginning with the second sura, which is 286 verses long, they decrease in length down to the final sura, which contains only 5 verses. Some of the suras were revealed at Mecca and others at Medina. Various writers have sought to reorganize the Qur'an to present the suras in historical sequence, but much of this is educated guessing. The Qur'an's total length is just slightly less than that of the New Testament.

The Emergence of Hadith and Sunna

In the centuries following Muhammad's death, Islam spread into an immense empire with laws and techniques of governing which were far more complex than those required when Muhammad was leading the community. Where was guidance to be found? The Qur'an, of course, was the most prestigious and authoritative source, but the methodology for developing an effective legal and administrative system based on the Holy Book was not yet well developed. So, for a while, the young Muslim empire simply followed the laws and practices of the areas it conquered and left much of the day-to-day government in the hands of the local population.

But this was not a satisfactory solution. As problems arose, many Muslims began to wonder what Muhammad, the prophet, would do in like situations. They began to gather information about what, in fact, he had done and said on almost any question that could be imagined. Eventually, this information took the form of reports called *hadith*, or, as the word is often (if not very precisely) translated, "traditions." Six multivolume collections of hadith were eventually recognized as canonical in Islam and are used as the basis for determining the prophet's customs and exemplary conduct (sunna). Next to the Qur'an, the sunna of the prophet is the most important source of normative action and belief in the Islamic community.

It is largely on the basis of these hadith that the all-inclusive legal code of Islam, called shari'a, was constructed. Actually, it is somewhat misleading to call it a legal code, since it regulates things which are far removed from anything that would be recognized as "law" in the Christian West. Not only does it deal with crimes, inheritance, marriage, and divorce, but it lays down rules on prayer, fasting, etiquette, table manners, dress and grooming, personal hygiene, and virtually every other aspect of human existence.

THE FIVE PILLARS OF ISLAM

Every religious community espouses core doctrines that define the essence of its message and determine its ethos, identity, and direction in the world. That pivotal set of teachings in Christianity might be the Sermon on the Mount; in Judaism, the Ten Commandments or Maimonides' Thirteen Articles of Faith; and in Buddhism, the Four Noble Truths and Eightfold Middle Path. Islamic life revolves around five basic principles that all observant Muslims, whether Sunni or Shi'ite, agree on as binding and normative. These *Five Pillars of Islam* are designated in the Qur'an and the hadith as the witness of faith, prayer, almsgiving, pilgrimage to Mecca, and fasting.

Inherent in Islamic liturgy are several principles that observers of Muslim religious life often overlook but that are crucial for understanding how Muslims view and practice the Five Pillars of their faith. The principle of righteous intent—*niyya* in Arabic—dictates that performance of any religious duty or ritual is ineffectual unless it is done for the right reason and with pure motive. It is similar to the injunction in the Book of Mormon that "ye must not perform any thing unto the Lord save in the first place ye shall pray . . . that he will consecrate thy performance unto thee, that thy performance may be for the welfare of thy soul" (2 Ne. 32:9). A second principle is that all rites of worship must be performed in a state of personal purity (*tahara*), which normally involves a process of ritual cleansing and washing that is meticulously described in Islamic law. Flexibility is a third essential dimension in observance of the Five Pillars. While Islamic rituals demand significant sacrifice and commitment on the part of observant Muslims, Islamic law provides many exceptions to the prescribed rules in order to make worship as pleasant and uplifting as possible. Muslims often point out that the Qur'an refers to Islam as the religion of ease, not difficulty, meaning that Allah is merciful and does not desire to place unnecessary burdens on the shoulders of the believers (2:185). Worship, in the Islamic tradition, is not intended to be a source of affliction, but of spiritual peace, joy, and equilibrium.

Witness of Faith (Shahada)

The witness of faith is a two-part declaration that embodies the central beliefs of Islam: "I witness that there is no god but Allah, and I witness that Muhammad is the messenger of Allah." To be or become a Muslim, one must embrace this statement as inviolable and recite it with conviction. The centrality of the *shahada* in Islamic religious life is evident in many rituals: five times each day it is broadcast from the tops of the mosques to call the faithful to prayer; it is sunna for a father to whisper the call to prayer, which includes the shahada, into the ear of his newborn infant; and it is every Muslim's hope that the last thing one utters before death is the shahada.

The phrase "no God but Allah" states succinctly the cardinal tenet of Islam: strict monotheism, the uncompromising unity of God, which Muslims call tawheed. God is one, eternal, uncreated, and totally other than anything human finiteness can comprehend or describe. It follows, then, that polytheism is anathema in Islam. Muslims refer to this heresy as *shirk*, which means ascribing partners to God, and the Qur'an repeatedly enjoins believers to accept tawheed and avoid shirk.

The Qur'an is said to enumerate ninety-nine "beautiful names" of God that, taken together, reveal the Divine Personality and Nature. For example, the opening phrase of every sura except the ninth begins with the phrase *Bismillah al-Rahman al-Raheem,* "In the name of Allah, the Merciful, the Compassionate." This brief invocation is ubiquitous in Muslim culture: it is recited during ritual prayers five times each day, uttered before eating food or beginning any endeavor, printed at the top of government forms, and inscribed above gateways and portals of schools, houses, and office buildings. These practices reinforce the principles of God's grace and mercy and the opportunity for repentance in Islamic religious life. Allah is portrayed as "Oft-Returning" (*tawwab* [2:37]), from the same Arabic root as the word for repentance, *tawba,* which means "turning" and implies turning away from sin and toward God. The process of repentance outlined in the Qur'an requires "that ye set your whole selves [to Allah] at every time and place of prayer, and call upon Him, making your devotion sincere. . . . So shall ye return" (7:29). The Qur'anic commentary elaborates: "For repentance, three things are necessary: the sinner must acknowledge his wrong; he must give it up; and he must resolve to eschew it for the future. Man's nature is weak, and he may have to return again and again for mercy. So long as he does it sincerely, Allah is Oft-Returning, Most Merciful."[11]

Other names of Allah describe him as Just, Forgiving, Almighty, Omniscient, Creator, Provider, Protector, Helper, King of the Judgment Day, and Lord of the Worlds. The Qur'an says that the purpose of life is to surrender one's will to God: "I have only created Jinns and men, that they may serve me" (51:56). Another verse dispels the idea of some critics that the God of Islam is a distant and detached being: "It was We who created man, and We know what suggestions his soul makes to him: for We are nearer to him than (his) jugular vein" (50:16).

The quintessential message of God's unity is reinforced not only in Islamic ritual and scripture, but in daily conversation and in the conception of æsthetics and sacred space. Qur'anic phrases like *al-hamdulillah* ("praise or thanks to God") and *insha'allah* ("if God wills") punctuate everyday speech—constant reminders that nothing happens without God's knowledge and permission. Muslims almost automatically say "al-hamdullilah" when mentioning something favorable and "insha'allah" when stating assertions or speaking of future events.[12] Linguistic subtleties that evoke thoughts of tawheed permeate Islamic discourse: for instance, in some countries the Arabic word for the index finger is *al-shahid*, "the witness."

Devotion to tawheed has uniquely shaped the development of Islamic art and architecture, a fact that is readily apparent when one contrasts the decoration of Christian buildings (such as St. Peter's Basilica and the Sistine Chapel in Rome, or the Latter-day Saint Visitors Center on Temple Square in Salt Lake City) with Muslim buildings (such as Dome of the Rock Mosque in Jerusalem or Sultan Ahmet Mosque in Istanbul). One clearly observes that the focus in Western religious art, architecture, and sculpture is on the human form, an outgrowth of the Christian concept of the Word of God made flesh. In contrast, Islamic art and architecture are characterized by severe iconoclasm in keeping with Qur'anic denunciation of the anthropomorphic nature of God and the human tendency to worship the creature instead of the Creator. Muslim artisans, obliged to avoid the use of representational images, developed alternative motifs for decorating sacred space, employing as integral elements the order and symmetry of columns and arches, elaborate geometric patterns, delicate vegetal designs, and Qur'anic quotes sculpted in exquisite Arabic calligraphy. The unique æsthetic features of Islamic art achieve with stunning impact the goals of all sublimely rendered religious art: instruction, edification, and uplifting of the soul of the spiritual seeker, while invoking a sense of awe and reverence in the Divine Presence.

Implicit in the witness of faith in Allah are a variety of related theological tenets. Belief in Allah entails, certainly, acceptance of an invisible Qur'anic cosmology. This unseen world includes angels—personages created from light who surround God, pay continuous devotions to Him, and interact with human beings in all dimensions of life. The jinn (from which the word genie is derived)—invisible creatures of fire, one of whom is Satan—often tempt humans to evil and create mischief in the world.

The Qur'an teaches that Allah created the world and all things in it and that in time he will bring the world to an end. Then all human beings will be resurrected, judged according to their deeds and observance of tawheed, and assigned to a paradise or hell for eternity. Paradise is portrayed in Islamic literature as a place of endless delights, pleasures, and rest, where every pious desire of the believers, both men and women, will be fulfilled. Hell is portrayed as a place of endless torment and punishment for those who oppressed other people, performed evil deeds, and denied the Oneness of Allah. The question of who goes to heaven—an elusive one in virtually every religion—is addressed with candor and wit in a delightful anecdote from Shi'ite tradition:

Two Iranian scholars were discussing religion. One of them asked the other, "In the last analysis, who goes to paradise?" The other, a poet well known for his sense of humor, answered, "Well, it is really very simple. First, all religions other than Islam are obviously false, so we do not have to consider them. That leaves Islam. But among Muslims, some are Shi'ites and some Sunnis, and we all know that the Sunnis have strayed from the right path and will be thrown into hell. That leaves the Shi'ites. But among Shi'ites, there are the common people and the ulama. Everyone knows that the common people don't care about God and religion, so they will burn in the Fire. That leaves the ulama. But the ulama have become ulama in order to lord it over the common people. That leaves you and me. And I am not so sure about you."[13]

The most common attitude of Muslims concerning who will be saved, whether Muslim or non-Muslim, is expressed in the phrase *Allahu a'lam:* "only God knows."

The second half of the witness of faith, belief in Muhammad's prophethood, implies acceptance of a broad view of God's relationship to humanity throughout history. For Muslims, Islam is God's revelation to humanity "for all times and all places," as they are fond of saying. Allah's communication did not begin with Muhammad's prophetic call in the cave at Mount Hira in 610 C.E.; rather, he has spoken to many prophets beginning with Adam and including Abraham, Moses, Jesus, and many others mentioned in the Bible. Often, however, the details of these "Stories of the Prophets" differ from their biblical counterparts. In the case of Abraham's sacrifice of his son, for example, the Qur'an portrays both father and son discussing God's command and agreeing to go through with the sacrifice: "O my son! I have seen in a dream that I offer thee in sacrifice: now see what is thy view?"—to which the son replies, "O my father! Do as thou art commanded." They then "both submitted (to Allah)" (37:102–5). Though the Qur'an does not mention the name of Abraham's son in this quintessential example of submission to God's will, contemporary Islamic tradition clearly identifies him as Ishmael, not Isaac as in Judeo-Christian tradition.[14] The Qur'an also mentions many prophetic figures unknown in biblical history, and Islamic tradition holds that there have been 313 messengers (sing. rasul) to whom God has revealed the true religion, Islam, and a holy book, and 120,000 prophets (sing. nabi) throughout history who have sought to guide people to that true religion.[15] According to the Qur'an, Allah has sent messengers and prophets to every people (10:47, 16:46), teaching them the message of tawheed in their own language (14:4). Believers are cautioned not to distinguish between these messengers, for they all came to confirm the truth (61:6, 3:3, 2:136).

The view of sacred history in Islam is, in many respects, analogous to the idea of dispensations in Latter-day Saint doctrine. Before the time of Muhammad, distortions and corruptions—apostasy—had gradually eroded the pristine revelation of each prophet of God, necessitating the raising up of another prophet who would reestablish tawheed as the only true form of worship. In witnessing that Muhammad is the prophet of God, Muslims accept the truths taught by previous prophets and sacred books, including the Torah and the Gospels in their original "pure" versions. But Muslims hold that Muhammad is the last and greatest of all in the prophetic pantheon—the "seal of the prophets" (Qur'an 33:40)—and that Allah revealed to him a complete and perfect Qur'an that will never be corrupted, eliminating the need for any future prophets or scriptures.

The Qur'an refers to Muhammad as "a mercy to the worlds" (21:107) and "an excellent exemplar" (33:21), and therefore his sunna is regarded as an impeccable source of guidance to happiness and success in all aspects of life. Contrary to the Western stereotype of Muhammad as a ruthless tyrant, Muslim sources portray a man of unfailing humility, kindness, good humor, generosity, and simple tastes. Though he smiled often, he seldom laughed because, as one famous hadith states, "If you knew what I know you would cry much and laugh little." His gentle sense of humor is evident in the following story: "One day a little old woman came to him to ask whether old wretched women would also go to Paradise. 'No,' answered the Prophet, 'there are no old women in Paradise!' And then, looking at her grieved face, he continued with a smile: 'They will all be transformed in Paradise for there, there is only one youthful age for all!'" He dispensed wise and practical advice to followers: When a man asked

if, since he already trusted in God's help and protection, he needed to tie his camel up, Muhammad replied: I'qilha wa tawakkal ("First tether it, and then trust in God.") Some reports indicate that Muhammad's family was poor and often hungry, only able to afford coarse bread at times. His statement Faqri fakhri ("My poverty is my pride,") reveals his joy in simple pleasures, and this saying was later adopted as a slogan by some of the Sufi ascetics. Muhammad's gentleness and kindness extended to all beings. He was especially fond of children, allowing his two young grandsons, Hasan and Husayn, to climb on his back while he was performing prayers. A man once criticized him for kissing his grandson Hasan, saying, "I have ten boys but have never kissed any of them." Muhammad answered, "He who does not show mercy will not receive mercy."[16]

With this view of Muhammad in mind, it is not difficult to understand why Muslims bless his name each time it is mentioned in speech or writing, invoke his name in conversations, and (in most countries) celebrate his birthday. Pious Muslims strive to emulate his sunna in their mode of dress; style of grooming; table manners; rituals of prayer; and gentleness and kindness to women, children, and animals. It is little wonder, then, that the name "Muhammad," meaning "highly praised," is more widespread than any other name in the world.

Prayer (Salat)

Islam teaches that God is to be remembered at all times and in all places, and the Qur'an encourages Muslims to pray frequently and to await Allah's answer: "And your Lord says: 'Call on Me; I will answer your (prayer)'" (40:60). A prophetic hadith suggests that believers supplicate God in their every need, no matter how small: "Ask Allah for all your needs, even for the thong of your sandal when it breaks." Muslims engage in many forms of prayer: sometimes they are informal, private, and intensely personal; sometimes they are more formal in nature and address specific communal needs, as in the case of special prayers for rain during seasons of drought. Simple, formulaic prayers are normally uttered before and after a meal.

But the centerpiece of Islamic worship is the ritual prayer called salat that is conducted five times each day and involves a prescribed set of physical movements designed to turn heart and mind toward

God. In preparation to perform salat, a Muslim must first have righteous intent (niyya) in his or her heart and must perform a symbolic washing of face, hands, and feet that signifies one's purity and readiness to approach God in prayer. The times of prayer are determined by the position of the sun in the sky and therefore vary somewhat according to season of the year, geographical location, and daylight-saving schedules. But generally speaking, the five prayer times are dawn, midday, late afternoon, sunset, and early evening.

Islamic law (shari'a) recommends that ritual prayer be performed, if possible, in a mosque together with other believers. The English word mosque is a garbled version of the Arabic *masjid,* meaning "place of prostration," and this can be any suitable location, whether inside a sacred building or outside in an open space. Performing salat with other worshipers in a mosque is not mandatory, however, and Muslims commonly pray wherever they happen to be when the call to prayer is sounded and wherever they can find a small, clean space: in stores, factories, offices, and homes; by the side of the highway; in the fields and open spaces; and on downtown sidewalks. Islam designates Friday as a special day when the faithful are required to gather in the mosque to listen to a sermon and to perform the noon prayer together as a community. Thus, Friday in the Islamic world is similar to the "Sabbath Day" in Judaism and Christianity, when schools and government offices are closed.[17]

The performance of salat is rich in spiritual symbolism and meaning. The preliminary washing, as noted before, refocuses the mind and heart from things mundane to things spiritual. White caps for men and head coverings for women denote humility before God. Whenever two or more of the faithful pray together, one person stands in front of the others and acts as the imam, or prayer leader. Those behind the imam line up shoulder to shoulder in rows, everyone facing toward the Ka'aba in Mecca, signifying the egalitarianism, fellowship, and worldwide unity of the Muslim community: all worshipers, no matter what their socioeconomic status outside the mosque, are equals before Allah. The prayer proceeds with recitations from the Qur'an and with a series of bowings, kneelings, and prostrations that end with the faithful gently touching their foreheads in unison to the floor of the mosque. This is the symbolic moment of utter submission to the will of the Almighty.

In addition to its role as a place of prayer, worship, and Qur'an study, a mosque often serves as a kind of Muslim community center for socializing, discussing and organizing political activities, providing courses in Islamic education and adult literacy, and offering health care for the poor. Mosque complexes frequently include space for people to sleep, soup kitchens to feed the hungry, and societies to assist the poor in improving their economic status. They are usually open to non-Muslims. Every mosque has several distinctive features. Near the entrance, one normally finds a water fountain used for performing the ritual ablution that precedes prayer. The *mihrab,* a curved niche in one wall that is often richly ornamented, indicates the direction of the Ka'aba, and its concave shape helps amplify the voice of the imam as he leads the prayer and recites the Qur'an. Visitors to mosques sometimes erroneously suppose that the mihrab is a kind of idol. Large mosques also have an elevated platform with steps leading up to it, called a *minbar.* The imam ascends these steps each Friday and gives a sermon preceding the congregational prayer. The exterior tower attached to the mosque is called a *minaret,* anglicized from the Arabic *manara.* From this tower faithful Muslims are summoned to prayer five times each day. Recorded calls to prayer broadcast by loudspeakers are becoming more and more frequent, replacing the call recited in person by a *muezzin,* or prayer-caller. The melodious sound of the muezzin's voice at prayer time is one of the most distinctive and enchanting dimensions of Islamic society. The call to prayer, always recited in Arabic, is as follows:

Allahu akbar ("God is greater [than all else]").
[Recited four times]
Ashhadu anna la ilaha illa Allah ("I testify that there is no god but Allah"). [Twice]
Ashhadu anna Muhammadan rasul Allah ("I testify that Muhammad is the messenger of God"). [Twice]
Hayya 'ala al-salat ("Come to prayer"). [Twice]
Hayya 'ala al-falah ("Come to salvation and prosperity"). [Twice]
Allahu akbar ("God is greater [than all else]"). [Twice]
La ilaha illa Allah ("There is no god but Allah").

For the early morning prayer, the phrase *al-sala khayr min al-nawm* ("Prayer is better than sleep") is added as a gentle reminder to the believer who might be inclined to roll over in bed rather than roll out to pray.

Muhammad referred to salat as the *mi'raj*, or spiritual ascent, of each individual believer, alluding to his own heavenly ascent to the Divine Presence and suggesting that every Muslim can enjoy the peace and ecstacy of personal communion with God several times daily. In short, salat is the focus of personal and communal worship in Islam, a powerful ritual that binds the umma together worldwide despite differences of language, nationality, or religious interpretation.

Almsgiving (Zakat)

The principle of *zakat*, or almsgiving, is designed to care for the poor, to foster empathy and compassion in the community of believers, and to provide for the building and maintenance of mosques and other Islamic institutions. The Qur'an states that charity and compassion, as opposed to mere mechanical observance of rituals, define one's worthiness in God's sight:

It is not righteousness that ye turn your faces towards East or West; but it is righteousness to believe in Allah and the Last Day, and the Angels, and the Book, and the Messengers; to spend of your substance, out of love for Him, for your kin, for orphans, for the needy, for the wayfarer, for those who ask, and for the ransom of slaves; to be steadfast in prayer, and give Zakat, to fulfill the contracts which ye have made; and to be firm and patient, in pain (or suffering) and adversity, and throughout all periods of panic. Such are the people of truth, the God-fearing. (2:177)

Service to God and service to human beings are inseparable precepts in the Qur'an and incumbent on all the faithful: "Serve Allah, and . . . do good— to parents, kinsfolk, orphans, those in need, neighbors who are of kin, neighbors who are strangers, the Companion by your side, the way-farer (ye meet), and what your right hands possess: for Allah loveth not the arrogant, the vainglorious" (4:36). The hadith also advocate in clear terms the practice of charity:

None of you [truly] believes until he wishes for his brother what he wishes for himself.

Each person's every joint must perform a charity every day the sun comes up: to act justly between two people is a charity; to help a man with his mount, lifting him onto it or hoisting up his belongings onto it is a charity; a good word is a charity; every step you take to prayers is a charity; and removing a harmful thing from the road is charity.

Charity extinguishes sin as water extinguishes fire.

Smiling to another person is an act of charity.

"By God, he's not a believer. By God, he's not a believer. By God, he's not a believer." The people said: "Whom are you speaking about, O messenger of God?" He replied: "He who sleeps with a full stomach, knowing that his neighbor is hungry."[18]

Islam distinguishes between two forms of charitable giving: zakat, a legal duty obligatory for all Muslims, and *sadaqa,* a free-will offering that is spontaneous and intended specifically to help the poor and those in need. According to Islamic law, zakat is to be paid at the end of each year, and the amount is designated as 2.5 percent of a person's personal wealth. In many Islamic countries, collection and distribution of religious donations has historically been handled by a government ministry. But in more recent times, the trend has been toward private giving in local mosques. These individual, informal contributions take many forms. Residents of a neighborhood may pool their savings to build a new mosque or an addition to an existing mosque. An individual or family may contribute money to buy books or new furnishings for the mosque. A family may "adopt" a needy individual or family in the neighborhood, buying them food and clothing, paying for school fees and supplies for their children, and giving them gifts during Muslim holidays. Many Muslims opt to give their zakat and sadaqa offerings to support charitable organizations providing care for orphans, the disabled, the homeless, and the poor.

It would be a mistake to view zakat too narrowly as simply a financial transaction mandated by religious law. The contribution of 2.5 percent of one's personal possessions is paralleled by the principle of tithing in Latter-day Saint thought, that of *seva* in Sikhism, and like customs in many other religious communities. As in these other faiths, the stipulated donation is merely a beginning point, a minimum. God is less interested in teaching the faithful to calculate precise percentages of their income than in inculcating a spirit of benevolence and concern for the welfare of other people. In this sense, zakat becomes, not a mechanical performance, but a state of mind and heart, an impulse to expand one's sphere of influence for good, and a community ethos that promotes the well-being and safety of every individual.

Fasting (Sawm)

Fasting plays a central role in individual spirituality and in the annual cycle of Muslim religious festivals.

The Qur'an and the sunna of Muhammad emphasize the efficacy of frequent fasting (*sawm*) as a means of achieving islam—complete submission to Allah—and of promoting individual and communal well-being: "O ye who believe! Fasting is prescribed to you as it was prescribed to those before you, that ye may (learn) self-restraint" (see Qur'an 2:183–88). Statements of Allah, quoted by Muhammad but not found in the Qur'an, extol the benefits of fasting: "Fasting is a protection and a shield"; "Every deed that a person performs is for him except fasting, and that is done for Me, and I will reward him for it"; "The bad breath of one who fasts is sweeter to God than the fragrance of musk."[19] It was Muhammad's custom to fast regularly throughout the year in addition to the thirty-day fast required during *Ramadan*: on Monday and Thursday each week and on the "white days" (the thirteenth, fourteenth, and fifteenth) of each month.[20] Muslims view sawm as having a dual purpose: to bring about a state of humility and surrender of one's soul to God, and to foster compassion and care for the indigent in the community. Thus, sawm and zakat go hand in hand: denying of oneself cannot be complete without giving of oneself.

The tandem relationship between fasting and alsmgiving is most clearly in evidence during the month-long ritual called Ramadan. The hadith make it clear that fasting during Ramadan is intended to be a time for spiritual introspection, seeking forgiveness of sins, and taking care of the poor: "When there comes the month of Ramadan, the gates of mercy are opened, and the gates of Hell are locked and the devils are chained"; "The best charity is that in Ramadan."[21] The entire month is holy for Muslims because the Qur'an and sunna prescribe fasting for the faithful from sunrise to sunset (twelve to sixteen hours depending on the season of the year) for thirty days in a row. But the last ten days of Ramadan are particularly auspicious because it was during this time that the angel Gabriel first appeared to Muhammad and revealed the opening verses of the Qur'an. No one knows the precise date of the initial revelation and prophetic call, but traditionally the twenty-seventh night of Ramadan is designated the "Night of Power." It is believed that on this evening the heavens draw closer to the earth than at any other time in the year, and the mosques are therefore crowded with worshipers seeking the blessings and forgiveness of Allah. Sura 97 of the Qur'an describes

this night as "better than a thousand months," one in which spiritual peace and power descend from Allah upon the believers in rich abundance.

The fast begins with the dawn prayer and ends with the sunset prayer. During the daytime hours between those prayers, physical gratifications of any kind—eating, drinking, chewing gum, smoking, and sexual relations—are to be avoided. When the call to prayer sounds at sunset signaling the end of the fast each day, an observant Muslim eats a date or two and drinks some fruit juice (in adherence to Muhammad's sunna) before going to the mosque to perform salat. After the sunset prayer is completed, the main meal is consumed and then further devotions are carried out in the mosque: supererogatory prayers and reading from the Qur'an. Customs for breaking the fast and performing evening devotions vary somewhat from country to country. Just before the dawn prayer, faithful Muslims awaken to eat a light meal and prepare for another day of fasting.

It is considered meritorious for those who can afford it to provide food for the poor as often as possible during Ramadan. Therefore, poor families can be seen going door to door seeking and obtaining plentiful donations of food; and in some countries like Egypt, enormous tables are set up in the streets to feed thousands of needy people at the evening *iftar,* or "breakfast."

It is impossible to describe adequately the sense of anticipation, excitement, joy, and spiritual renewal that accompany the advent of Ramadan in the Muslim community. An apt comparison to Christian tradition is that Ramadan is like Christmas, Easter, and Thanksgiving all rolled into one and observed simultaneously for thirty consecutive days. It has the magic and wonder of Christmas, with the display of decorations and lights; preparation of special candies, fruit drinks, and foods; viewing of new television programs produced especially for the season; and a tradition of gift-giving. It carries the spiritual significance of Easter in that it celebrates the defining moment in Islamic history: the beginning of God's final revelation to his last and greatest prophet. It resembles Thanksgiving, at least at the level of popular religious tradition, in its emphasis on large family gatherings and sumptuous feasting after the fasting each day.

One of the two major religious holidays in the Islamic world, *'Aeed al-Fitr* ("The Feast of Breaking the Fast"), is observed at the end of the month of

Ramadan. It normally lasts three days into the new lunar month and is a time of rejoicing and celebration. Children customarily receive gifts of clothing and money from their relatives; families gather for reunions and picnics in the countryside; and special prayers are held in the mosques.

For Muslims the observance of fasting, especially during Ramadan, strengthens one's relationship with God, affirms one's religious identity in the umma, and promotes social harmony and equality. Muslims who consistently fast say that they look forward to the approach of Ramadan and feel sad when its end draws near. Hakeem Olajuwon, a well-known American Muslim athlete, captures the feelings of many Muslims when he describes the personal benefits of his decision to fast during Ramadan while playing professional basketball: "I feel much better. I feel lighter, faster, much more mentally focused. When God prescribes something, it is for your best interest. . . . Your whole body goes through a change. It's like rebirth."[22]

Pilgrimage to Mecca (Hajj)

Every Muslim who is physically and financially able is required to go on the pilgrimage to Mecca at least once in his or her lifetime (Qur'an 2:196–203, 3:97, 5:98). The *hajj* is the highest act of devotion for a Muslim. It is a time of spiritual reflection, of rededication to Allah and the Islamic faith, of purity and self-denial, and of peace with one's fellow beings. The coming together of more than two million people from myriad nations and from every walk of life, all dressed in white robes, all worshiping Allah in unison, reaffirms powerfully the unity and diversity of the worldwide umma and reinforces the faith and identity of individual pilgrims. The hajj is in a very real sense the Muslim equivalent of the Latter-day Saint endowment combined with the communal aspects of general conference, for it reminds Muslims of who they are and what God has done and still does for them. Muslims who have performed the hajj describe it as a profoundly moving, ineffable experience that changes their life, solidifies their faith, and deepens their spiritual enjoyment.[23] Those who make the hajj are given the honorific title *hajj* or *hajji* (for a man) or *hajja* (for a woman), and they and their families acquire heightened respect in the community. A charming form of folk art has arisen out of the hajj tradition: the

homes of pilgrims are often painted in bright colors with pictures of the Ka'aba, Mecca, airplanes, or other scenes from the pilgrimage experience. It is interesting to note that the hajj can be experienced vicariously as well. Islamic law allows for a son or daughter to act as proxy in performing the hajj on behalf of a father or mother who passed away before having the opportunity or means to go to Mecca.

The sacred precinct surrounding Mecca is a spiritual sanctuary for the Muslim faithful who arrive annually to visit the holy sites and to perform the greater or the lesser pilgrimage.[24] It is designated as a place of perfect peace in which violence or ill-will of any kind is prohibited, and pilgrims are even instructed to be careful not to pluck up plants or to kill animals within the grounds of the sanctuary (Qur'an 5:94–100). In recent years, much to the dismay of Muslims themselves, the hajj has become a staging ground—even a battleground at times—for Muslim activists who want to promote a political cause. Shi'ite pilgrims, mostly from Iran, have attempted to distribute political literature denouncing the Sunni Saudi Arabian ruling family, and heavy fighting between government security forces and Shi'ite militants has taken a high toll in casualties and marred the sanctity of the hajj season.

Only Muslims are permitted to enter the area around the holy cities of Mecca and Medina, and thus non-Muslims are generally unfamiliar with the remarkable religious ritual that takes place there every year. Special clothing requirements are observed: men don two pieces of simple white cloth, called the *ihram,* and women are specifically forbidden to veil their faces while performing the hajj. Beginning on the first day of the month called *Dhu al-Hijja,* the pilgrims engage in a series of physically demanding rituals that reenact sacred historical events. Circling the Ka'aba seven times reminds participants of Abraham's faithfulness in submitting to God and building a house of worship. The running back and forth between the hills of Safwa and Marwa and the presence of the well of Zamzam evoke memories of Hagar's desperate search for water to save her son, Ishmael, and Allah's mercy in causing a well to spring up as the infant kicked his heels in the desert sand. The multitudes move en masse from Mecca to Mina and the plains of 'Arafat, where they are accommodated in a vast tent city as they contemplate the sacrifice and obedience of Abraham and his son Ishmael. The hajj culminates on the ninth day with the standing at Mount 'Arafat. On this holy day of atonement, the masses of Muslim pilgrims and the Muslim community throughout the world express their repentance and submission to Allah, seek his forgiveness and blessings, and emerge with a renewed sense of spiritual purity and peace. Leaving 'Arafat, the pilgrims move on to Muzdalifa, where they throw pebbles at several columns, symbolizing their renunciation of Satan's evil temptations and recalling Abraham's and Ishmael's rejection of Satan's whisperings to disobey God's command.

The most important religious holiday in the Islamic world, 'Aeed al-Adha ("Feast of Sacrifice"), begins the next day, when the faithful who can afford to do so sacrifice an animal (usually a sheep or goat, but often a cow or camel) in commemoration of Abraham's willingness to sacrifice his son Ishmael (see Qur'an 37:100–111). The meat from the sacrifice is divided into thirds: one-third for the immediate family, one-third as a gift to neighbors and friends, and one-third as a zakat offering for the poor. Muslims throughout the world join with the pilgrims in Mecca in celebrating this rite, and the holiday lasts for at least three days as families and friends congregate for exchanging gifts, sharing meals, and enjoying picnics and games. The sacrifice completes the official hajj ritual, but many participants in the hajj feel their pilgrimage is incomplete without a visit to Medina (about 125 miles north of Mecca) to honor the memory of Muhammad by performing salat at the mosque where he is buried.

JIHAD

Muslims sometimes speak of the principle of *jihad* as a sixth pillar of Islam. The word is usually mistranslated in English as "holy war," but the Arabic root does not denote holiness or war. The literal meaning is "struggle" or "striving," meaning to exert oneself in the service of Allah. The Qur'an teaches that jihad involves violent struggle only under certain well-defined and restricted circumstances, such as defending family, home, religion, and innocent people against outside aggression. In everyday practice, jihad is a word that encompasses virtually every aspect of a Muslim's life and signifies the daily striving for self-improvement and the prosperity of the umma by various means, such as performing charitable deeds, giving money, speaking truth, working for justice. "Those who believe, and

emigrate and strive with might and main, in Allah's cause, with their goods and their persons, have the highest rank in the sight of Allah: they are the people who will achieve (salvation)" (Qur'an 9:20). A familiar hadith states that Muhammad, while returning from a battle with the Meccans, informed the Muslim combatants that they were leaving behind the "lesser jihad" (military struggle) and taking up again the "greater jihad" (the struggle against the evil inclinations of the soul).

WOMEN AND FAMILY LIFE IN ISLAM

One of the most fascinating but neglected issues in the study of world religions is the status of women in various religious communities. Gender role differentiation has been a feature of nearly every faith tradition in the world, and with the rise of the feminist movement during the past three decades it has become an ever more controversial question at the forefront of religious discourse. The issue, simply stated, is this: To what extent is religion a facilitating or debilitating factor in women's historical struggle to achieve equal status, treatment, opportunities, and rights in society?

Islam has long occupied a prominent position in this wider debate on the role of women in religion.[25] Muslim practices are regularly condemned in feminist debate—by both Muslim and non-Muslim intellectuals—as anachronistic and mysogynistic, and Western mass media and scholarship have typically portrayed Muslim women as anonymous entities bereft of rights, identity, intelligence, personality, or a significant role to play in society. These views of women's role in Islam form the nub of one of the sharpest contentions between the Muslim East and the Christian West. Western criticism of Islamic family life and gender roles strikes Muslims as hypocritical. They point to the high rate of sexual promiscuity, divorce, drug abuse, crime, and teenage pregnancy as proof that the avowed superiority of liberal Christian mores is a delusion and that such permissiveness only erodes the family and social structure of the nation. Yes, Muslims respond, our religion advocates a more traditional form of family life in which men and women have complementary, equally important roles. Generally speaking, men are the breadwinners and protectors; women are the homemakers and nurturers. But the fundamental requirements and rewards of Allah are the same for both men and women. Islam seeks to build marriages and families that foster faith, kindness, hard work, cooperation, and prosperity. Islam does not condone abuse of wife and children, as suggested in literature and movies in the West.[26] On the contrary, the Qur'an and sunna admonish men, women, and children to be kind, gentle, and respectful in their family relations.

Muslim sources point out that Islam greatly elevated the status of women in ancient Arabia and in many other cultures: the Qur'an condemns the practice of female infanticide, apparently quite common in pre-Islamic Arabian culture, and allots to women certain rights in marriage and inheritance that they did not enjoy before the advent of Islam. One can say that the Qur'an permits polygamy but does not recommend it. It limits to four the number of wives that a man can legally marry (in pre-Islamic Arabia, the number was unlimited), and this permission is given in the context of verses dealing with orphaned women and widows. It adds the condition that if the husband cannot "deal justly with them," then only one wife is permissible (4:3). The vast majority of Muslims interpret these verses to mean that, since it is virtually impossible for a man to care equitably and justly for four wives, Allah's intent is that Muslims be monogamous; and in fact only a small percentage of Muslims practice polygyny.

To Westerners, the practice of veiling found in most Muslim societies is tangible evidence that Islam discriminates against women. As always, however, the reality beneath the surface of sociocultural appearances is complex and defies facile conclusions. Muslims themselves have widely divergent views on the issue of veiling. Opinions and practices have varied at different times and in different places, and social, cultural, and political conditions heavily influence veiling trends. Many devout Muslims hold that the veil is not required at all in Islam, arguing that Muslim women during the time of Muhammad did not veil and that the practice became a part of Muslim culture only after non-Arab peoples who had a tradition of veiling entered Islam in large numbers. The more mainstream contemporary view is that veiling is required as a means of fostering modesty and morality in society, although the question of just what constitutes a proper veil is a matter of personal interpretation. Full-length robe, gloves, and face mask with only small slits for vision are required

of women in some countries and families, but most Muslims consider this practice too extreme. The majority of women who veil wear a head scarf over their hair and an ankle-length, long-sleeved robe, but no mask or gloves.

An eminent anthropologist who has spent years living among Muslim women cautions against drawing conclusions based on superficial impressions:

We [non-Muslims] tend to believe that those who look out (through the veil) suffer from the same exclusion as those of us who look at the veil and its hidden contents. However, we have no right to make such an assumption. Much depends on who makes the decision to veil—whether it is imposed or self-selected. . . . [Veiling] is "an outward sign of a complex reality." . . . [It] relates to the individual's sense of belonging to a group, and to the individual's sense of her own identity. . . . Women stress repeatedly . . . that the choice to wear Islamic dress is one they make themselves, and it must come "from inner religious conviction." The majority of women . . . see themselves as making a statement or taking action that strengthens their own position within the society.[27]

A nursing student from Brigham Young University, after living for a semester with Muslim women in Amman, Jordan, found similarities between her roommates' attitudes toward veiling and her own religious experience:

My roommate Rana stated that there's a time in every Muslim woman's life when she must decide to "mature" and wear [the veil]. She sat down and described how she felt as she put it on each day: "It makes my true self come out." She feels happier, more mature, doesn't laugh or act like a child, but she feels humble and acts humble. [She says] that no one should wear the veil unless they are ready because it's a disgrace to see girls acting so childish and flirting with boys when they have the veil on. I couldn't help but compare this to some of the covenants we make in the temple or even the clothes we wear. I related to [Rana] because when I started wearing garments, I too had to change my wardrobe but I felt a great peace and responsibility to live the highest standards of the Gospel—all because some article of clothing reminds me.[28]

Most Latter-day Saints consider standards of dress to be a necessary, reasonable, and comfortable part of their religious life, while outside observers describe these same standards as rigid and repressive. Muslims also feel that their requirements for dress, including veiling for women, are a necessary, reasonable, and comfortable norm for human society, even while outside observers denounce these norms as oppressive to women. In reality, the sometimes acrimonious debate about religious clothing is merely one dimension of the wider dialectic about gender roles and women's status in world religions. But by seeking to understand the issue from the perspective of those who practice the faith, making fair comparisons to one's own religious experience, and remaining open to the possibility of gaining new spiritual insights from interfaith discourse, it is possible to look past the acrimony toward a deeper level of comprehension.

CONTEMPORARY ISSUES AND CHALLENGES IN THE MUSLIM WORLD

Since the latter half of the nineteenth century, Muslims have been engaged in an intense internal debate about the status of their religion and community in the modern world. Colonization of nearly the entire Islamic world by Western powers, beginning with Napoleon's invasion of Egypt in 1798, and the political and economic subjugation that followed precipitated a crisis among Muslims similar to the spiritual, psychological, and intellectual angst that has surfaced in other world religions that espouse a doctrine of "chosenness." In Judaism it was the Holocaust, and in Shinto it was Japan's defeat and the emperor's humiliation in World War II that forced agonizing reflection on this question: "If we are God's chosen people, then why has this happened to us?" That is essentially the existential dilemma that has impelled Muslims to search for answers to two basic questions: What brought about the military, economic, and spiritual decline of the Islamic community following more than one thousand years of supremacy in the world? What should be done to bring about renewal and reform? The issue for Muslims is not Islam's viability as a set of spiritual truths and religious practices; the core of the conflict is the extent to which Islamic ideals should be permitted to govern not only religious matters in society, but political, economic, social, and educational domains of life as well.

The renewed push by Muslims to reform their societies according to Islamic principles of equity and justice is often referred to by scholars as the "Islamist Movement." The complexity and diversity of this movement defy easy explanation, as it comprises a multiplicity of groups, ideologies, and activities that are often at cross-purposes with each other. Virtually all Islamist factions agree on the goals for solving the problems of internal decline and external domination: first, cleansing their societies from within and returning to Islam; second, minimizing the impact of Western secular influences and resisting further neocolonial attempts to weaken and humiliate them. The slogan "Islam is the solution" has become ubiquitous in the Islamic world, whether in literature, Friday sermons, daily conversations, or graffiti spray-painted on public buildings. A publication of the influential Muslim Brotherhood states: "There is no cure for the widespread disease of poverty, ignorance, sickness, and moral and national corruption except a return to the laws of Islam."[29] The ultimate goal of all Islamists is the establishment of an Islamic state that applies Islamic laws and principles in every phase of public and private life, including economics, politics, education, and family relations.

The various groups in the Islamist movement are deeply divided, however, on what methods should be adopted to achieve these goals. The vast majority of Muslims advocate a peaceful, moderate approach that emphasizes social and political activism to bring about reform: participating in the political process and election campaigns; establishing mosques, institutes, and newspapers to educate the masses and shape public opinion; and providing jobs and social services (like health care, adult literacy programs, and day-care centers) for the poor. On the other hand, a minority of Muslims have concluded that peaceful, gradual agitation for change is doomed to failure because the Muslim politicians, military officers, businessmen, and intellectuals who control the country are corrupt, anti-Islamic puppets of Christian and Jewish neocolonial powers. Militant groups assert, therefore, that violent means are justified to throw off the oppressive yoke and to obtain the freedom and prosperity that a true Islamic state would provide. They view themselves in a desperate war for survival against apostates and infidels, the outcome of which will determine the fate of the Islamic community. From the perspective of militant Islam, violence is justified by the Qur'anic principles of jihad because the fighters are defending innocent Muslims against hostilities, aggression, and suffering. Assassinating corrupt leaders, shooting intellectuals and newspaper editors, struggling violently to overthrow an oppressive regime, or bombing Western-sponsored institutions are viewed as a religious duty, the performance of which reaps Allah's rewards (even an automatic place in paradise if one dies and thus becomes a martyr while carrying out this duty).

Mainstream Muslims denounce this kind of radical ideology as a gross misinterpretation of Islamic principles and antithetical to Islam's historical advocacy of tolerance and peace. An American Muslim explains: "Islam is against compulsion in religion, as Allah says in the Qur'an: 'There is no compulsion in religion.' . . . As to the relationship between Muslims and non-Muslims, Allah ordained a peaceful co-existence and a mutual understanding, as He said in the Qur'an: 'Say: O People of the Scripture [Jews and Christians]! Come to an agreement between us and you. . . . And argue not with the People of the Scripture, except in the best way.'"[30] A Pakistani student at Brigham Young University expressed the attitude of many Muslims toward religious extremism in an insightful editorial following an attack by Muslim militants:

The Muslim students at BYU join the rest of the nation in condemning the recent terrorist attack on the World Trade Center in New York City. We also condemn the possible involvement of Muslims in this heinous crime. We regret the loss of innocent lives in this incident and hope the real culprits are subjected to exemplary punishment. These senseless acts have nothing to do with Islam and are against the spirit of the religion that emphasizes the concept of peace more than anything else. . . . The incident in New York City is not any more representative of Islam than the people in Waco, Texas [the cult of extremists led by David Koresh] are representative of mainstream Christianity. Cody Judy [who briefly held President Howard W. Hunter hostage] does not represent Mormonism any better than do the Palestinian suspects of the New York bombing represent Islam. Acts of a handful of derelicts are not true representatives of the faith they adhere to.[31]

The Islamist Movement, in its moderate and extreme manifestations, will continue to shape economic, social, and political developments throughout the world. Even though Islamist rhetoric couches the problems of Muslims in religious terms, it must be understood that the seedbed of religious extremism is prolonged suffering, humiliation, and despair arising from extreme sociopolitical conditions: poverty, hunger, unemployment, illiteracy, and political disenfranchisement. When exposed long enough to desperate circumstances, even moral, intelligent people sometimes resort to desperate measures, and religion is often invoked to acquire support and legitimacy. Religious militancy is not a uniquely

Islamic phenomenon reflecting, as some Westerners seem to suppose, a theological flaw or inherent Muslim predisposition toward fanaticism. Extremists who rationalize violence in the name of God can be found in the history of every religious tradition, including that of Latter-day Saints. The point is not to justify violent acts of religious extremists, but to encourage students to analyze and understand the conditions that create one of the great paradoxes in the study of world religions: the growth of hatred, bigotry, and violence in the same spiritual soil that produces love, tolerance, and peace.

LATTER-DAY SAINT REFLECTIONS

In the Qur'an, Christians are generally spoken of in a positive light. They are numbered among the "People of the Book," religious groups (including Jews) that enjoy favored status because they practice monotheism and have received a sacred scripture. The Qur'an gives Jesus prominent status among the prophets of God, acknowledging the many miracles associated with his life (including his virgin birth to Mary) and the supernatural powers he possessed from a young age. However, it emphatically denies that he died on the cross, was resurrected, and is therefore divine, the Son of God and a member of a Godhead or Trinity: "Say: He is Allah, the One! Allah, the Eternal, Absolute; He begetteth not, nor is He begotten; and there is none like unto Him" (112:1–4). In the Islamic view, these ideas are incompatible with monotheistic worship as practiced and taught by the Qur'anic Jesus and represent the efforts of later generations of Christians to deify him. The Qur'an teaches that, rather than allowing Jesus to die an ignominious death on the cross, God "raised him up" alive to heaven, where he resides at present (4:157–59). According to the hadith, Jesus' descent to the world at the end of time will be an eschatological sign of the Day of Resurrection and Judgment.

Despite the favored status of Christians in Islamic doctrine, the history of relations between Christianity and Islam has often been characterized by rivalry, confrontation, and hostility. As a result, interaction today between countries of the Christian West and countries of the "Islamic heartland"—the Muslim majority countries of the Middle East—continues to be problematic. Most Islamic countries prohibit proselyting by Christian missionaries, and even the churches that managed to establish an official presence in the Middle East before the end of the colonial period and the emergence of the current political landscape have had very limited success in establishing a viable presence. Christian groups who have tried to make inroads in the past twenty years have been virtually excluded because of increased pressure from extreme Islamist groups in these countries who violently oppose the corrupting and oppressive presence (as they see it) of Western interests. They lump together under one heading Zionists, Communists, Christian crusaders (modern missionaries), and other European or American ideologies that work against the realization of their goal: the establishment of a truly Islamic society.

This legacy of conflict, suspicion, and resentment between the Muslims and the "Christian West" will continue to present formidable obstacles in Muslim-Christian dialogue. Taken together, these historical, political, and doctrinal forces create an atmosphere of hostility, suspicion, and resistance that Christians find frustrating and bewildering.

Much has been written over the years about the similarities between Islam and The Church of Jesus Christ of Latter-day Saints. Most of these writings have been malicious in tone and intent, produced by non–Latter-day Saint Christian authors attempting to disparage Joseph Smith and the church by making superficial comparisons to the arch-rival of Western civilization, Muhammad, the prophet of Islam.[32] One example is the work of the prominent German scholar Eduard Meyer, who became fascinated with what he viewed as striking parallels between the two religions. He was convinced that careful study of the Latter-day Saint experience in nineteenth-century America would shed much light on the development of the Muslim community in eighth-century Arabia. These writings typically dwell on themes of plural marriage; the humble origins and charismatic leadership of two false prophets, both dangerous enemies of Christianity; persecution and exodus; the sensuous, literal, "unspiritual" nature of Latter-day Saint and Muslim theology; and the ideas of covenant and community. Fortunately, more balanced, well-informed analysis of Muslim–Latter-day Saint issues has been carried out in recent years (see bibliography).

Careful examination of Latter-day Saint and Islamic doctrine reveals that there are indeed remarkable similarities between the two traditions and much common ground upon which to build solid relations. As early as the 1850s Latter-day Saint leaders noted commonalities between the faiths. Speaking in general conference, George A. Smith and Parley P. Pratt both treated extensively and in complimentary terms the role of Islam in religious history. Elder Smith stated that Muhammad "preached the moral doctrines which the Savior taught . . . and was no doubt raised up by God to scourge the world for their idolatry." Elder Pratt, who acknowledged that "Mahometanism" (a variant spelling of "Muhammadanism," the archaic term for Islam) was regarded with prejudice by Westerners, noted that "the followers of Mahomet did not take the sword . . . until compelled to do so by the persecutions of their enemies" and asserted that Muslims "upon the whole . . . have better morals and better institutions than many Christian nations."[33] Even though these comparisons were based on sketchy knowledge of Islamic history and doctrine and were made in part to discredit pre-Restoration Christianity, they are nevertheless remarkable (given the vitriolic tone of most Christian literature on Islam during that time period) in the degree of understanding and sympathy evinced for the figure of Muhammad and the religion he taught.

Part of the interest of these Latter-day Saint leaders in Islam probably stems from the many points of commonality in the history and teachings of the two religions. Following is a representative, though not exhaustive, list of some of the main precepts shared by Muslims and Latter-day Saints:

1. Faith in a God who is omniscient, omnipotent, and eternally concerned about the welfare of all human beings. He is a God of justice but also of mercy, anxious to forgive men and women who are willing to repent of wrongdoing and submit their wills to His will. By following the path outlined by God—faith, humility, obedience, repentance, morality, and compassion—individuals can achieve peace and prosperity in this life and enter into restful existence with God in the hereafter.

2. Belief in prophets whom God has raised up in every place and time in world history to teach humanity about the path of happiness through submission to God. Both Latter-day Saints and Muslims have their own "modern" scriptures—the Book of Mormon and the Qur'an respectively—but both groups accept previous revelations such as the Bible and the Torah "so far as they are translated correctly"

(that is, so far as they are congruent with orthodox doctrine in each tradition).

3. Observance of religious rituals and acts of worship such as prayer, fasting, and charitable giving. Both groups encourage frequent communication with God through individual and group prayers (some of which are spontaneous, while others are said by rote), abstaining from food and drink during certain periods to increase spiritual awareness and commitment, and giving of one's material substance to help the poor and needy in society and to strengthen the religious community.

4. Emphasis on strong family life. Latter-day Saints and Muslims are adamant in their views about the sanctity and importance of families as the basis for achieving peace, happiness, and prosperity. Consequently, both religions prescribe chastity before marriage, fidelity after marriage, and traditional roles for fathers and mothers unless circumstances require the mother to work. Men and women are encouraged to dress in modest clothing (even though within each community the standards used to define modesty vary). Islam and The Church of Jesus Christ of Latter-day Saints, in short, are both family-centered religions that cherish familial ties and extol the virtues of love at home.

5. Adherence to high standards of moral and ethical conduct. Muslims and Latter-day Saints are taught, both in holy scripture and by the example of founding prophets, to practice principles of honesty, hard work, frugality, generosity, and politeness in dealings with others. The ethical, orthopraxic emphasis of both religions has engendered similar positions on contemporary social and political issues: abortion is generally prohibited (though there are exceptions and divergent views), and birth control, though discouraged, is a matter to be decided by a wife and husband;[34] crime must be vigorously opposed, and punishments like the death penalty are permissible for murder and other such crimes; social justice, in the form of equality of access to educational and employment opportunities, is an ideal that the faithful must work for; and pornography and immoral media influences must be resisted and even eliminated when possible.

6. Observance of a dietary code intended to promote physical health as a means to spiritual well-being. Faithful Muslims refrain from drinking alcohol and eating pork or pork products, which are forbidden by God—*haraam,* as Muslims say. Some Muslims believe that the list of proscribed substances includes tobacco. Tea and coffee, however, are not forbidden in Islam.

In relations with Muslims, Latter-day Saints need to keep in mind both the convergences and the divergences of belief. That is, while recognizing and building on the common ground as a basis for promoting friendship and cooperation, one must also be aware that some of the most fundamental, deeply cherished theological tenets of Latter-day Saints are diametrically opposed to those of Muslims. These points of theological divergence, and some other issues that carry potential for friction between the two communities, can be summarized as follows.

1. Nature of God. Muslims are strictly monotheistic, meaning they believe that there always has been, is now, and always will be only one God— Allah. Any person, thing, or idea that compromises this cardinal principle of monotheism is considered polytheism, the gravest form of heresy in Islam. Hence, Christian teachings about the divinity of Jesus Christ and certainly the Latter-day Saint doctrines of eternal progression and anthropomorphism would be labeled as blasphemies by Muslims. As a result, Muslims will generally take a dim view of religious art that emphasizes themes of God's physical nature or man's divine nature as exemplified in statues and paintings that adorn Latter-day Saint temples, visitors centers, and chapels. Another aspect of this issue is that, in Islam, God is the creator and human beings are referred to as his creatures (though they are the highest form of all creation— God's vicegerents). In orthodox Islamic thought God is not spoken of as a Father, and therefore humans are not his children, as Latter-day Saints and other Christians are apt to say. This terminology is, in fact, repugnant to most Muslims because it implies an anthropomorphic conception of God that Islam rejects. Having noted this, it is important to point out that holding different views of the nature of God and referring to him by different names does not justify the conclusion (put forth by some Latter-day Saint authors) that the Muslims worship a different God than do Latter-day Saints. "Allah" is the general name for God used by all native speakers of Arabic, whether Muslim, Jewish, or Christian. It is also the term used in Arabic-speaking Latter-day Saint branches in the Middle East and in the Arabic translations of Latter-day Saint scripture.

2. Modern prophets and continuing revelation. The second most important principle for Muslims, next to belief in the one God, is belief that Muhammad is the last and greatest of all prophets. With the revelation of the perfect and complete Qur'an to him, God's need to communicate his message through prophets ceased. Therefore, Latter-day Saint declarations that God has revealed modern scriptures and that the process of revelation continues through modern prophets will obviously be difficult concepts for Muslims to agree with.

3. Views on religious pluralism. The history of relations among Muslims, Christians, and Jews shows that Muslim governments generally have been more tolerant in their treatment of religious minorities than have Christian governments. However, it is also true that Islam discourages or in many cases prohibits proselyting by non-Muslim groups and that there are severe strictures against Muslims converting to other faiths. Most Muslims view this Islamic policy as necessary to preserve stability and unity in their communities, but Westerners tend to see it as an anachronistic, repressive practice that denies religious minorities basic human and civil rights. In sum, one might say that Islam believes in religious tolerance but not in religious pluralism, a fact that will continue to be a source of friction between Christians and Muslims.

4. Dietary practices. As stated above, Muslims are forbidden to drink alcohol and to eat pork or pork products (some extremely devout Muslims even refuse to eat in homes or restaurants where pork products are served). In hosting Muslim guests and acquaintances, it is important to try to ensure that no pork products are served: bacon bits in the green salad and chicken cordon bleu stuffed with pieces of ham, for example. Again, if an innocent, inadvertent mistake is made, Muslims will not be seriously offended; rather, they will politely abstain from eating these foods.

The Church of Jesus Christ of Latter-day Saints is virtually unknown in the Islamic world, and without a proper introduction to Latter-day Saint beliefs and practices, Muslims would tend to view the church as simply another Christian sect. But it is also true that whenever Muslims and Latter-day Saints become acquainted, a bond of admiration and mutual respect is quickly established. Muslims, whose stereotypical view is that most Westerners are faithless, wealthy, and immoral, are pleasantly surprised on first encountering Latter-day Saints to learn of their faith in God, belief in prophets, emphasis on families, restrictions against alcohol and tobacco, and conservative dress and dating standards. Many Muslim students at Brigham Young University (and their parents) have mentioned that they came there because they heard of its reputation for high moral and academic standards and because they feel comfortable in a Latter-day Saint environment: "It is similar to our lifestyle at home" is a typical comment.

Establishing a relationship of mutual respect between Christians and Muslims depends on the ability of individuals in each group to demonstrate accurate, sympathetic understanding of each other's religion and way of life. Muslims are always pleased to find non-Muslims who have made an honest effort to become acquainted with the values and lifestyle of Islam and who understand that the vast majority of Muslims are intelligent, compassionate individuals who work hard, love their families, have faith in God, abide by the laws of their country, and seek peaceful relations with their neighbors.

Islam is a world religion in every sense of the word. From humble beginnings, it successfully transcended boundaries of space, time, culture, ethnicity, gender, and language to become a faith tradition of worldwide scope and impact. Despite the negative image of Islam in the West, it continues to be a dynamic, rapidly growing religion, providing spiritual comfort and guidance to millions of people in nearly every country in the world. Studies of converts to Islam indicate that two factors are uniformly attractive: the simplicity and power of the doctrine of tawheed—one God—and the sense of egalitarianism and acceptance that pervades the Muslim community.

How might Latter-day Saints regard Islam and Muhammad? The best approach is to recognize, emphasize, and rejoice in shared truths and values, even while acknowledging that sharp theological differences exist. Certainly Latter-day Saints cannot accept Islamic doctrines that deny the divinity of Jesus Christ, the need for modern prophets, or the principle of eternal progression; but they can gain beneficial insight from Islamic teachings about the necessity for faith, prayer, fasting, repentance, compassion, modesty, and strong families as cornerstones of individual spirituality and community life. Latter-day Saints can affirm with Muslims that the secret of human happiness and progress lies ultimately in bringing about spiritual change within the souls of men and women. As the Qur'an says: "Verily, never will Allah change the condition of a people until they change what is in themselves" (13:11). Moreover, it is an official part of Latter-day Saint doctrine that Heavenly Father has revealed eternal truths to his children of every nation, and the First Presidency's statement of February 1978 specifically mentions Muhammad as one of the great historical founders who received "a portion of God's light" and "moral truths . . . to enlighten whole nations and to bring a higher level of understanding to individuals." The thirteenth Article of Faith states that Latter-day Saints seek after "anything virtuous, lovely, or of good report or praiseworthy," and Joseph Smith taught that "we should gather all the good and true principles in the world and treasure them up, or we shall not come out true 'Mormons.'"[35] Latter-day Saint philosophy, then, holds that God—not Satan—inspired Muhammad and revealed to him a significant degree of eternal truth that Latter-day Saints should seek to understand and benefit from. A perceptive question that students sometimes pose is: Why did Muhammad (or any of the other religious figures in history) receive "a portion of God's light" but not a fulness? A satisfactory answer to this question

is elusive, for mortals cannot fully comprehend God's "inscrutable designs in relation to the human family."[36] But some hints appear in Latter-day Saint teachings. The Book of Mormon states that "the Lord doth grant unto all nations . . . all that he seeth fit that they should have" (Alma 29:8), and the prophet Joseph Smith declared that God deals with the peoples of the earth on the basis of "their means of obtaining intelligence, the laws by which they are governed, [and] the facilities afforded them of obtaining correct information."[37] Elder B. H. Roberts offers this insight:

God raises up wise men and prophets here and there among all the children of men, of their own tongue and nationality, speaking to them through means that they can comprehend; not always giving a fulness of truth . . . ; but *always giving that measure of truth that the people are prepared to receive.* Mormonism holds, then, that all the great teachers are servants of God; . . . inspired men, appointed to instruct God's children according to the conditions in the midst of which he finds them.[38]

In short, Latter-day Saints can enjoy positive, amicable relations with Muslims by acknowledging the spiritual truth and beauty that are found in Islam, emphasizing the similarities in belief and lifestyle, and agreeing to disagree agreeably on the differences.

Glossary of Islamic Names and Terms

'AEED AL-ADHA. "The Feast of Sacrifice"; the most important religious holiday in the Islamic world. It begins the day after the Hajj, when the faithful who can afford to do so sacrifice an animal in commemoration of Abraham's willingness to sacrifice his son Ishmael.

'AEED AL-FITR. "The Feast of Breaking the Fast"; a major religious holiday observed at the end of Ramadan, the month of fasting.

ALLAH. Contraction of an Arabic term that means "the God"; the word used by Muslims and Arabic-speaking Christians and Jews to refer to God.

BARAKA. "Blessing power" which comes from God into creation for the benefit of human beings.

CALIPHS. The successors of Muhammad to the leadership of the Muslim community who are not, however, considered prophets.

FIVE PILLARS OF ISLAM. The fundamental beliefs and practices for Muslims: the witness of faith, prayer, fasting, almsgiving, and pilgrimage to Mecca.

HADITH. A reported saying or action of Muhammad. The canonical collections of hadith are used to determine the sunna of the prophet.

HAJJ. The pilgrimage to Mecca, which is to be made once in a person's lifetime if financially and physically possible; one of the five pillars of faith.

HIJRA. Muhammad's emigration from Mecca to Yathrib (Medina) in 622 C.E. This turning point in Islamic history marks the beginning of the Muslim Hijri calendar.

IMAM. In Sunni tradition, the leader of salat prayer; in Shi'ite thought, the umma's divinely guided leader.

ISLAM. Literally, "submission" or "surrender" to God. The term is used in the Qur'an to describe true monotheistic worship as revealed to Muhammad and other prophets before him; it is also commonly used as the name of the religion practiced by Muslims.

JIHAD. Literally means "striving" or "struggling" to serve God and the umma. In a narrower sense, it sometimes involves armed struggle against outside aggression and is therefore sometimes translated as "holy war."

KA'ABA. The black-draped cubicle structure in Mecca which contains the black stone and which, according to legend, was first built by Abraham and his son Ishmael.

MAHDI. Messianic figure who, according to tradition, will appear at the end of history to prepare the world for final judgment by God.

MECCA. Most sacred place of Islam; birthplace of Muhammad and location of the Ka'aba.

MEDINA. Shortened form of Madinat Al-Nabi, meaning "city of the prophet"; the second holiest site in Islam. This is the place, first known as Yathrib, to which Muhammad fled in 622 C.E. and where many of the basic institutions of Islam were established. Muhammad is buried here.

MINARET. A tower associated with a mosque from which the call to prayer is given.

MOSQUE. From the Arabic word *masjid*, meaning "place of prostration" for ritual prayer. Mosques are the centers of Islamic communal life where prayers are held, religious education conducted, and charitable services provided.

MUEZZIN. Individual who gives the call to prayer.

MUHAMMAD (570–632 C.E.). The founder of Islam and the prophetic figure through whom Allah revealed the Qur'an.

MUSLIM. A person who practices Islam; means literally "one who submits to God."

QUR'AN. Means "recitation"; the name of the holy book of Islam, which is the mind and will of Allah delivered to Muhammad through the angel Gabriel; sometimes Anglicized "Koran."

RAMADAN. The month in which Muhammad received his initial call and the month in which faithful Muslims fast during daylight hours; the ninth lunar month of the Muslim calendar.

SALAT. Ritual prayer that is conducted five times each day and involves performing a prescribed set of physical movements designed to turn heart and mind toward God; one of the five pillars of faith.

SAWM. Fasting as a means of promoting individual spirituality and communal well-being; one of the five pillars of faith.

SHAHADA. The Muslim confession of faith: "There is no god but God, and Muhammad is His Messenger"; the first of the five pillars of faith.

SHARI'A. The all-inclusive legal code of Islam.

SHI'ITES. Muslims who believe that leadership of the community should have passed to Muhammad's son-in-law 'Ali and should be hereditary. Shi'a means "the party or sect."

SHIRK. The heresy of ascribing partners to God, or believing in more than one deity; opposite of tawheed.

SUFI. An adherent of the branch of Islam that emphasizes internal spiritual experience rather than external ritual forms and seeks mystical union with God in this life.

SUNNA. The customs and exemplary behavior of Muhammad. Next to the Qur'an, the sunna is the most important epistemological source in Islam.

SUNNI. The majority sect of Islam, who believe in consensual leadership and reject the Shi'ite claim that heredity or lineage determines a person's right to lead the umma.

TAWHEED. The doctrine of the uncompromised unity of God: "There is no god but Allah."

'ULAMA. Religious scholars or clergy who are the authoritative interpreters of Islamic law.

UMMA. The worldwide community of Muslims.

ZAKAT. The practice of giving 2.5 percent of one's accumulated wealth to support the umma; embodiment of the principle of charitable giving and one of the five pillars of faith.

Notes

I want to thank the following individuals, who read early drafts of this chapter and made valuable comments: Abdul-Rahman Fitzgerald, of Marrakesh, Morocco; Saleh Al-Zu'bi, of Amman, Jordan; Lee Wohlgemuth, of Brussels, Belgium; and Donna Lee Bowen and Richard Frost of Provo, Utah. Thanks also to Daniel C. Peterson of Brigham Young University, for his contributions to the section on pre-Islamic history, which is drawn from the previous edition of this text.

1. Two of the best Muslim sources on the early life of Muhammad are Martin Lings, *Muhammad: His Life Based on the Earliest Sources* (London: George Allen and Unwin and The Islamic Texts Society, 1983); and Muhammad Husayn Haykal, *The Life of Muhammad*, trans. by Isma'il al-Faruqi (N.p.: North American Trust Publications, 1976).

2. All Qur'anic quotes and references in this chapter are from the translation by Abdullah Yusuf 'Ali entitled *The Holy Qur'an: English Translation of the Meanings and Commentary* (Medina, Saudi Arabia: The Custodian of the Two Holy Mosques King Fahd Complex for the Printing of The Holy Qur'an, 1413 hijri [1992/3 C.E.]).

3. Haykal, *The Life of Muhammad,* 75.

4. Quoted in Steven Barboza, *American Jihad: Islam after Malcolm X* (New York: Doubleday, 1993), 357–58. *A History of Turkey* was published in 1854.

5. Ameer 'Ali, *The Spirit of Islam* (London: Chatto and Windus, 1890 [11th impression, 1978]), 218.

6. Dallin H. Oaks, "Joseph, the Man and the Prophet," *Ensign*, May 1996, 72.

7. Annemarie Schimmel, *Islam in the Subcontinent* (Leiden: E. J. Brill, 1980), 10.

8. Frederick Mathewson Denny, *An Introduction to Islam,* 2d ed. (New York: Macmillan, 1994), 86. Bernard Lewis, in his study of Jewish status under Islamic rule, concluded that "Islamic practice on the whole turned out to be gentler than Islamic precept—the reverse of the situation in Christendom" (*The Jews of Islam* [Princeton, N.J.: Princeton University Press, 1984], 24).

9. Denny, *Introduction to Islam,* 93–94.

10. 'Ali, *The Holy Qur'an: English Translation,* iv–v.

11. Ibid., 17–18 n. 55.

12. Some observers of Islam have criticized the concept of insha'allah as giving rise to a perceived attitude of passivity, recklessness, and fatalism among Muslims. While it is true that most Muslims hold to the idea that Allah is in control of their lives, this does not mean that indolence or carelessness is justified in Islam. The Islamic notion of "if God wills," as I understand it, is almost identical to the biblical precept of "if the Lord will" as explained in James 4:13–15. It is an acknowledgment that nothing in life happens except by His will.

13. Sachiko Murata and William C. Chittick, *The Vision of Islam* (New York: Paragon House, 1994), 175.

14. Yusuf 'Ali's commentary provides the rationale for this view. The boy mentioned in these verses "was, according to Muslim tradition, the first-born son . . . Isma'il. The name itself is from the root *sami'a* , to hear, because Allah had heard Abraham's prayer. . . . Our version may be compared with the Jewish-Christian version of the present Old Testament. The Jewish tradition . . . refers this sacrifice to Isaac (Gen. 22:1–18). Now Isaac was born when Abraham was 100 years old (Gen. 21:5), while Isma'il was born to Abraham when Abraham was 86 years old (Gen. 16:16). Isma'il was therefore 14 years older than Isaac. During his 14 years Isma'il was the *only* son of Abraham; at no time was Isaac the *only* son of Abraham. Yet, in speaking of the sacrifice, the Old Testament says (Gen. 22:2): 'And He said, Take now thy son, thine *only* son Isaac, whom thou lovest, and get thee into the land of Moriah: and offer him there for a burnt offering. . . .' This slip shows at any rate which was the older version, and how it was overlaid, like the present Jewish records, in the interests of a tribal religion" ('Ali, *The Holy Qur'an: English Translation,* 1356–57 nn. 4096 and 4101).

15. These figures are from a standard Muslim source written in Arabic: Abu Bakr al-Jaza'iri, *Minhaj al-Muslim* (Medina: n.p., 1964), 32.

16. One of the most thoroughly researched and enlightening books on the subject of Muhammad's life, as viewed by Muslims, is Annemarie Schimmel, *And Muhammad Is His Messenger: The Veneration of the Prophet in Islamic Piety* (Chapel Hill: University of North Carolina Press, 1985). The examples in this paragraph are derived from pp. 46–49.

17. In accordance with local tradition, Friday is also the day when Latter-day Saints living in Muslim countries hold their worship services.

18. The first three hadith cited here are from Ezzedin Ibrahim and Denys Johnson-Davies, trans., *Al-Arba'in al-Nawawiyya/Nawawi's Forty Hadith* (Beirut: The Holy Koran Publishing House, 1976), 56, 88, 98. The last two hadith, like several other examples in this essay that have no reference, were recounted to me during conversations with Muslim friends and acquaintances.

19. These extra-Qur'anic divine utterances, referred to as *hadith qudsi,* "holy sayings," are cited in Mahmoud al-Sirtawi, "Ramadaniyat: Al-Sawm Junna," *Al-Ajniha,* February 1996, 15–16. See also Mahmoud Matraji's English translation of *Sahih Muslim* (Beirut: Dar El-Fikr, 1993), 2:355.

20. Abu Bakr al-Jaza'iri, *Methodology of the Muslim* (Beirut: Dar el-Fikr, 1994), 372–73.

21. Matraji, *Sahih Muslim,* 2:275; al-Jaza'iri, *Methodology of the Muslim,* 376.

22. "Rigors of NBA Do Not Deter Olajuwon from Ramadan Fast," *Jordan Times,* February 10, 1996, 10.

23. In describing the spiritual rewards of hajj, Muslims often use terminology that is familiar to Christians. For example, a Jordanian friend said that the effect is "as if you are born a second time, feeling the purity and happiness and innocence of a small child."

24. The formal pilgrimage is performed only once each year during the month of *Dhu al-Hijja.* However, many Muslims visit Mecca at other times of the year to perform *'umra,* an abbreviated version of the hajj ritual. 'Umra, however, does not satisfy the obligation to perform the complete hajj outlined in Islamic law.

25. Two excellent sources on the role of women in Islam from the perspective of Western scholarship are Leila Ahmed, *Women and Gender in Islam* (New Haven, Conn.: Yale University Press, 1992), and Donna Lee Bowen and Evelyn A. Early, eds., *Everyday Life in the Muslim Middle East* (Bloomington: Indiana University Press, 1993), part 2: "Gender Relations."

26. One widely viewed film, *Not without My Daughter,* portrays Islamic family life as oppressive to women and Muslim men as brutal wife-beaters. Muslims who have seen the film are outraged that the story, a true account of an American woman's experience in Iran, implies that violence against women is sanctioned in Islam and that Muslim husbands and fathers are tyrannical. They point out that one can find

examples of spouse abuse in every religion and that it is inappropriate to judge the lives of an entire religious community based on the wrongdoings of a few misguided individuals.

27. Elizabeth W. Fernea, "The Veiled Revolution," in Bowen and Early, *Everyday Life in the Muslim Middle East,* 119–22.

28. Student interview conducted in November 1995 in Amman, Jordan; copy in my possession.

29. Statement by the founding committee of the Muslim Brethren, one of the most influential groups in the Islamist Movement, quoted in their official newspaper, *Al-Ikhwan al-Muslimun,* 7 May 1946.

30. Qur'an 3:64 and 29:46. In Assad Nimer Busool's pamphlet *Islamic Fundamentalism?* (Chicago: American Islamic Educational Foundation, 1993), 4, 18.

31. S. Waqar Ahmad, "Terrorist Bombing Contradicts Islam," *Daily Universe* [Brigham Young University], March 16, 1993.

32. A thoughtful overview and analysis of this issue is presented by Arnold H. Green in his article "The Muhammad–Joseph Smith Comparison: Subjective Metaphor or a Sociology of Prophethood," in Spencer J. Palmer, ed., *Mormons and Muslims: Spiritual Foundations and Modern Manifestations,* Religious Studies Monograph Series, no. 8 (Provo, Ut.: Religious Studies Center, Brigham Young University, 1983), 63–84.

33. G. A. Smith, "The History of Mahomedanism," September 23, 1855, in Brigham Young et al., *Journal of Discourses,* 26 vols. (1842–96; reprint, Salt Lake City: n.p., 1967), 3:31–32; Parley P. Pratt, "Mahometanism and Christianity," September 23, 1855, in ibid., 3:38, 41.

34. See Donna Lee Bowen, "Pragmatic Morality: Islam and Family Planning in Morocco," in Bowen and Early, *Everyday Life in the Muslim Middle East,* 91–101; Donna Lee Bowen, "Abortion, Islam, and the 1994 Cairo Population Conference," *International Journal of Middle East Studies* 29, no. 2 (May 1997): 161–84.

35. Joseph Fielding Smith, comp., *Teachings of the Prophet Joseph Smith* (Salt Lake City: Deseret Book, 1979), 316.

36. Ibid., 218.

37. Ibid.

38. B. H. Roberts, *Defense of the Faith and the Saints,* 2 vols. (Salt Lake City: Deseret News, 1907), 1:512 (emphasis added). More of this quotation may be found at superscript 21 in the chapter on religious similarities in this book.

Part Five
Reflections

In this book, we have walked down many paths of faith. We have examined the beliefs and world views of the vast majority of the world's peoples. In our presentation of the faiths of others we have always tried to be objective, detailing the very best that is to be found within each religion. Still, because no one is ever wholly objective, we have reflected from a Latter-day Saint perspective on specific issues raised in the various religious traditions, so that Latter-day Saint students might be tactfully guided in their reflections about the beliefs of others.

It is now time, however, to lay aside the objective stance and to ask how Latter-day Saints should finally view the religious traditions of others. Membership in The Church of Jesus Christ of Latter-day Saints is, after all, based on belief that it is only faith in which the fulness of the Christian gospel may be found, because it is the only one in which God's authoritative priesthood resides. In the same spirit of openness that has existed in the previous chapters, we invite all—Latter-day Saint and non–Latter-day Saint alike—to explore this final arena with us.

Religious Similarities

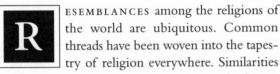

Spencer J. Palmer

ESEMBLANCES among the religions of the world are ubiquitous. Common threads have been woven into the tapestry of religion everywhere. Similarities and parallels between the restored gospel of Jesus Christ and the other great religions have been repeatedly referenced in the chapters of this book. For example, in many of the great religions there is a vivid eschatology which includes magnificent messianic personages who will appear at the end of time to assist in rescuing humankind—Kalki in Hinduism, Maitreya in Buddhism, Saoshyant in Zoroastrianism, al-Mahdi in Islam, the Messiah in Judaism, and Jesus in Christianity. Other common themes include premortal life, oracles or prophetic figures, resurrection or survival after death, and ecstasy from ultimate union with the divine.

At the sociological level, Howard Christy has given special attention to the second part of Jesus' Great Commandment, sometimes known as the Golden Rule, as a preeminent and inclusive leitmotif in world religion. Citing H. T. D. Rost,[1] a Baha'i scholar, and Bahagavan Das,[2] an Indian writer, Christy points out that virtually all the great religions of the world, including (in addition to Christianity) Confucianism, Hinduism, Jainism, Buddhism, Taoism, Zoroastrianism, Sikhism, Judaism, and Islam, regard the Golden Rule as fundamentally important.[3] He cites the following examples:

1. In Christianity, Jesus said, "Thou shalt love thy neighbor as thyself" (Matt. 19:19) and "Whatsoever ye would that men should do unto you, do ye even so unto them . . ." (Matt. 7:12).

2. In Confucianism, when asked by his disciple Tzu Kung, "Is there any one maxim which ought to be acted upon throughout one's life?" Confucius replied: "Surely the maxim of charity is such: 'Do not unto others what you would not they should do unto you.'"[4]

3. In Hinduism, from the Mahabharata: "Do not to others what ye do not wish Done to yourself; and wish for others too What ye desire and long for, for yourself—This is the whole Dharma, heed it well."[5]

4. In Islam, one of the *hadith* quotes Muhammad as saying: "None of you [truly] believes until he wishes for his brother what he wishes for himself."[6]

5. In Judaism, in the Babylonian Talmud (Shabbath 3la), is the story of a heathen (or gentile) who approached Shammai, one of the chief pharisaic scribes in Jerusalem, and asked him to "make me a proselyte, on the condition that you teach me the whole Torah while I stand on one foot." Shammai "repulsed him." The heathen then approached the great Rabbi Hillel with the same proposition. Hillel answered, "What is hateful to you do not to your neighbor; that is the whole Torah, while the rest is the commentary thereof; go and learn it."

What is the explanation for the numerous similarities and parallels in the religions of the world? What view should Latter-day Saints take of the resemblances between their own religion and other world faiths; between Christ and other savior figures; between Joseph Smith and other prophets; between the truths, teachings, symbols, ceremonies, and textual statements of The Church of Jesus Christ of Latter-day Saints in the modern scriptures and the other great religious traditions described in this book? Are these parallels and agreements simply imaginary? Are they only accidental coincidences? Are they simply remarkable illustrations of poetic license or results of distortions of language and culture at the hands of faulty translators? Should they be explained by reference to the similarity of circumstances under which their founders—Christ and the Buddha, or Christ and Lao Tzu, or Joseph Smith and Zarathustra, or Joseph Smith and Confucius—taught?

Is it possible to explain all the similarities by purportedly showing either historical borrowing or historical impact? Which came first, the Rig Veda or the Gatha poems; and does the answer make any real difference to the credibility of Hinduism or Zoroastrianism? Is it critical to prove that Zoroastrianism influenced Jewish doctrine during the Exile, and is Jewish credibility compromised if influence can be shown? The same could be asked about commonalities between Judaism and Islam and the implications of Old Testament influences on Muhammad.

Must Christians admit that certain of their beliefs have derived from earlier Buddhist sources simply because some commonalities appear, or should all parties involved in these comparative studies look to other sources that are earlier than any of them? Should religious resemblances in world religions be looked upon as the work of humans, God, or the devil? For Latter-day Saints, what are the implications of the recognition and acceptance of "golden threads" in the religions of humanity? Are such linkages between "us" and "them" a benefit or a disadvantage to the expansion of The Church of Jesus Christ of Latter-day Saints in the world today?

In The Church of Jesus Christ of Latter-day Saints the relationship of Christ to his prophets is clear. But Christ's relationship to the Buddha, Muhammad, Mahavira, Zarathustra, Confucius, or Lao Tzu is not so well defined. We may ask ourselves if religious truths which seem harmonious or even universal spring from a common source which may be traced to Adam; does that explanation resolve the problem, or are there other valid explanations that we must also keep in mind?

This chapter suggests five possible ways in which Latter-day Saints have responded to the above series of questions.

Diffusion

Among Latter-day Saints the most common explanation of religious resemblances is the belief that religious elements that seem harmonious or even universal spring from a common source: the pure gospel of Jesus Christ as once known to all our fathers. Adam, the first man, received the fulness of the gospel and in turn taught it to his descendants. But they, yielding to the temptations of the Evil One, sinned and departed from the truth. To use Thomas Romney's words, "The original, true doctrine was changed and warped to suit the appetites of evil, ambitious [persons]." Thus, in Romney's

diffusionist view, the principles of the gospel have appeared in a more or less modified form in the various religions of humankind.

Further, in this view, in the days of Jesus Christ the gospel was once again presented to the world in its purity. Again, willful individuals altered the doctrine, bringing into being a myriad of differing Christian parties. The many religions now extant among the human family, both Christian and non-Christian, testify to the number and magnitude of the apostasies, wrought through human pride, which have altered the plain and easily understood revelations of God.[7]

Consistent with the diffusionist approach, Romney concludes that doctrines of the Trinity reach back into the remote past and are widely espoused. The numerous examples of a triune godhead among Egyptians, Mesopotamians, Babylonians, and Sumerians are all reflections of an original authentic model: the Father, Son, and Holy Ghost.[8] Romney also argues that both blood and bloodless sacrificial offerings to the Vedic gods of India (Indra, Agni, Varuna, Vishnu, and Krishna); the libations to Confucius in the traditional ceremonies of the state cult of China; the sacrificial offerings to the gods of the ancient Greeks and Romans—as well as those many Jewish sacrifices for the purpose of placating the wrath of deity or of putting the worshipers in accord with unseen and ineffable powers—are all evidences of "common bonds of union," universal religious patterns that, in the main, at least, "sprang originally from a common source."[9] Anciently, people offered sacrifices without really knowing that the roots of the practice lay in the original sacrifices of Adam and his posterity. Adam's sacrifices were a similitude of the sacrifice of the Lamb of God, Jesus Christ, as the scripture explains:

And after many days an angel of the Lord appeared unto Adam, saying: Why dost thou offer sacrifices unto the Lord? And Adam said unto him: I know not, save the Lord commanded me. And then the angel spake, saying: This thing is a similitude of the sacrifice of the Only Begotten of the Father, which is full of grace and truth. (Moses 5:6–7)

In like manner, Romney argues that the doctrine of reincarnation in Hinduism, Buddhism, Jainism, and Sikhism is actually a modified type of immortality, rather than accepting the more commonly held conclusion in the academic world that reincarnation explains a historic attempt to deal with why people are different, or why ethnic and cultural differences were institutionalized after the Aryan conquest of the Dravidians. Alvin R. Dyer, another spokesman for the diffusionist view, has concluded that Hinduism, Zoroastrianism, Confucianism, Taoism, and Islam are replete with fragmentary examples of gospel principles and doctrines that have come about through adulteration of original truths, or departures from the "high theories" once held by the founders of world religions.[10]

The most influential Latter-day Saint diffusionist is Professor Hugh Nibley of Brigham Young University. Nibley holds that God, in his dealings with man, follows a constant pattern. God repeatedly reveals his will, his unchanging truth, to selected peoples of the earth. Resemblances and ties which seem to exist among all the religions of antiquity reappear in history primarily because of this pattern of divine restorations, followed by human apostasies. Since the teachings and powers of God to chosen peoples have often been deliberately imitated or disseminated among humanity, a diffusion of truth from a single center has to recur continuously. What has been done in one dispensation has often been foreshadowed in another. Nibley traces an eschatological pattern of history which he sees as prominent in Jewish and Christian scriptures and in apocryphal writings as well. The pattern includes

the periodic repetition of certain characteristic events—a "visitation," as it was called, from heaven; the making of a covenant; the corruption and the wickedness of men, leading to the breaking of the covenant; the bondage of sin, then the coming of a prophet with a call to repentance; the making of a new covenant; and so around the cycle.[11]

God is at the helm of history. Thus, at the base, religious parallels are rooted in the mind and will of God through repeated revelations.

Nibley points out that parallels between the history of The Church of Jesus Christ of Latter-day Saints and the doings of the ancients are not consciously contrived imitations. The obvious analogies between the sufferings, wanderings, and spiritual aspirations of the Latter-day Saint pioneers and those of the people of ancient Israel cannot be drawn because the Latter-day Saints wanted it so; "they were . . . pushed and driven around entirely against their own will." All along, the whole history of the church has been the will of God. Resemblances to earlier beliefs and experiences have an extraordinary force among Latter-day Saints, because they see in these similarities the fulfillment of prophecy.[12]

Faced with resemblances between the Latter-day Saint temple endowment ceremony and ancient Egyptian endowment rites, Nibley looks at these as an example of countless parallels, many of them instructive, among the customs and religions of humankind. But he sees them as imitations of earlier gospel models and little more. The Egyptian rites "are a parody, an imitation, but as such not to be despised. For all the great age and consistency of their rites and teachings, which certainly command respect, the Egyptians did not have the real thing, and they knew it."[13]

COMMON HUMAN PREDICAMENT

There are Latter-day Saints who believe that the diffusion theory explains religious parallels only in a limited way. They readily agree that God revealed the original principles and ordinances of the gospel and bestowed the authority and power of the priesthood on Adam. They agree that in the course of time, as populations expanded and as peoples moved away from one another and became independent, they took with them some of their original features and applied them in new settings. But to these Latter-day Saints this is a convenient explanation that fails to cover much of the ground. At best, such a view explains common religious forms only within limited geographical areas.

It can be argued that certain experiences are fundamental to all human beings—arising out of the common human predicament—that explain many of the similarities of thought and practice so widely found here on earth. All humans face problems of birth, life, sex, disease, death, joy, disappointment, and grief. All ask, Why must we die? Why must we be sick? Why must we grow old? Why must we suffer? What happens after death? Thus, common beliefs and practices arise from the common predicaments faced by people; for parallels to Job's experience are everywhere.

This polygenetic view—that religious beliefs and rituals have arisen spontaneously and independently in various countries but have generally followed uniform patterns of development—offers special insight into the uses of religious symbols, rituals, and ordinances among humankind. In expounding upon the views of Mircea Eliade, Merlin G. Myers explains that "human actions have no intrinsic value" and "become valuable only insofar as they unfold according to divine patterns," thus surmounting the human predicament and becoming associated with "the transcendental." For this reason, people the world over hold festivals and participate in rituals.[14] Referring to Victor Witter Turner's description of these performances as "periods of 'timeless' time," Myers explains that ritual uses its own form of symbolic language to invest human relationships, institutions, and social structures with meaning of an otherworldly nature.[15] Religious symbols provide this means, and peoples of all cultures utilize them; similarities in practice are therefore bound to occur. The frustration and pain that form an inevitable part of human existence are relieved largely through these rituals and symbolic expressions.

Obviously, continues Myers, the God who created humankind has not limited himself to a single time period in history or to a single group of his children. However, as the cultures of various peoples differ, so will the "cultural idioms" in which these peoples express the fundamental principles of their worship. Latter-day Saints searching other world religions for similar expressions of belief may not find them; but those who look for shared principles will discover much common ground. Thus, he observes, the "symbolic vehicles" of the various world religions "can provide valid functions and services" for those who believe in them, but in order to conform to "the celestial order of things" they must in time be adapted to meet the principles of truth underlying them in a way that will leave no room for misunderstanding. Within the restored Church of Jesus Christ there are instrumentalities through which the necessary levels of insight are achieved—among them, revelation from God and the authority to receive it.

John A. Widtsoe repeatedly emphasized that "we live in a world of symbols," some more beautiful and pleasing than others, but that their forms are of relatively little consequence. In the end, it is what they suggest and teach that counts. "No man or woman can come out of the temple endowed as he should be, unless he has seen, beyond the symbol, the mighty realities for which the symbols stand."[16]

For those Latter-day Saints who give credence to "the common human predicament," there is superiority in the rites and ordinances of the priesthood but also recognition that peoples all over the world are trying to accomplish similar goals within the frameworks of their own world views. They have their symbols and ordinances, too; and through these symbols they seek to transcend their earthly predicament, to break through this mundane realm and realize the supernatural.

All human beings bear the stamp of the human condition. The similarities of their concerns and their responses to the needs and conditions of this life are not essentially determined by either divine or nefarious forces emanating from another world. Rather, they are determined by the harsh realities of this world.

PRIMORDIAL IMAGES

In Latter-day Saint theology, human predispositions of thought and feeling may be viewed as "echoes of eternity,"[17] since all men lived together under common conditions with God in a premortal spirit world. After quoting Wordsworth's famous "Ode: Intimations of Immortality," which suggests that the minds and spirits of mankind come to earth

> Not in entire forgetfulness, . . .
> But trailing clouds of glory do we come
> From God, who is our home,

Joseph Fielding Smith comments that "there may be times when flashes of remembrance of these former days come to us."[18] He later quotes Orson F. Whitney, a member of the Council of the Twelve, who explains that "more than once, upon hearing a noble sentiment expressed, though unable to recall that I had ever heard it until then, I have found myself in sympathy with it, was thrilled by it, and felt as if I had always known it." Elder Whitney refers to the Savior's statement that "[m]y sheep hear my voice" (John 10:27), concluding that those things which are true and beautiful appeal to men everywhere because we were all acquainted with the gospel in our premortal life, and it is this prior exposure which makes it seem familiar.[19] President Joseph F. Smith "heartily endorse[s]" Elder Whitney's observation that common experiences in the antemortal spiritual life predispose, influence, and guide human thoughts and preferences in this life, for "we often catch a spark from the awakened memories of the immortal soul, which lights up our whole being as with the glory of our former home."[20]

This truth should not be confused with Carl Jung's view of the "collective unconscious," but there is much in his discussion of "basic archetypes" that nonetheless seems congruent with the Latter-day Saint view of premortal existence and that might well help explain resemblances of thought and belief among humankind. Jung postulates that a symbol can express itself simultaneously among large and diverse groups of people. He draws parallels between mythological motifs and the unconscious thinking of his patients. For instance, a very young child once recounted a dream that paralleled some ancient Persian myth. Since very few people other than classical scholars knew anything of such a myth, the child could not have been taught it. After considerable study and deliberation, Jung notes that cultural heritages with no possible history of contact contain myths that are virtually identical in general outline. He concludes that all people, both civilized and primitive, share an instinctual disposition to symbolize the same themes in their religious myths.

Why are the story lines of religious fantasy and experience so common among all people? In 1919 Jung developed the term archetype to account for these expressions of "collective psyche." He does not suggest universal symbolism, but he does suggest universal archetypes. He does not see these archetypes as conscious images of the mind; instead, they lie in the deepest reaches of the unconscious. He calls them "primordial images"—images inherently existent in the mind of any human being at birth—believing that the mind has inherited the tendency to work in a particular way. According to him, the psyche is not passive but is actively involved in forming one's perceptions of meaning.[21]

From the vantage point of Latter-day Saint theology, ways of thinking and acting can easily be interpreted as brought with us from our existence with God. Perhaps the so-called psychic unity of humanity that has been argued by so many may indeed go back to our pre-earth existence, to our primordial native intelligence. President Smith, Elder Whitney, and so many others in the church have, from time to time, talked about "glimmers" and the "thin veil," saying that thoughts rise in the mind to make members feel that they have experienced this, felt that, or believed something else. And such "echoes of eternity" seem to be the common experience of humanity. Having common beginnings in the premortal existence, naturally we should expect—if only at times in faint and wistful ways—common manifestations of those beginnings with God. In his Commissioner's Lecture of 1973, Truman Madsen concludes that "only something of such magnitude . . . can account for the full phenomenon and power of conscience" and of other faculties inherent in mortal experience, and though presently a veil is drawn over specific images of that realm—we do not now recall our name, rank, and serial number—there is built in us and not quite hidden a "collective unconscious" that is superracial in character, a pool of such vivid effect, such residual power in us, that our finite learnings and recoveries are at best a tiny aftermath.[22] It is in this collective unconscious that one should be able to find explanations for resemblances in the beliefs and religious experiences of humankind.

DIVINE INSPIRATION

Latter-day Saints believe that the spiritual influence which emanates from God is not confined to selected nations, races, or groups. All people share an inheritance of divine light. Christ himself is the light of the world. Even those who have never heard of Christ are granted the Spirit and Light of Christ.[23] In the Book of Mormon, Christ told the brother of Jared, "In me shall all humankind have life" (Ether 3:14). In a revelation to Joseph Smith, the Lord explained:

[W]hatsoever is light is Spirit, even the Spirit of Jesus Christ. And the Spirit giveth light to every man that cometh into the world; and the Spirit enlighteneth every man through the world, that hearkeneth to the voice of the Spirit. (D&C 84:45–46)

In the "Olive Leaf" revelation of 1832 we are told that this Light of Christ

proceedeth forth from the presence of God to fill the immensity of space—The light . . . which is the law by which all things are governed, even the power of God who sitteth upon his throne, who is in the bosom of eternity, who is in the midst of all things. (D&C 88:12–13)

If people act according to this inspiration, they progress from grace to grace, learning precept upon precept, until they receive full enlightenment (see D&C 93:19–20; 98:11–12). That every person ever born enjoys the Light of Christ was reiterated by Brigham Young, who taught that there has never been "a man or woman upon the face of the earth, from the days of Adam to this day, who has not been enlightened, instructed, and taught by the revelations of Jesus Christ."[24] This allows each individual to recognize truth, and the associated results often lift these individuals to new and higher insights than were traditionally known among a given people.

Since God has thus inspired human beings of all cultures and creeds, the possibilities are staggering. Such religious reformers as Martin Luther and John Wesley—despite their personal frailties and errors— may be looked upon as instruments of God's will. Likewise, a whole continuum of Christian mystics in medieval European history (some of whose ideas seem at times to resemble so closely gospel teachings today) show the extent to which they have been guided by Christ's light. These include Saint Francis of Assisi and Saint Bernard de Clairvaux, to name only two. Also, Christian devotionalism, represented by Thomas à Kempis's *The Imitation of Christ* (1426), expresses a diffusion of Christ's inspiration. The works of Manuel Tamayo, Francisco Goya, and Diego Velázquez in the fields of literature and painting are celebrated worldwide for their illumination and beauty. Miguel de Cervantes's classic *Don Quixote* has provided inspiring insights for people of all lands.

The Book of Mormon indicates that Columbus was moved upon by the "Spirit of God" to sail to the New World (1 Ne. 13:12). Among those who inhabited the Americas, contributions to civilization also seemingly inspired by God are monumental and countless. Called the "Greeks of the New World" because of their advanced culture, the Maya Indians created a calendar that has the reputation of being more nearly perfect than any devised elsewhere in the world, including the Gregorian calendar we use today. Mexican achievements in establishing the first university in North America and in publishing the first book in the Western Hemisphere (in 1539 by Juan Pablos) have been a great blessing to all those who have been able to come under their influence. Artists and writers such as Diego Rivera and Octavio Paz have made fine contributions in more recent times. Similarly, in North America, the Founding Fathers and the framers of the Constitution of the United States received guidance through the same divine Spirit (D&C 101:80). Scientists, artists, and poets have likewise been inspired.[25]

God has raised up inspired teachers and great reformers in various cultures throughout history—

not just Jewish and Christian spokespersons. In this view, all peoples and even all religions possess significant elements of truth. To illustrate, as has been previously pointed out, all of the following religions or philosophies profess a statement of moral principle in essentially the same wording as the Christian Golden Rule: Judaism, Hinduism, Buddhism, Sikhism, Zoroastrianism, Islam, Shinto, Socratic philosophy, Confucianism, Taoism, and Jainism. John Taylor affirms: "The Catholics have many pieces of truth; so have the Protestants, the Mahometans, and Heathens."[26] George Albert Smith reiterated this theme,[27] and Brigham Young observed:

"Do you suppose the Hindoos have the light of the Spirit of Christ?" I know they have; and so have the Hottentots, and so has every nation and kingdom upon the face of the earth, even though some of them may be cannibals.[28]

Just as the Spirit of Christ has led the above persons, so also Christ inspired the thinkers of Greece and Rome. Likewise, artists and thinkers in Asia have been moved by inspiration from God: Ferdosi of Persia; Kalidasa, Asoka, and Gandhi of India; Mencius, Tu Fu, and Po Chiu-I of China; Sejong and Chong Mong-ju of Korea; Basho and Chikamatsu of Japan; and José Rizal of the Philippines, to name only a few. Brigham Young comments that virtue is to be found among all peoples, even those he terms "idolatrous."[29]

Orson F. Whitney teaches that Zarathustra, the Buddha, and Confucius "were servants of the Lord in a lesser sense, and were sent to those pagan or heathen nations to give them the measure of truth that a wise Providence had allotted to them." These leaders, along with many others, "have been used from the beginning to help along the Lord's work—mighty auxiliaries in the hands of an Almighty God, carrying out his purposes, consciously or unconsciously."[30] B. H. Roberts summarizes:

While the Church of Jesus Christ of Latter-day Saints is established for the instruction of men; and is one of God's instrumentalities for making known the truth yet he is not limited to that institution for such purposes, neither in time nor place. God raises up wise men and prophets here and there among all the children of men, of their own tongue and nationality, speaking to them through means that they can comprehend; not always giving a fulness of truth such as may be found in the fulness of the gospel of Jesus Christ; but always giving that measure of truth that the people are prepared to receive. Mormonism holds, then, that all the great teachers are servants of God;

among all nations and in all ages. They are inspired men, appointed to instruct God's children according to the conditions in the midst of which he finds them. Hence it is not obnoxious to Mormonism to regard Confucius, the great Chinese philosopher and moralist, as a servant of God, inspired to a certain degree by him to teach those great moral maxims which have governed those millions of God's children for lo! these many centuries. It is willing to regard Gautama, Buddha as an inspired servant of God, teaching a measure of the truth, at least giving to these people that twilight of truth by which they may somewhat see their way. So with the Arabian prophet, that wild spirit that turned the Arabians from worshiping idols to a conception of the Creator of heaven and earth that was more excellent than their previous conception of Deity. And so the sages of Greece and of Rome. So the reformers of early Protestant times. Wherever God finds a soul sufficiently enlightened and pure; one with whom his Spirit can communicate, lo! he makes of him a teacher of men. While the path of sensuality and darkness may be that which most men tread, a few, to paraphrase the words of a moral philosopher of high standing, have been led along the upward path; a few in all countries and generations have been wisdom seekers, or seekers of God. They have been so because the Divine Word of Wisdom has looked upon them, choosing them for the knowledge and service of himself.[31]

As mentioned in the chapter on Islam, George A. Smith believes that Muhammad "was no doubt raised up by God on purpose to scourge the world for their idolatry."[32] Parley P. Pratt, in a general conference address, declares that

with all my prejudices of early youth, and habits of thought and reading, my rational faculties would compel me to admit that the Mahometan history and Mahometan doctrine was a standard raised against the most corrupt and abominable idolatry that ever perverted our earth, found in the creeds and worship of Christians, falsely so named.[33]

Moses Thatcher, another member of the Council of the Twelve of the church, is "struck by the profound philosophy, pure morality, and comprehensiveness exhibited in the writings of Confucius and Mencius and the Chinese sages" as "divinely inspired, far-reaching and heavenly doctrines."[34] Likewise, in a KSL radio address in 1927, Elder Matthew Cowley expressed his belief that "Confucius understood the doctrine of repentance" and that on the basis of his teachings on purity and virtue "one would almost believe that the gospel was borrowed from Confucius."[35]

Thus, in this Latter-day Saint view, God has inspired men to think and write according to the conditions in the midst of which he finds them.

Islam, Hinduism, Taoism, Confucianism, Shinto, Jainism, Sikhism, Zoroastrianism, Buddhism, and others have within them inspired principles; and the peoples of all lands and cultures will be judged by God in accordance with their individual willingness to abide by them. All humankind will ultimately be judged by that which they have received by inspiration direct from God, at least until a fulness of the gospel has been provided.[36]

THE DEVIL INVENTION THEORY

Milton R. Hunter points out that Justin Martyr (ca. 150 C.E.), an early Christian apologist, and Tertullian (160–220 C.E.), another early Christian leader and theologian, both saw in the rituals of the pagan religions of their day copies of the sacred ordinances of the Christian church. Justin Martyr saw in the religion of Mithra certain rites that could be related to communion. Tertullian saw those who worshiped idols using rituals that involved baptism for the remission of their sins. Thirteen hundred years later, a Catholic priest named Las Casas saw in the rites and rituals of many New World Indians such close similarities to gospel practices and beliefs that he concluded that Satan must have reached the Americas ahead of the gospel.[37]

Latter-day Saints who accept this view feel that Satan seeks to lead humanity away from light and truth, sponsoring all manner of deceitful false doctrines. In the words of Elder Hunter, the devil "has exerted a powerful influence upon mortal beings . . . in counterfeiting the true principles and ordinances of the gospel."[38] He has fostered many clever and attractive imitations in the religions of the world in an effort to lull humanity into satisfaction with partial truths, to weaken the appeal of the fulness of the restored gospel and the Lord's divinely authorized teachers. Jacob, the Book of Mormon prophet, has explained that people can become angels to the devil; for Satan, who beguiled our first parents, is capable of stirring up the hearts of their posterity to participate in works of darkness by transforming himself "nigh unto an angel of light" (2 Ne. 9:9). Thus, for Latter-day Saints who subscribe to the "devil invention view," apparent similarities to the restored gospel found in the religions of the world should be considered as satanic substitutes—counterfeit attractions mistakenly suggesting, among other possibilities, that all roads lead to heaven.

Conclusion

Each of the five views elaborated in this chapter can provide useful and meaningful insights into questions of religious resemblances. But no view by itself covers the whole ground, and all together fall short of explaining all parallels. For Latter-day Saints, only inspiration from the Lord can provide the answers as to which of these five possibilities is dominant in a particular case. Regardless of the relative importance of each of the five in a particular setting, members of the church must decide from a tactical point of view whether the evangelical mission of the church can be accomplished more effectively by emphasizing the diabolic nature of the specious similarities between the gospel and the native faiths or by emphasizing the common heritage of the pre-earth life, the influence of the Light of Christ, the partially accurate deposit of faith and truth from ancient times, and so forth. This much is certain: the view its membership takes has important implications for the future growth of the church.

For Latter-day Saints, reactions to religious similarities influence not merely perceptions of the religions of the world (are they intrinsically valuable or not?) but also of the restored gospel (is it comprehensive and global in scope and application?). Members with even superficial familiarity with other religions can be much impressed by what seem to be replications of elements otherwise assumed to be unique or confined to the restored gospel. To come upon these parallels in the remains of cultures long dead (Assyrian, Egyptian, Roman, Babylonian, Ugaritic, and others) is one thing. To come upon them in the scriptures and daily contemporary experience of living world faiths which compete for the hearts and minds of men and women may be more difficult to handle. Familiarity with non-Christian religions by Latter-day Saints whose testimonies are not strong or who are not otherwise prepared to face the realities of religion in the world at large can breed confusion, disillusionment, or indifference, for some may be tempted to turn to sheer relativism—the belief that one faith is as good as another or that all faiths express the same truth in variant cultural trappings.

For some, this may become a major pitfall associated with the polygenetic "human predicament" and "Light of Christ" approaches to the problem of religious resemblances. Some have seized upon the resemblance of Christ to other messianic hero figures of all time, or upon resemblances between Joseph Smith and Muhammad or some other religious leader, to prove that these were simply representations of many others who have been inspired. This runs the risk of making the Lord Jesus Christ and the prophet Joseph Smith much easier to explain—they are just two of many equally important personalities.

Hugh Nibley has warned us that by diligent research it may be possible to match all the Christian teachings with the teachings of others. These have been pointed to repeatedly by students of comparative religion "in order to bring Christ [and his prophets] down to the level of everyday experience and supplant the miraculous and embarrassing by the commonplace and reassuring." Contemplating the process of gaining a sure knowledge of the Lord and his prophet, Nibley's colorful and cryptic statement quite accurately applies:

One does not compose music with a sliderule, and the divinity and truthfulness of Christ were never meant to be proved by history, since we are told from the beginning that knowledge comes to one only by direct revelation from the Father in heaven.[39]

Speaking personally, of the five approaches suggested in this chapter I find the diffusionist approach to be the most persuasive explanation of religious similarities in world religions, although in some cases the view that God inspires, loves, and intervenes in behalf of his children everywhere through the influence of the Light of Christ is also compelling. However, there is one aspect of the diffusionist approach which is particularly challenging for Latter-day Saint students. Diffuisonists believe that the human story is essentially a conflict between two states of mind, between those who have been rebellious or indifferent or hostile to God and those who have been custodians of truth—the lovers of God. This is the standard by which the world religions may be measured. Therefore, in each case it must be considered how much the religion has preserved of original revelation and how closely linked the religion may be to the original. Assuming that the Old Testament and Judaism are still very viable in preserving original values and original inspiration, how should the other great religions be ranked? Should first place be assigned to Zoroastrianism, because it passes on a tradition of great antiquity, strict truth, and high morality? Should Zarathustra be followed by the rishis of the Vedas who, though somewhat impaired, are still devoted to God's service, as E. L. Allen has contended?[40] Or, on the other hand, can it be agreed that, among the nations of antiquity who stood nearest to—or at least very near to—the source of ancient revelations from God, the Chinese must hold a distinguished place? Are there not many remarkable vestiges of great truths to be found in their classical works and in their time-honored religious traditions? As Latter-day Saints begin to investigate the source of Japanese religion seriously and find extraordinary links between them and the peoples of the Old Testament and Book of Mormon, does this not require a significant revision of our perceptions of that people's place in the unfolding of God's work in the latter days?[41]

Among Latter-day Saints who underscore the manifestation of God's influence among all people on an independent and personal basis—either through his spirit or in response to common needs and problems in the human condition—the universality of God is stressed. The whole race of humankind in every land, of every color, and at every stage of culture is not only the offspring of God but is, in the vast compass of his providence, being supported by his love, which reaches from within the limits of humanity's powers to knowledge supreme. Not only is God thought of as having a more universal and direct involvement in the lives of all his children on an individual basis, but also the sense of community among human beings is enhanced. On the other hand, diffusionists tend to stress the eternal struggle between truth and error, between eternal truth and local culture, between God's chosen people and those who are not so chosen, between the revelations of God and the ways in which Latter-day Saints are different from others, rather than upon their common humanity or their dependence on a common Father. Among Latter-day Saint diffusionists there is always the temptation to construe a narrow, exclusive, and arrogant view of themselves and of the church, a view that militates against true brotherhood, the pure love of Christ, the expansion of Zion to the "nethermost" places in the earth, the full acceptance of gospel values in "alien" cultures, and full recognition that the God of Israel is also the God of the whole earth.

By contrast, for those who seem ready to see God's handiwork throughout the world in the lives of wise teachers, poets, philosophers, and scientists and who are happy to believe that all these have a work and mission under an overruling Providence, there are cautions to be made. First, although the Spirit and power of Christ are manifest worldwide, this is not to suggest that the founders and teachers of the great religions of humankind have a full endowment of either light or power. They have not. In Latter-day Saint belief they did not receive the gift of the Holy Ghost or the keys and authority of the holy priesthood, and without these they could not receive revelation and authority to exercise more than preparatory beliefs and practices.[42]

Latter-day Saints believe that God has a living prophet who heads up his kingdom on the earth—and that kingdom is The Church of Jesus Christ of Latter-day Saints. The president of the church is God's mouthpiece—a universal mouthpiece, endowed with the keys of presidency over all affairs dealing with a fulness of God's power and authority throughout the earth.

Still, despite this belief, Latter-day Saints cannot categorically dismiss a religion like Buddhism as a false faith; it, too, has been influenced and illuminated by the Spirit of the Lord, and so have its followers. But there is danger here, also. A friendly and appreciative approach to non–Latter-day Saint Eastern religions carries with it an intrinsic temptation to think that in places like Thailand we must symbolically, if not literally, dress church members like Buddhist monks. Recognition of religious parallels does not imply the need or advisability of such a course. In seeking for that which is "virtuous, lovely, . . . [and] praiseworthy" (Article of Faith 13) within the native faiths, we should not be seeking accommodation or compromise. Others have tried this with no effective benefit. There is no value to either the church or the people of Asia in allowing Jehovah to be accepted into the Buddhist pantheon. There is no gospel benefit in having Jesus Christ identified as an avatar of a Hindu god, as an incarnation of the Buddha, or in any way less than the Son of God, the "[only] name . . . given among men, whereby we must be saved" (Acts 4:12). But despite the prospect of this negative result, the positive implications of using good things in the religions of the world as building blocks for bringing people into a full realization of their own spiritual possibilities must not be ignored.

Notes

This chapter is a revision of my essay originally published under the title "Mormon Views of Religious Resemblances," in *Brigham Young University Studies* 16, no. 4 (Summer 1976): 660–81.

1. H. T. D. Rost, *The Golden Rule: A Universal Ethic* (Oxford: George Ronald, 1986).

2. Bahagavan Das, *The Essential Unity of All Religions* (Banaras, India: Ananda Publishing House, 1947), 272–309.

3. Howard A. Christy, "The Great Commandment: Principle or Platitude?" (unpublished personal essay, Provo, Ut., 1996), 5.

4. From Lionel Giles, *The Analects of Confucius: Translated from the Chinese, with an Introduction and Notes,* collector's ed. (Norwalk, Conn.: Easton Press, 1976), 37.

5. Das, *Essential Unity,* 262.

6. Ezzeddin Ibrahim and Denys Johnson-Davies, trans., *Al-Arba'in al-Nawawiyya/Nawawi's Forty Hadith* (Beirut: The Holy Koran Publishing House, 1976), 56. According to Nawawi, each of the hadith in his collection is one of the "great precepts of religion" and is classified as "sound" in the canonical hadith collections; he adds that "every person wishing to attain the Hereafter should know these Hadith because of the important matters they contain" (23–24). Christy acknowledges James Toronto's help in locating this source.

7. See John A. Widtsoe's introduction to Thomas Cottam Romney, *World Religions in the Light of Mormonism* (Independence, Mo.: Press of Zion's Printing and Publishing Co., 1946), v.

8. Romney, *World Religions,* 64–65.

9. Ibid., 217.

10. Alvin R. Dyer, *This Age of Confusion . . .* (Salt Lake City: Deseret Book, 1965), esp. 15n.

11. Hugh Nibley, *The World and the Prophets* (Salt Lake City: Deseret Book, 1954), 213–14.

12. Ibid., 214–15.

13. Hugh Nibley, *The Message of the Joseph Smith Papyri: An Egyptian Endowment* (Salt Lake City: Deseret Book, 1975), xii.

14. See Mircea Eliade, *Cosmos and History: The Myth of the Eternal Return,* trans. Willard R. Trask (New York: Harper Brothers, Harper Torch Books, 1959), esp. 3–6.

15. Victor Witter Turner, *The Drums of Affliction: A Study of Religious Processes among the Ndembu of Zambia* (London: Oxford University Press, 1968), 5–8.

16. John A. Widtsoe, "Temple Worship," *Utah Genealogical and Historical Magazine* 12 (April 1921): 62.

17. Quoted in Joseph Fielding Smith, *The Way to Perfection,* 12th ed. (Salt Lake City: Deseret Book, 1963), 45.

18. Ibid., 30.

19. Ibid., 45.

20. Joseph F. Smith, *Gospel Doctrine,* 8th ed. (Salt Lake City: Deseret Book, 1949), 12–14.

21. J. F. Rychlak, *Introduction to Personality and Psychotherapy: A Theory-Construction Approach* (Boston: Houghton Mifflin, 1973), 143–47; see also C. G. Jung, *The Collected Works of C. G. Jung,* ed. Herbert Read, Michael Fordham, and Gerhard Adler, 17 vols. (London: Routledge and Kegan Paul, 1953–73), particularly vol. 9, *The Archetypes and the Collective Unconscious* (1959), and vol. 11, *Psychology and Religion: West and East* (1958).

22. Truman G. Madsen, *Conscience and Consciousness,* Commissioner's Lecture Series (Provo, Ut.: Brigham Young University Press, 1973), 5.

23. See Charles W. Penrose, "Partaking of the Lord's Supper, Etc." May 1, 1880, in Brigham Young et al., *Journal of Discourses,* 26 vols. (1842–96; reprint, Salt Lake City: n.p., 1967), 22:85 [hereafter cited as *JD*].

24. Brigham Young, "Spiritual Gifts, Etc.," December 3, 1854, in *JD,* 2:139.

25. Emphasized by Charles W. Penrose, "Revealed Religion," January 14, 1883, in *JD,* 23:346.

26. John Taylor, "Motives and Feelings of the Saints," June 12, 1853, in *JD,* 1:155.

27. George Albert Smith, untitled address, in *One Hundred and Second Semi-annual Conference of The Church of Jesus Christ of Latter-day Saints* (Salt Lake City: The Church of Jesus Christ of Latter-day Saints, 1931), 120.

28. Young, "Spiritual Gifts, Etc.," in *JD,* 2:140.

29. Brigham Young, "Idolatry, Etc.," February 7, 1858, in *JD,* 6:194.

30. Orson F. Whitney, untitled address, in *Ninety-first Annual Conference of The Church of Jesus Christ of Latter-day Saints* (Salt Lake City: The Church of Jesus Christ of Latter-day Saints, 1921), 33. See also Forace Green, comp., *Cowley and Whitney on Doctrine* (Salt Lake City: Bookcraft, 1963), 293.

31. B. H. Roberts, *Defense of the Faith and the Saints,* 2 vols. (Salt Lake City: Deseret News, 1907), 1:512–13.

32. George A. Smith, "The History of Mahomedanism," September 23, 1855, in *JD,* 3:32.

33. Parley P. Pratt, "Mahometanism and Christianity," September 23, 1855, in *JD,* 3:40.

34. Moses Thatcher, "Chinese Classics," *Contributor* 8, no. 8 (June 1887): 301.

35. Matthew Cowley, "The Gospel of Repentance" (address given on KSL radio, July 31, 1927; photocopy of transcript in Special Collections, Harold B. Lee Library, Brigham Young University, Provo, Ut.), 1.

36. Compare 2 Ne. 29:7–12.

37. See Milton R. Hunter, *The Gospel through the Ages* (Salt Lake City: Stevens and Wallis, 1945), 40.

38. Ibid.

39. Nibley, *World and the Prophets*, 16–17.

40. E. L. Allen, *Christianity among the Religions* (Boston: Beacon Press, 1961), 61–62.

41. This is a popular theme among some Japanese Latter-day Saints, and particularly among nisei Japanese and missionaries returned from Japanese fields of labor. Some of the ramifications are suggested in my article "Did Christ Visit Japan?" *Brigham Young University Studies* 10, no. 2 (Winter 1970): 135–58.

42. Spencer J. Palmer, *The Expanding Church* (Salt Lake City: Deseret Book, 1978), 11–12.

Joseph Smith, Jr.

Restoration Fulness 14

Roger R. Keller

As remarked by Lanier Britsch in the foreword to this book, there are so many fine introductory texts on the religions of the world that could be used in any class on world religions that there is little justification for another text, unless there is something unique about it. The authors of this text believe that there is a uniqueness within the pages of this book—a uniqueness that is captured in the title *Religions of the World: A Latter-day Saint View*. The second phrase recognizes the fact that no one really comes to the study of another person's religion with absolute objectivity.

Whether expressed or unexpressed, there is always a dialogue taking place between an author and the religion about which he or she writes. In the prior chapters, we, the authors of this text, have tried to state as objectively and clearly as we possibly could what members of any of the religions would have said about themselves and their faith. We hope we have been successful in that effort. But at the same time, we have recognized that we are Latter-day Saints and that we hold a particular belief system of our own; thus, we want our Latter-day Saint readers to reflect upon the similarities and differences between their own faith and the faiths they are studying. Consequently, each chapter has ended with a section entitled "Latter-day Saint Reflections."

This chapter now seeks to bring those reflections to a culmination. It is written by a Latter-day Saint for Latter-day Saints. It makes no claim to be non-partisan, but seeks to state clearly how Latter-day Saints may appreciate the truth and beauty of other religious faiths while at the same time holding firmly to their own understandings and convictions about God, humankind, the plan of salvation, Jesus Christ, the Atonement, prophets, ordinances, and other gospel matters—or, in a nutshell, hold to the fulness of the gospel as revealed through Joseph Smith.

Persons of other faith traditions are more than welcome to listen in on this inside conversation. We hope that those who do will seek to appreciate our beliefs about our unique place in the realm of religion as we have sought to appreciate their place in that same world. We will assume that it is not necessary to restate what has been said in the prior chapters, and we will not attempt to provide in this limited space a full synopsis of Latter-day Saint theology. There are many sources from which that can be derived. We intend solely to draw attention to the way in which we believe Latter-day Saint thought to be the capstone to the various issues to which human beings have sought answers for millennia.

JOSEPH SMITH

Any discussion of Latter-day Saint contributions to the issues raised by the religions of the world must begin with Joseph Smith, Jr., the first president and prophet of The Church of Jesus Christ of Latter-day Saints, for Latter-day Saints believe that his first vision marks the beginning of God's last interventions on behalf of the human race before Jesus' second coming and the end of the world as we now know it. Latter-day Saints believe that he was an instrument in the hands of God in restoring a fulness of the gospel of Jesus Christ. After he was martyred by a mob at Carthage, Illinois, in June of 1844, John Taylor, who had witnessed the event, made this remarkable statement: "Joseph Smith, the Prophet and Seer of the Lord, has done more, save Jesus only, for the salvation of men in this world, than any other man that ever lived in it" (D&C 135:3).

In comparison with other great religious founders or reformers—Moses, Zarathustra, Gautama, Mahavira, Lao Tzu, Confucius, Muhammad, and Guru Nanak—Joseph Smith was the youngest and most recent. He was born in Sharon, Vermont, on

December 23, 1805. He had little formal education, and his family had little social standing. They were hard-working and God-fearing but not economically well situated. In religious affiliation, some of his family members were Methodists and others were Presbyterians. Although Joseph himself did not formally belong to any church, he reportedly favored Methodism (see JS–H 1:3, 7–8).

Joseph Smith's life did not follow the pattern of most of the other great religious leaders. Most were from wealthy or prominent families. Except for Zarathustra, who was martyred when he was seventy-seven, most of the founders died natural deaths at advanced ages. Moses apparently lived to the age of one hundred and twenty, though the particulars of his death are not known. Lao Tzu's date and place of death are unknown, but he is credited with advanced age. Mahavira died at seventy-two, Gautama at eighty, Confucius at seventy-two, Guru Nanak at seventy, and Muhammad at sixty-two. By contrast, Joseph Smith was thirty-eight—in the prime of life—and his public ministry had lasted only fifteen years when he was martyred.

Joseph Smith's beginnings were humble, but his life was an open book. The events of his life, his experiences, and pronouncements he made are clearly set forth. He was straightforward, unassuming, and consistent. It requires no elaborate interpretations to know where he stood in doctrine and practice. His religious revelations are authenticated not only by an abundance of documents but also by the personal testimony of reliable witnesses, some of whom shared in his experiences.

In 1844, the year Joseph Smith was killed, John Taylor predicted that "from age to age" Joseph Smith's name would "go down to posterity" classed as a "gem . . . for the sanctified," that as "an ambassador of Jesus Christ" he would "touch the hearts of honest men among all nations" (D&C 135:6, 7). As The Church of Jesus Christ of Latter-day Saints has spread across the earth through its missionary efforts, this prophecy has more than been fulfilled. Yet what does it mean that Joseph Smith was an instrument in the hands of God in bringing about a "Restoration fulness"? The Lord answers the question in this way:

> Wherefore, I the Lord, knowing the calamity which should come upon the inhabitants of the earth, called upon my servant Joseph Smith, Jun., and spake unto him from heaven, and gave him commandments . . . that every man might speak in the name of God the Lord, even the Savior of the world; That faith also might increase in the earth; That mine everlasting covenant might be established; That the fulness of my gospel might be proclaimed by the weak and the simple unto the ends of the world, and before kings and rulers. (D&C 1:17, 20–23)

Does this mean that Latter-day Saints are parochial and uninterested in anything God may have done before or apart from the Restoration? Of course not, for that would be to close our eyes to the many truths and the light that we have discovered in the religious traditions explicated in this book. Instead of splendid isolation, we seek after "anything virtuous, lovely, or of good report or praiseworthy" (Article of Faith 13).

GOD'S WORK IN THE WORLD

Latter-day Saints often speak of belonging to the one true church, sometimes implying that all other traditions are at best incomplete and at worst without truth. Perhaps a more productive way of looking at the relationship between the Latter-day Saint fulness of the gospel and the truths found in other religions is to realize that the restored gospel encompasses all truth. President Brigham Young stated:

> For me, the plan of salvation must . . . circumscribe [all] the knowledge that is upon the face of the earth, or it is not from God. Such a plan incorporates every system of true doctrine on the earth, whether it be ecclesiastical, moral, philosophical, or civil: it incorporates all good laws that have been made from the days of Adam until now; it swallows up the laws of nations, for it exceeds them all in knowledge and purity; it circumscribes the doctrines of the day, and takes from the right and the left, and brings all truth together in one system, and leaves the chaff to be scattered hither and thither.[1]

In addition, President Spencer W. Kimball taught that all persons are on a pathway to the fulness of the gospel. He stated, "[W]e believe that God has given and will give to all peoples sufficient knowledge to help them on their way to eternal salvation, either in this life or in the life to come."[2] He knew that all people are children of God. Again, he stated:

> Based upon ancient and modern revelation, The Church of Jesus Christ of Latter-day Saints gladly teaches and declares the Christian doctrine that all men and women are brothers and sisters, not only by blood relationship from common mortal progenitors but also as literal spirit children of an Eternal Father.[3]

Thus, God leaves none of his children without guidance. All are given opportunities in life to grow, and all are given guidance sufficient for that growth, if they choose to follow it.

It is dangerous to speculate, based on appearances, why some are born into The Church of Jesus Christ of Latter-day Saints while others are born into Hindu, Buddhist, Protestant, or Roman Catholic homes. If externals are the basis upon which judgments about valiancy in the premortal life are made, then many of the great martyrs of the Judeo-Christian tradition would appear to be failures. There were no outward signs of success as Jeremiah was imprisoned, as Jesus died on the cross, as Paul was beheaded, as Peter was crucified upside down, or as Joseph and Hyrum Smith were martyred in Carthage. Behind surface appearances in each case lay the mystery of the hand of God moving inexorably toward his chosen ends.

Just as surely, the hand of God must move in the lives of all of God's children. B. H. Roberts is undoubtedly correct when he says that the situation in life to be sought most diligently is the one which will enable a person to grow the most.[4] While speculative, it would appear that Heavenly Father places all his children in situations that maximize their potential for growth. In whatever situations persons may find themselves, then, they are there to grow closer to their Heavenly Father and to be more like Christ through the workings of the Holy Ghost. Human beings, with their limited perspectives and understandings, cannot fathom the intricacies of God's plan for each of his children. We should be satisfied to know that he desires none to be lost but leads all toward himself, so long as persons are willing to follow his guidance. He does not abrogate agency, but neither is his time human time. His guidance begins in the premortal life, is present throughout mortality, and continues into the postmortal existence. Because there are many who are taught and receive the fulness of the gospel after death (D&C 138), it is imperative that Latter-day Saints do temple work for the dead. By that very act, Latter-day Saints recognize the truth of President Kimball's statement that all persons can be on the path to eternal salvation. Therefore, no human being has the right to judge another or to be arrogant in his or her faith. Only God can judge the human heart. President Howard W. Hunter stated:

In the gospel view, no man is alien. No one is to be denied. There is no underlying excuse for smugness, arrogance, or pride. Openly scorning the pettiness and intolerance of rival religious groups, the Prophet Joseph Smith said in an editorial:

"While one portion of the human race is judging and condemning the other without mercy, the Great Parent of the universe looks upon the whole of the human family with a fatherly care and paternal regard; He views them as His offspring, and without any of those contracted feelings that influence the children of men, causes 'His sun to rise on the evil and on the good, and sendeth rain on the just and on the unjust.' He holds the reins of judgment in His hands; He is a wise Lawgiver, and will judge all men, not according to the narrow, contracted notions of men, but, 'according to the deeds done in the body whether they be good or evil,' or whether these deeds were done in England, America, Spain, Turkey, or India."[5]

Taking this view, it is best that we assume God's hand to be in all the traditions we have examined, that their adherents are children whom God loves, and that he desires them to be with him. That being the case, we should rejoice in the truths to be found in those faiths, while simultaneously recognizing the responsibility we possess as Latter-day Saints to share the fulness of the gospel with all of God's children. That fulness is found only in Jesus Christ, who is accessed completely only through The Church of Jesus Christ of Latter-day Saints.

Therefore, what does the restored gospel have to say about the topics which have been discussed in each of the preceding chapters? This final chapter explores how the restored gospel completes or clarifies truths found in the world's other great religions.

KNOWLEDGE OF THE ULTIMATE

The Religions of the World

Some of the religions examined have no belief in a deity. Even so, they are all concerned with what they consider to be ultimate reality, whether that reality concerns the world in which we live (traditional Confucianism, philosophical Taoism) or looks beyond the forms of this world (Jainism, Buddhism). Thus, the issue for the nontheistic traditions is the question of how people come to a knowledge of the ultimate, however that ultimate may be defined. For those religions that are theistic (Hinduism, Sikhism, Shinto, religious Taoism, Zoroastrianism, Judaism, Christianity, Islam) the concern is with how persons may gain knowledge of the will of God or the gods who are ultimate for them.

In the nontheistic world of Confucianism and philosophical Taoism, knowledge comes through individual teachers such as Confucius or Lao Tzu. The teachings of Confucius were written and codified by disciples after his day, and those writings, insights, and subsequent traditions continue to guide persons who live by the Confucian values today. In contrast, the mystical nature of philosophical Taoism leaves great latitude for individual exploration and comprehension—so much latitude, in fact, that the number of those who have been able to follow the way, or find the ultimate, seems to have been limited.

Buddhism stands as a middle ground between the nontheistic and the theistic traditions. Adherents of Theravada Buddhism, the form that the Buddha himself taught, gain knowledge of the way by following the Buddha's example and teachings. However, access to the ultimate comes only through individual effort. Mahayana Buddhism, on the other hand, has a plethora of enlightened helping beings who, at a minimum, may show the way or who, at the other extreme, may actually become incarnate in order to guide people. The obvious example of the latter is the Dalai Lama, the incarnation of Avalokitesvara.

In the theistic realm, the will of God may be made known through scriptures, through spiritual mentors (gurus, rabbis, rebbes), through divinely appointed persons like the pope, or through ecclesiastical councils. Few of these traditions clearly agree about the way in which knowledge of the ultimate can be acquired. Opinions are numerous and may vary widely, both between religions and within them, as shown in the preceding chapters.

Latter-day Saints

Revelation

In contrast to the above, Latter-day Saint thought states clearly how knowledge of ultimate things is obtained. It comes through revelation, the most dramatic example being Joseph Smith's first vision. As Joseph sought knowledge of God's will, the Father and the Son appeared to him. Thus, much of the knowledge of God for Latter-day Saints, particularly about the nature of God, is derived from Joseph's experience in the Sacred Grove and from later revelations.

At the personal and perhaps the most important level, Latter-day Saints also know that individuals may receive direct revelation from God for themselves or for those areas over which they have stewardship. However, individual revelation is always checked against corporate (ecclesiastical) revelation. In the church, there is a creative tension between individual and ecclesiastical revelation. Organizational leaders are supplied with counselors, so that there are checks and balances, as well as consensus on what the Lord desires. Decisions are sustained by those directly affected. Problems are solved by studying the depository of revelation (the scriptures), by seeking direct guidance from the Lord, and by counseling with others.

In the end, Latter-day Saints know that God has placed one man at a time on the earth to be his spokesperson for the whole church. Certain things are left to individual discretion, but on the things that really matter in life there is clear guidance from a living prophet and a quorum of twelve apostles under his direction. Thus, the Restoration fulness provides the faithful with a clear knowledge of God's will for them as they align themselves with the prophet and apostles. Such clarity is unique within the religious world.

Scripture

The revelations received by previous prophets and apostles have been recorded over time and are captured in what Latter-day Saints call the Standard Works. Because God never ceases to speak, there may well be new additions to the Standard Works. It is this openness of the canon that marks Latter-day Saints as unique among the world's religions and is the realm in which Joseph Smith left his greatest personal mark. Through his hands and by the power of God, we have received the Doctrine and Covenants, the Pearl of Great Price, and the Book of Mormon, the latter being characterized by Joseph Smith as "the most correct of any book on earth, and the keystone of our religion, and a man would get nearer to God by abiding by its precepts, than by any other book."[6] Because the content of these books was given directly by revelation and not through limited human powers of translation, much as Muslims believe the Qur'an was given, they hold a special place within Latter-day Saint thought. They are perfect and without error in their original English form. They are authoritative for all Latter-day Saints, and their precepts may be altered or enhanced only by the living prophet of the church. They contain the critical doctrines of the Restoration, which state with greater clarity than any other writings the central doctrines related to Jesus Christ, the plan of salvation, the Atonement, and doctrines of the future.

THE DIVINE

The Religions of the World

The purpose of both scripture and revelation in any faith is to lead persons to a clearer understanding of and closer contact with the divine. As mentioned, concepts of deity in the religions of the world range from no deities through traditions with multiple gods to traditions with a pronounced monotheism. Jainism, Theravada Buddhism, philosophical Taoism, and traditional Confucianism have no deities or helping beings in their scheme of things. Essentially, the benefits of these religions derive from human exertions.

On the other end of the spectrum lie Judaism and Islam, with clear concepts of one all-powerful divine figure. This God controls beginnings and endings. He summons all people to himself, but only those who live by the commandments which he gives are ultimately admitted to his presence or become one with him.

In between these two extremes are those traditions which have multiple helping beings or concepts of a godhead with more than one person within it. Within Mahayana and Vajrayana Buddhism, there is a recognition that frail human beings need some form of assistance. Thus, the heavenly bodhisattvas and dyani buddhas provide that assistance. However, they are not themselves the ultimate, and no concept of an ultimate divine being of any variety is to be found in Buddhism.

Within Shinto are the kami. They are a divine power within the natural world which can be individualized and whose assistance may be sought. However, they are not ultimate beings. Even Amaterasu, the sun goddess, does not fill that role, for she comes from kami who existed prior to her. In addition, the kami do not prescribe ethical norms for their followers. Purity seems to be their fundamental concern—a purity which falls within the realm of ritual rather than ethics. The values by which the people of Japan have lived have been found more within the bushido code than in demands made by the kami.

Hinduism offers a different perspective on the divine. Some Hindus talk about one divine entity—Brahman—behind all things, but normally Brahman is not personalized. Whatever personhood Brahman may have is manifest in divine figures who are extensions of the impersonal Brahman, thereby accommodating the inability of humans to comprehend the abstract Brahman. According to some currents of Hindu belief, these gods may involve themselves directly in human life, as Vishnu did through his avatars, or as Shiva might do in destroying evil. When they do, there are usually guiding principles for life which derive from them. However, in the end—and keeping in mind that there is no normative Hinduism—Brahman still remains abstract and distant for most Hindus.

Zoroastrianism, while traditionally viewed as purely monotheistic, has in its history blurred that line. Sometimes the dualism between Ahura Mazda and Angra Mainyu or the distinction between Ahura Mazda and the Amesha Spentas appears to create a multiplicity of deities. However, assuming that Ahura Mazda is in control of all things, he is a God who gives ethical directions to humans. In that way, he is like Jehovah within Judaism, Allah within Islam, or True Name within Sikhism. All give ethical and moral directions to their followers, and the followers are judged against those directions. All four deities have revealed themselves to prophetic figures and delivered their will through these prophets—a will which is codified in a scriptural form.

Christians continue the tradition of Judaism, but the understanding of God becomes modified. As has been seen, traditional trinitarian Christians believe there is one God who has made himself known in Jesus Christ. In doing so, however, Christians gain a unique knowledge about the divine. God is one, but at the same time the Father, Jehovah, has a Son, Jesus, who entered this world, died for its sins, and was raised from the dead. He is present with the community through the Holy Ghost. This God is composed of three persons of the same essence, as defined by the word homoousios.

Latter-day Saints

As a result of Joseph Smith's first vision, Latter-day Saints hold a different understanding of the nature of the Godhead from other Christians, one that does not depend on the philosophical concept of homoousios. Two distinct personages appeared to Joseph and identified themselves as the Father and the Son; both of them had physical form, a revelation that profoundly alters the perceptions of God in traditional Christianity, Judaism, and Islam. In addition, Latter-day Saints understand that the God of the Old Testament is not Jehovah, the Father, as held by the majority of Christians. The Son, the second person of the Godhead, is Jehovah. This means that the unique knowledge Christians gain through Jesus Christ, according to Latter-day Saint Christians, is that the God of the Old Testament, Jehovah, *has a Father!* Thus, while humanity has never been separated from the Son (Jehovah) and the Holy Ghost, the fall of Adam and Eve cut human beings off from the Father. This separation was rectified through the Atonement made by the incarnate Jehovah, who is Jesus Christ. This identification between Jesus and Jehovah has not been made in traditional Christian theology, although Jesus claims for himself the divine name of I Am, delivered in Exodus 3:14, throughout the Gospel of John (see, for example, John 8:58–59).

Another area of difference between Latter-day Saints and the monotheistic faiths lies in the realm of God's creative activity. Jews, Muslims, and traditional Christians generally hold that God creates everything out of nothing—the doctrine of *creatio ex nihilo.* Latter-day Saints, however, claim that matter, energy, and intelligence, as well as the members of the Godhead, are eternal—that is, they have no beginning or end. Thus, God does not create in the absolute sense, but organizes already pre-existing elements. It is through the organization of these elements that the world, for example, was brought into being.

In the end, Latter-day Saints have a great deal in common with all Christians in their beliefs about deity, but they clarify speculation concerning the relationships between the members of the Godhead, as well as clarifying the natures of those members. The creative activity of God is also clarified as being a process of organizing the elements of the universe, rather than bringing them into being from nothing. All this leads to a concept of deity with some striking differences from that of mainstream Christians.

These differences have led some traditional Christians to claim that Latter-day Saints are not Christians. Such a charge fails to recognize the absolute centrality of Christ and his atonement in Latter-day Saint thought—the very elements which

should be the determining criteria of who is Christian. As has been stated, the doctrine of the Trinity with its accompanying emphasis on homoousios is a philosophical construct that Latter-day Saints do not believe can be defended on the basis of scripture. Thus, they deny its validity. By contrast, Latter-day Saints find it difficult to get around the anthropomorphic language of the scriptures, thus leading them to believe in a God who possesses physical form. They see Joseph Smith's first vision as doing away with philosophical speculation about God, because God made himself visible to all who will hear the witness of those who have seen him. Joseph's vision simply confirms Stephen's vision as he was martyred (Acts 7:56). These differences, however, do not change the central reality of Christ and his atoning sacrifice. Consequently, Latter-day Saints find themselves puzzled over the charge that they are not Christians.

HUMAN BEINGS

Perhaps the greatest contribution of Latter-day Saint theology is to the understanding of the human being. It is characteristic of Latter-day Saint doctrine to answer three questions: From whence do people come? Why are they living mortal lives? Where will they go after death? Every religion tries to answer these questions, but Latter-day Saint answers have a consistency and a clarity that is not always found in other religious traditions. To explore the Latter-day Saint contributions to the understanding of who and what human beings are, Latter-day Saint categories will be used as headings. Reflections from other traditions will be utilized as they are appropriate to the category.

Premortality

Among the religions which have their roots in India—Hinduism, Jainism, Buddhism, and Sikhism—there is the belief that people enter this mortal life having had previous existences. They may have been gods, humans, animals, or even vegetation at some time in their prior lives. This doctrine is known as reincarnation. Fundamentally, what it seeks to answer are the questions surrounding the inequities of life. Why are some persons born to poverty, while others are born to wealth? Why do some people die young, while others live to an old age? Why do some persons suffer from debilitating diseases, while others are healthy all their lives? In addition, the doctrine of reincarnation deals with the reality that human beings do not attain perfection in a single mortal lifespan. Thus, the Indian answer to the question "From whence do we come?" is that we come from a previous life and probably from many previous existences.

The monotheistic faiths of Zoroastrianism, Judaism, Christianity, and Islam, however, all hold that human life, the wedding of spirit and body, starts at conception or shortly thereafter, with no prior existence. The possible exception to this may be Zoroastrianism. Thus, the differences in life between persons are a product of their existence in mortality, rather than the result of goodness or badness in some former existence.

In contrast with both the reincarnational and theistic traditions, Latter-day Saints understand that they are eternal beings with intelligence coeternal with God's, beings who existed in spirit form in a premortal world. They believe that they lived with their Heavenly Father in that world and began the process of growth there. This was the beginning of their progression. Further, like the Indian-based religions, Latter-day Saints understand that perfection is not attained in a single mortal lifetime; however, their answer to that imperfection is not reincarnation. Instead, they speak of eternal progression. They hold that growth begins in premortality (D&C 138:56) and continues both in mortality and in a postmortal life. However, that growth is rendered possible by the Atonement; hope for attaining perfection lies in Christ's perfection, not in people's own abilities. Lehi tells his son Jacob:

Wherefore, how great the importance to make these things known unto the inhabitants of the earth, that they may know that there is no flesh that can dwell in the presence of God, save it be through the merits, and mercy, and grace of the Holy Messiah, who layeth down his life according to the flesh, and taketh it again by the power of the Spirit, that he may bring to pass the resurrection of the dead, being the first that should rise. (2 Ne. 2:8)

Additionally, a premortal existence does not necessarily account directly for the differences between people, as does the law of karma. Despite some views to the contrary, it is not possible to look at the external circumstances of people and attribute their suffering or misfortune to something they did in their premortal lives. Good people do suffer, and the book of Job was written for the express purpose of making that point clear. In modern times, President Howard W. Hunter suffered greatly, yet he was undoubtedly a righteous man. All that can be said with certainty is that all persons who enter this world have proven themselves valiant for Christ in the premortal life. It may also be stated that certain persons were foreordained to leadership roles in the church in their premortal lives (D&C 138:55), but even so, that did not abrogate their agency nor remove their responsibility to reaffirm their acceptance of those roles as mortals. Beyond these points, one cannot safely go. Little is said clearly or unequivocally in the Standard Works on this issue.

It is a unique contribution of Latter-day Saint theology to the Christian world to affirm the premortal existence of human beings in the heavenly realms. That affirmation gives greater meaning to mortality than is found in other Christian communions, if it is realized that mortality is the second step in the growth of a human being. While there is much truth in the Shorter Catechism's statement that the "chief end of man is to enjoy God and glorify him forever,"[7] Latter-day Saints understand that glorification takes place through the growth of the human being from eternity to eternity.

Created in the Image of God

It is within the Judeo-Christian-Islamic world that one finds the concept that human beings are created in the image of God. Yet among all three traditions, God is normally held to be without form. Thus, the "image" which human beings bear has often been defined as reason, the ability to comprehend symbolic meanings, or the ability to relate with one another and with God. Latter-day Saints, however, maintain that the image of God is in fact a physical image. Based on knowledge derived from Joseph Smith's first vision and subsequent revelations, both the Father and the Son have bodies of flesh and bones.

The two positions are not mutually exclusive, and both contain truth which should be examined. Clearly, the first vision of Joseph Smith establishes that both the Father and the Son have physical form. Thus, humans are created in the physical image of God. However, it is not just the shape of human beings that makes them truly human. Without the ability to reason and to relate to one another and to the members of the Godhead, human beings would be no more than just another species of animal. The "image of God," then, must capture the attributes of reason and relationships, as well as form, in order to differentiate humans from the animal world. The viewpoints of Latter-day Saint Christians and persons of the Jewish, traditional Christian, and Islamic faiths are all worthy of consideration as one ponders what it means to be created "in the image of God."

Purpose of Mortality

None of the religions studied has seen life as a fruitless, pointless affair. It may be hard, but it is not pointless. The major goal in life for the Indian religions is to gain release from the round of rebirths, generally through loss of oneself either in Brahman or in nirvana. In philosophical Taoism and traditional Confucianism, the purpose of life is to live harmoniously in a secular society, while in Shinto the goal is to live in harmony with the kami in this life. In these three traditions there is no particular sense of life beyond death, for life is to be lived for the present moment. To gain a sense of an afterlife, they usually combine their thinking with Mahayana or Vajrayana Buddhism. However, religious Taoism brings in the thought of some kind of life after death.

The monotheistic religions present to their adherents the goal to live in the presence of God after the death of the mortal body. Thus, life's purpose is to live in such a way that one may gain the presence of God. For each, this means living an ethical life as defined by God. When persons fall short of that goal, each of these religions believes that sinners may turn to God in repentance and be forgiven.

Christians, however, add the dimension of the Atonement. If God's law is broken, Christians do not believe that repentance alone is sufficient to atone for the breaking of that law. If God commands and that command is broken, then justice must have its due. A penalty beyond mere repentance must be paid. For Christians who turn to Christ, who believe that he can remove their sins, and who repent with a broken heart and a contrite spirit, the Atonement becomes effective and pays for their sins. Thus, justice is paid by Christ's sufferings, and mercy is given to sinners through Christ's substitutionary atonement.

Latter-day Saints, however, carry this process further. While agreeing with all that has been said above about the Atonement, they add more to a discussion that has exercised Christians for centuries. It has been asked whether the Atonement is *unconditionally* effective for all persons or whether it is only *conditionally* effective for those who turn to Christ. The Latter-day Saint answer is that it is both unconditional and conditional. To understand this, however, we need to examine the nature of the Fall.

The Fall

For Latter-day Saints, the fall of Adam and Eve was not a disaster, as it is held to be in all other Christian traditions, but rather was the absolute prerequisite to human growth and development. Premortal humans had to leave their heavenly home, enter mortality, receive a body, be tempted and tried so that they might grow, come to their savior Jesus Christ, and fulfill his commandments for living a righteous life. If they were to do that, the path back to the Father would be open for them. First, however, the way to mortality had to be opened. This was the contribution which Adam and Eve made to the human family. They blazed the path to mortal life through the Fall.

While they were yet in the premortal realm, Adam and Eve were commanded to "[b]e fruitful, and multiply, and replenish the earth, and subdue it, and have dominion over the fish of the sea, and over the fowl of the air, and over every living thing that moveth upon the earth" (Moses 2:28). Upon being placed in the Garden of Eden, Adam was given a second command: "Of every tree of the garden thou mayest freely eat, But of the tree of the knowledge of good and evil, thou shalt not eat of it" (Moses 3:16–17). But with this second command, Adam was given a choice: "[N]evertheless, thou mayest choose for thyself, for it is given unto thee; but, remember that I forbid it, for in the day thou eatest thereof thou shalt surely die" (Moses 3:17).

What were Adam and Eve to do? They could remain in the Garden of Eden as long as they did not eat of the tree of the knowledge of good and evil, but they could not fulfill the prior command to replenish the earth if they did. Thus, they exercised the choice given them by God and ate of the fruit, thereby forcing their eviction from the garden and from the presence of the Father, as well as bringing upon themselves and their posterity the death of the mortal body. Eve sums up the necessity of the Fall when she says, "Were it not for our transgression we never should have had seed, and never should have known good and evil, and the joy of our redemption, and the eternal life which God giveth unto all the obedient" (Moses 5:11). Their decision, however, brought upon all their posterity two consequences: temporal death and spiritual death. Temporal death means that all persons must die physically. Spiritual death means that all persons are separated from the presence of God the Father, but not from the presence of the other two members of the Godhead—Jehovah and the Holy Ghost (D&C 29:41–42).

The Unconditional Effects of the Atonement

It is the universal consequences of Adam and Eve's choice for which Christ's suffering, death, and resurrection atone *unconditionally*. The second Article of Faith states: "We believe that men will be punished for their own sins, and not for Adam's transgression." In order for this to be true, Christ must have abolished for all humanity, whether they wanted it or not, the effects of both temporal and spiritual death. Latter-day Saints believe that he did precisely that. By his resurrection he assures that all persons who have ever lived will have their bodies and souls reunited and that they will have immortality. Secondly, by his substitutionary atonement, he reopened the way to God the Father for all persons unconditionally. All will return to the Father for judgment. The only question will be whether they will be permitted to stay in his presence.

The Conditional Effects of the Atonement

The purpose of mortal life was for persons to grow before God. To do so meant separation from God the Father and the death of the body. As discussed, those effects have been unconditionally removed by Christ. He did not, however, remove unconditionally the effects of people's own sins. These they must deal with themselves, *unless* they draw upon his atonement. The *conditional* effects of the Atonement may pay for the sins of individuals *if* they fill the requirements necessary to appropriate them.

People may stand before God either with arrogant pride or with abject humility. The parable of the Pharisee and the tax collector is a good example of these two stances. The Pharisee boasted in pride before God, while the tax collector beat his breast in sorrow and repentance. According to Jesus, the latter went away justified (Luke 18:9–14). If persons stand before God in humility, they will want to do what God asks of them. Latter-day Saints believe that God has some specific requirements, if persons wish to avail themselves of the Atonement to cover their own sins. The first requirement is that persons must have faith in Jesus Christ as their Savior and Lord. If they have such faith, then humble repentance for past sins—the second requirement—will immediately follow. If persons have faith and repent, then they will want to enter the kingdom of God through the ordinance of baptism for the remission of sins—the third step—under the hands of a person holding God's authority to baptize. Fourth, they will want to receive the Holy Ghost, as they are commanded to do, through another authorized representative of the Lord, who lays his hands upon their heads as he confirms them members of The Church of Jesus Christ of Latter-day Saints. Finally, they will want to endure to the end of their lives in faithfulness to Christ as they live in a way that reflects Christ's life; this sort of life would include serving as saviors on Mount Zion through participation in temple work. All these elements together are called the fulness of the gospel of Christ (see 2 Ne. 31; 3 Ne. 27:13–22).

If persons do these things, then the Atonement becomes fully effective for them. Justice is satisfied because Christ pays the penalty for their sins, and a fulness of joy in the presence of the Father and the Son is open to them. If, however, persons choose to oppose God's will and try to attain salvation through some path other than the first principles of the gospel, which include the prescribed saving ordinances as performed by those holding proper authority, the conditional portion of the Atonement will not be effective for them. They will suffer for their own sins. Justice will be only partially satisfied, because persons cannot fully atone for all their sins. As a consequence, a fulness of joy with the Father will not be open to them.

This pattern is accepted by most Christians, who believe in the conditional character of the Atonement. However, Latter-day Saints differ from their Christian brothers and sisters in one specific area. All Christians believe that persons appropriate the Atonement into their lives through faith and repentance. Only Latter-day Saints believe that God has prescribed certain priesthood ordinances which people must receive or fulfill to demonstrate their faith and obedience to God. Those ordinances are baptism by immersion, the laying on of hands to receive the Holy Ghost, additional temple ordinances which point to Christ, and endurance in faith to the end of one's mortal life. Latter-day Saints believe so completely in the essential nature of these ordinances that they maintain that they must be done by proxy even for the dead. In addition, the ordinances for both the living and the dead can only be done by those holding the authority from God to perform them. That authority may be found only within The Church of Jesus Christ of Latter-day Saints, as will be discussed under the next main heading.

Postmortal Life

Most of the religions studied assume that there is some sort of existence after death. It may be another life on earth, as in the Indian religions which believe in reincarnation. It may be an existence with a heavenly figure, as in the monotheistic faiths or as in Mahayana Buddhism. It may be a more shadowy, less well defined existence, as in religious Taoism. Obviously, in their beliefs about the afterlife Latter-day Saint Christians are closest to Christians of other traditions. However, Catholics and Protestants do not have as much information about life after death as do Latter-day Saints, who possess the Restoration scriptures.

Based on the information in the Bible, Protestants generally hold that following death persons either go to be with God in heaven or are separated from him spiritually in some way, perhaps going to a place of eternal torment called hell. Most hold also that there will be a literal resurrection of all the dead and that they will continue in either heaven or hell as embodied beings, although some do doubt the doctrine of a literal resurrection.

Roman Catholics have a more complex view of life after death. To the realities of the resurrection and of heaven and hell, their theology adds two places known as purgatory and limbo. Limbo is a place of natural joy and until recently was generally believed to be the place to which unbaptized infants went. This doctrine has been undergoing revision. Purgatory is a place of cleansing for those who are not yet prepared to enter heaven, their ultimate destination. Prayers of the faithful may help those residing in this realm to prepare themselves.

Because of latter-day revelations, Latter-day Saints have a clearer understanding of what awaits persons after death. First, they know that there is a spirit world composed of paradise and spirit prison into which all persons enter. Those persons who have heard and accepted the fulness of the gospel with its ordinances will enter paradise (Alma 40:12, 14; D&C 138:12). These persons then have the privilege of spreading the gospel to those in spirit prison, who upon acceptance of the gospel will await the completion of their proxy temple work. Once their ordinance work is done, they will then be able to enter paradise to await the last judgment (D&C 76:73; 138:8–10, 18–21, 28–37). In the meantime, they will probably continue the missionary work in spirit prison (D&C 138). It appears that there may be different grades of spirit prison, the lowest being a hell where people suffer for their sins, but not without the hope of future release (D&C 76:84, 106).

Generally, Latter-day Saints speak of the "first resurrection" as being at the time of Jesus' second coming. However, Alma points out to Corianton that he does not know how many resurrections there may be, though he does know that all will rise (Alma 40:5). In reality, the first resurrection was at the time of Jesus' resurrection, when righteous persons who lived before him were raised from the dead (Matt. 27:52–53). There will also be a resurrection of the righteous at the time of Jesus' return in glory (D&C 29:13; 76:50–53). A final resurrection of the unjust will occur at the time of the last judgment, so that all will stand before the Father and the Son as resurrected beings (D&C 29:26–27; 76:85). They will then be judged and given the final state which they have desired by their relationship to Christ and by their actions (Alma 29:4; 41:5).

The additional understanding that Latter-day Saints possess about the life following the final judgment is that there are three degrees of glory in which resurrected beings will dwell: the celestial, the terrestrial, and the telestial. Those persons who come to the Father through Christ and the ordinances and have lived as Christ has called upon them to live will dwell in the celestial kingdom as gods, having eternal life, as do the Father and the Son. Those who have been honorable but have chosen not to appropriate the conditional effects of the Atonement in the manner in which the Father has prescribed will dwell in terrestrial glory, there enjoying the presence of the Son. Lastly, those who have lived evil lives will dwell in telestial glory, where the Holy Ghost is accessible. Some very few, known as "the sons of perdition," may be assigned to outer darkness, but what this classification entails is not specifically stated (D&C 76). In essence, Latter-day Saints equate salvation with celestial glory, where the full potential of people as children of God is realized. In a sense, those who enter any lower degree are damned, for they are banished from the presence of the Father. Even so, even the telestial glory is greater than anyone can possibly imagine (D&C 76:109–12).

It is dangerous to try to assign persons to the degrees of glory, for only God knows a person's heart and soul. However, the Latter-day Saint contribution to the understanding of life after death is that there is a God who is both just and merciful and wills to give to his children whatever they honestly seek for themselves. In the final analysis, both spirit prison (including hell) and paradise give up their dead to the resurrection. The final judgment gives some degree of glory to virtually all except the sons of perdition, thus making the Latter-day Saint concept of grace more all-encompassing than that of almost any other religious tradition.

AUTHORITY

Priesthood

As has been seen throughout this book, few of the religious traditions studied put great stress on a centralized authority embodied in a single person. Hindus may follow a guru, but there are many gurus and many paths, all of which may be equally efficacious. Jainism and Buddhism both have founders as models. Buddhism has individual teachers, and the monastic structure may have a central authority within a country, but not over Buddhism as a whole. Today, the nearest individual to a spokesperson for Buddhism would be the Dalai Lama, but that is more a tribute to his personality and character than to any designated authoritative role within Buddhism. No central authority exists in Confucianism, Taoism, or Shinto, although certain individuals may be respected.

Within the monotheistic world, centralized authority to lead or rule in the name of God is rare. Zoroastrians may respect the priests of an ancient fire temple, but those men have little general authority. Judaism has no central governing figure, nor do Islam and Sikhism. Authority for all three lies more within books and traditions than with specific people. Within Christianity, only the Roman Catholics and the Latter-day Saints have worldwide, authoritative structures with a central figure at their heads. Both realize that authority must be passed by legitimate priesthood holders from generation to generation. Just as the Latter-day Saints trace their roots back through the current prophet to Joseph Smith, to Peter, James, and John, and to Christ, so also the Catholics trace their authority back from the current pope to Peter and to Christ.

Who is correct? Do both Catholics and Latter-day Saints hold the full authority to act on behalf of God? Certainly God is active through the Catholic church, for no other church today is as close to Latter-day Saints on critical issues of morality and social conduct as the Catholics. Where, then, lies the point of difference? In part, it is in the very structure of the churches. Latter-day Saints believe that Jesus, during his earthly life, actually showed the world what his church's structure should be. The Church must have, at a minimum, twelve apostles or special witnesses of the Lord at all points in its history. That unique element vanished from the early church toward the end of the first century C.E.

Roman Catholics, however, believe that, although the twelve apostles were foundational to the church, the apostolic structure was never intended to be final because of the continuing guidance of God. As the church grew under the guidance of the bishop of Rome (the pope), necessary changes were made to accommodate its worldwide character. Thus, the College of Cardinals has tended to encompass the responsibilities which lie with the Quorum of Twelve and the Quorums of Seventy in the Latter-day Saint communion. Latter-day Saints claim that the failure to maintain Christ's established structure, with the Twelve as special witnesses of Christ and the continuing foundation of the church, broke the authoritative thread of priesthood. Thus, apostasy occurred through the loss of the quorum and its authority. Consequently, the Roman Catholic structure does not hold the authority from God that Catholics claim for it. Perhaps one indication of this, from a Latter-day Saint perspective, is the disunity that one finds within the Catholic church over certain central issues like birth control and the authority of the pope. Despite its centralized organization, the Catholic church does not seem to be uniformly moving in the same direction. Latter-day Saints see this as a sign of the loss of priesthood authority. They believe that the bestowal of the Aaronic and Melchizedek priesthoods on Joseph Smith, as part of the Restoration, returned to mankind the legitimate authority to act in God's behalf.

Living Prophet

Many of the traditions examined have had prophets or charismatic leaders as founders. None of these, with the exception again of Roman Catholicism, has a central figure at its head today. For most traditions, the past controls the present. Nothing new can be injected, except as the community is moved by a majority. Even the pope seems to be only one voice among many in today's Roman Catholic church.

Within The Church of Jesus Christ of Latter-day Saints, however, God speaks to the whole church on issues critical to its faith and actions through one voice: that of the living prophet. He is held by the membership to be the one person on earth who can speak to the entire church in the name of God. To prevent the disorder apparent in other religious traditions, God has made it clear how he will communicate with his church: he will speak through a prophet, as he did in olden days (D&C 1:14; 43:3–4). Latter-day Saints are fond of saying that the Lord is not the master of confusion. The only way to avoid this is to have a central voice speak to all. Granted, there are some Latter-day Saints who do not wish to listen; but that very act puts them on the edge of the church rather than in its mainstream. Such people cease to be vibrant contributors to the church's life and marginalize themselves into positions of no influence. This is the beauty of "following the brethren." All move together in the same direction in unity, love, and fellowship.

Continuing Revelation

The expression "continuing revelation" implies a divine figure who guides his people. There are bhakti traditions within Hinduism which believe that gods give more information to the spiritually mature. Neither Jews nor Muslims believe that God continues to give revelation beyond the revelation at Sinai or that given in the Qur'an. Even within the Christian world, while not denying the continuing guidance of God, most theologians see the once-for-all revelation of God being given in Jesus Christ, and all later work as explication of this original revelation. Latter-day Saints accept that the ultimate revelation of God is found in Jesus Christ, but they do not agree that God has ceased to make new things known to his people through living prophets. Thus, there are many revelations which expand the knowledge of the faithful about the things of God. It is precisely for this reason that the Latter-day Saint canon of scripture remains open, while all other canons are closed.

If God has more to say to his people, then there must be a place to record it and make it authoritative in the life of the Church. There is no book of scripture in any other religious tradition comparable to the Doctrine and Covenants, for that book remains always open, always ready to record a new word from God as it is given through the prophet. Thus, Latter-day Saints live on the cutting edge of revelation, always expectant, always yearning to learn more of the ways and works of the one whom they know to be the God of the universe.

SACRED SPACE

The Religions of the World

All the religions studied have places that they consider to be sacred or special places of worship and learning. Hindus go to their temples to "see the gods" through the images. Jains visit temples to be inspired by the images of the Tirthankaras. Theravada Buddhists visit temples for learning and meditation, while Mahayana and Vajrayana Buddhists may go to temples to worship and seek assistance in daily life. Confucian temples are places of learning, exams, and remembrance, while Taoist temples express variety and individuality in worship. The Shinto temples are places of prayer and union with the kami. Within the monotheistic faiths, Zoroastrian fire temples, Jewish synagogues, Christian churches, Muslim mosques, and Sikh gurdwaras are all places of worship before the one God. Islam, however, has a special place that is so sacred that no one but Muslims may enter there: Mecca. Here they pass through a series of events rooted in scriptural history that teach them about themselves and the God they worship. In Mecca and at Mount 'Arafat, heaven and earth come together as the Muslim stands in the presence of his or her God during the Hajj.

Latter-day Saints

Latter-day Saints, too, have sacred space that only members in good standing may enter. They, too, have places where they can come into the presence of their God and learn through drama the events of sacred history. These places are the Latter-day Saint temples. Their uniqueness lies in the fact that there can be no salvation for anyone, living or dead, without them. They are an extension of the authority found only in the restored priesthood of The Church of Jesus Christ of Latter-day Saints. The ordinances which take place within the temples are essential for salvation.

Like the Muslim Hajj or the Catholic mass, the temple ceremonies bind word and symbol together. One must seek their meaning through the Spirit of God, and that meaning focuses entirely on Jesus Christ and his work for us. Whether persons experience baptism for the dead, washings and anointings, the endowment, or celestial marriage, they are participants in the plan of salvation as God extends power and salvation to the living directly or to the dead by proxy.

The crown of the temple is found in celestial marriage, where a couple is married for time and eternity by a sealer who can bind on earth that which will be recognized in heaven. Only among Latter-day Saints is it recognized clearly that salvation must be shared, first with a spouse and then with all other children of God whom we can influence either through missionary work or proxy work in the temple. There is no individual salvation. The temple teaches that salvation is corporate; we must enter God's presence with our brothers and sisters—his sons and daughters. While other traditions have sacred edifices and sacred space which may point in this direction, God's fully authorized edifices for his saving work are found only among the Latter-day Saints.[8] Marion D. Hanks sums up the temple's importance in these words:

The first and the last of Temple work relates to him [Christ]—the cleansing through his redeeming love (and the blessing), the symbolic journey back into the presence of the divine—all of this coming through the atoning sacrifice of the Savior who declared, "no man cometh unto the Father, but by me" [John 14:6]—and the culminating moment at the altar when clasped hands point toward the indescribable love of the Lord in what he did and what he paid and what he suffered—in all of this

there is only one theme, so far as I am concerned. Every stop along the way where we learn principles and make covenants relates us directly to him and the way he lived and the principles central in his holy life.[9]

Thus, Jesus Christ *is* the temple, for he is the plan of salvation. He is the gospel. He is the one and only way into the presence of the Father. President Ezra Taft Benson has said that the Book of Mormon leads people to Christ and the Doctrine and Covenants leads them to the church.[10] It is the temple and its ordinances that bring them to the Father.

"FALLING AWAY" AND "RESTITUTION OF ALL THINGS"

Non-Christians

Wherefore, all things which are good cometh of God; and that which is evil cometh of the devil; for the devil is an enemy unto God, and fighteth against him continually, and inviteth and enticeth to sin, and to do that which is evil continually. But behold, that which is of God inviteth and enticeth to do good continually; wherefore, every thing which inviteth and enticeth to do good, and to love God, and to serve him, is inspired of God. (Moro. 7:12–13)

All the religions studied have sought to lead people to better, fuller lives. In all of them there are people who do not live up to the ideal, but many lead lives very much in harmony with gospel principles. What is the source of their knowledge of good? The chapter discussing religious similarities offers a variety of suggestions to explain the truths found in various religions. One is that they came from a common root: the gospel as it was made known to Adam. Over time the fulness of the gospel became corrupted, yet much that was true remained in various traditions. Further, God continues to guide his children. He gives them that which they are capable of receiving and adds to it as appropriate. President Howard W. Hunter made the following statement:

Elder Orson F. Whitney, in a conference address, explained that many great religious leaders were inspired. He said: "[God] is using not only his covenant people, but other peoples as well, to consummate a work, stupendous, magnificent, and altogether too arduous for this little handful of Saints to accomplish by and of themselves. . . .

"All down the ages men bearing the authority of the Holy Priesthood—patriarchs, prophets, apostles and others, have officiated in the name of the Lord, doing the things that he required of them; and outside the pale of their activities other good and great men, not bearing the Priesthood, but possessing profundity of thought, great wisdom, and a desire to uplift their fellows, have been sent by the Almighty into many nations, to give them, not the fulness of the Gospel, but that portion of truth that they were able to receive and wisely use."[11]

Spencer W. Kimball similarly stated: "The great religious leaders of the world such as Muhammad, Confucius, and the Reformers, as well as philosophers including Socrates, Plato, and others, received a portion of God's light. Moral truths were given to them by God to enlighten whole nations and to bring a higher level of understanding to individuals."[12]

God also gives his word to all nations and peoples and expects them to record in writing what he gives them.

For behold, thus saith the Lord God: I will give unto the children of men line upon line, precept upon precept, here a little and there a little; and blessed are those who hearken unto my precepts, and lend an ear unto my counsel, for they shall learn wisdom; for unto him that receiveth I will give more; and from them that shall say, We have enough, from them shall be taken away even that which they have. . . . For I command all men, both in the east and in the west, and in the north, and in the south, and in the islands of the sea, that they shall write the words which I speak unto them; for out of the books which shall be written I will judge the world, every man according to their works, according to that which is written. For behold, I shall speak unto the Jews and they shall write it; and I shall also speak unto the Nephites and they shall write it; and I shall also speak unto the other tribes of the house of Israel, which I have led away, and they shall write it; and I shall also speak unto all nations of the earth and they shall write it. (2 Ne. 28:30; 29:11–12)

It would appear that God's goodness and grace know no national or religious boundaries. Yet, despite the universality of God's love, the fulness of the gospel exists nowhere but among Latter-day Saints. It is true that all are on the way toward it, as President Kimball has said. Given that, Latter-day Saints are beginning to look more for the golden threads of truth that God has preserved in the religions of the world than for the falsehoods which may be found therein. If we seek truths, we may better see how God was and is preparing his children for the reception of the fulness of the gospel, and how we may best present it to them. If persons seek truth with all their hearts, they will ultimately be led by God himself to Jesus Christ, who is "the way, *the*

truth, and the life" (John 14:6; emphasis added). Perhaps it could be said that the religions of the world are God's Eliases, or forerunners, to the fulness of the gospel which is to be found in The Church of Jesus Christ of Latter-day Saints. All the good that is found in these other religions, according to Mormon in the passage quoted from the book of Moroni at the beginning of this section, comes from God. If so, God can use that truth to draw his children of all faiths to him.

If this were not true, the work for the dead that Latter-day Saints do in their temples would be meaningless. In order for that work to be valid, it has to be assumed that people of all faiths have the potential to enter the celestial kingdom and that the ordinances by proxy are essential for them to attain that goal. We are taught that persons take into the next life all the intelligence that they gain in mortality (D&C 130:18–19). As Westerners, Latter-day Saints usually view that statement in the context of informational intelligence. However, the Indian religions teach that there is a reality beyond sheer propositional truths. The intelligence that should be gained in this life is not solely factual knowledge about God, as important as that may be. Rather, real intelligence is derived from a relationship with God. It is that relationship, be it shallow or deep, that is carried into the postmortal world. It is this path of relationship with God that all religions of the world walk. People who seek ultimate reality in mortal life are all on the path toward the Father. Those who wish to find that relationship in its fulness will have to come to Christ, either in this life or in the spirit world. Whatever relationship they may have developed with God through their native religions will serve as the foundation for the reception of the fulness of the gospel. Thus, though the religion into which people are born may be incomplete, it can still serve as the springboard to the full gospel for those who follow God's truths as they are made known to them, either in this life or in the next.

Christians

Commonalities

When the relationship between Latter-day Saint Christians and Christians of the Catholic and Protestant traditions is considered, a different set of considerations comes to the fore. The commonality between Latter-day Saints and other Christians is immense. We all claim Christ as Lord. We all believe in a Godhead composed of the Father, the Son, and the Holy Ghost. We all believe that Jesus was the Son of God who suffered and died to work out a substitutionary atonement for the sins of all humanity. We all believe that he was laid in a tomb and that he rose on the third day to rule and reign at the right hand of the Father. With these central truths proclaimed by Catholics and Protestants down through the centuries and held dear by Latter-day Saints, where, then, lie the differences, and what does "falling away" mean in this Christian context?

Differences

One major difference becomes evident when the central nature of ordinances is examined. Attached to that, however, is a second major difference which concerns the loss of priesthood authority. Latter-day Saints hold, as do all other Christians, that Christ established his church when he was on the earth. With Catholics, they agree that the keys of the kingdom were given to Peter. With Protestants, they agree that the church is founded on the confession of faith that Jesus is the Christ, the Son of the living God. They also add, as do most other Christians, that there can be no church without continued guidance by God. What additional news does the Restoration have to proclaim to the world about authority?

The central issue seems to be whether Christ established an authoritative organization that was to be continued, or whether he merely began a church whose organization could be fluid. Both Catholics and Protestants hold that the organization was fluid. In the Roman Catholic tradition, the pope stands as the vicar of Christ at the head of the church. However, there was no attempt to keep a Quorum of Twelve or a Quorum of Seventy. The functions of both of these have been subsumed under the cardinals of the Roman Catholic church, as noted above. Cardinals fill the central role of leadership in the Roman Curia, as well as being the authoritative extension of the pope across the world.

Protestants have structures of all kinds. Some are episcopal in nature—that is, with bishops and a hierarchy—but none of these is worldwide in scope. Most Protestant denominations have their roots in the scriptures of the Old and New Testaments, where they find their prophetic and apostolic authority. This authority may be manifested, however, through a myriad of organizational structures.

The message of the Restoration is that Christ not only established his church on the earth, *but he also defined its authoritative structure.* The church's structure is always to contain a quorum of twelve apostles (compare Luke 6:13–16; John 15:16; 1 Cor. 12:28; Eph. 4:11–16; Acts 1:21–26) to comprise the guiding body of the church, along with a quorum of seventy (Luke 10:1) to act as the missionary arm of the church. Without these authoritative bodies, the church cannot exist with its proper authority. Interestingly, Eusebius, a historian of the Christian church writing in the early fourth century C.E., affirms that Jesus appointed the Twelve and the Seventy:

Our Lord and Saviour, Jesus Christ, not very long after the commencement of his public ministry, elected the twelve, whom he called Apostles, by way of eminence over the rest of his disciples. He also appointed seventy others beside these, whom he sent, two and two, before him into every place and city whither he himself was about to go.[13]

In addition to these two bodies, there is to be a First Presidency, which is drawn out of the Quorum of Twelve, at the head of which stands the living prophet of God. The first to fill this position was Peter.

Loss of Structure

If this was Christ's intent, what happened to the structure? Did he not know that it would vanish in the persecutions of the times? If Paul knew that there would be a falling away (2 Thess. 2:3–4), surely Jesus knew. In fact, Jesus did know that the structure of the church as he established it would be lost; but his intention was to show the world how the church would be structured *when the time came for it to be present in its fulness.* However, that time was not to be in the centuries immediately following his resurrection.

The early Christian era was not the time for the church in its fulness because there was no way, given persecution and the state of transportation and communication, for the church to be unified under one prophetic voice or to maintain its authoritative structure. Thus, Jesus came to work the Atonement and to prepare people for the dispensation when the church could lift its voice through the living prophet to the entire population of the world. That time would come only when a special land had been discovered, when a special nation was established, and when the seeds of worldwide transportation and communication were beginning to bear fruit.

With the close of the first century C.E., the Quorum of Twelve Apostles had vanished from the earth. These men had traveled to the ends of the known world, and many had been martyred. Others probably died in distant lands, there being no possibility of filling their places in the quorum at their deaths. With their deaths and the failure to fill their places, the authority of the Melchizedek priesthood was removed from the earth.

That loss constitutes the heart of the "falling away," sometimes called the "great apostasy," among Latter-day Saints. With the loss of the priesthood came the loss of divine authority to perform the saving ordinances and a concomitant loss of much truth. Again, Eusebius reminds us of this fact:

The same author [Hegesippus], relating the events of the times, also says, that the church continued until then [the early second century] as a pure and uncorrupt virgin; whilst if there were any at all, that attempted to pervert the sound doctrine of the saving gospel, they were yet skulking in dark retreats; but when the sacred choir of apostles became extinct, and the generation of those that had been privileged to hear their inspired wisdom, had passed away, then also the combinations of impious error arose by the fraud and delusions of false teachers. These also, as there was none of the apostles left, henceforth attempted, without shame, to preach their false doctrine against the gospel of truth. Such is the statement of Hegesippus.[14]

However, so that the essential truths of the gospel would not be lost, the Lord permitted and to some extent guided the establishment of the Catholic and Protestant churches, which for seventeen centuries carried the golden threads of the gospel, preparing the way for the dispensation of the church in its fulness, the dispensation of the last days. Without the Catholic and Protestant work of preservation, there could have been no Restoration. With their work of preservation, there was a prepared people, a people seeking for the church of the New Testament, a people seeking God's full authority on earth. Even today, the Catholic and Protestant churches still fulfill this preparatory role. Latter-day Saint missionaries still find that their greatest success is among those peoples who have already met Jesus Christ through the Catholic and Protestant churches.

This fact was dramatically affirmed when Professor Dale LeBaron of Brigham Young University conducted a study in 1988 of African blacks who joined The Church of Jesus Christ of Latter-day Saints immediately following the 1978 revelation on priesthood. Of the 400 converts he interviewed, 398 were already Christians before becoming Latter-day Saints. Two had been Muslims. Without the Catholic and Protestant missionary efforts in black Africa prior to the Latter-day Saint presence, it is safe to say that few of the 400 would have become Latter-day Saints. They were prepared for the fulness of the gospel through the dedicated efforts of Catholic and Protestant missionaries, ministers, and priests.[15]

Even so, the witness of the Restoration is that other Christian traditions, even with the sanction God gave them to keep the flame of the gospel alive, are incomplete and do not possess the full and final authority of God to bind and to loose on earth and in heaven. The testimony of Latter-day Saints is that this power was returned to the earth through Joseph Smith and the establishment of The Church of Jesus Christ of Latter-day Saints.

Preliminary Events for the Restoration

A PREPARED LAND. Essential events had to precede this return. First, there had to be a place in which the Restoration could take place. Non-Christian countries could not fulfill that purpose, even though, like India, they may have had several millennia of spiritual experiences. The Restoration demanded a knowledge of Jesus Christ, and that knowledge did not exist in the non-Christian world. However, in the Christian world, most of the religious traditions were bound to governments. Only certain denominations were welcome in many countries. Thus, a country was needed where religious freedom and pluralism could exist, with no established religion being tied to the governmental forces. The land kept in trust for this very purpose was America (2 Ne. 2:5–9).

With the Declaration of Independence, the Constitution, and the Bill of Rights, the foundation was laid in the United States for the environment which could nurture the Restoration. Yet, despite the country's stated commitment to religious freedom, for a time the Latter-day Saints had to flee the boundaries of the United States and settle the Great Basin in order to practice their faith. Even in the land of religious freedom, religious tolerance ran only so deep. If that was the case in the United States, it is clear how much worse the persecutions would have been in other countries of the world.

COMMUNICATION AND TRANSPORTATION. The second essential factor for the Restoration had to be an improvement in communication and transportation, the very factors—in conjunction with savage persecution—that permitted the dissolution of the Quorum of Twelve in the first century C.E. By the time of Joseph Smith, steam power was beginning to enhance transportation both by rail and by water. In 1838 the telegraph came into being. Postal services were beginning to assure the delivery of mail. Advances such as these made it possible, following Joseph Smith's death on June 27, 1844, to bring the entire Quorum of Twelve back together within about a month. The leadership of the restored church did not falter or fail.

From that time, communication and transportation have only improved worldwide. Today the living prophet can do what was impossible in the first century—speak to the entire church, scattered though it is across the face of the earth. General Authorities can be almost anywhere in the world within twenty-four hours. Phone calls shunted through satellites permit church leaders to communicate instantly concerning any problem or opportunity. Computers permit instant communication; but perhaps even more importantly, they permit the storage of vast amounts of data, especially data related to names of deceased persons, thereby dramatically aiding the work of the temples. The means are now present for a worldwide church organization to exist and to address the needs of people, both living and dead.

The Dispensation of the Church

What was created by the Restoration was the dispensation of the church. These latter days are the time when the Lord intended his church to be on the earth in its fulness. How do we know? Because the structure which the Lord showed us in his lifetime has returned. We see once again the organization of the early church with its First Presidency, its Quorum of Twelve, and its Quorums of Seventies. No other religious organization in the world has this form except The Church of Jesus Christ of Latter-day Saints. With the structure came the full authority of the Melchizedek priesthood and the keys of gathering, binding, and loosing, as well as the restoration of lost truths. While others may claim the fulness of divine authority, Latter-day Saints claim that true authority is tied to a particular, divinely instituted form of government which is found in the New Testament and reconstituted in

these latter days in The Church of Jesus Christ of Latter-day Saints.

Through that structure comes continuing divine revelation dealing with all aspects of life. Through that organization Christ guides his church across the whole earth, giving new truths as needed. Through that organization there is unity and harmony in the church, something found in no other ecclesiastical or religious organization. The living prophet can give guidance and instruction to all members, as can the other General Authorities. Through the organization has arisen the largest full-time volunteer missionary force in the world, which preaches the fulness of the gospel of Jesus Christ to all who will listen, be they Christians or non-Christians. These missionaries tell the world that, while there is much truth preserved by God in their individual religious traditions, those traditions point beyond themselves to a fuller, more complete truth that includes Jesus Christ as Lord, the essential ordinances of salvation, temple work for the dead, missionary work to the living, and a living prophet who does in fact give additional revelation from God to people as they are prepared to hear it. The Church of Jesus Christ of Latter-day Saints is the Restoration fulfillment of all the religious truth which is found in all the traditions we have studied. Nowhere else does the fulness dwell, for nowhere else is found the full authority of God to bless the nations of the earth.

OTHERS' GIFTS TO US

If the fulness of the gospel exists only in The Church of Jesus Christ of Latter-day Saints, why bother to study other religious traditions at all? A good answer is that if Latter-day Saints are to be knowledgeable citizens of the world, we need to understand and appreciate the things nearest and dearest to the hearts of our religiously diverse brothers and sisters. But there is also another answer. By learning about other people's faith, we also learn about our own. The important elements in other religions enrich the tapestry of ours as we are reminded of truths of which we may have lost sight, even though they are present in our own tradition.

For example, no one can study Hinduism or Buddhism and not remember that true religion demands that we lose ourselves in the will of God. If we are to become one with the Father as Christ is one with the Father, then our egos and our desires must be swallowed up and lost in the will and desires of God for us. While a Hindu or a Buddhist would not frame the loss of self as has just been done here, their emphasis on the loss of individuality induces Latter-day Saints to consider what we believe about the relationship between the ego and God. In doing so, we may see an element of our own faith that we would not have seen had we not first observed it in the beliefs of our Hindu or Buddhist brothers and sisters.

Similarly, no one can study Sikhism, Judaism, or Islam without being required to examine questions of ethical living, of duty to God and neighbor. There are correct ways of living. There are moral norms. There are things that God expects and demands of each of us. Likewise, these faiths point to the greatness and otherness of God, a corrective that we, who sometimes become too familiar with the divine, need to hear. God is great! God does control the entire universe! We are to seek to become more like him, not to lower him to becoming more like us.

Philosophical Taoism reminds us that the present is the only moment we have. We cannot live in the past, nor can we live in the future. Life is that we might have joy now (2 Ne. 2:25). We should learn to enjoy each moment for what it holds. There should be a spirit of equanimity that permeates our being, that cannot be shaken or taken from us despite the storms which may whirl around us. We are to live by the Spirit, permitting God to guide us each moment of the day, just as the philosophical Taoist sought to live in harmony with the Tao day by day.

Traditional Confucianism reminds us that we live in a society of human beings and that no society, religious or otherwise, can endure without norms of behavior and standards which define relationships. Every human society has them, including the church. Are Latter-day Saint practices the same as those prescribed by Confucius? Yes, some are; but others are given for our time and place by God through his living prophet. There must be harmony in all societies. Of this Confucius reminds us.

Conclusion

As has been shown, the Restoration fulness completes and enhances the truths found in the religions of the world. It teaches that the knowledge of God must come through revelation, not human reason alone. We learn that there are three separate persons in the Godhead—not of one essence, but one in will and purpose. They are our Heavenly Father, a being of flesh and bones; Jehovah, the Son, who becomes incarnate as Jesus Christ; and the Holy Ghost. We also learn that matter, energy, and intelligence are eternal, and thus the members of the Godhead organize pre-existing materials rather than creating from nothing.

The Restoration teaches that human beings have a premortal existence as eternally intelligent beings clothed by the Father with spirit form. They begin the path of eternal progression in the premortal world and continue that growth into mortality, postmortality, and some degree of glory. Human beings are created in the image of God, meaning that they have the same physical form as the Father and the Son—a truth that adds to the understanding of a human being as one who is defined by reasoning powers.

The Restoration clarifies the effects of the Atonement and how it is to be appropriated. We learn that the Atonement unconditionally covers the effects of the fall of Adam and Eve, an event which was not a disaster but was essential for human progress. Both spiritual and physical death, the products of the Fall, are removed for all persons. However, the Atonement's effects on individual sins are conditional. It removes the sins of those who humble themselves before God and receive the Atonement through faith in the Lord Jesus Christ, repentance, and essential saving ordinances under the hands of persons bearing the authority to perform them. This latter stance concerning the essential nature of ordinances is what separates Latter-day Saints from all other traditions, both Christian and non-Christian. The ordinances are so essential that they are done even for the dead by proxy in the sacred space of the temple.

Latter-day revelation teaches that persons pass at death into a world of spirits, where those who have received the gospel may participate in a missionary effort to those who have not. Following the final judgment, virtually all persons will receive some degree of glory, but only those who have appropriated the Atonement as God has prescribed will be gods, sharing in the eternal life which the Father and the Son live. The Latter-day Saint clarity about the afterlife, even though much is unknown, adds to the knowledge that other Christians have.

Latter-day revelation also teaches us of the essential character of the church's organization and authority.

Authority must reside in one person who has been designated to speak for God. He must be drawn from the Quorum of Twelve Apostles, which, with the First Presidency, holds the essential keys to administer the saving ordinances. Without this central structure, there is no authority and there is no church of Christ. Through this channel comes God's continuing revelation of his will and his ways as people are ready to receive those revelations. A general falling away during the early Christian era stemmed from the loss of these essential elements. While others may have pieces and parts of the gospel, only The Church of Jesus Christ of Latter-day Saints contains all the essential elements and truths of the kingdom of God which have been delivered to the earth in the latter days.

This knowledge of the fulness of the gospel found in The Church of Jesus Christ of Latter-day Saints should not breed arrogance or exclusiveness. We should simply be grateful to have been given the opportunity to be God's spokespersons in the last days. But the truths Latter-day Saints teach often have been given in a preparatory way to many people who are not Latter-day Saints. All the religions examined in this text possess gospel truths. Wherever truth is found, we should rejoice, for there the hand of God has been at work. Where there is truth, we should build on it, strengthen it, and deepen it. Latter-day Saints should rejoice in all that is beautiful and good, for that is the essence of the last sentence of the thirteenth Article of Faith: "If there is anything virtuous, lovely, or of good report or praiseworthy, we seek after these things."

Likewise, we should learn the lesson Ammon exemplified as he explained the gospel to Lamoni: first, find the common ground, and then present God's additional truths to enrich the lives of all our brothers and sisters (Alma 18:24–28). This is our calling as participants in the fulness of the gospel found in The Church of Jesus Christ of Latter-day Saints, and so it has been stated at the outset of this book. Here at its conclusion, that calling is reaffirmed. President Howard W. Hunter, in quoting and expanding on President George Albert Smith's words, expresses it thus:

In our humble efforts to build brotherhood and to teach revealed truth, we say to the people of the world what President George Albert Smith so lovingly suggested: "We have come not to take away from you the truth and virtue you possess. We have come not to find fault with you nor to criticize you. We have not come here to berate you because of things you have not done; but we have come here as your brethren . . . and to say to you: 'Keep all the good that you have, and let us bring to you more good, in order that you may be happier and in order that you may be prepared to enter into the presence of our Heavenly Father.'" . . .

Ours is a perennial religion based on eternal, saving truth. Its message of love and brotherhood is lodged in scripture and in the revelations of the Lord to his living prophet. It embraces all truth. It circumscribes all wisdom—all that God has revealed to man, and all that he will yet reveal. Of that eternal revelation, I bear testimony in the name of Jesus Christ, amen.[16]

Notes

1. Brigham Young, "Government of God," May 22, 1859, in Brigham Young et al., *Journal of Discourses*, 26 vols. (1842–96; reprint, Salt Lake City: n.p., 1967), 7:148; quoted by President Howard W. Hunter in "The Gospel—A Global Faith," *Ensign,* November 1991, 18.

2. President Spencer W. Kimball, First Presidency Statement, February 15, 1978; quoted in Carlos E. Asay, "God's Love for Mankind," in Spencer J. Palmer, ed., *Mormons and Muslims: Spiritual Foundations and Modern Manifestations,* Religious Studies Monograph Series, no. 8 (Provo, Ut.: Religious Studies Center, Brigham Young University, 1983), 208.

3. Ibid.

4. B. H. Roberts, *The Gospel and Man's Relationship to Deity* (Salt Lake City: Deseret Book, 1924), 289.

5. Joseph Smith, *History of the Church of Jesus Christ of Latter-day Saints,* 7 vols. (1949; reprint, Salt Lake City: Deseret Book, 1970), 4:595–96; quoted in Hunter, "Global Faith," 18.

6. Smith, *History of the Church,* 4:461.

7. "The Shorter Catechism," in *Book of Confessions* (New York: Office of the General Assembly of the Presbyterian Church [USA], 1983), 7.001.

8. For those who want more detailed information on the temple or about baptism for the dead, washings and anointings, the endowment, or celestial marriage, there are several excellent sources. Relevant articles in Daniel H. Ludlow et al., eds., *Encyclopedia of Mormonism,* 5 vols. (New York: Macmillan, 1992), can be consulted. Joseph Fielding McConkie has an excellent book on symbolism: *Gospel Symbolism* (Salt Lake

City: Bookcraft, 1985). For discussion of the temple and the endowment, consult James E. Talmage, *The House of the Lord: A Study of Holy Sanctuaries, Ancient and Modern* (Salt Lake City: Deseret Book, 1968), and Boyd K. Packer, *The Holy Temple* (Salt Lake City: Bookcraft, 1968).

9. Marion D. Hanks, letter to Spencer J. Palmer, July 17, 1989.

10. Ezra Taft Benson, *A Witness and a Warning: A Modern-day Prophet Testifies of the Book of Mormon* (Salt Lake City: Deseret Book, 1988), 30.

11. Hunter, "Global Faith," 19. Elder Whitney's remarks first appeared in *Ninety-First Annual Conference of The Church of Jesus Christ of Latter-day Saints* (Salt Lake City: The Church of Jesus Christ of Latter-day Saints, 1921), 32–33.

12. Kimball, Statement; quoted in Asay, "God's Love for Mankind," 208.

13. Eusebius Pamphilus, *The Ecclesiastical History . . . ,* trans. and intro. by Christian Frederick Cruse (Grand Rapids, Mich.: Baker Book House, 1955), 40.

14. Ibid., 118.

15. These facts were conveyed orally to the author by E. Dale LeBaron. See the anthology he edited, *"All Are Alike unto God"* (Salt Lake City: Bookcraft, 1990), for this account of God's work among the African people.

16. Hunter, "Global Faith," 19. The internal quotation, "Let Us Bring You More Good," is found in George Albert Smith, *Sharing the Gospel with Others: Excerpts from the Sermons of President Smith*, comp. Preston Nibley (Salt Lake City: Deseret News Press, 1948), 12–13.

Bibliography

THE following bibliography reflects the major works cited in this text. In addition, it includes a number of references which may be found in the Harold B. Lee Library at Brigham Young University or which, in our judgment, should be present in a bibliography dealing with the religions of the world.

GENERAL WORKS

Antoun, Richard T., and Mary Elaine Hegland, eds. *Religious Resurgence: Contemporary Cases in Islam, Christianity, and Judaism.* Syracuse, N.Y.: Syracuse University Press, 1987.

Bach, Marcus. *Major Religions of the World.* New York: Abingdon, 1959.

de Bary, William Theodore. *Sources of Indian Tradition.* 2 vols. New York: Columbia University Press, 1958.

Eliade, Mircea, et al., eds. *The Encyclopedia of Religion.* 16 vols. New York: Macmillan, 1987.

Graham, William A. *Beyond the Written Word: Oral Aspects of Scripture in the History of Religion.* Cambridge, Engl.: Cambridge University Press, 1987.

Ham, Wayne. *Man's Living Religions.* Independence, Mo.: Herald, 1966.

Hopfe, Lewis M. *Religions of the World.* 6th ed. New York: Macmillan College Publishing, 1994.

Hume, Robert Ernest. *The World's Living Religions . . . .* Rev. ed. New York: Charles Scribner's Sons, 1959.

Noss, David S., and John B. Noss. *Man's Religions.* 7th ed. New York: Macmillan, 1984.

Smart, Ninian. *The Religious Experience of Mankind.* 3d ed. New York: Charles Scribner's Sons, 1969.

HINDUISM

Chatterjee, Satishchandra. *The Fundamentals of Hinduism.* Calcutta: Das Gupta, 1950.

Ghurye, G. S. *Caste and Class in India.* 2d ed. Bombay: Popular Book Depot, 1957. Originally published as *Caste and Race in India* (1932).

Kinsley, David R. *Hinduism: A Cultural Perspective.* Prentice-Hall Series in World Religions. Englewood Cliffs, N.J.: Prentice-Hall, 1982.

Monier-Williams, Monier. *Hinduism.* Non-Christian Religious Systems, vol. 1. New York: Macmillan, 1919.

Richards, Glyn, ed. *A Source-Book of Modern Hinduism.* London: Curzon Press, 1985.

Zaehner, Robert C. *Hinduism.* London: Oxford University Press, 1962.

Zimmer, Heinrich. *Philosophies of India.* Ed. Joseph Campbell. Bollingen Series, no. 26. New York: Meridian Books, 1957.

Sacred Texts

Bose, Abinash Chandra, trans. *Hymns from the Vedas.* New York: Asia Publishing House, 1966.

Buitenen, J. A. B. van, trans. and ed. *The Mahabharata.* 3 vols. Chicago: University of Chicago Press, 1973.

Edgerton, Franklin, trans. *Bhagavad Gita.* Cambridge, Mass.: Harvard University Press, 1972.

MacDonell, A. A., ed. *Hymns from the Rigveda.* London: Association Press, 1922.

Mascaro, Juan, trans. *Bhagavad Gita.* Baltimore: Penguin Books, 1962.

Narayan, R. K., trans. and ed. *The Ramayana: A Shortened Modern Prose Version of the Indian Epic.* New York: Penguin Books, 1977.

O'Flaherty, Wendy Doniger, sel. and trans. *The Rig Veda: An Anthology.* Harmondsworth, Engl.: Penguin Books, 1981.

Pereira, José, ed. *Hindu Theology: A Reader.* Garden City, N.Y.: Image Books, 1976.

Radhakrishnan, S., ed. and trans. *The Principal Upanishads.* New York: Harper and Brothers, 1953.

Thomas, Edward J., trans. *Vedic Hymns.* London: John Murray, 1923.

JAINISM

Chatterjee, Asim Kumar. *A Comprehensive History of Jainism up to 1000 A.D.* Calcutta: Firma KLM, 1978.

Jain, Muni Uttam Kamal. *Jaina Sects and Schools.* New Delhi, India: Concept, 1975.

Jaini, Jagmanderlal. *Outlines of Jainism.* Ed. F. W. Thomas. 1940. Reprint. Westport, Conn.: Hyperion, 1982.

Jaini, Padmanabh S. *The Jaina Path of Purification.* Berkeley: University of California Press, 1979.

277

Lalwani, K. C. *Sramana Bhagavan Mahavira: Life and Doctrine.* Calcutta: Minerva Associates, 1975.

Sacred Texts

Stevenson, J., trans. *The Kalpa Sutra and Nava Tatva: Two Works Illustrative of the Jain Religion and Philosophy.* London: Oriental Translation Fund of Great Britain and Ireland, 1848.

Thomas, F. W., trans. *The Flower-Spray of the Quodammodo Doctrine: Sri Mallisenasuri Syad-Vada-Mañjari.* Delhi, India: Motilal Banarsidass, 1968.

BUDDHISM

Asvaghosha. *Discourse on the Awakening of Faith in the Mahayana.* Trans. Daisetz T. Suzuki. Chicago: Open Court, 1900.

Bechert, Heinz, and Richard Gombrich, eds. *The World of Buddhism: Buddhist Monks and Nuns in Society and Culture.* London: Thames and Hudson, 1984.

Blofeld, John. *Bodhisattva of Compassion: The Mystical Tradition of Kuan Yin.* Boston: Shambhala, 1988.

Chalmers, Lord, trans. *Further Dialogues of the Buddha.* 2 vols. London: Oxford University Press, 1926. (The two volumes of this work comprise vols. 5 and 6 of *Sacred Books of the Buddhists,* ed. Mrs. Rhys Davids.)

Coomaraswamy, Ananda. *Buddha and the Gospel of Buddhism.* New Hyde Park, N.Y.: University Books, 1964.

Dumoulin, Heinrich, and John C. Maraldo, eds. *Buddhism in the Modern World.* 1st American ed., newly rev. New York: Macmillan, 1976. Originally published as *Buddhismus der Gegenwart* (1970).

Eliot, Charles. *Hinduism and Buddhism: An Historical Sketch.* 3 vols. New York: Barnes and Noble, 1954.

Getty, Alice. *The Gods of Northern Buddhism: Their History, Iconography, and Progressive Evolution through the Northern Buddhist Countries.* 2d ed. rev. Rutland, Vt.: Charles E. Tuttle, 1962.

Herold, A. Ferdinand. *The Life of Buddha: According to the Legends of Ancient India.* Trans. Paul C. Blum. Rutland, Vt.: Charles E. Tuttle, 1954.

Hopkins, Jeffrey. *The Tantric Distinction: An Introduction to Tibetan Buddhism.* Ed. Anne C. Klein. London: Wisdom Publications, 1984.

Kapleau, Philip, comp. and ed. *The Three Pillars of Zen: Teaching, Practice, and Enlightenment.* Boston: Beacon Press, 1967.

Lloyd, Arthur. *The Creed of Half Japan: Historical Sketches of Japanese Buddhism.* London: Smith, Elder, 1911.

Pye, Michael. *The Buddha.* London: Duckworth, 1979.

Rockhill, W. Woodville, trans. *The Life of the Buddha and the Early History of His Order . . . .* Popular ed. Trübner's Oriental Series. London: Kegan Paul, Trench, Trübner, 1884.

Saint-Hilaire, J. Barthélemy. *The Buddha and His Religion.* London: Kegan Paul, 1914.

Suzuki, Beatrice Lane. *Mahayana Buddhism: A Brief Outline.* New York: Macmillan, 1956.

Suzuki, Daisetz T. *Outlines of Mahayana Buddhism.* 1907. Reprint. New York: Schocken Books, 1963.

Takakusu, Junjiro. *The Essentials of Buddhist Philosophy.* Ed. Wing-tsit Chan and Charles A. Moore. Westport, Conn.: Greenwood Press, 1973.

Woodward, F. L., and E. M. Hare, trans. *The Book of the Gradual Sayings . . . .* 5 vols. Pali Text Society Translation Series, no. 22. London: Luzac and Co., 1960.

Sacred Texts

Fox, Douglas A., trans. and ed. *The Heart of Buddhist Wisdom: A Translation of the Heart Sutra with Historical Introduction and Commentary.* Studies in Asian Thought and Religion, vol. 3. Lewiston, N.Y.: Edwin Mellen, 1985.

Kato, Bunno, et al., trans. *The Threefold Lotus Sutra . . . .* New York: Weatherhill, 1975.

Kaviratna, Harischandra, trans. *Dhammapada: Wisdom of the Buddha.* English-Pali ed. Pasadena, Calif.: Theosophical University Press, 1980.

Mullin, Glenn H., ed. and trans. *Selected Works of the Dalai Lama.* 2 vols. Ithaca, N.Y.: Snow Lion, 1985.

Niwano, Nikkyo. *Buddhism for Today: A Modern Interpretation of the Threefold Lotus Sutra.* New York: Weatherhill, 1976.

Sekida, Katsuki, trans. *Two Zen Classics: Mumonkan and Hekiganroku.* Ed. A. V. Grimstone. New York: Weatherhill, 1977.

Warren, Henry Clarke, trans. *Buddhism in Translations: Passages Selected from the Buddhist Sacred Books . . . .* Student's ed. Cambridge, Mass.: Harvard University Press, 1953.

SIKHISM

Cole, W. Owen. *Sikhism and Its Indian Context, 1469–1708 . . . .* London: Darton, Longman, and Todd, 1984.

———. *The Guru in Sikhism.* London: Darton, Longman, and Todd, 1982.

Kapur, Rajiv A. *Sikh Separatism: The Politics of Faith.* London: George Allen and Unwin, 1986.

Kaur, Gundindar. *The Guru Granth Sahib: Its Physics and Metaphysics.* New Delhi, India: Sterling, 1981.

McLeod, W. H. *Early Sikh Tradition: A Study of the Janamsakhis.* Oxford, Engl.: At the Clarendon Press, 1980.

———. *The Evolution of the Sikh Community: Five Essays.* London: Oxford University Press, 1976.

———. *Guru Nanak and the Sikh Religion.* London: Oxford University Press, 1968.

Singh, Gopal. *A History of the Sikh People: 1469–1978.* New Delhi, India: World Sikh University Press, 1979.

Singh, Gurmit. *A Critique of Sikhism.* New Delhi, India: Ishar Singh Satnam Singh, 1964.

Singh, Harbans. *Guru Gobind Singh.* Chandigarh, India: The Guru Gobind Singh Foundation, 1966.

———. *Guru Nanak and Origins of the Sikh Faith*. Bombay: Asia, 1969.

Singh, Ranbir. *Glimpses of the Divine Masters*. New Delhi, India: International Traders Corporation, 1965.

Sacred Texts

McLeod, W. H., trans. and ed. *Textual Sources for the Study of Sikhism*. Manchester, Engl.: Manchester University Press, 1984.

Singh, Gopal. *Sri Guru Granth Sahib: English Version*. 4 vols. New York: Taplinger, 1965.

TAOISM

Creel, Herrlee G. *What Is Taoism? and Other Studies in Chinese Cultural History*. Chicago: University of Chicago Press, 1970.

Hoff, Benjamin. *The Tao of Pooh*. New York: Penguin Books, 1983.

Liu, Xiaogan. "Taoism." In Arvind Sharma, ed. *Our Religions*. New York: HarperCollins, 1993.

Palmer, Spencer J. "Uses of the Five Elements in East Asia." *Brigham Young University Studies* 6, nos. 3 and 4 (Summer 1976): 123–34.

Thompson, Laurence G. *Chinese Religion: An Introduction*. 4th ed. Belmont, Calif.: Wadsworth Publishing, 1989.

Welch, Holmes. *Taoism: The Parting of the Way*. Rev. ed. Boston: Beacon Press, 1966.

Welch, Holmes, and Anna Seidel, eds. *Facets of Taoism: Essays in Chinese Religion*. New Haven, Conn.: Yale University Press, 1979.

Yutang, Lin, ed. *The Wisdom of China and India*. New York: Random House, 1942.

Sacred Texts

Feng, Gia-fu, and Jane English, trans. and eds. *Tao Te Ching*. New York: Vintage Books, 1972.

Waley, Arthur, trans. and ed. *The Way and Its Power: A Study of the Tao Te Ching and Its Place in Chinese Thought*. New York: Grove Press, 1958.

Wing, R. L., trans. *The Tao of Power: A Translation of the Tao Te Ching by Lao Tzu*. Garden City, N.Y.: Dolphin Books, Doubleday, 1986.

Yutang, Lin, ed. and trans. *The Wisdom of Laotse*. New York: Modern Library, Random House, 1948.

CONFUCIANISM

Dawson, Raymond. *Confucius*. Oxford, Engl.: Oxford University Press, 1981.

Nivison, David S., and Arthur F. Wright, eds. *Confucianism in Action*. Stanford, Calif.: Stanford University Press, 1959.

Palmer, Spencer J. *Confucian Rituals in Korea*. Religions of Asia Series, no. 3. Berkeley, Calif.: Asian Humanities Press, [1980].

Taylor, Rodney L. *The Way of Heaven: An Introduction to the Confucian Religious Life*. Iconography of Religions, sec. 12, fasc. 3. Leiden: E. J. Brill, 1986.

Sacred Texts

Chai, Ch'u, and Winberg Chai, trans. and eds. *The Sacred Books of Confucius and Other Confucian Classics*. New Hyde Park, N.Y.: University Books, 1965.

Legge, James, trans. *Confucian Analects, The Great Learning, and The Doctrine of the Mean*. Vol. 1 of *The Chinese Classics*. 5 vols. Hong Kong: Hong Kong University Press, 1960.

Waley, Arthur, trans. *The Analects of Confucius*. New York: Vintage Books, 1938.

SHINTO

Anesaki, Masaharu. *Religious Life of the Japanese People*. Rev. Hideo Kishimoto. Series on Japanese Life and Culture, vol. 4. Tokyo: Kokusai Bunka Shinkokai [The Society for International Cultural Relations], 1961.

Creemers, Wilhelmus H. M. *Shrine Shinto after World War II*. Leiden: E. J. Brill, 1968.

Herbert, Jean. *Shinto: At the Fountain-head of Japan*. New York: Stein and Day, 1967.

Kato, Genchi. *A Historical Study of the Religious Development of Shinto*. Trans. Shoyu Hanayama. Tokyo: Japan Society for the Promotion of Science, 1973.

Ono, Sokyo, with William P. Woodward. *Shinto: The Kami Way*. Rutland, Vt.: Charles E. Tuttle, 1976.

Picken, Stuart D. B. *Shinto: Japan's Spiritual Roots*. Tokyo: Kodansha International, 1980.

Piggott, Juliet. *Japanese Mythology*. Rev. ed. New York: P. Bedrick, 1983.

Sacred Texts

Aston, William George, trans. *Nihongi: Chronicles of Japan from the Earliest Times to A.D. 697*. London: George Allen and Unwin, 1956.

Philippi, Donald L., trans. *Kojiki*. Tokyo: University of Tokyo Press, 1968.

ZOROASTRIANISM

Bode, Dastur Framroze A. *Man, Soul, Immortality in Zoroastrianism*. Bombay: n.p., 1960.

Boyce, Mary. *A Persian Stronghold of Zoroastrianism*. Oxford, Engl.: At the Clarendon Press, 1977.

———. *Zoroastrians: Their Religious Beliefs and Practices*. London: Routledge and Kegan Paul, 1979.

Duchesne-Guillemin, Jacques. *Symbols and Values in Zoroastrianism: Their Survival and Renewal*. New York: Harper and Row, Harper Torch Books, 1970.

Jafarey, Ali A. *The Passing Away of Asho Zarathustra: A Treatise Based on Available Sources in Avesta, Pahlavi, Arabic, and Persian Scriptures*. Teheran: n.p., 1980.

Mehta, P. D. *Zarathushtra: The Transcendental Vision.* Longmead, Engl.: Element Books, 1985.

Pangborn, Cyrus R. *Zoroastrianism: A Beleaguered Faith.* New York: Advent Books, 1983.

Pavry, Jal Dastur Cursetji. *The Zoroastrian Doctrine of a Future Life: From Death to the Individual Judgment.* 2d ed. Columbia University Indo-Iranian Series, vol. 11. New York: AMS Press, 1965.

Zaehner, Robert C. *The Teachings of the Magi: A Compendium of Zoroastrian Beliefs.* Ethical and Religious Classics of East and West, no. 14. London: George Allen and Unwin, 1956.

Sacred Texts

Boyce, Mary, ed. and trans. *Textual Sources for the Study of Zoroastrianism.* Manchester, Engl.: Manchester University Press, 1984.

Duchesne-Guillemin, Jacques, trans. *The Hymns of Zarathustra: Being a Translation of the Gathas Together with Introduction and Commentary.* Boston: Beacon Press, 1952.

Insler, S., trans. *The Gathas of Zarathustra.* Vol. 1 of Textes et mémoires, 3d series of *Acta Iranica: Encyclopédie permanente des études iraniennes . . . .* Teheran: Bibliothèque Pahlavi, 1975.

Mills, Lawrence H., trans. and ed. *A Study of the Five Zarathustrian (Zoroastrian) Gathas with Texts and Translations . . . .* Erlangen, Ger.: University Press, 1894.

Judaism

Buber, Martin. *I and Thou.* Trans. Ronald Gregor Smith. 2d ed. New York: Charles Scribner's Sons, 1958.

Finkelstein, Louis. *The Jews: Their Religion and Culture.* New York: Schocken Books, 1971.

Fishbane, Michael A. *Judaism: Revelation and Traditions.* San Francisco: Harper and Row, 1987.

Goldberg, David J., and John D. Rayner. *The Jewish People: Their History and Their Religion.* New York: Viking Press, 1987.

Guttman, Julius. *Philosophies of Judaism: The History of Jewish Philosophy from Biblical Times to Franz Rosenzweig.* Trans. David W. Silverman. New York: Holt, Rinehart, and Winston, 1964.

Heschel, Abraham Joshua. *God in Search of Man: A Philosophy of Judaism.* 1955. Reprint. Northvale, N.J.: Jason Aronson, 1987.

Jacobs, Louis. *The Book of Jewish Belief.* New York: Behrman House, 1984.

———. *The Book of Jewish Practice.* New York: Behrman House, 1987.

Roth, Cecil, et al. *Encylopædia Judaica.* Corrected ed. 17 vols. Jerusalem: Keter, [1974?].

Tcherikover, Victor. *Hellenistic Civilization and the Jews.* Trans. S. Applebaum. Philadelphia: Jewish Publication Society of America, 1959.

Trepp, Leo. *Judaism: Development and Life.* 3d ed. Belmont, Calif.: Wadsworth, 1982.

———. *The Complete Book of Jewish Observance: A Practical Manual for the Modern Jew.* New York: Behrman House, 1980.

Sacred Texts

Danby, Herbert, trans. *The Mishnah.* Oxford, Engl.: Oxford University Press, 1933.

Epstein, I., ed. *The Babylonian Talmud: Seder Tohoroth.* 18 vols. London: Soncino Press, 1948–52.

Neusner, Jacob, trans. and ed. *Invitation to the Talmud: A Teaching Book.* Rev. ed. San Francisco: Harper and Row, 1984.

———, ed. *The Modern Study of the Mishnah.* Leiden: E. J. Brill, 1973.

Christianity

Augustine. *The City of God.* Trans. Marcus Dods. New York: The Modern Library, Random House, 1950.

Bainton, Roland H. *Here I Stand: A Life of Martin Luther.* New York: Mentor Books, The New American Library, 1950.

Cross, F. L., ed. *The Early Christian Fathers.* London: Gerald Duckworth and Co., 1960.

Enslin, Morton Scott. *Christian Beginnings.* New York: Harper and Brothers, 1938.

Gilby, Thomas, sel. and trans. *Saint Thomas Aquinas: Philosophical Texts.* 1951. Reprint. Durham, N.C.: Labyrinth, 1982.

Kelly, J. N. D. *Early Christian Doctrines.* Rev. ed. San Francisco: Harper and Row, 1978.

Latourette, Kenneth Scott. *A History of Christianity.* New York: Harper and Brothers, 1953.

———. *A History of the Expansion of Christianity.* 7 vols. New York: Harper and Brothers, 1937–45.

Leff, Gordon. *Medieval Thought: Saint Augustine to Ockham.* Baltimore: Penguin Books, 1958.

Lietzmann, Hans. *A History of the Early Church.* Trans. Bertram Lee Woolf. 4 vols. 1937–51. Reprint (4 vols. in 2). New York: Meridian Books, 1961.

Walker, Williston, et al. *A History of the Christian Church.* 4th ed. New York: Charles Scribner's Sons, 1985.

Islam

Ayoub, Mahmoud M. *The Qur'an and Its Interpreters.* 2 vols. Albany: State University of New York Press, 1984–92.

Cragg, Kenneth, and R. Marston Speight. *Islam from Within: Anthology of a Religion.* The Religion of Man Series. Belmont, Calif.: Wadsworth, 1980.

Esposito, John L. *Islam: The Straight Path.* New York: Oxford University Press, 1988.

Faruqi, Isma'il R. *Islam.* Brentwood, Md.: International Graphics, 1984.

Hourani, Albert. *Islam in European Thought.* Cambridge, Engl.: Cambridge University Press, 1991.

Nasr, Seyyed Hossein. *Islamic Life and Thought*. Albany: State University of New York Press, 1981.

Schimmel, Annemarie. *Mystical Dimensions of Islam*. Chapel Hill: University of North Carolina Press, 1975.

Smith, Wilfred Cantwell. *Islam in Modern History*. Princeton, N.J.: Princeton University Press, 1957.

Waddy, Charis. *The Muslim Mind*. 2d ed. London: Longman, 1982.

Watt, William Montgomery. *Muslim-Christian Encounters: Perceptions and Misperceptions*. London: Routledge, 1991.

Sacred Texts

'Ali, Abdullah Yusuf, trans. *The Meaning of the Glorious Qur'an*. 2 vols. Cairo: Dar al-Kitab al-Masri, n.d.

Pickthall, Mohammed Marmaduke, trans. *The Meaning of the Glorious Koran: A Bilingual Edition with English Translation, Introduction, and Notes*. London: George Allen and Unwin, 1976.

LATTER-DAY SAINT PERSPECTIVES

Blomberg, Craig L., and Stephen E. Robinson. *How Wide the Divide? A Mormon and an Evangelical in Conversation*. Downers Grove, Ill.: InterVarsity Press, 1997.

Dyer, Alvin R. *This Age of Confusion . . . .* Salt Lake City: Deseret Book, 1965.

Hunter, Howard W. "All Are Alike unto God." In *1979 Devotional Speeches of the Year: BYU Devotional and Fireside Addresses*. Provo, Ut.: Brigham Young University Press, 1980. Reprinted in *Ensign,* June 1979, 72–74.

Hunter, Milton R. *The Gospel through the Ages*. Salt Lake City: Stevens and Wallis, 1945.

Keller, Roger R. *Reformed Christians and Mormon Christians: Let's Talk*. Ann Arbor, Mich.: Pryor Pettengill, 1986.

Ludlow, Daniel H., et al., eds. *Encyclopedia of Mormonism*. 5 vols. New York: Macmillan, 1992.

Mayfield, James B. "Ishmael, Our Brother." *Ensign*, June 1979, 24–32.

Nibley, Hugh. *The World and the Prophets*. Salt Lake City: Deseret Book, 1954.

Palmer, Spencer J. *The Church Encounters Asia*. Salt Lake City: Deseret Book, 1970.

———. "Did Christ Visit Japan?" *Brigham Young University Studies* 10, no. 2 (Winter 1970): 135–58.

———. *The Expanding Church*. Salt Lake City: Deseret Book, 1978.

———. "Israel in Asia." *Ensign,* January 1971, 70–75.

———. "Mormon Views of Religious Resemblances." *Brigham Young University Studies* 16, no. 4 (Summer 1976): 660–81.

———, ed. *Deity and Death: Selected Symposium Papers*. Religious Studies Monograph Series, no. 2. Provo, Ut.: Religious Studies Center, Brigham Young University, 1978.

———, ed. *Mormons and Muslims: Spiritual Foundations and Modern Manifestations*. Religious Studies Monograph Series, no. 8. Provo, Ut.: Religious Studies Center, Brigham Young University, 1983.

Peterson, Daniel C. *Abraham Divided: An LDS Perspective on the Middle East*. Rev. ed. Salt Lake City: Aspen Books, 1995.

Platt, Joseph B. "Our Oasis of Faith." *Ensign*, April 1988, 39–41.

Romney, Thomas Cottam. *World Religions in the Light of Mormonism*. Independence, Mo.: Press of Zion's Printing and Publishing Co., 1946.

Smith, George Albert. *Sharing the Gospel with Others: Excerpts from the Sermons of President Smith*. Comp. Preston Nibley. Salt Lake City: Deseret News Press, 1948.

Smith, Joseph. *History of the Church of Jesus Christ of Latter-day Saints*. 7 vols. 1949. Reprint. Salt Lake City: Deseret Book, 1970.

Smith, Joseph Fielding, comp. *Teachings of the Prophet Joseph Smith*. Salt Lake City: Deseret Book, 1979.

Index

*Terms following in parentheses are alternate forms. Page numbers in **bold type** indicate illustrations.*

Aaron, 170, 191
'Abd al-Mutallib, 214
Abhidhamma Pitaka, 54, 55
Abraham, xiii, xv, 163–64, 166, 169, 170, 173, 181, 187, 191, 208, 214, 217, 225, 230, 231, 238, 239, 240
Abu Bakr, 220–21
Abu Talib, 214
Adam, 20, 42, 157, 160, 166, 190, 193, 207, 225, 246, 247, 250, 258, 262, 264–65, 269, 274
Adi Granth. *See* Granth
Adultery, 155, 181. *See also* Sexual relations, unlawful
Advent, 195, 209
'Aeed Al-Adha, 231, 238
'Aeed Al-Fitr, 229–30, 238
Afikomen, 171, 172, 183
Africa, 10, 213, 218
Afterlife, 85, 87, 153–54, 157, 264, 266–67, 274. *See also* Brahman; Nirvana, in Mahayana Buddhism; Reincarnation
Agamas, 40
Agency. *See* Choice, freedom of
Aggadah, 164, 179, 183
Agni, 18, 24, 30, 151, 246
Agnus Dei, 194, 209
Ahasuerus, 157, 172
Ahimsa, 15, 22, 30, 37, 38–40, 42–46, 53, 66, 69
Ahura Mazda (Ohrmazd, Asura), 57, 148, 149, 150–52, 153, 154, 158, 159, 160, 261
Akal Purakh, 79, 82. *See also* Ik Oankar
Alchemy, 92, 93, 96
Alcohol, 53, 54, 76, 92–93, 94, 220, 236
Alexander the Great, 56, 187
'Ali, 220–21

Allah, 80, 213, 214, 216–18, 222, 224–28, 229, 230, 231, 233, 236, 238, 239, 240, 261. *See also* God; Tawheed
Almsgiving. *See* Zakat
Amar Das, Guru, 80, 82
Amaterasu, 59, 112–13, 115, 116, 117, 120, 261
Ambition, 89, 90
Ameretat, 150
Americas, 272
Amesha Spentas, 55, 150, 153, 159, 261
Amina, 215
Amitabha (Amida, Omit'ofu), 57–59, 60, 61, 68, **127, 128**
Amrit, 76, 78
Amritsar, 76, 80, 81, 82, 129
Analects (Lun Yu), 89, 99, 101, 102, 105, 106, 108; paraphrased, 102; quoted, 99, 101–4
Analogia Entis, 188, 209
Analogia Fidei, 188, 209
Ananda, 55
Anand Karaj (Ceremony of Bliss), 82
Ancestors. *See* Dead, ordinance work for; Family; Filial piety; Hsiao
Angabahya, 40, 46
Angad, Guru, 75, 80, 82
Angas, xv, 40, 46
Angels, 147, 152, 157, 188, 225
Anglicans. *See* England, Church of
Angra Mainyu (Ahriman), 151, 153, 154, 155, 158, 159, 261
Animals, 28, 29, 38, 39, 42–45, 46, 168, 176, 190, 226, 230, 262. *See also* Sacrifice, animal
Animism, 6, 17, 76, 111, 214
Anointing, 109. *See also* Unction
Anti-Nephi-Lehies, 45, 46
Antiochus IV, 172, 187
Antiwar. *See* Pacifism
Apocrypha, 197, 209
Apostasy, 8, 9, 226, 246, 247, 271–72, 275
Apostles, 8, 11, 193, 196, 205, 216, 260, 267, 269, 271, 272, 273, 275

Apostles' Creed, 199, 200, 209
Aquinas, Saint Thomas, 188, 207
Arabians, 3, 164, 176, 183, 217, 218, 219, 220, 251; pre-Islamic, 214, 231
Arabic language, 220, 222, 225, 231, 236, 238
'Arafat: Mount (Mount of Mercy), 231, 268; plains of, 230
Aranyakas, 24, 32
Archetypes, 249
Arhats, 54, 59, 67, 69, 70
Arians and Arianism, 189, 210
Aristotle, Golden Mean of, 103, 108
Arjasp, 150
Arjun, Guru, 75, 79–82
Arjuna, 20, 23, 24–25, 31, 57
Armaiti, 150
Artaxerxes, 157
Articles of Faith, Thirteen (Jewish), 223. *See also* Pearl of Great Price, quoted
Arts, æsthetic, and architecture, 49, 225, 236, 250. *See also* Hymns; Literature; Music; Temples
Aryans, xv, 17–18, 19, 30, 35, 52, 147–48, 150, 151, 159, 247
Asceticism, 35, 36, 37, 38, 40, 41, 50, 51, 64, 74, 79, 159, 173, 226
Asha, 148, 150, 151, 159
Ashkenazim, 176, 183
Ashram, 27, 30
Asia, 10, 250; central, 17, 147, 213, 220; east, 54, 85; south, 15; southeast, 49, 52, 218; southwest, 7, 145. *See also names of countries and regions*
Asita, 50, 66
Asoka, xv, 39, 56, 218, 250
Assimilation, 208; of Jews, 176–77, 180, 181, 182
Assyrians, 164, 165, 252
Asvaghosha, 56
Atman, 22, 23, 30, 31. *See also* Brahman-Atman
Atonement, 29, 30, 118, 157, 182, 188, 190, 191, 192, 194, 195–96, 199, 209, 231, 261, 262, 263, 264, 265, 271, 274. *See also* Yom Kippur

Augustine, Saint, 207

Austin, Ann, 207

Authority, 192–93, 202, 248, 253, 265, 266, 267–68, 272, 273, 274–75. *See also* Priesthood

Avalokitesvara, 57, 58, 59, 60, 65, 69, **128**, 260. *See also* Kuan Yin (Kannon)

Avatansaka. *See* Kegon Sutra

Avatar, 19–20, 29, 30, 57, 73, 124, 261. *See also names of various avatars*

Avesta, xv, 148, 149, 152, 154, 158, 159, 160; Later, 153, 154

Az, 152

Baal Shem Tov (Israel ben Eliezer, Besht), 177

Babylon, 147, 164, 173, 179, 187, 246, 252

Bali (demon king), 20

Banaras, 26, 124

Bangkok, 127, 128

Baptism, 76, 78, 188, 190, 193–94, 209, 210, 251, 265; by immersion, 194, 204, 266; infant, 194, 204

Baptists, 6, 195, 204

Baraka, 238

Bar Kochba rebellion, 165

Bar mitzvah, **138**, 155, 174, 183

Barth, Karl, 188

Bat mitzvah, 155, 174, 181, 183

Becket, Thomas à, 206

Benevolence, 55, 93, 102, 150–51. *See also* Charity; Compassion; Golden Rule; Kindness

Benjamin, King, 95, 107

Benson, Ezra Taft, 269

Bernard, Saint, de Clairvaux, 250

Bethlehem, 139

Bhagavad Gita, 20, 23, 24–25, 28, 30, 31

Bhairava, 69

Bhaisajyaguru, 57

Bhakti, 21, 23, 24, 30, 57, 73, 79, 268

Bhutatathata, 56

Bible, 21, 89, 95, 157, 197–98, 199, 209, 222, 225, 235, 266; translations of, xv, 11, 197–98, 201, 210. *See also* Old Testament; New Testament

Bill of Rights, 272

Bishop, 193, 210

Blue Mosque, **141**

Bodhi (fig) tree, 51, 56, 62, 63, 66, 69

Bodhidharma, 63, 64, 69

Bodhisattva, 55, 57, 58–61, 65, 67, 69, 104, 261. *See also* Buddhas

Body, 27, 28, 29, 67, 68, 81, 92, 93, 148, 152, 153, 159, 192, 199, 262, 263, 264, 266, 274

Book of Mencius. *See* Mencius, book of

Book of Mormon, xiii, xv, 41, 90, 214, 223, 235, 253, 254, 260, 269; paraphrased, 29, 45, 67, 90, 95, 107, 119, 250, 265, 266, 272, 274, 275; quoted, xiii, 12, 13, 23, 28, 29, 82, 95, 106, 157, 158, 159, 223–24, 238, 249, 251, 263, 269, 270

Brahma, 19, 25, 30, 31, 32, **125**

Brahman, 22, 23, 24, 30, 31, 40, 41, 261, 264. *See also* Brahman-Atman

Brahmanas, 24, 32, 67

Brahman-Atman, 19, 23, 31, 32, 79, 125

Brahmin, 18, 20, 21, 22, 24, 27, 31, 49, 51, 63, 67, 81

Browne, Robert, 204

Buddha, the, 12, 49–51, 53–54, 55, 56, 61, 63, 68–69, 70, 78, 88, 149, 245, 246, 250, 251, 260; as avatar of Vishnu, 20, 30; images of, 56–57; similarities between Jesus and, 66–67; teachings of, 53–54, 67. *See also* Gautama, Siddhartha

Buddha-nature, 61, 63, 70

Buddhas, 55, 57–61, 65, 69; dyani, 261; manushi, 58. *See also* Bodhisattva; Buddha, the

Buddhism, xv, 2, 3, 5, 6, 7, 15, 35, 38, 39–40, 45, 49–70, 77, 87, 111, 112, 116, 117, 118, 127, 130, 223, 245, 246, 250, 251, 259, 260, 261, 262, 267, 273–74; Jodo Shu, Jodo Shinshu (True Land, True Pure Land), 59, 61, 69, 70; Mahayana, 6, 15, 52, 55–64, 66, 67, 69, 70, 260, 261, 264, 266, 268; Nichiren Shoshu, 61, 63, 64, 69, 70; Nyingmapa, 64, 70; Shingon (Chen Yen; mystery school), 64; Tendai (T'ein-t'ai; rationalist school), 63–64; Theravada (Hinayana), 6, 15, 51, 52, 53–55, 58, 64, 66, 67, 68, 69, 70, 78, 260, 261, 268; Vajrayana (Lamaism, Mantrayana, Tantrayana), xv, 6, 15, 52–53, 57, 58, 61, 64–65, 66, 69, 70, 261, 264, 268; Zen (Ch'an, Dhyana, Jhana, Son), 55, 63, 64, 69, 70, 111

Bulgaria, 201

Burial, 75, 81, 87, 137, 153

Burma, 58

Bushido, 112, 115–16, 118, 120, 261

Byzantine Empire, 200–201, 214, 218

Cairo, 142, 219, 220

Calendar: Hebrew, 169; Hijri (Islamic), 217, 238; liturgical,

Christian, 195–96, 209, 210; Mayan, 250

Caliph, caliphate, 220, 238

Calvin, John, 188, 203, 207, 209, 210

Cambodia, 52

Canaan, 45, 103, 163, 164, 181. *See also* Palestine

Cannon, George Q., quoted, 44

Caste system, 15, 18, 20, 21–22, 23, 25, 30, 31, 32, 40, 76, 78, 219. *See also names of various castes*

Cathedrals, 7, **141**

Catholicism, Roman, xv, 3, 5, 6, 9, 187, 188–202, 205, 206, 207, 208–9, 210, 250, 266, 267, 268, 270–71, 272

Celibacy, 37, 65, 193, 206, 207

Cellarius, Martin, 204

Chanting, 63, 65

Charity, 228, 229, 231, 236. *See also* Seva; Zakat

Charlemagne, 206, 218

Chastity, 37, 38, 119, 236

Cheng ming, 103, 107, 108

Ch'i, 104, 108

Chien, Ssu-ma, 89, 100

China, xv, 8, 85, 93; Buddhism in, 49, 52, 55, 56, 57, 58, 59, 60, 63, 64, 66, 68; Confucianism in, 103, 106, 116; Islam in, 220, 222; Taoism in, 87; Zoroastrianism in, 149

Chinese canon, Chinese classics, Confucian classics, xv, 88, 96, 104–5, 106, 108, 116, 253. *See also names of works*

Chinvat Bridge, 153, 154, 160

Choice, freedom of, 151–52, 166, 190–91, 259, 263

Chosen people, 167, 179–80, 182, 191, 233, 253. *See also* Covenant

Chou, 89, 106

Christ. *See* Jesus Christ; Light of Christ

Christianity, xv, 2, 3, 6, 7, 9, 38, 49, 105, 111, 139, 145, 150, 154, 155, 156, 157, 173, 181, 187–210, 214, 245, 246, 247, 250, 251, 259, 261, 263, 264, 267, 268, 270–71, 272, 274; and ahimsa, 42; and Buddhism, 57, 59, 66; and Islam, 213, 217, 219, 222, 223, 225–26, 227, 229, 231, 233, 234–35, 236, 237. *See also* Catholicism, Roman; Orthodox church, Eastern; Protestantism; *names of various denominations*

Christmas, 173, 195

Chuang Tzu, 89

Chu Hsi, 100, 104, 105, 108

Ch'un Ch'iu, 88, 101, 105, 108

Chung yung, 101, 103, 104, 105, 106, 108

Chun tzu, 96, 101, 104, 107, 108

Church of Jesus Christ of Latter-day Saints, The, xv, 12, 118, 182, 208, 243, 245–47, 250, 253, 258, 259, 265, 266, 268, 269, 270, 272, 273, 275; and Islam, 235–38; views of, on ahimsa, 42–46. *See also* Latter-day Saints

Church of the Holy Sepulchre, **140**

Church of the Nativity, **139**

Chushingura, 116

Cinnabar, Fields of. *See* Fields of Cinnabar

Circumambulation (ritual walk), 6, 56, 80, 81, 174. *See also* Tawaf

Circumcision, 163, 172, 173, 177, 183

Cleanliness, ritual. *See* Purity, ritual

Clergy, 193, 206. *See also* Priesthood; Priests; *names of offices*

Clothing, 10, 35, 37, 40, **129,** 152, 155, 158–59, 177, 180, 227, 230, 232–33, 236, 237. *See also* Phylacteries; Prayer shawl; Veiling; Yarmulka

"Collective unconscious," "collective psyche," 249

Columbus, Christopher, 250

Common human predicament, 247–48, 252, 253

Communication, 8–9, 271, 272–73

Communion, Holy. *See* Eucharist

Communism, 103, 206, 235

Compassion, 19, 20, 38, 49, 54, 58, 60, 66, 79, 107, 172, 228, 229, 235, 237

Confession, 190, 194

Confessions of faith, 165, 194, 199–200, 271. *See also* Shahada

Confirmation, 193, 194, 209, 210

Confucian classics. *See* Chinese canon

Confucianism, xv, 2, 5, 8, 85, 87, 88, 92, 93, 94, 98–109, 111, 112, 116, 245, 247, 250, 251, 259, 260, 261, 264, 267, 268, 274; and Buddhism, 56, 66, 104; five social relationships of, 88, 102; in Japan, 117, 118; political philosophy of, 103–4; and Taoism, 93, 104. *See also* Neo-Confucianism

Confucius (K'ung Ch'iu, K'ung Fu-tzu, Koshi), xv, 8, 35, 59, 85, 89, 96, 99–101, 102, 104–8, 133, 139, 149, 245, 246, 250, 251, 257, 258, 260, 270, 274; statue of, **133;** Temple of, **132;** Tomb of, **133**

Congregationalists, 203–4, 210

Conscience, 46, 249

Constantine, Emperor of Rome, 206

Constantinople (Istanbul), 200, 201, 214, 218, 220, 225

Constitution of the United States, 250, 272

"Conventional religions," 6

Council on Church Union (CCU), 205, 209

Courage, 148

Covenant, 163–64, 166, 173, 191, 195, 208, 247, 269. *See also* Chosen people

Cow, sanctity of, 39, 46

Cowley, Matthew, quoted, 251

Creation, 113, 114, 150, 152–53, 168

Credo, 194, 209

Creeds, 199–200

Cremation, 75, 81, 148, 153

Cross, 190, 196

Crucifix, 5, **140,** 196, 209

Crucifixion, 29, 140, 189, 234, 259

Crusades, 201

Cyril, Saint, 201

Cyrus, xv, 157, 160, 161, 187

Daeva, 158

Dagobas, 70

Dai-Gohonzon, 61, 63, 69, 70

Dakhma ("tower of silence"), **137,** 148, 153, 160

Dalai Lama, 58, 60, 65, 260, 267

Darius, 157, 160

David (king of Israel), 157, 167, 170, 188

Deacon (diaconate), 193, 210

Dead, ordinance work for, 107, 230, 259, 266, 269, 270, 273

Death, 50, 93, 236, 264; Aryan view of, 148; Buddhist view of, 59; Chinese view of, 59, 87; Christian view of, 192, 196; Hindu view of, 25; Jewish view of, 173, 174–75; Latter-day Saint view of, 29, 46, 264–65, 274; Shinto view of, 112; Sikh customs at, 81; Zoroastrian view of, 153

Declaration of Independence, 203, 272

Deer Park, 51, 52

Deities. *See* Gods

Demons, 19, 20, 24, 64, 150, 152, 154, 158

Denominations, 25, 40, 75, 120, 193, 198, 199, 200–205, 220

Devadatta, 51

Devil, 29, 246, 251, 252. *See also* Angra Mainyu; Lucifer; Satan

Dhammapada, 54

Dhanna, 80

Dharma, 17, 20, 22, 25, 30, 31, 63, 68, 245

Dharmakaya, 55, 66

Dhyana, 59, 63. *See also* Buddhism, Zen

Diamond Sutra, 64

Diaspora (scattering of Israel), 170, 174, 181, 183, 184, 191

Dietary laws, 45, 92, 93, 94, 95, 167, 170, 176, 177, 180, 183, 236, 237. *See also* Alcohol; Fasting; Meat; Tobacco; Vegetarianism; Word of Wisdom

Diffusionism, 246–47, 252, 253

Discipleship, concept of, in Sikhism, 79–80

Discrimination. *See* Intolerance

Disobedience, 166, 190, 191. *See also* Obedience

Divination, 88, 91, 92, 93, 104, 111, 114, 117

Divorce, 118, 174, 181, 183, 223, 231

Divyavadana, 60

Doctrine and Covenants, xv, 43–44, 107, 200, 209, 222, 223, 260, 268, 269; paraphrased, 8, 9, 11, 30, 94, 250, 259, 263, 265, 266, 267, 268; quoted, 3, 10, 27, 30, 45, 67, 68, 94, 103, 118, 197, 249, 258

Dome of the Rock. *See* Mosque of Omar

Dravidians, 17–18, 19, 30, 31, 247

Dualism, 68, 77, 151, 154, 158, 261. *See also* Yang; Yin

Durga, 19, 31, 124

Duty, 30, 103. *See also* Dharma

Dyer, Alvin R., quoted, 247

Earth, 41, 152, 153

Easter, 196

Eastern culture and traditions, 6–7, 9, 12, 38, 49

Eastern Orthodox church. *See* Orthodox church, Eastern

Ecumenism, 204–5, 210

Eden, garden of, 152, 264

Education, 91, 101, 103, 105–6, 181, 219, 222, 233, 258

Egalitarianism, 41, 81, 82, 169, 227, 237; of sexes, 94, 107

Egypt and Egyptians, 9, 102–3, 163, 164, 165, 169, 183, 218, 219, 229, 233, 246, 247, 252

Eightfold Middle Path, 53–54, 55, 66, 69, 223

Elders, 203

Elijah, 171

Elohim, 214. *See also* God, the Father

Emerald Buddha, Temple of the, **128**

Emperors of Japan, 114, 115, 116

Endowment, temple, 167, 230, 247, 248, 269

England, Church of, 195, 196, 202, 206

Enlightenment, 37, 46, 49, 50, 51, 53, 55, 56, 58, 61, 63, 64, 66, 249

Epiphany, 195, 210

Episcopal denominations, 195, 202–3, 206, 208, 210, 271

Episcopalians, 6, 192, 193, 202, 205, 206

Eschatology, 87, 118, 225, 245, 247. *See also* Jesus Christ, second coming of; Judgment, final; Resurrection

Esther, 157, 172, 183

Eternal progression, 29. *See also* Salvation, plan of

Ethics, 90, 91

Eucharist (Holy Communion, Lord's Supper), 190, 193, 194, 195, 202, 204, 206, 210, 251. *See also* Sacrament

Eusebius, quoted, 271, 272

Eve, 160, 166, 190, 193, 196, 207, 262, 264–65, 274

Evil, 19, 27, 28, 38, 68, 150, 151, 152, 153, 154, 157, 158, 166, 167, 168, 172, 180, 190, 222, 225, 231, 261, 266, 269

Exclusivism, ix, 253

Exercise, 92, 93. *See also* Yoga

Exile, Babylonian, xv, 147, 157–58, 164, 165, 166, 246

Exodus, the, 7, 151, 164, 165, 168, 170–71, 181

Exorcism, 6, 64, 87, 91, 92

Extremism, 233–35

Ezekiel, 35, 151, 164, 165, 179, 182

Ezra, 164, 165

Fa-Hsien, 59

Faith, 28, 58, 63, 79, 145, 190, 232, 235, 237, 265; in Jesus Christ, 188, 191, 192, 194, 201, 203, 208, 274; witness of, 223, 224–26, 239. *See also* Confessions of faith; Shahada

Fall, the, 190, 262, 264–65, 274; Zoroastrian view of, 152

Family: in Buddhism, 63, 65, 66; in Christianity, 205, 206; in Confucianism, 56, 99, 102, 105–6, 107; in Hinduism, 23, 25; in Islam, 231–32, 233, 236, 237, 240–41; in Jainism, 40; in Judaism, 174, 180, 181, 182; Latter-day Saint view of, 68; in Shinto, 116; in Sikhism, 81, 82; in Taoism, 93–94; in Zoroastrianism, 154, 159. *See also* Filial piety

Farohar, **136,** 152, 160

Fasting, 25, 38, 169, 173, 174, 223, 228–30, 236, 237, 238. *See also* Ramadan

Fatihah, 223

Fertility cult, 18, 19, 31, 111, 163

Festivals: Jewish, 167–73, 179, 180; Muslim, 228, 229–30, 231. *See also* Matsuri

Fields of Cinnabar, 92–93, 96

Fig tree. *See* Bodhi tree

Filial piety, 8, 66, 87, 92, 93–94, 102, 106, 107. *See also* Family; Hsiao

Fire, 18, 30, 81, 147, 148, 150, 151, 153, 155

Fire temples. *See* Temples, Zoroastrian fire

First Council, 54, 55

First vision. *See* Smith, Joseph, first vision of

Fisher, Mary, 207

Five Classics of Confucianism, 104. *See also* Chinese classics

Five Elements. *See* Wu-hsing

Five Pillars of Islam, 223–31, 238, 239

"Folk religions." *See* "Popular religions"

Founding Fathers, 107, 250

Four Books of Confucianism, 99, 104, 106, 108. *See also* Chinese classics

Four Noble Truths, 50, 51, 53, 55, 67, 69, 223

Francis, Saint, of Assisi, 42, 250

Fravashi, 152, 159

Freedom, 191; religious, 272. *See also* Choice, freedom of; Rights, human; Tolerance

Fundamentalism, 26–27. *See also* Extremism

Funerals, 81, 118, 153, 158

Gabars, 156, 159. *See also* Zoroastrianism and Zoroastrians

Gabriel (angel), 216, 217, 229, 239

Galilee, Sea of, **139**

Gambling, 76

Gandhi, Mohandas K. (Mahatma), 18, 23, 31, 39, 250; quoted, 21

Ganesha, 18, 31, **125**

Ganges River, 17, **26,** 36, 80

Garden Tomb, **140**

Garments, sacred. *See* Clothing

Garuda, 20, 31

Gathas, 149, 150, 152, 153, 154, 160, 161, 246

Gautama, Siddhartha, xv, 32, 35, 50–51, 55, 58, 61, 62, 66, 257, 258. *See also* Buddha, the

Gaya, 51, 53, 61, 62, 63

Gayomart, 152, 160

Gemara, 175, 183, 184

Geomancy, 6, 91

Get, 181, 183

Gloria, 194, 210

Glory, degrees of, 159, 208, 274

Gobind Singh, Guru, 75, 76, 77, 82, 83

God, 5, 11–12, 22, 28, 38, 42, 67, 68, 73–82, 94, 106, 145, 149, 163, 164, 167, 168, 170, 175, 189, 190, 191, 194, 196, 197, 198, 203, 210, 237, 246, 247, 248, 250, 259, 260, 264, 268, 269, 270; as Creator, 7, 38, 43, 67, 68, 77, 79, 118–19, 145, 150, 151, 163, 165–66, 168, 171, 189, 190, 193, 199, 207, 224, 225, 257, 262, 263, 274; the Father, 30, 59, 159, 188, 246, 258–59, 260, 262, 263, 265, 266, 267, 269, 271, 273, 274; image of, 263–64; Jewish conception of, 165–66, 169, 177, 180, 182; Latter-day Saint view of, 182, 238, 253; nature of, 190, 199, 204, 225, 235; Sikh conception of God, 73, 77–79. *See also* Ahura Mazda; Allah; Ik Oankar; Love

Godhead, 29, 81, 118–19, 182, 200, 208, 210, 234, 246, 261–62, 264, 265, 271, 274. *See also* Trinity

Gods, deities, 5, 54, 61, 76, 85, 260, 261; Aryan, 18–19, 148; Chinese, 87, 99; Hindu, 19–20, 23, 262, 268; Mahayana Buddhist, 61; Middle Eastern, 163, 214; Roman, 199; Taoist, 91; Vajrayana Buddhist, 65. *See also* Bodhisattvas; Buddhas; Kami

Golden Rule, 4, 5, 93, 245, 250

Golden Temple, 76, 80, 81, 82, **128**

Golgotha, **140**

Good, 5, 68, 93, 150, 152, 153, 157, 158, 159, 166, 168, 190, 269

Gospel of Jesus Christ, 30, 43, 95, 107, 118, 205, 243, 246, 257, 265, 266; restored, 8–10, 119, 156, 187, 245, 252. *See also* Restoration

Government, 88, 91, 99, 101, 103–4, 107

Grace, 21, 25, 77, 79, 190, 191, 193, 194, 195, 196, 201, 202, 209, 223, 267, 270

Grand Mosque, Mecca, **142**

Grant, Heber J., 119; quoted, 45

Granth (Adi Granth, Guru Granth Sahib), xv, 75, 76, 77, 80–81, 82, 129; quoted, 79

Grave, 87, 94, 103, 106, 140. *See also* Burial; Death; Funeral

Great Commandment. *See* Golden Rule

Great Learning, the. *See* Ta Hsueh
Greece and Greeks, 9, 35, 57, 59, 103, 107, 149, 201, 214, 220, 246, 250, 251. *See also* Hellenistic Empire; Neo-Platonic thought
Greed, 90, 94, 152
Greek Orthodox. *See* Orthodox church, Eastern
Gurdwara, 80, 82, **129, 130,** 268
Guru, 5, 25, 73, 75, 77, 78, 80, 81, 82, 260, 267. *See also names of various Sikh gurus*
Gurumantra, 78
Guyart, Marie, 207
Gwalior, 126

Hadith, 223, 226, 229, 234, 238, 245, 254
Hafiz, 222
Hagar, 163, 230
Haggadah, 171, 172, 183
Hajj, 143, 223, 230–31, 238, 240, 268, 269; painting, **143,** 230
Hajji (hajja), 230
Halacha, 179, 183
Halima, 215
Haman, 157, 172
Hanks, Marion D., quoted, 269
Hanukkah, 172–73, 183
Haoma, 147, 148, 151, 160. *See also* Soma
Harai, 114, 120. *See also* Pollution; Purity, ritual
Haraiguishi, 120
Hare Krishna movement. *See* International Society for Krishna Consciousness (ISKCON)
Hargobind, Guru, 75, 82
Harijan, 18, 31
Hari Krishan, Guru, 80, 82
Hari Rai, Guru, 82
Harmony, 8, 63, 69, 85, 88, 90, 92, 94, 103, 104, 107, 108, 119, 164, 193, 207, 213, 264, 273
Hasan, 221, 226
Hasidism. *See* Judaism, Hasidic
Hasmoneans, 172, 187. *See also* Maccabees
Haumai, 79, 82
Haurvatat, 150
Healing, 6, 19, 81, 91, 117, 118. *See also* Medicine
Heart Sutra, 64
Heaven, 20, 78, 99, 100, 105, 159, 193, 208, 217, 266; mandate of, 105. *See also* Glory, degrees of; Paradise; P'eng-lai; T'ien; Western Land
Hell, 20, 78, 192, 225, 229, 266, 267
Hellenistic Empire, 172, 189

Henry II, King of England, 206
Henry VIII, King of England, 202, 206
Herai Mura myth, 119
Herod the Great, 187
Herzl, Theodore, 181
Hijra, 7, 217, 238
Hillel, Rabbi, quoted, 166, 245
Himsa 39, 46. *See* Ahimsa; Violence
Hinayana. *See* Buddhism, Theravada (Hinayana)
Hinckley, Gordon B., quoted, ix–x, 4
Hinduism, 2, 3, 5, 6, 7, 15, 17–32, 36, 38, 45, 49, 53, 57, 65, 76, 77, 148, 159, 160, 173, 219, 245, 246, 247, 250, 251, 259, 261, 262, 267, 268, 273–74; and Islam, 219; sects of, in United States, 27; and Sikhism, 73, 75, 79, 80, 82
Hira, Mount, 216, 225
Hirohito, Emperor of Japan, 114
Holocaust, the, 165, 172, 173, 180, 181, 191, 233
Holy Communion. *See* Eucharist
Holy Ghost, Holy Spirit, 30, 94, 150, 182, 188, 189, 193, 195, 196, 198, 200, 204, 210, 246, 253, 259, 261, 262, 265, 266, 271, 274
Holy Land. *See* Palestine
Holy orders, 193, 210. *See also* Ordination; Priests, Christian
Holy Roman Empire, 206
Homoiousios, 189, 210
Homoousios, 189, 210, 261, 262
Homosexuality, 155
Hompa Hongwanji, 61
Honesty, 116, 119, 215, 216, 236. *See also* Lying
Hoshana Rabba, 170, 183
Hsiao, 101, 102–3, 104, 105, 108. *See also* Family; Filial piety
Hsiao Ching, 102
Hsien, 92, 96
Hsuan-tsang, 59
Hsun Tzu, 101
Human beings, purpose of, 151–52, 166, 190–92, 236
Humility, 1, 28, 60, 79, 90, 94, 102, 214, 226, 227, 229, 235, 265
Hunafa', 214
Hunter, Howard W., 234, 263; quoted, 259, 269–70, 275
Hunter, Milton R., quoted, 251
Hunting, 44, 46
Husayn, 221, 226
Hygiene school, 92, 94–95, 96; Interior Gods, 92
Hymns, songs, 74, 75, 79, 80, 81, 82, 104, 149, 150, 153, 154, 160, 161, 168, 170, 172

I Ching (Book of Changes), 64, 88, 96, 101, 104, 106, 108
Icons, 5, 196, 201, 210, 214
Idols and idolatry, 79, 214, 216, 218, 250, 251. *See also* Images
Ignorance, 19, 151, 152
Ihram, 230
Ik Oankar (One True Name), 76, 82, 261
Illusion. *See* Maya
Images, 5, 268. *See also* Idols and idolatry
Imam, 221, 227, 238
Immortality, 6, 43, 59, 85, 92–93, 96, 151, 159, 246, 265
Impurity, ritual, 114, 118, 154, 155, 175. *See also* Pollution; Purity, ritual
Incarnation, 36, 55, 58, 60, 61. *See also* Reincarnation
Inclusivism, ix
Independent Christian denominations, 202, 204
India, 7, 17–18, 27, 35, 73, 214, 262, 272; Buddhism in, 49, 52, 54, 56, 58, 60, 63; Islam in, 75, 218, 219, 220; religions of, 15; resurgence of religion in, 26–27; Sikhism in, 81; Zoroastrianism in, 147, 149, 151, 156, 159, 160
Indian mythology, 25
Indo-Aryans. *See* Aryans
Indonesia, 213, 220
Indra, 18, 24, 31, 32, 246
Indus Valley, 17–18, 31
Infanticide, female, 25, 216, 232
Inner-Trinitarian Decree, 189–90, 210
Inspiration, divine, 249–51
Intelligence, 43. *See also* Knowledge
International Society for Krishna Consciousness (ISKCON), 27, 30, 31
Intolerance, 3–5, 182, 213, 218. *See also* Tolerance
Iran, 17, 149, 151, 156, 159, 220, 221, 230, 241
Iraq, 219
Isaac, 164, 169, 170, 225, 240
Isaiah, 154, 158, 164, 165, 174, 179, 182
Ise, Grand Shrine of, 6, 111, 114, 120
Ishmael, 164, 214, 225, 230, 231, 238, 239, 240
Islam and Muslims, xv, 2, 3, 5, 6, 7, 38, 49, 145, 147, 150, 151, 156, 197, 213–41, 245, 246, 247, 250, 251, 259, 260, 261, 263, 264, 267, 268, 274; and Christianity, 213, 217, 219, 222, 223, 225–26, 227, 229, 231, 233, 234–35, 236, 237;

Islam and Muslims *(continued),*
  contributions of, to civilization,
  219–20, 222; Five Pillars of,
  223–31, 238, 239; and Judaism,
  214, 217, 219, 220, 223, 225–26,
  227, 233, 234, 236, 237; Shi'ite, 6,
  220–21, 223, 225, 230, 238, 239;
  and Sikhism, 73, 75, 76; Sufi, 77,
  226, 239; Sunni, 6, 220–21, 223,
  225, 230, 238, 239
Israel: house of, xiii, 45, 158, 164,
  165, 166, 167, 169, 176, 182, 191,
  208, 247; lost tribes of, 12, 67, 270;
  modern nation of, 165, 173, 177,
  180, 181, 184. *See also* Jacob (Israel)
Izanagi and Izanami, 113, 117, 120

Jacob (Israel), 102–3, 164, 170, 191
Jade Emperor, 92
Jain caves, **126**
Jainism, xv, 2, 7, 15, 35–46, 53, 77,
  126, 245, 246, 250, 251, 259, 261,
  262, 267, 268; Digambara, 15, 36,
  37, 40, 41, 46; Svetambara, 15, 36,
  40, 41, 46
Jai Ram, 74, 82
James (apostle), 267
Janam-sakhis, 74, 82, 83
Japan, 40, 58, 63, 68, 85, 118, 233,
  253; Buddhism in, 39–40, 49, 52,
  55, 56, 57, 58, 59, 60, 61, 63, 64,
  66, 111; Christianity in, 111;
  Confucianism in, 100, 106; and
  Judaism, 119; mythological origin
  of, 113–14; Shinto in, 111, 115,
  116, 135; Taoism in, 111
Japji, 80, 82
Jashan ceremony, **136**
Jataka tales, 55, 69; Kalingabodhi, 56
Jehovah, 151, 164, 261, 262, 265,
  274. *See also* God; Jesus Christ
Jen, 101, 102, 103, 104, 107, 108
Jeremiah, 35, 164, 165, 179, 182, 259
Jerome, Saint, 198, 210
Jerusalem, 137, 138, 140, 142, 165,
  170, 172, 173, 177, 187, 191, 217,
  220, 225
Jesus Christ, xv, 7, 12, 28, 29, 30, 94,
  119, 139, 140, 188–92, 194–97,
  199, 200, 202–8, 217, 222, 225,
  249, 250, 259, 261, 266–74; and
  the Buddha, 49; divinity of, 200,
  204, 237; as God of the Old
  Testament, 45; and Japan, 119; as
  Messiah, 12, 181, 187, 245, 252,
  263; Muslim view of, 234; quoted,
  4, 45, 67, 95, 245; as Savior, 12, 30,
  189, 190, 191, 195, 196, 199, 203,
  205, 208, 264; second coming of,
  67, 257, 266; the Son, 22, 30, 145,

182, 189, 197, 210, 246, 260, 262,
  263; status of, 193, 253. *See also*
  Crucifixion; Light of Christ;
  Resurrection, of Jesus Christ
Jihad, 231, 233, 238
Jimmu, 114, 120
Jina, 36, 46
Jinn, 214, 224, 225
Jiriki, 63
Jiva, 36, 41, 46
Job, 28, 247, 263
Jodo Shu, Jodo Shinshu. *See* Bud-
  dhism, Jodo Shu, Jodo Shinshu
John (apostle), 43, 267; Gospel of,
  196, 197, 262
John XXIII, Pope, 201, 210
John Paul II, Pope, 201
Joseph (son of Jacob), 102–3, 164, 170
Joshua, 218
Judaism and Jews, xv, 2, 3, 5, 6, 7,
  12, 38, 67, 145, 163–84, 233, 245,
  246, 247, 250, 252, 259, 261, 263,
  264, 267, 268, 270, 274; Ashkenazi,
  176; and Christianity, 187–88,
  189, 191, 197, 202, 208; Conservative, 6, 174, 175, 177, 181, 183;
  Hasidim, 176, 177, 183; and Islam,
  214, 217, 219, 220, 223, 225–26,
  227, 233, 234, 236, 237; and Japan,
  119; Mitnagdim, 177, 183; Orthodox (modern), 6, 169, 174, 175,
  176–77, 180–81, 182, 183, 184;
  Reformed, 6, 174, 175, 176, 177,
  181, 183; Sephardi, 176; Ultra-
  Orthodox, 138, 174, 175–76, 177,
  180, 181; Zoroastrian influences
  on, 150, 154, 155, 157. *See also*
  Assimilation, of Jews
Judgment, final, 87, 145, 147, 155,
  192, 224, 225, 234, 239, 251,
  266–67, 274; general, 221;
  individual, 154, 169. *See also*
  Eschatology
Jung, Carl G., 7, 249
Justice, 20, 116, 150–51, 163, 167,
  169, 180, 197, 207, 216, 231, 234,
  236, 264, 265, 267. *See also* Asha
Justin Martyr, 251
Jyana, 20, 22–23, 29–30

Ka'aba, 74, **142,** 214, 216, 217, 227,
  230, 239
Kabbalah, 157, 170
Kabir, 80, 82
Kachh, 76, 82
Kaddish, 174–75, 183
Kali, 19, 26, 31, 38
Kalki, 20, 30, 31, 245
Kalpa, 7, 19, 31, 41
Kamakura, 127

Kambun, Mani, quoted, 60
Kami, 56, 111, 112–15, 116, 118, 119,
  120, 133, 261, 264, 268
Kami-dana, 114, 118, 120
Kami no Michi. *See* Shinto
Kangha, 76, 82
Kapilavastu, 50, 52
Kara, 76, 82
Karma, 15, 17, 20, 21–22, 27–28, 31,
  36–37, 38, 51, 63, 68, 263
Karma-matter, 36–37, 46
Karttikeya, 19
Kashi, 26
Kashyapa, 54, 63
Kegon Sutra (Avatansaka), 64
Kesh, 76, 82
Ketuvim (Writings), 179, 183, 184,
  197
Kevala-jñana, 36, 46
Khadija, 216
Khalsa, 75–76, 82, 129
Kiddush, 168
Killing, 27, 37, 38, 39, 40, 44–46, 53,
  54, 66, 230
Kimball, Heber C., quoted, 43
Kimball, Spencer W., 9, 259; quoted,
  4, 44, 258, 270
Kindness, 226, 232. *See also* Benevo-
  lence; Charity; Compassion;
  Golden Rule
Kippah. *See* Yarmulka
Kirpan, 76, 82
Knowledge, 10–11, 22, 40, 43, 46,
  152, 192, 252, 258, 259–61, 270,
  274
Knowledge, Way of. *See* Jyana;
  Kevala-jñana
Knox, John, 203
Koans, 63, 69
Kobo Daishi, 60
Ko Hung, 92, 93, 96
Kojiki, 113, 120
Kol Nidre, 169, 183
Korea, 40, 58, 116; Buddhism in,
  39–40, 49, 52, 55, 56, 57, 58, 60,
  63, 64, 68, 127; Confucianism in,
  100, 106, 132, 133; Shinto in, 111
Kosen-rufu, 63, 68
Kosher, 176, 183
Koya, Mount, 60
Krishna, 20, 23, 24–25, 27, 30, 31,
  32, 57, 73, 79, **124,** 246. *See also*
  Rama; Vishnu; *names of other
  avatars*
Kshathhra, 150
Kshatriyas, 18, 20, 21, 22, 24, 25, 31,
  32, 50
Kuan Yin (Kannon), 60, 65, 67. *See
  also* Avalokitesvara
Kuei, 87, 92, 96

Kukkutapada, Mount, 61
Kumarajiva, 59
Kurma, 20, 30, 31
Kushinara, 51
Kusti, 155, 158, 160
Kyoto, 128, 134, 135
Kyrie, 194, 210

Lakshmi, 24, **124**. *See also* Radha; Sita
Lamaism. *See* Buddhism, Vajrayana
Lamanites, 119
Lamas, 53, 57. *See also* Buddhism,
    Vajrayana; Monks, Buddhist;
    Priests, Buddhist
Langar, 81, 130
Lankavatara Sutra, 64
Lao Tzu, xv, 12, 35, 89, 90, 91, 95,
    96, 149, 245, 246, 257, 258, 260
Las Casas (Catholic priest), 251
Latter-day Saints, ix, xii–xiv, 1, 3–4,
    78, 79, 145, 147, 167, 192, 200,
    219, 234, 257–75; and ahimsa,
    42–46; and Apocrypha, 197; and
    Buddhism, 66–68; and Christian-
    ity, 188, 199, 208–9, 262, 266, 271;
    and Confucianism, 106–7; and
    Hinduism, 27–30; and Islam, 222,
    223, 226, 228, 230, 233, 234–38,
    240; and Jainism, 41–46; and
    Judaism, 163, 167, 181–82; and
    Shinto, 118–19; and Sikhism,
    81–82; study of religions by, ix–x,
    xii–xiv, 1, 3–12, 187, 243, 245–75;
    and Taoism, 94–95; and Zoroastri-
    anism, 152, 156–59. *See also*
    Church of Jesus Christ of Latter-
    day Saints, The
Law, 223; of the harvest, 21, 27–28;
    of Moses, 164, 165, 166, 179, 182.
    See also Pentateuch; Shari'a; Torah
Laws (Code, Ordinances) of Manu.
    See Manu, Laws of
Leadership, 104
Lehi, 35, 41, 119, 157, 214, 263
Lent, 195–96, 210
Leo I, Pope, 201
Li (rational principle), 104, 108
Li (ritual), 101, 102, 103, 104, 105,
    107, 108
Libations, 147, 246
Li Chi (Book of Ritual), 105, 106,
    108
Lies and lying, 37, 38, 53, 54, 66, 116,
    151, 158. *See also* Honesty; Truth
Life, reverence for. *See* Ahimsa;
    Pacifism; Violence; War
Light of Christ, 30, 94, 249, 252
Limbo, 266
Lindsay, Richard P., quoted, 4
Lingam, 19, 31

Literature, 49, 104, 117, 222, 250
Liturgical calendar. *See* Calendar,
    liturgical, Christian
Lord's Supper. *See* Eucharist
Lotus, 19, 20, 59, 60, 63, 66, 69, 70, 80
Lotus Sutra (Saddharmapundarika),
    59, 60, 61, 63, 66, 69, 70
Love, 20, 60, 68, 79, 81, 94, 95, 107,
    124, 150, 199, 234; for God, 82,
    163, 269; of God, 12, 78, 80, 191,
    197, 253; of Jesus Christ, 29
Loyalty, 93, 102, 115, 148
Lu, 100, 101, 105, 108
Lucifer, 158. *See also* Devil; Satan
Lun Yu. *See* Analects
Luther, Martin, xv, 190, 198, 201,
    202, 203, 204, 207, 210, 250
Lutherans, 195, 203, 204–5, 210

Maccabees, 173, 187. *See also*
    Hasmoneans
Magic, 20, 49, 64, 65, 91
Magus, magi, 149, 157, 160
Mahabharata, 20, 23, 24, 25, 30, 32;
    quoted, 245
Mahakasyapa, 61
Maha-mantra, 27, 31
Maha Maya, 50
Mahavira, Vardhamana, xv, 35–36,
    39, 40, 41, 42, 46, 88, 149, 246,
    257, 258
Mahayana. *See* Buddhism, Mahayana
Mahdi, 221, 239, 245
Maidhyomanha, 149
Maimonides, Moses (Rambam), 223
"Mainstream religion." *See*
    "Conventional religions"
Maitreya, 20, 57, 59, 60, 61, 68, 70,
    127, 128, 245
Mala, 79, 82
Malli, 41
Mana, 112
Mandala, 61, 65, 68, 70
Mantras, 58, 65, 68, 70
Mantrayana. *See* Buddhism, Vajrayana
Manu, 20, 31; Laws (Code,
    Ordinances) of, 24, 25, 27, 31, 32
Manushi buddhas. *See* Buddhas,
    manushi
Maps, 2, 52, 215
Mara, 51, 66
Marananda, 56
Mardana the Bard, 74, 81, 82
"Marketplace, the." *See* "Popular
    religions"
Marriage, 7, 88; celestial, 269; in
    Christianity, 193, 205, 206, 207,
    210; in Hinduism, 25, 81; in Islam,
    223, 232; in Jainism, 36; in Judaism,
    173, 174, 180, 182; in Sikhism, 76,

80, 81, 82; in Vajrayana Buddhism,
    64–65; in Zoroastrianism, 155,
    161
Martyrs, 149–50, 234, 257, 258, 259,
    262
Mary (mother of Jesus), 196, 210, 234
Mashye and Mashyane, 152, 153, 160
Mass, 190, 194, 195, 196–97, 201,
    209, 210, 269
Matrimony. *See* Marriage, in
    Christianity
Matsuri, 115, 120
Matsya, 20, 30, 31
Maya (illusion), 7, 19, 23, 31, 68,
    79, 82
Maya Indians, 250
Mazzah, 171, 172, 183
McKay, David O., 9
Meals, ritual, 167–68, 171–72. *See
    also* Eucharist; Langar; Naorai;
    Sacrament
Meat, 27, 39–40, 92–93, 94, 176,
    236. *See also* Vegetarianism
Mecca, viii, 7, 74, 80, 142, 214, 215,
    216, 217, 220, 223, 227, 230–31,
    238, 239, 268
Medicine, 57, 69, 92. *See also* Healing
Medina (Madinat al-Nabi, Yathrib),
    7, 74, 217, 220, 221, 223, 230, 231,
    238, 239
Meditation, 5, 7, 19, 23, 31, 37, 38,
    51, 58, 59, 63, 64, 65, 70, 73, 78,
    92, 93, 111, 197, 216, 268
Megillah, 172, 183
Meiji regime of Japan, 112, 135
Mencius (Meng Tzu), 101, 102, 104,
    108, 250, 251; Book of, 105, 106,
    108
Mennonites, 204
Menorah, 172–73, 183
Mercy, 21, 29, 79, 169, 180, 194, 197,
    223, 224, 226, 267
Meru, Mount, 19
Mesopotamia, 163, 246
Messiah figures, 12, 20, 118, 245,
    252; Jewish, 167, 171, 181, 187,
    188, 245. *See also* Jesus Christ, as
    Messiah; Kalki; Mahdi; Maitreya;
    Saoshyant
Methodists, 6, 195, 202–3, 205, 206,
    258
Mexico, 250
Mezuzah, 176, 183
Middle East, 3, 10, 220, 234–35. *See
    also names of countries*
Midrash, 179, 183
Mihrab, 74, 75, 227
Mikoshi, **134**
Mikveh, 175, 177, 183

Militarism, 45; and Islam, 218, 233–35; and Shinto, 111, 112, 113, 115–16, 118; and Sikhism, 73, 75. *See also* Bushido; Shinto, state

Millennium, Latter-day Saint view of, 45, 46

Mina, 230

Minaret, **141,** 227, 239

Minyan, 175, 177, 181, 183

Miracles, 213, 234

Misery. *See* Suffering

Mishnah, 164, 179, 183, 184

Missionary work, 9–10, 205, 207, 234–35, 258, 259, 266, 269–75

Mithra, 153, 160, 251

Mitnagdim. *See* Judaism, Mitnagdim

Miyajima, 134

Moderation, 103, 105. *See also* Eight-fold Middle Path

Mohel, 173, 183

Moksha, 17, 22, 23, 24, 25, 28, 31, 37, 264. *See also* Mukti; Reincarnation

Monad, 26, 41, 46

Monasteries: Buddhist, 56; Taoist, **131**

Mongolia and Mongols, 49, 56, 57, 64, 69

Monism, 7, 15, 23, 36, 38, 77

Monks and monasticism: Buddhist, 50, 54, 56, 65, 66, 67, 70, 80, **127,** 159, 173; Christian, 197, 206; Hindu, 51; Jain, 36, 39, 41. *See also* Arhat; Sadhus; Sangha

Monotheism, 7, 15, 38, 77, 117, 145, 189, 214, 234, 236, 239, 261, 263; ethical, 106, 114, 145, 261

Morality, morals, 53, 68, 87, 91, 93, 104, 106, 107, 108, 159, 182, 204, 207–8, 232, 235, 236, 237, 253, 267, 274

Morality play, 198

Mordecai, 157, 172

Mormon, Book of. *See* Book of Mormon

Mormonism. *See* Church of Jesus Christ of Latter-day Saints, The

Moses, xiii, xv, 22, 68, 157, 164, 165, 170, 179, 181, 217, 218, 225, 257, 258. *See also* Law, of Moses

Mosque (masjid), 5, 6, **141, 142,** 224, 225, 227, 228, 229, 230, 231, 233, 239, 268. *See also names of mosques*

Mosque of Omar (Dome of the Rock), **137,** 217, 225

Mourning, 81, 100, 101, 102, 106, 173, 174–75, 183, 184

Mu'awiyah, 221

Muezzin, **142,** 227, 239

Mughals. *See* India, Islam in

Muhammad, xv, 12, 49, 213, 214–18, 220–21, 222, 223, 225, 226, 227–28, 229, 236, 237, 238, 239, 245, 246, 251, 252, 257, 258, 270

Mukti, 73, 77, 79, 82. *See also* Moksha

Music, 49, 88, 194, 195, 202. *See also* Hymns, songs

Muslims. *See* Islam and Muslims

Mysticism. *See* Islam, Sufism in; Kabbalah

Myth, 249; Chinese, 87; Hindu, 19–20, 24, 26, 40; Indo-Aryan, 150; Shinto, 113–14

Nam-myoho-renge-kyo, 63

Nanak, Guru, xv, 12, 73–75, 77, 79, 80, 81, 82, 83, 257, 258

Nandi, 19, 31

Nankana Sahib (Talwandi), 74

Naorai, 114, 115, 120. *See also* Meals, ritual

Narasimha, 20, 30, 31

Nataputta, Nigantha, 35, 46. *See also* Mahavira, Vardhamana

Nataraja, 19, 31

Nath tradition, 73, 82

Nature, 7, 38, 60, 63, 69, 85, 163, 170; in Shinto tradition, 111, 112, 118, 261; in Taoist tradition, 87, 88, 89, 90

Navjote, 155, 156, 160

Nazis. *See* Third Reich

Neo-Confucianism, 100, 104, 108, 112

Neo-Platonic thought, 189, 192, 199, 210

Nephites, 12, 45, 119, 270; Three, 67

Nevi'im (Prophets), 183, 197

"New religions," in Japan, 117, 118

New Testament, xv, 66, 157, 174, 196, 197–98, 199, 222, 226, 271, 272, 273; paraphrased, 187, 189, 196, 240, 262, 265, 266, 271; quoted, 3, 4, 12, 28, 29, 42, 45, 46, 67, 95, 155, 188, 191, 192, 196, 207, 245, 248, 253, 269, 270. *See also* John, Gospel of; Paul, letters of

Nibley, Hugh, quoted, 11, 247, 252

Nicaea, Council of, 199

Nicene Creed, 189, 199, 200

Nichiren Daishonin, 61, 63, 70

Nichiren Shoshu. *See* Buddhism, Nichiren Shoshu

Nicholas of Hereford, 198

Night Journey and Ascension, 217

Nihongi (Nihon Shoki), 113, 120

Niiname Matsuri, 115, 120

Ninigi, 114, 120

Nirang, 148, 160

Nirvana, 49, 67, 264; in Hinduism, 21, 23, 31, 53, 54, 70; in Mahayana

Buddhism, 56, 58, 59, 61, 65, 66; in Theravada Buddhism, 51, 68

Noah, 20, 157

Norito, 114, 115, 120

Nuns: Buddhist, 51, 54, 65, 118; Christian, 197, 206; Jain, 36, 37, 41

Nyingmapa. *See* Buddhism, Nyingmapa

Oaks, Dallin H., quoted, 219

Obedience, 93, 102, 118, 159, 235, 266

Offerings, 56, 118, 124, 128, 246. *See also* Sacrifice; Shinsen

Oharai, 115, 120

Ohira, Masayoshi, 111

Old Testament, xv, 42, 45, 119, 148, 157, 163, 166, 176, 179, 184, 197–98, 199, 209, 223, 246, 252, 253, 262, 271; paraphrased, xiii, 102, 158, 163, 164, 166, 168, 169, 170, 171, 172, 173, 175, 262; quoted, 28, 42, 45, 67, 103, 165, 170, 176, 240

Omizuya, 114, 120

Ordinances, 208, 247, 248, 265–66, 272, 273, 274, 275

Ordination, 193, 206, 209

Original sin. *See* Sin, original

Orthodox church, Eastern, xv, 5, 6, 187, 189, 192–97, 200–201, 203, 206, 209, 210

Pacifism, 35, 38, 45, 204

Padma Sambhava, 64, 70

Pagodas, 56

Pahlavi, 149, 160

Pakistan, 218, 220

Palestine and Palestinians, 179, 187, 219

Pali, 55, 64, 68, 70

Pantheism, 117

Parables: Jain, 41–42; of Jesus, 3, 5, 265

Paradise, 225, 226, 233, 266, 267. *See also* Heaven; P'eng-lai; Western Land

Parasraya, 20

Parasurama, 20, 30, 31

Parsis, 5, 32, 156, 160. *See also* Zoroastrianism and Zoroastrians

Parvati, 19, 30, 31

Passover, 170–72, 183

Patna, 36, 46

Patriarchs, 11, 269; eastern Orthodox, 192–93, 200–201

Patriotism, 85, 115

Paul (apostle), xv, 196, 206–7, 259, 271; letters of, 197, 205; quoted, 45, 155, 191

Paul VI, Pope, 201, 210

Pava, 36

Peace, 78, 81, 85, 90, 99, 101, 105, 108, 168, 181, 194, 213, 216, 224, 228, 230, 231, 234, 235, 236

Pearl of Great Price, xv, 260; paraphrased, xiii, 8, 28, 41, 118, 158, 258; quoted, ix, 4, 22, 29, 43, 118, 157, 199, 238, 246, 253, 258, 264, 265, 275

Penance, 190, 193, 209, 210

P'eng-lai, 92, 96

Pentateuch, xv, 166, 179, 184

Pentecost, 196, 210

Pentecostal churches, 195

Perfect Wisdom (Prajnaparamita), 64

Persecution, 156, 165, 180, 182, 191, 216, 219, 272, 273. See also Intolerance

Persian empire and culture, 148, 149, 155, 157, 172, 187, 214, 218, 220

Peter (apostle), 67, 192–93, 201, 259, 267, 271

Pharisees, 3, 66, 67, 165, 187, 245, 265

Philanthropy, 38

Phylacteries (tefillin), 5, **138**, 175, 184

Pilgrimage, xiii, 25, 79, 217. See also Hajj

Pioneers, Latter-day Saint, xiii, 247

Pius IX, Pope, 192

Plan of salvation. See Salvation, plan of

Plants, 28, 29, 43, 46, 190, 230, 262

Plato, 107, 149, 270. See also Neo-Platonic thought

Plotinus, 210

Pluralism, ix, 180, 205, 237, 252, 272

Pogroms, 165, 183

Pollution, 119, 153. See also Harai; Impurity, ritual; Purity, ritual

Polytheism, 150, 154, 214, 216, 224, 236. See also Gods, deities

Pool of Immortality, 76, 81, **129**

Poor, giving to, 21, 172. See also Seva; Zakat

Pope, 192, 200, 201, 208, 260, 267, 268, 271. See also names of various popes

"Popular religions," 6, 117

Prabhupada, A. C. Bhaktivedanta Swami, 27; quoted, 39

Prajnaparamita. See Perfect Wisdom

Pratt, Orson, quoted, 43

Pratt, Parley P., quoted, 235, 251

Prayer, 5, 85, 268; in Buddhism, 57, 65, 70; call to, in Islam, 224, 227, 229; in Christianity, 194, 197, 206; in Hinduism, 23, 25; in Islam (salat), 216, 217, 223, 224, 226, 229, 230, 236, 237, 238; in Judaism, 165, 168, 170, 172, 173, 174–75, 177, 183; shawl (tallit), 175, 184; in

Shinto, 111; in Sikhism, 79; in Zoroastrianism, 153, 155, 160. See also Norito; Salat

Predestination, 203

Prejudice. See Intolerance

Premortal existence, 28–29, 147, 152, 158, 208, 245, 248–49, 252, 259, 263, 274

Presbyterians, 195, 203, 204–5, 210, 258

Pride, 79, 90, 191, 246, 259, 265. See also Haumai

Priesthood, 11–12, 94, 190, 192, 193, 203, 243, 247, 248, 253, 267–68, 269–70, 271; Melchizedek, 164, 268, 272, 273; restoration of, 268. See also Authority; Priests

Priests, 5; Buddhist, 112; Christian, 193, 194, 197, 198, 202, 203, 206, 210; Israelite, 191; Shinto, 112, 118, **135;** Taoist, 193; Zoroastrian, **136,** 267. See also Magus, magi; Priesthood

Prophets, 5, 11, 67, 149, 151, 157, 164–65, 167, 179, 182, 183, 216, 217, 226, 234, 235, 236, 238, 245, 247, 250, 261, 268, 269; modern, 208, 209, 237, 260–61, 268, 271, 273, 274; school of the, 10. See also Nevi'im (Prophets); names of various prophets

Protestantism, xv, 3, 6, 9, 187, 188–200, 201, 202–9, 250, 266, 270–71, 272. See also Prayer, in Buddhism

Puja, 57. See also Prayer, in Buddhism

Punjab, 3, 73, 83, 129, 160

Puranas, 20, 24, 25, 32

Purgatory, 202, 266

Purim, 157, 172, 183

Purity, 20, 81, 85, 113, 148, 160, 231; ritual, 111, 113, 117, 175, 222, 224, 227, 261. See also Harai; Impurity, ritual; Pollution

Purvey, J., 198

Qur'an (Koran), xv, 151, 197, 213, 218, 219, 221–23, 225, 226, 227, 229, 230, 231, 232, 234, 235, 237, 238, 239, 260, 268; quoted, 216, 222, 223, 224, 225, 226, 228, 229, 231, 232, 234, 238

Rabbi, 164, 165, 166, 167, 170, 174, 177, 179, 181, 182, 183, 260

Radha, 26, 31, **124**. See also Lakshmi; Sita

Rahula, 50

Rama, 20, 23, 24, 30, 31, 32, 73, 80. See also Krishna; Vishnu

Ramadan, 229–30, 238, 239

Ramayana, 20, 23, 24, 25, 31, 32

Ram Das, Guru, 80, 83

Rashnu, 154

Rashtriya Swayamsevak Sangh (RSS), 26–27

Ratnapani, 58

Ravana, 20, 24

Reason, rationality, 188, 209

Rebbe, 177, 183, 260

Rebirths, round of. See Reincarnation

Redemption, 29, 171, 203; of first-born son, 173–74

Red Hat Lamaism. See Buddhism, Nyingmapa

Reformation and Reformers, 190, 198, 199, 201, 202, 203, 204, 210, 251, 270. See also names of Reformers

Reformed Christian denominations, 202, 203–4, 210

Reincarnation, 15, 20–22, 24, 27, 28–29, 36, 37, 41, 49, 54, 55, 57, 61, 73, 79, 246, 262–63, 266. See also Moksha; Mukti; Nirvana

Relativism. See Pluralism

Relics, 56

Repentance, 29, 76, 145, 169, 188, 208, 209, 224, 231, 235, 237, 247, 251, 264, 265, 274

Restoration, 8, 12, 68, 94, 187, 188, 208. See also Book of Mormon; Doctrine and Covenants; Gospel of Jesus Christ, restored; Pearl of Great Price; Smith, Joseph

Resurrection, 29, 43, 67, 92, 118, 147, 148, 153, 154, 157, 159, 192, 225, 234, 245, 263, 264, 266, 267; of Jesus Christ, 188, 189, 190, 194, 195, 196, 206, 234, 266, 271

Revelation, 20, 165, 182, 188, 192, 200, 209, 216, 221, 237, 252, 253, 260, 261, 266, 268, 273, 274, 275

Righteousness, 28, 29, 79, 81, 102, 150, 151, 154, 163, 264

Rights, human, 218, 219, 231, 237. See also Freedom, of religion; Intolerance; Tolerance

Rig Veda, 17, 24, 31, 148, 154, 246; quoted, 18, 19

Rinzai, 63, 70. See also Buddhism, Zen

Rita. See Asha

Rituals, 5, 79, 82, 87, 91, 94, 99, 105, 107, 111, 113, 114, 155, 164, 167, 169, 173, 175–76, 182, 228, 236, 251; function of, in religion, 11, 247–48

Roberts, B. H., 259; quoted, 238, 250–51

Roman Catholicism. See Catholicism, Roman

Romania, 201

Rome and Romans, 9, 173, 187, 188, 190, 191, 198, 200, 214, 250, 251, 252

Rosary, 5, 82, 150. *See also* Mala

Rosh Hashanah, 168–69, 170, 173, 183, 184

Roshi, 63, 70

Round of rebirths. *See* Moksha; Mukti; Reincarnation

Rudra, 19, 31

Russia, 201

Sabbath, 166, 167–68, 171, 172, 173, 174, 175, 176, 177, 180, 227

Sacrament, 195, 222. *See also* Eucharist

Sacraments, 190, 195, 196; Seven, 194, 209, 210

Sacred thread, Hindu, 23, 74, 173

Sacrifice, 35, 87, 100, 148, 151, 195, 246; of Abraham, 164, 225, 230, 231, 238, 240; animal, 18, 38, 171, 231

Sadaqa, 228

Sad Dar, 159

Saddharmapundarika. *See* Lotus Sutra

Sadhus, 37, 40, 41, 46. *See also* Monks

Saint, 67; Catholic, 196. *See also* Arhat; *names of saints*

Sakaki, 114, 120

Sakya, Sakyamuni, 51. *See also* Buddha, the

Salat, 226–28, 231, 239. *See also* Prayer, in Islam

Salvation, 20–23, 25, 30, 37, 54, 55, 56, 57, 58, 67, 153, 159, 189, 193, 194, 202, 205, 259, 265, 269, 273; plan of, 28, 157, 189, 195, 210, 258–59, 261, 269, 274

Samadhi, 23, 31, 80. *See also* Enlightenment

Samantabhadra, 58

Samsara, 21, 31

Samurai, 112, 115–16, 120

Sanctus (Sanctus Benedictus), 194, 210

Sangat, 78, 83

Sangha, 54, 55, 70

Sanskrit, 24, 64, 68

Sant tradition, 73, 78, 83

Saoshyant, 153, 160, 245

Sarab-loh (All-steel), 82. *See also* Ik Oankar

Sarah, 163–64

Sarasvati, 19, 31

Sarnath, 51, 52, 126, 128

Sassanians, 153, 214

Satan, 29, 66, 147, 157, 225, 231, 238, 251. *See also* Devil; Lucifer

Satnam, 78, 83. *See also* Ik Oankar

Satori, 63, 70. *See also* Enlightenment

Sawm, 228–30, 239

Scattering of Israel. *See* Diaspora

Scriptures and writings, 5, 6, 76, 80, 82, 226, 234, 235, 236, 260, 261; Buddhist, 54–55, 64; Christian, 193, 195, 197–200, 203, 209; Confucian, 104–5; Hindu, 24–25; Islamic, 221–23, 235–36; Jain, 40; Jewish, 179; new, revelation of, 268; of Restoration (Standard Works), 260–61, 263, 266; Shinto, 113–14; Sikh, 80–81; Taoist, 89; Zoroastrian, 154. *See also* Chinese classics; *names of various sacred writings*

Sealing, 209

Seder, 171–72, 183

Selfishness, 53, 90, 116

Sephardim, 183

Septuagint, 198, 210

Service, 31, 82, 206, 228, 231, 269. *See also* Seva

Sesha, 19, 20, 32

Seton, Elizabeth Ann, 207

Seva, 76, 78, 79, 82, 83, 228

Seventy, quorums of, 271, 273

Sexual relations, 54, 66, 92, 155, 169, 173, 175, 229; unlawful, 38, 53, 76. *See also* Adultery; Chastity

Shahada, 224–26, 239

Shakti, Shaktism, 19, 26, 32

Shamans, shamanism, 5, 6, 64, 93, 94, 111, 117, 118

Shang Ti, 92

Shari'a, 219, 223, 227, 239

Shema, 165, 176, 183

Shemini Atzeret, 170, 183, 184

Shen, 87, 92, 96

Sheol, 148

Shi'a. *See* Islam and Muslims, Shi'ite

Shih Chi, 100

Shih Ching (Book of Poetry), 101, 104, 106, 108

Shinran Shonin, 61, 70

Shinsen, 114–15, 120

Shinto (Kami no Michi), 2, 85, 111–121, 233, 250, 251, 259, 261, 264, 267, 268; sect, 116–17; state, 112, 113, 116, 117

Shirk, 224, 239

Shiva (Hindu god), 18, 19, 23, 25, 26, 30, 32, 57, 124, **125**, 261

Shiva (Jewish mourning), 174–75, 184

Shofar, 169, 184

Shoguns, 112, 120

Sho-Hondo, 61, 70

Shotoku Taishi, 56, 111

Shrines, 5; Buddhist, 56; Confucian, 5; Shinto, 114–15, 117, 118, 120

Shruti, 24, 32

Shu Ching (Book of History), 88, 96, 101, 102, 104, 106, 108

Siddha, 37

Siddhanta, 40, 46

Siddhartha (father of Mahavira), 35

Siddhartha Gautama. *See* Gautama, Siddhartha; *see also* Buddha, the

Sikhism and Sikhs, xv, 2, 3, 15, 73–82, 129, 130, 228, 245, 246, 250, 251, 259, 261, 262, 267, 274

Similarities among religions, 245–54

Simons, Menno, 204

Simran, 78–79, 82

Sin, 28, 45, 119, 145, 151, 166, 188, 189, 191, 194, 208, 224, 228, 229, 247, 264, 265, 269, 274; original, 190, 193

Sinai, Mount, 68, 164, 179, 181, 182, 268

Sinhat Torah, 170, 184

Sita, 20, 24, 31. *See also* Lakshmi; Radha

Smith, George A., quoted, 235, 251

Smith, George Albert, 250; quoted, 4, 275

Smith, Joseph, xv, 9, 22, 43, 199, 208, 219, 235, 245, 252, 257–58, 259, 267, 268, 272, 273; first vision of, 260, 261–62, 263; on plan of salvation, 29; quoted, ix, 4, 5, 9, 29, 44, 238, 260; on reincarnation, 29; on resurrection, 29

Smith, Joseph F., 249; quoted, 43, 248

Smith, Joseph Fielding, quoted, 43, 46, 248

Smoking. *See* Tobacco

Smriti, 24, 32

Smyth, John, 204

Snow, Lorenzo, quoted, 44

Social relations, five, of Confucianism, 88, 102

Socrates, 149, 250, 270

Soma, 18, 24, 32, 147. *See also* Haoma

Sorcery, 6, 91

Soto, 63, 70. *See also* Buddhism, Zen

Soul, 46, 148. *See also* Jiva; Monad; Spirit

Spain, 176, 183, 218

Spirit, 27, 28, 29, 41, 46, 67, 68, 79, 87, 94, 152, 159, 160, 191, 199, 263, 274; prison, 266, 267; world, 266. *See also* Paradise

Spirit of Christ. *See* Light of Christ

Spring and Autumn Annals. See
    Ch'un Ch'iu
Sraosha, 154
Sri Lanka, 3, 20, 49, 52, 58, 74
sRong-Tsan-Gam-Po, 60, 63
Stealing, 37, 38, 53, 54, 66, 74
Stephen, 262
Stupa, 56, **62**, 70, **128**
Succoth, 169–70, 183, 184
Suddhodana, 50, 68
Sudra, 18, 22, 25, 32
Sudre, 155, 158, 160
Suffering, 21, 24, 27, 28, 41, 42, 49,
    50, 53, 54, 60, 69, 149, 151, 167,
    171, 180, 182, 189, 234, 247–48,
    263
Sufi. See Islam and Muslims, Sufi
Suiko, Empress of Japan, 56
Sukhavati-heaven, 58, 59. See also
    Western Land
Sukkah, 170, 184
Sumerians, 246
Sundo, 56
Sunna, 223, 224, 226, 229, 232, 238,
    239
Sunnis. See Islam and Muslims,
    Sunnis
Surabhi, 39, 46
Susano, 113, 114, 120
Sutra, 50, 65, 70. See also names of
    various sutras
Sutta Pitaka, 54, 55
Symbols and symbolism, 5, 42, 56,
    82, 245, 247–49, 269
Synagogue, 165, 168, 169, 170, 172,
    174, 175, 177, 183, 268
Syria, 172, 183, 219

Taboo, 6, 161
Ta Hsueh (The Great Learning), 99,
    105, 106, 108
Taiwan, 130, 131; Buddhism in, 52,
    57, 67, 130; Confucianism in, 100;
    Taoism in, 94
Tallit (prayer shawl), 175, 184
Talmage, James E., quoted, 119
Talmud, xv, 164, 174, 179, 184, 245
Talwandi. See Nankana Sahib
Tanak, 179, 184
Tantras, 65
Tantrayana. See Buddhism, Vajrayana
Tao, 89, 90, 91, 92, 94, 95, 96, 102,
    104, 274
Taoism, xv, 2, 6, 78, 85, 86–97, 100,
    104, 111, 130, 245, 247, 250, 251,
    267, 268; and immortality, 92–93;
    philosophical (tao chia), 88,
    89–91, 94, 96, 259, 260, 261, 264,
    274; religious, 89, 91–93, 94–95,
    96, 131, 259, 264, 266

Tao Te Ching, xv, 6, 89, 90–91, 94,
    96; paraphrased, 93; quoted, 90,
    91, 95
Tash lich, 169, 184
Tawheed, 216, 224–26, 237, 239
Taylor, John, quoted, 43, 250, 257,
    258
Tefillin. See Phylacteries
Tegh Bahadur, Guru, 81, 83
"Temple, the." See "Conventional
    religions"
Temple Mount, **137, 138**
Temples, 5, 187; Buddhist, 66, 94,
    97, **128, 130,** 268; Confucian, 94,
    100, **132,** 268; Hindu, 27, **124,
    125,** 268; Jain, 35, **126,** 268; Jew-
    ish, 137, 165, 166, 170, 171, 172,
    173, 174, 183, 217; Latter-day
    Saint, xiii, 107, **141,** 236, 248, 265,
    269, 270, 273, 274; Shinto, 268;
    Sikh, 78, 80, 81; Taoist, 97, 268;
    Zoroastrian fire, **136,** 148, 150,
    151, 153, 154, 155, 267, 268. See
    also Confucius, Temple of; Dead,
    ordinance work for; Endowment,
    temple; Golden Temple
Ten Commandments, 68, 223
Tenri-kyo, 116, 117
Tertullian, 251
Tevijja Sutta, quoted, 67
Thailand, 52, 58, 127
Thatcher, Moses, quoted, 251
Theism, 7, 68
Theology, 198–99
Third eye, 59, 60
Third Reich, 173, 180, 206
Thomas à Kempis, 250
Three Immortals, **131**
Tibet, xv; Buddhism in, 49, 53, 55,
    57, 60, 64, 69; Sikhism in, 74
T'ien, 99–100, 108. See also Heaven
Time, end of. See also Eschatology;
    Judgment, final; Kalpa
Tirthankara, 36, 41, 46, 126, 268
Tisha Be'av, 173
Tithes, 76, 78, 82, 228. See also Seva;
    Zakat
Tobacco, 76, 173, 229, 236
Tokugawa clan, 112
Tolerance, 119, 213, 234, 237, 240,
    272. See also Intolerance;
    Persecution
Torah, 164, 165, 166–67, 170, 171,
    173, 174, 177, 179, 181, 183, 184,
    197, 222, 226, 235, 245; scroll, xv,
    138
Torii, 114, 120, **134, 135**
"Tower of silence." See Dakhma
Tradition, 200
Trances, 6, 53

Transmigration, 35. See also
    Reincarnation
Transportation (travel), 8–9, 271,
    272–73
Transubstantiation, 195, 210
Trent, Council of, 199, 201
Trimurti, Hindu, 19, 25, 30, 32, 125.
    See also Brahma; Shiva; Vishnu
Trinity, 189–90, 204, 210, 234, 246,
    261, 262; Buddhist, in Western
    Land, 58–61, **128;** season of, 196,
    210. See also Godhead; Trimurti,
    Hindu
Tripitaka, xv, 54, 55, 56, 64, 70, 71
Trisala, 35
Truth, 63, 73, 82, 95, 148, 150, 151,
    154, 158, 226, 231, 238, 247, 248,
    250–51, 252, 253, 258, 259, 270,
    273, 274, 275; pursuit of, 10–12
Truthfulness. See Honesty
Tso Chuan, 102, 105, 106, 108
Tsuki-yomi, 113, 120
Turkey, 220, 221
Tushita-heaven, 58
Tzitzit, 175, 184
Tzu-lu, 99

Udayana, 56
Ujigami, 113
Ulama, 239
Uma, 19, 32
'Umar, 221
Umayyads, 221
Umma, 220, 228, 230, 231, 238, 239
'Umra (lesser pilgrimage), 230, 240
'Uthman, 221
Unction, 193
Unitarians, 204
United Church of Christ. See
    Congregationalists
United States of America, 156
Upanishads, 22, 23, 24, 30, 32, 35,
    36; Chandogya, quoted, 22
Urna, 59
Urvan, 153, 160
Ushnisha, 59

Vairocana, 57, 59, 63, 68
Vaishyas, 18, 21, 32
Vajra, 18, 32, 66, 70
Vajrapani, 58
Vajrayana. See Buddhism, Vajrayana
Vamana, 20, 30, 32
Varaha, 20, 30, 32
Vardhamana Mahavira. See Mahavira,
    Vardhamana
Varuna, 18, 19, 32, 246
Vatican II, 201, 207, 210
Vedas, 17, 19, 23, 24, 32, 35, 66, 154,
    246, 253. See also Rig Veda

Vegetarianism, 27, 38–39, 45
Veiling, **143,** 213, 230, 232
Vendidad, 154, 160
Vinaya Pitaka, 54, 55
Violence, 19, 39, 45–46, 234. *See also* Extremism; Intolerance; War
Virtue, 20, 99, 107, 108, 119, 148, 251
Vishnu, 19, 20, 23, 24, 25, 30, 31, 32, 57, 73, 79, **124, 125,** 246, 261. *See also names of avatars*
Vistaspa, 149, 150, 160
Visvapani, 58
Vizaresha, 154
Vohu Manah, 149, 150
Vritra, 18, 31, 32
Vulgate, 198, 210

Wailing Wall. *See* Western Wall
War, 24, 25, 27, 38, 39, 45–46, 81, 88, 213, 214, 218, 219, 221. *See also* World War I; World War II
Washing, 155, 172. *See also* Purity, ritual
Water, 91, 147, 148, 153, 170. *See also* Purity, ritual
Weddings: Hindu, 81; Jewish, 174; Shinto, 118; Sikh, 81, 82; Zoroastrian, 155
Wen, King in China, 76
Wesley, Charles, 202
Wesley, John, 202, 250
Western culture and traditions, 6–7, 9, 38, 42, 54, 60, 87, 105, 156, 205, 219, 233, 234–35
Western Land, 58, 59, 60, 61, 69
Western Wall, **137, 138, 178**

Westminster Confession of Faith, 199, 200
White, Ellen, 207
Whitney, Orson F., 249; quoted, 11, 248, 250, 269–70
Widtsoe, John A., quoted, 11, 45, 248
Willard, Frances, 207
Williams, Roger, 204
Winchester Cathedral, **141**
Women, 15; in Buddhism, 59, 60, 65–66, 118; in Christianity, 204, 206–7, 209; in Confucianism, 93, 105, 107; in Hinduism, 20, 25–26; in Islam, 213, 225, 226, 230, 231–33, 240–41; in Jainism, 37, 40–41; in Judaism, 166, 175, 176, 177, 180–81, 182; in Shinto, 117–18; in Sikhism, 81; in Taoism, 93, 94; in Zoroastrianism, 154, 155
Word of Wisdom, 45, 94, 182
Work ethic, 82, 181, 203, 215, 216, 232, 236, 237, 258
Works, salvation through, 201. *See also* Karma
World War I, 180, 221
World War II, 45, 85, 112, 114, 117, 118, 191, 233
Worship, Way of. *See* Bhakti
Wu-hsing, 88, 90, 92, 96
Wu-wei, 88, 89, 90–91, 92, 93, 94, 96
Wycliffe, John, 198

Yajna, 57
Yamato clan, 114
Yang, 87–88, 89, 90, 93, 94, 96
Yarmulka (kippah), 5, 175–76, 184
Yashts, 154, 160

Yasna, 149, 154, 160; paraphrased, 152, 158; quoted, 150, 152. *See also* Gathas
Yasodhara, 50
Yasukuni Shrine, 113
Yathrib. *See* Medina
Yazid, 221
Yeshiva rabbinic students, **137**
Yin, 87–88, 89, 90, 93, 94, 95, 96
Yoga, 70, 92; hatha, 73, 82
Yom ha-Atzma'ut, 173
Yom ha-Shoa, 173
Yom ha-Zikaron, 173
Yom Kippur, 169, 170, 173, 174, 183, 184
Yom Yerushalayim, 173
Young, Brigham, 249; quoted, 11, 250, 258
Yueh (Book of Music), 101
Yushima Shrine, **133**

Zadspram, 149
Zakat (almsgiving), 223, 228, 229, 231, 238, 239
Zamzam, 214, 230
Zarathustra (Zoroaster), xv, 12, 17, 147, 148–50, 151, 152, 154, 158, 160–61, 245, 246, 250, 253, 257, 258
Zazen, 63. *See also* Buddhism, Zen
Zealots, 187, 188
Zen Buddhism. *See* Buddhism, Zen
Zionism, 181, 184
Zoroastrianism and Zoroastrians, xv, 2, 7, 17, 38, 57, 59, 136, 145–61, 245, 246, 247, 250, 251, 252–53, 259, 261, 263, 267; and Islam, 156, 160, 214

About the Authors

Spencer J. Palmer

Spencer John Palmer, professor emeritus of Church history and doctrine at Brigham Young University, graduated from Eastern Arizona College in 1947 and received a B.A. in fine arts from Brigham Young University in 1948, an M.A. in East Asian studies from University of California at Berkeley in 1958, and a Ph.D. in Asian history and religion from the University of California at Berkeley in 1964. He has taught world religion classes at BYU for more than thirty years, as well as in Jerusalem and Beijing. He also held a fellowship at Harvard University's Religions of the World Institute. Noted for creative scholarship and publications in fields of Asian history and culture, Asian religions, and Latter-day Saint history and doctrine, he has authored or edited more than a dozen books and numerous monographic articles and essays. He is married to Shirley Hadley Palmer. They have three children—Dwight, Jennette, and James—and twelve grandchildren.

Roger R. Keller

Roger R. Keller, associate professor of Church history and doctrine at Brigham Young University, holds a B.Mus. from the University of Colorado, a M.Div. from Princeton Theological Seminary, and a Ph.D. from Duke University. His academic training focused on biblical studies and twentieth-century Christian theology, with an emphasis in hermeneutics. However, he has taught primarily world religions over the past twenty years. He has served in teaching and/or administrative positions at Duke University, Peace College, Pikeville College, Scarritt Graduate School, and Brigham Young University. As a former Presbyterian minister, he has also served Presbyterian and Methodist churches in North Carolina and Arizona. He has traveled widely and has taught for one year in Israel. Dr. Keller is the author of three books and a number of articles. He is married to the former Flo Beth Lindsay, and they have three children—Marta, Evan, and Kirsten.

Dong Sull Choi

Dong Sull Choi, professor of Church history and doctrine at Brigham Young University, received a Th.D. degree from Choong Theological Seminary in Seoul. He joined The Church of Jesus Christ of Latter-day Saints in Korea in 1981, having previously served as a Presbyterian minister and a professor of Hebrew, Greek, Latin, Christian history, and comparative religion. He returned to studies at BYU and received a Master's degree in 1984 in Asian studies and a Ph.D. in 1990 in American history and comparative religion. As an Asian professor in religious education at BYU for nearly a decade, he has been popular among students for his unusual ability to bridge religious and cultural gaps between Asian thought and the Western world. Dr. Choi has been a productive scholar, having delivered papers before numerous international conferences and symposia. He is married to Kyung Ae Shin, and they have two sons—Young Shik and Young Hoon.

James A. Toronto

James A. Toronto, assistant professor of Church history and doctrine at Brigham Young University, earned his B.A. in English and history from Brigham Young University in 1975, his M.A. in Middle Eastern studies from Harvard University in 1984, and his Ph.D. in Islamic studies from Harvard University in 1992. He has been a teacher and school administrator in Saudi Arabia, studied Arabic, and worked on international development projects in Egypt, as well as traveling extensively in Africa, Asia, and Europe. He is currently serving as director of the Center for Cultural and Educational Affairs in Amman, Jordan, coordinating BYU's programs in the Arab countries of the Middle East. His research and publications are in the areas of contemporary Islamic society, religious freedom and pluralism, and church history in Italy. With his wife, Diane, and two children, Joseph and Jenna, he has lived ten years in the Middle East.